Instant Pot Duo Crisp Cookbook for Beginners

1001 Recipes

to Fry, Bake, Grill and Roast with Your

Instant Pot Duo Crisp Pressure Cooker

Carmen Mitchell

CONTENTS

INTRODUCTION

The Instant Pot That Air Fries: The hottest new multi-cooker from the makers of the all-time bestselling Duo series, the Instant Pot Duo Crisp is a pressure cooker and air fryer with 2 convenient, removable lids

11-In-1 1-Touch Cooking Programs: Put cooking on autopilot with delicious results; Pressure cooks, sautés, steams, slow cooks, sous vides, warms, air fries, roasts, bakes, broils and dehydrates

Tender Juicy Meals with a Crisp Golden Finish: Innovative Even Crisp technology ensures a perfect crunch every time; Imagine biting into fall-off-the-bone ribs with a perfect air fried crust

Air Fryer Accessories: The multi-level air fryer basket with dehydrating and broiling tray is designed for optimal air flow; The protective pad is great for storage and countertop use

Dishwasher Safe Stainless-Steel Cookware: Cook for up to 8 people with the premium quality (18/8) stainless-steel inner pot; Healthy and BPA-PFOA-PTFE-free

Advanced Safety: 10 plus built-in safety features include automatic pressure and temperature control and overheat protection; New Easy Seal lid automatically seals for pressure cooking and the pressure release button vents steam from a distance

Family Meals Fast: The powerful 1500W heating element reduces preheating time and cooks up to 70% faster — from frozen to golden in minutes

Pressure cooking and air frying are fantastic ways to help you save time and energy when cooking healthy meals, and the Instant Pot Duo Crisp plus Air Fryer is one hot pot that you won't want to miss cook and crisp all in one place by swapping out the pressure cooker lid for the innovative air fryer lid, and add a whole new set of cooking techniques to your culinary collection. All the same taste and texture of your deep-fried favorites, but made with as little as 2 tablespoons of oil. Save space by replacing your pressure cooker, slow cooker, saute pan, steamer, sous vide cooker, warmer, air fryer, roaster, oven, broiler and dehydrator — it's like having 11 appliances in 1. Use the pressure cooker lid to easily pressure cook, saute, steam, slow cook, sous vide and warm your meals. The air fryer lid is useful to quickly air fry, roast, bake, broil and dehydrate all your favorites. Chow down on juicy chicken wings, crispy fries and onion rings, perfectly crunchy spring rolls and much more, up to 70% faster than other cooking methods. Simplify mealtime with one-touch controls and preset cooking programs. Bright, easy-to-read dual display with large font. Customizable temperature range of 70°C (21°C) to 400°F (201°F), varying by smart program. Automatic and manual keep warm to ensure that dishes stay at ready-to-eat temperatures. Delay cooking up to 24 hours. Prepare delicious, heart-healthy meals at home, at your home-away-from-home, or wherever life takes you.

Troubleshoot: (1) Air fryer lid is in place but will not turn on - *The connection between the air fryer lid and pressure cooker base is loose or broken *Bad power connection or no power *Electrical fuse has blown *Micros witch is dirty grease or damaged (2) Black smoke is coming from the air fryer lid - *Using an oil with a low smoke point *Food residue on the bottom of the inner pot or around the element on the air fryer lid *Appliance malfunction (3) White Smoke is coming from the air fryer lid - * Cooking foods with a high fat content, such as bacon, sausage, and hamburger * Food is moist * Seasoning on food has blown into element.

BREAKFAST AND BRUNCH RECIPES

Spinach and Eggs

Ingredients: Servings: 4 Cooking Time: 30 Mins

3 C. baby spinach
12 eggs; whisked
1 tbsp. Olive oil
½ tsp. Smoked paprika
Salt and black pepper to taste.

Directions:
Take a bowl and mix all the ingredients except the oil and whisk them well. Heat up your air fryer at 360°f, add the oil, heat it up, add the eggs and spinach mix, cover, cook for 20 minutes. Divide between plates and serve

Spinach Muffins

Ingredients: Servings: 6 Cooking Time: 15 Mins

5 eggs
1 C. spinach, chopped
1/4 tsp. garlic powder
1 bacon slice, cooked and crumbled
1/4 tsp. onion powder
1/2 C. mushrooms, chopped
Pepper
Salt

Directions:
In a bowl, whisk eggs with garlic powder, onion powder, pepper, and salt. Add spinach, mushrooms, and bacon and stir well. Pour egg mixture into the 6 silicone muffin molds. Place the dehydrating tray in a multi-level air fryer basket and place basket in the instant pot. Place muffin molds on dehydrating tray. Seal pot with air fryer lid and select bake mode then set the temperature to 400 F and timer for 15 minutes. Serve and enjoy.

Cajun Chicken

Ingredients: Servings: 2 Cooking Time: 15 Mins

2 chicken breasts, boneless & skinless
3 tbsp. Cajun spice

Directions:
Season chicken breasts with Cajun spice from both the sides. Place the dehydrating tray in a multi-level air fryer basket and place basket in the instant pot. Place chicken breasts on dehydrating tray. Seal pot with air fryer lid and select air fry mode then set the temperature to 350 F and timer for 15 minutes. Serve and enjoy.

Tropical Oatmeal

Ingredients: Servings: 4 Cooking Time: 4 Mins

1 C. steel-cut oats
3 tbsp. hemp seeds
1/2 papaya, chopped
1/2 C. coconut cream
2 C. of water

Directions:
Add oats, coconut cream, and water into the instant pot and stir well. Seal pot with lid and cook on manual high pressure for 4 minutes. Once done then allow to release pressure naturally for 10 minutes then release using the quick-release method. Open the lid. Stir in hemp seeds and papaya. Serve and enjoy.

Cheesy Sausage Balls

Ingredients: Servings: 16 Cooking Time: 15 Mins

1 lb. Pork breakfast sausage
1 oz. Full-fat cream cheese; softened.
1 large egg.
½ C. shredded cheddar cheese

Directions:
Mix all ingredients in a large bowl. Form into sixteen (1-inchballs). Place the balls into the air fryer basket. Adjust the temperature to 400 degrees f and set the timer for 12 minutes. Shake the basket two-or three-times during cooking Sausage balls will be browned on the outside and have an internal temperature of at least 145 degrees f when completely cooked.

Cranberry Farro

Ingredients: Servings: 8 Cooking Time: 20 Mins

15 oz farro
1/2 C. dried cranberries
1 tsp. lemon extract
1/2 C. brown sugar
4 1/2 C. water
1/4 tsp. salt

Directions:
Add farro, lemon extract, brown sugar, water, and salt into the instant pot and stir well. Seal pot with lid and cook on high pressure for 20 minutes. Once done then allow to release pressure naturally for 10 minutes then release using the quick-release method. Open the lid. Add cranberries and stir well. Serve and enjoy.

Healthy Air Fryer Granola

Ingredients: Servings: 8 Cooking Time: 15 Mins

2 C. Rolled Oats
1/2 C. Toasted Wheat Germ
1/4 C. Dried Cherries
1/8 C. Dried Cranberries
1/4 C. Dried Blueberries
1/8 C. Pepitas
1/8 C. Sunflower Seeds
1 Tbsp Flaxseed
1/8 C. Chopped pecans
1/8 C. Chopped Almonds
1/8 C. Chopped Walnuts
1/8 C. Chopped Hazelnuts.
2 tbsp. Honey or Agave Extract
1/2 tsp. Vanilla extract
1/4 C. Maple Syrup
6 tbsp. Olive Oil
1/2 tsp. Ground Cinnamon
1/8 tsp. Ground Cloves

Directions:
Combine all the dry ingredients in a large or a medium bowl. Mix the agave or honey with the oil and maple syrup. Thoroughly mix the syrup mix with the dry ingredients, stirring well to fully coat all of the ingredients. Choose the Air Fry option from the Instant Pot Duo Crisp Air Fryer and set the temperature to 350°F. Press start and let it preheat. Add the food to the Air Fryer and Air Fry at 350°F for 15 minutes, stirring every 5 minutes until the granola is golden brown. Let it cool and store for up to three weeks in an airtight container

Keto Ribs

Ingredients: Servings: 6 Cooking Time: 35 Mins

3.5 lbs pork baby back ribs about 2 racks of ribs
1/3 C. spicy dry rub
1/2 C. Keto BBQ sauce
1 C. Zevia Cola or Chicken Broth

Directions:
Season the pork ribs on the both sides with the dry rub. Marinate the ribs for at least 4 hours. Set the ribs in the Instant Pot Duo Crisp Air Fryer. Pour the chicken broth or keto-friendly Cola soda at the bottom of the pot. Close the Air Fryer lid and cook the ribs for 25-30 minutes at 390°F. Place them into the Instant Pot Duo Crisp Air Fryer Basket. Top the ribs with BBQ sauce. Select the option Air Fryer. Close the Air Fryer lid and cook for about 5 minutes.

Banana Buckwheat Porridge

Ingredients: Servings: 4 Cooking Time: 6 Mins

1 C. raw buckwheat grouts, rinsed
1/4 C. raisins
1 banana, sliced
3 C. almond milk
1/2 tsp. vanilla
1 tsp. cinnamon

Directions:
Add all ingredients into the inner pot of instant pot duo crisp and stir well. Seal the pot with pressure cooking lid and cook on high for 6 minutes. Once done, allow to release pressure naturally. Remove lid. Serve and enjoy.

Steak Kebabs

Ingredients: Servings: 4 Cooking Time: 12 Mins

1 lb sirloin steak cut into 1-inch chunks
¼ C. olive oil
¼ C. of soy sauce
1 Tbsp garlic minced
1 tsp. brown sugar
8 oz Baby Bella mushrooms stem removed
½ tsp. ground cumin
¼ tsp. black pepper
1 red onion chopped into 1-inch pieces
1 Green Bell Pepper chopped into 1-inch pieces
salt and pepper to taste

Directions:
Mix together soy sauce, garlic, cumin, salt, steak, olive oil, and black pepper. Allow marinating for around 30 minutes. While preparing for cooking, select the Air Fry option. Adjust the temperature to 390°F and press start to begin preheating. Once the preheating temperature is reached, place the marinated meat, baby Bella mushrooms, green pepper, and red onion on the Instant Pot Duo Crisp Air Fryer tray. Place the tray inside of Instant Pot Duo Crisp Air fryer. Air Fry for 10-12 minutes while flipping halfway.

Bacon and Croissant

Ingredients: Servings: 2 Cooking Time: 10 Mins

Thick-cut bacon – 4 pieces
Croissants – 2, sliced
Eggs – 2
Butter – 1 tbsp.
For the sauce
Apple cider vinegar – 2 tbsps.
Ketchup – ½ cup
Brown sugar – 1 tbsp.
Molasses – 1 tbsp.
Worcestershire sauce – ½ tbsp.
Onion powder – ¼ tsp.
Mustard powder – ¼ tsp.
Liquid smoke – ¼ tsp.

Directions:
Preheat the air fryer to 390F. Mix all the sauce ingredients in a saucepan and heat until sauce thickens slightly. Place the bacon cuts flat on a tray and brush them with sauce on one side. Transfer to the air fryer basket with the brushed side up. Cook for 5 minutes then flip. Brush the other side with sauce and cook for 5 minutes more. Melt the butter in a pan and fry the eggs. Then place the eggs at the bottom of each croissant. Top them with two bacon slices each and close the croissant top. Serve.

Carrot and Pineapple Oatmeal (pressure Cook)

Ingredients: Servings: 8 Cooking Time: 10 Mins

4½ C. water
2 C. shredded carrots
1 C. steel-cut oats
1 (20-ounce / 567-g) can crushed pineapple, undrained
1 C. raisins
2 tsp. ground cinnamon
1 tsp. pumpkin pie spice
Cooking spray
Brown sugar (optional)

Directions:
Spritz the bottom of the Instant Pot with cooking spray. Place the water, carrots, oats, raisins, pineapple, cinnamon, and pumpkin pie spice into the Instant Pot and stir to combine. Secure the lid. Select the Pressure Cook and set the cooking time for 10 minutes at High Pressure. Once cooking is complete, do a natural pressure release for 10 minutes, then release any remaining pressure. Carefully open the lid. Let the oatmeal stand for 5 to 10 minutes. Sprinkle with the brown sugar, if desired. Serve warm.

Traditional Scotch Eggs

Ingredients: Servings: 4 Cooking Time: 18 Mins

1 C. water
4 eggs
12 oz. Italian sausage patties
1 C. panko breadcrumbs
2 tbsps. melted unsalted butter

Directions:
Pour 1 C. of water into the inner pot. Put in the reversible rack place the eggs on the rack. Seal the pressure lid, choose Pressure, set to High, and the cook time to 3 minutes. Press Start. After cooking, perform a quick pressure release, and carefully open the lid. Use tongs to pick up the eggs into an ice bath. Allow cooling for 3 to 4 minutes. Peel the eggs to keep the egg whites intact and blot dry with a clean napkin. Pour the water out of the inner pot and return the pot to the base. Grease the reversible rack with cooking spray and place in the pot. Preheat your cooker by closing the crisping lid; choose Air Fry, set the temperature to 360 F and the timer to 4 minutes. Press Start. Meanwhile, place an egg on each sausage patty. Carefully pull the sausage around the egg and seal the edges. In a bowl, mix breadcrumbs with melted butter. One at a time,

dredge sausage-covered eggs in crumbs while pressing into the breadcrumbs for a coat. Open the crisping lid and place the eggs on the rack. Close the crisping lid; choose Air Fry, adjust the temperature to 360 F, and the cook time to 15 minutes. Press Start to start crisping. When the timer has ended, carefully remove the eggs and allow cooling for several minutes. Slice the eggs in half and serve.

Cinnamon Sweet Potato Chips (air Fryer)

Ingredients: Servings: 6 To 8 Cooking Time: 8 Mins

2 tbsp. olive oil
1 to 2 tsp. ground cinnamon
1 small sweet potato, cut into ⅜ inch-thick slices

Directions:
Preheat the air fryer to 390°F (199°C). Add the sweet potato slices and olive oil in a bowl and toss to coat. Fold in the cinnamon and stir to combine. Arrange the sweet potato slices in a single layer in the air fryer basket. Air fry for 8 minutes, or until the chips are crisp. Shake the basket halfway through. Remove from the air fryer basket and allow to cool for 5 minutes before serving.

Breakfast Fish Tacos

Ingredients: Servings: 4 Cooking Time: 13 Mins

Big tortillas – 4
Red bell pepper – 1, chopped
Yellow onion – 1, chopped
Whitefish fillets – 4, skinless, and boneless
Corn – 1 cup
Salsa – ½ cup
Mixed romaine lettuce, spinach, and radicchio – 1 handful
Parmesan – 4 tbsps. grated

Directions:
Put fish fillets in the air fryer and cook at 350F for 6 minutes. Meanwhile, heat up a pan over medium-high heat; add corn, onion, and bell pepper — Stir-Fry for 2 minutes. On your work surface, arrange tortillas. and build your tacos with all the ingredients. Roll the tacos, place them in the preheated air fryer and cook at 350F for 6 minutes more. Divide fish tacos between plates and serve.

Ham and Egg Toast Cups

Ingredients: Servings: 4 Cooking Time: 15 Mins

Toast slices – 8
Ham slices – 2, cut into 8 strips
Eggs – 4
Butter – 2 ounces
Ground black pepper and salt to taste
Cheese – 4 ounces

Directions:
Grease 4 ramekins with butter. with a rolling pin, flatten the toast to the maximum level. Now line each ramekin with 2 toast slices. Then line each ramekin with 2 ham strips. Now on each toast cup, crack one egg per toast cup. Season with salt and pepper. Then place cubed cheese. Place the C. in the air fryer basket and cook at 320F for 15 minutes. Serve.

Simple & Easy Breakfast Casserole

Ingredients: Servings: 4 Cooking Time: 20 Mins

2 1/2 C. egg whites
1/2 C. mexican blend cheese
1/4 C. cream cheese
1/2 C. onion, chopped
1 C. bell pepper, chopped
1/2 tsp. onion powder
1/4 tsp. garlic powder
1/4 tsp. pepper
1/4 tsp. salt

Directions:
Spray instant pot from inside with cooking spray. Add onion and bell pepper to the pot and cook until softened, about 5 minutes. Transfer onion and bell pepper to the baking dish. Add egg whites, seasonings, and cream cheese and stir well. Top with mexican blend cheese. Pour 1 C. of water into the instant pot then place the trivet in the pot. Place baking dish on top of the trivet. Seal pot with lid and cook on manual mode for 15 minutes. Once done then release pressure using the quick-release method than open the lid. Slice and serve.

Herbed Cheddar Frittata (air Fryer)

Ingredients: Servings: 4 Cooking Time: 20 Mins

½ C. shredded Cheddar cheese
½ C. half-and-half
2 tbsp. chopped scallion greens
2 tbsp. chopped fresh parsley
4 large eggs
½ tsp. kosher salt
½ tsp. ground black pepper
Cooking spray

Directions:
Preheat the air fryer to 300°F (149°C). Spritz a baking pan with cooking spray. Whisk together all the ingredients in a large bowl, then pour the mixture into the prepared baking pan. Set the pan in the preheated air fryer and bake for 20 minutes or until set. Serve immediately.

Creamy Polenta

Ingredients: Servings: 3 Cooking Time: 5 Mins

1/2 C. polenta
1 C. of coconut milk
1 C. of water
1/2 tbsp. butter
1/4 tsp. salt

Directions:
Set instant pot on sauté mode. Add milk, water, and salt in a pot and stir well. Once milk mixture begins to boil then add polenta and stir to combine. Seal pot with lid and cook on high pressure for 5 minutes. Once done then allow to release pressure naturally then open the lid. Stir and serve.

Tasty Chicken Tenders

Ingredients: Servings: 4 Cooking Time: 18 Mins

1 lb chicken tenders
2 tbsp. sesame oil
6 tbsp. pineapple juice
2 tbsp. soy sauce
1 tsp. ginger, minced
4 garlic cloves, minced

Directions:
Add all ingredients except chicken in a bowl and mix well. Add chicken and coat well. Cover and place in the refrigerator for 2 hours. Place the dehydrating tray in a multi-level air fryer basket and place basket in the instant pot. Place marinated chicken tenders on dehydrating tray. Seal pot with

air fryer lid and select air fry mode then set the temperature to 350 F and timer for 18 minutes. Turn chicken halfway through. Serve and enjoy.

Sizzling Turkey Fajitas Platter

Ingredients: Servings: 2 Cooking Time: 20 Mins

6 Tortilla Wraps
3.5oz Leftover Turkey Breast
1 Large Avocado
1 Large Yellow Pepper
1 Large Red Pepper
1 Large Green Pepper
½ Small Red Onion
5 Tbsp Soft Cheese
3 Tbsp Cajun Spice
2 Tbsp Mexican Seasoning
1 Tsp Cumin
Salt & Pepper
1/2 C. Fresh Coriander

Directions:
Start by slicing the salad. Chop the avocado to little wedges. Dice the red onion. Slice the peppers into thin slices. Chop up the turkey breast into small little chunks. Place the turkey, peppers, and onions into a bowl and mix with all the seasonings along with the soft cheese and then place in silver foil. Place all of them in Instant Pot Duo Crisp Air Fryer tray and then close the lid. Select the Air Fry option. Cook for 20 minutes at 390°F. Once done, serve them hot.

Loaded Cauliflower Bake

Ingredients: Servings: 4 Cooking Time: 30 Mins

2 scallions, sliced on the bias
1 C. shredded medium cheddar cheese.
1 medium avocado; peeled and pitted
¼ C. heavy whipping cream.
12 slices sugar-free bacon; cooked and crumbled
1 ½ C. chopped cauliflower
6 large eggs.
8 tbsp. Full-fat sour cream.

Directions:
Take a medium bowl, whisk eggs and cream together. Pour into a 4-cup round baking dish. Add cauliflower and mix, then top with cheddar Place dish into the air fryer basket. Adjust the temperature to 320 degrees f and set the timer for 20 minutes. When completely cooked, eggs will be firm and cheese will be browned. Slice into four pieces Slice avocado and divide evenly among pieces. Top each piece with 2 tbsp. Sour cream, sliced scallions and crumbled bacon.

Air Fryer Garlic Bread

Ingredients: Servings: 4 Slices Cooking Time: 5 Mins

4 slices Ciabatta
¼ C. Parmesan, freshly grated
1 tbsp. salted butter
3 cloves garlic, crushed
A few pinches of dried parsley

Directions:
Preheat your air fryer to 360 degrees F. Put the butter in a small bowl and microwave for 10 seconds or until softened. Add the cheese, garlic and dried parsley to the bowl of butter. Spread the garlic mixture to both sides of Ciabatta slices. Assemble the slices in the air fryer basket and air-fry for about 3-5 minutes. Serve warm.

Quick & Easy Farro

Ingredients: Servings: 4 Cooking Time: 10 Mins

1 C. pearl farro
2 C. vegetable broth
1 tsp. olive oil
1/4 tsp. salt

Directions:
Add all ingredients into the instant pot and stir well. Seal pot with lid and cook on manual mode for 10 minutes. Once done then allow to release pressure naturally for 5 minutes then release using the quick-release method. Open the lid. Stir well and serve.

Delicious Egg Brulee

Ingredients: Servings: 8 Cooking Time: 10 Mins

8 large Eggs
1 tsp. Sugar
Salt to taste
1 C. Water
Ice Bath

Directions:
Open the cooker, pour the water in, and fit the reversible rack in it. Put the eggs on the rack in a single layer, close the lid, secure the pressure valve, and select Pressure on High Pressure for 5 minutes. Press Start. Once the timer has ended, do a quick pressure release, and open the pot. Remove the eggs into the ice bath and peel the eggs. Put the peeled eggs in a plate and slice them in half. Sprinkle a bit of salt on them and then followed by the sugar. Lay onto your crisp basket fryer basket. Select Air Fry mode, set the temperature to 390 F and the time to 3 minutes.

Air Fryer Breakfast Frittata

Ingredients: Servings: 2 Cooking Time: 18 Mins

4 eggs
¼ lb. breakfast sausage, cooked.
2 tablespoons, red bell pepper, chopped
½ C. cheddar cheese, grated
1 green onion, finely chopped
¼ tsp. ground cayenne pepper
¼ tsp. salt
Cooking spray

Directions:
Beat the eggs in a large bowl. Crumble the sausages. In bowl, combine beaten egg, crumbled sausages, grated cheddar cheese, onion, salt, and cayenne pepper thoroughly. Take an Instant Pot Air Fryer compatible non-stick pan and spritz some cooking spray. Pour the egg mix into the tray and place it in the air fryer basket in the inner pot. Close the crisp lid. Set the temperature 350°C and timer for 18 minutes in the AIR FRYER mode. Press START to begin the cooking. Remove the Frittata when the cooking stops. Serve hot.

Easy Poached Eggs On Heirloom Ripe Tomatoes

Ingredients: Servings: 4 Cooking Time: 3 Mins

4 large Eggs
2 large Heirloom
1 C. Water
1 tsp. chopped Fresh

Ripe Tomatoes, halved crosswise	Herbs, of your choice
Salt and Black Pepper to taste	2 tbsp. grated Parmesan Cheese
	Cooking Spray

Directions:
Pour the water into the cooker and fit the reversible rack. Grease the ramekins with the cooking spray and crack each egg into them. Season with salt and pepper. Cover the ramekins with aluminum foil. Place the C. on the trivet. Seal the lid. Select Steam mode for 3 minutes on High pressure. Press Start. Once the timer goes off, do a quick pressure release. Use a napkin to remove the ramekins onto a flat surface. In serving plates, share the halved tomatoes and toss the eggs in the ramekin over on each tomato half. Sprinkle with salt and pepper, parmesan, and garnish with chopped herbs.

Avocado and Bacon Breakfast Burger (pressure Cook)

Ingredients: Servings: 2 Cooking Time: 10 Mins

2 tbsp. coconut oil	½ C. shredded full-fat Cheddar cheese
2 eggs, lightly beaten	1 C. shredded lettuce
3 slices no-sugar-added bacon	1 avocado, halved and pitted
½ tsp. kosher salt	2 tbsp. sesame seeds
½ tsp. freshly ground black pepper	

Directions:
Press the Sauté button on the Instant Pot and melt the coconut oil. Fold in the beaten eggs, bacon, cheese, salt, and pepper and stir thoroughly and continuously. When cooked, remove the egg mixture from the pot to a bowl. Assemble the burger: Place an avocado half on a clean work surface and top with the egg mixture and shredded lettuce, and finish with the other half of the avocado. Scatter the sesame seeds on top and serve immediately.

Air Fryer Baked Eggs

Ingredients: Servings: 2 Cooking Time: 6 Mins

2 large eggs	Salt and freshly ground black pepper, to taste
2 tbsp. half-and-half	Cooking spray
2 tsp. shredded Cheddar cheese	

Directions:
Preheat the air fryer to 330°F (166°C). Spritz 2 ramekins lightly with cooking spray. Crack an egg into each ramekin. Top each egg with 1 tbsp. of half-and-half and 1 tsp. of Cheddar cheese. Sprinkle with salt and black pepper. Stir the egg mixture with a fork until well combined. Place the ramekins in the air fryer basket and bake for 6 minutes until set. Check for doneness and cook for 1 minute as needed. Allow to cool for 5 minutes in the basket before removing and serving.

Cheesy Egg Cup

Ingredients: Servings: 1 Cooking Time: 15 Mins

2 eggs	2 tbsp. cheddar cheese, shredded
2 tbsp. half and half	Pepper
1 tbsp. parmesan cheese, grated	Salt

Directions:
Spray a ramekin with cooking spray and set aside. In a small bowl, whisk eggs and a half and half. Stir in cheddar cheese, parmesan cheese, pepper, and salt. Pour egg mixture into the prepared ramekin. Place the dehydrating tray in a multi-level air fryer basket and place basket in the instant pot. Place ramekin on dehydrating tray. Seal pot with air fryer lid and select bake mode then set the temperature to 380 F and timer for 15 minutes. Serve and enjoy.

Banana Oatmeal

Ingredients: Servings: 2 Cooking Time: 5 Mins

1 C. oatmeal	1 C. almond milk
1 banana, sliced	1 tbsp. maple syrup
1 C. of water	1 1/2 tsp. cinnamon

Directions:
Spray instant pot inner pot with cooking spray. Add water, oatmeal, and almond milk and stir well. Add maple syrup, cinnamon, and banana and stir well. Seal the pot with pressure cooking lid and cook on high for 5 minutes. Once done, allow to release pressure naturally. Remove lid. Stir and serve.

Cheesy Air Fryer Spaghetti

Ingredients: Servings: 6 Cooking Time: 14 Mins

1 lb. ground beef	½ C. Parmesan cheese grated
1 (24 oz.) jar spaghetti sauce	2 C. beef broth
8 oz. spaghetti noodles, broken into thirds	1 onion, diced
	1 green onion, diced (optional)
1½ C. Mozzarella cheese, grated and divided	2 tbsps. olive oil
	¼ tsp. salt

Directions:
Set the instant pot to SAUTE then drizzle the bottom of the steel pot with olive oil. Sauté the onions and ground beef then season with salt. Continue to cook until the ground beef is no longer pink. Evenly spread the cooked meat to cover the bottom of the pot entirely. Pour the spaghetti sauce then add the broth into the jar. Put the lid back on and shake the jar to mix the meat and broth with the remaining sauce. Pour the broth into the pot but do not stir. Sprinkle the broken spaghetti noodles on top of the liquid. Using a spoon spatula, gently submerge the noodles into the sauce but do not stir. Place the pressure cooker lid and close the steam valve. Pressure cook on HIGH for 9 minutes. Quick-release and remove the lid. Stir in one C. of mozzarella cheese until it melts. Sprinkle the remaining half C. of the mozzarella cheese plus the parmesan on top of the spaghetti. Top with the diced green onions then closes the pot with air fryer lid. Air fry at 400degrees F for 5 minutes, until the cheese melts and gets golden brown on top. Serve and enjoy.

Sweet Potato Hash

Ingredients: Servings: 6 Cooking Time: 15 Mins

Large sweet potato –	Dried dill weed – 1

2, chopped
Bacon – 2 slices
Olive oil – 2 tbsps.
Paprika – 1 tbsp. smoked
tsp.
Ground black pepper – 1 tsp.
Salt – 1 tsp.

Directions:
Preheat the air fryer at 390F for 5 minutes. In a bowl, add everything and mix. Place in the air fryer. Cook at 390F for 12 minutes. Stir the potatoes 2 to 3 times during the cooking process. Serve.

Air-fried Scotch Eggs

Ingredients: Servings: 6 Cooking Time: 15 Mins

1 egg, lightly beaten
1 lb. bulk sausage, uncooked
1 tbsp. mustard or hot sauce
5 hard-boiled eggs
Oil spray, for coating
1 C. almond flour or coconut flour

Directions:
Peel the hard-boiled eggs and set aside. Meanwhile, divide the sausage into 6 equal parts and flatten to form a 4-inch wide patty. Lay the boiled eggs in the center and wrap the patty around it. Repeat the process until you have used up all the eggs and sausage patties. Dip each sausage-wrapped patty in the beaten egg and then into almond flour for coating. Spray evenly all sides with oil. Place wrapped patties in the air fryer, making sure they aren't overcrowded. You may use the second layer of the air fryer basket to accommodate all patties. Attach the instant pot duo crisp Air Fryer Lid and air fry at 400 degrees F for 12-16 minutes, turning halfway through cooking. Once done, cut in halves and serve with mustard on top. You may also serve it with hot sauce.

Air Fryer Hard Boiled Eggs

Ingredients: Servings: 3 Cooking Time: 15 Mins

6 large eggs

Directions:
Select the Air Fry option on the Instant Pot Duo Crisp Air Fryer. Adjust the temperature to 390°F and press start to begin preheating. Once the preheating is complete, place the eggs on the Air Fryer tray in the Air Fryer basket and close the lid. Air Fry on 300°F for 15 minutes. Once the set time is over, remove the eggs from the Instant Pot Duo Crisp Air Fryer tray and place them in a bowl filled with ice water for 5 minutes. Remove and peel the eggs for eating.

Air Fryer Hot Dogs

Ingredients: Servings: 6 Cooking Time: 8 Mins

6 Hot Dogs
6 Hot Dog Buns

Directions:
Simply place the hot dogs in the Instant Pot Duo Crisp Air Fryer basket and close the lid. Select the Air Fry option and Air Fry on 400°F for 4-6 minutes. Remove the hot dogs and put them in buns. Place them back in Air Fryer basket and cook on 400°F for two more minutes. Remove and top with your favorite toppings.

Potato Fish Cakes

Ingredients: Servings: 4 Cooking Time: 15 Mins

2 C. white fish
1 tsp. coriander
1 tsp. Worcestershire sauce
2 tsp. chili powder
1 C. potatoes, mashed
1 tsp. mix herbs
1 tsp. mix spice
1 tsp. milk
1 tsp. butter
1 small onion, diced
1/4 C. breadcrumbs
Pepper
Salt

Directions:
Add all ingredients into the bowl and mix well to combine. Make small patties from mixture and place in the refrigerator for 2 hours. Place the dehydrating tray in a multi-level air fryer basket and place basket in the instant pot. Place patties on dehydrating tray. Seal pot with air fryer lid and select air fry mode then set the temperature to 400 F and timer for 15 minutes. Turn patties halfway through. Serve and enjoy.

Tomato Pepper Frittata

Ingredients: Servings: 2 Cooking Time: 15 Mins

1/4 C. tomato, sliced
1/4 C. pepper, sliced
1 C. egg whites
2 tbsp. milk
Pepper
Salt

Directions:
Add all ingredients into the large bowl and whisk until well combined. Pour bowl mixture into the baking dish. Place steam rack into the instant pot then place baking dish on top of the rack. Seal pot with air fryer lid and select air fry mode and set the temperature to 320 F and timer for 15 minutes. Serve and enjoy.

Bacon and Egg Bread Cups (air Fryer)

Ingredients: Servings: 4 Cooking Time: 8 To 12 Mins

4 (3-by-4-inch) crusty rolls
4 thin slices Gouda or Swiss cheese mini wedges
5 eggs
2 tbsp. heavy cream
3 strips precooked bacon, chopped
½ tsp. dried thyme
Pinch salt
Freshly ground black pepper, to taste

Directions:
Preheat the air fryer to 330°F (166°C). On a clean work surface, cut the tops off the rolls. Using your fingers, remove the insides of the rolls to make bread cups, leaving a ½-inch shell. Place a slice of cheese onto each roll bottom. Whisk together the eggs and heavy cream in a medium bowl until well combined. Fold in the bacon, thyme, salt, and pepper and stir well. Scrape the egg mixture into the prepared bread cups. Transfer the bread C. to the basket and bake for 8 to 12 minutes, or until the eggs are cooked to your preference. Serve warm.

Spinach Frittata

Ingredients: Servings: 4 Cooking Time: 15 Mins

6 eggs
1/4 C. bacon, cooked
1 tsp. Italian seasoning

and chopped
1 tomato, chopped
1/4 tsp. garlic powder
3/4 C. fresh spinach
1 tbsp. heavy cream
1/4 tsp. pepper
1/4 tsp. salt

Directions:
In a bowl, whisk eggs with spices and heavy cream. Spray a 7-inch baking dish with cooking spray. Add bacon, tomato, and spinach to the prepared dish. Pour egg mixture over the bacon mixture. Cover dish with foil. Pour 1 1/2 C. of water into the inner pot of instant pot then place steamer rack in the pot. Place baking dish on top of the steamer rack. Seal the pot with pressure cooking lid and cook on high for 15 minutes. Once done, release pressure using a quick release. Remove lid. Serve and enjoy.

Speedy Pork Roast Sandwich with Slaw

Ingredients: Servings: 8 Cooking Time: 15 Mins

2 lb Chuck Roast
¼ C. Sugar
1 tsp. Spanish Paprika
1 tsp. Garlic Powder
1 White Onion, sliced
2 C. Beef Broth
Salt to taste
2 tbsp. Apple Cider Vinegar
Assembling:
4 Buns, halved
1 C. White Cheddar Cheese, grated
4 tbsp. Mayonnaise
1 C. Red Cabbage, shredded
1 C. White Cabbage, shredded

Directions:
Place the pork roast on a clean flat surface and sprinkle with paprika, garlic powder, sugar, and salt. Use your hands to rub the seasoning on the meat. Open the cooker, add beef broth, onions, pork, and apple cider vinegar. Close the lid, secure the pressure valve, and select Pressure mode on High pressure for 12 minutes. Press Start. Once the timer has ended, do a quick pressure release. Remove the roast to a cutting board, and use two forks to shred them. Return to the pot, close the crisping lid, and cook for 3 minutes on Air Fry at 300 F. In the buns, spread the mayo, add the shredded pork, some cooked onions from the pot, and shredded red and white cabbage. Top with the cheese.

Healthy Kale Muffins

Ingredients: Servings: 8 Cooking Time: 30 Mins

6 large eggs
1/2 C. almond milk
1/4 C. chives, chopped
1 C. kale, chopped
Pepper
Salt

Directions:
Add all ingredients into the bowl and whisk well. Pour egg mixture into the 8 silicone muffin molds. Place the dehydrating tray in a multi-level air fryer basket and place basket in the instant pot. Place 6 muffin molds on dehydrating tray. Seal pot with air fryer lid and select bake mode then set the temperature to 350 F and timer for 30 minutes. Bake remaining muffins using the same method. Serve and enjoy.

Creamy Chicken

Ingredients: Servings: 4 Cooking Time: 4 Hours

1 lb chicken breasts, skinless and boneless
1 tbsp. garlic, minced
2 tbsp. olive oil
1 tsp. chicken bouillon
1/2 C. water
1/2 C. ricotta cheese
4 oz cream cheese
1/2 tsp. ground pepper
1 tsp. oregano, dried
1 tsp. thyme, dried
1 tsp. rosemary, dried

Directions:
Place chicken into the inner pot of instant pot. Top with cream cheese and ricotta cheese. Pour water, oregano, thyme, basil, thyme, rosemary, garlic, oil, bouillon, and pepper over the chicken. Seal the pot with pressure cooking lid and select slow cook mode and cook on high for 4 hours. Serve and enjoy.

Pumpkin Cranberry Oatmeal

Ingredients: Servings: 4 Cooking Time: 3 Mins

1 C. steel-cut oats
2 tbsp. honey
1/2 C. dried cranberries
3/4 C. pumpkin puree
1 C. milk
2 C. of water
1 1/2 tsp. pumpkin pie spice
Pinch of salt

Directions:
Add oats, cranberries, pumpkin puree, milk, water, pumpkin pie spice, and salt and stir well. Seal pot with lid and cook on manual high pressure for 3 minutes. Once done then release pressure using the quick-release method than open the lid. Add honey and stir well. Serve and enjoy.

Spinach and Cheese Omelette

Ingredients: Servings: 2 Cooking Time: 8 Mins

Shredded cheese – ½ cup
Chopped fresh spinach – 2 tbsps.
Eggs – 3
Salt and pepper to taste

Directions:
Whisk the eggs and with salt and pepper and place in a flat dish. Add the cheese and spinach. Do not stir. Cook at 390F for 8 minutes in the air fryer. Check the consistency of the omelette. Cook for another 2 minutes if a browner omelette is desired. Enjoy.

Maple Walnut Pancake (air Fryer)

Ingredients: Servings: 4 Cooking Time: 20 Mins

3 tbsp. melted butter, divided
1 C. flour
2 tbsp. sugar
1½ tsp. baking powder
¼ tsp. salt
1 egg, beaten
¾ C. milk
1 tsp. pure vanilla extract
½ C. roughly chopped walnuts
Maple syrup or fresh sliced fruit, for serving

Directions:

Preheat the air fryer to 330°F (166°C). Grease a baking pan with 1 tbsp. of melted butter. Mix together the flour, sugar, baking powder, and salt in a medium bowl. Add the beaten egg, milk, the remaining 2 tbsp. of melted butter, and vanilla and stir until the batter is sticky but slightly lumpy. Slowly pour the batter into the greased baking pan and scatter with the walnuts. Place the pan in the air fryer basket and bake for 20 minutes until golden brown and cooked through. Let the pancake rest for 5 minutes and serve topped with the maple syrup or fresh fruit, if desired.

Creamy Cauliflower Mashed

Ingredients: Servings: 4 Cooking Time: 15 Mins

1 medium cauliflower head, cut into florets
2 tbsp. heavy cream
1/4 tsp. garlic powder
1/4 tsp. onion powder
4 tbsp. butter
1 1/2 tbsp. ranch seasoning
1 C. of water

Directions:
Pour water into the instant pot. Add cauliflower florets into the steamer basket and place basket in the pot. Seal the pot with pressure cooking lid and cook on high for 15 minutes. Once done, release pressure using a quick release. Remove lid. Transfer cauliflower florets into the mixing bowl. Add remaining ingredients and mash cauliflower mixture until smooth. Serve and enjoy.

Easy Cheese Bake

Ingredients: Servings: 3 Cooking Time: 25 Mins

6 eggs
1/4 tsp. dry mustard
1/4 lb cheddar cheese, grated
2 tbsp. butter, melted
1/2 C. milk
Pepper
Salt

Directions:
Spray a baking dish with cooking spray and set aside. In a bowl, whisk eggs with milk, mustard, pepper, and salt. Stir in grated cheese. Pour egg mixture into the prepared baking dish. Place steam rack into the instant pot then place baking dish on top of the rack. Seal pot with air fryer lid and select bake mode then set the temperature to 350 F and timer for 25 minutes. Serve and enjoy.

Coconut Lime Breakfast Quinoa

Ingredients: Servings: 5 Cooking Time: 1 Min

1 C. quinoa, rinsed
1/2 tsp. coconut extract
1 lime juice
1 lime zest
2 C. of coconut milk
1 C. of water

Directions:
Add all ingredients into the instant pot and stir well. Seal pot with lid and cook on manual high pressure for 1 minute. Once done then allow to release pressure naturally for 10 minutes then release using the quick-release method. Open the lid. Stir well and serve.

Almond Coconut Risotto

Ingredients: Servings: 4 Cooking Time: 5 Mins

1 C. arborio rice
3 tbsp. almonds, sliced and toas ted
2 tbsp. shredded coconut
1 C. of coconut milk
2 C. almond milk
1/2 tsp. vanilla
1/3 C. coconut sugar

Directions:
Add coconut and almond milk in instant pot and set the pot on sauté mode. Once the milk begins to boil then add rice and stir well. Seal pot with lid and cook on manual high pressure for 5 minutes. Once done then allow to release pressure naturally then open the lid. Add remaining ingredients and stir well. Serve and enjoy.

Shrimp Croquettes

Ingredients: Servings: 4 Cooking Time: 8 Mins

Shrimp – 2/3 pound, cooked, peeled, deveined and chopped
Bread crumbs – 1 ½ cups
Lemon juice – 2 tbsps.
Egg – 1, whisked
Green onions – 3, chopped
Basil – ½ tsp. dried
Salt and black pepper to taste
Olive oil – 2 tbsps.

Directions:
Mix half of the bread crumbs with lemon juice, and egg in a bowl and stir well. Add shrimp, salt, pepper, basil, and green onions. Stir well. In another bowl, mix the rest of the bread crumbs with the oil and toss well. Shape round balls out of the shrimp mix, dredge them in bread crumbs. Place them in the preheated air fryer and cook for 8 minutes, at 400F. Serve.

Morning Churros

Ingredients: Servings: 4 Cooking Time: 5 Mins

1/4 C. butter
1/2 C. milk
1 pinch salt
1/2 C. all-purpose flour
2 eggs
1/4 C. white sugar
1/2 tsp. ground cinnamon

Directions:
Melt butter in a 1-quart saucepan and add salt and milk. Stir cook the butter mixture to a boil then stir in flour. Mix it quickly. Remove the butter-flour mixture from the heat and allow the flour mixture to cool down. Stir in egg and mix to get choux pastry and transfer the dough to a pastry bag. Put a star tip on the pastry bag and pine the dough into straight strips in the Air Fryer Basket. Set the Air Fryer Basket in the Instant Pot Duo. Put on the Air Fryer lid and seal it. Hit the "Air fry Button" and select 5 minutes of cooking time, then press "Start." Once the Instant Pot Duo beeps, remove its lid. Mix sugar with cinnamon in a mini bowl and drizzle over the churros. Serve.

Smoky-sweet Air Fryer Chickpeas

Ingredients: Servings: 4 Cooking Time: 16 Mins

1 (15 ounces) can chickpeas
1 tbsp. maple syrup
2 tsp. smoked paprika
2 tbsp. aquafaba from chickpeas
1 1/2 tsp. garlic powder
1/2 tsp. sea salt

Directions:

Drain the chickpeas while reserving aquafaba obtained. Don't rinse chickpeas. Add chickpeas to the Instant Pot Duo Crisp Air Fryer basket, shake to a single layer, place inside the Air Fryer. Choose the Air Fry function and close the lid. Air Fry at 390°F for at least 8 minutes. While the chickpeas cook, whisk together 2 tbsp. aquafaba, maple syrup, smoked paprika, garlic powder, and salt in a mixing bowl (Save the remaining aquafaba for further use.) Add chickpeas fresh from the Instant Pot Duo Crisp Air Fryer and stir to coat them completely. Return the flavored chickpeas to the air fryer basket and using a spatula to get every last bit of the sauce. Return chickpeas to the Instant Pot Duo Crisp Air Fryer. Air Fry at 390°F for 5 more minutes. Shake the basket, return to the Fryer for another 3-5 minutes, until chickpeas are crisp. Transfer to a serving bowl. Serve warm or at room temperature.

Breakfast Muffins

Ingredients: Servings: 6 Cooking Time: 25 Mins

4 large eggs
2 tbsp. butter
4 oz cream cheese
1 scoop whey protein

Directions:

In a bowl, melt cream cheese and butter. Add eggs and whey protein in a bowl and beat until well combined. Pour batter into the 6 silicone muffin molds. Place the dehydrating tray in a multi-level air fryer basket and place basket in the instant pot. Place muffin molds on dehydrating tray. Seal pot with air fryer lid and select air fry mode then set the temperature to 350 F and timer for 25 minutes. Serve and enjoy.

Stuffed Poblanos

Ingredients: Servings: 4 Cooking Time: 15 Mins

½ lb. Spicy ground pork breakfast sausage
4 large poblano peppers
4 large eggs.
½ C. full-fat sour cream.
4 oz. Full-fat cream cheese; softened.
¼ C. canned diced tomatoes and green chiles, drained
8 tbsp. Shredded pepper jack cheese

Directions:

In a medium skillet over medium heat, crumble and brown the ground sausage until no pink remains. Remove sausage and drain the fat from the pan. Crack eggs into the pan, scramble and cook until no longer runny Place cooked sausage in a large bowl and fold in cream cheese. Mix in diced tomatoes and chiles. Gently fold in eggs Cut a 4"–5" slit in the top of each poblano, removing the seeds and white membrane with a small knife. Separate the filling into four serving and spoon carefully into each pepper. Top each with 2 tbsp. Pepper jack cheese Place each pepper into the air fryer basket. Adjust the temperature to 350 degrees f and set the timer for 15 minutes. Peppers will be soft and cheese will be browned when ready. Serve immediately with sour cream on top.

Breakfast Soufflé

Ingredients: Servings: 4 Cooking Time: 8 Mins

Heavy cream – 4 tbsps.
Red chili pepper – 1 pinch crushed
Parsley – 2 tbsps. chopped
Eggs – 4, whisked
Chives – 2 tbsps. chopped
Salt and black pepper to taste

Directions:

In a bowl, mix eggs with chives, parsley, red chili pepper, heavy cream, salt, and pepper. Mix well and divide into 4 soufflé dishes. Arrange dishes in the air fryer and cook at 350F for 8 minutes. Serve hot.

Western Omelet (pressure Cook)

Ingredients: Servings: 2 Cooking Time: 20 Mins

2 tbsp. avocado oil
¼ C. red bell pepper, finely chopped
¼ C. green bell pepper, finely chopped
½ C. shredded full-fat Cheddar cheese
2 slices no-sugar-added bacon, cooked and finely cut (optional)
¼ C. onion, chopped
6 eggs
½ tsp. dried parsley
½ tsp. dried basil
½ tsp. kosher salt
½ tsp. crushed red pepper
½ tsp. freshly ground black pepper
Cooking spray
1 C. filtered water

Directions:

Press the Sauté button on your Instant Pot. Add and heat the oil. Add the bell pepper and onion and sauté for 4 minutes. Mix together the eggs, cheese, bacon (if desired), parsley, basil, salt, and pepper in a medium bowl and stir well. Spray a glass dish with cooking spray and pour in the mixture. Fold in the sautéed bell pepper and onion, scraping the bits from the pot, and mix well. Add 1 C. of filtered water to the inner pot of the Instant Pot and then place the trivet in the bottom of the pot. Carefully lower the dish into the Instant Pot with a sling. Secure the lid. Press the Pressure Cook on the Instant Pot and set the cooking time for 20 minutes at High Pressure. When the timer beeps, use a natural pressure release for about 10 minutes and then release any remaining pressure. Carefully open the lid. Remove the dish and serve.

Hot Dogs

Ingredients: Servings: 6 Cooking Time: 8 Mins

Hot dogs – 6
Hot dog buns - 6

Directions:

Place the hot dogs in the air fryer basket and close the lid. Cook at 400F for 4 to 6 minutes. Then remove and put them in the buns. Cook again for 2 minutes at 400F. Serve.

Hard-boiled Eggs

Ingredients: Servings: 3 Cooking Time: 15 Mins

6 eggs

Directions:

Preheat the air fryer at 390F. Then place the eggs in the air fryer basket and close. Air fry for 15 minutes at 300F. Then remove the eggs and place them in icy water. Serve.

Hash Browns with Pancetta

Ingredients: Servings: 3 Cooking Time: 30 Mins

5 slices pancetta, chopped
1 white onion, diced
2 potatoes, peeled and grated
1 tsp. sweet paprika
1 tsp. pink salt
1 tsp. ground black pepper
1 tsp. garlic powder
3 eggs

Directions:

Choose Sear/Sauté and set to High to preheat your cooker. Place in the pancetta and cook for 5 minutes, or until crispy. Stir in the onion, potatoes, eggs, the sweet paprika, pink salt, black pepper, and garlic powder. Press the hash brown mixture. Close the crisping lid, choose Bake and cook for 25 minutes at 350 F. Once the timer goes off, ensure the hash brown is perfectly golden brown on top. Serve immediately.

Air Fried Kale Crisps

Ingredients: Servings: 2-4 Cooking Time: 10 Mins

1 bunch Tuscan kale, stems and ribs removed, leaves cut into 2-inch (5-cm) pieces
2 Tbsp. olive oil
1/2 tsp. kosher salt, plus more, to taste
1/4 tsp. freshly ground pepper

Directions:

Preheat Instant Pot Duo Crisp Air Fryer to 390°F. In a large bowl, toss together kale, olive oil, 1/2 tsp. salt, and pepper. In batches, place the kale in the air fry basket and insert it into the Instant Pot Duo Crisp Air Fryer. Cook until the kale gets crisp, about 5 minutes. Transfer the chips to a bowl and season with salt. Serve warm or at room temperature.

Baked Cod Fillet

Ingredients: Servings: 4 Cooking Time: 20 Mins

1 lbs cod fillet
1 tsp. Italian seasoning
1/4 C. olives, sliced
1 tbsp. olive oil
1 C. cherry tomatoes, halved
Pepper
Salt

Directions:

Line instant pot multi-level air fryer basket with foil. Coat fish fillet with oil and season with Italian seasoning, pepper, and salt. Place fish fillet into the air fryer basket and place basket into the instant pot. Add cherry tomatoes and olives on top fo fish fillet. Seal pot with air fryer lid and select air fry mode then set the temperature to 400 F and timer for 20 minutes. Serve and enjoy.

Zucchini Fritters

Ingredients: Servings: 4 Cooking Time: 12 Mins

2 eggs; whisked
8 oz. Zucchinis; chopped.
2 spring onions; chopped.
¼ tsp. Sweet paprika; chopped.
Cooking spray
Salt and black pepper to taste.

Directions:

Take a bowl and mix all the ingredients except the cooking spray, stir well and shape medium fritters out of this mix Put the basket in the air fryer, add the fritters inside, grease them with cooking spray and cook at 400°f for 8 minutes. Divide the fritters between plates and serve for breakfast.

Bell Pepper & Salmon Cakes

Ingredients: Servings: 4 Cooking Time: 30 Mins

2 (5 oz) packs Steamed Salmon Flakes
1 Red Onion, chopped
Salt and Black Pepper to taste
1 tsp. Garlic Powder
2 tbsp. Olive Oil
1 Red Bell Pepper, seeded and chopped
4 tbsp. Butter, divided
3 Eggs, cracked into a bowl
1 C. Breadcrumbs
4 tbsp. Mayonnaise
2 tsp. Worcestershire Sauce
¼ C. chopped Parsley

Directions:

Turn on the cooker and select Sear/Sauté on High pressure. Heat oil and add half of the butter. Once it has melted, add the onions and the chopped red bell peppers. Cook for 6 minutes while stirring occasionally. Press Start. In a mixing bowl, add salmon flakes, sautéed red bell pepper and onion, breadcrumbs, eggs, mayonnaise, Worcestershire sauce, garlic powder, salt, pepper, and parsley. Use a spoon to mix well while breaking the salmon into the tiny pieces. Use your hands to mold 4 patties out of the mixture. Add the remaining butter to melt, and when melted, add the patties. Fry for 4 minutes, flipping once. Close the crisping lid, select Bake mode and bake for 4 minutes on 320 F. Remove them onto a wire rack to rest. Serve.

Cherry Risotto

Ingredients: Servings: 4 Cooking Time: 10 Mins

1 1/2 C. arborio rice
1/2 C. dried cherries
3 C. of milk
1 C. apple juice
1/3 C. brown sugar
1 1/2 tsp. cinnamon
2 apples, cored and diced
2 tbsp. butter
1/4 tsp. salt

Directions:

Add butter into the instant pot and set the pot on sauté mode. Add rice and cook for 3-4 minutes. Add brown sugar, spices, apples, milk, and apple juice and stir well. Seal pot with lid and cook on manual high pressure for 6 minutes. Once done then release pressure using the quick-release method than open the lid. Stir in dried cherries and serve.

Air-fried Shrimps with Lemon

Ingredients: Servings: 2-4 Cooking Time: 15 Mins

¼ tsp. garlic powder
A dash of vegetable oil or cooking spray, for coating
A pinch of parsley or chili flakes, optional
1 lb. raw shrimps, peeled and deveined
Black pepper and salt to taste
2 lemon wedges, juiced

Directions:

In a bowl, combine shrimps with oil and add salt, pepper and garlic. Toss thoroughly to mix well. Place shrimps in the air fryer basket and insert the basket inside the instant pot. Attach the air fryer lid and set to air-fry at 400 degrees F for 10-14 minutes. Gently shake the air fryer basket to flip halfway through cooking. Once done, transfer the shrimp dish to a bowl and drizzle lemon juice over it. Sprinkle parsley or chili flakes on top and serve hot.

Perfect Bacon & Croissant Breakfast

Ingredients: Servings: 2 Cooking Time: 10 Mins

4 pieces thick-cut bacon
2 croissants, sliced
2 eggs
1 tbsp. butter
For the bacon barbecue sauce:
2 tbsps. apple cider vinegar
½ C. ketchup
1 tbsp. brown sugar
1 tbsp. molasses
½ tbsp. Worcestershire sauce
¼ tsp. onion powder
¼ tsp. mustard powder
¼ tsp. liquid smoke

Directions:
Preheat your air fryer to 390 degrees F. Meanwhile, incorporate all the barbecue sauce ingredients in a small saucepan. Place the pan over medium heat and bring it to a simmer until the sauce thickens slightly. Place the bacon cuts flat on a tray and brush them with barbecue sauce on one side. Transfer to the air fryer basket with the brushed-side up. Cook for about 4-5 minutes then flip the bacon. Brush the other side with bacon sauce and cook for another 5 minutes (or until your desired doneness is achieved). In a medium-size frying pan, melt the butter and fry the eggs according to your preference. Once done, place the eggs at the bottom of each croissant. Top them with two bacon slices each and close with the croissant on top. Serve with your favorite breakfast beverage.

Dutch Pancake

Ingredients: Servings: 4 Cooking Time: 15 Mins

Unsalted butter – 2 tbsps.
Eggs – 3
Flour – ½ cup
Milk – ½ cup
Vanilla – ½ tsp.
Sliced fresh strawberries – 1 ½ cups
Powdered sugar – 2 tbsps.

Directions:
Preheat the air fryer with a pan in the basket at 330F. Add the butter and melt. Meanwhile, beat the eggs, milk, flour, and vanilla in a bowl until frothy. Remove from the air fryer. Pour in the batter and tilt, so the butter covers the bottom of the pan and put back in the fryer. Bake at 330F until the pancake is puffed and golden brown, about 12 to 16 minutes. Remove and top with strawberries and powdered sugar. Serve.

Tuna and Zucchini Tortillas

Ingredients: Servings: 4 Cooking Time: 10 Mins

Butter – 4 tbsps. soft
Canned tuna – 6 ounces, drained
Zucchini – 1 cup, shredded
Corn tortillas – 4
Mayonnaise – 1/3 cup
Mustard – 2 tbsps.
Cheddar cheese – 1 cup, grated

Directions:
Spread butter on tortillas. Put them in the air fryer basket and cook them at 400F for 3 minutes. Meanwhile, in a bowl, mix tuna with mustard, mayo, and zucchini and stir. Split this mixture on each tortilla, top with cheese and roll tortillas. Cook at 400F for 4 minutes more. Serve.

Creamy Spinach Spread

Ingredients: Servings: 4 Cooking Time: 30 Mins

3 C. spinach leaves
2 tbsp. Bacon, cooked and crumbled
2 tbsp. Coconut cream
2 tbsp. Cilantro
Salt and black pepper to taste.

Directions:
In a pan that fits the air fryer, combine all the ingredients except the bacon, put the pan in the machine and cook at 360°f for 10 minutes Transfer to a blender, pulse well, divide into bowls and serve with bacon sprinkled on top.

Tomato Mozzarella Quiche

Ingredients: Servings: 6 Cooking Time: 30 Mins

8 eggs
1 red pepper, chopped
1/2 C. almond flour
1/2 C. almond milk
1 1/2 C. mozzarella cheese, shredded
2 tbsp. green onions, chopped
1 C. tomatoes, chopped
1/4 tsp. pepper
1/4 tsp. salt

Directions:
Pour 1 1/2 C. of water to the instant pot then place steamer rack in the pot. In a large bowl, whisk eggs, almond flour, milk, pepper, and salt. Add vegetables and cheese and stir to combine. Pour egg mixture into the baking dish. Cover dish with foil and place on top of the steamer rack. Seal the pot with pressure cooking lid and cook on high for 30 minutes. Once done, allow to release pressure naturally for 10 minutes then release remaining pressure using a quick release. Remove lid. Serve and enjoy.

Tuna and Spring Onions Salad

Ingredients: Servings: 4 Cooking Time: 15 Mins

14 oz. Canned tuna, drained and flaked
2 spring onions; chopped.
1 C. arugula
1 tbsp. Olive oil
A pinch of salt and black pepper

Directions:
In a bowl, all the ingredients except the oil and the arugula and whisk. Preheat the air fryer over 360°f, add the oil and grease it. Pour the tuna mix, stir well and cook for 15 minutes In a salad bowl, combine the arugula with the tuna mix, toss and serve.

Kale Crips

Ingredients: Servings: 2 Cooking Time: 10 Mins

Kale – 1 bunch, stems and ribs removed; leaves chopped
Olive oil – 2 tbsps.
Salt and pepper to taste

Directions:
Preheat the air fryer to 390F. In a bowl, mix kale, olive oil, salt and pepper. Bake the kale mix in the air fryer in batches, about 5 minutes each time. Serve.

Mixed Berry Muffins

Ingredients: Servings: 8 Cooking Time: 15 Mins

Flour – 1 1/3 cups, plus 1 tbsp.
Baking powder – 2 tsps.
White sugar – ¼ cup
Brown sugar – 2 tbsps.
Eggs – 2
Whole milk – 2/3 cup
Safflower oil – 1/3 cup
Mixed fresh berries – 1 cup

Directions:
Combine the 1 1/3 C. flour, brown sugar, white sugar, and baking powder in a bowl and mix well. Combine the milk, eggs, and oil in another bowl and beat until mixed. Stir the egg mix into the dry ingredients. Mix until just combined. In another bowl, toss the mixed berries with the remaining 1 tbsp. flour until coated. Stir gently into the batter. Fold 16 foil muffin C. to make 8 cups. Put 4 C. into the basket and fill ¾ full with the batter. Bake at 320F until cooked, about 12 to 17 minutes. Repeat with the remaining batter and muffin cups. Cool and serve.

Brazilian Mini Turkey Pies

Ingredients: Servings: 8 Cooking Time: 10 Mins

8 Slices Filo Pastry
1.76oz Shredded Turkey
1 Small Egg beated
1.6oz ml Coconut Milk
1.6oz Whole Milk
7 oz Homemade Tomato Sauce
1 oz Turkey Stock
1 Tsp Oregano
1 Tbsp Coriander
Salt & Pepper

Directions:
Place your wet ingredients into a mixing bowl apart from the egg and mix well. You will now have a pale looking sauce that will be the stock for your pie. Add the turkey and seasoning and mix again. Put to one side. Line your little pie cases with a little flour to stop them sticking and then line with the filo pastry. Aim for one sheet of filo for each pie you are doing and have it centered so that you can then fold over the spare pastry for the top of the pie. Add the mixture to each mini pie pot so that they are ¾ full. Cover the top with the remaining pastry and then brush the egg along the top. Place them into the Instant Pot Duo Crisp Air Fryer Basket. Close the Air Fryer lid and cook for ten minutes at 350°F.

Creamy Mac N Cheese

Ingredients: Servings: 8 Cooking Time: 5 Mins

15 oz elbow macaroni
1 C. milk
1/2 C. parmesan cheese, shredded
1 C. mozzarella cheese, shredded
2 C. cheddar cheese, shredded
1 tsp. garlic powder
1 tsp. hot pepper sauce
2 tbsp. butter
4 C. vegetable broth
1/4 tsp. pepper
1/2 tsp. salt

Directions:
Add macaroni, garlic powder, hot sauce, butter, broth, pepper, and salt into the instant pot and stir well. Seal pot with lid and cook on manual high pressure for 5 minutes. Once done then release pressure using the quick-release method than open the lid. Add cheese and milk and stir until cheese is melted. Serve and enjoy.

Egg Bites with Cheese (pressure Cook)

Ingredients: Servings: 2 To 4 Cooking Time: 10 Mins

1 C. filtered water
½ C. shredded full-fat Cheddar cheese
½ C. bell peppers, finely chopped
½ C. spinach, finely chopped
6 eggs
½ tsp. dried cilantro
½ tsp. kosher salt
½ tsp. freshly ground black pepper
Cooking spray

Directions:
Place the trivet in the bottom of your Instant Pot and add the water. Mix together the eggs, cheese, bell peppers, spinach, cilantro, salt, and pepper in a large bowl. Stir well. Spritz a silicone egg mold with cooking spray and ladle the mixture into the impressions in the mold. Put the mold on the trivet with a sling and wrap loosely in aluminum foil. Secure the lid and select Press the Pressure Cook on the Instant Pot and set the cooking time for 10 minutes at High Pressure. When the timer beeps, use a quick pressure release. Carefully open the lid. Remove the egg mold from the pot. Remove the foil and allow to cool for 5 minutes. Scoop the egg bites out of the mold with a spoon and transfer to a serving dish. Serve.

Yogurt Omelet

Ingredients: Servings: 4 Cooking Time: 12 Mins

1 ½ C. greek yogurt
1 tbsp. Cilantro; chopped.
1 tbsp. Chives; chopped.
4 eggs; whisked
Cooking spray
Salt and black pepper to taste.

Directions:
Take a bowl and mix all the ingredients except the cooking spray and whisk well. Now, take a pan that fits in your air fryer and grease it with the cooking spray, pour the eggs mix, spread well, put the pan into the machine and cook the omelet at 360°f for 20 minutes. Divide between plates and serve for breakfast

Glazed Strawberry Toast (air Fryer)

Ingredients: Servings: 4 Cooking Time: 8 Mins

4 slices bread,
1 C. sliced

½-inch thick
1 tsp. sugar
strawberries
Cooking spray

Directions:
Preheat the air fryer to 375°F (191°C). On a clean work surface, lay the bread slices and spritz one side of each slice of bread with cooking spray. Place the bread slices in the air fryer basket, sprayed side down. Top with the strawberries and a sprinkle of sugar. Air fry for 8 minutes until the toast is well browned on each side. Remove from the air fryer basket to a plate and serve.

Cheesy Chicken and Spinach Breakfast (pressure Cook)

Ingredients: Servings: 4 Cooking Time: 10 Mins

2 tbsp. coconut oil
1 lb. (454 g) ground chicken
1 C. shredded full-fat Cheddar cheese
2 tbsp. sugar-free or low-sugar salsa
½ C. chopped spinach
1 tsp. curry powder
½ tsp. dried basil
½ tsp. dried parsley
½ tsp. dried cilantro
1 tbsp. hot sauce
½ tsp. kosher salt
½ tsp. freshly ground black pepper
1 C. filtered water

Directions:
Press the Sauté button on the Instant Pot and heat the coconut oil. Fold in the ground chicken, cheese, salsa, spinach, curry powder, basil, parsley, cilantro, hot sauce, salt, and pepper and stir thoroughly. Pour in the water. Secure the lid. Select the Pressure Cook and set the cooking time for 10 minutes at High Pressure. Once cooking is complete, do a quick pressure release. Carefully open the lid. Serve warm.

Simple & Easy Mac and Cheese

Ingredients: Servings: 6 Cooking Time: 25 Mins

2½ C. macaroni
2⅔ C. sharp cheddar or pepper jack, shredded
1 C. bread crumbs
2 C. chicken stock
1¼ C. heavy cream
⅓ C. Parmesan cheese, shredded
8 tbsps. butter, melted and divided
¼ tsp. garlic powder
Salt and pepper to taste

Directions:
Place the metal inner pot in your instant pot and add the chicken broth. Also add the heavy cream, 4 tbsp. of butter and macaroni. Pressure cook on HIGH for about 20 minutes or until al dente. Combine the bread crumbs with the remaining butter in a mixing bowl. Quick-release the pressure and stir in 2 C. of sharp cheddar (or pepper jack), salt, pepper and garlic powder. Top with the remaining ⅔ C. of sharp cheddar (or pepper jack), ⅓ C. of Parmesan cheese, and breadcrumb mixture. Air fry at 400 degrees F for about 5 minutes or until browned. Transfer into serving plates and enjoy!

Baked Eggs

Ingredients: Servings: 4 Cooking Time: 20 Mins

Eggs – 4
Baby spinach – 1 pound, torn
Ham – 7 ounces, chopped
Milk – 4 tbsps.
Olive oil – 1 tbsp.
Cooking spray
Salt and black pepper to taste

Directions:
Heat oil in a pan over medium heat. Add baby spinach and stir-fry for 2 minutes and remove from heat. Use cooking spray to grease 4 ramekins and divide ham and baby spinach in each. Crack an egg in each ramekin. Also divide milk, and season with salt and pepper. Place ramekins in the preheated air fryer at 350F and bake for 20 minutes. Serve.

Spicy Cabbage

Ingredients: Servings: 6 Cooking Time: 5 Mins

1 cabbage head, chopped
2 tbsp. olive oil
1 tsp. chili powder
3 tbsp. soy sauce
1/2 onion, diced
1 tsp. paprika
1/2 tsp. garlic salt
1 C. vegetable stock
1/2 tsp. salt

Directions:
Add oil into the inner pot of instant pot duo crisp and set pot on sauté mode. Add cabbage and sauté for 1-2 minutes. Add remaining ingredients and stir everything well. Seal the pot with pressure cooking lid and cook on high for 3 minutes. Once done, release pressure using a quick release. Remove lid. Stir and serve.

Sausage Patties

Ingredients: Servings: 4 Cooking Time: 10 Mins

Sausage patties – 1 (12-ounce) packet
Non-stick cooking spray

Directions:
Grease the air fryer basket and place in the patties. Do not overcrowd the basket. Spray some cooking oil on top of the patties. Cover and cook at 400F for 5 minutes. Serve.

Turkey Fajitas Platter

Ingredients: Servings: 3 Cooking Time: 20 Mins

Tortilla wraps – 6
Leftover turkey breast – 3.5 oz.
Avocado – 1, chopped
Bell peppers – 3, chopped
Small red onions – ½
Soft cheese – 5 tbsps.
Cajun spice – 3 tbsps.
Mexican seasoning – 2 tbsps.
Cumin – 1 tsp.
Salt and pepper to taste
Fresh coriander – ½ cup

Directions:
Slice the vegetables and chop the turkey breast into small chunks. Place everything in a bowl and mix. Place in silver foil and them place all of them in the air fryer basket. Close the lid. Cook on Air Fry more at 390F for 20 minutes. Serve.

Air Fryer Cheeseburgers

Ingredients: Servings: 4 Cooking Time: 8 Mins

Ground beef – 1 pound
Soy sauce – 1 tbsp.
Mayonnaise – 4 tbsps.
Red onion – ½ cup,

low-sodium
Garlic – 2 cloves, chopped
American cheese – 4 slices
Hamburger buns – 4 sliced
Salt – ½ tsp.
Ground black pepper – ½ tsp.
Lettuce – 2 ounces

Directions:
Combine soy sauce, garlic, and beef in a bowl. Make 4 patties. Then season with salt and pepper. Place in the air fryer basket and cover. Cook at 380F for 8 minutes on Air Fryer mode. After 4 minutes, open and top it with a cheese sliced and cook. Arrange the burgers and serve.

Mixed Berry Dutch Baby Pancake (air Fryer)

Ingredients: Servings: 4 Cooking Time: 12 To 16 Mins

1 tbsp. unsalted butter, at room temperature
1 egg
2 egg whites
½ C. 2% milk
½ C. whole-wheat pastry flour
1 tsp. pure vanilla extract
1 C. sliced fresh strawberries
½ C. fresh raspberries
½ C. fresh blueberries

Directions:
Preheat the air fryer to 330°F (166°C). Grease a baking pan with the butter. Using a hand mixer, beat together the egg, egg whites, milk, pastry flour, and vanilla in a medium mixing bowl until well incorporated. Pour the batter into the pan and bake in the preheated air fryer for 12 to 16 minutes, or until the pancake puffs up in the center and the edges are golden brown. Allow the pancake to cool for 5 minutes and serve topped with the berries.

Mushroom Frittata

Ingredients: Servings: 2 Cooking Time: 15 Mins

4 eggs
1 1/2 C. water
1/4 tsp. garlic powder
4 oz mushrooms, sliced
1/8 tsp. white pepper
1/8 tsp. onion powder
2 tsp. heavy cream
2 Swiss cheese slices, cut each slice into 4 pieces
1/4 tsp. salt

Directions:
In a bowl, whisk eggs with spices and heavy cream. Spray a 7-inch baking dish with cooking spray. Add sliced mushrooms to the dish then pour egg mixture over the mushrooms. Arrange cheese slices on top of the mushroom and egg mixture. Cover dish with foil. Pour 1 1/2 C. of water to the instant pot then place steamer rack in the pot. Place dish on top of the steamer rack. Seal the pot with pressure cooking lid and cook on high for 15 minutes. Once done, release pressure using a quick release. Remove lid. Serve and enjoy.

Ranchero Brunch Crunch Wraps

Ingredients: Servings: 2 Cooking Time: 15 Mins

2 tofu scramble (or vegan egg)
2 large flour tortillas
2 small corn tortillas
½ C. classic ranchero sauce
½ avocado, peeled and sliced
⅓ C. pinto beans, cooked
2 fresh jalapeños, stemmed and sliced

Directions:
Assemble the large tortillas on a work surface. Arrange the crunch wraps by stacking the following ingredients in order: tofu or egg scramble, jalapeños, ranchero sauce, corn tortillas, avocado, and pinto beans. You can add more ranchero sauce if desired. Fold the large flour tortilla around the fillings until sealed completely. Place one crunch wrap in the air fryer basket and set the basket on top of the trivet. Air-fry each crunch wrap at 350 degrees F (or 180°C) for 6 minutes. Remove from the basket and transfer to a plate. Repeat step 3 and 4 for the other crunch wrap.

Air-fried Crumbed Fish

Ingredients: Servings: 4 Cooking Time: 12 Mins

¼ C. vegetable oil
1 egg, beaten
4 flounder fillets
1 C. dry breadcrumbs
1 lemon, sliced

Directions:
In a mixing bowl, mix oil and breadcrumbs. Stir to combine. Dredge fillets into the egg, shaking off excess liquid. Dip fillets into the breadcrumbs to coat evenly on all sides. Lay coated fillets on the air fryer basket and place inside the instant pot. Attach the air fryer lid and cook at 350 degrees F for about 12 minutes. Flip halfway through cooking. Garnish with lemon slices and serve.

Pumpkin Oatmeal (pressure Cook)

Ingredients: Servings: 6 Cooking Time: 10 Mins

3 C. water
1½ C. 2% milk
1¼ C. steel-cut oats
3 tbsp. brown sugar
1½ tsp. pumpkin pie spice
1 tsp. ground cinnamon
¾ tsp. salt

Directions:
1 (15-ounce / 425-g) can solid-pack pumpkin Place all the ingredients except the pumpkin into the Instant Pot and stir to incorporate. Secure the lid. Select the Pressure Cook and set the cooking time for 10 minutes at High Pressure. Once cooking is complete, do a natural pressure release for 10 minutes, then release any remaining pressure. Carefully open the lid. Add the pumpkin and stir well. Allow the oatmeal to sit for 5 to 10 minutes to thicken. Serve immediately.

Homemade Giant Pancake

Ingredients: Servings: 6 Cooking Time: 15 Mins

3 C. All-purpose Flour
¾ C. Sugar
5 Eggs
⅓ C. Olive Oil
⅓ C. Sparkling Water
⅓ tsp. Salt
1 ½ tsp. Baking Soda
2 tbsp. Maple Syrup
A dollop of Whipped Cream to serve

Directions:
Start by pouring the flour, sugar, eggs, olive oil, sparkling water, salt, and baking soda into a food processor and blend until smooth. Pour the batter into the cooker and let it sit in there

for 15 minutes. Close the lid and secure the pressure valve. Select the Pressure mode on Low pressure for 10 minutes. Press Start. Once the timer goes off, press Cancel, quick-release the pressure valve to let out any steam and open the lid. Gently run a spatula around the pancake to let loose any sticking. Once ready, slide the pancake onto a serving plate and drizzle with maple syrup. Top with the whipped cream to serve.

Ham and Cheese Toast (air Fryer)

Ingredients: Servings: 1 Cooking Time: 6 Mins

1 tsp. butter, at room temperature
Salt and freshly ground black pepper, to taste
1 slice bread
1 egg
2 tsp. diced ham
1 tbsp. grated Cheddar cheese

Directions:
Preheat the air fryer to 325°F (163°C). On a clean work surface, use a 2½-inch biscuit cutter to make a hole in the center of the bread slice with about ½-inch of bread remaining. Spread the butter on both sides of the bread slice. Crack the egg into the hole and season with salt and pepper to taste. Transfer the bread to the air fryer basket. Air fry for 5 minutes. Scatter the cheese and diced ham on top and continue to cook for an additional 1 minute until the egg is set and the cheese has melted. Remove the toast from the basket to a plate and let cool for 5 minutes before serving.

Ham Egg Muffins

Ingredients: Servings: 6 Cooking Time: 25 Mins

6 eggs
6 tbsp. cheddar cheese, shredded
1/4 tsp. garlic powder
1/2 C. milk
1 green onion, sliced
4 oz ham, cubed
Pepper
Salt

Directions:
In a large bowl, whisk eggs with milk, garlic powder, pepper, and salt. Add green onion, ham, and cheese and stir well. Place the dehydrating tray in a multi-level air fryer basket and place basket in the instant pot. Place muffin molds on dehydrating tray. Seal pot with air fryer lid and select bake mode then set the temperature to 350 F and timer for 25 minutes. Serve and enjoy.

Egg Frittata

Ingredients: Servings: 2 Cooking Time: 15 Mins

4 eggs
½ C. milk
2 green onions chopped
¼ C. baby Bella mushrooms chopped
¼ C. spinach chopped
¼ C. red bell pepper chopped
¼ C. cheddar cheese
½ tsp. salt
½ tsp. black pepper
Dash of hot sauce

Directions:
Grease a 6x3 inch round or square pan with butter and set it aside. Whisk the eggs and milk in a large bowl until they are thoroughly blended. Stir in green onions, mushrooms, salt, black pepper, spinach, red bell pepper, cheddar cheese, and hot sauce. Pour the egg mixture into a greased pan. Place in the Instant Pot Duo Crisp Air Fryer and close the lid. Cook on 360°F for 15-18 minutes, or until a toothpick comes out clean.

Shrimp Frittata

Ingredients: Servings: 4 Cooking Time: 15 Mins

Eggs – 4
Basil – ½ tsp. dried
Salt and black pepper to taste
Shrimp – ½ cup, cooked, peeled, deveined, and chopped
Cooking spray
Rice – ½ cup, cooked
Baby spinach – ½ cup, chopped
Monterey jack cheese – ½ cup, grated

Directions:
In a bowl, mix eggs with basil, pepper, and salt. Whisk well. Grease the air fryer's basket with cooking spray and add shrimp, spinach, and rice. Add egg mix, sprinkle cheese all over and cook in the air fryer at 350F for 10 minutes. Serve.

Air Fryer Omelet

Ingredients: Servings: 2 Cooking Time: 8 Mins

Eggs – 2
Milk – ¼ cup
Green onions – ¼ cup, diced
Bell pepper – 2, chopped
Mushrooms – ¼ cup, chopped
Ham – 4 ounces, chopped
Breakfast seasoning – 1 tsp.
Cheese – ¼ cup, grated
Salt to taste
Oil – 1 tbsp.

Directions:
Mix milk and egg in a bowl. Season with salt. Put all the veg and ham into the mix and mix. Pour the mix into a pan. Place the pan in the air fryer basket and cover. Cook at 350F for 8 minutes. After 4 minutes, open the lid and sprinkle the breakfast seasoning and cheese. Cover and finish cooking. Serve.

Crunchy Breakfast Nuggets

Ingredients: Servings: 4 Cooking Time: 30 Mins

1 lb. boneless, skinless chicken breasts
⅔ C. whole wheat panko bread crumbs
⅓ C. Parmesan cheese, freshly grated
¼ C. whole wheat flour
2 tsps. dried parsley flakes
1 large egg
Olive oil spray
¼ tsp. salt or to taste
¼ tsp. black pepper
For dipping sauce (optional):
1 tbsp. marinara
1 tbsp. ranch dressing
1 tbsp. barbecue sauce

Directions:
Preheat your air fryer 400 degrees F for about 8-10 minutes. Meanwhile, slice the chicken breasts into 1-inch cubes. Prepare three shallow bowls; mix the flour, salt, and pepper in the first bowl. Lightly beat the egg in the second and combine the parmesan, panko, and parsley flakes in the third. Working one piece at a time, dredge the chicken in the flour mixture and

press lightly to adhere. Next, dip it into the egg, removing the excess egg as needed. Finally, coat with the Panko mixture, pressing lightly to help evenly coat the chicken. Arrange the nuggets in the air fryer basket in a single layer. Liberally spritz them with cooking spray to help them get crispy and golden brown. Air-fry each batch for about 7 minutes or until the internal temperature reaches 165 degrees F (or 74°C). Monitor them to make sure that they're not overcooked. Serve with your favorite dip and your favorite side dish.

Coconut Blueberry Oatmeal

Ingredients: Servings: 6 Cooking Time: 30 Mins

2 1/4 C. oats
1 C. blueberries
1/4 C. gluten-free flour
1/2 tsp. vanilla
3 C. of water
14 oz coconut milk
6 tbsp. brown sugar
1/8 tsp. salt

Directions:
Add all ingredients into the instant pot and stir well. Seal pot with lid and cook on manual mode for 30 minutes. Once done then release pressure using the quick-release method than open the lid. Stir well and serve.

Tuna Sandwiches

Ingredients: Servings: 4 Cooking Time: 5 Mins

Canned tuna – 16 ounces, drained
Mayonnaise – ¼ cup
Mustard – 2 tbsps.
Green onions – 2, chopped
Lemon juice - 1 tbsp.
English muffins – 3, halved
Butter – 3 tbsps.
Provolone cheese - 6

Directions:
In a bowl, mix mayo, tuna, lemon juice, mustard, and green onions. Grease muffin halves with butter. Place them in the preheated air fryer and bake them at 350F for 4 minutes. Add tuna mix on muffin halves, then top each with cheese. Return sandwiches to air fryer and bake 4 minutes more. Serve.

Air Fried Mac and Cheese

Ingredients: Servings: 4 Cooking Time: 35 Mins

1 C. Elbow Macaroni
1/2 C. Broccoli or Cauliflower (equal size small florets)
1/2 C. Milk (Warmed)
1 1/2 C. Cheddar Cheese (grated)
Salt and Pepper
1 tbsp. Parmesan Cheese (grated)

Directions:
Preheat the Instant Pot Duo Crisp Air Fryer at 390°F. Boil some water over high heat, and reduce the heat to med and add macaroni & vegetables. Simmer it until macaroni is al dente & vegetables are tender but not mushy (for about 7-10 minutes). Drain the vegetables and pasta, & return them to the basket. Add Cheddar cheese and milk to the macaroni and vegetables, and toss to combine. Season with pepper and salt. Pour pasta mixture into an ovenproof dish. Then sprinkle the Parmesan cheese over top of it. Place the dish onthe Instant Pot Duo Crisp Air Fryer Basket and adjust the temperature at 350°F. Close the Air Fryer lid and cook for bake it for fifteen minutes (the pasta will be bubbling). Allow it to sit for 5-10 minutes in the Instant Pot Duo Crisp Air Fryer before serving.

Chorizo Cheese Cake

Ingredients: Servings: 6 Cooking Time: 10 Mins

8 Eggs, cracked into a bowl
8 oz Chorizo Sausage, chopped
3 Bacon Slices, chopped
1 large Green Bell Pepper, chopped
1 large Red Bell Pepper, chopped
½ C. Milk
1 C. chopped Green Onion
1 C. grated Cheddar Cheese
1 tsp. Red Chili Flakes
Salt and Black Pepper to taste
4 slices Bread, cut into ½ -inch cubes

Directions:
Add the eggs, sausage chorizo, bacon slices, green and red bell peppers, green onion, chili flakes, cheddar cheese, salt, pepper, and milk to a bowl and use a whisk to beat them together. Grease a bundt pan with cooking spray and pour the egg mixture into it. After, drop the bread slices in the egg mixture all around while using a spoon to push them into the mixture. Open the cooker, pour in 2 C. water, and fit the rack at the center of the pot. Place bundt pan on the rack and seal the pressure lid. Select Pressure mode on High pressure for 6 minutes, and press Start. Once the timer goes off, press Cancel, do a quick pressure release. Run a knife around the egg in the bundt pan, close the crisping lid and cook for another 4 minutes on Bake on 380 F. When ready, place a serving plate on the bundt pan, and then, turn the egg bundt over. Cut the egg into slices. Serve.

Chicken Sandwiches

Ingredients: Servings: 4 Cooking Time: 10 Mins

Chicken breasts – 2, skinless, boneless, and cubed
Red onion – 1, chopped
Red bell pepper – 1, sliced
Thyme – ½ tsp. dried
Italian seasoning – ½ cup
Butter lettuce – 2 cups, torn
Pita pockets – 4
Cherry tomatoes – 1 cup, halved
Olive oil – 1 tbsp.

Directions:
In the air fryer, mix chicken with oil, Italian seasoning, bell pepper, onion, toss and cook at 380F for 10 minutes. Transfer chicken mixture to a bowl, add cherry tomatoes, butter lettuce, and thyme. Toss well. Stuff pita pockets with this mixture and serve.

Honey-mustard Sausage Weenies

Ingredients: Servings: 4 Cooking Time: 7 Mins

20 Hot Dogs, cut into 4 pieces
Salt and Black Pepper to taste
1 tsp. Dijon Mustard
1 ½ tsp. Soy Sauce
¼ C. Honey
¼ C. Red Wine Vinegar
½ C. Tomato Puree
¼ C. Water

Directions:
Add the tomato puree, red wine vinegar, honey, soy sauce, Dijon mustard, salt, and black pepper in a medium bowl. Mix them with a spoon. Put sausage weenies in the crisp basket, and close the crisping lid. Select Air Fry mode. Set the temperature to 370 F and the timer to 4 minutes. Press Start. At the 2-minute mark, turn the sausages. Once ready, open the lid and pour the sweet sauce over the sausage weenies. Close the pressure lid, secure the pressure valve, and select Pressure mode on High for 3 minutes. Press Start. Once the timer has ended, do a quick pressure release. Serve and enjoy.

Cheese Eggs with Prosciutto

Ingredients: Servings: 4 Cooking Time: 25 Mins

4 eggs, beaten
1 C. milk
1 orange bell pepper, seeded and chopped
Salt and black pepper to taste
1 C. shredded Monterey Jack cheese
8 oz. prosciutto, chopped
1 C. water

Directions:
In a bowl, put the almond milk, eggs, pink salt, and black pepper and whisk until evenly combined and a creamy color has formed. Stir in the Monterey Jack Cheese. Arrange the bell pepper and prosciutto onto a baking dish. Then, pour over the egg mixture, cover the pan with aluminum foil and put on the reversible rack. Add the water into the pot, put the rack with the dish in the pot. Then, seal the pressure lid, choose Pressure and set to High. Set the time to 20 minutes. Choose Start. When done cooking, perform a quick pressure release and carefully remove the lid. Take out the dish from the pot and place it on a cooling rack. Cool for 5 minutes and serve.

Peppered Maple Bacon Knots (air Fryer)

Ingredients: Servings: 6 Cooking Time: 7 To 8 Mins

1 lb. (454 g) maple smoked center-cut bacon
1/4 C. maple syrup
1/4 C. brown sugar
Coarsely cracked black peppercorns, to taste

Directions:
Preheat the air fryer to 390°F (199°C). On a clean work surface, tie each bacon strip in a loose knot. Stir together the maple syrup and brown sugar in a bowl. Generously brush this mixture over the bacon knots. Working in batches, arrange the bacon knots in the air fryer basket. Sprinkle with the coarsely cracked black peppercorns. Air fry for 5 minutes. Flip the bacon knots and continue cooking for 2 to 3 minutes more, or until the bacon is crisp. Remove from the basket to a paper towel-lined plate. Repeat with the remaining bacon knots. Let the bacon knots cool for a few minutes and serve warm.

Air-fried Cinnamon & Sugar Doughnuts

Ingredients: Servings: 9 Cooking Time: 8 Mins

2 1/4 + 1/4 C. all-purpose flour
3/4 + 1/3 C. white sugar
2 egg yolks, large
2 1/2 tbsp. butter kept in room temperature
1 1/2 tsp. baking powder
1/2 C. sour cream
2 tbsp. butter, melted
1 tsp. cinnamon
1 tsp. salt

Directions:
In a bowl combine, 2 1/2 tbsp. butter kept in room temperature with 3/4 C. white sugar, until it takes a crumbly shape. Now add the egg yolk and mix thoroughly. Put the all-purpose flour, salt, and baking powder in a medium bowl and combine. Put one-third of the flour mixture into the egg-sugar mix and combine thoroughly. Add the remaining flour and sour cream and mix well. Refrigerate the mixture for 3-4 hours. Mix cinnamon and 1/3 C. of white sugar in another medium bowl. Keep ready your kitchen working table and spread some flour on it. Take out the refrigerated dough and spread it into 1/2" thick sheet. Cut it into 9 large dough using a dough dye cutter and make a small circle in the center of each dough, to make it look like a dough. Place the air fryer basket in the inner pot of the Instant Pot Air Fryer. Close the crisp cover of your Instant Pot Air Fryer and preheat at 340°F for 3 minutes in the AIR FRYER mode. Press START to begin preheating. Apply melted butter on both sides of the doughnut before placing it in the air fryer. Place the doughs in the basket without overlapping. If space is not enough, use the separator and place the remaining dough on it. Close the crisp lid. Set the timer to 8 minutes and temperature at 340°F. Press START for cooking. Brush the melted butter on the cooked doughnuts and dredge it into the cinnamon-sugar mixture. Your doughnuts are ready to serve.

Sausage and Cheese Quiche (air Fryer)

Ingredients: Servings: 4 Cooking Time: 25 Mins

12 large eggs
1 C. heavy cream
12 oz. (340 g) sugar-free breakfast sausage
Salt and black pepper, to taste
2 C. shredded Cheddar cheese
Cooking spray

Directions:
Preheat the air fryer to 375°F (191°C). Coat a casserole dish with cooking spray. Beat together the eggs, heavy cream, salt and pepper in a large bowl until creamy. Stir in the breakfast sausage and Cheddar cheese. Pour the sausage mixture into the prepared casserole dish and bake for 25 minutes, or until the top of the quiche is golden brown and the eggs are set. Remove from the air fryer and let sit for 5 to 10 minutes before serving.

Saucy Eggs Bake

Ingredients: Servings: 4 Cooking Time: 35 Mins

1 1/2 lb. plum tomatoes
2 garlic cloves, smashed
2 tbsp. olive oil
8 large eggs
Salt and ground pepper
1 tsp. oregano, chopped
2 tbsp. Parmigiano-Reggiano cheese, grated

Directions:
Place the tomatoes in the Instant Pot Duo and add garlic, olive oil, salt, and black pepper on top. Put on the Air Fryer lid and seal it. Hit the "Roast Button" and select 20 minutes of cooking time, then press "Start." Once the Instant Pot Duo beeps, remove its lid. Transfer the tomatoes to a blender and

puree them with oregano. Take a suitable baking pan and spread the sauce in it. Whisk eggs with salt and black pepper then pour over the sauce. Top it with shredded cheese. Place the egg pan in the Instant Pot Duo. Put on the Air Fryer lid and seal it. Hit the "Bake Button" and select 15 minutes of cooking time, then press "Start." Once the Instant Pot Duo beeps, remove its lid. Serve.

Lemon Butter Brussels Sprouts

Ingredients: Servings: 4 Cooking Time: 5 Mins

1 lb Brussels sprouts, trimmed and washed
1/4 C. parmesan cheese, grated
1 fresh lemon juice
1/4 tsp. garlic powder
2 tbsp. butter
1 C. of water

Directions:
Pour water into the inner pot of instant pot duo crisp. Add Brussels sprouts into the steamer basket and place basket in the pot. Seal the pot with pressure cooking lid and cook on high for 2 minutes. Once done, release pressure using a quick release. Remove lid. Drain Brussels sprouts well and place in mixing bowl. Clean the pot. Add butter into the pot and set the pot on sauté mode. Add cooked Brussels sprouts, garlic powder, and lemon juice and sauté for 2-3 minutes. Top with cheese and serve.

Sweet and Smokey Chickpeas

Ingredients: Servings: 4 Cooking Time: 16 Mins

Chickpeas – 1 (15-ounce) can
Aquafaba from chickpeas – 2 tbsps.
Maple syrup – 1 tbsp.
Smoked paprika – 2 tsps.
Garlic powder - 1 ½ tsps.
Sea salt – ½ tsp.

Directions:
Drain the chickpeas while reserving aquafaba obtained. Do not rinse chickpeas. Add chickpeas to the air fryer basket and shake to a single layer. Choose the air fryer function and close the lid. Air fry at 390F for 8 minutes. Meanwhile, whisk together 2 tbsps. of aquafaba, maple syrup, smoked paprika, garlic powder, and salt in a bowl. When cooked, add the chickpeas in this mixture and coat. Return the coated chickpeas with the sauce to the air fryer basket and air fryer at 390F for 5 minutes more. Shake the basket and cook again for 3 to 5 minutes. Serve.

Pumpkin and Pecan Porridge (pressure Cook)

Ingredients: Servings: 2 To 4 Cooking Time: 10 Mins

¼ C. unsweetened coconut flakes
2 C. filtered water
2 C. full-fat coconut milk
1 C. organic pumpkin purée
1 C. pecans, chopped
¼ C. organic coconut flour
½ tsp. ground cinnamon
½ tsp. ginger, finely grated
Swerve, to taste (optional)

Directions:
Press the Sauté button on your Instant Pot and toast the coconut flakes, stirring occasionally. Pour in the filtered water and milk. Secure the lid. Press the Pressure Cook on the Instant Pot and set the cooking time for 0 minutes at High Pressure. Once cooking is complete, use a natural pressure release for about 10 minutes and then release any remaining pressure. Carefully remove the lid. Fold in the pumpkin, pecans, flour, cinnamon, ginger, and Swerve (if desired). Let stand for 2 to 4 minutes until desired consistency, stirring occasionally. Ladle the porridge into bowls and serve warm.

Pepperoni Pasta

Ingredients: Servings: 8 Cooking Time: 25 Mins

16 oz. rigatoni pasta
1 lb. Italian sausage
6 oz. pepperoni, sliced
1 (28 oz.) can diced Italian tomatoes, with juice
1 (28 oz.) can tomato puree
8 oz. Mozzarella cheese, shredded
2 C. chicken stock
1 C. red wine
1 medium onion, chopped
2 tbsps. garlic, minced
½ tsp. oregano
½ tsp. basil
¼ tsp. red pepper, crushed
¼ tsp. ground black pepper
½ tsp. salt

Directions:
Set the instant pot to SAUTE then cook the onions, sausage and garlic until browned. Stir in the spices, salt, pepper, the chicken stock, red wine, and half of the pepperoni. Make sure that everything is well combined. Add the tomato puree and tomatoes and stir lightly. Pour in the pasta, gently pressing down to ensure that it's covered with liquid. Don't stir so that the pasta will be kept at the bottom of the pot. Pressure cook on HIGH for about 6 minutes or until al dente. Quick-release and remove the lid. Add in ⅓ of the cheese then stir well. Add the remaining cheese on top and layer the rest of the pepperoni on top of the cheese. Attach the air fryer lid to the instant pot and air-fry at 400 degrees F for 5 minutes. Once cooked, remove the lid and serve the pepperoni pasta.

Breakfast Frittata

Ingredients: Servings: 2 Cooking Time: 18 Mins

Breakfast sausage – ¼ pound, cooked and crumbled
Red bell pepper – 2 tbsps. chopped
Cheddar cheese – ½ cup, grated
Eggs – 4, beaten
Green onion – 1, chopped
Ground cayenne pepper – ¼ tsp.
Salt to taste and cooking spray

Directions:
In a bowl, combine the egg, sausage, grated cheddar cheese, onion, salt, and cayenne pepper. Mix well. Grease the air fryer basket with cooking spray. Pour the egg mix into the basket and cover. Close the lid and cook at 350F for 18 minutes. Serve.

Farro Breakfast Risotto

Ingredients: Servings: 4 Cooking Time: 12 Mins

1 tsp. Italian seasoning
1/2 C. parmesan cheese, grated
1/2 C. mozzarella
1 C. farro
2 tbsp. heavy whipping cream
2 C. vegetable stock
1 tbsp. butter

cheese, grated

Directions:

Add butter into the instant pot and set the pot on sauté mode. Add farro and cook for 2 minutes. Add stock and stir everything well. Seal pot with lid and cook on manual high pressure for 10 minutes. Once done then allow to release pressure naturally for 10 minutes then release using the quick-release method. Open the lid. Add remaining ingredients and stir well. Serve and enjoy.

Mozzarella Sticks

Ingredients: Servings: 6 Cooking Time: 8 Mins

Mozzarella sticks – 6 (8-ounces) each
Panko breadcrumbs - 1 cup
All-purpose flour – 3 tbsps.
Eggs – 2
Crushed black pepper – ½ tsp.
Salt – ½ tsp.
Marinara sauce – ¼ cup

Directions:

Freeze the mozzarella in the freezer. Beat the eggs in a bowl. Place the breadcrumbs in another bowl. Keep the all-purpose flour in another bowl. Dredge the mozzarella sticks in the flour and shake off excess. Then dip in the beaten egg and then dredge in the panko bread crumbs. Lastly, dip in the egg liquid. Line the air fryer basket with parchment and place in the mozzarella sticks. Cover and cook at 400F for 8 minutes. Serve with marinara sauce.

Lemony Raspberries Bowls

Ingredients: Servings: 2 Cooking Time: 12 Mins

1 C. raspberries
2 tbsp. Butter
2 tbsp. Lemon juice
1 tsp. Cinnamon powder

Directions:

In your air fryer, mix all the ingredients, toss, cover, cook at 350°f for 12 minutes Divide into bowls and serve for breakfast

Cheesy Arugula Frittata (pressure Cook)

Ingredients: Servings: 2 Cooking Time: 5 Mins

3 eggs, beaten
¼ C. loosely packed arugula
¼ red onion, chopped
¼ C. feta cheese crumbles
¼ tsp. garlic powder
Kosher salt, to taste
Freshly ground black pepper, to taste
1 C. water

Directions:

Stir together the eggs, arugula, onion, feta cheese crumbles, garlic powder, salt, and pepper in a medium bowl. Pour the egg mixture into a greased round cake pan and cover with foil. Add the water and trivet to the Instant Pot, then place the cake pan on top of the trivet. Lock the lid. Select the Pressure Cook and set the cooking time for 5 minutes at High Pressure. Once cooking is complete, do a natural pressure release for 10 minutes, then release any remaining pressure. Carefully open the lid. Let the frittata rest for 5 minutes in the pan before cutting and serving.

Kale Frittata (air Fryer)

Ingredients: Servings: 2 Cooking Time: 11 Mins

1 C. kale, chopped
1 tsp. olive oil
4 large eggs, beaten
Kosher salt, to taste
2 tbsp. water
3 tbsp. crumbled feta
Cooking spray

Directions:

Preheat the air fryer to 360°F (182°C). Spritz an air fryer baking pan with cooking spray. Add the kale to the baking pan and drizzle with olive oil. Arrange the pan in the preheated air fryer. Broil for 3 minutes. Meanwhile, combine the eggs with salt and water in a large bowl. Stir to mix well. Make the frittata: When the broiling time is complete, pour the eggs into the baking pan and spread with feta cheese. Reduce the temperature to 300°F (149°C). Bake for 8 minutes or until the eggs are set and the cheese melts. Remove the baking pan from the air fryer and serve the frittata immediately.

Tasty Ham with Collard Greens

Ingredients: Servings: 4 Cooking Time: 5 Mins

20 oz Collard Greens, washed and cut
2 cubes of Chicken Bouillon
4 C. Water
½ C. diced Sweet Onion
2 ½ C. diced Ham

Directions:

Place the ham at the bottom of the inner pot. Add collard greens and onion. Then, add chicken cubes to the water and dissolve it. Pour the mixture into the pot. Close the lid, secure the pressure valve, to seal properly. Select Steam mode on High pressure for 5 minutes. Press Start. Once the timer has ended, do a quick pressure release, and open the lid. Spoon the vegetables and the ham with sauce into a serving platter. Serve with a side of steak dish of your choice.

Cinnamon Toast

Ingredients: Servings: 6 Cooking Time: 5 Mins

Butter – 1 stick, soft
Bread – 12 slices
Sugar – ½ cup
Vanilla extract – 1 ½ tsps.
Cinnamon powder – 1 ½ tsps.

Directions:

In a bowl, mix soft butter with cinnamon, vanilla, and sugar, and whisk well. Spread this on bread slices. Place them in the air fryer and cook at 400F for 5 minutes. Serve.

Cinnamon Apple Butter (pressure Cook)

Ingredients: Servings: 5 Cooking Time: 3 Mins

4 lb. (1.8 kg) large apples, cored and quartered
¾ to 1 C. sugar
3 tsp. ground cinnamon
¼ tsp. ground cloves
¼ C. water
¼ tsp. ground allspice
¼ tsp. ground nutmeg
¼ C. creamy peanut butter

Directions:

Combine all the ingredients except the butter in the Instant Pot. Secure the lid. Select the Pressure Cook and set the cooking time for 3 minutes at High Pressure. Once cooking is complete, do a natural pressure release for 5 minutes, then release any remaining pressure. Carefully open the lid. Blend the mixture with an immersion blender. Add the peanut butter and whisk until smooth. Let the mixture cool to room temperature. Serve immediately.

Spaghetti Squash Fritters

Ingredients: Servings: 4 Cooking Time: 12 Mins

2 C. cooked spaghetti squash
2 stalks green onion, sliced
¼ C. blanched finely ground almond flour.
1 large egg.
2 tbsp. Unsalted butter; softened.
½ tsp. Garlic powder.
1 tsp. Dried parsley.

Directions:
Remove excess moisture from the squash using a cheesecloth or kitchen towel. Mix all ingredients in a large bowl. Form into four patties Cut a piece of parchment to fit your air fryer basket. Place each patty on the parchment and place into the air fryer basket Adjust the temperature to 400 degrees f and set the timer for 8 minutes. Flip the patties halfway through the cooking time. Serve warm.

Ranchero Wraps

Ingredients: Servings: 2 Cooking Time: 8 Mins

Egg scramble – 2 servings
Flour tortillas – 2-large
Corn tortillas – 2-small
Pinto beans – 1/3 cup, cooked
Ranchero sauce – ½ cup
Avocado – ½, peeled and sliced
Fresh jalapenos – 2, stemmed and sliced

Directions:
Assemble the large tortillas on a work surface. Arrange the crunch wraps by stacking the following ingredients in order: egg scramble, jalapeno, ranchero sauce, corn tortillas, avocado, and pinto beans. Fold to seal completely. Place one crunch wrap in the air fryer basket and cook at 350F for 6 minutes. Repeat and serve.

Mini Frittata

Ingredients: Servings: 4 Cooking Time: 15 Mins

1/2 small onion, chopped
1/2 bell pepper, chopped
3 bacon slices, chopped
6 eggs
1/4 C. cheddar cheese, shredded
1/4 C. coconut milk
1/4 tsp. black pepper
1/2 tsp. sea salt

Directions:
Add bacon slices on the bottom of each silicone muffin mold. Add chopped vegetables on top of the bacon. In a bowl, whisk eggs with pepper and salt. Pour egg mixture over vegetables. Sprinkle shredded cheddar cheese on top. Place silicone muffin molds into the instant pot air fryer basket and place basket in the pot. Seal the pot with pressure cooking lid and select bake mode and cook at 350 F for 10-15 minutes. Serve and enjoy.

Easy Lemon Garlic Chicken Breast

Ingredients: Servings: 1 Cooking Time: 15 Mins

1 chicken breast, boneless and skinless
1 lemon juice
1 tsp. garlic, minced
1 tbsp. chicken seasoning
Pepper
Salt

Directions:
Season chicken with pepper and salt. Mix together lemon juice, garlic, and chicken seasoning and rub all over chicken breast. Place the dehydrating tray in a multi-level air fryer basket and place basket in the instant pot. Place chicken on the dehydrating tray. Seal pot with air fryer lid and select air fry mode then set the temperature to 350 F and timer for 15 minutes. Turn chicken halfway through. Serve and enjoy.

Tarragon and Parmesan Scramble

Ingredients: Servings: 4 Cooking Time: 30 Mins

8 eggs; whisked
¼ C. coconut cream
2 tbsp. Parmesan; grated
2 tbsp. Tarragon; chopped.
Salt and black pepper to taste.

Directions:
Take a bowl and mix the eggs with all the ingredients and whisk. Pour this into a pan that fits your air fryer, introduce it in the preheated fryer and cook at 350°f for 20 minutes, stirring often Divide the scramble between plates and serve for breakfast.

Air Fryer Granola

Ingredients: Servings: 8 Cooking Time: 15 Mins

Rolled oats – 2 cups
Toasted wheat germ – ½ cup
Dried cherries – ¼ cup
Dried cranberries – 1/8 cup
Dried blueberries – ¼ cup
Pepitas – 1/8 cup
Sunflower seeds – 1/8 cup
Flaxseed – 1 tbsp.
Chopped pecans – 1/8 cup
Chopped almond – 1/8 cup
Chopped walnuts – 1/8 cup
Chopped hazelnuts – 1/8 cup
Honey – 2 tbsps.
Vanilla extract – ½ tsp.
Maple syrup – ¼ cup
Olive oil – 6 tbsps.
Ground cinnamon – ½ tsp.
Ground cloves – 1/8 tsp.

Directions:
Combine all the dry ingredients in a bowl. Mix the honey with oil and maple syrup. Mix the syrup mix with the dry ingredients. Preheat the air fryer at 350F. Add the mix to the air fryer basket and cook for 15 minutes. Stirring after every 5 minutes. Cool and serve.

Gruyere & Bacon Grits

Ingredients: Servings: 4 Cooking Time: 10 Mins

3 slices smoked Bacon, diced
1 ½ C. grated Gruyere Cheese
1 C. ground Grits
2 tsp. Butter
Salt and Black Pepper
½ C. Water
½ C. Milk

Directions:
To preheat the cooker, select Sear/Sauté mode and set to HIGH pressure. Cook bacon until crispy, about 5 minutes. Set aside. Add the grits, butter, milk, water, salt, and pepper to the pot and stir using a spoon. Close the pressure lid and secure the pressure valve. Choose the Pressure mode and cook for 3 minutes on High. Press Start. Once the timer has ended, turn the vent handle and do a quick pressure release. Add in cheddar cheese and give the pudding a good stir with the same spoon. Close crisping lid, press BAKE button and cook for 8 minutes on 370 F. Press Start key. When ready, dish the cheesy grits into serving bowls and spoon over the crisped bacon. Serve right away with toasted bread.

Herbed Eggs

Ingredients: Servings: 4 Cooking Time: 30 Mins

½ C. cheddar; shredded
2 tbsp. Chives; chopped.
2 tbsp. Basil; chopped.
10 eggs; whisked
2 tbsp. Parsley; chopped.
Cooking spray
Salt and black pepper to taste.

Directions:
Take a bowl and mix the eggs with all the ingredients except the cheese and the cooking spray and whisk well Preheat the air fryer at 350°f, grease it with the cooking spray and pour the eggs mixture inside Sprinkle the cheese on top and cook for 20 minutes. Divide everything between plates and serve.

Rice Lentil Porridge

Ingredients: Servings: 4 Cooking Time: 21 Mins

1/2 C. yellow lentils, soaked for 15 minutes and drained
1 C. rice, soaked for 15 minutes and drained
6 C. vegetable stock
1 bay leaf
1 tsp. turmeric
1 1/2 tsp. cumin seeds
2 tbsp. olive oil
1 1/2 tsp. salt

Directions:
Add oil into the inner pot of instant pot duo crisp and set pot on sauté mode. Add cumin seeds and bay leaf and sauté for 30 seconds. Add lentils, turmeric, rice, salt, and stock. Stir well. Seal the pot with pressure cooking lid and cook on high for minutes. Once done, allow to release pressure naturally for 10 minutes then release remaining pressure using a quick release. Remove lid. Stir and serve.

SNACKS, DESSERTS AND APPETIZERS

Fried Peaches

Ingredients: Servings: 4 Cooking Time: 15 Mins

4 ripe peaches (1/2 a peach = 1 serving)
1 1/2 C. flour
Salt
2 egg yolks
3/4 C. cold water
1 1/2 tbsp. olive oil
2 tbsp. brandy
4 egg whites
Cinnamon/sugar mix

Directions:
Preparing the Ingredients. Mix flour, egg yolks, and salt in a mixing bowl. Slowly mix in water, then add brandy. Set the mixture aside for 2 hours and go do something for 1 hour 45 minutes. Boil a large pot of water and cut and X at the bottom of each peach. While the water boils fill another large bowl with water and ice. Boil each peach for about a minute, then plunge it in the ice bath. Now the peels should basically fall off the peach. Beat the egg whites and mix into the batter mix. Dip each peach in the mix to coat. Air Frying. Close air fryer lid and cook at 360 degrees for 10 Minutes. Prepare a plate with cinnamon/sugar mix, roll peaches in mix and serve.

Lemon Ricotta Cake (air Fryer)

Ingredients: Servings: 6 Cooking Time: 25 Mins

17.5 oz. (496 g) ricotta cheese
5.4 oz. (153 g) sugar
3 eggs, beaten
3 tbsp. flour
1 lemon, juiced and zested
2 tsp. vanilla extract

Directions:
Preheat the air fryer to 320°F (160°C). In a large mixing bowl, stir together all the ingredients until the mixture reaches a creamy consistency. Pour the mixture into a baking pan and place in the air fryer. Bake for 25 minutes until a toothpick inserted in the center comes out clean. Allow to cool for 10 minutes on a wire rack before serving.

Mini Lava Cakes

Ingredients: Servings: 3 Cooking Time: 20 Mins

Egg – 1
Sugar – 4 tbsps.
Olive oil – 2 tbsps.
Milk – 4 tbsps.
Flour – 4 tbsps.
Cocoa powder – 1 tbsp.
Baking powder – ½ tsp.
Orange zest – ½ tsp.

Directions:
In a bowl, mix oil, sugar, milk, egg, flour, salt, cocoa powder, baking powder, and orange zest. Mix well and pour into greased ramekins. Add ramekins to the air fryer and cook at 320F for 20 minutes. Serve.

Classic Cheesecake (pressure Cook)

Ingredients: Servings: 4 Cooking Time: 40 Mins

2 C. graham crackers, crushed
3 tbsp. brown sugar
2 (8 oz. / 227-g) cream cheese, softened
½ C. granulated sugar
¼ C. butter, melted
2 tbsp. all-purpose flour
1 tsp. vanilla extract
3 eggs
1 C. water
1 C. caramel sauce

Directions:
Make the crust: Mix the crushed crackers with brown sugar and butter. Spread the mixture at the bottom of a springform pan and use a spoon to press to fit. Freeze in refrigerator for 10

minutes. In a bowl, whisk the cream cheese and sugar until smooth. Mix in the flour and vanilla. Whisk in the eggs. Remove the pan from refrigerator and pour mixture over crust. Cover the pan with foil. Pour the water in Instant Pot, then fit in a trivet and place the pan on top. Seal the lid, select the Pressure Cook and set the timer for 40 minutes at High Pressure. When cooking is complete, allow a natural pressure release for 10 minutes, then release any remaining pressure. Open the lid. Carefully remove the cake pan and take off the foil. Let cool for 10 minutes. Pour the caramel sauce over and refrigerate for 3 hours. Remove the pan from the refrigerator and invert the cheesecake on a plate. Slice and serve.

Cookies and Cream Cheesecake

Ingredients: Servings: 6 Cooking Time: 40 Mins

1 C. Water
2 tbsp. unsalted butter melted
1 tsp. vanilla extract
1/2 C. full-fat sour cream
1/2 C. granulated sugar
16 oz cream cheese softened
26 cream-filled chocolate sandwich cookies divided
2 large eggs room temperature

Directions:
Grease 7 inch push pan and set it aside. Place 16 chocolate cookies in a zip-lock bag and seal it. with a rolling pin roll it until crumbs are formed. Take a small bowl then mix the crushed cookies and the melted butter together. Press the cookie crust into the bottom and halfway up sides of the greased Push Pan. Place the pan in the freezer till you prepare the cheesecake batter. with an electric mixer, cream together cream cheese, sugar, and vanilla. Beat it for around 2 minutes until it is light and fluffy. Slowly mix in the sour cream. Add the eggs - one at a time, beating after each addition. Only mix until it is combined. Do not overmix. Chop remaining cookies and fold half of them into the cheesecake batter. Reserve remaining chopped cookies for topping. Choose the Bake option from the Instant Pot Duo Crisp Air Fryer settings and push the start button after setting the temperature to 360°F. Pour batter into the push pan. Once preheated, put the pan on the tray of the Air Fryer. Close the Air Fryer lid and bake for 40 minutes. When the timer beeps, unlock the lid and remove it. Carefully remove the pan from Air Fryer Tray. Place on a cooling rack and let cool to room temperature. Cover it with a plastic wrap and refrigerate for 8 hours minimum. Top the cheesecake with the remaining cookies crumbs and serve.

Sweet Potato Fries with Mayonnaise (air Fryer)

Ingredients: Servings: 2 To 3 Cooking Time: 20 Mins

1 large sweet potato (about 1 lb. / 454 g), scrubbed
1 tsp. vegetable or canola oil
Salt, to taste
¼ C. light mayonnaise
Dipping Sauce:
½ tsp. sriracha sauce
1 tbsp. spicy brown mustard
1 tbsp. sweet Thai chili sauce

Directions:
Preheat the air fryer to 200°F (93°C). On a flat work surface, cut the sweet potato into fry-shaped strips about ¼ inch wide and ¼ inch thick. You can use a Food Slicer to slice the sweet potato quickly and uniformly. In a medium bowl, drizzle the sweet potato strips with the oil and toss well. Transfer to the air fryer basket and air fry for 10 minutes, shaking the basket twice during cooking. Remove the air fryer basket and sprinkle with the salt and toss to coat. Increase the air fryer temperature to 400°F (204°C) and air fry for an additional 10 minutes, or until the fries are crispy and tender. Shake the basket a few times during cooking. Meanwhile, whisk together all the ingredients for the sauce in a small bowl. Remove the sweet potato fries from the basket to a plate and serve warm alongside the dipping sauce.

Chicken Tenders

Ingredients: Servings: 12 Cooking Time: 16 Mins

1 lb. skinless, chicken tenders or chicken breast cut into strips
1/2 C. grated Parmesan cheese
1/2 C. Panko breadcrumbs or other breadcrumbs of choice
1/3 C. all-purpose flour
2 eggs
1/2 C. milk or Buttermilk (preferred)
1 tsp. Italian Seasoning
Salt and pepper to taste
Cooking oil spray (avocado oil)

Directions:
Choose the Air Fry option on the Instant Pot Duo Crisp Air Fryer and set the temperature to 400°F. Push start and begin the preheating. Put the chicken tenders in a bag with a ziplock or bowl and coat them with milk Combine the breadcrumbs, salt and pepper,seasoning and Parmesan cheese in a deep bowl. Place the egg in the other bowl and flour in a separate bowl. Dig the tenders through the flour followed by dipping in egg, post dredge through the breadcrumb mix. Once preheated, sprinkle the Air Fryer trays or basket with oil and place the tenders on the tray. Do not crowd or overlap the tenders. Drizzle the chicken tenders with some oil. Close the Air fryer lid and Air Fry for about 5 minutes, then turn the tenders over and spray them with oil again. Switch the tray positions in case you are using multiple trays. Repeat step 8 again. Air fry for another 6 minutes or until the chicken tenders are golden brown and internal temperature is at least 165°F, flipping the tenders or switching trays as necessary.

Blackberry Chocolate Cake (air Fryer)

Ingredients: Servings: 8 Cooking Time: 22 Mins

½ C. butter, at room temperature
2 oz. (57 g) Swerve
4 eggs
1 C. almond flour
1 tsp. baking soda
⅓ tsp. baking powder
½ C. cocoa powder
1 tsp. orange zest
⅓ C. fresh blackberries

Directions:
Preheat the air fryer to 335°F (168°C). with an electric mixer or hand mixer, beat the butter and Swerve until creamy. One at a time, mix in the eggs and beat again until fluffy. Add the almond flour, baking soda, baking powder, cocoa powder, orange zest and mix well. Add the butter mixture to the almond flour mixture and stir until well blended. Fold in the

blackberries. Scrape the batter to a baking pan and bake in the preheated air fryer for 22 minutes. Check the cake for doneness: If a toothpick inserted into the center of the cake comes out clean, it's done. Allow the cake cool on a wire rack to room temperature. Serve immediately.

Coconutty Lemon Bars

Ingredients: Servings: 12 Cooking Time: 25 Mins

¼ C. cashew
¼ C. fresh lemon juice, freshly squeezed
¾ C. coconut milk
¾ C. erythritol
1 C. desiccated coconut
1 tsp. baking powder
2 eggs, beaten
2 tbsp. coconut oil
A Instant Crisp Air Fryer of salt

Directions:

Preparing the Ingredients. Preheat the Instant Crisp Air Fryer for 5 minutes. In a mixing bowl, combine all ingredients. Use a hand mixer to mix everything. Pour into a baking dish that will fit in the Instant Crisp Air Fryer. Air Frying. Close the air fryer Lid. Select Bake and cook for 25 minutes at 350°F or until a toothpick inserted in the middle comes out clean.

Cinnamon Cream Puffs

Ingredients: Servings: 8 Cooking Time: 6 Mins

Almond flour – ½ cup
Vanilla protein powder – ½ cup
Granular erythritol – ½ cup
Baking powder – ½ tsp.
Egg – 1
Unsalted butter – 5 tbsps. melted
Full-fat cream cheese – 2 ounces
Powdered erythritol – ¼ tsp.
Ground cinnamon – ¼ tsp.
Heavy whipping cream – 2 tbsps.
Vanilla extract – ½ tsp.

Directions:

Mix butter, egg, baking powder, granular erythritol, protein powder, and flour in a bowl to make a dough. Keep the dough in the freezer for 20 minutes. Roll the dough with wet hands to make eight balls. Line the air fryer basket with parchment. Place the dough balls into the air fryer basket. Cook at 380F for 6 minutes. Flip halfway through the cooking time. Remove and cool the puffs. In a bowl, beat cream, cream cheese, powdered erythritol, cinnamon, and vanilla until fluffy. Cut a small hole in the bottom of each puff and fill with some of the cream mixtures. Serve.

Apple Bread

Ingredients: Servings: 6 Cooking Time: 40 Mins

Apples – 3, cored and cubed
Sugar – 1 cup
Vanilla – 1 tbsp.
Apple pie spice – 1 tbsp.
Eggs – 2
White flour – 2 cups
Baking powder – 1 tbsp.
Butter – 1 stick
Water – 1 cup

Directions:

In a bowl, mix 1 stick butter, eggs, apple pie spice, and sugar and stir with a mixer. Add apples and stir well. In another bowl, mix flour and baking powder. Combine the 2 mixtures. Stir and pour into a springform pan. Put springform pan in the air fryer and cook at 320F for 40 minutes. Slice and serve.

Chicken Empanadas

Ingredients: Servings: 6 Cooking Time: 10 Mins

2 lb. shredded chicken
Package of chicken taco seasoning (or another seasoning mix of choice,Frontera Chicken skillet)
1 C. shredded cheese of choice (cheddar)
2 frozen pie crusts, thawed
1/2 onion diced
A dusting of flour (to roll out the crust)
Spray cooking oil of choice (coconut or avocado oil)
garnishes (sour cream, salsa, guacamole)

Directions:

Push the Air Fry button on the Instant Pot Duo Crisp Air Fryer. Set the prescribed temperature and push start to begin preheating. Shred the meat properly Take a medium bowl and mix the meat along with onion, sauce, and cheese Roll out to each pie crust over the dusting of flour Using a ramekin or small bowl to make a circle imprint on the dough Cut out the circle finely Cut additional circles by re-rolling the dough Add a small amount of filling on each circle and fold over to form a half-circle shape Pinch or crimp the dough and shut using a fork Once the appliance is preheated, add food to the Air Fry tray and Close the lid. Air fry for around 10 minutes, turning the empanadas half way though Garnish with salsa and sour cream and/or guacamole

Cheesecake Bites

Ingredients: Servings: 2 Cooking Time: 7 Mins

Cream cheese – 8 oz. softened
Erythritol – ½ cup, plus 2 tbsps.
Almond flour – ½ cup
Vanilla extract – ½ tsp.
Heavy cream – ½ packet

Directions:

Mix the cream cheese with ½ packet heavy cream, ½-cup erythritol, and vanilla extract until smooth. Scoop the mixture onto a parchment paper-lined baking sheet. Freeze for 30 minutes for the best results. Mix the almond flour with 2 tbsps. of erythritol in a bowl. Roll the frozen bites into the almond flour mixture. Place the cheesecake bites into the air fryer basket and cook for 7 minutes at 370F.

Choco Fudge

Ingredients: Servings: 8 Cooking Time: 15 Mins

5 eggs
1/2 C. cocoa powder
1/2 C. dark chocolate, chopped
1/2 tsp. vanilla
2 tbsp. erythritol
3/4 tsp. baking powder

2 C. almond flour	1/2 C. almond milk
1 tsp. baking soda	Pinch of salt

Directions:
Add all dry ingredients into the large bowl and mix to combine. Add remaining ingredients and beat using a blender until well combined. Pour 2 C. of water into the inner pot of instant pot duo crisp then place steamer rack in the pot. Pour batter in the oven-safe baking dish and place on top of the steamer rack. Seal the pot with pressure cooking lid and cook on high for 15 minutes. Once done, release pressure using a quick release. Remove lid. Serve and enjoy.

Hot Lava Cake

Ingredients: Servings: 8 Cooking Time: 29 Mins

1 C. Butter	Powdered sugar to garnish
4 tbsp. Milk	7 tbsp. All-purpose Flour
4 tsp. Vanilla Extract	5 Eggs
1 ½ C. Chocolate Chips	1 C. Water
1 ½ C. Sugar	

Directions:
Grease the cake pan with cooking spray and set aside. Open the cooker, fit the reversible rack at the bottom of it, and pour in the water. In a medium heatproof bowl, add the butter and chocolate and melt them in the microwave for about 2 minutes. Remove it from the microwave. Add sugar and stir well. Add the eggs, milk, and vanilla extract and stir again. Finally, add the flour and stir until smooth. Pour the batter into the greased cake pan and use the spatula to level it. Place the pan on the trivet in the pot, close the lid, secure the pressure valve, select Pressure on High for 15 minutes. Press Start. Once the timer has gone off, do a natural pressure release for 10 minutes. Remove the pan to a flat surface. Put a plate over the pan and flip the cake over into the plate. Pour the powdered sugar in a fine sieve and sift it over the cake. Use a knife to cut the cake into 8 slices and serve immediately (while warm).

Coconut Cookies

Ingredients: Servings: 10 Cooking Time: 12 Mins

Egg – 1	Vanilla extract – 1 tsp.
Dried coconut – 3 tbsps.	Chocolate – 2 oz. no sugar added
Butter – 3 oz.	Almond flour – 5 oz.
Erythritol – 2 oz. powdered	

Directions:
In a bowl, beat butter and erythritol until fluffy. Add one egg, vanilla extract and stir to combine. Crush the chocolate into small pieces. Add them to the mixture. Roll small balls with hands. Roll these balls in the dried coconut. Place balls on the baking sheet. Preheat the air fryer to 370F. Bake coconut balls for 8 minutes. Shake once. Lower temperature to 280 to 300F and cook for 4 minutes more. Serve.

Sweet Potato Tots

Ingredients: Servings: 4 Cooking Time: 16 Mins

2 sweet potatoes, peeled	olive oil cooking spray
1/2 tsp. Cajun seasoning	sea salt to taste

Directions:
Add sweet potatoes to boiling water in a pot and cook for 15 minutes until soft. Drain the boiled sweet potatoes and allow them to cool down. Grate the potatoes into a bowl and stir in Cajun seasoning and salt. Mix well and make small tater tots out of this mixture. Place these tater tots in the Air Fryer Basket and spray them with cooking oil. Set the Air Fryer Basket in the Instant Pot Duo. Put on the Air Fryer lid and seal it. Hit the "Air fry Button" and select 16 minutes of cooking time, then press "Start." After 8 minutes, flip all the tots and spray them again with cooking oil then resume cooking. Once the Instant Pot Duo beeps, remove its lid. Serve fresh.

Brazilian Snack Pao De Queijo

Ingredients: Servings: 4 Cooking Time: 20 Mins

2 C. All-purpose flour	A pinch of salt
1 C. Milk	2 C. grated Parmesan Cheese
2 Eggs, cracked into a bowl	½ C. Olive Oil

Directions:
Grease the crisp basket with cooking spray and set aside. Put the cooker on Medium and select Sear/Sauté mode. Add the milk, oil, and salt, and let boil. Add the flour and mix it vigorously with a spoon. Let the mixture cool. Once cooled, use a hand mixer to mix the dough well, and add the eggs and cheese while still mixing. the dough should be thick and sticky. Use your hands to make 14 balls out of the mixture, and put them in the greased basket. Put the basket in the pot and close the crisping lid. Select Air Fry, set the temperature to 380 F and set the timer to 15 minutes. At the 7-minute mark, shake the balls. Serve with lemon aioli, garlic mayo or ketchup.

Chocolate Mayo Cake

Ingredients: Servings: 6 Cooking Time: 25 Mins

Salted butter – ¼ cup, melted	Almond flour – 1 cup
Granular erythritol – ½ cup, plus 1 tbsp.	Full-fat mayonnaise – ¼ cup
Vanilla extract – 1 tsp.	Unsweetened cocoa powder – ¼ cup
	Eggs – 2

Directions:
Mix all the ingredients in a bowl until smooth. Pour batter into a round baking pan. Place the pan into the air fryer basket. Cook at 300F for 25 minutes. Cool and serve.

Crab Sticks

Ingredients: Servings: 4 Cooking Time: 12 Mins

Crabsticks – 10, halved	Cajun seasoning – 2 tsps.
Sesame oil – 2 tsps.	

Directions:
Put crab sticks in a bowl. Add seasoning and sesame oil. Toss and place in the air fryer basket. Cook at 350F for 12 minutes. Serve.

Easy Muffuletta Sliders with Olives (air Fryer)

Ingredients: Servings: 8 Cooking Time: 5 To 7 Mins

¼ lb. (113 g) thinly sliced deli ham
¼ lb. (113 g) thinly sliced pastrami
4 oz. (113 g) low-fat Mozzarella cheese, grated
8 slider buns, split in half
1 tbsp. sesame seeds
Cooking spray
Olive Mix:
½ C. sliced green olives with pimentos
¼ C. sliced black olives
¼ C. chopped kalamata olives
1 tsp. red wine vinegar
¼ tsp. basil
⅛ tsp. garlic powder

Directions:

Preheat the air fryer to 360°F (182°C). Combine all the ingredients for the olive mix in a small bowl and stir well. Stir together the ham, pastrami, and cheese in a medium bowl and divide the mixture into 8 equal portions. Assemble the sliders: Top each bottom bun with 1 portion of meat and cheese, 2 tbsp. of olive mix, finished by the remaining buns. Lightly spritz the tops with cooking spray. Scatter the sesame seeds on top. Working in batches, arrange the sliders in the air fryer basket. Bake for 5 to 7 minutes until the cheese melts. Transfer to a large plate and repeat with the remaining sliders. Serve immediately.

Perfect Cinnamon Toast

Ingredients: Servings: 6 Cooking Time: 5 Mins

2 tsp. pepper
1 ½ tsp. vanilla extract
½ C. sweetener of choice
1 ½ tsp. cinnamon
1 C. coconut oil
12 slices whole wheat bread

Directions:

Preparing the Ingredients. Melt coconut oil and mix with sweetener until dissolved. Mix in remaining ingredients minus bread till incorporated. Spread mixture onto bread, covering all area. Air Frying. Place coated pieces of bread in your Instant Crisp Air Fryer. Close air fryer lid and cook 5 minutes at 400 degrees. Remove and cut diagonally. Enjoy!

Air-fried Pickles

Ingredients: Servings: 3 Cooking Time: 10 Mins

¼ C. Parmesan, freshly grated
1 tsp. garlic powder
2 C. dill pickle slices
½ C. bread crumbs
1 large egg, whisked with a tbsp. of water
1 tsp. dried oregano
A dash of ranch for dipping

Directions:

Pat pickle chips dry using paper towels. In a medium-size mixing bowl, add Parmesan, bread crumbs, garlic powder, and oregano. Stir to mix. One by one, dredge pickle chips in egg and then in the breadcrumb mixture. Work in batches to avoid overcrowding in the air fryer basket. Arrange chips in a single layer. Place air fryer basket inside the instant pot and attach the air fryer lid. Cook at 400 degrees F for 10 minutes. Serve while warm with ranch for the dip.

Raspberry Cream Rol-ups

Ingredients: Servings: 4 Cooking Time: 25 Mins

1 C. of fresh raspberries, rinsed and patted dry
½ C. of cream cheese, softened to room temperature
¼ C. of brown sugar
¼ C. of sweetened condensed milk
1 tsp. of corn starch
1 egg
6 spring roll wrappers (any brand will do, we like Blue Dragon or Tasty Joy, both available through Target or Walmart, or any large grocery chain)
¼ C. of water

Directions:

1 Preparing the Ingredients. Cover the basket of the Instant Crisp Air Fryer with a lining of tin foil, leaving the edges uncovered to allow air to circulate through the basket. Preheat the Instant Crisp Air Fryer to 350 degrees. In a mixing bowl, combine the cream cheese, brown sugar, condensed milk, cornstarch, and egg. Beat or whip thoroughly, until all ingredients are completely mixed and fluffy, thick and stiff. Spoon even amounts of the creamy filling into each spring roll wrapper, then top each dollop of filling with several raspberries. Roll up the wraps around the creamy raspberry filling, and seal the seams with a few dabs of water. Place each roll on the foil-lined Instant Crisp Air Fryer basket, seams facing down. 2 Air Frying. Close air fryer lid. Set the Instant Crisp Air Fryer timer to 10 minutes. During cooking, shake the handle of the fryer basket to ensure a nice even surface crisp. After 10 minutes, when the Instant Crisp Air Fryer shuts off, the spring rolls should be golden brown and perfect on the outside, while the raspberries and cream filling will have cooked together in a glorious fusion. Remove with tongs and serve hot or cold.

Apple Chips In Instant Pot Air Fryer

Ingredients: Servings: 2 Cooking Time: 20 Mins

16 oz. (2 Nos.) apple, large
2 tsp. sugar
½ tsp. ground cinnamon

Directions:

Wash, dry apple, and thinly slice. Mix the apple pieces with sugar and cinnamon in a large bowl. Place the coated apple slices in the air fryer basket without overlapping. Put the air fryer basket in the inner pot of the Instant Pot Air Fryer. Close the crisp lid. Set the temperature at 350°F and timer for 12 minutes in the ROAST mode. Press START to begin the roasting. Halfway through the roasting, open the crisp lid and shake the air fryer basket for even cooking. Close the crisp lid to resume the roasting. Keep checking in between to confirm the desired crisp. Note – the apple slices will continue to crisp as they cool down.

Broccoli Tots

Ingredients: Servings: 4 Cooking Time: 25 Mins

1 lb broccoli, chopped
1/4 C. ground flaxseed
1/2 tsp. garlic powder
1/2 C. flour
1 tsp. salt

Directions:

Add broccoli into the microwave-safe bowl and microwave for 3 minutes. Transfer steamed broccoli into the food processor and process until it looks like rice. Transfer broccoli to a large bowl. Add remaining ingredients into the bowl and mix until well combined. Place the dehydrating tray in a multi-level air fryer basket and place basket in the instant pot. Make small tots from broccoli mixture and place on dehydrating tray. Seal pot with air fryer lid and select air fry mode then set the temperature to 375 F and timer for 12 minutes. Turn halfway through. Serve and enjoy.

Chickpeas Snack

Ingredients: Servings: 4 Cooking Time: 10 Mins

Canned chickpeas – 15 ounces, drained
Cumin – ½ tsp. ground
Olive oil – 1 tbsp.
Smoked paprika – 1 tsp.
Salt and black pepper to taste

Directions:
In a bowl, mix chickpeas with oil, salt, pepper, paprika, and cumin. Toss to coat and place in the air fryer basket. Cook at 390F for 10 minutes. Serve.

Chocolaty Banana Muffins

Ingredients: Servings: 12 Cooking Time: 25 Mins

¾ C. whole wheat flour
¾ C. plain flour
¼ C. cocoa powder
¼ tsp. baking powder
1 tsp. baking soda
¼ tsp. salt
2 large bananas, peeled and mashed
1 C. sugar
1/3 C. canola oil
1 egg
½ tsp. vanilla essence
1 C. mini chocolate chips

Directions:
Preparing the Ingredients. In a large bowl, mix together flour, cocoa powder, baking powder, baking soda and salt. In another bowl, add bananas, sugar, oil, egg and vanilla extract and beat till well combined. Slowly, add flour mixture in egg mixture and mix till just combined. Fold in chocolate chips. Preheat the Instant Crisp Air Fryer to 345 degrees F. Grease 12 muffin molds. Air Frying. Transfer the mixture into prepared muffin molds evenly, close the air fryer Lid. Select Bake, set the temperature to 390°F, and set the time to 20 minutes or till a toothpick inserted in the center comes out clean. Select Start to begin. Remove the muffin molds from Instant Crisp Air Fryer and keep on wire rack to cool for about 10 minutes. Carefully turn on a wire rack to cool completely before serving.

Fast Crème Brulee

Ingredients: Servings: 4 Cooking Time: 23 Mins

3 C. Heavy Whipping Cream
6 tbsp. Sugar
7 large Egg Yolks
2 tbsp. Vanilla Extract
2 C. Water

Directions:
In a mixing bowl, add the yolks, vanilla, whipping cream, and half of the swerve sugar. Use a whisk to mix them until they are well combined. Pour the mixture into the ramekins and cover them with aluminium foil. Open the cooker, fit the reversible rack into the pot, and pour in the water. Place 3 ramekins on the rack and place the remaining ramekins to sit on the edges of the ramekins below. Close the lid, secure the pressure valve, and select Pressure mode on High for 8 minutes. Press Start. Once the timer has stopped, do a natural pressure release for 10 minutes, then a quick pressure release to let out the remaining pressure. with a napkin in hand, remove the ramekins onto a flat surface and then into a refrigerator to chill for at least 6 hours. After refrigeration, remove the ramekins and remove the aluminium foil. Equally, sprinkle the remaining sugar on it and return to the pot. Close the crisping lid, select Bake mode, set the timer to 4 minutes on 380 F. Serve the crème brulee chilled with whipped cream.

Simple Shrimp Kabobs

Ingredients: Servings: 2 Cooking Time: 8 Mins

1 C. shrimp
1 garlic clove, minced
1 lemon juice
Pepper
Salt

Directions:
Add shrimp, lemon juice, garlic, pepper, and salt into the bowl and toss well. Spray instant pot multi-level air fryer basket with cooking spray. Thread shrimp onto the soaked wooden skewers and place them into the air fryer basket and place basket into the instant pot. Seal pot with air fryer lid and select air fry mode then set the temperature to 350 F and timer for 8 minutes. Stir halfway through. Serve and enjoy.

Air Fried Chocolate Chips

Ingredients: Servings: 8 Cooking Time: 12 Mins

1 C. chocolate chips or chunks
½ tsp. baking soda
½ C. butter, softened
1 egg
1 tsp. vanilla
½ C. light brown sugar
1½ C. all-purpose flour
¼ tsp. salt
A scoop of vanilla ice cream to serve

Directions:
Line 2 layers of the air fryer basket with parchment paper. Cream altogether the butter and brown sugar. Then add the egg and vanilla along with the baking soda, flour, and salt. Stir in chocolate chunks. Press cookie dough into the bottom of the air fryer. Attach the air fryer lid and bake for 10-12 minutes until edges are lightly browned. Top with a scoop of vanilla ice cream to serve.

Peanut Butter Cookies

Ingredients: Servings: 8 Cooking Time: 8 Mins

Smooth peanut butter – 1 cup
Granular erythritol – 1/3 cup
Egg – 1
Vanilla extract – 1 tsp.

Directions:
Mix all the ingredients in a bowl until smooth. Continue to stir until the mixture begins to thicken. Roll the mixture into eight balls and press gently down to flatten into 2-inch round disks.

Line the air fryer basket with parchment. Place the cookies onto the parchment. Work in batches if necessary. Cook at 320F for 8 minutes. Flip the cookies at the 6-minute mark. Serve.

Chocolate Souffle

Ingredients: Servings: 2 Cooking Time: 15 Mins

2 egg whites
2 egg yolks
1/2 tsp. vanilla
3 oz chocolate, melted
3 tbsp. sugar
2 tbsp. flour
1/4 C. butter, melted

Directions:
Spray two ramekins with cooking spray and set aside. In a bowl, beat egg yolks with vanilla and sugar. Stir in flour, melted chocolate, and butter. In a separate bowl, beat egg whites and until stiff peak forms. Slowly fold egg white mixture into the egg yolk mixture. Pour batter into the prepared ramekins. Place the dehydrating tray in a multi-level air fryer basket and place basket in the instant pot. Place ramekins on a dehydrating tray. Seal pot with air fryer lid and select bake mode then set the temperature to 330 F and timer for 15 minutes. Serve and enjoy.

Spicy Spinach Artichoke Dip

Ingredients: Servings: 6 Cooking Time: 10 Mins

Frozen spinach – 10 ounces, drained and thawed
Artichoke hearts – 1 (14-ounce) can, drained and chopped
Chopped pickled jalapenos – ¼ cup
Full-fat cream cheese – 8 ounces, softened
Full-fat sour cream – ¼ cup
Full-fat mayonnaise – ¼ cup
Garlic powder – ½ tsp.
Grated Parmesan cheese – ¼ cup
Shredded pepper jack cheese – 1 cup

Directions:
Mix all ingredients in a baking bowl. Place into the air fryer basket. Cook at 320F for 10 minutes. Serve warm.

Coconut Chicken Bites

Ingredients: Servings: 4 Cooking Time: 13 Mins

Garlic powder – 2 tsps.
Salt and black pepper to taste
Panko bread crumbs – ¾ cup
Eggs – 2
Coconut – ¾ cup, shredded
Cooking spray
Chicken tenders – 8

Directions:
Mix eggs with garlic powder, salt, and pepper in a bowl and whisk well. In another bowl, mix coconut with panko and stir well. Dip chicken tenders in the eggs mix and then coat in coconut thoroughly. Spray chicken bits with cooking spray. Place them in the air fryer basket and cook them at 350F for 10 minutes. Serve.

Cinnamon & Vanilla Balls

Ingredients: Servings: 4 Cooking Time: 10 Mins

⅔ C. all-purpose flour
½ tsp. baking powder
3 tbsps. white sugar
1 tbsp. ground cinnamon
A pinch of salt
2 tbsp. cold butter, cubed
¼ C. sour cream
1 tbsp. vanilla powder

Directions:
Mix the all-purpose flour, baking powder, 1 tbsp. of sugar, ¼ tsp. of cinnamon, and the salt in a medium bowl. Add the butter and use a pastry cutter to cut into the butter to be broken into pieces. Pour in the sour cream and mix until the dough forms into a ball. Knead the dough on a flat surface until a smooth both is achieved. Divide the dough into 8 pieces and roll each piece into a ball. Coat the preheated Cook & Crisp basket with cooking spray. Put the balls in the basket with space in between each ball and oil the balls with cooking spray. Close the crisping lid. Choose Air Fry, set the temperature to 350 F, and set the time to 10 minutes. Press Start. In a medium mixing bowl, combine the remaining sugar and cinnamon, and vanilla powder. When done baking, toss the dough balls in the vanilla-cinnamon and sugar mixture.

Air-fried Toasted Sticks

Ingredients: Servings: 6 Cooking Time: 8 Mins

⅓ C. heavy cream
2 large eggs
⅓ C. whole milk
¼ tsp. ground cinnamon
1 tsp. maple syrup
3 tbsps. granulated sugar
6 thick pullman slices, cut into 3 parts (alternative: brioche or white loaf)
½ tsp. pure vanilla extract
Kosher salt to taste

Directions:
Beat eggs and add sugar, milk, cream, vanilla, cinnamon with salt in a large shallow baking dish. Coat bread with the mixture, turning for even coating at all sides. Line air fryer basket with parchment paper before arranging French toasts sticks inside. Avoid overcrowding and work in batches when necessary. Place the basket inside the instant pot, attach the air fryer lid to the pressure cooker and set to cook at 370 degrees F for 8 minutes, tossing halfway through for even cooking. Drizzle maple syrup over toast and serve warm.

Pumpkin Pie

Ingredients: Servings: 9 Cooking Time: 15 Mins

Sugar – 1 tbsp.
Flour – 2 tbsps.
Butter – 1 tbsp.
For the pumpkin pie filling
Pumpkin flesh – 3.5 ounces, chopped
Water – 2 tbsps.
Mixed spice – 1 tsp.
Nutmeg – 1 tsp.
Water – 3 ounces
Egg – 1, whisked
Sugar – 1 tbsp.

Directions:
Put 3 oz. of water in a pot. Bring to a boil and add pumpkin, 1 tbsp. of sugar, egg, spice, and nutmeg. Stir and boil for 20 minutes. Remove from the heat and blend with a hand mixer. In a bowl, mix butter, flour, 2 tbsps. of water, 1 tbsp. sugar and knead the dough well. Grease a pie pan with butter. Press dough into the pan. Fill with pumpkin pie filling. Place in the air fryer's basket and cook at 360F for 15 minutes. Serve.

Sweet and Salty Snack Mix (air Fryer)

Ingredients: Servings: 10 Cooking Time: 10 To 12 Mins

3 tbsp. butter, melted
½ C. honey
1 tsp. salt
2 C. granola
2 C. crispy corn puff cereal
2 C. sesame sticks
2 C. mini pretzel crisps
1 C. cashews
1 C. pepitas
1 C. dried cherries

Directions:
In a small mixing bowl, mix together the butter, honey, and salt until well incorporated. In a large bowl, put the granola, sesame sticks, corn puff cereal and pretzel crisps, cashews, and pepitas. Drizzle with the butter mixture and toss until evenly coated. Preheat the air fryer to 370°F (188°C). Transfer the snack mix to the air fryer basket. You may need to cook in batches depending on the size of your air fryer basket. Air fry for 10 to 12 minutes until lightly toasted, shaking the basket a few times during cooking for even cooking Remove from the basket and allow to cool completely. Repeat with the remaining snack mix. Scatter with the dried cherries and mix well. Serve immediately.

Garlic Edamame (air Fryer)

Ingredients: Servings: 4 Cooking Time: 16 To 20 Mins

2 tbsp. olive oil, divided
1 (16-ounce / 454-g) bag frozen edamame in pods
½ tsp. salt
½ tsp. garlic salt
¼ tsp. freshly ground black pepper
½ tsp. red pepper flakes (optional)

Directions:
Preheat the air fryer to 375°F (191°C). Grease the air fryer basket with 1 tbsp. of olive oil. Place the edamame in a medium bowl and drizzle the remaining 1 tbsp. of olive oil over the top. Toss to coat well. Stir together the garlic salt, salt, pepper, and red pepper flakes (if desired) in a small bowl. Pour the mixture into the bowl of edamame and toss until the edamame is fully coated. Arrange the edamame in the greased basket. You may need to cook in batches to avoid overcrowding. Air fry for 8 to 10 minutes, shaking the basket halfway through, or until the edamame is crisp. Remove from the basket to a plate and repeat with the remaining edamame. Serve warm.

Apple Snack

Ingredients: Servings: 4 Cooking Time: 5 Mins

Big apples – 3, cored, peeled and cubed
Pecans – ¼ cup, chopped
Lemon juice – 2 tsps.
Dark chocolate chips – ½ cup
Clean caramel sauce – ½ cup

Directions:
Mix apples and lemon juice in a bowl. Add to a dish that fits in the air fryer. Add pecans, chocolate chips, and drizzle the caramel sauce. Toss to coat. Cook at 320F for 5 minutes in the air fryer. Serve.

Orange Toast (pressure Cook)

Ingredients: Servings: 4 Cooking Time: 15 Mins

2 large eggs
1 C. milk
2 tsp. vanilla extract
1 tsp. ground cinnamon
Zest of 1 orange
6 bread slices, cubed
1 C. water
Maple syrup, for topping

Directions:
Beat the eggs with the milk, vanilla extract, cinnamon and orange zest in a mixing bowl. Add the bread cubes and mix to coat. Pour the mixture into a greased baking pan and cover with aluminium foil. Pour the water into the Instant Pot and fit in a trivet. Place the covered pan on top. Seal the lid, select the Pressure Cook and set the cooking time for 15 minutes at High Pressure. When cooking is complete, perform a quick pressure release. Unlock the lid, remove the pan, and take off the foil. Let cool for 5 minutes. Drizzle with maple syrup to serve.

Mexican Chicken Fajitas with Guacamole

Ingredients: Servings: 4 Cooking Time: 20 Mins

2 lb Chicken Breasts, skinless and cut in 1-inch slices
½ C. Chicken Broth
1 Yellow Onion, sliced
1 Green Bell Pepper, seeded and sliced
1 Yellow Bell Pepper, seeded and sliced
1 Red Bell Pepper, seeded and sliced
2 tbsp. Cumin Powder
2 tbsp. Chili Powder
Salt to taste
Half a Lime
Cooking Spray
Fresh cilantro, to garnish
Assembling:
Tacos, Guacamole, Sour Cream, Salsa, Cheese

Directions:
Grease the inner pot with cooking spray and line the bottom with the peppers and onion. Lay the chicken on the bed of peppers. Sprinkle with salt, chili powder, and cumin powder. Squeeze some lime juice and pour in chicken broth. Close the lid, secure the pressure valve, and select Pressure mode on High pressure for 15 minutes. Press Start. Once the timer has ended, do a quick pressure release, and open the lid. Close the crisping lid and cook for 5 minutes on Roast mode at 370 F. Dish the chicken with the vegetables and juice onto a large serving platter. Add sour cream, cheese, guacamole, salsa, and tacos in one layer on the side of the chicken.

Creamy Potato

Ingredients: Servings: 2 Cooking Time: 1 Hour 20 Mins

Big potato – 1
Bacon strips – 2, cooked and chopped
Cheddar cheese – 1/3 cup, shredded
Green onions – 1 tbsp. chopped
Olive oil – 1 tsp.
Salt and black pepper to taste
Butter – 1 tbsp.
Heavy cream – 2 tbsps.

Directions:
Rub potato with oil, season with salt and pepper. Place in the preheated air fryer and cook at 400F for 30 minutes. Flip

potato, and cook for 30 minutes more. Transfer to a cutting board. Cool and slice in half lengthwise and scoop pulp in a bowl. Add salt, pepper, green onions, heavy cream, butter, cheese, and bacon. Stir well and stuff potato skins with this mix. Return potato to the air fryer and cook them at 400F for 20 minutes. Divide among plates and serve.

Cheeseburger Dip

Ingredients: Servings: 6 Cooking Time: 10 Mins

Full-fat cream cheese – 8 ounces
Full-fat mayonnaise – 1/4 cup
Full-fat sour cream – 1/4 cup
Garlic powder – 1 tsp.
Worcestershire sauce -1 tbsp.
Chopped onion – 1/4 cup
Shredded cheddar cheese – 1 1/4 cups, divided
Cooked 80/20 ground beef – 1/2 pound
Bacon – 6 slices, cooked and crumbled
Large pickle spears – 2, chopped

Directions:
Place cream cheese in a bowl, and microwave for 45 seconds. Stir in sour cream, mayonnaise, onion, garlic powder, 1-cup cheddar, and Worcestershire sauce. Add cooked bacon and ground beef. Sprinkle remaining cheddar on top. Place in a bowl and put into the air fryer basket. Cook at 400F for 10 minutes. the dip is done when the top is golden and bubbling. Sprinkle pickles over the dish. Serve warm.

Raspberry Bites

Ingredients: Servings: 10 Cooking Time: 5 Mins

2 oz. Full-fat cream cheese; softened.
1 large egg.
1 C. blanched finely ground almond flour.
3 tbsp. Granular swerve.
1 tsp. Baking powder.
10 tsp. Sugar-free raspberry preserves.

Directions:
Mix all ingredients except preServing in a large bowl until a wet dough form. Place the bowl in the freezer for 20 minutes until dough is cool and able to roll into a ball. Roll dough into ten balls and press gently in the center of each ball. Place 1 tsp. PreServing in the center of each ball. Cut a piece of parchment to fit your air fryer basket. Place each danish bite on the parchment, pressing down gently to flatten the bottom. Adjust the temperature to 400 degrees f and set the timer for 7 minutes. Allow to cool completely before moving, or they will crumble.

Dulce De Leche & Chocolate Brownies

Ingredients: Servings: 6 Cooking Time: 54 Mins

8 oz. dark chocolate
8 tbsps. unsalted butter
1 C. sugar
2 tsps almond extract
A pinch of salt
2 large eggs, at room temperature
3/4 C. flour
1/2 C. dulce de leche
1/2 C. toasted walnuts

Directions:
Put chocolate and butter in a small bowl and pour 1 C. of water into the inner pot. Place in the reversible rack put the bowl on top. Close the crisping lid, choose Bake; adjust the temperature to 375 F and cook time to 10 minutes. Press Start. Check after 5 minutes and stir. Remove the bowl from the pot. Use a small spatula to transfer the chocolate mixture into a medium bowl and stir in the almond extract, sugar, and salt. One after another, crack each egg into the bowl and whisk after each addition. Mix in the flour until smooth, about 1 minute. Grease a round cake pan with cooking spray. Pour the batter into the prepared pan and place on the rack. Close the crisping lid and choose Bake; adjust the temperature to 250 F and the cook time to 40 minutes. Press Start. Once the time is up, open the lid. Generously drizzle the dulce de leche on top of the brownies and scatter the walnuts on top. Close the crisping lid again and adjust the temperature to 325 F and the cook time to 4 minutes. Press Start. Allow the brownies cool and serve

Sausage Balls with Cheese (air Fryer)

Ingredients: Servings: 8 Cooking Time: 10 To 11 Mins

12 oz. (340 g) mild ground sausage
1½ C. baking mix
1 C. shredded mild Cheddar cheese
3 oz. (85 g) cream cheese, at room temperature
1 to 2 tbsp. olive oil

Directions:
Preheat the air fryer to 325°F (163°C). Line the air fryer basket with parchment paper. Mix together the ground sausage, baking mix, Cheddar cheese, and cream cheese in a large bowl and stir to incorporate. Divide the sausage mixture into 16 equal portions and roll them into 1-inch balls with your hands. Arrange the sausage balls on the parchment, leaving space between each ball. You may need to work in batches to avoid overcrowding. Brush the sausage balls with the olive oil. Bake for 10 to 11 minutes, shaking the basket halfway through, or until the balls are firm and lightly browned on both sides. Remove from the basket to a plate and repeat with the remaining balls. Serve warm.

Green Beans

Ingredients: Servings: 4 Cooking Time: 25 Mins

Green beans – 1 1/2 pounds, trimmed and steamed for 2 minutes
Salt and black pepper to taste
Shallots – 1/2 pound, chopped
Almonds – 1/4 cup, toasted
Olive oil – 2 tbsps.

Directions:
Mix green beans with oil, almonds, shallots, salt, and pepper in the air fryer basket. Toss well and cook at 400F for 25 minutes. Divide among plates and serve.

Chocolate Peppermint Cheesecake (air Fryer)

Ingredients: Servings: 6 Cooking Time: 18 Mins

Crust:
1/2 C. butter, melted
1/2 C. coconut flour
Topping:
1 C. mascarpone cheese, at room

2 tbsp. stevia
Cooking spray
4 oz. (113 g) unsweetened baker's chocolate
temperature
1 tsp. vanilla extract
2 drops peppermint extract

Directions:

Preheat the air fryer to 350°F (177°C). Lightly coat a baking pan with cooking spray. In a mixing bowl, whisk together the butter, flour, and stevia until well combined. Transfer the mixture to the prepared baking pan. Place the baking pan in the air fryer and bake for 18 minutes until a toothpick inserted in the center comes out clean. Remove the crust from the air fryer to a wire rack to cool. Once cooled completely, place it in the freezer for 20 minutes. When ready, combine all the ingredients for the topping in a small bowl and stir to incorporate. Spread this topping over the crust and let it sit for another 15 minutes in the freezer. Serve chilled.

Tasty Chicken Wings

Ingredients: Servings: 6 Cooking Time: 25 Mins

3 lb Chicken Wingettes
3 tbsp. Cajun Garlic Powder
Salt to taste
1/4 C. Barbecue Sauce
1/2 C. Hot Sauce
1/4 C. Butter, melted
1/2 C. Water

Directions:

Pat the wingettes dry with a paper towel and put them in a bowl. Season them with Cajun garlic powder and salt. Open the cooker, pour in the water, and fit in the reversible rack. Arrange the wingettes on top, close the lid, secure the pressure valve, and select Pressure mode for 5 minutes. Press Start to start cooking. Once the timer has ended, do a natural pressure release for 10 minutes, and then a quick pressure release to let out any more steam. Open the lid. Remove the wings with tongs to a crisp basket and add the butter, half of the hot sauce and half of the barbecue sauce. Stir the chicken until well coated in the sauce. Insert the basket in the pot and close the crisping lid. Select Air Fry, set to 380 F, and cook for 10 minutes. Select Start. Once nice and crispy, remove them to a bowl, and top with the remaining barbecue and hot sauces. Stir and serve the chicken with a cheese dip.

Prosciutto-parmesan Asparagus

Ingredients: Servings: 4 Cooking Time: 10 Mins

Asparagus – 1 pound
Prosciutto – 12 (0.5 ounce) slices
Coconut oil – 1 tbsp. melted
Lemon juice – 2 tsps.
Red pepper flakes – 1/8 tsp.
Grated Parmesan cheese – 1/3 cup
Salted butter – 2 tbsps. melted

Directions:

On a clean work surface, place a few asparagus spears onto a sliced of prosciutto. Drizzle with lemon juice and coconut oil. Sprinkle Parmesan and red pepper flakes across asparagus. Roll prosciutto around asparagus spears. Place into the air fryer basket. Repeat. Cook at 375F and 10 minutes. Drizzle the asparagus rolls with butter before serving.

Bacon-wrapped Onion Rings

Ingredients: Servings: 4 Cooking Time: 10 Mins

Large onion – 1, sliced into 1/4 inch thick slices
Sriracha – 1 tbsp.
Bacon – 8 slices

Directions:

Brush sriracha over the onion slices. Take two slices of onion and wrap bacon around the rings. Repeat with the remaining onion and bacon. Place into the air fryer basket. Cook at 350F for 10 minutes. Flip the onion rings halfway through the cooking time. Serve warm.

Herby Chicken Thighs

Ingredients: Servings: 4 Cooking Time: 25 Mins

2 lb Chicken Thighs, bone in and skin on
2 tbsp. Olive Oil
Salt and Pepper, to taste
1 1/2 C. diced Tomatoes
3/4 C. Yellow Onion
2 tsp. minced Garlic
1/2 C. Balsamic Vinegar
3 tsp. chopped fresh Thyme
1 C. Chicken Broth
2 tbsp. chopped Parsley

Directions:

With paper towels, pat dry the chicken and season with salt and pepper. Select Sear/Sauté mode. Warm the olive and add the chicken with skin side down. Cook to golden brown on each side, for about 9 minutes. Remove onto a clean plate. Then, add onions and tomatoes to the pot and sauté for 3 minutes, stirring occasionally with a spoon. Add in garlic and cook for 30 seconds, until fragrant. Pour the chicken broth, and add some salt, thyme, and balsamic vinegar. Stir them using a spoon. Add the chicken back to the pot. Close the lid, secure the pressure valve, and select Pressure mode on High pressure for 15 minutes. Press Start to start cooking. When ready, do a quick pressure release. Close the crisping lid and cook on Air Fry mode for 5 minutes at 400 F. Garnish with parsley and serve with thyme roasted tomatoes, carrots, and sweet potatoes.

Vanilla Pumpkin Pudding

Ingredients: Servings: 6 Cooking Time: 20 Mins

2 eggs
1/2 C. almond milk
1/2 tsp. pumpkin pie spice
1/2 tsp. vanilla
14 oz pumpkin puree
1/4 C. sugar

Directions:

Grease 6-inch baking dish with cooking spray and set aside. In a large bowl, whisk eggs with remaining ingredients. Pour mixture into the prepared dish and cover with foil. Pour 1 1/2 C. of water into the inner pot of instant pot duo crisp then place a steamer rack in the pot. Place dish on top of the steamer rack. Seal the pot with pressure cooking lid and cook on high for 20 minutes. Once done, allow to release pressure naturally for 10 minutes then release remaining pressure using a quick release. Remove lid. Carefully remove dish from the pot and let it cool completely then place in the refrigerator for 5 hours before serving. Serve and enjoy.

Air Fried Cheeseburgers

Ingredients: Servings: 4 Cooking Time: 8 Mins

4 hamburger buns
1 tbsp. low-sodium soy sauce
2 cloves garlic, minced
4 slices American cheese
Freshly ground black pepper to taste
1 lb. ground beef
1 red onion, thinly sliced
4 lettuce
4 tsp. mayonnaise
4 sliced tomatoes
Kosher salt to taste

Directions:
Combine Beef with soy sauce, salt, pepper and garlic in a large mixing bowl. Mix thoroughly so the mixture can seep through the beef. Shape marinated ground beef into patties and arrange in a single layer in the air fryer basket. If there's not enough space to accommodate all patties, cook in batches. Put the air fryer basket on top of the metal trivet inside the instant pot. Attach the air fryer lid and cook at 375 degrees F for about 4 minutes. Turn over for even cooking and cook for another 4 minutes. Once done, remove the burgers quickly and top every burger with a slice of cheese. Cook the remaining patties using the same procedure. Spread mayo on hamburger buns and then arrange its filling using lettuce as the base followed by a burger with cheese, tomatoes, and onions on top. Serve immediately while warm.

Corn On the Cob

Ingredients: Servings: 8 Cooking Time: 4 Mins

8 ears corn on the cob, remove husk and silk
4 tbsp. butter
Pepper
Salt

Directions:
Pour 2 C. of water into the instant pot then place rack in the pot. Place corn on the rack. Seal pot with lid and cook on manual high pressure for 4 minutes. Once done then allow to release pressure naturally then open the lid. Remove corn from pot and season with pepper and salt. Top with butter and serve.

Curried Fries

Ingredients: Servings: 3 Cooking Time: 20 Mins

2 small sweet potatoes, peel and cut into fry's shape
1/2 tsp. curry powder
2 tbsp. olive oil
1/4 tsp. coriander
1/4 tsp. sea salt

Directions:
Add all ingredients into the large mixing bowl and toss well. Spray instant pot multi-level air fryer basket with cooking spray. Transfer sweet potato fries into the air fryer basket and place basket into the instant pot. Seal pot with air fryer lid and select air fry mode then set the temperature to 370 F and timer for 20 minutes. Stir halfway through. Serve and enjoy.

Mini Buffalo Chicken Balls with Roquefort Sauce

Ingredients: Servings: 4 Cooking Time: 24 Mins

1 lb Ground Chicken
2 tbsp. Buffalo wing sauce
1 Egg, beaten
Salt and Pepper to taste
2 tbsp. Minced Garlic
2 tbsp. Olive Oil
5 tbsp. Hot Sauce
2 tbsp. chopped Green Onions + extra for garnish
For the sauce:
½ C. Roquefort Cheese, crumbled
¼ tbsp. Heavy Cream
2 tbsp. Mayonnaise
Juice from ½ Lemon
Select Air Fry, set the temperature to 385 F and the time to 14 minutes. At the 7-minute mark, turn the meatballs.
2 tbsp. Olive Oil
Meanwhile, add the hot sauce and butter to a bowl and microwave them until the butter melts. Mix the sauce with a spoon. Pour the hot sauce mixture and a half C. of water over the meatballs. Close the lid, secure the pressure valve, and select Sear/Sauté mode on High Pressure for 10 minutes. Press Start. Once the timer has ended, do a quick pressure release. Dish the meatballs. Garnish with green onions, and serve with Roquefort sauce.

Directions:
Mix all salsa

White Chocolate Cookies (air Fryer)

Ingredients: Servings: 10 Cooking Time: 11 Mins

8 oz. (227 g) unsweetened white chocolate
2 eggs, well beaten
¾ C. butter, at room temperature
1⅔ C. almond flour
½ C. coconut flour
¾ C. granulated Swerve
2 tbsp. coconut oil
⅓ tsp. grated nutmeg
⅓ tsp. ground allspice
⅓ tsp. ground anise star
¼ tsp. fine sea salt

Directions:
Preheat the air fryer to 350ºF (177ºC). Line the air fryer basket with parchment paper. Combine all the ingredients in a mixing bowl and knead for about 3 to 4 minutes, or until a soft dough forms. Transfer to the refrigerator to chill for 20 minutes. Make the cookies: Roll the dough into 1-inch balls and transfer to parchment-lined basket, spacing 2 inches apart. Flatten each with the back of a spoon. Bake for about 11 minutes until the cookies are golden and firm to the touch. Transfer to a wire rack and let the cookies cool completely. Serve immediately.

Broccoli Nuggets

Ingredients: Servings: 4 Cooking Time: 15 Mins

2 C. broccoli florets, cooked until soft
1/4 C. almond flour
1 C. cheddar cheese, shredded
2 egg whites
1/8 tsp. salt

Directions:
Add cooked broccoli into the bowl and using masher mash broccoli into the small pieces. Add remaining ingredients to

the bowl and stir to combine. Place the dehydrating tray in a multi-level air fryer basket and place basket in the instant pot. Make nuggets from broccoli mixture and place on dehydrating tray. Seal pot with air fryer lid and select air fry mode then set the temperature to 425 F and timer for 15 minutes. Turn halfway through. Serve and enjoy.

Cauliflower Fritters

Ingredients: Servings: 6-8 Cooking Time: 8 Mins

1/3 C. shredded sharp cheddar cheese
½ C. chopped parsley
1 C. Italian breadcrumbs
3 chopped scallions
1 head of cauliflower, cut into florets
1 egg
2 minced garlic cloves

Directions:

Blend the florets into a blender to make the rice like structure. Add in a bowl. Mix in the pepper, salt, egg, cheeses, breadcrumbs, garlic, and scallions. Prepare 15 patties from the mixture. Coat them with some cooking spray. Place Instant Pot Air Fryer Crisp over kitchen platform. Press Air Fry, set the temperature to 400°F and set the timer to 5 minutes to preheat. Press "Start" and allow it to preheat for 5 minutes. In the inner pot, place the Air Fryer basket. In the basket, add the patties. Close the Crisp Lid and press the "Air Fry" setting. Set temperature to 390°F and set the timer to 8 minutes. Press "Start." Halfway down, open the Crisp Lid, shake the basket and close the lid to continue cooking for the remaining time. Open the Crisp Lid after cooking time is over. Serve warm.

Instant Pot Chocolate Chip Cookie In Air Fryer

Ingredients: Servings: 2 Cooking Time: 10 Mins

2 large eggs
16 oz. cream cheese, softened at room temperature
½ tsp. lemon juice
2 tbsps. sour cream
1 tsp. vanilla extract
¾ C. zero-calorie sweetener

Directions:

Add eggs, vanilla, sweetener and lemon juice in a blender. Process until smooth and add the sour cream along with the cheese. Continue to free until silky and free of lumps. the creamier, the better. Line the air fryer basket with parchment paper and pour the batter into it. Place inside the instant pot and cover with the air fryer lid. Bake for 8-10 minutes at 350 degrees F. Allow to cool in a wire rack and leave in the fridge overnight or at least 2-3 hours.

Zucchini Cakes

Ingredients: Servings: 12 Cooking Time: 12 Mins

Cooking spray
Dill – ½ cup, chopped
Whole wheat flour – ½ cup
Salt and black pepper to taste
Egg – 1
Yellow onion – 1, chopped
Garlic cloves – 2, minced
Zucchinis – 3, grated

Directions:

In a bowl, mix zucchinis with dill, egg, salt, pepper, flour, onion, and garlic. Mix thoroughly. Make small patties with the mix and spray them with cooking spray. Place them in the air fryer basket and cook at 370F for 6 minutes on each side. Serve.

Fluffy Baked Donuts

Ingredients: Servings: 6 Cooking Time: 8 Mins

2 eggs
2 tbsp. butter, melted
1 tsp. vanilla
3/4 C. buttermilk
1/4 tsp. cinnamon
1/4 tsp. nutmeg
2 tsp. baking powder
3/4 C. sugar
2 C. flour
1 tsp. salt

Directions:

In a mixing bowl, whisk eggs, butter, vanilla, and buttermilk until well combined. In a large bowl, mix together flour, cinnamon, nutmeg, baking powder, sugar, and salt. Pour egg mixture into the flour mixture and mix until well combined. Pour batter into the 6 silicone donut molds. Place the dehydrating tray in a multi-level air fryer basket and place basket in the instant pot. Place 4 silicone donut molds on dehydrating tray. Seal pot with air fryer lid and select bake mode then set the temperature to 325 F and timer for 8 minutes. Bake remaining donut using the same method. Serve and enjoy.

Chocolate Oreo Cookie Cake (pressure Cook)

Ingredients: Servings: 6 Cooking Time: 35 Mins

12 Oreo cookies, smoothly crushed
2 tbsp. salted butter, melted
16 oz. (454 g) cream cheese, softened
½ C. granulated sugar
2 large eggs
1 tbsp. all-purpose flour
¼ C. heavy cream
2 tsp. vanilla extract
16 whole Oreo cookies, coarsely crushed
1½ C. water
1 C. whipped cream
2 tbsp. chocolate sauce, for topping

Directions:

Line a springform pan with foil, then spritz with cooking spray. Make the crust: In a bowl, combine smoothly crushed Oreo cookies with butter, then press into bottom of pan. Freeze for 15 minutes. In another bowl, add cream cheese, and beat until smooth. Add sugar to whisk until satiny. Beat in the eggs one by one until mixed. Whisk in flour, heavy cream, and vanilla. Fold in 8 coarsely crushed cookies and pour the mixture onto the crust in the springform pan. Cover pan tightly with foil. Pour the water in the Instant Pot and fit in a trivet. Place the pan on trivet. Seal the lid, set to the Pressure Cook and set the cooking time for 35 minutes at High Pressure. When cooking is complete, allow a natural pressure release for 10 minutes, then release any remaining pressure. Carefully open the lid. Remove the trivet with cake pan from the pot. Remove foil and transfer to a cooling rack to chill. Refrigerate for 8 hours. Top with whipped cream, remaining cookies, and chocolate sauce. Slice and serve.

Mozzarella Balls

Ingredients: Servings: 12 Cooking Time: 10 Mins

2 C. fresh grated mozzarella	1 tbsp. oregano
3 tbsp. cornstarch	1 1/2 tsp. garlic powder
1 egg	1 tsp. salt
1 C. Italian seasoned breadcrumbs	1 1/2 tbsp. Parmesan

Directions:
Choose the Air Fry option and set the temperature of the Instant Pot Duo Crisp Air Fryer to 400°F. Line a baking sheet with the parchment. Make a thorough mixture of cornstarch and Parmesan to shredded cheese. Roll the cheese into the bite-size balls and put it in the freezer (45- 60 mins). Beat your egg in a small bowl. Combine salt, garlic powder, and bread crumbs and mix well in another bowl. Immerse your cheese balls in the egg and coat them well. Roll the egg coated balls in bread crumbs and place them back on a baking sheet. Put this in the freezer for around 20 mins. Repeat the egg and bread steps and place it in the Air Fryer basket. Close the lid. Cook on 400°F for around 10 minutes while making sure to rotate frequently. When the balls begin to melt, transfer them back to your baking sheet. Let rest for a couple of minutes.

Tater Tots

Ingredients: Servings: 2 Cooking Time: 10 Mins

16 oz frozen tater tots	1 tbsp. olive oil
	Salt

Directions:
Drizzle tater tots with olive oil and season with salt. Spray instant pot multi-level air fryer basket with cooking spray. Add tater tots into the air fryer basket and place basket into the instant pot. Seal pot with air fryer lid and select air fry mode then set the temperature to 400 F and timer for 10 minutes. Stir halfway through. Serve and enjoy.

Panko Chicken Croquettes

Ingredients: Servings: 6 Cooking Time: 25 Mins

1 lb. ground chicken	¼ C. crumbled queso fresco
1 green bell pepper, minced	¼ C. panko breadcrumbs
2 celery stalks, minced	1 egg
¼ C. hot sauce	2 tbsps. melted butter
	½ C. water

Directions:
In a bowl, combine the chicken, bell pepper, celery, queso fresco, hot sauce, breadcrumbs, and egg. Form balls (approximately the size of golf balls) out of the mixture. Choose Sear/Sauté on the pot and set to High. Pour in the melted butter and fry the meatballs in batches until lightly browned on all sides. Use a slotted spoon to remove the meatballs onto a plate. Put the Cook & Crisp basket in the pot. Pour in the water and put all the meatballs in the basket. Seal the pressure lid, choose Pressure, set to High, and set the timer to 5 minutes. Hit Start. When done cooking, perform a quick pressure release and carefully open the lid. Close the crisping lid, press Air Fry button set the temperature to 360 F and set the time to 10 minutes. Choose Start. At the 5-minute mark, shake the meatballs. Serve.

Parmesan Truffle Fries

Ingredients: Servings: 2 Cooking Time: 15 Mins

2 large gold potatoes, peeled	1 tsp. black pepper, crushed
1 tbsp. parsley flakes	1/2 tsp. truffle salt
1/2 tsp. garlic powder	2 tbsp. parmesan cheese
olive oil spray	

Directions:
Use a mandoline with a French fry setting, slice the whole potato using the spring-form handle to slice into French fries. Place sliced potatoes in a bowl and spray with olive spray for about 3 seconds. Add garlic powder, black pepper, and parsley flakes. Place all of them into the Instant Pot Duo Crisp Air Fryer Basket. Close the Air Fryer lid and cook for about 5 minutes at 390°F. Take out the basket and flip fries in order to evenly cook the fries. Cook another 8 minutes and remove from the Air Fryer and add to a bowl. Sprinkle with truffle salt and parmesan cheese.

Paprika Potato Chips (air Fryer)

Ingredients: Servings: 3 Cooking Time: 22 Mins

2 medium potatoes, preferably Yukon Gold, scrubbed	¼ tsp. paprika
Cooking spray	¼ tsp. plus ⅛ tsp. sea salt
2 tsp. olive oil	¼ tsp. freshly ground black pepper
½ tsp. garlic granules	Ketchup or hot sauce, for serving

Directions:
Preheat the air fryer to 392ºF (200ºC). Spritz the air fryer basket with cooking spray. On a flat work surface, cut the potatoes into ¼-inch-thick slices. Transfer the potato slices to a medium bowl, along with the olive oil, garlic granules, paprika, salt, and pepper and toss to coat well. Put the potato slices in the air fryer basket and air fry for 22 minutes until tender and nicely browned. Shake the basket twice during the cooking process for even cooking. Remove from the basket and serve alongside the ketchup for dipping.

Molten Lava Cakes

Ingredients: Servings: 4 Cooking Time: 12 Mins

Self-raising flour – 1.5 tbsps.	Unsalted butter – 3.5 oz.
Baker's sugar – 3.5 tbsps.	Dark chocolate – 3.5 oz. chopped
Eggs – 2	

Directions:
Preheat the air fryer to 375F. Grease and flour 4 ramekins. Melt butter and dark chocolate in the microwave. Stirring throughout. Mix sugar and egg until frothy and pale. Pour melted chocolate mixture into the egg mixture. Stir in flour and mix everything. Fill the ramekins about ¾ full with batter. Bake in the air fryer at 375F for 10 minutes. Remove, cool and serve.

Air-fried Donuts

Ingredients: Servings: 8 Cooking Time: 10 Mins

2 C. all-purpose flour
¼ C. warm water, 100-110 degrees F
¼ C. whole milk at room temperature
1 tsp. active dry yeast
¼ tsp. salt
¼ C. granulated sugar
2 tbsps. unsalted butter, melted
1 C. powdered sugar
1 large egg, beaten
4 tsps. tap water

Directions:

In a small bowl, add the yeast, water, and half a tsp. of the granulated sugar. Stir well to combine and let it stand for about 5 minutes until it becomes foamy. In a medium-size mixing bowl, combine flour, salt and the remaining granulated sugar. Add the yeast mixture along with butter, milk, and egg. Stir the mixture using a wooden spoon until it forms into a soft dough and no longer sticks to the sides of the bowl. Place dough on a lightly floured surface and knead until it becomes smooth, about 1-2 minutes. Transfer the dough to a lightly greased bowl and cover with a plastic wrap. Allow the dough to rise until doubles in volume, about an hour. As soon as the dough becomes double in size, transfer to a lightly floured surface. Roll it to about 1/4-inch in thickness. Using a 3-inch round cutter, cut into 8 doughnuts. Use a 1-inch cutter for the hole at the center. Make sure that the area where you place the doughnuts and doughnut holes is lightly floured to avoid doughnuts sticking to each other. Cover with plastic wrap and allow standing until doubles in size, about 30 minutes. Place 2 doughnuts and 2 doughnut holes in the air fryer basket and place inside the instant pot duo crisp. Attach the air fryer lid and cook at 350 degrees F until golden brown. Repeat the process with the remaining doughnuts and doughnut holes. To make the glaze, add powdered sugar and tap water in a medium bowl and whisk them together until smooth. Dip each doughnut and doughnut holes in the glaze before placing them on a wire rack to drip off. Allow cooling for the glaze to harden (about 10 minutes) before serving.

Easy Salmon Bites

Ingredients: Servings: 4 Cooking Time: 12 Mins

1 lb salmon fillets, boneless and cut into chunks
2 tsp. olive oil
1/4 tsp. cayenne
1/2 tsp. chili powder
1 tsp. dried dill
Pepper
Salt

Directions:

Add salmon and remaining ingredients into the large bowl and toss well. Spray instant pot multi-level air fryer basket with cooking spray. Add salmon chunks into the air fryer basket and place basket into the instant pot. Seal pot with air fryer lid and select air fry mode then set the temperature to 350 F and timer for 12 minutes. Turn salmon chunks halfway through. Serve and enjoy.

Stuffed Mushrooms

Ingredients: Servings: 4-6 Cooking Time: 30 Mins

1/4 C. grated Pecorino-Romano
1 tsp. chopped fresh mint
1 clove garlic, minced
1/4 C. breadcrumbs
36 white button mushrooms (about 1 1/2 pounds), stemmed
4 tbsp. olive oil
1 tbsp. chopped fresh parsley
Kosher salt and freshly ground black pepper
2 tbsp. shredded mozzarella

Directions:

In a medium bowl, combine the mozzarella, parsley, mint, garlic, 2 tbsp. of olive oil, breadcrumbs, Pecorino-Romano, 1/2 tsp. salt, and 1/4 tsp. pepper, and toss to blend. In a large bowl, toss the mushrooms with the remaining 2 tbsp. of olive oil and arrange on a small baking sheet or plate with the cavities facing up. Divide the breadcrumb mixture among the mushrooms while filling the cavities and pressing down gently to secure. Place half the mushrooms in a single layer in the basket of the Instant Pot Duo Crisp Air Fryer. Set the Air Fryer to 360°F and close the lid. Cook until the filling is bubbling and browned about 10 minutes. Repeat with the remaining mushrooms.

Cinnamon Rolls with Dip

Ingredients: Servings: 8 Cooking Time: 15 Mins

Bread dough – 1 pound
Cinnamon – 1 ½ tbsps. ground
Butter – ¼ cup, melted
For the cream cheese dip
Brown sugar – ¾ cup
Butter – 2 tbsps.
Cream cheese – 4 ounces
Sugar – 1 ¼ cups
Vanilla – ½ tsp.

Directions:

Roll dough on a floured working surface, shape a rectangle and brush with ¼ C. butter. Mix sugar and cinnamon in a bowl. Sprinkle this over the dough. Roll dough into a log. Seal well and cut into 8 pieces. Leave rolls to rise for 2 hours. Place them in the air fryer basket. Cook at 350F for 5 minutes. Then flip and cook 4 minutes more. Transfer to a platter. In a bowl, mix butter, cream cheese, sugar, and vanilla. Whisk well. Serve cinnamon rolls with this cream cheese dip.

Fried Bananas with Chocolate Sauce

Ingredients: Servings: 2 Cooking Time: 10 Mins

1 large egg
¼ C. plain bread crumbs
3 bananas, halved crosswise
¼ C. cornstarch
Cooking oil
Chocolate sauce (see Ingredient tip)

Directions:

1 Preparing the Ingredients. In a small bowl, beat the egg. In another bowl, place the cornstarch. Place the bread crumbs in a third bowl. Dip the bananas in the cornstarch, then the egg, and then the bread crumbs. Spray the Instant Crisp Air Fryer basket with cooking oil. Place the bananas in the basket and spray them with cooking oil. 2 Air Frying. Close the air fryer Lid. Cook for 5 minutes. Open the Instant Crisp Air Fryer and flip the bananas. Cook for an additional 2 minutes. Transfer the bananas to plates. Drizzle the chocolate sauce over the bananas, and serve. You can make your own chocolate sauce using 2 tbsp. milk and ¼ C. chocolate chips. Heat a saucepan over medium-high heat. Add the milk and stir for 1 to 2 minutes.

Add the chocolate chips. Stir for 2 minutes, or until the chocolate has melted.

Lemon Cupcakes

Ingredients: Servings: 12 Cooking Time: 15 Mins

2 eggs
1 tbsp. fresh lemon juice
1 tbsp. lemon zest, grated
1/4 C. milk
1 tsp. vanilla
3/4 C. sugar
1/4 C. butter
1 1/2 tsp. baking powder
1 1/4 C. all-purpose flour
1/4 tsp. salt

Directions:
In a small bowl, mix together flour, baking powder, and salt and set aside. In a mixing bowl, beat together sugar and butter until well combined. Add eggs, lemon juice, lemon zest, milk, and vanilla and beat until combined. Add flour mixture and stir to combine. Pour batter into the 12 silicone muffin molds. Place the dehydrating tray in a multi-level air fryer basket and place basket in the instant pot. Place 6 silicone muffin molds on dehydrating tray. Seal pot with air fryer lid and select bake mode then set the temperature to 350 F and timer for 15 minutes. Bake remaining cupcakes using the same method. Serve and enjoy.

Air Fried Turkey and Fajitas

Ingredients: Servings: 2 Cooking Time: 20 Mins

6 Tortilla Wraps
3.5oz Leftover Turkey Breast
1 Large Avocado
1 Large Yellow Pepper
1 Large Red Pepper
1 Large Green Pepper
½ Small Red Onion
5 Tbsp Soft Cheese
3 Tbsp Cajun Spice
2 Tbsp Mexican Seasoning
1 Tsp Cumin
Salt & Pepper
0.35oz Fresh Coriander

Directions:
Slice up the salad and chop the avocado into little wedges. Chop up the turkey breast into small little chunks. Place the turkey, peppers, and onions into a bowl and mix with all the seasonings along with the soft cheese. Then dice the red onion. Slice the peppers into thin slices. Place them into the Instant Pot Duo Crisp Air Fryer Tray. Close the Air Fryer lid and cook for 20 minutes on 390°F. Serve when ready.

Cinnamon Rolls

Ingredients: Servings: 8 Cooking Time: 15 Mins

1 ½ tbsp. cinnamon
¾ C. brown sugar
¼ C. melted coconut oil
1 lb. frozen bread dough, thawed
Glaze:
½ tsp. vanilla
1 ¼ C. powdered erythritol
2 tbsp. softened ghee
4 oz. softened cream cheese

Directions:
Preparing the ingredients. Preheat the unit by selecting Bake, setting the temperature to 300°F, and setting the time to 5 minutes. Press Start to begin. Lay out bread dough and roll out into a rectangle. Brush melted ghee over dough and leave a 1-inch border along edges. Mix cinnamon and sweetener together and then sprinkle over dough. Roll dough tightly and slice into 8 pieces. Let sit 1-2 hours to rise. To make the glaze, simply mix ingredients together till smooth. Finish the dish. Once rolls rise, place into the Instant Crisp Air Fryer. Close the air fryer Lid. Select Bake, set the temperature to 350°F, and set the time to 5 minutes. Select Start to begin. Serve rolls drizzled in cream cheese glaze. Enjoy

Hush Puppies (air Fryer)

Ingredients: Servings: 12 Cooking Time: 10 Mins

1 C. self-rising yellow cornmeal
½ C. all-purpose flour
1 tsp. sugar
1 tsp. salt
1 tsp. freshly ground black pepper
1 large egg
⅓ C. canned creamed corn
1 C. minced onion
2 tsp. minced jalapeño pepper
2 tbsp. olive oil, divided

Directions:
Thoroughly combine the cornmeal, flour, sugar, salt, and pepper in a large bowl. Whisk together the egg and corn in a small bowl. Pour the egg mixture into the bowl of cornmeal mixture and stir to combine. Stir in the minced onion and jalapeño. Cover the bowl with plastic wrap and place in the refrigerator for 30 minutes. Preheat the air fryer to 375°F (191°C). Line the air fryer basket with parchment paper and lightly brush it with 1 tbsp. of olive oil. Scoop out the cornmeal mixture and form into 24 balls, about 1 inch. Arrange the balls in the parchment paper-lined basket, leaving space between each ball. Air fry in batches for 5 minutes. Shake the basket and brush the balls with the remaining 1 tbsp. of olive oil. Continue cooking for 5 minutes until golden brown. Remove the balls (hush puppies) from the basket and serve on a plate.

Marble Cake

Ingredients: Servings: 6 Cooking Time: 17 Mins

Erythritol - 7 tbsps. powdered
Almond flour – ½ cup
Eggs – 4, whisked
Baking powder – 1 tsp.
Cocoa powder – 5 tsps.
Butter – 2/3 cup, melted
Lime juice – ½ tsp.

Directions:
Preheat the air fryer to 356F. Mix 3 tbsp. of melted butter with the cocoa powder to form a paste. Add the erythritol to the remaining butter and mix well. Stir in the eggs, almond flour, and baking powder and mix until smooth. Pour in the lime and stir. Place a greased baking pan into the air fryer and allow to heat for a minute. Pour some of the batter into the hot pan then add a layer of the chocolate mixture, then the batter, chocolate and lastly top with batter. Use a skewer to create a swirl. Place in the air fryer and bake for 17 minutes.

Mini Pies with Blueberries

Ingredients: Servings: 4 Cooking Time: 12 Mins

1 C. blueberries
2 tbsps. sugar
½ lemon, juiced
¼ tsp. salt
½ tsp. vanilla extract
½ tsp. cornstarch
4 frozen piecrusts; thawed
Nonstick cooking spray

Directions:
In a large mixing bowl, combine the blueberries, sugar, lemon juice, salt, and vanilla. Allow the mixture to stand for 10 minutes, then drain, and reserve 1 tbsp. of the liquid. In a small bowl, whisk the cornstarch into the reserved liquid and then, mix with the blueberry mixture. Put the piecrusts on a lightly floured surface and cut into 4. Spoon a tbsp. of blueberry mixture in the center of the circle, with ½ an inch's border around the dough. Brush the edges with water and fold the dough over the filling. Press the edges with a fork to seal. Cut 3 small slits on top of each pie and oil with cooking spray. Arrange the pies in a single layer in the basket. Close the crisping lid, choose Air Fry, set the temperature to 350 F, and set the time to 12 minutes. Press Start to begin baking. Once done baking, remove, and place the pies on a wire rack to cool.

Air Fryer Cinnamon Rolls

Ingredients: Servings: 8 Cooking Time: 5 Mins

1 ½ tbsp. cinnamon
¾ C. brown sugar
¼ C. melted coconut oil
1 lb. frozen bread dough, thawed
Glaze:
½ tsp. vanilla
1 ¼ C. powdered erythritol
2 tbsp. softened ghee
3 oz. softened cream cheese

Directions:
1 Preparing the Ingredients. Lay out bread dough and roll out into a rectangle. Brush melted ghee over dough and leave a 1-inch border along edges. Mix cinnamon and sweetener together and then sprinkle over dough. Roll dough tightly and slice into 8 pieces. Let sit 1-2 hours to rise. To make the glaze, simply mix ingredients together till smooth. 2 Air Frying. Once rolls rise, place into Instant Crisp Air Fryer. Close the air fryer Lid. Select Bake and cook 5 minutes at 350 degrees. Serve rolls drizzled in cream cheese glaze. Enjoy!

Dill Pickle Fries

Ingredients: Servings: 12 Cooking Time: 28 Mins

1½ (16-ouncesjars spicy dill pickle spears, drained and pat dried
1 C. all-purpose flour
1 egg, beaten
¼ C. milk
1 C. panko breadcrumbs
½ tsp. paprika

Directions:
Preheat the air fryer to 440 o f and grease an air fryer basket. Place flour and paprika in a shallow dish and whisk the egg with milk in a second dish. Place the breadcrumbs in a third shallow dish. Coat the pickle spears evenly in flour and dip in the egg mixture. Roll into the breadcrumbs evenly and arrange half of the pickle spears in an air fryer basket. Cook for about 14 minutes, flipping once in between. Repeat with the remaining pickle spears and dish out to serve warm.

Banana Cake

Ingredients: Servings: 4 Cooking Time: 30 Mins

Soft butter – 1 tbsp.
Egg – 1
Brown sugar – 1/3 cup
Honey – 2 tbsps.
Banana – 1, peeled and mashed
White flour – 1 cup
Baking powder – 1 tsp.
Cinnamon powder – ½ tsp.
Cooking spray

Directions:
Spray a cake pan with cooking spray and set aside. In a bowl, mix flour, baking powder, cinnamon, egg, honey, banana, sugar, and butter. Whisk. Pour the batter into the greased cake pan and cook in the air fryer at 350F for 30 minutes. Cool, slice and serve.

Christmas Chocolate Cheesecake

Ingredients: Servings: 8 Cooking Time: 25 Mins

Crust:
1 C. Graham Crackers Crumbs
1 tbsp. Sugar
3 tbsp. Cocoa Powder
3 tbsp. Butter, melted
Filling:
2 Eggs, room temperature, cracked
2 Egg Yolks, room temperature, cracked
20 oz Cream Cheese, room temperature
½ C. Granulated Sugar
½ C. Cocoa Powder
1 C. Heavy Cream
½ C. Sour Cream
2 tsp. Vanilla Extract
8 oz Baking Chocolate, melted

Directions:
Line a cake pan with parchment paper. In a mixing bowl, add the graham crackers crumbs, cocoa powder, and sugar. Mix evenly then add the melted butter and mix again until well incorporated. Spoon the mixture into the pan and tap it to firm using the spoon. Set aside. Using an electric mixer, beat the cream cheese and cocoa powder. While still mixing, add the eggs and egg yolks. Once combined and still mixing, add the sour cream, melted chocolate, heavy cream, and vanilla extract. Scrape the sides of the bowl as you mix. Once well combined, turn off the electric mixer, and spoon the filling mixture onto the crust in the springform pan. Use the spatula to smoothen it out. Fit A rack in the cooker and pour in 2 C. of water. Cover the pan with foil and place on the reversible rack. Close the lid, select pressure mode on High pressure for 25 minutes. Press Start. Once the timer has stopped, do a natural pressure release for 10 minutes, then a quick pressure release to let out the remaining steam. with napkins in both hands, hold the trivet's sling and lift it out with the spring form pan. Let the cake sit for an hour to cool and then refrigerate for 5 hours. Slice the cake to serve.

Air Fried Bananas

Ingredients: Servings: 2-3 Cooking Time: 10 Mins

½ C. all-purpose flour
3 egg whites
1 C. panko breadcrumbs
3 tbsp. cinnamon
8 ripe bananas, peeled and halved
3 tbsp. canola oil

Directions:
Place Instant Pot Air Fryer Crisp over kitchen platform. Press "Sauté," select "Hi" setting and press "Start." In the inner pot, add the oil and allow it to heat. Add the breadcrumbs and stir-cook for 2-3 minutes until evenly golden. Set aside in a bowl. Take two bowls, in one bowl beat the egg whites and in another, add the flour. Coat the bananas with egg mixture, flour mixture, and then with the crumbs. In the inner pot, place the Air Fryer basket. In the basket, add the bananas. Close the Crisp Lid and press the "Bake" setting. Set temperature to 280°F and set the timer to 10 minutes. Press "Start." Open the Crisp Lid after cooking time is over. Serve warm.

Easy Air Fryer Donuts

Ingredients: Servings: 8 Cooking Time: 5 Mins

Pinch of allspice
4 tbsp. dark brown sugar
1/3 C. granulated sweetener
½ - 1 tsp. cinnamon
3 tbsp. melted coconut oil
1 can of biscuits

Directions:
1 Preparing the Ingredients. Mix allspice, sugar, sweetener, and cinnamon together. Take out biscuits from can and with a circle cookie cutter, cut holes from centers and place into Instant Crisp Air Fryer. 2 Air Frying. Close the air fryer Lid and cook 5 minutes at 350 degrees. As batches are cooked, use a brush to coat with melted coconut oil and dip each into sugar mixture. Serve warm!

Pork Rind Tortillas

Ingredients: Servings: 4 Cooking Time: 5 Mins

Pork rinds – 1 ounce, ground
Shredded mozzarella cheese – ¾ cup
Full-fat cream cheese – 2 tbsps. chopped
Egg – 1

Directions:
Place mozzarella into a bowl. Add cream cheese then to the bowl. Microwave for 30 seconds, or until both types of cheese are melted. Add the egg and ground pork rinds to the cheese mixture. Stir and make a ball. Separate the dough into four small balls. Place each ball of dough between two sheets of parchment and roll into a ¼ flat layer. Place tortillas into the air fryer basket in a single layer. Set the temperature to 400F and cook for 5 minutes. Serve.

Blueberry Almond Mason Jar Cakes

Ingredients: Servings: 4 Cooking Time: 15 Mins

4 large eggs
2 tsp. pure vanilla extract
1/4 tsp. salt
1 C. blueberries
1 tsp. baking powder
1/4 C. erythritol
1/4 C. sliced almonds
1 1/3 C. almond flour

Directions:
Take a bowl and whisk eggs and vanilla extract. Add flour, erythritol, baking powder, and salt, then stir to combine. Fold in the blueberries. Spray four 6 oz. Mason jars with cooking oil. Divide the batter into the jars, top each jar with some of the almonds, and cover them with an aluminum foil. Pour 1 cup. Put the jars in the Instant Pot Duo Crisp Air Fryer tray. Close the lid. Press the Bake button before adjusting the time to 15 minutes. When you hear the timer beep, unlock the lid. Carefully remove the Mason jars from the inner pot and allow it to cool before serving.

Jalapeño Peanuts (pressure Cook)

Ingredients: Servings: 4 Cooking Time: 45 Mins

4 oz. (113 g) raw peanuts in the shell
1 jalapeño, sliced
1 tbsp. Creole seasoning
½ tbsp. cayenne pepper
½ tbsp. garlic powder
1 tbsp. salt

Directions:
Add all ingredients to the Instant Pot. Pour in enough water to cover. Stir to mix well. Use a steamer to gently press down the peanuts. Secure the lid. Choose the Pressure Cook and set the cooking time for 45 minutes at High pressure. Once cooking is complete, perform a natural pressure release for 15 minutes, then release any remaining pressure. Carefully open the lid. Transfer the peanut and the liquid in a bowl, then refrigerate for 3 hours before serving.

Bread Pudding with Cranberry

Ingredients: Servings: 4 Cooking Time: 45 Mins

1-1/2 C. milk
1/2 C. cranberries1 tsp. butter
1/4 C. and 2 tbsp. white sugar
1/4 C. golden raisins
1/8 tsp. ground cinnamon
3/4 C. heavy whipping cream
2-1/2 eggs
3/4 tsp. lemon zest
3/4 tsp. kosher salt
3/4 French baguettes, cut into 2-inch slices
3/8 vanilla bean, split and seeds scraped away

Directions:
1 Preparing the Ingredients. Lightly grease baking pan of Instant Crisp Air Fryer with cooking spray. Spread baguette slices, cranberries, and raisins. In blender, blend well vanilla bean, cinnamon, salt, lemon zest, eggs, sugar, and cream. Pour over baguette slices. Let it soak for an hour. Cover pan with foil. 2 Air Frying. close the air fryer Lid. Select Bake and cook for 35 minutes, cook on 330°F. Let it rest for 10 minutes. Serve and enjoy.

Nutty Asparagus

Ingredients: Servings: 4 Cooking Time: 11 Mins

1 ½ lb Asparagus, ends trimmed
Salt and Pepper, to taste
1 C. Water
1 tbsp. butter
½ C. chopped Pine Nuts
1 tbsp. Olive Oil to garnish

Directions:
Open the cooker, pour the water in, and fit the reversible rack at the bottom. Place the asparagus on the rack, close the crisping lid, select Air Fry mode, and set the time to 8 minutes on 380 F.

Press Start. At the 4-minute mark, carefully turn the asparagus over. When ready, remove to a plate, sprinkle with salt and pepper, and set aside. Select Sear/Sauté on your cooker, set to Medium and melt the butter. Add the pine nuts and cook for 2-3 minutes until golden. Scatter over the asparagus the pine nuts, and drizzle olive oil.

Cinnamon Fried Bananas

Ingredients: Servings: 2-3 Cooking Time: 10 Mins

1 C. panko breadcrumbs
3 tbsp. cinnamon
½ C. almond flour
3 egg whites
8 ripe bananas
3 tbsp. vegan coconut oil

Directions:
1 Preparing the Ingredients. Heat coconut oil and add breadcrumbs. Mix around 2-3 minutes until golden. Pour into bowl. Peel and cut bananas in half. Roll each bananas half into flour, eggs, and crumb mixture. 2 Air Frying. Place into the Instant Crisp Air Fryer. Close the air fryer Lid. Select Bake, and cook 10 minutes at 280 degrees. A great addition to a healthy banana split!

Paprika Crispy Wings

Ingredients: Servings: 4 Cooking Time: 20 Mins

½ C. water
½ C. sriracha sauce
2 tbsp. butter, melted
1 tbsp. lemon juice
8 chicken wings
½ tsp. hot paprika
Cooking spray

Directions:
Mix the water, sriracha, butter and lemon juice in the pot. In the Cook & Crisp basket, put the wings, and then the basket into the pot. Seal the pressure lid. Choose Pressure, set to High, set the timer at 5 minutes, and choose Start. When the timer is done reading, perform a quick pressure release, and carefully open the lid. Pour the paprika all over the chicken and oil with cooking spray. Cover the crisping lid. Choose Air Fry, set the temperature to 375 F, and the timer to 15 minutes. Choose Start to commence frying. After half the Cook Time, open the crisping lid, shake the wings. Oil the chicken again with cooking spray and return the basket to the pot. Close the lid and continue cooking until the wingettes are crispy.

Spiced Apple Chips (air Fryer)

Ingredients: Servings: 4 Cooking Time: 10 Mins

4 medium apples (any type will work), cored and thinly sliced
¼ tsp. nutmeg
¼ tsp. cinnamon
Cooking spray

Directions:
Preheat the air fryer to 360°F (182°C). Place the apple slices in a large bowl and sprinkle the spices on top. Toss to coat. Working in batches, place the apple slices in the air fryer basket in a single layer and spray them with cooking spray. Air fry for 10 minutes, shaking the basket halfway through, or until the apple chips are crispy. Transfer the apple chips to a paper towel-lined plate and rest for 5 minutes before serving.

Cocoa Cake

Ingredients: Servings: 6 Cooking Time: 17 Mins

Butter – 3.5 ounces, melted
Eggs – 3
Sugar – 3 ounces
Cocoa powder – 1 tsp.
Flour – 3 ounces
Lemon juice – ½ tsp.

Directions:
In a bowl, mix cocoa powder, with 1 tbsp. butter and whisk. In another bowl, mix the rest of the butter with lemon juice, flour, eggs, and sugar. Whisk well and pour half into a cake pan. Add half of the cocoa mix, spread, add the rest of the butter layer and top with the rest of the cocoa. Cook in the air fryer at 360F for 17 minutes. Cool, sliced and serve.

Ground Beef & Cabbage Dumplings

Ingredients: Servings: 8 Cooking Time: 12 Mins

8 oz. ground beef
½ C. grated cabbage
1 carrot, grated
1 large egg, beaten
1 garlic clove, minced
2 tbsp. coconut aminos
½ tbsp. melted ghee
½ tbsp. ginger powder
½ tsp. salt
½ tsp. freshly ground black pepper
20 wonton wrappers
2 tbsp. olive oil

Directions:
Close crisping lid. Preheat your cooker by choosing Air Fry at 390 F for 5 minutes. In a large bowl, mix beef, cabbage, carrot, egg, garlic, coconut aminos, ghee, ginger, salt, and pepper. Put wonton wrappers on a clean flat surface and spoon 1 tbsp. of the beef mixture into the middle of each wrapper. Run the edges of the wrapper with a little water; fold the wrapper to cover the filling into a semi-circle shape and pinch the edges to seal. Brush the dumplings with olive oil. Lay the dumplings in the preheated basket, choose Air Fry, set the temperature to 390 F, and set the time to 12 minutes. Choose Start. At the 6-minute mark, open the lid, pull out the basket and shake the dumplings. Return the basket to the pot and close the lid to continue frying until the dumplings are crispy to your desire.

Peanut Butter and Chocolate Tart (pressure Cook)

Ingredients: Servings: 4 To 6 Cooking Time: 25 Mins

5 tbsp. unsalted butter
1 C. granulated sugar
2 tbsp. peanut butter
1 tbsp. vegetable oil
¼ C. chocolate chips
½ C. peanut butter chips
⅓ C. cocoa powder
2 large eggs
1 C. all-purpose flour
1 tsp. baking powder
2 tsp. vanilla extract
½ tsp. salt
2 tbsp. water
5 oz. (142 g) chocolate chip cookie dough, rolled into teaspoon-size balls

Directions:
Combine the butter, sugar, and peanut butter in a microwave-safe bowl and microwave for a minute to melt and mix well. Add the vegetable oil to the bowl of butter mixture and whisk to combine. Whisk in the remaining ingredients, except for the cookie dough balls. Spritz a springform pan

with cooking spray. Line the with parchment paper, then spritz with another layer of cooking spray. Pour the mixture into the pan and use a spatula to level the top. Arrange the cookie-dough balls and slightly push them into the mixture and they're still visible on the surface. Pour 2 C. of water in the Instant Pot, then fit in a trivet. Place the pan on the trivet. Secure the lid, and select the Pressure Cook and set the cooking time for 25 minutes. When cooking is complete, do a natural pressure release for 10 minutes, then release any remaining pressure. Open the lid. Carefully remove the pan and trivet from the Instant Pot and let cool for 30 minutes before slicing and serving.

Sweet Pepper Poppers

Ingredients: Servings: 4 Cooking Time: 8 Mins

Mini sweet peppers – 8 (seeds and membranes removed)
Full-fat cream cheese – 4 ounces, softened
Bacon – 4 slices, cooked and crumbled
Shredded pepper jack cheese – ¼ cup

Directions:
In a bowl, mix bacon, cream cheese, and pepper jack. Place 3 tsps. of the mixture into each sweet pepper and press down firmly. Place in the air fryer basket. Cook at 400F for 8 minutes. Serve warm.

Healthy Eggplant Chips

Ingredients: Servings: 2 Cooking Time: 30 Mins

1 eggplant, sliced 1/4-inch thick
2 tbsp. rosemary, chopped
1/2 C. parmesan cheese, grated
Pepper
Salt

Directions:
Add eggplant slices, cheese, rosemary, pepper, and salt into the mixing bowl and toss well. Place the dehydrating tray in a multi-level air fryer basket and place basket in the instant pot. Arrange eggplant slices on the dehydrating tray. Seal pot with air fryer lid and select air fry mode then set the temperature to 400 F and timer for 30 minutes. Turn eggplant slices halfway through. Serve and enjoy.

Bread Pudding

Ingredients: Servings: 4 Cooking Time: 1 Hour

Glazed doughnuts – 6, crumbled
Cherries – 1 cup
Whipping cream – 1 ½ cups
Egg – 4 yolks
Raisins – ½ cup
Sugar – ¼ cup
Chocolate chips – ½ cup

Directions:
In a bowl, mix cherries, with egg yolks, and whipping cream and stir well. In another bowl, mix doughnuts, chocolate chips, sugar, and raisins. Mix. Combine 2 mixtures and transfer everything to a greased pan that fits in your air fryer and cook at 310F for 1 hour. Chill pudding before cutting and serve.

Crispy Air Fried Chicken Wings

Ingredients: Servings: 4 Cooking Time: 30 Mins

2 lbs chicken wings
¾ C. corn starch
1 tsp. garlic powder
1 tsp. onion powder
Korean Air Fried Chicken Sauce
2 Tbsp gochujang Korean chili paste
½ tsp. salt
3 Tbsp honey
2 Tbsp brown sugar
1 Tbsp soy sauce
1 tsp. ginger minced
1 tsp. garlic minced
½ tsp. salt

Directions:
Rinse chicken wings and dry them with a paper towel. Place them in a large bowl and season with garlic powder, onion powder, and ½ tsp. salt. Cover the chicken with corn starch and using kitchen tongs to stir, make sure that all chicken pieces are coated. Tap each piece on the side of the bowl (to remove excess starch) and place it in the Instant Pot Duo Crisp Air Fryer basket. Close the lid of the basket and choose the Air Fry option. Cook the chicken wings at 390°F for 30 minutes, turning and rotating chicken about every 10 minutes.

Instant Pot Duo Crisp Crisp-fried Cheeseburgers

Ingredients: Servings: 4 Cooking Time: 8 Mins

4 hamburger buns
1 lb. Ground beef
1 tbsp. Low-sodium soy sauce
2 cloves garlic, minced
4 slices American cheese
Freshly ground black pepper
Red onion (thinly sliced
Lettuce
Mayonnaise
Sliced tomatoes
Kosher salt

Directions:
Combine beef with soy sauce and garlic in a large mixing bowl. Mix thoroughly so the mixture can seep through the beef. Shape marinated ground beef into patties and arrange in a single layer in the air fryer basket. If there's not enough space to accommodate all patties, cook in batches. Put the air fryer basket on top of the metal trivet inside the instant pot. Attach the air fryer lid and cook at 375 degrees Fahrenheit for about 4 minutes. Turn it over for even cooking and cook for another 4 minutes. Once done, remove the burgers quickly and top every burger with a slice of cheese. Cook the remaining patties using the same procedure. Spread mayo on hamburger buns and then arrange its filling using lettuce as the base followed by a burger with cheese, tomatoes, and onions on top. Serve immediately while warm.

Pecan, Date, Sultana Stuffed Apples (pressure Cook)

Ingredients: Servings: 6 Cooking Time: 3 Mins

¼ C. toasted pecans, chopped
½ C. dates, chopped
1 tbsp. cinnamon powder
2 tbsp. brown sugar
¼ C. sultanas
4 tbsp. butter
6 red apples, whole and cored
4 tbsp. chocolate sauce, for topping

Directions:
In a bowl, mix the pecans, dates, sultanas, cinnamon, brown sugar, and butter. Stuff apples with mixture. Pour 1 C. of water in Instant Pot and place stuffed apples in water. Seal the lid, select the Pressure Cook and set the timer for 3 minutes at Low Pressure. When cooking is complete, do a natural pressure release for 5 minutes, then release any remaining pressure. Open the lid. Carefully remove apples onto plates and drizzle with chocolate sauce.

Strawberry Muffins

Ingredients: Servings: 12 Cooking Time: 14 Mins

1 egg
1 C. strawberries, diced
1/2 C. milk
1/3 C. olive oil
2 tsp. baking powder
3/4 C. sugar
1 1/2 C. all-purpose flour
1/2 tsp. salt

Directions:
In a large bowl, mix together flour, baking powder, sugar, and salt and set aside. In a small bowl, whisk together egg, milk, and oil. Pour egg mixture into the flour mixture and mix until well combined. Add strawberries and fold well. Pour batter into the 12 silicone muffin molds. Place the dehydrating tray in a multi-level air fryer basket and place basket in the instant pot. Place 6 silicone muffin molds on dehydrating tray. Seal pot with air fryer lid and select bake mode then set the temperature to 380 F and timer for 14 minutes. Bake remaining muffins using the same method. Serve and enjoy.

Air-fried Cinnamon Rolls

Ingredients: Servings: 6 Cooking Time: 10 Mins

For the Rolls
⅓ C. packed brown sugar
2 tbsps. melted butter (+ more for brushing)
½ tsp. ground cinnamon
8-oz. crescent rolls, tube-refrigerated
Kosher salt to taste
All-purpose flour for surface
For the Glaze
1 tbsp. whole milk (+ more if needed)
2 oz. cream cheese, softened
½ C. powdered sugar

Directions:
To make rolls, prepare by lining air fryer basket with parchment paper. Grease with butter. Add butter, cinnamon, brown sugar, and a pinch of salt. Mix thoroughly the ingredients until it turns smooth and fluffy. Sprinkle flour lightly over a flat surface and roll out crescent rolls in one piece. Fold in half and pinch seams together before rolling it to form a 9x7-inch rectangle. Spread butter mixture over it, keeping a 1/4 -inch border on all sides. Roll the dough up starting from its long edge and cut crosswise into six pieces. Arrange rolls inside the air fryer basket, space evenly with cut-side up. Place the air fryer basket inside the instant pot and attach the air fryer lid. Set the timer to 10 minutes and cook at 350 degrees F. To make the glaze, whisk milk and powdered sugar with cream cheese in a mixing bowl. If necessary, you may add more milk by a teaspoonful to thin glaze. Spread glaze over warm cinnamon before serving fresh from the air fryer.

Cinnamon Bread Pudding

Ingredients: Servings: 2 Cooking Time: 15 Mins

3 eggs, beaten
4 C. bread cube
3 tbsp. raisins
1 C. almond milk
1/2 tsp. cinnamon
1/2 tsp. vanilla
1 tsp. olive oil
Pinch of salt

Directions:
Place bread cubes in the oven-safe casserole dish. In a bowl, mix remaining ingredients and pour over bread cubes. Cover dish with foil. Pour 2 C. of water into the inner pot of instant pot duo crisp than place steamer rack in the pot. Place casserole dish on top of the steamer rack. Seal the pot with pressure cooking lid and cook on high for 15 minutes. Once done, allow to release pressure naturally for 10 minutes then release remaining pressure using a quick release. Remove lid. Serve and enjoy.

Ginger Cheesecake

Ingredients: Servings: 6 Cooking Time: 20 Mins

Butter – 2 tsps. melted
Ginger cookies – ½ cup, crumbled
Cream cheese – 16 ounces, soft
Eggs – 2
Sugar – ½ cup
Rum – 1 tsp.
Vanilla extract – ½ tsp.
Nutmeg – ½ tsp. ground

Directions:
Grease a pan with butter and spread cookie crumbs on the bottom. In a bowl, beat cream cheese, eggs, rum, vanilla, and nutmeg. Whisk well and spread over the cookie crumbs. Place in the air fryer and cook at 340F for 20 minutes. Cool and keep in the refrigerator. Slice and serve.

Air Fryer Chocolate Cake

Ingredients: Servings: 8-10 Cooking Time: 35 Mins

½ C. hot water
1 tsp. vanilla
¼ C. olive oil
½ C. almond milk
1 egg
½ tsp. salt
¾ tsp. baking soda
¾ tsp. baking powder
½ C. unsweetened cocoa powder
2 C. almond flour
1 C. brown sugar

Directions:
1 Preparing the Ingredients. Preheat your Instant Crisp Air Fryer to 356 degrees. Stir all dry ingredients together. Then stir in wet ingredients. Add hot water last. the batter will be thin, no worries. 2 Air Frying. Pour cake batter into a pan that fits into the fryer. Cover with foil and poke holes into the foil. Close the air fryer Lid. Select Bake, set the temperature to 356°F, and set the time to 35 minutes. Select Start to begin. Discard foil and then bake another 10 minutes.

Apple Pie In Air Fryer

Ingredients: Servings: 4 Cooking Time: 35 Mins

½ tsp. vanilla extract
1 beaten egg
1 large apple,
1 tbsp. ground cinnamon
1 tbsp. raw sugar

chopped
1 Pillsbury Refrigerator pie crust
1 tbsp. butter
2 tbsp. sugar
2 tsp. lemon juice
Baking spray

Directions:

1 Preparing the Ingredients. Lightly grease baking pan of Instant Crisp Air Fryer with cooking spray. Spread pie crust on bottom of pan up to the sides. In a bowl, mix vanilla, sugar, cinnamon, lemon juice, and apples. Pour on top of pie crust. Top apples with butter slices. Cover apples with the other pie crust. Pierce with knife the tops of pie. Spread beaten egg on top of crust and sprinkle sugar. Cover with foil. 2 Air Frying. Close air fryer lid. For 25 minutes, cook on 390°F. Remove foil cook for 10 minutes at 330oF until tops are browned. Serve and enjoy.

Buffalo Chicken Strips

Ingredients: Servings: 4 Cooking Time: 8 Mins

1/2 C. Greek yogurt
1/4 C. egg
1 ½ tbsp. hot sauce
1 C. panko breadcrumbs
1 tbsp. sweet paprika
1 tbsp. garlic pepper seasoning
1 tbsp. cayenne pepper
1-pound chicken breasts, cut into strips

Directions:

Mix Greek yogurt with hot sauce and egg in a bowl. Whisk breadcrumbs with garlic powder, cayenne pepper, and paprika in another bowl. First, dip the chicken strips in the yogurt sauce then coat them with the crumb's mixture. Place the coated strips in the Air Fryer Basket and spray them with cooking oil. Set the Air Fryer Basket inside the Instant Pot Duo. Put on the Air Fryer lid and seal it. Hit the "Air fry Button" and select 16 minutes of cooking time, then press "Start." Flip the chicken strips after 8 minutes of cooking then resume Air fearing. Once the Instant Pot Duo beeps, remove its lid. Serve.

Cheesecake

Ingredients: Servings: 15 Cooking Time: 15 Mins

Cream cheese – 1 pound
Vanilla extract – ½ tsp.
Eggs – 2
Sugar – 4 tbsps.
Graham crackers – 1 cup, crumbled
Butter – 2 tbsps.

Directions:

Mix crackers with the butter in a bowl. Press crackers mix on the bottom of a lined cake pan. Place in the air fryer and cook at 350F for 4 minutes. Meanwhile, in a bowl, mix eggs, cream cheese, sugar, and vanilla and whisk well. Spread filling over crackers crust and cook in the air fryer at 310F for 15 minutes. Cool and keep in the refrigerator for 3 hours. Slice and serve.

Baked Apple

Ingredients: Servings: 4 Cooking Time: 20 Mins

¼ C. water
¼ tsp. nutmeg
¼ tsp. cinnamon
1 ½ tsp. melted ghee
2 tbsp. raisins
2 tbsp. chopped walnuts
1 medium apple

Directions:

Preparing the Ingredients. Preheat your Instant Crisp Air Fryer to 350 degrees. Slice apple in half and discard some of the flesh from the center. Place into frying pan. Mix remaining ingredients together except water. Spoon mixture to the middle of apple halves. Pour water over filled apples. Air Frying. Place pan with apple halves into the Instant Crisp Air Fryer, close the air fryer Lid. Select Bake, bake 20 minutes.

Chocolate Cake Ii

Ingredients: Servings: 6 Cooking Time: 30 Mins

Eggs – 3
Sour cream – ½ cup
Flour – 1 cup
Sugar – 2/3 cup
Butter – 1 stick, room temperature
Cocoa powder – 1/3 cup
Baking powder – 1 tsp.
Baking soda – ½ tsp.
Vanilla – 2 tsps.

Directions:

Preheat air fryer to 320F. Mix the wet ingredients in a bowl and dry ingredients in another. Gradually pour the dry mixture into the wet. Lightly mix. Place in the air fryer basket. Cook for 25 minutes. Check if the cake is done, if not then cook for another 5 more minutes. Cool on a wire rack.

Radish Chips

Ingredients: Servings: 2 Cooking Time: 12 Mins

1/2 lb radishes, sliced thinly
1/2 tsp. red pepper flakes, crushed
1/2 tbsp. olive oil
1/2 tbsp. lime juice
Pepper
Salt

Directions:

Add radish slices and remaining ingredients into the mixing bowl and toss well. Spray instant pot multi-level air fryer basket with cooking spray. Add radish slices into the air fryer basket and place basket into the instant pot. Seal pot with air fryer lid and select air fry mode then set the temperature to 380 F and timer for 12 minutes. Stir halfway through. Serve and enjoy.

Easy Donuts

Ingredients: Servings: 8 Cooking Time: 5 Mins

Pinch of allspice
4 tbsp. dark brown sugar
1/3 C. granulated sweetener
½ - 1 tsp. cinnamon
3 tbsp. melted coconut oil
1 can of biscuits

Directions:

Preparing the ingredients. Preheat the unit by selecting Bake/Roast, setting the temperature to 300°F, and setting the time to 5 minutes. Press Start/Stop to begin. Mix allspice, sugar, sweetener, and cinnamon together. Take out biscuits from can and with a circle cookie cutter, cut holes from centers and place into Instant Crisp Air Fryer. Air Frying the Dish. Close the air fryer Lid. Select Bake, set the temperature to 350°F, and set the time to 5 minutes. Select Start to begin. As batches are cooked, use a brush to coat with melted coconut oil and dip each into sugar mixture. Serve warm!

Vanilla Brownie

Ingredients: Servings: 4 Cooking Time: 20 Mins

1 egg
1/4 C. cocoa powder
1 tsp. vanilla
2 tbsp. olive oil
1/3 C. flour
2 tbsp. sugar
1/4 C. chocolate chips

Directions:
Spray a baking dish with cooking spray and set aside. In a bowl, whisk egg, vanilla, oil, and sugar. In a mixing bowl, mix together flour and cocoa powder. Add egg mixture into the flour mixture and mix until well combined. Pour batter into the prepared baking dish. Place steam rack in the instant pot then place baking dish on top of the rack. Seal pot with air fryer lid and select bake mode then set the temperature to 320 F and timer for 20 minutes. Serve and enjoy.

Chocolate Cake

Ingredients: Servings: 6 Cooking Time: 25 Mins

Eggs – 3
Sour cream – ½ cup
Almond flour – 1 cup
Erythritol – 2/3 cup, powdered
Butter – 1 stick, room temperature
Cocoa powder – 1/3 cup
Baking powder – 1 tsp.
Baking soda – ½ tsp.
Vanilla – 2 tsps.

Directions:
Preheat air fryer to 320F. Mix the wet ingredients in a bowl and dry ingredients in another. Gradually pour the dry mixture into the wet. Lightly mix. Place in the air fryer basket. Cook for 25 minutes. Check if the cake is done, if not then cook for another 5 more minutes. Cool on a wire rack.

Sweet and Spicy Brussel Sprouts

Ingredients: Servings: 4 Cooking Time: 20 Mins

1 lb brussels sprouts cut in half
1 1/2 tbsp. vegetable oil
2 tbsp. honey
1 tbsp. gochujang
1/2 tsp. salt

Directions:
Mix honey, vegetable oil, gochujang, and salt in a bowl and stir thoroughly. Set aside 1 Tbsp of the sauce. Add the Brussels sprouts to a bowl and stir them until all sprouts are fully covered. Place your brussels sprouts in the Instant Pot Duo Crisp Air Fryer, ensuring that they are not overlapping with each other. Close the Air Fryer lid and choose the Air Fry option. Cook at 360°F for 15 minutes, shaking the basket halfway through or stir the ingredients for the uniform coooking. Once 15 minutes timer is up, increase the temperature to 390°F and cook for five more minutes. When sprouts are done, place in a bowl and cover with reserved sauce and stir.

Air Fryer Apple Fritters

Ingredients: Servings: 6 Cooking Time: 7 To 8 Mins

1 C. chopped, peeled Granny Smith apple
½ C. granulated sugar
1 tsp. ground cinnamon
1 C. all-purpose flour
1 tsp. salt
1 tsp. baking powder
2 tbsp. milk
2 tbsp. butter, melted
1 large egg, beaten
Cooking spray
¼ C. confectioners' sugar (optional)

Directions:
Mix together the apple, granulated sugar, and cinnamon in a small bowl. Allow to sit for 30 minutes. Combine the flour, baking powder, and salt in a medium bowl. Add the milk, butter, and egg and stir to incorporate. Pour the apple mixture into the bowl of flour mixture and stir with a spatula until a dough forms. Make the fritters: On a clean work surface, divide the dough into 12 equal portions and shape into 1-inch balls. Flatten them into patties with your hands. Preheat the air fryer to 350°F (177°C). Line the air fryer basket with parchment paper and spray it with cooking spray. Transfer the apple fritters onto the parchment paper, evenly spaced but not too close together. Spray the fritters with cooking spray. Bake for 7 to 8 minutes until lightly browned. Flip the fritters halfway through the cooking time. Remove from the basket to a plate and serve with the confectioners' sugar sprinkled on top, if desired.

Onion Rings

Ingredients: Servings: 4 Cooking Time: 6 Mins

1 Large Onion
2 Bread Maker Gluten Free Rolls
2 Large Eggs
4.23oz Oat Flour
1 Tbsp Basil
1 Tsp Garlic Puree
1 Tsp Paprika
½ Tsp Mustard Powder
Salt & Pepper

Directions:
Place eggs and garlic into a bowl and using a fork beat the eggs. Place them into a second bowl and mix oat flour along with salt, pepper, and mustard. Blend your gluten-free bread rolls and place them into a third bowl along with the rest of the seasonings. Make sure each bowl is well mixed with its seasonings. Slice your onion into rings. Place each of your onion rings into the oat flour bowl, the egg bowl, and the breadcrumbs bowl until it is well mixed. Shake off any excess batter Place the onion rings into the Instant Pot Duo Crisp Air Fryer Basket. Close the Air Fryer lid and select the Air Fry option and cook for 6 minutes at 400°F and serve with your favorite dipping sauce.

Marshmallow and Chocolate Sandwiched Graham Cracker

Ingredients: Servings: 2 Cooking Time: 5 Mins

2 Graham Crackers broken in half
2 marshmallows broken in half
2 small pieces of chocolate

Directions:
Place the Graham cracker halves on the tray of Instant Pot Duo Crisp Air Fryer. Take the sticky side of the broken marshmallow and place it on the Graham Cracker, push it so

that it sticks to the cracker. Close the Air Fryer lid and cook on 390°F for 5 to 7 minutes, or until the tops of the marshmallows get a nice golden color. Once this is done, add a piece of chocolate on top of the marshmallows, then put the other half of the graham cracker over it.

Cranberry Coconut Pudding

Ingredients: Servings: 6 Cooking Time: 20 Mins

1 C. brown rice, rinsed and drained
1/2 C. coconut milk
1 1/2 C. milk
1 C. cranberries
1/4 C. sugar
1/2 tsp. cinnamon
1/2 C. water

Directions:

Add all ingredients into the inner pot instant pot duo crisp and stir well. Seal the pot with pressure cooking lid and cook on high for 20 minutes. Once done, allow to release pressure naturally. Remove lid. Stir and serve.

Chocolate Donuts

Ingredients: Servings: 8-10 Cooking Time: 20 Mins

(8-ounce) can jumbo biscuits
Cooking oil
Chocolate sauce, such as Hershey's

Directions:

1 Preparing the Ingredients. Separate the biscuit dough into 8 biscuits and place them on a flat work surface. Use a small circle cookie cutter or a biscuit cutter to cut a hole in the center of each biscuit. You can also cut the holes using a knife. Spray the Instant Crisp Air Fryer basket with cooking oil. 2 Air Frying. Place 4 donuts in the Instant Crisp Air Fryer. Do not stack. Spray with cooking oil. Close the air fryer Lid and cook for 4 minutes. Open the Instant Crisp Air Fryer and flip the donuts. Cook for an additional 4 minutes. Remove the cooked donuts from the Instant Crisp Air Fryer, then repeat for the remaining 4 donuts. Drizzle chocolate sauce over the donuts and enjoy while warm.

Garlic Parmesan Chicken Wings

Ingredients: Servings: 4 Cooking Time: 25 Mins

Raw chicken wings – 2 pounds
Salt – 1 tsp.
Garlic powder – ½ tsp.
Baking powder – 1 tbsp.
Unsalted butter – 4 tbsps. melted
Grated Parmesan cheese – 1/3 cup
Dried parsley – ¼ tsp.

Directions:

Place chicken wings, salt, ½ tsp. garlic powder, and baking powder in a bowl. Coat and place wings into the air fryer basket. Cook at 400F for 25 minutes. Toss the basket two or 3 times during the cooking time. Combine butter, parmesan, and parsley in a bowl. Remove wings from the air fryer and place into a bowl. Pour the butter mixture over the wings and toss to coat. Serve warm.

Tortilla Chips

Ingredients: Servings: 6 Cooking Time: 6 Mins

8 corn tortillas, cut into triangles
Salt, to taste
1 tbsp. olive oil

Directions:

Preheat the air fryer to 390 o f and grease an air fryer basket. Drizzle the tortilla chips with olive oil and season with salt. Arrange half of the tortilla chips in the air fryer basket and cook for about 3 minutes, flipping in between. Repeat with the remaining tortilla chips and dish out to serve warm.

Pound Cake

Ingredients: Servings: 6 Cooking Time: 25 Mins

Almond flour – 1 cup
Salted butter – ¼ cup, melted
Granular erythritol – ½ cup
Vanilla extract – 1 tsp.
Baking powder – 1 tsp.
Full-fat sour cream – ½ cup
Full-fat cream cheese – 1 ounce, softened
Eggs – 2

Directions:

Mix erythritol, butter, and flour in a bowl. Add in cream cheese, sour cream, baking powder, and vanilla. Mix well. Add eggs and mix. Pour batter into a 6-inch round baking pan. Place the pan into the air fryer basket. Cook at 300F for 25 minutes. Cool and serve.

Blueberry Lemon Muffins

Ingredients: Servings: 12 Cooking Time: 10 Mins

1 tsp. vanilla
Juice and zest of 1 lemon
2 eggs
1 C. blueberries
½ C. cream
¼ C. avocado oil
½ C. monk fruit
2 ½ C. almond flour

Directions:

1 Preparing the Ingredients. Mix monk fruit and flour together. In another bowl, mix vanilla, egg, lemon juice, and cream together. Add mixtures together and blend well. Spoon batter into cupcake holders. 2 Air Frying. Place in Instant Crisp Air Fryer. Close the air fryer Lid. Select Bake, set the temperature to 320°F, and set the time to 10 minutes. Select Start to begin checking at 6 minutes to ensure you don't overbake them.

Sweet Potato Fries

Ingredients: Servings: 2 Cooking Time: 20 Mins

Sweet potatoes – 2, peeled and cut into medium fries
Salt and black pepper to taste
Olive oil – 2 tbsps.
Coriander – ¼ tsp. ground
Curry powder – ½ tsp.
Ketchup – ¼ cup
Mayonnaise – 2 tbsps.
Cumin – ½ tsp. ground
Ginger powder – 1 pinch
Cinnamon powder – 1 pinch

Directions:

In the air fryer's basket, mix sweet potato fries with salt, pepper, coriander, curry powder, and oil. Toss well. Cook at 370F for 20 minutes. Flipping once. Meanwhile, in a bowl, mix ketchup with cinnamon, ginger, cumin, and mayo. Whisk well. Divide fries on plates. Drizzle ketchup mix over them and serve.

Pumpkin Cake

Ingredients: Servings: 12 Cooking Time: 30 Mins

White flour – 3/4 cup
Whole wheat flour – 3/4 cup
Baking soda – 1 tsp.
Pumpkin pie spice – 3/4 tsp.
Sugar – 3/4 cup
Banana – 1, mashed
Baking powder – 1/2 tsp.
Canola oil – 2 tbsp.
Greek yogurt – 1/2 cup
Canned pumpkin puree – 8 ounces
Cooking spray
Egg – 1
Vanilla extract – 1/2 tsp.
Chocolate chips – 2/3 cup

Directions:
In a bowl, mix whole wheat flour, white flour, salt, baking soda, baking powder, and pumpkin spice and stir. In another bowl, mix egg, vanilla, pumpkin puree, yogurt, banana, oil, and sugar. Mix with a mixer. Combine the 2 mixtures, and add the chocolate chips. Pour this into a greased Bundt pan. Place in the air fryer and cook at 330F for 30 minutes. Cool, slice and serve.

Black and White Brownies

Ingredients: Servings: 8 Cooking Time: 20 Mins

1 egg
1/4 C. brown sugar
2 tbsp. white sugar
2 tbsp. safflower oil
1 tsp. vanilla
1/4 C. cocoa powder
1/3 C. all-purpose flour
1/4 C. white chocolate chips
Nonstick baking spray with flour

Directions:
1 Preparing the Ingredients. In a medium bowl, beat the egg with the brown sugar and white sugar. Beat in the oil and vanilla. Add the cocoa powder and flour, and stir just until combined. Fold in the white chocolate chips. Spray a 6-by-6-by-2-inch baking pan with nonstick spray. Spoon the brownie batter into the pan. 2 Air Frying. Close the air fryer Lid. Select Bake, and bake for 20 minutes or until the brownies are set when lightly touched with a finger. Let cool for 30 minutes before slicing to serve.

Raspberry Danish Bites

Ingredients: Servings: 10 Cooking Time: 7 Mins

Almond flour – 1 cup
Baking powder – 1 tsp.
Granular swerve – 3 tbsps.
Full-fat cream cheese – 2 ounces, softened
Egg – 1
Raspberry preserve – 10 tsps.

Directions:
Mix all ingredients except preserve in a bowl and make a dough. Place the bowl in the freezer for 20 minutes, then roll it to make 10 balls. Press gently in the center of each ball. Place 1 tsp. preserves in the center of each ball. Line the air fryer basket with parchment. Place each Danish bite on the parchment. Press down gently to flatten the bottom. Cook at 400F for 7 minutes. Cool and serve.

Cream Cheese and Zucchinis Bars

Ingredients: Servings: 12 Cooking Time: 20 Mins

3 oz. Zucchini, shredded
4 oz. Cream cheese
6 eggs
2 tbsp. Erythritol
3 tbsp. Coconut oil; melted
2 tsp. Vanilla extract
1/2 tsp. Baking powder

Directions:
In a bowl, combine all the ingredients and whisk well. Pour this into a baking dish that fits your air fryer lined with parchment paper, introduce in the fryer and cook at 320°f, bake for 15 minutes. Slice and serve cold

Cinnamon Maple Chickpeas

Ingredients: Servings: 4 Cooking Time: 12 Mins

14 oz can chickpeas, rinsed, drained and pat dry
1 tsp. ground cinnamon
1 tbsp. brown sugar
1 tbsp. maple syrup
1 tbsp. olive oil
Pepper
Salt

Directions:
Place the dehydrating tray in a multi-level air fryer basket and place basket in the instant pot. Spread chickpeas on dehydrating tray. Seal pot with air fryer lid and select air fry mode then set the temperature to 375 F and timer for 12 minutes. Stir halfway through. In a mixing bowl, mix together cinnamon, brown sugar, maple syrup, oil, pepper, and salt. Add chickpeas and toss well to coat. Serve and enjoy.

Pecan Brownies

Ingredients: Servings: 6 Cooking Time: 20 Mins

Almond flour – 1/2 cup
Powdered erythritol – 1/2 cup
Unsweetened cocoa powder – 2 tbsps.
Baking powder – 1/2 tsp.
Unsalted butter – 1/4 cup, softened
Egg – 1
Chopped pecans – 1/4 cup
Chocolate chips – 1/4 cup

Directions:
Mix almond flour, baking powder, cocoa powder, and erythritol in a bowl. Stir in egg and butter. Fold in chocolate chips and pecans. Scoop mixture into a baking pan and place the pan into the air fryer basket. Cook at 300F for 20 minutes. Cool, sliced and serve.

Simple Pepper & Salt Baby Potatoes

Ingredients: Servings: 4 Cooking Time: 10 Mins

1 lb. baby potatoes
1 1/2 C. water
Pepper
Salt

Directions:

Pour water into the instant pot the place trivet in the pot. Arrange baby potatoes on top of the trivet. Seal pot with lid and cook on manual high pressure for 10 minutes. Once done then allow to release pressure naturally then open the lid. Season potatoes with pepper and salt and serve.

Crispy Roasted Cashews

Ingredients: Servings: 3 Cooking Time: 6 Mins

1 C. cashews
1/4 tsp. onion powder
1/4 tsp. garlic powder
1/2 tsp. nutritional yeast
1 tbsp. rice flour
1 tbsp. olive oil
Pepper
Salt

Directions:
Add cashews and remaining ingredients into the large bowl and toss well. Place the dehydrating tray in a multi-level air fryer basket and place basket in the instant pot. Spread cashews on dehydrating tray. Seal pot with air fryer lid and select air fry mode then set the temperature to 350 F and timer for 6 minutes. Stir halfway through. Serve and enjoy.

Air Fried French Fries

Ingredients: Servings: 6 Cooking Time: 13 Mins

2 Potatoes Russett, medium or large in size
3/4 tbsp. Olive Oil
1/2 tsp. Salt
1/4 tsp. Black Pepper
1/2 tsp. Garlic powder

Directions:
Arrange the seasoned potato slices and place them at the bottom of your air fryer basket. Potatoes will be crispier if they'll be separated. Close the Air Fryer lid Select the option Air Fryer and cook fries at 360°F for 20 minutes. Toss the fries halfway through. If you want fries to be more crisper, allow to cook for 2 more additional minutes. Serve hot.

French Fries In Instant Pot Air Fryer

Ingredients: Servings: 4 Cooking Time: 12 Mins

2 lb. (6 nos.parsnips
¼ C. olive oil
¼ C. of water
¼ C. almond flour
1 tsp. salt
Olive oil cooking spray

Directions:
Wash, peel the parsnips and pat dry before you chop them into ½ inch sizes In a large bowl to mix the almond flour, water, salt, and olive oil. Combine it well until there are no lumps at all. Add the parsnips to this mix and stir it well until everything gets a proper coating. Place the coated parsnips in the air fryer basket and put the basket in the inner pot of the instant pot air fryer. Close the crisp cover. Now in the air fry mode and set the temperature at 390° f and keep the timer for 12 minutes. Press start to begin the frying. It is a good habit if you can open the crisp lid and shake the basket for even cooking. Spritz some cooking spray while shaking the basket, which can help to improve the crispness. Keep cooking 2 more minutes if you don't find it crispy enough. Serve it hot.

Zucchini Chips

Ingredients: Servings: 6 Cooking Time: 1 Hour

Zucchinis – 3, thinly sliced
Salt and black pepper to taste
Olive oil – 2 tbsps.
Balsamic vinegar – 2 tbsps.

Directions:
Mix vinegar, oil, salt, and pepper and whisk well. Add zucchini slices and toss to coat. Cook in the air fryer at 200F for 1 hour. Shake once. Serve.

Cardamom Yogurt Pudding (pressure Cook)

Ingredients: Servings: 4 Cooking Time: 15 Mins

1½ C. Greek yogurt
1 tsp. cocoa powder
2 C. sweetened condensed milk
1 tsp. cardamom powder
1 C. water
¼ C. mixed nuts, chopped

Directions:
Spritz 4 medium ramekins with cooking spray. Set aside. In a bowl, combine the Greek yogurt, cocoa powder, condensed milk, and cardamom powder. Pour mixture into ramekins and cover with foil. Pour the water into the Instant Pot, then fit in a trivet, and place ramekins on top. Seal the lid, select the Pressure Cook and set the cooking time for 15 minutes at High Pressure. When cooking is complete, perform a natural pressure release for 15 minutes, then release any remaining pressure. Unlock the lid. Remove the ramekins from the pot, then take off the foil. Top with mixed nuts and serve immediately.

Cocoa and Nuts Bombs

Ingredients: Servings: 12 Cooking Time: 20 Mins

2 C. macadamia nuts; chopped.
¼ C. cocoa powder
1/3 C. swerve
4 tbsp. Coconut oil; melted
1 tsp. Vanilla extract

Directions:
Take a bowl and mix all the ingredients and whisk well. Shape medium balls out of this mix, place them in your air fryer and cook at 300°f for 8 minutes. Serve cold

Lava Cakes

Ingredients: Servings: 4 Cooking Time: 10 Mins

3.5 oz dark chocolate, melted
1 1/2 tbsp. self-rising flour
2 eggs
3 tbsp. sugar
3.5 oz butter, melted

Directions:
Spray four ramekins with cooking spray and set aside. In a bowl, beat eggs and sugar until frothy. Add melted chocolate, flour, and butter and fold well. Pour batter into the prepared ramekins. Place the dehydrating tray in a multi-level air fryer basket and place basket in the instant pot. Place ramekins on a dehydrating tray. Seal pot with air fryer lid and select air fry

mode then set the temperature to 375 F and timer for 10 minutes. Serve and enjoy.

Fried Hot Dogs

Ingredients: Servings: 2 Cooking Time: 7 Mins

2 hot dogs
2 hot dog buns
2 tbsp. grated cheese

Directions:
Preheat Instant Pot Duo Crisp Air Fryer to 390°F. Place two hot dogs into the air fryer basket. Close the Air Fryer lid and cook for about 5 minutes. Remove the hot dog from the air fryer. Place the hot dog on a bun, add cheese if desired. Place dressed hot dog into the Instant Pot Duo Crisp Air Fryer, and cook for an additional 2 minutes.

Healthy Steamed Vegetables

Ingredients: Servings: 6 Cooking Time: 2 Mins

1/2 lb. yellow beans, cut into pieces
1/2 lb. green beans, cut into pieces
1 tbsp. butter
1 tsp. garlic powder
1/4 C. water
1 cauliflower head, cut into florets
Pepper
Salt

Directions:
Add all ingredients into the instant pot and stir well. Seal pot with lid and cook on manual high pressure for 2 minutes. Once done then release pressure using the quick-release method than open the lid. Stir well and serve with your favorite dip.

Vanilla Cream Cheese Filled Tart

Ingredients: Servings: 4 Cooking Time: 20 Mins

1 frozen piecrust, thawed
2 ½ C. fresh raspberries, divided
1 tbsp. arrowroot starch
¼ tsp. grated lemon zest
1 tsp. freshly squeezed lemon juice
¼ C. sugar
Cream Filling
1 tsp. vanilla extract
8 oz. cream cheese, at room temperature
½ C. confectioners' sugar
¼ C. heavy (whipping) cream

Directions:
Roll out the pie crust and fit into a tart pan. Prick all over the bottom of the dough. Place the reversible rack in the pot and put the tart pan on top. Close the crisping lid, choose Bake; adjust the temperature to 250 F and the cook time to 15 minutes. Press Start. Set the crust aside to cool. Fetch out 1 C. of berries into the inner pot. In a bowl, whisk arrowroot starch and 2 tbsps. water until mixed. Pour the slurry on the raspberries along with sugar, lemon zest, and lemon juice. Mix. Seal the pressure lid, choose Pressure; adjust the pressure to High and the cook time to 2 minutes. Press Start. Once done cooking, perform a quick pressure release and carefully open the lid. Add the remaining 1½ C. of raspberries, stirring to coat with the cooked mixture. Then, allow cooling. In a bowl and with a hand mixer, whisk the vanilla extract and cream cheese until evenly combined and smooth. Mix in confectioners' sugar and whisk again until the sugar has fully incorporated and the mixture is light and smooth. with clean whisks and in another bowl, beat the heavy cream until soft peaks form. Fold the heavy cream into the vanilla mixture. Spoon the cream filling into the piecrust and scatter the remaining raspberries on the cream. Chill for 30 minutes before serving.

Crunchy Zucchini Chips

Ingredients: Servings: 4 Cooking Time: 12 Mins

1 medium zucchini, thinly sliced
3/4 C. Parmesan cheese, grated
1 C. Panko breadcrumbs
1 large egg, beaten

Directions:
In a mixing bowl, add the Parmesan cheese and panko breadcrumbs. Combine the ingredients to mix well with each other. In a mixing bowl, beat the eggs. Coat the zucchini slices with the eggs and then with the crumb mixture. Spray the slices with some cooking spray. Place Instant Pot Air Fryer Crisp over kitchen platform. Press Air Fry set the temperature to 400°F and set the timer to 5 minutes to preheat. Press "Start" and allow it to preheat for 5 minutes. In the inner pot, place the Air Fryer basket. Line it with a parchment paper, add the zucchini slices. Close the Crisp Lid and press the "Air Fry" setting. Set temperature to 350°F and set the timer to 10-12 minutes. Press "Start." Halfway down, open the Crisp Lid, shake the basket and close the lid to continue cooking for the remaining time. Open the Crisp Lid after cooking time is over. Serve warm.

Turkey Bacon-wrapped Dates (air Fryer)

Ingredients: Servings: 6 Cooking Time: 5 To 7 Mins

16 whole dates, pitted
16 whole almonds
6 to 8 strips turkey bacon, cut in half
Special Equipment:
16 toothpicks, soaked in water for at least 30 minutes

Directions:
Preheat the air fryer to 390°F (199°C). On a flat work surface, stuff each pitted date with a whole almond. Wrap half slice of bacon around each date and secure it with a toothpick. Place the bacon-wrapped dates in the air fryer basket and air fry for 5 to 7 minutes, or until the bacon is cooked to your desired crispiness. Transfer the dates to a paper towel-lined plate to drain. Serve hot.

Buckwheat Cobbler

Ingredients: Servings: 6 Cooking Time: 12 Mins

1/2 C. dry buckwheat
2 1/2 lbs apples, cut into chunks
1/4 tsp. nutmeg
1/4 tsp. ground ginger
1 1/2 tsp. cinnamon
1 1/2 C. water
1/4 C. dates, chopped

Directions:
Add all ingredients into the inner pot instant pot duo crisp and stir well. Seal the pot with pressure cooking lid and cook on high for 12 minutes. Once done, release pressure using a quick release. Remove lid. Stir well and serve.

Banana Muffins

Ingredients: Servings: 12 Cooking Time: 15 Mins

2 eggs
1 1/2 C. flour
1 tsp. baking soda
1 1/2 tsp. cinnamon
1 tsp. vanilla
1/4 C. milk
1 C. mashed banana
1/3 C. maple syrup
4 tbsp. butter, melted
1/2 tsp. salt

Directions:
In a medium bowl, whisk eggs with vanilla, mashed banana, maple, syrup, and butter until well combined. Mix together flour, baking soda, cinnamon, and salt in a mixing bowl. Add egg mixture into the flour mixture and mix until well combined. Pour batter into the 12 silicone muffin molds. Place the dehydrating tray in a multi-level air fryer basket and place basket in the instant pot. Place 6 silicone muffin molds on dehydrating tray. Seal pot with air fryer lid and select bake mode then set the temperature to 350 F and timer for 15 minutes. Bake remaining muffins using the same method. Serve and enjoy.

Crispy Avocado Fries

Ingredients: Servings: 4 Cooking Time: 8 Mins

2 large eggs
1.2 C. all-purpose flour
1 tbsp. water
2 avocados, cut into 8 wedges
½ C. panko bread crumbs
1 tsp. canola mayonnaise
1½ tsps. black pepper
½ C. no-salt added ketchup
1 tbsp. Sriracha chili sauce
1 tbsp. apple cider vinegar
Cooking spray
Salt to taste

Directions:
Add flour and pepper in a shallow dish and stir to combine. Lightly beat eggs with water in a bowl. Place the panko bread crumbs in another dish. Dredge each avocado wedge first in the flour mixture and shaking off any excess coating. Then dip in the egg mixture, allowing to drip off before finally coating with the panko bread crumbs. Spray each wedge with the cooking spray. Place wedges on the air fryer basket lined with parchment paper. Place the basket inside the instant pot and cover with the air fryer lid. Cook at 400 degrees F and for 7-8 minutes, flipping halfway through for even cooking. Once done, remove wedges from the air fryer, transfer into a platter, and sprinkle with salt. Meanwhile, prepare the dip by whisking together mayonnaise, vinegar, Sriracha, and ketchup in a mixing bowl. Serve the avocado wedges with this dip.

Plum Cake

Ingredients: Servings: 8 Cooking Time: 8 Mins

4 plums, pitted and chopped.
1 ½ C. almond flour
½ C. coconut flour
¾ C. almond milk
½ C. butter, soft
3 eggs
½ C. swerve
1 tbsp. Vanilla extract
2 tsp. Baking powder
¼ tsp. Almond extract

Directions:
Take a bowl and mix all the ingredients and whisk well. Pour this into a cake pan that fits the air fryer after you've lined it with parchment paper, put the pan in the machine and cook at 370°f for 30 minutes. Cool the cake down, slice and serve

Mini Popovers

Ingredients: Servings: 4-7 Cooking Time: 20 Mins

1 C. milk room temperature
2 eggs room temperature
1 tbsp. butter melted
1 C. all-purpose flour
Salt and pepper Pinch of each

Directions:
Generously coat a heatproof silicone egg bite mold with nonstick spray. Add all ingredients to a blender and process at medium speed for 30 seconds. Fill each mold with a scant 2 tbsp. of batter. Place them into the Instant Pot Duo Crisp Air Fryer Basket. Select the option Air Fryer, Close the Air Fryer lid and cook at 400°F for 20 minutes. After twenty minutes place the egg bite mold on the lower tray of the Instant Pot Duo Crisp Air Fryer. After it gets cooked quickly pierce each popover with a sharp knife, then again place them in the Instant Pot Duo Crisp Air Fryer Basket and continue cooking for 1-2 minutes more. Serve immediately.

French Fries

Ingredients: Servings: 4 Cooking Time: 22 Mins

1-3 medium-sized russet potatoes cut into 1/2 inch fries
2 Tbsp olive oil

Directions:
Soak the potatoes in a bowl of water for one hour. Drain the potatoes and dry them with a paper towel. Then, place the potatoes in a dry bowl and add oil. Choose the Air Fry option and set the Instant Pot Duo Crisp Air Fryer to 400°F. Close the Instant Pot Duo Crisp Air Fryer lid and Air fry for 22-30 minutes. Shake the Air Fryer basket or stir the ingredients every 5 minutes for uniform cooking.

Key Lime Cheesecake

Ingredients: Servings: 8 Cooking Time: 65 Mins

1 tbsp. butter, melted
1½ C. Graham cracker crumbs
24 oz. cream cheese, softened
1 tbsp. cornstarch
1 C. white sugar
3 large eggs
2 C. key lime juice
1 tbsp. lime zest, grated

Directions:
Combine Graham cracker crumbs with butter and press the mix into the bottom of the air fryer basket lined with parchment paper. Refrigerate. Add the cream cheese, lime peel, sugar, and cornstarch in a large mixing bowl. Using an immersion blender, blend the ingredients until smooth and fluffy. Gradually add in eggs while continuously beating to blend until smooth. Also, add key lime juice with a mixer on low mode. Finish mixing with your hand. Avoid over blending lest your cake will crack when baked. Pour batter over the prepared base. Place the basket inside the instant pot duo unit and use

the air fryer lid to cover. Secure and set to bake at 300 degrees F for 65 minutes. Allow to cool and refrigerate overnight.

Peanut Butter Muffins

Ingredients: Servings: 12 Cooking Time: 20 Mins

1 egg
1 1/2 tsp. vanilla
1/4 C. oil
2/3 C. peanut butter
3/4 C. milk
2 1/2 tsp. baking powder
2/3 C. brown sugar
1 3/4 C. flour
1/4 tsp. salt

Directions:
In a mixing bowl, mix together flour, baking powder, brown sugar, and salt. In a small bowl, whisk egg, vanilla, oil, peanut butter, and milk. Pour egg mixture into the flour mixture and mix until well combined. Pour batter into the 12 silicone muffin molds. Place the dehydrating tray in a multi-level air fryer basket and place basket in the instant pot. Place 6 silicone muffin molds on dehydrating tray. Seal pot with air fryer lid and select bake mode then set the temperature to 350 F and timer for 20 minutes. Bake remaining muffins using the same method. Serve and enjoy.

Corn with Lime and Cheese

Ingredients: Servings: 2 Cooking Time: 15 Mins

Corns on the cob – 2, husks removed
A drizzle of olive oil
Juice from 2 limes
Feta cheese – ½ cup, grated
Sweet paprika – 2 tsps.

Directions:
Rub corn with oil and paprika. Place in the air fryer basket and cook at 400F for 15 minutes. Flip once. Divide corn on plates, sprinkle cheese on top. Drizzle with lime juice and serve.

Air Fried Cinnamon Rolls

Ingredients: Servings: 8 Cooking Time: 9 Mins

1 Pound frozen bread dough, thawed
¼ Cup butter, melted and cooled
¾ Cup brown sugar
1½ Tsp ground cinnamon
4 Oz cream cheese softened
2 Tbsp butter softened
1¼ Cups powdered sugar
½ Tbsp vanilla

Directions:
Bring the bread dough to room temperature. Over a lightly floured surface, roll up the dough to a thirteen-inch by 11-inch rectangle. Position the rectangle so the thirteen-inch side, so that it is facing you. Brush the liquid or melted butter over the dough, leaving one-inch border uncovered along the edge farthest away from you. Mix the brown sugar and cinnamon in a little bowl. Sprinkle the mixture over the buttered dough, keeping one-inch border uncovered. Start with the closest edge and roll the dough into a log by starting with the closest edge to you. Tightly roll the dough, and make sure to evenly roll and then push out any air pockets. When you reach the uncovered edge of the dough, press the dough onto the roll and seal it together. Cut the log into eight pieces, slicing it slowly with a sawing motion so you don't flatten the dough. Turn the slices on the sides and then cover it with a clean towel. Place the rolls in the hottest part of the kitchen for 1 to 2 hours to rise. For making the glaze, place the butter and cream cheese in a microwave-safe bowl. Soften the mixture in the microwave until it is easy to stir (30 sec). Gradually add the powdered sugar and stir it to combine. Add the vanilla extract and whisk it until smoothens. Set it aside. After the rise of the rolls, preheat the Instant Pot Duo Crisp Air Fryer at 350°F. Transfer four of the rolls to the Instant Pot Duo Crisp Air Fryer Basket. Close the Air Fryer lid and cook for about 5 minutes. Turn the rolls over and again air fry them for another 4 minutes. Repeat the steps with the remaining four rolls. Cooldown the rolls for a few minutes before glazing. Then spread large dollops of cream cheese glaze on top of the hot cinnamon rolls, and then allow some of the glaze to drip down the side of the rolls.

Carrot Cake

Ingredients: Servings: 6 Cooking Time: 45 Mins

Flour – 5 ounces
Baking powder – ¾ tsp.
Baking soda – ½ tsp.
Cinnamon powder – ½ tsp.
Allspice - ½ tsp.
Nutmeg – ¼ tsp. ground
Egg – 1
Yogurt – 3 tbsps.
Sugar – ½ cup
Pineapple juice – ¼ cup
Sunflower oil – 4 tbsps.
Carrots – 1/3 cup, grated
Pecans – 1/3 cup, toasted and chopped
Coconut flakes – 1/3 cup, shredded
Cooking spray

Directions:
In a bowl, mix flour, nutmeg, cinnamon, allspice, salt, baking soda, and powder and mix. In another bowl, mix the egg with coconut flakes, pecans, carrots, oil, pineapple juice, sugar, and yogurt. Combine the two mixtures and mix well. Pour this into a greased springform pan. Place the pan in the air fryer and cook at 320F for 45 minutes. Cool, slice and serve.

Crumbly Fruit Cakes

Ingredients: Servings: 4 Cooking Time: 15 Mins

4 oz. plain flour
2 oz. butter
1 oz. caster sugar
1 oz. gluten-free oats
4 plums, cored and chopped
1 small apple, cored and chopped
1 oz. brown sugar
1 small pear, cored and chopped
1 small peach, cored and chopped
handful blueberries, quartered
1 tbsp. honey

Directions:
Add all the fruits to a bowl and divide them into 4 ramekins. Drizzle honey and brown sugar over the fruits in each ramekin. Whisk flour with caster sugar and butter in a mixing bowl to get a crumbly mixture. Divide this crumble into the ramekins then place these ramekins in the Instant Pot Duo. Put on the Air Fryer lid and seal it. Hit the "Air fry Button" and select 10 minutes of cooking time, then press "Start." Once the Instant Pot Duo beeps, switch it Broil mode and broil for 5 minutes. Remove the lid and serve.

Lava Molten Cake

Ingredients: Servings: 4 Cooking Time: 13 Mins

1½ tbsps. self-rising flour
3.5 oz. unsalted butter
3½ tbsps. baker's sugar, not powdered
2 eggs
3.5 oz. dark chocolate, cut into pieces or chopped
A drizzle of raspberries to serve

Directions:

Prepare 4 safe-oven ramekins. Grease them with butter or cooking spray. Melt butter and dark chocolates for 3 minutes, level 7 on your microwave. Remove from heat before it is totally melted and stir thoroughly, allowing remaining heat from butter and chocolate to completely melt the mixture. Beat or whisk eggs and sugar in a mixing bowl until frothy and pour over the chocolate mixture into the egg mixture. Add in flour to combine thoroughly using a spatula. Fill each ramekin (about 3/4 full) with the cake mixture. Place over the trivet inside the instant pot and cover with the air fryer lid attachment. Set to 375 degrees F and cook for 10 minutes. Remove ramekins from the air fryer basket and allow to cool for about 2 minutes. Loosen edges with a knife and carefully turnover ramekin content into a serving plate while tapping its bottom. Serve with a drizzle of raspberries.

Air Fryer Zucchini Chips

Ingredients: Servings: 4 Cooking Time: 12 Mins

1 C. panko bread crumbs
1 medium zucchini, thinly sliced
1 large egg, beaten
¾ C. Parmesan cheese, grated
Cooking spray

Directions:

Combine Parmesan cheese and panko bread crumbs in a shallow dish. Break egg in a shallow dish or bowl and whisk. Dip zucchini slices in the egg, one at a time and then dip into bread crumbs to coat. Lightly spray the coated slices of zucchini with cooking spray and arrange them in the air fryer basket lined with parchment paper. Insert the air fryer basket into the instant pot duo crisp and attach the air fryer lid to cover. Attach the air fryer lid and air-fry at 350 degrees F for 10 minutes. Remove from the air fryer, flip for even cooking and cook for another 2 minutes.

Strawberry Donuts

Ingredients: Servings: 4 Cooking Time: 15 Mins

Flour – 8 ounces
Brown sugar – 1 tbsp.
White sugar – 1 tbsp.
Egg – 1
Butter – 2 ½ tbsps.
Whole milk – 4 ounces
Baking powder – 1 tsp.
For the strawberry icing
Butter – 2 tbsps.
Icing sugar – 3.5 ounces
Pink coloring – ½ tsp.
Strawberries – ¼ cup, chopped
Whipped cream – 1 tbsp.

Directions:

In a bowl, mix flour, 1 tbsp. white sugar, 1 tbsp. brown sugar, and butter and stir. In another bowl, mix the egg with 1 ½ tbsps. of butter and milk and stir well. Combine the 2 mixtures, stir, and shape donuts from this mix. Place them in the air fryer's basket and cook at 360F for 15 minutes. Put strawberry puree, whipped cream, food coloring, icing sugar, and 1 tbsp. butter and whisk well. Arrange the donuts on a platter and serve with strawberry icing on top.

Tomato Bacon Cheeseburger Dip

Ingredients: Servings: 10 Cooking Time: 5 Mins

½ C. chopped Tomatoes
10 oz shredded Monterey Jack Cheese
10 oz Cream Cheese
10 Bacon Slices, chopped roughly
1 C. Water

Directions:

Turn on the cooker and select Air Fry mode. Set the temperature to 370 F and the time to 8 minutes. Add the bacon pieces and close the crisping lid. Press Start. When ready, open the lid and add the water, cream cheese, and tomatoes. Do Not Stir. Close the lid, secure the pressure valve, and select Pressure mode on High for 5 minutes. Press Start. Once the timer has ended, do a quick pressure release, and open the lid. Stir in the cheddar cheese and mix to combine. Serve with a side of chips.

Parmesan Mushrooms

Ingredients: Servings: 3 Cooking Time: 15 Mins

Button mushroom caps – 9
Cream cracker slices – 3, crumbled
Parmesan – 2 tbsps. grated
Egg white – 1
Italian seasoning – 1 tsp.
Salt and black pepper
Butter – 1 tbsp. melted

Directions:

Mix crackers with butter, Parmesan, salt, pepper, seasoning, and egg white. Stir well and stuff mushrooms with this mix. Arrange mushrooms in the air fryer basket and cook them at 360F for 15 minutes. Divide among plates and serve.

Pumpkin Muffins

Ingredients: Servings: 18 Cooking Time: 15 Mins

Butter – ¼ cup
Pumpkin puree – ¾ cup
Flaxseed meal – 2 tbsps.
Flour – ¼ cup
Sugar – ½ cup
Nutmeg – ½ tsp. ground
Cinnamon powder – 1 tsp.
Baking powder – ½ tsp.
Egg – 1
Baking powder – ½ tsp.

Directions:

Mix butter, pumpkin puree and egg in a bowl and blend well. Add cinnamon, nutmeg, baking powder, baking soda, sugar, flour and flaxseed meal. Spoon this into a muffin pan. Bake in the air-fryer at 350F for 15 minutes. Serve.

Sweet and Spicy Bacon Wrapped Chicken

Ingredients: Servings: 4 Cooking Time: 13 Mins

1 lb chicken breast cut into 1-inch pieces
6 slices bacon cut into thirds*
1/3 C. brown sugar
1/2 Tbsp chili powder
1/8 tsp. cayenne pepper

Directions:
Place one piece of chicken on one end of a piece of bacon. Secure each one with a toothpick after rolling it up. Combine chili powder, brown sugar, and cayenne pepper in a bowl and stir.Use this mixture to coat each bacon-wrapped chicken piece. Place bacon-wrapped chicken pieces on the tray in the Instant Pot Duo Crisp Air Fryer Basket, make sure that they have enough space between them. Close the lid, choose the Air Fry option and cook at 390°F for 13-15 minutes.

Bacon-wrapped Jalapeno Poppers

Ingredients: Servings: 4 Cooking Time: 12 Mins

Jalapenos – 6, membrane and seeds removed (about 4" long each)
Full-fat cream cheese – 3 ounces
Shredded medium cheddar cheese – 1/3 cup
Garlic powder – ¼ tsp.
Bacon – 12 slices

Directions:
Place cream cheese, cheddar, and garlic powder in a bowl. Microwave for 30 seconds and stir. Spoon cheese mixture into hollow jalapenos. Wrap a slice of bacon around each jalapeno half, completely covering pepper. Place into the air fryer basket. Cook at 400F for 12 minutes. Flip once. Serve.

Beef Jerky

Ingredients: Servings: 6 Cooking Time: 1 Hour 30 Mins

Soy sauce – 2 cups
Worcestershire sauce – ½ cup
Black peppercorns – 2 tbsps.
Black pepper – 2 tbsps.
Beef round – 2 pounds, sliced

Directions:
In a bowl, mix Worcestershire sauce, black pepper, black peppercorns, and soy sauce and whisk well. Add beef slices. Coat and keep in the refrigerator for 6 hours to marinate. Cook in the air-fryer at 370F for 1 hour and 30 minutes. Transfer to a bowl and serve.

Ranch Chickpeas

Ingredients: Servings: 4 Cooking Time: 12 Mins

14 oz can chickpeas, rinsed, drained and pat dry
Pepper
1 1/2 tsp. ranch seasoning mix
Salt

Directions:
Add chickpeas, ranch seasoning, pepper, and salt into the mixing bowl and toss well. Place the dehydrating tray in a multi-level air fryer basket and place basket in the instant pot. Spread chickpeas on dehydrating tray. Seal pot with air fryer lid and select air fry mode then set the temperature to 375 F and timer for 12 minutes. Stir halfway through. Serve and enjoy.

Currant Cream

Ingredients: Servings: 4 Cooking Time: 8 Mins

7 C. red currants
6 sage leaves
1 C. water
1 C. swerve

Directions:
In a pan that fits your air fryer, mix all the ingredients, toss, put the pan in the fryer and cook at 330°f for 30 minutes Discard sage leaves. Divide into C. and serve cold.

Angel Food Cake

Ingredients: Servings: 12 Cooking Time: 30 Mins

¼ C. butter, melted
1 C. powdered erythritol
1 tsp. strawberry extract
12 egg whites
2 tsp. cream of tartar
A pinch of salt

Directions:
1 Preparing the Ingredients. Preheat the Instant Crisp Air Fryer for 5 minutes. Mix the egg whites and cream of tartar. Use a hand mixer and whisk until white and fluffy. Add the rest of the ingredients except for the butter and whisk for another minute. Pour into a baking dish. 2 Air Frying. Place in the Instant Crisp Air Fryer basket, close air fryer lid and cook for 30 minutes at 400°F or if a toothpick inserted in the middle comes out clean. Drizzle with melted butter once cooled.

Moist Chocolate Cake

Ingredients: Servings: 8 Cooking Time: 25 Mins

1 egg
1 tsp. baking soda
1 tsp. baking powder
3 tbsp. cocoa powder
1 C. all-purpose flour
1 C. of sugar
1 tsp. vanilla
1/4 C. butter
1 C. boiling water
1/4 tsp. salt

Directions:
Spray a baking dish with cooking spray and set aside. Add butter and boiling water in a mixing bowl and beat until butter is melted. Add vanilla and egg and beat until well combined. In a medium bowl, mix together flour, baking soda, baking powder, cocoa powder, sugar, and salt. Add egg mixture into the flour mixture and beat until well combined. Pour batter in prepared baking dish. Place steam rack in the instant pot then places a baking dish on top of the rack. Seal pot with air fryer lid and select bake mode then set the temperature to 350 F and timer for 25 minutes. Serve and enjoy.

Yellow Pineapple Cake (pressure Cook)

Ingredients: Servings: 4 Cooking Time: 18 Mins

1 (18.5-ounce / 524-g) box yellow cake mix
2 tbsp. butter, melted
¼ C. brown sugar
1 C. pineapple slices
1 C. water

Directions:

In a medium bowl, prepare the cake mix according to the instructions on box. Set aside. Grease a springform pan with butter, sprinkle the brown sugar at the bottom of the pan and place the pineapple slices on top. Pour the cake batter all over and cover the pan with foil. Pour the water in the Instant Pot, then fit in a trivet, and place the pan on top. Seal the lid, select the Pressure Cook and set the timer for 18 minutes at High Pressure. When cooking is complete, do a natural pressure release for 10 minutes, then release any remaining pressure. Carefully remove cake pan, take off foil and let cool for 10 minutes. Turn cake over onto a plate. Slice and serve.

Baked Plums

Ingredients: Servings: 6 Cooking Time: 20 Mins

6 plums; cut into wedges
10 drops stevia
Zest of 1 lemon, grated
2 tbsp. Water
1 tsp. Ginger, ground
½ tsp. Cinnamon powder

Directions:
In a pan that fits the air fryer, combine the plums with the rest of the ingredients, toss gently. Put the pan in the air fryer and cook at 360°f for 20 minutes. Serve cold

Coconut Donuts

Ingredients: Servings: 4 Cooking Time: 20 Mins

8 oz. Coconut flour
4 oz. Coconut milk
1 egg, whisked
2 tbsp. Stevia
2 ½ tbsp. Butter; melted
1 tsp. Baking powder

Directions:
Take a bowl and mix all the ingredients and whisk well. Shape donuts from this mix and place them in your air fryer's basket and cook at 370°f for 15 minutes. Serve warm

Chocolate Chip Cookie

Ingredients: Servings: 4 Cooking Time: 9 Mins

Softened butter – 3 tbsps.
Erythritol – ¼ C. plus 1 tbsp. powdered
Ground white chocolate – 2 tbsps. no sugar added
Egg yolk – 1
Almond flour – ½ cup
Baking soda – ¼ tsp.
Vanilla – ½ tsp.
Chocolate chips – ¾ cup, no sugar added

Directions:
In a medium bowl, beat the butter and erythritol together until fluffy. Stir in egg yolk. Add the vanilla, baking soda, white chocolate, and flour. Mix well. Stir in the chocolate chips. Line a baking pan with the parchment paper. Spray the parchment paper with nonstick baking spray. Spread the batter into the prepared pan, leaving a ½-inch border on all sides. Bake at 300F for 9 minutes or until cookie is lightly brown and just barely set. Remove the pan from the air fryer and let cook for 10 minutes. Remove the cookie from the pan, remove the parchment paper and let cool on a wire rack.

Vanilla White Chocolate Cheesecake

Ingredients: Servings: 8 Cooking Time: 31 Mins

4 oz. graham crackers, crushed
2 tbsps. unsalted butter, melted
16 oz. cream cheese, room temperature
½ C. sugar
2 tbsps. heavy cream
2 tsps vanilla extract
2 tbsps. sour cream
2 large eggs
3 oz. white chocolate chips, melted

Directions:
In a small bowl, mix the cookie crumbs and butter. Spoon the crumbs into a spring form pan and press all around with a spoon. Place the reversible rack in the inner pot and put the spring form pan on top. Close the crisping lid and choose Air Fry; adjust the temperature to 350 F and the cook time to 6 minutes. Press Start and bake until fragrant and set. Remove the pan and let the crumbs cool. In a medium bowl and using a hand mixer, beat the cream cheese until smooth, add the sugar, and beat further until smooth. Pour in the heavy cream, vanilla extract, and sour cream. Whisk again and crack the eggs into the bowl one after the other while whisking after each egg is added. Spoon ½ C. of the cream mixture into a bowl and mix in the chocolate chips. Pour the remaining cream mixture into the spring form pan, drop spoonfuls of the chocolate mixture with even distance on the filling and run the tip of a skewer through each chocolate drop to marbleize the top of the filling. Cover the filling with aluminium foil. Pour 1 C. of water into the inner pot. Fix in the reversible rack in the pot and put the spring form pan on top. Seal the pressure lid, choose Pressure; adjust the pressure to High and the cook time to 25 minutes. Press Start. After cooking, perform a natural pressure release for 10 minutes. Take off the foil. Chill the cheesecake before serving.

Mixed Berries with Pecan Streusel Topping (air Fryer)

Ingredients: Servings: 3 Cooking Time: 17 Mins

½ C. mixed berries
Cooking spray
Topping:
3 tbsp. almonds, slivered
3 tbsp. chopped pecans
2 tbsp. chopped walnuts
1 egg, beaten
3 tbsp. granulated Swerve
2 tbsp. cold salted butter, cut into pieces
½ tsp. ground cinnamon

Directions:
Preheat the air fryer to 340ºF (171ºC). Lightly spray a baking dish with cooking spray. Make the topping: In a medium bowl, stir together the beaten egg, nuts, Swerve, butter, and cinnamon until well blended. Put the mixed berries in the bottom of the baking dish and spread the topping over the top. Bake in the preheated air fryer for 17 minutes, or until the fruit is bubbly and topping is golden brown. Allow to cool for 5 to 10 minutes before serving.

Air Fryer Crispy Tofu Buffalo Bites

Ingredients: Servings: 6 Cooking Time: 15 Mins

13oz Extra-firm Tofu
1/2 C. Franks Hot sauce
1/2cup Chickpea flour
1 1/2 C. Panko breadcrumbs (Gluten-free version)
1/2 tsp. Garlic powder
salt to taste
1/4 C. Rice flour
Few Tbsp water to make a thick batter
oil spray

Directions:
Press the tofu for thirty minutes. (Drain tofu and then wrap in paper towels or clean tea towel, and place heavy items on top to press. Combine in a bowl chickpea flour, garlic powder, and salt. Add in a little water to make the batter thick. Cut the tofu into the sticks or nugget sized pieces. Coat tofu with rice flour then in the chickpea flour batter Coat it with the panko breadcrumbs. Place the tofu into the Instant Pot Duo Crisp Air Fryer Basket. Spray oil on the tofu. Select the option Air Fryer. Close the Air Fryer lid and cook at 400°F for a total of 15 minutes. Turn them after seven minutes until browned and crispy. Repeat with remaining tofu. Put the Air-fryer tofu in a large mixing bowl and toss with the buffalo sauce to coat. Serve immediately with celery and ranch sauce.

Apple Hand Pies

Ingredients: Servings: 6 Cooking Time: 8 Mins

15-ounces no-sugar-added apple pie filling
1 store-bought crust

Directions:
1 Preparing the Ingredients. Lay out pie crust and slice into equal-sized squares. Place 2 tbsp. filling into each square and seal crust with a fork. 2 Air Frying. Place into the Instant Crisp Air Fryer Instant Crisp Air Fryer. Close the air fryer Lid. Select Bake, set the temperature to 390°F, and set the time to 8 minutes until golden in color. Select Start to begin.

Creamy Banana Pudding (pressure Cook)

Ingredients: Servings: 4 Cooking Time: 5 Mins

1 C. whole milk
2 C. half-and-half
¾ C. plus 1 tbsp. granulated sugar, divided
4 egg yolks
3 tbsp. cornstarch
2 tbsp. cold butter, cut into 4 pieces
1 tsp. vanilla extract
2 medium banana, peeled and sliced
1 C. heavy cream

Directions:
Set the Instant Pot to Sauté mode. Mix the milk, half-and-half, and ½ C. of sugar in the pot. Heat for 3 minutes or until sugar dissolves. Stir constantly. Meanwhile, beat the egg yolks with ¼ C. of sugar in a medium bowl. Add cornstarch and mix well. Scoop ½ C. of milk mixture into egg mixture and whisk until smooth. Pour mixture into Instant Pot. Seal the lid, select the Pressure Cook and set the cooking time for 2 minutes at High Pressure. When cooking is complete, do a quick pressure release and unlock the lid. Stir in butter and vanilla. Lay banana pieces into 4 bowls and top with pudding. In a bowl, whisk heavy cream with remaining sugar; spoon mixture on top of pudding. Refrigerate for 1 hour before serving.

Banana Bread

Ingredients: Servings: 4 Cooking Time: 35 Mins

1/2 C. all-purpose flour
1/4 C. wheat germ or whole-wheat flour
1/2 tsp. kosher salt
1/4 tsp. baking soda
1/2 C. granulated sugar
2 ripe bananas
1/4 C. vegetable oil
1/4 C. plain yogurt (not Greek)
1/2 tsp. pure vanilla extract
1 large egg
1 to 2 tbsp. turbinado sugar, optional

Directions:
Whisk together flour, wheat germ, salt and baking soda in medium bowl. Mash the bananas until very smooth in a separate medium bowl. Add granulated sugar, oil, yogurt, vanilla and egg to the banana and whisk until smooth. Sift the dry ingredients over the wet and fold together with a spatula until just combined. Scrape batter into a 7-inch round air fryer insert, metal cake pan or foil pan and smooth the top. Sprinkle the top of the batter with the turbinado sugar if desired, for a crunchy, sweet topping. Put the pan in the Instant Pot Duo Crisp Air Fryer and close the lid. Select the Air Fry option and cook at 310°F, turning the pan halfway through, until a toothpick inserted in the middle of the bread comes out clean for 30 to 35 minutes. Transfer the pan to a rack to cool for 10 minutes. Unmold the banana bread from the pan and let cool completely on a rack before slicing into wedges to serve.

Kale & Artichoke Bites

Ingredients: Servings: 8 Cooking Time: 15 Mins

¼ C. chopped kale
¼ C. chopped artichoke hearts
¼ C. ricotta cheese
2 tbsp. grated Parmesan cheese
¼ C. goat cheese
1 large egg white
1 lemon, zested
Salt and black pepper to taste
4 sheets frozen phyllo dough, thawed
1 tbsp. olive oil

Directions:
In a bowl, mix the kale, artichoke hearts, ricotta cheese, parmesan cheese, goat cheese, egg white, lemon zest, salt, and pepper. Close the crisping lid, choose Air Fry, set the temperature to 370 F, and the time to 5 minutes. Press Start. Then, place a phyllo sheet on a clean flat surface. Brush with olive oil, place a second phyllo sheet on the first, and brush with oil. Continue layering to form a pile of four oiled sheets. Working from the short side, cut the phyllo sheets into 8 strips. Cut the strips in half to form 16 strips. Spoon 1 tbsp. of filling onto one short side of every strip. Fold a corner to cover the filling to make a triangle; continue folding repeatedly to the end of the strip, creating a triangle-shaped phyllo packet. Repeat the process with the other phyllo bites. Open the Ccisping lid and place the bites in the basket in one layer. Close the lid, choose Air Fry, set the temperature to 350 F, and the timer to 10 minutes. Press Start to begin baking. At the 5-minute mark, open the lid, and flip the bites. Return the basket to the pot and close the lid to continue baking. Once the timer beeps, check to ensure the bites are cooked all the way through.

Wrapped In Prosciutto Asparagus with Been Dip

Ingredients: Servings: 6 Cooking Time: 10 Mins

1 lb Asparagus, stalks trimmed
10 oz Prosciutto, thinly sliced
For the Dip:
1 C. canned white beans
1 medium onion, diced
2 cloves of garlic, minced
2 medium jalapeños, chopped
1 C. crushed Tomatoes
1 C. vegetable broth
1 ½ tbsp. olive oil
1 tsp. paprika
¾ tsp. sea salt
½ tsp. chili powder
Grease the crisp basket with cooking spray, and add in the wrapped asparagus. Close the crisping lid, select Air Fry mode at 370 F and set the time to 8 minutes. Press Start. At the 4-minute mark, turn the bombs. Serve.

Directions:
Open the cooker and add the white beans, onion, jalapeños, garlic, tomatoes, broth, oil, paprika, chili powder, and salt. Close the lid, secure the pressure valve, and select Pressure mode on High for 8 minutes. Press Start. Once the timer has ended, do a quick pressure release, and open the pot. Transfer the

Apple Crisp

Ingredients: Servings: 3 Cooking Time: 9 Mins

4 large apples, cored and sliced
1/4 C. water
For topping:
1/4 C. butter, melted
1 1/2 tsp. ground cinnamon
1/2 tsp. nutmeg
1/2 C. all-purpose flour
1/2 C. brown sugar
1 C. old fashioned oats
1/2 tsp. salt

Directions:
Add water and apple slices into the instant pot. Mix together all topping ingredients and sprinkle over apple mixture. Seal the pot with pressure cooking lid and cook on high pressure for 5 minutes. Once done, allow to release pressure naturally for 5 minutes then release remaining pressure using quick release. Remove lid. Seal pot with air fryer lid and select broil mode and set timer for 4 minutes. Serve and enjoy.

Beet Chips

Ingredients: Servings: 6 Cooking Time: 15 Mins

4 medium beetroots, peeled and thinly sliced
½ tsp. salt
¼ tsp. smoked paprika
2 tbsp. olive oil

Directions:
Preheat the air fryer to 325 o f and grease an air fryer basket. Mix together all the ingredients in a bowl until well combined. Arrange the beet slices in the air fryer basket and cook for about 15 minutes. Dish out and serve warm.

Banana Snack

Ingredients: Servings: 2 Cooking Time: 5 Mins

Chocolate chips – ¾ cup
Banana – 1, peeled and sliced in 16 pieces
Peanut butter – ¼ cup
Vegetable oil – 1 tbsp.
Other
16 baking C. crust

Directions:
Melt the chocolate chips in a small pot over a low heat or in the microwave. In a bowl, mix coconut oil with peanut butter and whisk well. Spoon 1 tsp. chocolate mix in a cup, add 1 banana sliced and top with 1 tsp. butter mix. Repeat with the rest of the cups; place them all into a dish that fits the air fryer. Cook at 320F for 5 minutes. Cool, freeze and serve.

Air Fryer Banana Bread

Ingredients: Servings: 8 Cooking Time: 35 Mins

2 medium ripe bananas, mashed
½ C. granulated sugar
2 large eggs, lightly beaten
⅓ C. plain nonfat yogurt
3/4 C. white whole wheat flour
¼ tsp. baking soda
1 tsp. cinnamon
½ tsp. Kosher salt
2 tbsps. vegetable oil
2 tsps. toasted walnuts, roughly chopped
1 tsp. vanilla extract
Cooking spray

Directions:
Line with parchment a 6-inch round cake pan and grease with cooking spray. In a medium-size mixing bowl, add flour, baking soda, cinnamon, and salt. Set aside. In another bowl, add eggs, mashed bananas, yogurt, oil, sugar, and vanilla, and whisk to blend. Slowly pour wet ingredients into the flour mixture and continue stirring to completely combine all ingredients. Pour batter into the pan and sprinkle walnuts over it. Insert a trivet into your instant pot and put the pan on top of it. Attach the air fryer lid and cook at 310 degrees F for about 30-35 minutes. Once done, remove the pan with the bread and transfer to a wire rack to cool for about 15 minutes. Transfer the bread to a platter and slice to serve.

Easy Baked Chocolate Mug Cake

Ingredients: Servings: 3 Cooking Time: 15 Mins

½ C. cocoa powder
½ C. stevia powder
1 package cream cheese, room temperature
1 C. coconut cream
1 tbsp. vanilla extract
3 tbsp. butter

Directions:
1 Preparing the Ingredients. Preheat the Instant Crisp Air Fryer for 5 minutes. In a mixing bowl, combine all ingredients. Use a hand mixer to mix everything until fluffy. Pour into greased mugs. Place the mugs in the fryer basket. 2 Air Frying. Close air fryer lid and bake for 15 minutes at 350°F. Place in the fridge to chill before serving.

Brownies

Ingredients: Servings: 6 Cooking Time: 20 Mins

Almond flour – ½ cup
Powdered erythritol – ½ cup
Unsweetened cocoa powder – 2 tbsps.
Baking powder – ½ tsp.
Unsalted butter – ¼ cup, softened
Egg – 1
Chopped pecans – ¼ cup
Chocolate chips – ¼ cup

Directions:
Mix almond flour, baking powder, cocoa powder, and erythritol in a bowl. Stir in egg and butter. Fold in chocolate chips and pecans. Scoop mixture into a baking pan and place the pan into the air fryer basket. Cook at 300F for 20 minutes. Cool, slice and serve.

Pizza Pasta

Ingredients: Servings: 8 Cooking Time: 25 Mins

1/2 lb to 1 lb Italian sausage
6 oz pepperoni (sliced)
1 medium onion
2 Tbsp minced garlic
1/2 tsp. oregano
1/2 tsp. basil
1/4 tsp. ground black pepper
1/2 tsp. salt
1/4 tsp. crushed red pepper
2 C. chicken stock
1 C. red wine (or substitute chicken stock)
1 28 oz can dice Italian tomatoes, whit juice
1 28 oz can tomato puree
16 oz pasta (I used rigatoni)
8 oz shredded Italian or Mozzarella cheese

Directions:
Mix Italian sausage, onion, and garlic in Instant Pot Duo Crisp Air Fryer basket. Add the spices and stir well. Add half of the pepperoni, the chicken stock, and red wine. Add the tomatoes and tomatoes puree. Stir lightly. Pour the pasta on top of the liquid and gently press down until the pasta is covered with liquid. Do not stir. the idea is to keep most of the pasta off of the bottom of the pot. Select the option Air Fryer. Close the Air Fryer lid and cook for 6 minutes. Stir in 1/3 of the cheese and place the rest on top of the pasta mix. Layer the remaining pepperoni on top of the cheese. Close the Air Fryer lid and cook at 400°F for 5 minutes. Remove the air fryer lid and serve!

Delicious Lime Pudding

Ingredients: Servings: 4 Cooking Time: 3 Mins

1/4 C. coconut milk
3/4 tsp. lime zest, grated
1/2 tsp. orange extract
1 tbsp. swerve
1/4 C. heavy whipping cream
1/4 C. coconut cream
1 tsp. agar powder
1 tbsp. coconut oil

Directions:
Add coconut oil into the inner pot of instant pot duo crisp and set the pot on sauté mode. Add coconut milk, whipping cream, and coconut cream to the pot and stir constantly. Add orange extract, swerve and agar powder. Stir constantly and cook for 2-3 minutes. Turn off the pot and pour pot mixture into the ramekins. Sprinkle lime zest on top of each ramekin. Place ramekins in the fridge for 1-2 hours. Serve and enjoy.

Cherry-choco Bars

Ingredients: Servings: 8 Cooking Time: 15 Mins

¼ tsp. salt
½ C. almonds, sliced
½ C. chia seeds
½ C. dark chocolate, chopped
½ C. dried cherries, chopped
½ C. prunes, pureed
½ C. quinoa, cooked
¾ C. almond butter
1/3 C. honey
2 C. old-fashioned oats
2 tbsp. coconut oil

Directions:
1 Preparing the Ingredients. Preheat the Instant Crisp Air Fryer to 375°F. In a mixing bowl, combine the oats, quinoa, chia seeds, almond, cherries, and chocolate. In a saucepan, heat the almond butter, honey, and coconut oil. Pour the butter mixture over the dry mixture. Add salt and prunes. Mix until well combined. Pour over a baking dish that can fit inside the Instant Crisp Air Fryer. 2 Air Frying. Close the air fryer Lid. Select Bake, Cook for 15 minutes at 375°F. Let it cool for an hour before slicing into bars.

Spicy Tortilla Chips (air Fryer)

Ingredients: Servings: 4 Cooking Time: 8 To 12 Mins

½ tsp. ground cumin
½ tsp. paprika
½ tsp. chili powder
½ tsp. salt
Pinch cayenne pepper
8 (6-inch) corn tortillas, each cut into 6 wedges
Cooking spray

Directions:
Preheat the air fryer to 375°F (191°C). Lightly spritz the air fryer basket with cooking spray. Stir together the cumin, paprika, chili powder, salt, and pepper in a small bowl. Working in batches, arrange the tortilla wedges in the air fryer basket in a single layer. Lightly mist them with cooking spray. Sprinkle some seasoning mixture on top of the tortilla wedges. Air fry for 4 to 6 minutes, shaking the basket halfway through, or until the chips are lightly browned and crunchy. Repeat with the remaining tortilla wedges and seasoning mixture. Let the tortilla chips cool for 5 minutes and serve.

Stuffed Bell Peppers

Ingredients: Servings: 4 Cooking Time: 36 Mins

4 large bell peppers, cut in half
1/4 C. feta cheese, crumbled
2 tsp. dried oregano
2 C. of water
3 tbsp. pine nuts, roasted
1 C. couscous
1/4 tsp. pepper
1 tsp. salt

Directions:
Add water and couscous into the instant pot and stir well. Seal pot with lid and cook on manual high pressure for 3 minutes. Once done then allow to release pressure naturally then open the lid. Add remaining ingredients except for bell peppers to

the pot and cook on sauté mode for 3 minutes. Stuff couscous mixture into the bell peppers and place on a baking tray. Bake at 375 f for 30 minutes. Serve and enjoy.

Banana-choco Brownies

Ingredients: Servings: 12 Cooking Time: 30 Mins

2 C. almond flour
2 tsp. baking powder
½ tsp. baking powder
½ tsp. baking soda
½ tsp. salt
1 over-ripe banana
3 large eggs
½ tsp. stevia powder
¼ C. coconut oil
1 tbsp. vinegar
1/3 C. almond flour
1/3 C. cocoa powder

Directions:
1 Preparing the Ingredients. Preheat the Instant Crisp Air Fryer for 5 minutes. Combine all ingredients in a food processor and pulse until well-combined. Pour into a baking dish that will fit in the Instant Crisp Air Fryer. 2 Air Frying. Place in the Instant Crisp Air Fryer basket. Close the air fryer Lid. Select Bake, set the temperature to 350°F, and set the time to 30 minutes or if a toothpick inserted in the middle comes out clean. Select Start to begin.

Yummy Broccoli Popcorn

Ingredients: Servings: 4 Cooking Time: 6 Mins

2 C. broccoli florets
4 eggs yolks
2 C. coconut flour
Pepper
Salt

Directions:
In a small bowl, whisk eggs with pepper and salt. In a shallow dish, add coconut flour. Spray instant pot multi-level air fryer basket with cooking spray. Dip broccoli floret with egg and coat with coconut flour and place it into the air fryer basket and place basket into the instant pot. Seal pot with air fryer lid and select air fry mode then set the temperature to 400 F and timer for 6 minutes. Serve and enjoy.

MEAT RECIPES

Teriyaki Pork

Ingredients: Servings: 4 Cooking Time: 40 Mins

2 lb. pork loin
1/2 tsp. onion powder
1 tsp. ground ginger
2 tbsp. brown sugar
1/2 C. water
1/4 C. soy sauce
1 C. chicken stock
1 1/2 tbsp. honey
2 garlic cloves, crushed

Directions:
In a small bowl, mix together all ingredients except meat and stock. Pour the stock into the instant pot. Place meat into the pot then pour bowl mixture over the pork. Seal pot with lid and cook on manual high pressure for 45 minutes. Once done then allow to release pressure naturally then open the lid. Serve and enjoy.

Honey-mustard Chicken Breasts

Ingredients: Servings: 6 Cooking Time: 20 Mins

6 oz. boneless and skinless chicken breasts
2 tbsps. fresh rosemary, minced
3 tbsps. honey
1 tbsp. Dijon mustard
¼ tsp. ground black pepper
¾ tsp. salt

Directions:
Combine the honey, Dijon mustard, black pepper, rosemary, and salt in a bowl. Rub the chicken breasts with the honey-mustard mixture. Spritz the air fryer basket generously with cooking spray. Arrange the chicken breasts inside the basket in a single layer (work in batches if necessary). Place the trivet inside the pot and place the basket on top. Air-fry at 350 degrees F for about 20-24 minutes or until the thermometer inserted at the center of the chicken reads 165 degrees F. Transfer the chicken breasts to a platter. Serve with green veggies, rice, or quinoa.

Steak Tips with Potatoes

Ingredients: Servings: 2 Cooking Time: 20 Mins

1/2 lb steak, cut into 1/2-inch cubes
1/4 lb potatoes, cut into 1/2-inch cubes
1/4 tsp. garlic powder
1/2 tsp. Worcestershire sauce
1 tbsp. butter, melted
Pepper
Salt

Directions:
Cook potatoes into the boiling water for 5 minutes. Drain well and set aside. In a mixing bowl, toss together steak cubes, potatoes, garlic powder, Worcestershire sauce, butter, pepper, and salt. Spray instant pot multi-level air fryer basket with cooking spray. Add steak potato mixture into the air fryer basket and place basket into the instant pot. Seal pot with air fryer lid and select air fry mode then set the temperature to 400 F and timer for 20 minutes. mix halfway through. Serve and enjoy.

Juicy Pork Ribs Ole

Ingredients: Servings: 4 Cooking Time: 25 Mins

1 rack of pork ribs
1/2 C. low-fat milk
1 tbsp. envelope taco seasoning mix
1/2 tsp. ground black pepper
1 can tomato sauce
1 tsp. seasoned salt
1 tbsp. cornstarch
1 tsp. canola oil

Directions:
Preparing the Ingredients. Place all ingredients in a mixing dish; let them marinate for 1 hour. Air Frying. Close air fryer lid. Cook the marinated ribs approximately 25 minutes at 390 degrees F Work with batches. Enjoy

Vietnamese Pork Chops

Ingredients: Servings: 6 Cooking Time: 7 Mins

1 tbsp. olive oil
1 tbsp. fish sauce
1 tsp. low-sodium dark soy sauce
1 tsp. pepper
3 tbsp. lemongrass
1 tbsp. chopped shallot
1 tbsp. chopped garlic
1 tbsp. brown sugar
2 pork chops

Directions:

1 Preparing the Ingredients. Add pork chops to a bowl along with olive oil, fish sauce, soy sauce, pepper, lemongrass, shallot, garlic, and brown sugar. Marinade pork chops 2 hours. Ensure your Instant Crisp Air Fryer is preheated to 400 degrees. Add pork chops to the basket. 2 Air Frying. Close air fryer lid. Set temperature to 400°F, and set time to 7 minutes. Cook making sure to flip after 5 minutes of cooking. Serve alongside steamed cauliflower rice.

Ginger, Garlic and Pork Dumplings

Ingredients: Servings: 8 Cooking Time: 15 Mins

¼ tsp. crushed red pepper
½ tsp. sugar
1 tbsp. chopped fresh ginger
1 tbsp. chopped garlic
1 tsp. toasted sesame oil
1 tsp. canola oil
18 dumpling wrappers
2 tbsp. rice vinegar
2 tsp. soy sauce
4 C. bok choy, chopped
4 oz. ground pork

Directions:

1 Preparing the Ingredients. Heat oil in a skillet and sauté the ginger and garlic until fragrant. Stir in the ground pork and cook for 5 minutes. Stir in the bok choy and crushed red pepper. Season with salt and pepper to taste. Allow to cool. Place the meat mixture in the middle of the dumpling wrappers. Fold the wrappers to seal the meat mixture in. Place the bok choy in the grill pan. 2 Air Frying. Close air fryer lid. Cook the dumplings in the Instant Crisp Air Fryer at 330°F for 15 minutes. Meanwhile, prepare the dipping sauce by combining the remaining Ingredients in a bowl.

Citrusy Chicken Tacos (pressure Cook)

Ingredients: Servings: 12 Cooking Time: 20 Mins

¼ C. olive oil
12 chicken breasts, skin and bones removed
8 cloves of garlic, minced
⅔ C. orange juice, freshly squeezed
⅔ C. lime juice, freshly squeezed
2 tbsp. ground cumin
1 tbsp. dried oregano
1 tbsp. orange peel
Salt and pepper, to taste
¼ C. cilantro, chopped

Directions:

Set your Instant Pot to Sauté. Add and heat the oil. Add the chicken breasts and garlic. Cook until the chicken pieces are lightly browned. Add the orange juice, lime juice, cumin, oregano, orange peel, salt, and pepper. Stir well. Secure the lid. Select the Poultry mode and cook for 15 minutes at High Pressure. Once cooking is complete, do a quick pressure release. Carefully remove the lid. Serve garnished with the cilantro.

Wonton Taco Cups

Ingredients: Servings: 8 Cooking Time: 10 Mins

1/2 lb. ground pork, browned and drained
1/2 lb. ground beef, browned and drained
1 envelope taco seasoning
1 (10-ounce) can tomatoes with chilies, diced and drained
1 bell pepper, seeded and chopped
32 wonton wrappers
1 C. Cheddar cheese, shredded

Directions:

1 Preparing the Ingredients. Combine the pork, beef, taco seasoning, diced tomatoes, and bell pepper; mix well. Line all the muffin C. with wonton wrappers. Spritz with a nonstick cooking oil. Divide the beef filling among wrappers; top with the shredded cheese. 2 Air Frying. Close air fryer lid. Bake at 370 degrees F for about 10 minutes or until heated through.

Chorizo and Beef Burger

Ingredients: Servings: 4 Cooking Time: 15 Mins

80/20 ground beef – ¾ pound
Ground chorizo – ¼ pound
Pickled jalapenos – 5 slices, chopped
Chopped onion – ¼ cup
Chili powder – 2 tsps.
Minced garlic -1 tsp.
Cumin – ¼ tsp.

Directions:

Mix all the ingredients in a bowl. Make four burger patties from the mixture. Place burger patties into the air fryer basket. Cook at 375F for 15 minutes. Flip once. Serve.

Browned Chicken with Veggies (pressure Cook)

Ingredients: Servings: 4 Cooking Time: 25 Mins

2 tbsp. olive oil
1 yellow onion, chopped
2 chicken breasts, skinless, boneless and cubed
1 C. cubed tomato
1 C. cubed mixed bell peppers
1 C. chicken stock
1 tsp. Creole seasoning
A pinch of cayenne pepper

Directions:

Set your Instant Pot to Sauté and heat the olive oil until hot. Add the onion and chicken cubes and brown for 5 minutes. Stir in the remaining ingredients. Secure the lid. Select the poultry mode and set the cooking time for 20 minutes at High Pressure. Once cooking is complete, do a natural pressure release for 10 minutes, then release any remaining pressure. Carefully open the lid. Serve warm.

Carrot and Beef Cocktail Balls

Ingredients: Servings: 10 Cooking Time: 20 Mins

1 lb. ground beef
2 carrots
1 red onion, peeled and chopped
2 cloves garlic
1/2 tsp. dried rosemary, crushed
1/2 tsp. dried basil
1 tsp. dried oregano
1 egg
3/4 C. breadcrumbs
1/2 tsp. salt
1/2 tsp. black pepper, or to taste
1 C. plain flour

Directions:

1 Preparing the Ingredients. Place ground beef in a large bowl. In a food processor, pulse the carrot, onion and garlic; transfer

the vegetable mixture to a large-sized bowl. Then, add the rosemary, basil, oregano, egg, breadcrumbs, salt, and black pepper. Shape the mixture into even balls; refrigerate for about 30 minutes. Roll the balls into the flour. 2 Air Frying. Close air fryer lid. Then, air-fry the balls at 350 degrees F for about 20 minutes, turning occasionally; work with batches. Serve with toothpicks.

Crispy Breaded Pork Chops

Ingredients: Servings: 8 Cooking Time: 15 Mins

1/8 tsp. pepper
¼ tsp. chili powder
½ tsp. onion powder
½ tsp. garlic powder
1 ¼ tsp. sweet paprika
2 tbsp. grated parmesan cheese
1/3 C. crushed cornflake crumbs
½ C. panko breadcrumbs
1 beaten egg
6 center-cut boneless pork chops

Directions:
Preparing the Ingredients. Ensure that your Instant Crisp Air Fryer is preheated to 400 degrees. Spray the basket with olive oil. with ½ tsp. salt and pepper, season both sides of pork chops. Combine ¾ tsp. salt with pepper, chili powder, onion powder, garlic powder, paprika, cornflake crumbs, panko breadcrumbs and parmesan cheese. Beat egg in another bowl. Dip pork chops into the egg and then crumb mixture. Add pork chops to Instant Crisp Air Fryer and spritz with olive oil. Air Frying. Close Air Fryer Lid. Set temperature to 400°F, and set time to 12 minutes. Cook 12 minutes, making sure to flip over halfway through cooking process. Only add 3 chops in at a time and repeat the process with remaining pork chops.

Lemony Chicken with Potatoes (pressure Cook)

Ingredients: Servings: 4 Cooking Time: 21 Mins

2 lb. (907 g) chicken thighs
1 tsp. fine sea salt
½ tsp. ground black pepper
2 tbsp. olive oil
¼ C. freshly squeezed lemon juice
¾ C. low-sodium chicken broth
2 tbsp. Italian seasoning
2 to 3 tbsp. Dijon mustard
2 to 3 lb. (907 to 1361 g) red potatoes, quartered

Directions:
Sprinkle the chicken with the salt and pepper. Add the oil to your Instant Pot. Select the Sauté mode. Add the chicken and sauté for 3 minutes until browned on both sides. Meanwhile, make the sauce by stirring together the lemon juice, chicken broth, Italian seasoning, and mustard in a medium mixing bowl. Drizzle the sauce over the chicken. Fold in the potatoes. Secure the lid. Press the Pressure Cook on the Instant Pot and cook for 15 minutes at High Pressure. Once cooking is complete, do a quick pressure release. Carefully remove the lid. Transfer the chicken to a serving dish and serve immediately.

Chicken Fillet

Ingredients: Servings: 3 Cooking Time: 25 Mins

3 chicken breast fillets
¾ C. chicken stock, divided
2 tbsps. olive oil, divided
1 tsp. Italian seasoning
½ tsp. ground coriander
½ tsp. paprika
½ tsp. garlic, minced
½ tsp. ground ginger
Salt and pepper to taste

Directions:
Mix the Italian seasoning, coriander, paprika, garlic, ginger, pepper, salt, 2 tbsp. chicken stock, and 1 tbsp. olive oil in a small bowl. Put the chicken into a bowl and pour the paste to the chicken. Rub the breasts with the paste to coat completely. Press the SAUTE setting of your instant pot and add the oil into the pot. Add the chicken breasts and cook for 2 minutes per side or until they're browned on both sides. Transfer the chicken breasts to a plate and set aside. Add the remaining chicken stock to the instant pot. Use a wooden or silicon spoon to scrape the fond at the bottom of the pot. Set the trivet inside and arrange the chicken fillets on top of it. Pressure cook on HIGH for 5 minutes. Once done, let it naturally release the pressure for about 8-10 minutes before quick releasing. Remove the chicken and the trivet from the pot; transfer the stock to a container. Set the trivet in the inner pot again and place the chicken breasts on top. Attach the air fryer lid to the instant pot and air-fry at 350 degrees F for 20 minutes, flipping the chicken halfway through the cooking process. Transfer to a serving plate and serve with your favorite greens or side dish.

Cuban Pork

Ingredients: Servings: 6 Cooking Time: 8 Hours 10 Mins

3 lbs pork shoulder roast
1 tsp. oregano, dried
1 tsp. cumin
1/2 C. fresh lime juice
1/2 C. orange juice
1 bay leaf
1 onion, sliced
1 1/2 garlic cloves, crushed
1/4 tsp. red chili flakes
2 tbsp. olive oil
1/8 tsp. pepper
1 1/2 tsp. salt

Directions:
In a bowl, mix together garlic, pepper, chili flakes, lime juice, orange juice, oil, oregano, cumin, and salt, Place pork into the inner pot of instant pot duo crisp. Pour bowl mixture over pork. Add bay leaf. Seal the pot with pressure cooking lid and select slow cook mode and cook on low for 8 hours. Remove meat from pot and shred using a fork. Clean the pot. Add shredded meat into the air fryer basket and place basket into the pot. Seal the pot with air fryer lid and select broil mode and cook for 10 minutes. Serve and enjoy.

Party Stuffed Full Chicken

Ingredients: Servings: 6 Cooking Time: 47 Mins

4 lb Whole Chicken
1 tbsp. Herbes de Provence Seasoning
Salt and Black Pepper to season
2 cloves Garlic, peeled
1 tbsp. Olive Oil
1 tsp. Garlic Powder
1 Yellow Onion, peeled and quartered
1 Lemon, quartered
1 ¼ C. Chicken Broth

Directions:
Put the chicken on a clean flat surface and pat dry using paper towels. Sprinkle the top and cavity of the chicken with salt, black pepper, Herbes de Provence, and garlic powder. Stuff the onion, lemon quarters, and garlic cloves into the cavity. In the cooker, fit the reversiblerack. Pour the broth in and place the chicken on the rack. Seal the lid, and select Pressure mode on High for 25 minutes. Press Start to start cooking. Once ready, do a natural pressure release for about 10 minutes, then a quick pressure release to let the remaining steam out, and press Stop. Close the crisping lid and broil the chicken for 5 minutes on Broil mode, to ensure that it attains a golden brown color on each side. Dish the chicken on a bed of steamed mixed veggies. Right here, the choice is yours to whip up some good veggies together as your appetite tells you.

Simple Whole Chicken Bake (air Fryer)

Ingredients: Servings: 2 To 4 Cooking Time: 1 Hour

½ C. melted butter
3 tbsp. garlic, minced
Salt, to taste
1 tsp. ground black pepper
1 (1-pound / 454-g) whole chicken

Directions:
Preheat the air fryer to 350°F (177°C). Combine the butter with garlic, salt, and ground black pepper in a small bowl. Brush the butter mixture over the whole chicken, then place the chicken in the preheated air fryer, skin side down. Bake the chicken for an hour or until an instant-read thermometer inserted in the thickest part of the chicken registers at least 165°F (74°C). Flip the chicken halfway through. Remove the chicken from the air fryer and allow to cool for 15 minutes before serving.

Provolone Cheeseburgers

Ingredients: Servings: 4 Cooking Time: 60 Mins

1 tbsp. Olive Oil
1 (14 oz) can French Onion Soup
1 lb Chuck Beef Roast
1 Onion, sliced
2 tbsp. Worcestershire Sauce
2 Cups Beef Broth
Salt and Black Pepper to taste
1 tsp. Garlic Powder
3 Slices Provolone Cheese
3 Hoagies, halved
3 tsp. Mayonnaise

Directions:
Season the beef with garlic powder, salt, and pepper. On cooker, select Sear/Sauté mode. Heat the olive oil and brown the beef on both sides for about 5 minutes. Remove the meat onto a plate. Into the pot, add the onions and cook until soft. Then, pour the beef broth and stir, while scraping the bottom off every stuck bit. Add the onion soup, Worcestershire sauce, and beef. Close the lid, secure the pressure valve, and select Pressure mode on High pressure for 20 minutes. Press Start. Once the timer has stopped, do a natural pressure release for 10-15 minutes, and then a quick pressure release to let out any remaining steam. Use two forks to shred the meat. Close the crisping lid and cook on Bake for 10 minutes at 350 F. When ready, open the lid and strain the juice of the pot through a sieve into a bowl to be used as "Au Jus" for serving. Assemble the burgers by slathering mayo on halved hoagies, spoon the shredded meat over and top each hoagie with cheese. Serve with the "Au Jus" as a dip.

Red Wine Pork Neck Bones

Ingredients: Servings: 6 Cooking Time: 35 Mins

3 lb Pork Neck Bones
4 tbsp. Olive Oil
Salt and Black Pepper to taste
2 cloves Garlic, smashed
1 tbsp. Tomato Paste
1 tsp. dried Thyme
1 White Onion, sliced
½ C. Red Wine
1 C. Beef Broth

Directions:
Open the lid and select Sear/Sauté mode. Warm the olive oil. Meanwhile, season the pork neck bones with salt and pepper. After, place them in the oil to brown on all sides. Work in batches. Each batch should cook in about 5 minutes. Then, remove them onto a plate. Add the onion and season with salt to taste. Stir with a spoon and cook the onions until soft, for a few minutes. Then, add garlic, thyme, pepper, and tomato paste. Cook them for 2 minutes, constant stirring to prevent the tomato paste from burning. Next, pour the red wine into the pot to deglaze the bottom. Add the pork neck bones back to the pot and pour the beef broth over it. Close the lid, secure the pressure valve, and select Pressure mode on High pressure for 10 minutes. Press Start to start cooking. Once the timer has ended, let the pot sit for 10 minutes before doing a quick pressure release. Close the crisping lid and cook on Broil mode for 5 minutes, until nice and tender. Dish the pork neck into a serving bowl and serve with the red wine sauce spooned over and a right amount of broccoli mash.

Herb Rack of Lamb

Ingredients: Servings: 2 Cooking Time: 20 Mins

Whole rack of lamb – 1 pound
Rosemary – 2 tbsps. dried
Thyme – 1 tbsp. dried
Garlic – 2 tsps. minced
Salt and pepper to taste
Olive oil – 4 tbsps.

Directions:
In a bowl, mix everything except for the lamb. Rub the lamb with the herb mixture and coat well. Cook in the air fryer at 360F for 10 minutes. Flip once at the halfway mark. Serve.

Lamb and Brussels Sprouts

Ingredients: Servings: 4 Cooking Time: 70 Mins

Leg of lamb – 2 pounds, scored
Rosemary - 1 tbsp. chopped
Lemon thyme – 1 tbsp. chopped
Garlic – 1 clove, minced
Olive oil – 2 tbsps.
Brussels sprouts – 1 ½ lb. trimmed
Butter – 1 tbsp. melted
Sour cream – ½ cup
Salt and black pepper to taste

Directions:
Season the leg of lamb with rosemary, thyme, salt, and pepper. Brush with oil, and place in the air fryer basket. Cook at 300F for 1 hour. Flip once at the halfway mark. Transfer to a plate and keep warm. In a pan, mix Brussels sprouts with sour cream,

butter, garlic, salt, and pepper. Mix well and cook at 400F for 10 minutes. Divide lamb on plates, add Brussels sprouts on the side and serve.

Spicy Thai Beef Stir-fry

Ingredients: Servings: 4 Cooking Time: 9 Mins

1 lb. sirloin steaks, thinly sliced
2 tbsp. lime juice, divided
⅓ C. crunchy peanut butter
1 tbsp. olive oil
½ C. beef broth
1½ C. broccoli florets
2 cloves garlic, sliced
1 to 2 red chile peppers, sliced

Directions:
1 Preparing the Ingredients. In a medium bowl, combine the steak with 1 tbsp. of the lime juice. Set aside. Combine the peanut butter and beef broth in a small bowl and mix well. Drain the beef and add the juice from the bowl into the peanut butter mixture. In a 6-inch metal bowl, combine the olive oil, steak, and broccoli. 2 Air Frying. Close air fryer lid. Cook for 3 to 4 minutes or until the steak is almost cooked and the broccoli is crisp and tender, shaking the basket once during cooking time. Add the garlic, chile peppers, and the peanut butter mixture and stir. Cook for 3 to 5 minutes or until the sauce is bubbling and the broccoli is tender. Serve over hot rice.

Rogan Josh

Ingredients: Servings: 4 Cooking Time: 35 Mins

1 lb leg of lamb, cut into cubes
2 garlic cloves, minced
1/4 tsp. ground cinnamon
1 small onion, diced
1 tbsp. tomato paste
1/2 C. yogurt
1/4 C. water
1/2 tsp. turmeric
1 tsp. paprika
2 tsp. garam masala
1/4 C. cilantro, chopped
1/2 tsp. cayenne pepper
2 tsp. ginger, minced
1 tsp. salt

Directions:
Add all ingredients into the bowl and stir well. Place bowl in the refrigerator for 2 hours. Add marinated meat with marinade into the instant pot. Seal pot with lid and cook on manual high pressure for 20 minutes. Once done then allow to release pressure naturally for 10 minutes then release using the quick-release method. Open the lid. Serve and enjoy.

Juicy Pork Chops

Ingredients: Servings: 2 Cooking Time: 15 Mins

Chili powder – 1 tsp.
Garlic powder – ½ tsp.
Cumin – ½ tsp.
Ground black pepper – ¼ tsp.
Dried oregano – ¼ tsp.
Boneless pork chops – 2 (4-ounce)
Unsalted butter – 2 tbsps. divided

Directions:
Mix oregano, pepper, cumin, garlic powder, and chili powder in a bowl. Rub dry rub onto pork chops. Place pork chops into the air fryer basket. Cook at 400F for 15 minutes. Serve each chop topped with 1 tbsp. butter.

Crispy Chicken-vegetable Rolls

Ingredients: Servings: 6 Cooking Time: 50 Mins

2 tbsps. vegetable oil
1 lb. ground chicken
3 cloves garlic, minced
1 tbsp. soy sauce
1 large egg
1 package egg roll wrappers or Spring roll pastry
Olive oil or oil spray for coating
½ tsp. salt to taste
½ tsp. sesame seed oil
Freshly grated black pepper to taste
½ C. carrot, grated
2 C. cabbage, sliced thinly
3 green onions, chopped
1 tsp. freshly grated ginger root, optional
For Hoisin-Peanut Dip:
½ tsp. chili hot sauce or Sriracha sauce, optional
½ tsp. sesame oil to taste
¼ C. peanut butter
½ C. hoisin sauce
2 tsps. vinegar
½ C. water

Directions:
To make egg roll filling, add garlic and ginger (optional) to the inner pot of the instant pot duo crisp. Cover with the pressure cooker lid and set to sauté function. Cook for about a minute or until lightly brown. Add the ground chicken along with the sesame seed oil, season with soy sauce, salt, and pepper to taste. Cook for 1-2 minutes until chicken turns slightly brown and tender. Add in green onions, cabbage, and carrots and cook for another 1-2 minutes until vegetables soften but still crisp. Stir in the egg and continue cooking for another 30 minutes. Remove from heat, strain to drain excess juice. Leave to cool. To make the Hoisin-Peanut dip, combine peanut butter, sesame oil, hot sauce, rice vinegar, and water in a bowl. Whisk altogether. You may use a blender to blend all ingredients. Note that some hoisin brands are very thick that you need more water. Lay egg roll wrapper on a flat surface and add 1 tbsp. or 2 of the chicken filling. Tuck and roll tightly. Seal edges using beaten eggs or water. Repeat the process until all fillings are used up. Spray each chicken roll with oil and arrange them inside the air fryer basket. Dislodge the pressure cooker lid from the instant pot and replace with the air fryer lid. Air fry at 380 degrees F for 15 minutes, flipping halfway through for even cooking until they become crispy and light brown. Serve immediately while warm with the hoisin-peanut dip.

Pork Chop Salad

Ingredients: Servings: 2 Cooking Time: 10 Mins

2 (4-oz. pork chops; chopped into 1-inch cubes
½ C. shredded monterey jack cheese
¼ C. full-fat ranch dressing
4 C. chopped romaine
1 medium roma tomato; diced
1 medium avocado; peeled, pitted and diced
1 tbsp. Chopped cilantro
1 tbsp. Coconut oil
½ tsp. Garlic powder.
¼ tsp. Onion powder.
2 tsp. Chili powder
1 tsp. Paprika

Directions:
Take a large bowl, drizzle coconut oil over pork. Sprinkle with chili powder, paprika, garlic powder and onion powder. Place pork into the air fryer basket. Adjust the temperature to 400 degrees f and set the timer for 8 minutes. Pork will be golden and crispy when fully cooked Take a large bowl, place romaine, tomato and crispy pork. Top with shredded cheese and avocado. Pour ranch dressing around bowl and toss the salad to evenly coat. Top with cilantro. Serve immediately.

Red Onion Beef Brisket Stew with Vegetables

Ingredients: Servings: 4 Cooking Time: 55 Mins

2 lb Brisket, cut into 2-inch pieces
4 C. Beef Broth
Salt and Black Pepper to taste
1 tbsp. Dijon Mustard
1 lb small Potato, quartered
¼ lb Carrots, cut in 2-inch pieces
1 tbsp. Olive Oil
1 large Red Onion, quartered
3 cloves Garlic, minced
1 Bay Leaf
2 fresh Thyme sprigs
2 tbsp. Cornstarch
3 tbsp. chopped Cilantro to garnish

Directions:
Pour broth, cornstarch, mustard, ½ tsp. salt, and ½ tsp. pepper in a bowl. Whisk them and set aside. Season the beef with salt and pepper. On the cooker, select Sear/Sauté mode. Add the olive oil, and once heated, add the beef strips. Flip halfway through to brown evenly. That should take 7 to 10 minutes. Then, add potato, carrots, onion, garlic, thyme, mustard mixture, and bay leaf. Stir once more. Close the lid, secure the pressure valve, and select Pressure mode on High pressure for 35 minutes. Press Start. Once the timer has ended, do a quick pressure release. Stir the stew and remove the bay leaf. Season the stew with pepper and salt. Close the crisping lid and cook for 10 minutes on Broil mode. Serve the soup with a bread of your choice.

Rustic Pork Ribs

Ingredients: Servings: 4 Cooking Time: 15 Mins

1 rack of pork ribs
3 tbsp. dry red wine
1 tbsp. soy sauce
1/2 tsp. dried thyme
1/2 tsp. onion powder
1/2 tsp. garlic powder
1/2 tsp. ground black pepper
1 tsp. smoke salt
1 tbsp. cornstarch
1/2 tsp. olive oil

Directions:
Preparing the Ingredients. Begin by preheating your Instant Crisp Air Fryer to 390 degrees F. Place all ingredients in a mixing bowl and let them marinate at least 1 hour. Air Frying. Lock the air fryer lid. Cook the marinated ribs approximately 25 minutes at 390 degrees F. Serve hot.

Pork Neck with Salad

Ingredients: Servings: 2 Cooking Time: 12 Mins

For Pork:
1 tbsp. soy sauce
1 tbsp. fish sauce
½ tbsp. oyster sauce
1 scallion, chopped
1 bunch fresh cilantro leaves
For Dressing:
½ lb. pork neck
For Salad:
1 ripe tomato, sliced tickly
8-10 Thai shallots, sliced
1 bunch fresh basil leaves
3 tbsp. fish sauce
2 tbsp. olive oil
1 tsp. apple cider vinegar
1 tbsp. palm sugar
2 bird eye chili
1 tbsp. garlic, minced

Directions:
1 Preparing the Ingredients. For pork in a bowl, mix together all ingredients except pork. Add pork neck and coat with marinade evenly. Refrigerate for about 2-3 hours. Preheat the Instant Crisp Air Fryer to 340 degrees F. 2 Air Frying. Place the pork neck onto a grill pan. Close air fryer lid and cook for about 12 minutes. Meanwhile in a large salad bowl, mix together all salad ingredients. In a bowl, add all dressing ingredients and beat till well combined. Remove pork neck from Instant Crisp Air Fryer and cut into desired slices. Place pork slices over salad.

Chicken Meatballs Primavera

Ingredients: Servings: 4 Cooking Time: 20 Mins

1 lb Ground Chicken
1 Egg, cracked into a bowl
Salt and Black Pepper to taste
2 tbsp. chopped Basil + Extra to garnish
1 tbsp. Olive Oil + ½ tbsp. Olive Oil
1 ½ tsp. Italian Seasoning
6 tsp. Flour
1 Red Bell Pepper, seeded and sliced
2 C. chopped Green Beans
½ lb chopped Asparagus
1 C. chopped Tomatoes
1 C. Chicken Broth

Directions:
In a mixing bowl, add the chicken, egg, flour, salt, pepper, 2 tbsps. of basil, 1 tbsp. of olive oil, and Italian seasoning. Mix them well with hands and make 16 large balls out of the mixture. Set the meatballs aside. Select Sear/Sauté mode. Heat half tsp. of olive oil, and add peppers, green beans, and asparagus. Cook for 3 minutes, stirring frequently. After 3 minutes, use a spoon the veggies onto a plate and set aside. Pour the remaining oil in the pot to heat and then fry the meatballs in it in batches. Fry them for 2 minutes on each side to brown them lightly. After, put all the meatballs back into the pot as well as the vegetables. Also, pour the chicken broth over it. Close the lid, secure the pressure valve, and select Pressure mode on High pressure for 10 minutes. When ready, do a quick pressure release. Close the crisping lid and select Air Fry. Cook for 5 minutes at 400 F, until nice and crispy. Dish the meatballs with sauce into a serving bowl and garnish it with basil. Serve with overcooked tagliatelle pasta.

Chicken Tikka Kebab

Ingredients: Servings: 4 Cooking Time: 15 Mins

1½ lbs. chicken breasts, pat dry
2 C. mixed peppers
1 medium red onion, sliced
For the marinade:
½ tsp. Garam masala
For the mint-cilantro chutney:
½ C. cilantro
¼ C. mint leaves
2 small green chilies

½ C. plain yogurt
2 tbsps. garlic paste
1 tbsp. oil
½ tbsp. lemon juice
2 tsps. cornstarch
1½ tsps. Kosher salt
1 tsp. green chili
1 tsp. ginger
1 tsp. ground white pepper
1 clove garlic
2 tbsps. unsweetened coconut
1 tbsp. lemon juice
1 tsp. sugar
1 tsp. Kosher salt
½ tsp. cumin seeds
2 tbsp. of water

Directions:
Cut the chicken, mixed peppers, and red onion into 1½-inch slices. Add all the marinade ingredients in a medium-size bowl and mix well. Add the chicken slices and mix well to coat. Marinate for at least 4 hours (preferably overnight) in the refrigerator. Thread the chicken, peppers, and onion slices in the skewers. Spritz them with cooking spray. Spritz the fryer basket with cooking spray and place the kebabs in it. Place the tall trivet into the instant pot and put the basket on top of it. Attach the air fryer lid to the instant pot and cook the kebabs at 400 degrees F for 15 minutes. Meanwhile, make the chutney by processing everything in a blender with 2 tbsp. of water. You can add a bit of water if necessary. Once the kebabs are cooked, transfer them to a platter or tray. Serve with the mint-cilantro chutney on the side. Enjoy.

Lamb Shanks Provençal

Ingredients: Servings: 6 Cooking Time: 40 Mins

2 large (12-ounce) lamb shanks
1 tsp. kosher salt, plus additional for seasoning
Freshly ground black pepper
1 tbsp. olive oil
1 C. sliced onion
2 medium plum tomatoes, coarsely chopped, or ½ C. diced canned tomatoes, drained
2 garlic cloves, finely minced
½ C. dry white wine or dry white vermouth
1 C. Chicken Stock or low-sodium broth
1 bay leaf
1 lemon, sliced very thin
⅓ C. pitted Kalamata olives
2 tbsp. coarsely chopped fresh parsley

Directions:
Preparing the Ingredients. Sprinkle the lamb shanks with 1 tsp. of kosher salt and several grinds of pepper. the longer ahead of the cooking time you can do this, the better. Cover and let sit for 20 minutes to 2 hours at room temperature or refrigerate for up to 24 hours. Heat the vegetable oil in the Instant Crisp Air Fryer using the "Sauté" function, until the oil is shimmering and flows like water. Add the lamb shanks, and brown on all sides, about 6 minutes total. Remove them to a plate. Add the onion and garlic, and sprinkle with a pinch or two of kosher salt. Cook, stirring, for about 3 minutes, or until the onions just begin to brown. Add the tomatoes, and cook until most of their liquid evaporates. Add the white wine, and stir, scraping up the browned bits from the bottom of the cooker. Cook for 2 to 3 minutes, or until the wine reduces by about half; then add the Chicken Stock and bay leaf. Return the lamb shanks to the cooker, and place the lemon slices over them. High pressure for 40 minutes. Lock the pressure cooking lid on the Instant Crisp Air Fryer and then cook for 40 minutes. To get 40-minutes cook time, press "Pressure" button and adjust the time. Pressure Release. After cooking, use the natural method to release pressure. Finish the dish. Remove the lid from the Instant Crisp Air Fryer. Close air fryer lid. Select AIR FRY, set temperature to 375°F, and set time to 18 minutes. Check after 10 minutes, cooking for an additional 8 minutes if dish needs more browning. Transfer the lamb to a cutting board or plate, and tent it with aluminum foil. Strain the sauce into a fat separator, and let it rest until the fat rises to the surface. If you don't have a fat separator, let the sauce sit for a few minutes, then spoon or blot off any excess fat from the top and discard. Pour the defatted sauce back into the cooker along with the strained vegetables. If you want a thicker sauce, simmer the liquid for about 5 minutes, or until it reaches the desired consistency. Stir in the olives and parsley. Place the shanks in shallow bowls, pour the sauce and vegetables over the lamb, and serve. Lamb shanks benefit from salting in advance, which makes them much more flavorful and helps them brown beautifully. If you have the time, salt them up to 24 hours in advance. Place them on a tray and refrigerate, covered loosely with foil.

Herbed Vegetable Beef

Ingredients: Servings: 6 Cooking Time: 60 Mins

3 lbs. beef
2 medium onions, sliced
2 carrots, chopped
2 sticks celery, chopped
1 bulb. of garlic, peeled cloves
1 bunch mixed fresh herbs (thyme, rosemary, bay, sage)
olive oil

Directions:
Add all the vegetables to the Instant Pot Duo Crisp. Top the veggies with the beef roast, olive oil, and herbs. Put on the Air Fryer lid and seal it. Hit the "Bake Button" and select 60 minutes of cooking time, then press "Start." Once the Instant Pot Duo beeps, remove its lid. Serve.

Mediterranean Lemon Chicken

Ingredients: Servings: 4 Cooking Time: 21 Mins

4 Chicken Thighs
1 ½ tbsp. Olive Oil
½ tsp. Garlic Powder
Salt and Black Pepper to taste
½ tsp. Red Pepper Flakes
1 small Onion, chopped
2 cloves Garlic, sliced
½ tsp. Smoked Paprika
½ C. Chicken Broth
1 tsp. Italian Seasoning
1 Lemon, zested and juiced
1 ½ tbsp. Heavy Cream
Lemon slices to garnish
Chopped parsley to garnish

Directions:
Preheat the cooker by selecting Sear/Sauté. Warm olive oil and add chicken thighs; cook to brown on each side for 3 minutes. Remove onto a plate. Melt the butter in the pot, then, add garlic, onions, and lemon juice. Deglaze the bottom of the pot and cook for 1 minute. Add the Italian seasoning, chicken broth, lemon zest, and the chicken. Close the pressure lid, secure the pressure valve, select Pressure mode on High for 10 minutes.

Press Start. When ready, do a quick pressure release. Open the lid. Stir in the heavy cream. Close the crisping lid and select Broil mode. Set the time to 5 minutes. Serve with the steamed kale and spinach mix. Garnish with lemons slices and parsley.

Greek Lamb Chops

Ingredients: Servings: 4 Cooking Time: 10 Mins

1 lb lamb chops
1 tsp. garlic, minced
1 tsp. dried oregano
2 tbsp. lemon juice
2 tbsp. olive oil
Pepper
Salt

Directions:
Add lamb chops into the mixing bowl. Add remaining ingredients and coat well. Place the dehydrating tray in a multi-level air fryer basket and place basket in the instant pot. Place lamb chops on dehydrating tray. Seal pot with air fryer lid and select air fry mode then set the temperature to 400 F and timer for 10 minutes. Turn lamb chops halfway through. Serve and enjoy.

Instant Pot Rotisserie Chicken

Ingredients: Servings: 4 Cooking Time: 60 Mins

1 whole chicken, cleaned and patted dry
2 tbsps. olive oil
1 tbsp. seasoned salt

Directions:
Make sure that the giblet packet from the chicken cavity is removed. Rub the oil all over the chicken and generously season with salt. Put the chicken with the breast-side down in your air fryer basket. Cook for 30 minutes at 350 degrees F. Once done, flip the chicken over and cook for another 30 minutes or until the internal temperature reads 165 degrees F. Once cooked, let the chicken rest for about 10 minutes and serve.

Fried Chicken Wings

Ingredients: Servings: 4 Cooking Time: 30 Mins

2 lbs. chicken wings
Black pepper and Kosher salt to taste
Optional: garlic salt to taste

Directions:
Cleanse and pat dry chicken wings. Season with salt and pepper to taste. Add garlic salt if desired but this is optional. Place them in the instant pot air fryer basket. Attach air fryer lid and set to air frying. Cook at 400 degrees F for 30-35 minutes, flipping about three times for even cooking. Serve with desired sauce for a dip.

Pork Roast

Ingredients: Servings: 4 Cooking Time: 10 Mins

1 lb. Pork tenderloin, trimmed
2 tbsp. Balsamic vinegar
3 tbsp. Mustard
2 tbsp. Olive oil
A pinch of salt and black pepper

Directions:
Take a bowl and mix the pork tenderloin with the rest of the ingredients and rub well. Put the roast in your air fryer's basket and cook at 380°f for 30 minutes. Slice the roast, divide between plates and serve.

Dijon Chicken Stew

Ingredients: Servings: 4 Cooking Time: 31 Mins

4 Chicken Breasts, diced
1 ¼ lb White Button Mushrooms, halved
3 tbsp. Olive Oil
1 large Onion, sliced
5 cloves Garlic, minced
Salt and Black Pepper to taste
1 ¼ tsp. Cornstarch
½ C. Spinach, chopped
1 Bay Leaf
1 ½ C. Chicken Stock
1 tsp. Dijon Mustard
1 ½ C. Sour Cream
3 tbsp. Chopped Parsley

Directions:
Select Sear/Sauté mode and set to medium High to preheat. Heat olive oil then include the onion and sauté for 3 minutes until soft. Add the mushrooms, chicken, garlic, bay leaf, salt, pepper, Dijon mustard, and chicken broth. Stir well. Close the lid, secure the pressure valve, and press Pressure mode on High pressure for 15 minutes. Press Start. Once ready, do a natural pressure release for 5 minutes and carefully open the lid. Stir the stew, remove the bay leaf, and scoop some of the liquid into a bowl. Add the cornstarch to the liquid and mix them until completely lump free. Pour the liquid into the sauce, stir it, and let the sauce thicken to your desired consistency. Top it with the sour cream, close the crisping lid and select Broil mode. Cook for 2 minutes. Garnish with parsley and serve.

Chinese Salt and Pepper Pork Chop Stir-fry

Ingredients: Servings: 4 Cooking Time: 15 Mins

Pork Chops:
Olive oil
¾ C. almond flour
¼ tsp. pepper
½ tsp. salt
1 egg white
Pork Chops
Stir-fry:
¼ tsp. pepper
1 tsp. sea salt
2 tbsp. olive oil
2 sliced scallions
2 sliced jalapeno peppers

Directions:
1 Preparing the Ingredients. Coat the Instant Crisp Air Fryer basket with olive oil. Whisk pepper, salt, and egg white together till foamy. Cut pork chops into pieces, leaving just a bit on bones. Pat dry. Add pieces of pork to egg white mixture, coating well. Let sit for marinade 20 minutes. Put marinated chops into a large bowl and add almond flour. Dredge and shake off excess and place into Instant Crisp Air Fryer. 2 Air Frying. Close air fryer lid. Set temperature to 360°F, and set time to 12 minutes. Cook 12 minutes at 360 degrees. Turn up the heat to 400 degrees and cook another 6 minutes till pork chops are nice and crisp. To make stir-fry, remove jalapeno seeds and chop up. Chop scallions and mix with jalapeno pieces. Heat a skillet with olive oil. Stir-fry pepper, salt, scallions, and jalapenos 60 seconds. Then add fried pork pieces to skills and toss with scallion mixture. Stir-fry 1-2 minutes till well coated and hot.

Sugar-and-spice Beef Empanadas

Ingredients: Servings: 4 Cooking Time: 15 Mins

6 oz. of raw, lean ground beef
1/4 C. of raw white onions, sliced and finely diced
1 tsp. of cinnamon
1/2 tsp. of nutmeg
1/2 tsp. of ground cloves
1 small pinch of brown sugar
2 tsp. of red chilli powder
pre-made empanada dough shells

Directions:
Preparing the Ingredients. In a deep stovetop saucepan, crumble and cook the ground beef at medium heat. Add in the onions, stirring continuously with a wooden spoon, then add the cinnamon, nutmeg and cloves. Break up the ground beef as it cooks, so it doesn't form large clumps. Remove the saucepan from the stovetop as soon as the beef is fully cooked, the onions are soft, and the spices are releasing their fragrances. Do not overcook, you want the meat to remain moist and juicy. Cover the saucepan and let stand on a heatsafe surface for a few minutes. Lay empanada shells flat on a clean counter. Spoon the spiced cooked beef from the saucepan into the empanada shells – a heaping spoonful on each, though not so much that the mixture spills over the edges. Fold the empanada shells over so that the spiced beef is fully covered. Seal edges with water and press down with a fork to secure. Sprinkle brown sugar over the still-wet seams of the empanadas, for an extra sweet crunch. Cover the basket of the Instant Crisp Air Fryer with a lining of tin foil, leaving the edges uncovered to allow air to circulate through the basket. Air Frying. Place the empanadas in the foil-lined Instant Crisp Air Fryer basket, close air fryer lid and set at 350 degrees for 15 minutes. Halfway through, slide the frying basket out and flip the empanadas using a spatula. Remove when golden, and serve directly from the basket onto plates.

Pork Tenderloin with Braised Apples

Ingredients: Servings: 4 Cooking Time: 45 Mins

For the Brine (optional)
1/2 C. Diamond Crystal kosher salt, or 1/4 C. fine table salt
1/4 C. granulated sugar
2 C. very hot tap water
2 C. ice water
For the Pork and Apples
1 (1-pound) pork tenderloin, trimmed of silver skin and halved crosswise
Kosher salt, for salting and seasoning
2 tbsp. unsalted butter
1 C. thinly sliced onion
1 medium Granny Smith apple, or another tart apple, peeled and cut into 1/4-inch slices
3/4 C. apple juice, cider, or hard cider
1/2 C. low-sodium chicken broth
2 tbsp. heavy (whipping) cream
1 tsp. Dijon mustard, plus additional as needed

Directions:
Preparing the Ingredients. -To make the brine (if using) In a large stainless steel or glass bowl, dissolve the salt and sugar in hot water; then stir in the ice water. Submerge the pork in the brine, and refrigerate for 2 to 3 hours. Drain and pat dry. -To make the pork and apples If you choose not to brine the pork, sprinkle it liberally with kosher salt. Set to "Sauté" heat the butter just until it stops foaming. Add the pork halves, browning on all sides, about 4 minutes total. Transfer to a plate or rack, and set aside. Add the onion slices to the cooker, and cook, stirring, for 2 to 3 minutes, or until they just start to brown. Add the apple slices, and cook for 1 minute. Add the apple juice, and scrape the browned bits from the bottom of the pot. Bring to a simmer, and cook for 2 to 3 minutes, or until the juice has reduced by about one-third. Add the chicken broth, and return the pork tenderloin to the cooker, placing the pieces on top of the apples and onions. High pressure for 45 minutes. Lock the pressure cooking lid on the Instant Crisp Air Fryer and then cook for 45 minutes. To get 45-minutes cook time, press "Pressure" button and use the adjust button to adjust the cook time to 45 minutes. Pressure Release. Use the quick-release method. Finish the dish. Close air fryer lid. Discard the bay leaves. Select AIR FRY, set temperature to 375°F, and set time to 10 minutes. Check after 5 minutes, cooking for an additional 5 minutes if dish needs more browning. Transfer the pork to a plate or rack, and tent it with aluminum foil while you finish the sauce. Turn the Instant Crisp Air Fryer to "Sauté", simmer for about 6 minutes, or until the liquid is reduced by about half. Stir in the heavy cream and mustard, and taste, adding kosher salt or more mustard as needed. Slice the pork into 3/4-inch pieces, and place on a serving platter. Spoon the apples, onions, and sauce over the pork, and serve.

Lamb Roast

Ingredients: Servings: 2 Cooking Time: 15 Mins

10 oz lamb leg roast
1 tsp. dried thyme
1 tsp. dried rosemary
1 tbsp. olive oil
Pepper
Salt

Directions:
Coat lamb roast with olive oil and rub with thyme, rosemary, pepper, and salt. Place the dehydrating tray in a multi-level air fryer basket and place basket in the instant pot. Place lamb roast on dehydrating tray. Seal pot with air fryer lid and select air fry mode then set the temperature to 360 F and timer for 15 minutes. Serve and enjoy.

Creamy Tuscan Chicken

Ingredients: Servings: 4 Cooking Time: 20 Mins

4 Chicken Thighs, cut into 1-inch pieces
1 tbsp. Olive Oil
1 1/2 C. Chicken Broth
10 chopped Sun-Dried Tomatoes with Herbs
2 tbsp. Italian Seasoning
Salt to taste
2 C. Baby Spinach
1/4 tsp. Red Pepper Flakes
6 oz softened Cream Cheese, cubed
1 C. shredded Pecorino Cheese

Directions:
Pour the chicken broth into the pressure cooker, and add the Italian seasoning, chicken, tomatoes, salt, and red pepper flakes. Stir with a spoon. Close the lid, secure the pressure valve, and select Pressure mode on High for 12 minutes. Press Start. Once the timer has ended, do a quick pressure release, and open the lid. Add and stir in the spinach, parmesan cheese,

and cream cheese until the cheese melts and is fully incorporated. Close the crisping lid and cook on Broil mode for 5 minutes. Dish the chicken over a bed of zoodles or a side of steamed asparagus.

Air Fryer Beef Steak

Ingredients: Servings: 4 Cooking Time: 15 Mins

1 tbsp. olive oil
Pepper and salt
2 lb. of ribeye steak

Directions:

1 Preparing the Ingredients. Season meat on both sides with pepper and salt. Rub all sides of meat with olive oil. Preheat Instant Crisp Air Fryer to 356 degrees and spritz with olive oil.
2 Air Frying. Close air fryer lid. Set temperature to 356°F, and set time to 7 minutes. Cook steak 7 minutes. Flip and cook an additional 6 minutes. Let meat sit 2-5 minutes to rest. Slice and serve with salad.

Pork Chops with Asparagus

Ingredients: Servings: 4 Cooking Time: 25 Mins

Salt and Pepper to taste
2 tbsp. canola oil
1 tbsp. creole seasoning
1 1/2 tsp. minced thyme
1 tbsp. garlic, minced
½ tbsp. Dijon mustard
4 pork chops, bone-in
1 tsp. Worchester sauce
2-3 tbsp. brown sugar
2 tbsp. parsley, for garnish
1-pound potatoes, cubed
1-pound asparagus, chopped

Directions:

Whisk ½ of the creole seasoning with thyme, garlic, mustard, sugar, oil, and Worcestershire sauce in a bowl. Season the pork chops with this creole mixture and place them in the Air Fryer Basket. Season the potatoes with remaining creole seasoning, oil, and salt. Place these potatoes around the pork chops in the Air Fryer Basket. Set the Air basket in the Instant Pot Duo. Put on the Air Fryer lid and seal it. Hit the “Bake Button” and select 22 minutes of cooking time, then press “Start.” Once the Instant Pot Duo beeps, switch it to Broil mode and cook for 3 minutes. Garnish with parsley and enjoy.

Thai Curry Beef Meatballs (air Fryer)

Ingredients: Servings: 4 Cooking Time: 15 Mins

1 lb. (454 g) ground beef
1 tbsp. sesame oil
2 tsp. chopped lemongrass
Cooking spray
1 tsp. red Thai curry paste
1 tsp. Thai seasoning blend
Juice and zest of ½ lime

Directions:

Preheat the air fryer to 380°F (193°C). Spritz the air fryer basket with cooking spray. In a medium bowl, combine all the ingredients until well blended. Shape the meat mixture into 24 meatballs and arrange them in the air fryer basket. Air fry for 15 minutes, or until well browned. Flip halfway through to ensure even cooking. Transfer the meatballs to plates. Let cool for 5 minutes before serving.

Fajita Flank Steak Rolls

Ingredients: Servings: 6 Cooking Time: 10 Mins

2 lb. Flank steak
4 (1-oz. slices pepper jack cheese
1 medium red bell pepper; seeded and sliced into strips
¼ C. diced yellow onion
1 medium green bell pepper; seeded and sliced into strips
2 tbsp. Unsalted butter.
1 tsp. Cumin
½ tsp. Garlic powder.
2 tsp. Chili powder

Directions:

In a medium skillet over medium heat, melt butter and begin sautéing onion, red bell pepper and green bell pepper. Sprinkle with chili powder, cumin and garlic powder. Sauté until peppers are tender, about 5–7 minutes. Lay flank steak flat on a work surface. Spread onion and pepper mixture over entire steak rectangle. Lay slices of cheese on top of onions and peppers, barely overlapping with the shortest end toward you, begin rolling the steak, tucking the cheese down into the roll as necessary. Secure the roll with twelve toothpicks, six on each side of the steak roll. Place steak roll into the air fryer basket Adjust the temperature to 400 degrees f and set the timer for 15 minutes. Rotate the roll halfway through the cooking time. Add an additional 1–4 minutes depending on your preferred internal temperature (135 degrees f for medium When timer beeps, allow roll to rest 15 minutes, then slice into six even pieces. Serve warm.

Garlic Pork Carnitas In Lettuce Cups

Ingredients: Servings: 6 Cooking Time: 20 Mins

3 lb Pork Shoulder
2 tbsp. Olive Oil
1 head Butter Lettuce, leaves removed, washed and dried
2 Limes, cut in wedges
2 Carrots, grated
1 ½ C. Water
1 Onion, chopped
½ tsp. Cayenne Pepper
½ tsp. Coriander Powder
1 tsp. Cumin Powder
1 tsp. Garlic Powder
1 tsp. White Pepper
2 tsp. dried Oregano
1 tsp. Red Pepper Flakes
Salt to taste

Directions:

In a bowl, add onion, cayenne, coriander, garlic, cumin, white pepper, dried oregano, red pepper flakes, and salt. Mix them well with a spoon. Drizzle over the pork and rub to coat. Then, wrap the meat in plastic wrap and refrigerate overnight. On the next day, open the cooker lid, and select Sear/Sauté mode. Pour 2 tbsps. of olive oil in the pot and while heating, take the pork out from the fridge, remove the wraps and place it in the pot. Brown it on both sides for 6 minutes and then pour the water. Close the lid, secure the pressure valve, and select Pressure mode on High pressure for 15 minutes. Press Start to start cooking. Once the timer has stopped, do a quick pressure release.Use two forks to shred the pork, inside the pot. Close the crisping lid, and select Bake mode. Set for 10 minutes at 350 F. When ready, turn off the heat and begin assembling. Arrange double layers of lettuce leaves on a flat surface, make a bed of grated carrots in them, and spoon the pulled pork on them. Drizzle a sauce of choice (I used mustardy sauce) over them, and serve with lime wedges for freshness.

Air Fryer Beef with Homemade Marinade

Ingredients: Servings: 3 Cooking Time: 45 Mins

1-pound beef sirloin
½ C. red onion slices
½ C. green onion slices
1 yellow bell pepper, cut into strips
1 green pepper, cut into strips
1 red bell pepper, cut into strips
1½ lb. broccoli florets
1 tbsp. vegetable oil
For the marinade:
¼ C. of water
1 tsp. minced ginger
1 tbsp. soy sauce
1 tbsp. sesame oil
2 tsp. finely grated garlic
¼ C. hoisin sauce

Directions:

Wash and pat dry the beef. Cut the beef sirloin into 2-inch strips. For making the marinade, add the hoisin sauce, garlic, sesame oil, soy sauce, finely grated ginger, and water in a bowl and mix thoroughly. Add the meat in the marinade and mix to coat for perfect seasoning. Cover the bowl and refrigerate for 20 minutes. Put all the vegetables in a large bowl and add one tsp. vegetable oil into it and mix thoroughly for even coating. Transfer the oil-coated vegetables into the air fryer basket and place it in the inner pot of the instant pot air fryer. Close the crisp lid. In the air fry mode, select temperature 200°f and set the timer to 5 minutes. Press start to begin the cooking. After the vegetables become soft, transfer it into a bowl. Now place the marinated meat in the air fryer basket. Close the crisp cover and set the temperature at 360°f on air fry mod. Set the timer to 40 minutes. Press start to begin cooking. After 20 minutes, open the air fryer and flip the meat. To resume cooking for the remaining period, close the crisp cover. Serve it with salad.

Keto Parmesan Crusted Pork Chops

Ingredients: Servings: 8 Cooking Time: 15 Mins

3 tbsp. grated parmesan cheese
1 C. pork rind crumbs
2 beaten eggs
¼ tsp. chili powder
½ tsp. onion powder
1 tsp. smoked paprika
¼ tsp. pepper
½ tsp. salt
4-6 thick boneless pork chops

Directions:

1 Preparing the Ingredients. Ensure your Instant Crisp Air Fryer is preheated to 400 degrees. with pepper and salt, season both sides of pork chops. In a food processor, pulse pork rinds into crumbs. Mix crumbs with other seasonings. Beat eggs and add to another bowl. Dip pork chops into eggs then into pork rind crumb mixture. 2 Air Frying. Spray down Instant Crisp Air Fryer with olive oil and add pork chops to the basket. Lock the air fryer lid. Set temperature to 400°F, and set time to 15 minutes.

Cheesy Lamb Chops

Ingredients: Servings: 3 Cooking Time: 18 Mins

3 lamb chops
1/2 tsp. garlic powder
3/4 C. parmesan cheese
1 tbsp. olive oil
1 C. of water
1/4 tsp. dried oregano, crushed
1/4 tsp. dried basil, crushed
Pepper
Salt

Directions:

Season lamb chops with pepper, garlic powder, and salt. Place lamb chops into the instant pot and cook for 4 minutes on each side. Remove lamb chops from pot and place on a plate. Pour water to the pot then place a trivet in the pot. Place lamb chops on the trivet. Seal pot with lid and cook on manual high pressure for 10 minutes. Once done then release pressure using the quick-release method than open the lid. Serve and enjoy.

Beef Korma

Ingredients: Servings: 6 Cooking Time: 20 Mins

½ C. yogurt
1 tbsp. curry powder
1 tbsp. olive oil
1 onion, chopped
2 cloves garlic, minced
1 tomato, diced
½ C. frozen baby peas, thawed

Directions:

1 Preparing the Ingredients. In a medium bowl, combine the steak, yogurt, and curry powder. Stir and set aside. In a 6-inch metal bowl, combine the olive oil, onion, and garlic. 2 Air Frying. Close air fryer lid. Cook for 3 to 4 minutes or until crisp and tender. Add the steak along with the yogurt and the diced tomato. Cook for 12 to 13 minutes or until steak is almost tender. Stir in the peas and cook for 2 to 3 minutes or until hot.

Spicy Pork Chops with Carrots and Mushrooms (air Fryer)

Ingredients: Servings: 4 Cooking Time: 15 To 18 Mins

2 carrots, cut into sticks
1 C. mushrooms, sliced
2 garlic cloves, minced
2 tbsp. olive oil
1 lb. (454 g) boneless pork chops
1 tsp. dried oregano
1 tsp. dried thyme
1 tsp. cayenne pepper
Salt and ground black pepper, to taste
Cooking spray

Directions:

Preheat the air fryer to 360°F (182°C). Spritz the air fryer basket with cooking spray. In a mixing bowl, toss together the carrots, mushrooms, garlic, olive oil and salt until well combined. Add the pork chops to a different bowl and season with oregano, thyme, cayenne pepper, salt and black pepper. Lower the vegetable mixture in the prepared air fryer basket. Place the seasoned pork chops on top. Air fry for 15 to 18 minutes, or until the pork is well browned and the vegetables are tender, flipping the pork and shaking the basket once halfway through. Transfer the pork chops to the serving dishes and let cool for 5 minutes. Serve warm with vegetable on the side.

Sumptuous Lamb Casserole (pressure Cook)

Ingredients: Servings: 2 To 4 Cooking Time: 41 Mins

1 lb. (454 g) lamb
2 tbsp. red wine

stew meat, cubed
1 tbsp. olive oil
3 cloves garlic, minced
2 tomatoes, chopped
2 carrots, chopped
1 onion, chopped
1 lb. (454 g) baby potatoes
1 celery stalk, chopped
2 C. chicken stock
2 tbsp. ketchup
1 tsp. ground cumin
1 tsp. sweet paprika
¼ tsp. dried rosemary
¼ tsp. dried oregano
Salt and ground black pepper, to taste

Directions:

Press the Sauté button on the Instant Pot and heat the oil. Add the lamb to the pot and sear for 5 minutes, or until lightly browned. Add the garlic and sauté for 1 minute. Add all the remaining ingredients to the pot. Set the lid in place. Select the Pressure Cook and set the cooking time for 35 minutes at High Pressure. Once cooking is complete, perform a natural pressure release for 10 minutes, then release any remaining pressure. Carefully open the lid. Serve hot.

Classic Minestrone Soup

Ingredients: Servings: 4 Cooking Time: 12 Mins

1 (15.5 oz) can Cannellini Beans
1 Potato, peeled and diced
1 Carrot, peeled and chopped
1 C. chopped Butternut Squash
2 small Red Onions, cut in wedges
1 tbsp. chopped Fresh Rosemary
1 C. chopped Celery
8 Sage Leaves, chopped finely
1 Bay Leaf
4 C. Vegetable Broth
Salt and Pepper, to taste
2 tsp. Olive Oil
2 tbsp. chopped fresh Parsley

Directions:

Add the potato, carrot, squash, onion, celery, rosemary, sage leaves, bay leaf, vegetable broth, salt, pepper, and olive oil to the pot of your cooker. Close the lid, secure the pressure valve, and select Pressure mode on High pressure for 7 minutes. Press Start. Once the timer has ended, do a quick pressure release and open the lid. Add the cannellini beans and stir with a spoon. Close the crisping lid and cook for 5 minutes on Broil mode. Use a soup spoon to fetch the soup into soup bowls. Garnish with fresh parsley and serve with a side of crusted bread.

Dijon Garlic Pork Tenderloin

Ingredients: Servings: 6 Cooking Time: 10 Mins

1 C. breadcrumbs
Pinch of cayenne pepper
3 crushed garlic cloves
2 tbsp. ground ginger
2 tbsp. Dijon mustard
2 tbsp. raw honey
4 tbsp. water
2 tsp. salt
1 lb. pork tenderloin, sliced into 1-inch rounds

Directions:

1 Preparing the Ingredients. with pepper and salt, season all sides of tenderloin. Combine cayenne pepper, garlic, ginger, mustard, honey, and water until smooth. Dip pork rounds into honey mixture and then into breadcrumbs, ensuring they all get coated well. Place coated pork rounds into your Instant Crisp Air Fryer. 2 Air Frying. Close air fryer lid, set temperature to 400°F, and set time to 10 minutes. Cook 10 minutes at 400 degrees. Flip and then cook an additional 5 minutes until golden in color.

Rice and Meatball Stuffed Bell Peppers

Ingredients: Servings: 4 Cooking Time: 15 Mins

1 tbsp. olive oil
1 small onion, chopped
2 cloves garlic, minced
1 C. frozen cooked rice, thawed
4 bell peppers
16 to 20 small frozen precooked meatballs, thawed
½ C. tomato sauce
3 tbsp. Dijon mustard

Directions:

1 Preparing the Ingredients. To prepare the peppers, cut off about ½ inch of the tops. Carefully remove the membranes and seeds from inside the peppers. Set aside. In a 6-by-6-by-2-inch pan, combine the olive oil, onion, and garlic. 2 Air Frying. Close air fryer lid. Bake in the Instant Crisp Air Fryer for 2 to 4 minutes or until crisp and tender. Remove the vegetable mixture from the pan and set aside in a medium bowl. Add the rice, meatballs, tomato sauce, and mustard to the vegetable mixture and stir to combine. Stuff the peppers with the meat-vegetable mixture. Place the peppers in the Instant Crisp Air Fryer basket and bake for 9 to 13 minutes or until the filling is hot and the peppers are tender.

Air Fryer Beef Fajitas

Ingredients: Servings: 6 Cooking Time: 20 Mins

Beef:
1/8 C. carne asada seasoning
2 lb. beef flap meat
Diet 7-Up
Fajita veggies:
1 tsp. chili powder
1-2 tsp. pepper
1-2 tsp. salt
2 bell peppers, your choice of color
1 onion

Directions:

1 Preparing the Ingredients. Slice flap meat into manageable pieces and place into a bowl. Season meat with carne seasoning and pour diet soda over meat. Cover and chill overnight. Ensure your Instant Crisp Air Fryer is preheated to 380 degrees. Place a parchment liner into the Instant Crisp Air Fryer basket and spray with olive oil. Place beef in layers into the basket. Cook 8-10 minutes, making sure to flip halfway through. Remove and set to the side. Slice up veggies and spray Instant Crisp Air Fryer basket. Add veggies to the fryer and spray with olive oil. 2 Air Frying. Close air fryer lid. Set temperature to 400°F, and set time to 10 minutes. Cook 10 minutes at 400 degrees, shaking 1-2 times during cooking process. Serve meat and veggies on wheat tortillas and top with favorite keto fillings!

Pork, Green Beans, and Corn (pressure Cook)

Ingredients: Servings: 4 Cooking Time: 35 Mins

2 lb. (907 g) pork
2 garlic cloves,

shoulder, boneless and cubed
1 C. green beans, trimmed and halved
1 C. corn
1 C. beef stock
minced
1 tsp. ground cumin
A pinch of salt and black pepper

Directions:
Combine all the ingredients in the Instant Pot. Secure the lid. Select the Pressure Cook and set the cooking time for 35 minutes at High Pressure. Once cooking is complete, do a natural pressure release for 10 minutes, then release any remaining pressure. Carefully open the lid. Divide the mix among four plates and serve.

Air Fryer Meatloaf

Ingredients: Servings: 4 Cooking Time: 25 Mins

1-pound lean beef
1 egg, medium, lightly beaten
3 tbsp. breadcrumbs
1 onion, small, finely chopped
1 tbsp. fresh thyme, chopped
1 tsp. kosher salt
½ tsp. ground black pepper
2 mushrooms, medium, sliced
1 tbsp. olive oil

Directions:
Wash beef and pat dry. In a medium-large bowl, combine beef, egg, breadcrumbs, salt, thyme, onion, and pepper. Knead and mix the ingredients well. Transfer this mix into a baking pan and place the mushroom on top of the mix. Coat this mix with olive oil and place the pan in the air fryer basket. Now put the air fryer basket in the inner pot of instant pot air fryer. Close the crisp cover. Under the roast mode, set the timer for 25 minutes and let the meatloaf roast. the smart roast option will automatically select the temperature to 380°f. Press the start button to resume the cooking. After cooking, allow the meatloaf to settle down the heat before you can slice and serve it. Slice it into small portions and serve.

Brisket with Veggies

Ingredients: Servings: 6 Cooking Time: 60 Mins

2 tbs. olive oil
5 or 6 red potatoes
2 lb. or larger regular brisket, rinsed and patted dry
Fresh ground black pepper
3 tbs. heaping chopped garlic
1 lg. yellow onion
2-½ c. homemade beef broth, or make from Knorr Beef Base
2 c. large chunks carrots
3 tbs. Worcestershire Sauce
4 bay leaves
5 or 6 red potatoes
Granulated garlic
Knorr Demi-Glace sauce
½ c. dehydrated onion
2 stalks celery in 1" chunks

Directions:
Preparing the Ingredients. Put the Instant Crisp Air Fryer on the sauté setting. Put in 1 tbs. (more if needed) of the oil and caramelize the onions. Once golden, remove from pot, put in a bowl, and set aside. But keep the Instant Crisp Air Fryer on the "Sauté" setting. Rub the freshly ground pepper on both sides of the brisket. Do the same with the granulated garlic. Add 1tbs. olive oil (or more) and only lightly sear the brisket on all sides. Add back the onions, garlic, Worcestershire sauce, bay leaves, dehydrated onion and beef broth. High pressure for 50 minutes. Close the pressure cooking lid and the pressure valve and then cook for 50 minutes. To get 50-minutes cook time, press "Pressure" button and use the Time Adjustment button to adjust the cook time to 50 minutes. While the meat is cooking, peel and cut up all the veggies. When the meat is done, use the quick pressure release feature, and then remove the lid. Add all of the veggies, replace the lid and cook at high pressure for to 10 minutes. To get 10-minutes cook time, press "Steam" button Pressure Release. When the time is up, turn the pot off, use the quick release again, and remove the lid. Finish the dish. Close air fryer lid. Select BROIL, and set time to 8 minutes. Check after 5 minutes, cooking for an additional 3 minutes if dish needs more browning. Use a platter to remove the veggies and meat. Use the "Sauté" setting and bring the broth to a boil, then add the Knorr Demi-Glace mixing with a Wisk. Adjust seasonings as needed. Serve with Cole Slaw or other salad, homemade rolls or Italian garlic bread. Be sure to remove the bay leaves before serving. Serve and Enjoy

Beef Steaks with Mushrooms (pressure Cook)

Ingredients: Servings: 2 Cooking Time: 25 Mins

2 beef steaks, boneless
Salt and black pepper, to taste
2 tbsp. olive oil
4 oz. (113 g) mushrooms, sliced
½ onion, chopped
1 garlic clove, minced
1 C. vegetable soup
1½ tbsp. cornstarch
1 tbsp. half-and-half

Directions:
Rub the beef steaks with salt and pepper on a clean work surface. Set the Instant Pot to Sauté mode and warm the olive oil until shimmering. Sear the beef for 2 minutes per side until browned. Transfer to a plate. Add the mushrooms and sauté for 5 minutes or until soft. Add the onion and garlic and sauté for 2 minutes until fragrant. Return the steaks to the pot and pour in the soup. Seal the lid, select the Pressure Cook, and set the time to 15 minutes at High Pressure. When cooking is complete, do a quick pressure release and unlock the lid and transfer the chops to a plate. Press the Sauté button. In a bowl, combine the cornstarch and half-and-half and mix well. Pour the mixture into the pot and cook until the sauce is thickened. Serve warm.

Beef Ribeye Steak

Ingredients: Servings: 4 Cooking Time: 20 Mins

1 tbsp. McCormick Grill Mates Montreal Steak Seasoning
4 (8-ounce) ribeye steaks
Salt
Pepper

Directions:
1 Preparing the Ingredients. Season the steaks with the steak seasoning and salt and pepper to taste. Place 2 steaks in the Instant Crisp Air Fryer. You can use an accessory grill pan, a layer rack, or the standard Instant Crisp Air Fryer basket. 2 Air Frying. Close air fryer lid. Cook for 4 minutes. Open the Instant Crisp Air Fryer and flip the steaks. Cook for an

additional 4 to 5 minutes. Check for doneness to determine how much additional cook time is need. Remove the cooked steaks from the Instant Crisp Air Fryer, then repeat steps 2 through 4 for the remaining 2 steaks. Cool before serving.

Crisp & Tasty Pork Chops

Ingredients: Servings: 4 Cooking Time: 15 Mins

4 pork chops, boneless
1/2 tsp. onion powder
1 tsp. paprika
1/4 C. parmesan cheese, grated
1 C. pork rind
2 eggs, lightly beaten
1/2 tsp. chili powder
1/4 tsp. pepper
1/2 tsp. salt

Directions:
Season pork chops with pepper and salt. Add pork rind in food processor and process until crumbs form. Mix together pork rind crumbs and seasoning in a large bowl. Place egg in a separate bowl. Dip pork chops in egg then coat with pork crumb. Place the dehydrating tray in a multi-level air fryer basket and place basket in the instant pot. Place coated pork chops on dehydrating tray. Seal pot with air fryer lid and select air fry mode then set the temperature to 400 F and timer for 15 minutes. Turn pork chops halfway through. Serve and enjoy.

Air-fried Garlic-rosemary Lamb Chops

Ingredients: Servings: 2 Cooking Time: 12 Mins

2 lamb chops
1 clove of garlic
2 tsps. olive oil
2 tsps. garlic puree
A sprig of fresh rosemary
Salt and pepper to taste

Directions:
Place lamb chops in a bowl and season with salt and pepper and brush or spray with olive oil. Top each lamb chop with garlic puree. Between each chops place fresh rosemary and unpeeled garlic. Leave the bowl with the lamb chops in the refrigerator for about an hour to marinate. Transfer the marinated lamb chops to the instant pot duo crisp air fryer basket and air-fry at 360 degrees F for 6 minutes. Flip lamb chops for even cooking and cook for another 6 minutes without changing the cooking temperature. Leave to rest for a minute or 2. Discard the fresh garlic and rosemary and serve.

Simple Steak

Ingredients: Servings: 2 Cooking Time: 14 Mins

Salt and freshly ground black pepper, to taste
½ lb. quality cuts steak

Directions:
Preparing the Ingredients. Preheat the Instant Crisp Air Fryer to 390 degrees F. Rub the steak with salt and pepper evenly. Air Frying. Place the steak in the Instant Crisp Air Fryer basket, close air fryer lid and cook for about 14 minutes crispy.

Pork Tenderloin and Coconut Rice

Ingredients: Servings: 4 Cooking Time: 15 Mins

2 tbsp. peanut oil
1 lb. pork tenderloin, cut into 4 pieces
1 small leek, white and pale green parts only, halved lengthwise, washed and thinly sliced
One 4½-ounce can chopped mild green chiles (about ½ cup)
1 tsp. dried thyme
1 tsp. ground cumin
¼ tsp. salt
½ tsp. ground coriander
¼ tsp. ground black pepper
One 15-ounce can black beans, drained and rinsed (about 1¾ cups)
1 C. chicken broth
1 C. regular or low-fat canned coconut milk
1 C. white long-grain rice, such as white basmati rice
2 tbsp. packed light brown sugar

Directions:
Preparing the Ingredients. Heat the oil in the Instant Crisp Air Fryer turned to the "Sauté" function. Add the pork tenderloin pieces; brown on all sides, occasionally turning, about 6 minutes. Transfer to a plate. Add the leek and chiles; cook, often stirring, until the leek softens, about 2 minutes. Stir in the thyme, cumin, coriander, salt, and pepper; cook until aromatic, less than half a minute. Stir in the beans, broth, coconut milk, rice, and brown sugar until the brown sugar dissolves. Nestle the pieces of pork in the sauce, submerging the meat and rice as much as possible in the liquid; pour any juices from the meat's plate into the cooker. High pressure for 15 minutes. Lock the pressure cooking lid on the Instant Crisp Air Fryer and then cook for 15 minutes. To get 15-minutes cook time, press "Pressure" Button and then adjust the time. Pressure Release. Use the quick-release method to bring the pot's pressure back to normal but do not open the cooker. Set the pot aside for 10 minutes to steam the rice. Finish the dish. Close air fryer lid and select Broil, set time to 7 minutes. Transfer the pork pieces to four serving plates; spoon the rice and beans around them

Beef Stroganoff

Ingredients: Servings: 4 Cooking Time: 14 Mins

9 Ozs Tender Beef
1 Onion, chopped
1 Tbsp Paprika
3/4 Cup Sour Cream
Salt and Pepper to taste
Baking Dish

Directions:
Preparing the Ingredients. Preheat the Instant Crisp Air Fryer to 390 degrees. Chop the beef and marinate it with the paprika. Add the chopped onions into the baking dish and heat for about 2 minutes in the Instant Crisp Air Fryer. When the onions are transparent, add the beef into the dish and cook for 5 minutes. Once the beef is starting to tender, pour in the sour cream and cook for another 7 minutes. At this point, the liquid should have reduced. Season with salt and pepper and serve.

Apricot Glazed Pork Tenderloins

Ingredients: Servings: 3 Cooking Time: 30 Mins

1 tsp. salt
1/2 tsp. pepper
2 tbsp. minced fresh
1-lb pork tenderloin
Apricot Glaze
Ingredients

rosemary or 1 tbsp. dried rosemary, crushed
2 tbsp. olive oil, divided
1 garlic cloves, minced
1 C. apricot preServings
1 garlic cloves, minced
4 tbsp. lemon juice

Directions:
1 Preparing the Ingredients. Mix well pepper, salt, garlic, oil, and rosemary. Brush all over pork. If needed cut pork crosswise in half to fit in Instant Crisp Air Fryer. Lightly grease baking pan of Instant Crisp Air Fryer with cooking spray. Add pork. 2 Air Frying. Lock the air fryer lid. For 3 minutes per side, brown pork in a preheated 390°F Instant Crisp Air Fryer. Meanwhile, mix well all glaze Ingredients in a small bowl. Baste pork every 5 minutes. Cook for 20 minutes at 330°F. Serve and enjoy.

Italian Stuffed Bell Peppers

Ingredients: Servings: 4 Cooking Time: 25 Mins

Ground pork Italian sausage – 1 pound
Garlic powder – ½ tsp.
Dried parsley – ½ tsp.
Diced Roma tomato – 1
Chopped onion – ¼ cup
Green bell pepper – 4
Shredded mozzarella cheese – 1 cup, divided

Directions:
Brown the ground sausage on Sauté in the Instant Pot until no longer pink. Drain fat. Add the onion, tomato, parsley, and garlic powder. Cook for 3 to 5 minutes more. Slice peppers in half and remove the seeds and white membrane. Spoon the meat mixture evenly into pepper halves. Top with mozzarella and place pepper halves into the air fryer basket. Cook at 350F for 15 minutes. Serve.

Russian Beef Bake

Ingredients: Servings: 6 Cooking Time: 60 Mins

1 (2 pounds) beef tenderloin
Salt and ground black pepper to taste
2 onions, sliced
1 1/2 C. Cheddar cheese, grated
1 C. milk
3 tbsp. mayonnaise

Directions:
Slice the beef into thick slices and lb. them with a mallet. Place these pounded slices in the Instant Pot Duo's pan. Top these slices with onion, salt, black pepper, cheese, milk, and mayonnaise. Put on the Air Fryer lid and seal it. Hit the "Bake Button" and select 60 minutes of cooking time, then press "Start." Crush the crackers and mix them well with 4 tbsp. melted butter. Once the Instant Pot Duo beeps, remove its lid. Serve.

Moroccan Lamb

Ingredients: Servings: 4 Cooking Time: 10 Mins

8 lamb cutlets
½ C. mint leaves
6 garlic cloves
4 tbsp. Olive oil
1 tbsp. Cumin, ground
3 tbsp. Lemon juice
1 tbsp. Coriander seeds
Zest of 2 lemons, grated
A pinch of salt and black pepper

Directions:
In a blender, combine all the ingredients except the lamb and pulse well. Rub the lamb cutlets with this mix, place them in your air fryer's basket and cook at 380°f for 15 minutes on each side. Serve with a side salad

Beef and Broccoli Stir-fry

Ingredients: Servings: 2 Cooking Time: 20 Mins

Sirloin steak – ½ pound, thinly sliced
Liquid aminos – 2 tbsps.
Grated ginger – ¼ tsp.
Finely minced garlic – ¼ tsp.
Coconut oil – 1 tbsp.
Broccoli florets – 2 cups
Crushed red pepper – ¼ tsp.
Xanthan gum – 1/8 tsp.
Sesame seeds – ½ tsp.

Directions:
In a bowl, add coconut oil, garlic, ginger, liquid aminos, and beef. Cover and marinate 1 hour in the refrigerator. Remove beef from the marinade, reserving marinade, and place the beef into the air fryer basket. Cook at 320F for 20 minutes. After 10 minutes, add broccoli and sprinkle red pepper into the air fryer basket and shake. Bring the marinade to a boil in a skillet, then reduce heat to simmer. Stir in xanthan gum and allow to thicken. When cooking is done, add the beef and broccoli from the air fryer to the skillet and toss. Sprinkle with sesame seeds and serve.

Fried Rice with Chicken & Mushrooms

Ingredients: Servings: 4 Cooking Time: 20 Mins

1 tbsp. ghee
1 onion, diced
4 garlic cloves, minced
1 lb boneless, skinless chicken breasts
Salt and black pepper, to taste
2 C. chicken broth
¼ C. coconut aminos
1 C. long grain rice
16 oz. frozen mixed mushrooms

Directions:
Choose Sear/Sauté on the pot and melt the ghee; sauté the onion for 5 minutes. Add garlic and cook until fragrant, about 1 minute. Season the chicken with salt and black pepper and place in the pot and. Cook for 5 minutes until browned. Pour in the chicken broth, coconut aminos, and rice. Seal the pressure lid, choose Pressure, set to High, and set the time to 3 minutes. Press Start. When the timer is done, perform a quick pressure and carefully open the lid. Pour the frozen mushrooms into the pot. Choose Sear/Sauté and set to High. Choose Start. Cook for 5 minutes while stirring occasionally. When ready, dish the fried rice with chicken and serve.

Cajun Pork Steaks

Ingredients: Servings: 6 Cooking Time: 20 Mins

4-6 pork steaks
1 tsp. low-sodium soy

BBQ sauce:
Cajun seasoning
1 tbsp. vinegar
sauce
½ C. brown sugar
½ C. vegan ketchup

Directions:
1 Preparing the Ingredients. Ensure your Instant Crisp Air Fryer is preheated to 290 degrees. Sprinkle pork steaks with Cajun seasoning. Combine remaining ingredients and brush onto steaks. Add coated steaks to Instant Crisp Air Fryer. 2 Air Frying. Close air fryer lid. Set temperature to 290°F, and set time to 20 minutes. Cook 15-20 minutes till just browned.

Green Cream Soup

Ingredients: Servings: 4 Cooking Time: 13 Mins

½ lb Kale Leaves, chopped
½ lb Spinach Leaves, chopped
½ lb Swiss Chard Leaves, chopped
1 tbsp. Olive Oil
4 cloves Garlic, minced
4 C. Vegetable Broth
1 Onion, chopped
1 ¼ C. Heavy Cream
Salt and Pepper, to taste
1 ½ tbsp. White Wine Vinegar
Chopped Peanuts to garnish
Spoon the soup into bowls, sprinkle with peanuts, and serve.

Directions:
Turn on the cooker and select Sear/Sauté mode on Medium. Add the olive oil, once it has heated add the onion and garlic and sauté for 2-3 minutes until soft. Add greens and vegetable broth. Close the lid, secure the pressure valve, and select Pressure mode on High pressure for 10 minutes. Press Start. Once the timer has ended, do a quick pressure release. Add the white wine vinegar, salt, and pepper. Use a stick blender to puree the

Air Fryer Steak Bites & Mushrooms

Ingredients: Servings: 4 Cooking Time: 20 Mins

8 oz. mushrooms, cleaned, washed and halved
1 lb. steaks, cut into 1-inch cubes and patted dry
2 tbsps. butter, melted
½ tsp. garlic powder
1 tsp. Worcestershire sauce
A dash of minced parsley for garnish
Optional: melted butter or chili flakes for finishing
Black pepper and salt to taste

Directions:
Add steak cubes and mushrooms in a bowl and coat with melted butter. Season the dish with garlic powder, Worcestershire sauce, salt and pepper to taste. Arrange mushrooms and steak cubes in the instant pot air fryer basket. Set to air fry at 400 degrees F for 10-18 minutes, flipping from time to time for even cooking. If you desire your steaks to be crispier, cook for an additional 2-5 minutes. Garnish with parsley and drizzle with melted butter or chili flakes if desired. Adjust seasoning with salt and pepper if needed. Serve warm.

Tasty Southern Pork Chops

Ingredients: Servings: 2 Cooking Time: 15 Mins

2 pork chops, wash and pat dry
2 tbsp. flour
1 1/2 tbsp. buttermilk
1/2 tsp. Montreal chicken seasoning
Salt

Directions:
Season pork chops with pepper and salt. Coat pork chops with buttermilk. Place pork chops in a zip-lock bag with flour and shake well to coat. Marinate pork chops for 30 minutes. Place the dehydrating tray in a multi-level air fryer basket and place basket in the instant pot. Place marinated pork chops on dehydrating tray. Seal pot with air fryer lid and select air fry mode then set the temperature to 380 F and timer for 15 minutes. Turn pork chops halfway through. Serve and enjoy.

Paprika Chicken with Cucumber Salad (pressure Cook)

Ingredients: Servings: 4 Cooking Time: 20 Mins

1 tbsp. olive oil
1 yellow onion, chopped
2 chicken breasts, skinless, boneless and halved
1 C. chicken stock
1 tbsp. sweet paprika
½ tsp. cinnamon powder
Salad:
2 cucumbers, sliced
1 tomato, cubed
1 avocado, peeled, pitted, and cubed
1 tbsp. chopped cilantro

Directions:
Press the Sauté button on the Instant Pot and heat the olive oil until it shimmers. Add the onion and chicken breasts and sauté for 5 minutes, stirring occasionally, or until the onion is translucent. Stir in the chicken stock, paprika, and cinnamon powder. Secure the lid. Select the Pressure Cook and set the cooking time for 15 minutes at High Pressure. Meanwhile, toss all the ingredients for the salad in a bowl. Set aside. Once cooking is complete, do a natural pressure release for 10 minutes, then release any remaining pressure. Carefully open the lid. Divide the chicken breasts between four plates and serve with the salad on the side.

Pork Meatloaf (pressure Cook)

Ingredients: Servings: 4 Cooking Time: 30 Mins

2 lb. (907 g) ground pork meat
½ C. tomato sauce
½ C. almond meal
½ C. coconut milk
2 eggs, whisked
1 yellow onion, minced
1 tbsp. chopped parsley
1 tbsp. chopped chives
A pinch of salt and black pepper
2 C. water

Directions:
Stir together all the ingredients except the water in a large mixing bowl until well incorporated. Form the mixture into a meatloaf and transfer to a loaf pan that fits the Instant Pot. Pour the water into the Instant Pot and insert a steamer basket. Place the loaf pan in the basket. Lock the lid. Select the Pressure Cook and set the cooking time for 30 minutes at High Pressure. Once cooking is complete, do a natural pressure release for 10 minutes, then release any remaining pressure.

Carefully open the lid. Allow to cool for 5 minutes before slicing and serving.

Indian Pork

Ingredients: Servings: 4 Cooking Time: 12 Mins

Ginger powder – 1 tsp.	Shallot – 1, chopped
Chili paste – 2 tsps.	Coconut milk – 7 ounces
Garlic cloves – 2, minced	Olive oil – 2 tbsps.
Pork chops – 14 ounces, cubed	Peanuts – 3 ounces, ground
Coriander – 1 tsp. ground	Soy sauce - 3 tbsps.
	Salt and black pepper to taste

Directions:

In a bowl, mix ginger with half the oil, half of the soy sauce, half of the garlic, and 1 tsp. chili paste. Whisk and add meat. Coat and marinate for 10 minutes. Cook the meat at 400F in the air fryer for 12 minutes. Meanwhile, heat up the pan with the rest of the oil and add the rest of the peanuts, coconut milk, coriander, rest of the garlic, rest of the chili paste, rest of the soy sauce, and shallot — Stir-Fry for 5 minutes. Divide pork on plates, spread coconut mix on top and serve.

Chicken-parmesan Wings

Ingredients: Servings: 4 Cooking Time: 15 Mins

2 lbs. chicken wings, cut into drumettes and wingettes	½ C. + 6 tbsps. Parmesan, freshly grated
1 tsp. Herbs de Provence	1 tsp. paprika
	Salt to taste

Directions:

Pat the chicken wings dry, put them in a bowl and set aside. Combine the Parmesan, Herbs de Provence, paprika, and salt in a small bowl. Coat the wings with the Parmesan mixture. Preheat your instant pot with the air fryer lid on at 350 degrees F. Spritz the air fryer basket with cooking spray. Arrange the wings in the basket in a single layer (work in batches as necessary). Set the trivet inside the pot and place the basket on top of it. Air-fry the chicken wings for 15 minutes, turning them halfway through. Garnish the wings with extra Parmesan and fresh herbs before serving.

Air-fried Breaded Chicken

Ingredients: Servings: 4 Cooking Time: 15 Mins

6-oz. boneless and skinless chicken breasts	⅛ tsp. paprika
¼ C. bread crumbs	¼ tsp. oregano
⅛ tsp. garlic powder	Salt and pepper to taste

Directions:

Preheat your air fryer to 390 degrees F. Mix the bread crumbs, garlic powder, paprika, salt, pepper and oregano in a medium bowl until well combined. Spritz the chicken breasts with cooking spray then dredge them one by one into the breadcrumb mixture. Shake off any extra breading and arrange them in the air fryer basket. Make sure to assemble them in a single layer, not over-crowding them. Work in batches if needed. Generously spritz the breaded chicken with cooking spray to help them crisp up. Air fry at 350 degrees F for 5 minutes. Flip the chicken and spritz some cooking spray on them. Continue to cook for additional 4-7 minutes or until they're golden brown. Remember, cooking time will depend on the thickness and size of the chicken breasts. Serve and enjoy.

Cheese-stuffed Meatballs

Ingredients: Servings: 4 Cooking Time: 10 Mins

⅓ C. soft bread crumbs	Freshly ground black pepper
3 tbsp. milk	1 lb. 95 percent lean ground beef
1 tbsp. ketchup	20 ½-inch cubes of cheese
1 egg	Olive oil for misting
½ tsp. dried marjoram	
Pinch salt	

Directions:

1 Preparing the Ingredients. In a large bowl, combine the bread crumbs, milk, ketchup, egg, marjoram, salt, and pepper, and mix well. Add the ground beef and mix gently but thoroughly with your hands. Form the mixture into 20 meatballs. Shape each meatball around a cheese cube. Mist the meatballs with olive oil and put into the Instant Crisp Air Fryer basket. 2 Air Frying. Close air fryer lid. Bake for 10 to 13 minutes or until the meatballs register 165°F on a meat thermometer.

Creamy Lamb

Ingredients: Servings: 8 Cooking Time: 1 Hour

Leg of lamb – 5 pounds	Garlic – 2 cloves, minced
Buttermilk – 2 cups	Salt and black pepper to taste
Mustard – 2 tbsps.	White wine – 1 cup
Butter – ½ cup	Cornstarch – 1 tbsp. mixed with 1 tbsp. water
Basil – 2 tbsps. chopped	Sour cream – ½ cup
Tomato paste – 2 tbsps.	

Directions:

Place lamb roast in a dish. Add buttermilk and toss to coat. Cover and marinate in the refrigerator for 24 hours. Pat dry lamb and put in a pan that fits in the air fryer basket. In a bowl, mix butter with garlic, salt, pepper, rosemary, basil, mustard, and tomato paste. Whisk well and spread over the lamb. Place in the air fryer and cook at 300F for 1 hour. Slice lamb, divide among plates. Heat up cooking juices from the pan on the stove. Add sour cream, salt, pepper, wine, and cornstarch mix. Remove from heat and drizzle lamb with this sauce. Serve.

Simple Air Fried Chicken Wings

Ingredients: Servings: 4 Cooking Time: 15 Mins

1 tbsp. olive oil	1 tsp. garlic powder
8 whole chicken wings	Freshly ground black pepper, to taste
Chicken seasoning or rub, to taste	

Directions:

Preheat the air fryer to 400°F (204°C). Grease the air fryer basket with olive oil. On a clean work surface, rub the chicken wings with chicken seasoning and rub, garlic powder, and ground black pepper. Arrange the well-coated chicken wings in the preheated air fryer. Air fry for 15 minutes or until the internal temperature of the chicken wings reaches at least 165°F (74°C). Flip the chicken wings halfway through. Remove the chicken wings from the air fryer. Serve immediately.

Festive Pork Loin with Vegetable Gravy

Ingredients: Servings: 4 Cooking Time: 28 Mins

2 lb Pork Loin Roast
Salt and Pepper, to taste
3 cloves Garlic, minced
1 medium Onion, diced
2 tbsp. Butter
3 stalks Celery, chopped
3 Carrots, chopped
1 C. Chicken Broth
2 tbsp. Worcestershire Sauce
½ tbsp. Sugar
1 tsp. Yellow Mustard
2 tsp. dried Basil
2 tsp. dried Thyme
1 tbsp. Cornstarch
¼ C. Water

Directions:
Select Sear/Sauté mode, and heat oil. Season the pork with salt and pepper. Sear the pork to golden brown on both sides. Then, add the garlic and onions, and cook them until soft, for about 4 minutes. Top with the celery, carrots, chicken broth, Worcestershire sauce, mustard, thyme, basil, and sugar. Close the lid, secure the pressure valve, and select Pressure mode on High pressure for 15 minutes. Press Start to start cooking. Once the timer is off, do a quick pressure release. Next, add the cornstarch to the water, in a bowl, and mix with a spoon, until nice and smooth. Add it to the pot, close the crisping lid, and cook on Broil mode, for 3 - 5 minutes, until the sauce becomes a slurry with a bit of thickness, and the pork is nice and tender. Adjust the seasoning, and ladle to a serving platter. Serve with a side of steamed almond garlicky rapini mix.

Lamb and Eggplant Pasta Casserole

Ingredients: Servings: 4 Cooking Time: 8 Mins

2 tbsp. olive oil
1 medium red onion, chopped
1 tbsp. minced garlic
1½ lb. lean ground lamb
One small eggplant (about ¾ pound), stemmed and diced
¾ C. dry red wine, such as Syrah
2¼ C. chicken broth
½ C. canned tomato paste
1 tsp. ground cinnamon
½ tbsp. dried oregano
½ tsp. dried dill
½ tsp. salt
½ tsp. ground black pepper
8 oz. dried spiral-shaped pasta, such as rotini

Directions:
Preparing the Ingredients. Heat the oil in the Instant Crisp Air Fryer turned to the "Sauté" function. Add the onion and cook, often stirring, until softened, about 4 minutes. Add the garlic and cook until aromatic, less than 1 minute. Crumble in the ground lamb; cook, stirring occasionally until it has lost its raw color, about 5 minutes. Add the eggplant and cook for 1 minute, often stirring, to soften a bit. Pour in the red wine and scrape up any browned bits in the pot as it comes to a simmer. Stir in the broth, tomato paste, cinnamon, oregano, dill, salt, and pepper until everything is coated in the tomato sauce. Stir in the pasta until coated. High pressure for 8 minutes. Lock the pressure cooking lid on the Instant Crisp Air Fryer and then cook for 8 minutes. To get 8-minutes cook time, press "Pressure" button and use the Time Adjustment button to adjust the cook time to 8 minutes. Pressure Release. Use the quick-release method. Remove the lid from the Instant Crisp Air Fryer. Close air fryer lid. Select BROIL, and set time to 5 minutes. Cooking for an additional 4 minutes if dish needs more browning. Unlock and open the pot. Stir well before serving.

Bell Pepper & Beef with Onion Gravy

Ingredients: Servings: 6 Cooking Time: 42 Mins

½ Green Bell Pepper, finely chopped
½ Red Bell Pepper, finely chopped
½ Yellow Bell Pepper, finely chopped
1 Yellow Onion, finely chopped
2 cloves Garlic, minced
2 lb Round Steak Pieces, about 6 to 8 pieces
Salt and Pepper, to taste
¼ C. All-purpose Flour
2 tbsp. Olive Oil
½ C. Water

Directions:
Wrap the steaks in plastic wrap, place on a cutting board, and use a rolling pin to lb. flat of about 2-inch thickness. Remove the plastic wrap and season them with salt and pepper. Set aside. Put the chopped peppers, onion, and garlic in a bowl, and mix them evenly. Spoon the bell pepper mixture onto the flattened steaks and roll them to have the peppers inside. Use some toothpicks to secure the beef rolls and dredge the steaks in all-purpose flour while shaking off any excess flour. Place in a plate. Select Sear/Sauté mode on cooker and heat the oil. Add the beef rolls and brown them on both sides, for about 6 minutes. Pour the water over the meat, close the lid, secure the pressure valve, and select Pressure mode on High pressure for 20 minutes. Press Start. Once the timer has stopped, do a natural pressure release for 10 minutes. Close the crisping lid and cook for 10 minutes on Broil mode. When ready, Remove the meat to a plate and spoon the sauce from the pot over. Serve the stuffed meat rolls with a side of steamed veggies.

Panko-breaded Pork Chops

Ingredients: Servings: 6 Cooking Time: 12 Mins

5 (3½- to 5-ounce) pork chops (bone-in or boneless)
Seasoning salt
Pepper
¼ C. all-purpose flour
2 tbsp. panko bread crumbs
Cooking oil

Directions:
Preparing the Ingredients. Season the pork chops with the seasoning salt and pepper to taste. Sprinkle the flour on both sides of the pork chops, then coat both sides with panko bread crumbs. Place the pork chops in the Instant Crisp Air Fryer.

Stacking them is okay. Air Frying. Spray the pork chops with cooking oil. Lock the air fryer lid. Cook for 6 minutes. Open the Instant Crisp Air Fryer and flip the pork chops. Cook for an additional 6 minutes Cool before serving. Typically, bone-in pork chops are juicier than boneless. If you prefer really juicy pork chops, use bone-in.

Zaatar Lamb Chops

Ingredients: Servings: 4 Cooking Time: 10 Mins

4 lamb loin chops
1/2 tbsp. Zaatar
1 tbsp. fresh lemon juice
1 tsp. olive oil
2 garlic cloves, minced
Pepper
Salt

Directions:
Coat lamb chops with oil and lemon juice and rubs with zaatar, garlic, pepper, and salt. Place the dehydrating tray in a multi-level air fryer basket and place basket in the instant pot. Place lamb chops on dehydrating tray. Seal pot with air fryer lid and select air fry mode then set the temperature to 400 F and timer for 10 minutes. Turn lamb chops halfway through. Serve and enjoy.

Beef and Green Onions

Ingredients: Servings: 4 Cooking Time: 20 Mins

Green onion - 1 cup, chopped
Soy sauce – 1 cup
Water – ½ cup
Brown sugar – ¼ cup
Sesame seeds – ¼ cup
Garlic – 5 cloves, minced
Black pepper – 1 tsp.
Lean beef – 1 pound

Directions:
In a bowl, mix the onion with water, soy sauce, garlic, sugar, sesame seeds, and pepper. Whisk and add meat. Marinate for 10 minutes. Drain beef. Cook in the preheated 390F air fryer for 20 minutes. Serve.

Italian Steak and Spinach Rolls (air Fryer)

Ingredients: Servings: 4 Cooking Time: 9 Mins

2 tsp. dried Italian seasoning
2 cloves garlic, minced
1 tbsp. vegetable oil
1 tsp. kosher salt
1 lb. (454 g) flank steak, ¼ to ½ inch thick
1 tsp. ground black pepper
1 (10-ounce / 284-g) package frozen spinach, thawed and squeezed dry
½ C. diced jarred roasted red pepper
1 C. shredded Mozzarella cheese
Cooking spray

Directions:
Combine the Italian seasoning, garlic, vegetable oil, salt, and ground black pepper in a large bowl. Stir to mix well. Dunk the steak in the seasoning mixture and toss to coat well. Wrap the bowl in plastic and marinate under room temperature for at least 30 minutes. Preheat the air fryer to 400°F (204°C). Spritz the air fryer basket with cooking spray. Remove the marinated steak from the bowl and unfold on a clean work surface, then spread the top of the steak with a layer of spinach, a layer of red pepper and a layer of cheese. Leave a ¼-inch edge uncovered. Roll the steak up to wrap the filling, then secure with 3 toothpicks. Cut the roll in half and transfer the rolls in the preheated air fryer basket, seam side down. Air fry for 9 minutes or until the steak is lightly browned and the internal temperature reaches at least 145°F (63°C). Remove the rolls from the air fryer and slice to serve.

Asian Pork Chops

Ingredients: Servings: 4 Cooking Time: 15 Mins

3 tbsp. cider vinegar
1 tbsp. Asian sweet chili sauce
1/4 tsp. garlic powder
1/2 C. hoisin sauce
4 (1/2-inch-thick) boneless pork chops
1 tsp. salt
1/2 tsp. pepper

Directions:
Preparing the Ingredients. Stir together hoisin, chili sauce, garlic powder, and vinegar in a large mixing bowl. Separate 1/4 C. of this mixture, then add pork chops to the bowl and marinate in the fridge for 2 hours. Remove the pork chops and place them on a plate. Sprinkle each side of the pork chop evenly with salt and pepper. Air Frying. Close air fryer lid. Cook at 360 degrees for 14 minutes, flipping half way through. Brush with reserved marinade and serve.

Crispy Breaded Pork Chop

Ingredients: Servings: 6 Cooking Time: 12 Mins

olive oil spray
6 3/4-inch thick center-cut boneless pork chops, fat trimmed (5 oz each)
kosher salt
1/2 C. panko crumbs, check labels for GF
1/3 C. crushed cornflakes crumbs
1 large egg, beaten
2 tbsp. grated parmesan cheese
1 1/4 tsp. sweet paprika
1/2 tsp. garlic powder
1/2 tsp. onion powder
1/4 tsp. chili powder
1/8 tsp. black pepper

Directions:
Preheat the Instant Pot Duo Crisp Air Fryer for 12 minutes at 400°F. On both sides, season pork chops with half tsp. kosher salt. Then combine cornflake crumbs, panko, parmesan cheese, 3/4 tsp. kosher salt, garlic powder, paprika, onion powder, chili powder, and black pepper in a large bowl. Place the egg beat in another bowl. Dip the pork in the egg & then crumb mixture. When the air fryer is ready, place 3 of the chops into the Instant Pot Duo Crisp Air Fryer Basket and spritz the top with oil. Close the Air Fryer lid and cook for 12 minutes turning halfway, spritzing both sides with oil. Set aside and repeat with the remaining.

Bacon Wrapped Pork Tenderloin

Ingredients: Servings: 4 Cooking Time: 15 Mins

Pork:
1-2 tbsp. Dijon mustard
3-4 strips of bacon
1 pork tenderloin

Apple Gravy:
1 tbsp. almond flour
2 tbsp. ghee
1 chopped onion
2-3 Granny Smith

½ - 1 tsp. Dijon mustard	apples
	1 C. vegetable broth

Directions:
1 Preparing the Ingredients. Spread Dijon mustard all over tenderloin and wrap meat with strips of bacon. 2 Air Frying. Place into the Instant Crisp Air Fryer, close air fryer lid, set temperature to 360°F, and set time to 15 minutes and cook 10-15 minutes at 360 degrees. Use a meat thermometer to check for doneness. To make sauce, heat ghee in a pan and add shallots. Cook 1-2 minutes. Then add apples, cooking 3-5 minutes until softened. Add flour and ghee to make a roux. Add broth and mustard, stirring well to combine. When sauce starts to bubble, add 1 C. of sautéed apples, cooking till sauce thickens. Once pork tenderloin I cook, allow to sit 5-10 minutes to rest before slicing. Serve topped with apple gravy. Devour!

Ranch Pork Chops

Ingredients: Servings: 6 Cooking Time: 30 Mins

6 pork chops, boneless	2 tbsp. ranch seasoning
1/4 C. olive oil	Pepper
1 tsp. dried parsley	Salt

Directions:
Line instant pot air fryer basket with parchment paper. Season pork chops with pepper and salt and place on parchment paper into the air fryer basket. Mix together olive oil, parsley, and ranch seasoning. Spoon oil mixture over pork chops. Place air fryer basket in the pot. Seal the pot with air fryer basket and select bake mode and cook at 400 F for 30 minutes. Serve and enjoy.

Paprika Chicken (pressure Cook)

Ingredients: Servings: 6 Cooking Time: 40 Mins

1¾ tbsp. olive oil	½ tsp. pepper
1½ tsp. salt	1 tsp. paprika
1 tsp. minced garlic	1 whole chicken
	1 C. chicken broth

Directions:
Stir together the olive oil, salt, pepper, garlic, and paprika in a small bowl. Rub the mixture all over the chicken until evenly coated. Pour the chicken broth into the Instant Pot and add the coated chicken. Secure the lid. Select the Poultry mode and set the cooking time for 40 minutes at High Pressure. Once cooking is complete, do a natural pressure release for 15 minutes, then release any remaining pressure. Carefully open the lid. Serve warm.

Creamy Chicken Chili with Cannellini Beans

Ingredients: Servings: 4 Cooking Time: 25 Mins

3 Chicken Breasts, cubed	1 tbsp. Butter
3 C. Chicken Broth	Salt and Black Pepper
1 White Onion, chopped	1 tsp. Cumin Powder
2 (14.5 oz) cans Cannellini beans, drained	1 tsp. dried Oregano
	½ C. heavy Whipping Cream
	1 C. Sour Cream

Directions:
Select Sear/Sauté mode and set to Medium. Melt the butter, and add onion and chicken. Stir and let cook the chicken for 6 minutes. Stir in the cannellini beans, cumin powder, oregano, salt, and pepper. Pour in the broth, stir, close the pressure lid, and secure the pressure valve.Select Pressure mode on High for 10 minutes. Press Start. Once the timer has ended, let the pot sit uncovered for 10 minutes, then do a quick pressure release. Stir in the whipping and sour cream. Close the crisping lid and select Broil mode. Cook for 2 minutes. Serve warm with a mix of steamed bell peppers and broccoli.

Heavenly Bangers with Mashed Potatoes & Onion Gravy

Ingredients: Servings: 4 Cooking Time: 35 Mins

2 lb Potatoes, peeled and halved	¼ C. + 2 tbsp. + 2 tbsp. Butter
4 Italian Sausages	1 tbsp. Cornstarch
1 C. Water + 2 tbsp. Water	3 tbsp. Balsamic Vinegar
⅓ C. Green Onion, sliced	1 Onion, sliced thinly
Salt and Pepper, to taste	1 C. + 2 tbsp. Beef Broth
4 tbsp. Milk	

Directions:
Put the potatoes in the inner pot and pour the water over. Seal the lid; select Steam mode on High for 15 minutes and press Start. Do a quick pressure release, and remove the potatoes to a bowl. Add in a quarter C. butter and use a masher to mash them until the butter is well mixed. Slowly add the milk and mix it using a spoon. Add the green onions, season with pepper and salt and fold it in with the spoon. Set aside. Pour out the liquid in the cooker, and use paper towels to wipe inside the pot dry. Select Sear/Sauté mode and melt two tbsps. of butter. Brown the sausages on each side for 3 minutes. Remove to the potato mash and cover with aluminium foil to keep warm. Set aside Back into the pot, add the two tbsps. of the beef broth to deglaze the bottom of the pot while stirring and scraping the bottom with a spoon. Add the remaining butter and onions; sauté the onions until translucent, then pour in the balsamic vinegar. Stir for another minute. In a bowl, mix the cornstarch with water and pour into the pot. Add the remaining beef broth. Allow the sauce to thicken and adjust the seasoning. Turn off the heat once a slurry is formed. Dish the mashed potatoes and sausages in serving plates. Spoon the gravy over it and serve immediately with steamed green beans.

Southern-style Chicken

Ingredients: Servings: 6 Cooking Time: 30 Mins

1 broiler or fryer chicken (about 4 lbs.), cut into pieces	1 large egg, beaten
	1 tsp. garlic salt
	1 tsp. paprika
2 C. bread crumbs	½ tsp. pepper
1 tbsp. fresh parsley, minced	¼ tsp. ground cumin
	¼ tsp. sage, rubbed

Directions:
Preheat your air fryer to 375 degrees F and spritz the fryer basket with cooking spray. Mix the bread crumbs, parsley, garlic salt, paprika, pepper, ground cumin, and sage in a

shallow bowl. Crack the egg in another bowl and whisk lightly. Dip the chicken cuts into the whisked egg then into the cracker mixture. Pat for the coating to stick to the chicken. Arrange the chicken pieces in a single layer in the basket and spritz the chicken with cooking spray. Working in batches, air fry for 10 minutes, then flip the chicken. Spritz them with more cooking spray to make them crispier. Continue to cook for 10-20 minutes longer until golden brown and the juices run clear. Serve warm.

Spicy Sausage and Chard Pasta Sauce

Ingredients: Servings: 6 Cooking Time: 6 Mins

2 tbsp. olive oil
1 medium red onion, chopped
Up to 3 small hot chiles, such as cherry peppers or Anaheim chiles, stemmed, seeded, and chopped
1 lb. mild Italian pork sausage meat, any casings removed
1 tbsp. minced garlic
½ C. dry red wine, such as Syrah
½ C. canned tomato paste
¼ C. chicken broth
1 tbsp. dried basil
2 tsp. dried oregano
4 C. stemmed and chopped Swiss chard

Directions:
Preparing the Ingredients. Heat the oil in an instant Crisp Air Fryer, turned to the sauté function. Add the onion and cook, often stirring, until softened, about 4 minutes. Add the chiles and garlic; cook until aromatic, stirring all the while, about 1 minute. Crumble in the sausage meat, breaking up any clumps with a wooden spoon. Stir until it loses its raw color. Stir in the wine, tomato paste, broth, basil, and oregano until the tomato paste dissolves. Add the chard and stir well. High pressure for 6 minutes. Lock the pressure cooking lid onto the cooker, set the machine's timer to cook at high pressure for 6 minutes. To get 6-minutes cook time, press the "Pressure" button and use the Time Adjustment button to adjust the cook time to 6 minutes. Pressure Release. Use the quick-release method to drop the pressure back to normal. Finish the dish. Remove the lid from the Instant Crisp Air Fryer. Close air fryer lid. Select BROIL, and set time to 5 minutes. Check after 4 minutes, cooking for an additional 4 minutes if dish needs more browning. Stir well before serving.

Pork Meatballs

Ingredients: Servings: 12 Cooking Time: 10 Mins

8 oz. ground Italian sausage, mild or hot
1 large egg
½ C. panko bread crumbs
12 oz. ground pork
½ tsp. dried paprika
1 tsp. dried parsley
1 tsp. salt

Directions:
In a large bowl, combine bread crumbs, sausage, pork, egg, paprika, and parsley. Season with salt. Mix to thoroughly combine all ingredients. Form into 12 meatballs of equal sizes, using an ice cream scoop. Place meatballs in an air fryer basket lined with parchment paper. You may use a two-layer of air fryer basket to accommodate all meatballs in a single batch. Place the air fryer basket in the instant pot duo crisp and attach the air fryer lid. Set to 350 degrees F and cook for 8 minutes. Shake basket and cook for another 2 minutes. Transfer to a platter and serve.

Beef Meatballs with Roasted Tomatoes (pressure Cook)

Ingredients: Servings: 4 Cooking Time: 16 Mins

2 tbsp. avocado oil
1 lb. (454 g) ground beef
½ tsp. dried basil
2 (14-ounce / 397-g) cans fire roasted tomatoes
½ tsp. crushed red pepper
½ tsp. ground cayenne pepper
½ tsp. kosher salt
½ tsp. freshly ground black pepper

Directions:
Set the Instant Pot to Sauté mode and heat the avocado oil. In a large bowl, mix the remaining ingredients, except for the tomatoes. Form the mixture into 1½-inch meatballs and place them into the Instant Pot. Spread the tomatoes evenly over the meatballs. Close the lid. Select the Pressure Cook, set the cooking time for 16 minutes at High Pressure. When timer beeps, perform a natural pressure release for 5 minutes, then release any remaining pressure. Open the lid and serve.

Rib Eye Steak

Ingredients: Servings: 4 Cooking Time: 20 Mins

Ribeye steak – 2 pounds
Salt and black pepper to taste
Olive oil – 1 tbsp.
For the rub
Sweet paprika – 3 tbsps.
Onion powder – 2 tbsps.
Garlic powder – 2 tbsps.
Brown sugar – 1 tbsp.
Oregano – 2 tbsps. dried
Cumin – 1 tbsp. ground
Rosemary – 1 tbsp. dried

Directions:
Mix cumin, salt, pepper, rosemary, oregano, sugar, garlic powder, onion powder and paprika in a bowl. Stir and rub steak with this mix. Season steak with salt, pepper, and rub again with the oil. Place in the air fryer and cook at 400F for 20 minutes. Flipping once. Slice and serve.

Creamy Pork

Ingredients: Servings: 6 Cooking Time: 22 Mins

Pork meat – 2 pounds, boneless and cubed
Yellow onions – 2, chopped
Olive oil – 1 tbsp.
Garlic – 1 clove, minced
Chicken stock – 3 cups
Sweet paprika – 2 tbsps.
Salt and black pepper to taste
White flour – 2 tbsps.
Sour cream – 1 ½ cups
Dill – 2 tbsps. chopped

Directions:
In a pan, mix pork with oil, salt, and pepper. Mix and place in the air fryer. Cook at 360F for 7 minutes. Add the sour

cream, dill, flour, paprika, stock, garlic, and onion and mix. Cook at 370F for 15 minutes more. Serve.

Lamb Kofta (air Fryer)

Ingredients: Servings: 4 Cooking Time: 10 Mins

1 lb. (454 g) ground lamb
1 tbsp. ras el hanout (North African spice)
½ tsp. ground coriander
1 tsp. onion powder
1 tsp. garlic powder
1 tsp. cumin
2 tbsp. mint, chopped
Salt and ground black pepper, to taste
Special Equipment:
4 bamboo skewers

Directions:
Combine the ground lamb, ras el hanout, coriander, onion powder, garlic powder, cumin, mint, salt, and ground black pepper in a large bowl. Stir to mix well. Transfer the mixture into sausage molds and sit the bamboo skewers in the mixture. Refrigerate for 15 minutes. Preheat the air fryer to 380°F (193°C). Spritz the basket with cooking spray. Place the lamb skewers in the preheated air fryer and spritz with cooking spray. Air fry for 10 minutes or until the lamb is well browned. Flip the lamb skewers halfway through. Serve immediately.

Roasted Char Siew (pork Butt)

Ingredients: Servings: 6 Cooking Time: 25 Mins

1 strip of pork shoulder butt with a good amount of fat marbling
Marinade:
1 tsp. sesame oil
4 tbsp. raw honey
1 tsp. low-sodium dark soy sauce
1 tsp. light soy sauce
1 tbsp. rose wine
2 tbsp. Hoisin sauce

Directions:
1 Preparing the Ingredients. Combine all marinade ingredients together and add to Ziploc bag. Place pork in bag, making sure all sections of pork strip are engulfed in the marinade. Chill 3-24 hours. Take out the strip 30 minutes before planning to cook and preheat your Instant Crisp Air Fryer to 350 degrees. Place foil on small pan and brush with olive oil. Place marinated pork strip onto prepared pan. 2 Air Frying. Close air fryer lid. Set temperature to 350°F, and set time to 20 minutes. Roast 20 minutes. Glaze with marinade every 5-10 minutes. Remove strip and leave to cool a few minutes before slicing.

Air Fryer Bacon Wrapped Hot Dogs

Ingredients: Servings: 4 Cooking Time: 15 Mins

For serving: mustards, ketchup, pickles, jalapenos, onions, and BBQ sauce
4 hot dogs
4 slices of bacon
4 hot dog buns

Directions:
Wrap hot dogs with bacon slices, making sure that they cover the tips of the hot dogs. Arrange in a single layer inside the instant pot duo crisp air fryer basket. Snugly wrap bacon slices around hot dogs and make sure that it covers the tips. Place hot dogs in the air fryer basket. Insert the air fryer basket to the instant pot and attach the air fryer lid. Air-fry at 380 degrees F for 8-10 minutes. If you want your hot dogs with bacon extra crispy, cook at 400 degrees F and adjust cooking time to 6-8 minutes. Serve bacon-wrapped hot dogs in the buns and then air-fry for a minute to keep bread crispy. Insert bacon-wrapped hot dogs in the hot dog buns and air-fry for another minute or until the bread is warm. Serve with your favorite toppings.

Garlic-cumin and Orange Juice Marinated Steak

Ingredients: Servings: 4 Cooking Time: 60 Mins

1 tsp. ground cumin
2 lb. skirt steak, trimmed from excess fat
2 tbsp. lime juice
¼ C. orange juice
2 tbsp. olive oil
4 cloves of garlic, minced
Salt and pepper to taste

Directions:
1 Preparing the Ingredients. Place all ingredients in a mixing bowl and allow to marinate in the fridge for at least 2 hours Preheat the Instant Crisp Air Fryer to 390°F. Place the grill pan accessory in the Instant Crisp Air Fryer. 2 Air Frying. Close air fryer lid. Grill for 15 minutes per batch and flip the beef every 8 minutes for even grilling. Meanwhile, pour the marinade on a saucepan and allow to simmer for 10 minutes or until the sauce thickens. Slice the beef and pour over the sauce.

Spicy Lamb Sirloin Steak

Ingredients: Servings: 4 Cooking Time: 15 Mins

Onion – ½, chopped
Ginger – 4 cubes, chopped
Garlic – 5 cloves, chopped
Garam masala – 1 tsp.
Fennel – 1 tsp. ground
Cinnamon – 1 tsp. ground
Cayenne powder – ½ tsp.
Salt – 1 tsp.
Lamb sirloin – 1-pound, boneless

Directions:
Add all the ingredients in a blender except for the lamb chops and blend until paste. Make strips over the lamb chops. Rub the paste on the chops and mix well. Marinate overnight. Grease the air fryer basket. Place the lamb steaks in the air fryer grease with cooking spray. Bake at 380F for 15 minutes. Flip the meat at the halfway mark. Serve.

Braised Pork

Ingredients: Servings: 4 Cooking Time: 40 Mins

Pork loin roast – 2 pounds, boneless and cubed
Butter – 4 tbsps. melted
Salt and black pepper to taste
Chicken stock – 2 cups
Garlic – 2 cloves, minced
Thyme – 1 tsp. chopped
Thyme spring – 1
Bay leaf – 1
Yellow onion – ½, chopped
White flour – 2 tbsps.

Dry white wine – ½ cup	Red grapes – ½ pound

Directions:

Season pork cubes with salt and pepper. Rub with 2 tbsps. melted butter and put in the air fryer. Cook at 370F for 8 minutes. Meanwhile, heat up a pan with 2 tbsps. of butter over a medium heat. Add onion and garlic, and stir-fry for 2 minutes. Add a bay leaf, flour, thyme, salt, pepper, stock, and wine. Mix well. Bring to a simmer and take off the heat. Add grapes and pork cubes. Cook in the air fryer at 360F for 30 minutes. Serve.

Coconut Chicken Curry

Ingredients: Servings: 4 Cooking Time: 20 Mins

4 Chicken Breasts	2 Red Bell Pepper, sliced
4 tbsp. Red Curry Paste	2 Yellow Bell Pepper, sliced
½ C. Chicken Broth	2 C. Green Beans, cut in half
2 C. Coconut Milk	2 tbsp. Lime Juice
4 tbsp. Sugar	
Salt and Black Pepper to taste	

Directions:

Add the chicken, red curry paste, salt, pepper, coconut milk, broth, and sugar, in the cooker inner pot. Close the pressure lid, secure the pressure valve, and select Pressure mode on High for 15 minutes. Press Start. Once the timer has ended, do a quick pressure release, and open the lid. Remove the chicken onto a cutting board and close the crisping lid. Select Broil mode. Add the bell peppers, green beans, and lime juice. Stir the sauce with a spoon and cook for 4 minutes. Slice the chicken with a knife, pour the sauce and vegetables over and serve warm.

Creamy Burger & Potato Bake

Ingredients: Servings: 3 Cooking Time: 55 Mins

salt to taste	1-1/2 C. peeled and thinly sliced potatoes
freshly ground pepper, to taste	1/2 C. shredded Cheddar cheese
1/2 (10.75 ounce) can condensed cream of mushroom soup	1/4 C. chopped onion
1/2-pound lean ground beef	1/4 C. and 2 tbsp. milk

Directions:

1 Preparing the Ingredients. Lightly grease baking pan of Instant Crisp Air Fryer with cooking spray. Add ground beef. For 10 minutes, cook on 360°F. Stir and crumble halfway through cooking time. Meanwhile, in a bowl, whisk well pepper, salt, milk, onion, and mushroom soup. Mix well. Drain fat off ground beef and transfer beef to a plate. In same Instant Crisp Air Fryer baking pan, layer ½ of potatoes on bottom, then ½ of soup mixture, and then ½ of beef. Repeat process. Cover pan with foil. 2 Air Frying. Close air fryer lid. Cook for 30 minutes. Remove foil and cook for another 15 minutes or until potatoes are tender. Serve and enjoy.

Strawberry-glazed Turkey (air Fryer)

Ingredients: Servings: 2 Cooking Time: 37 Mins

2 lb. (907 g) turkey breast	Salt and ground black pepper, to taste
1 tbsp. olive oil	1 C. fresh strawberries

Directions:

Preheat the air fryer to 375°F (191°C). Rub the turkey bread with olive oil on a clean work surface, then sprinkle with salt and ground black pepper. Transfer the turkey in the preheated air fryer and air fry for 30 minutes or until the internal temperature of the turkey reaches at least 165°F (74°C). flip the turkey breast halfway through. Meanwhile, put the strawberries in a food processor and pulse until smooth. When the frying of the turkey is complete, spread the puréed strawberries over the turkey and fry for 7 more minutes. Serve immediately.

Pork Loin with Potatoes

Ingredients: Servings: 2 Cooking Time: 25 Mins

1 tsp. fresh parsley, chopped	2 lb. pork loin
2 large red potatoes, chopped	½ tsp. red pepper flakes, crushed
½ tsp. garlic powder	Salt and freshly ground black pepper, to taste

Directions:

1 Preparing the Ingredients. In a large bowl, add all ingredients except glaze and toss to coat well. Preheat the Instant Crisp Air Fryer to 325 degrees F. Place the loin in the Instant Crisp Air Fryer basket. Arrange the potatoes around pork loin. 2 Air Frying. Close air fryer lid. Cook for about 25 minutes.

Crack Chicken with Bacon (pressure Cook)

Ingredients: Servings: 2 Cooking Time: 15 Mins

½ C. grass-fed bone broth	2 oz. (57 g) cream cheese, softened
½ lb. (227 g) boneless, skinless chicken breasts	3 slices bacon, cooked, chopped into small pieces
¼ C. tbsp. keto-friendly ranch dressing	½ C. shredded full-fat Cheddar cheese

Directions:

Add the bone broth, chicken, cream cheese, and ranch dressing to your Instant Pot and stir to combine. Secure the lid. Press the Pressure Cook and set the cooking time for 15 minutes at High Pressure. When the timer goes off, do a quick pressure release. Carefully open the lid. Add the bacon and cheese and stir until the cheese has melted. Serve.

Air Fried Herb Rack of Lamb

Ingredients: Servings: 2 Cooking Time: 20 Mins

1-pound whole rack of lamb	2 tsp. garlic, minced
2 tbsp. rosemary, dried	½ tsp. salt
1 tbsp. thyme, dried	½ tsp. pepper
	4 tbsp. olive oil

Directions:

Wash the lamb and pat dry. In a small bowl, mix all the herbs along with olive oil and keep it aside. Rub the herb mixture over the lamb rack and coat it thoroughly. Place the lamb in the air fryer basket and put it in the inner pot of instant pot air fryer. Close the crisp lid and set the temperature at 360° f in the air fry mode. Set the timer for 10 minutes. Press start to begin the cooking. Halfway through the cooking, open the crisp lid and flip the lamb for even cooking. After flipping, close the crisp lid, so that the appliance can automatically resume cooking for the remaining period. Once done, remove it from the air fryer and serve hot.

Chimichurri Skirt Steak

Ingredients: Servings: 2 Cooking Time: 8 Mins

2 x 8 oz Skirt Steak
1 C. Finely Chopped Parsley
1/4 C. Finely Chopped Mint
2 Tbsp Fresh Oregano (Washed & finely chopped)
3 Finely Chopped Cloves of Garlic
1 Tsp Red Pepper Flakes (Crushed)
1 Tbsp Ground Cumin
1 Tsp Cayenne Pepper
2 Tsp Smoked Paprika
1 Tsp Salt
1/4 Tsp Pepper
3/4 C. Oil
3 Tbsp Red Wine Vinegar

Directions:

1 Preparing the Ingredients. Throw all the ingredients in a bowl (besides the steak) and mix well. Put 1/4 C. of the mixture in a plastic baggie with the steak and leave in the fridge overnight (2–24hrs). 2 Air Frying. Leave the bag out at room temperature for at least 30 min before popping into the Instant Crisp Air Fryer. Preheat for a minute or two to 390° F before cooking until med-rare (8–10 min). Put 2 Tbsp of the chimichurri mix on top of each steak before serving.

Easy Chicken Fingers (air Fryer)

Ingredients: Servings: 12 Cooking Time: 30 Mins

1/2 C. all-purpose flour
2 C. panko bread crumbs
3 boneless and skinless chicken breasts, each cut into 4 strips
2 tbsp. canola oil
1 large egg
Kosher salt and freshly ground black pepper, to taste
Cooking spray

Directions:

Preheat the air fryer to 360°F (182°C). Spritz the air fryer basket with cooking spray. Pour the flour in a large bowl. Combine the panko and canola oil on a shallow dish. Whisk the egg in a separate bowl. Rub the chicken strips with salt and ground black pepper on a clean work surface, then dip the chicken in the bowl of flour. Shake the excess off and dunk the chicken strips in the bowl of whisked egg, then roll the strips over the panko to coat well. Arrange 4 strips in the air fryer basket each time and air fry for 10 minutes or until crunchy and lightly browned. Flip the strips halfway through. Repeat with remaining ingredients. Serve immediately.

Oregano-paprika On Breaded Pork

Ingredients: Servings: 4 Cooking Time: 30 Mins

1/4 tsp. dry mustard
1/2 tsp. black pepper
1/2 tsp. cayenne pepper
1/2 tsp. garlic powder
1/4 C. water
1/2 tsp. salt
1 C. panko breadcrumbs
1 egg, beaten
2 tsp. oregano
4 lean pork chops
4 tsp. paprika

Directions:

1 Preparing the Ingredients. Preheat the Instant Crisp Air Fryer to 390°F. Pat dry the pork chops. In a mixing bowl, combine the egg and water. Then set aside. In another bowl, combine the rest of the Ingredients. Dip the pork chops in the egg mixture and dredge in the flour mixture. 2 Air Frying. Place in the Instant Crisp Air Fryer basket, close air fryer lid and cook for 25 to 30 minutes until golden.

Lamb Casserole

Ingredients: Servings: 6-8 Cooking Time: 35 Mins

1 lb. of baby potatoes
1 lb. rack of lamb
2 carrots
1 large onion
1-2 tsp. of salt depending on the salt content of the chicken stock
2 medium size tomatoes
2 C. of chicken stock
3-4 large cloves of garlic
2 stalks of celery
2 tsp. of cumin powder
2 tsp. of Paprika
A pinch of dried rosemary
A pinch of dried oregano leaves
2 tbsp. of ketchup
3 tbsp. of sherry or red wine
A splash of beer if you have one in hand

Directions:

Preparing the Ingredients. Dice the tomatoes, onion, and garlic, cut potatoes, and carrots, cut the rack of lamb into two halves. Put all the ingredients, in the Instant Crisp Air Fryer. High pressure for 35 minutes. Lock the pressure cooking lid on the Instant Crisp Air Fryer and then cook for 35 minutes. To get 35-minutes cook time, press "Pressure" button and adjust the time. Pressure Release. Use Natural-Release Method for 10 minutes, and then Quick-Release. Remove the lid from the Instant Crisp Air Fryer. Close air fryer lid. Select AIR FRY, set temperature to 400°F, and set time to 15 minutes. Check after 10 minutes, cooking for an additional 5 minutes if dish needs more browning. Serve and Enjoy

Pulled Bbq Beef Sandwiches

Ingredients: Servings: 2-4 Cooking Time: 35 Mins

2 lb. – Beef of choice
2 cps – Water
4 cps – Finely shredded Cabbage (the secret ingredient and you'll never know it's in there.)
1/2 C. – of your favorite BBQ Sauce
1 C. – Ketchup
1/3 C. – Worcestershire Sauce
1 tblsp – Horse Radish
1 tblsp – mustard

Directions:
Preparing the Ingredients. Add and stir in ingredients to your Instant Crisp Air Fryer. High pressure for 35 minutes. Lock the pressure Cooking lid on the Instant Crisp Air Fryer and then cook for 35 minutes. To get 35-minutes cook time, press "Pressure" button and adjust the time. Pressure Release. Use natural release method. Finish the dish. Remove the lid from the Instant Crisp Air Fryer. Close air fryer lid. Select AIR FRY, set temperature to 390°F, and set time to 15 minutes. Check after 10 minutes, cooking for an additional 5 minutes if dish needs more browning. Set the beef aside. Set the Instant Crisp Air Fryer to a "Sauté" mode, Sauté the sauce until it reaches the desired consistency. Serve and Enjoy.

Air Fryer Pork Belly Bites

Ingredients: Servings: 4 Cooking Time: 20 Mins

1 lb. pork belly, rinsed and patted dry
1 tbsp. Worcestershire sauce or soy sauce
½ tsp. garlic powder
Black pepper and salt to taste
Optional: ¼ C. BBQ sauce

Directions:
Cleanse pork belly and remove the skin if any. Cut into ¾-inch cubes and place them in a bowl. Add seasonings and spread pork belly cubes in the air fryer basket. Put the air fryer inside the instant pot duo crisp. Attach the air fryer lid and air fry at 400 degrees F for 10-18 minutes. Shake and flip the air fryer basket for even coating twice through the cooking process, depending on desired crispiness. If you want it to be crispier, extend the cooking time up to 20 minutes. Drizzle with BBQ sauce if desired.

Bourbon Bacon Burger In the Air Fryer

Ingredients: Servings: 2 Cooking Time: 25 Mins

¾ lb. minced beef
3 strips bacon, cut into half
2 kaiser rolls
4 tbsp. barbeque sauce
¼ tsp. paprika
2 tbsp. mayonnaise
1 tsp. ground black pepper, fresh
1 tbsp. bourbon
1 tbsp. onion, finely chopped
2 tbsp. brown sugar
½ tsp. salt
½ lettuce, finely chopped (serving
1 tomato, chopped (serving

Directions:
In a small bowl, combine the bourbon and brown sugar. Brush this mixture over the bacon strips on both sides. Place the marinated bacon strips in the air fryer basket. Put the air fryer basket in the inner pot of the instant pot air fryer. Close the crisp cover. In the air fry mode, select the temperature to 390°f and set the timer to 10 minutes. Press start to begin the cooking. Halfway through the cooking, open the air fryer, and flip the bacon. Sprinkle the bourbon mixture on the bacon, if required and cook for the remaining period. While the cooking in progress, make the burger patties by combining the ground beef, bbq sauce, onion, salt, and pepper in a large bowl. Combine it thoroughly and make 2 patties out of the mixture. Remove the cooked bacon into a bowl and start the cooking process for burger patties. Place the patties in the air fryer basket and put in the inner pot of the instant pot air fryer. Close the crisp cover. In the air fry mode, select temperature 370°f and set the timer for 20 minutes. Press start to begin the cooking process. Now let us make the burger sauce by mixing bbq sauce, paprika, mayonnaise, and pepper in a bowl. Once the patties cooked, top it with cheese and air fry for one more minute. Spread the sauce in the kaiser rolls, place these burgers on rolls and top with the bourbon bacon, tomato, and lettuce. Serve it with additional sauces if needed.

Tuscan Air Fried Veal Loin (air Fryer)

Ingredients: Servings: 3 Cooking Time: 12 Mins

1½ tsp. crushed fennel seeds
1 tbsp. minced fresh rosemary leaves
1 tbsp. minced garlic
1½ tsp. lemon zest
1½ tsp. salt
½ tsp. red pepper flakes
2 tbsp. olive oil
3 (10-ounce / 284-g) bone-in veal loin, about ½ inch thick

Directions:
Combine all the ingredients, except for the veal loin, in a large bowl. Stir to mix well. Dunk the loin in the mixture and press to submerge. Wrap the bowl in plastic and refrigerate for at least an hour to marinate. Preheat the air fryer to 400°F (204°C). Arrange the veal loin in the preheated air fryer and air fry for 12 minutes for medium-rare, or until it reaches your desired doneness. Serve immediately.

Roast Beef

Ingredients: Servings: 6 Cooking Time: 40 Mins

2.5-pound Beef Roast (can go up to 4 pounds)
1 Tablespoon Olive Oil
Seasoning to taste (Montreal Steak seasoning)

Directions:
Tie the roast to make it fit in the Instant Pot Duo Crisp Air Fryer. Rub the roast with some olive oil. Add the seasoning as per your preference. Place the roast in the Air Fryer basket. Close the lid and select the Air fry option. Air Fry the beef at 360°F for approximately 15 minutes per lb. for medium-rare beef. Let the roast rest for around 5 minutes and serve.

Ginger Beef Curry

Ingredients: Servings: 4 Cooking Time: 33 Mins

1 ½ lb Beef Brisket, cut in cubes
1 tbsp. Olive Oil
2 cloves Garlic, minced
¼-inch Ginger, peeled and sliced
2 Bay Leaves
2 Star Anises
1 large Carrot, chopped
1 medium Onion, chopped
2 tbsp. Red Curry Paste
1 C. Milk
1 Potato, peeled and chopped
1 tbsp. Sugar
2 tsp. Oyster Sauce
2 tsp. Flour
3 tbsp. Water

Directions:
Select Sear/Sauté mode. Heat oil, add garlic, ginger, and red curry paste. Stir-fry them for 1 minute. Stir in onion and beef.

Cook for 4 minutes. Add the carrots, bay leaves, potato, star anises, sugar, and water. Stir. Close the lid, secure the pressure valve, and select Pressure on High for 25 minutes. Press Start. Once the timer goes off, do a quick pressure release. In a bowl, add the flour and 4 tbsps. of milk. Mix well with a spoon and pour it in the pot along with the oyster sauce and remaining milk. Stir it gently not to break the potato. Close the crisping lid and cook on Broil mode for about 3 minutes, until the sauce thickens and meat is tender. After, turn off the pot. Spoon the sauce into soup bowls and serve with a side of rice.

Easy Pork Roast

Ingredients: Servings: 6 Cooking Time: 8 Hours

3 lbs pork shoulder roast, boneless and cut into 4 pieces
1/2 tbsp. cumin
1 tbsp. fresh oregano
1 C. of grapefruit juice
Pepper
Salt

Directions:
Season meat with pepper and salt and place into the inner pot of instant pot duo crisp. Add oregano, cumin, and grapefruit juice into the blender and blend until smooth. Pour blended mixture over meat. Seal the pot with pressure cooking lid and select slow cook mode and cook on low for 8 hours. Remove meat from pot and shred using a fork. Return shredded meat into the pot and stir well. Serve and enjoy.

Tasty & Spicy Lamb

Ingredients: Servings: 4 Cooking Time: 35 Mins

1 lb lamb, cut into pieces
2 tbsp. lemon juice
1/2 C. fresh cilantro, chopped
2 onions, chopped
2 C. chicken stock
1 C. of coconut milk
3 tbsp. butter
1 C. grape tomatoes, chopped
1/2 tbsp. cumin powder
1 1/2 tsp. turmeric
2 tsp. garam masala
2 1/2 tbsp. chili powder
2 tbsp. apple cider
1 tsp. salt

Directions:
Set instant pot on sauté mode. Season meat with pepper and salt and place into the pot. Cook meat for 5 minutes. Add remaining ingredients and stir well. Seal pot with lid and cook on manual high pressure for 15 minutes. Once done then allow to release pressure naturally for 10 minutes then release using the quick-release method. Open the lid. Stir and serve.

Reuben Egg Rolls

Ingredients: Servings: 6 Cooking Time: 20 Mins

Swiss cheese
Sliced deli corned beef
Can of sauerkraut
Egg roll wrappers

Directions:
1 Preparing the Ingredients. Cut corned beef and Swiss cheese into thin slices. Drain sauerkraut and dry well. Take egg roll wrapper and moisten edges with water. Stack center with corned beef and cheese till you reach desired thickness. Top off with sauerkraut. Fold corner closest to you over the edge of filling. Bring up sides and glue with water. Add to the Instant Crisp Air Fryer basket and spritz with olive oil. 2 Air Frying. Close air fryer lid. Set temperature to 400°F, and set time to 4 minutes. Cook 4 minutes at 400 degrees, then flip and cook another 4 minutes.

Herbed Roast Beef

Ingredients: Servings: 6 Cooking Time: 20 Mins

½ tsp. fresh rosemary
1 tsp. dried thyme
¼ tsp. pepper
1 tsp. salt
4-pound top round roast beef
tsp. olive oil

Directions:
1 Preparing the Ingredients. Ensure your Instant Crisp Air Fryer is preheated to 360 degrees. Rub olive oil all over beef. Mix rosemary, thyme, pepper, and salt together and proceed to rub all sides of beef with spice mixture. Place seasoned beef into Instant Crisp Air Fryer. 2 Air Frying. Close air fryer lid. Set temperature to 360°F, and set time to 20 minutes. Allow roast to rest 10 minutes before slicing to serve.

Breaded Spam Steaks

Ingredients: Servings: 2 Cooking Time: 5 Mins

12 Oz Can Luncheon Meat
1 Cup All Purpose Flour
2 Eggs, beaten
2 Cups Italian Seasoned Breadcrumbs

Directions:
1 Preparing the Ingredients. Preheat the Instant Crisp Air Fryer to 380 degrees. Cut the luncheon meat into 1/4 inch slices. Gently press the luncheon meat slices into the flour to coat and shake off the excess flour. Dip into the beaten egg, then press into breadcrumbs. 2 Air Frying. Place the battered slices into the Instant Crisp Air Fryer tray, close air fryer lid and cook for 3 to 5 minutes until golden brown. Serve with chili or tomato sauce

Smoky Paprika Pork and Vegetable Kabobs (air Fryer)

Ingredients: Servings: 4 Cooking Time: 15 Mins

1 lb. (454 g) pork tenderloin, cubed
1 tsp. smoked paprika
Salt and ground black pepper, to taste
1 green bell pepper, cut into chunks
1 zucchini, cut into chunks
1 red onion, sliced
1 tbsp. oregano
Cooking spray
Special Equipment:
Small bamboo skewers, soaked in water for 20 minutes to keep them from burning while cooking

Directions:
Preheat the air fryer to 350°F (177°C). Spritz the air fryer basket with cooking spray. Add the pork to a bowl and season with the smoked paprika, salt and black pepper. Thread the seasoned pork cubes and vegetables alternately onto the soaked skewers. Arrange the skewers in the prepared air fryer basket and spray with cooking spray. Air fry for 15 minutes, or until the

pork is well browned and the vegetables are tender, flipping once halfway through. Transfer the skewers to the serving dishes and sprinkle with oregano. Serve hot.

Pigs In Blankets

Ingredients: Servings: 9 Cooking Time: 15 Mins

3 Large Brazilian Sausages
9 Back Bacon
Salt & Pepper

Directions:
Chop the sausages into three equal sizes so that they become mini sausages. Now that you have nine equal-sized pieces of sausage, wrap them in the bacon so that each piece of sausage has one rasher of bacon. Place them into the Instant Pot Duo Crisp Air Fryer Basket. Close the Air Fryer lid and cook at 350°F for 15 minutes and then sprinkle with salt and pepper Serve hot.

Air Fried Chicken Wings with Buffalo Sauce

Ingredients: Servings: 6 Cooking Time: 20 Mins

16 chicken drumettes (party wings)
Chicken seasoning or rub, to taste
1 tsp. garlic powder
Ground black pepper, to taste
¼ C. buffalo wings sauce
Cooking spray

Directions:
Preheat the air fryer to 400°F (204°C). Spritz the air fryer basket with cooking spray. Rub the chicken wings with chicken seasoning, garlic powder, and ground black pepper on a clean work surface. Arrange the chicken wings in the preheated air fryer. Spritz with cooking spray. Air fry for 10 minutes or until lightly browned. Shake the basket halfway through. Transfer the chicken wings in a large bowl, then pour in the buffalo wings sauce and toss to coat well. Put the wings back to the air fryer and cook for an additional 7 minutes. Serve immediately.

Saucy Beef & Broccoli

Ingredients: Servings: 4 Cooking Time: 30 Mins

2 lb Chuck Roast, boneless and cut into thin strips
4 cloves Garlic, minced
1 tbsp. Olive Oil
7 C. Broccoli Florets
1 C. Beef Broth
1 tbsp. Cornstarch
¾ C. Soy Sauce
Salt to taste

Directions:
Open the lid of cooker, and select Sear/Sauté mode. Add the olive oil, and once heated, add the beef and minced garlic. Cook the meat until brown. Stir in soy sauce and beef broth. Close the lid, secure the pressure valve, and select Pressure mode on High pressure for 10 minutes. Press Start to start cooking. Once the timer has ended, do a quick pressure release and remove the meat and set aside. Use a soup spoon to fetch out a quarter of the liquid into a bowl, add the cornstarch, and mix it until it is well dissolved. Pour the starch mixture into the pot and place the reversible rack. Place the broccoli florets on it and seal the pressure lid. Select Steam mode on LOW for 5 minutes. When ready, do a quick pressure release and open the lid. Remove the rack, stir the sauce, add the meat and close the crisping lid. Cook for 5 minutes on Broil mode. the sauce should be thick enough when you finish cooking. Dish the beef broccoli sauce into a serving bowl and serve with a side of cooked pasta.

Blue Cheese Chicken Soup

Ingredients: Servings: 4 Cooking Time: 30 Mins

4 Chicken Breasts, boneless and skinless
½ C. Hot Sauce
2 large White Onion, finely chopped
2 C. finely chopped Celery
1 tbsp. Olive Oil
1 tsp. dried Thyme
3 C. Chicken Broth
1 tsp. Garlic Powder
½ C. crumbled Blue Cheese + extra for serving
4 oz Cream Cheese, cubed in small pieces
Salt and Pepper, to taste

Directions:
Put the chicken on a clean flat surface and season with pepper and salt. Set aside. Select Sear/Sauté mode on High. Heat in olive oil, add onion and celery. Sauté them, constant stirring, until they are nice and soft, for about 5 minutes. Then, add garlic powder and thyme. Stir and cook for about a minute, and add the chicken, hot sauce, and chicken broth. Season with salt and pepper. Close the pressure lid, secure the pressure valve, and select Pressure mode on High for 15 minutes. Press Start. Meanwhile, put the blue cheese and cream cheese in a bowl, and use a fork to smash them together. Set the resulting mixture aside. Once the timer has ended, do a natural pressure release for 5 minutes. Take out the chicken on to a flat surface with a slotted spoon and use two forks to shred them. Return shredded chicken to the pot, close the crisping lid, select Broil mode and cook for 5 minutes. Add the cheese to the pot and stir until is slightly incorporated into the sauce. Sprinkle the remaining cheese over the soup and serve with sliced baguette.

Pork Carnitas

Ingredients: Servings: 6 Cooking Time: 9 Hours

3 lbs pork shoulder
3 tsp. cumin
2 orange juice
1/2 C. water
2 tsp. olive oil
2 tsp. ground coriander
2 tsp. salt

Directions:
Place the pork shoulder into the inner pot of instant pot duo crisp. Pour remaining ingredients over the pork shoulder. Seal the pot with pressure cooking lid and select slow cooker mode and cook on low for 9 hours. Remove meat from pot and shred using a fork. Serve and enjoy.

Beef Taco Fried Egg Rolls

Ingredients: Servings: 8 Cooking Time: 12 Mins

1 tsp. cilantro
2 chopped garlic cloves
1 C. shredded Mexican cheese
½ packet taco seasoning
1 tbsp. olive oil
½ can cilantro lime rotel
½ chopped onion
16 egg roll wrappers
1 lb. lean ground beef

Directions:

1 Preparing the Ingredients. Ensure that your Instant Crisp Air Fryer is preheated to 400 degrees. Add onions and garlic to a skillet, cooking till fragrant. Then add taco seasoning, pepper, salt, and beef, cooking till beef is broke up into tiny pieces and cooked thoroughly. Add rotel and stir well. Lay out egg wrappers and brush with water to soften a bit. Load wrappers with beef filling and add cheese to each. Fold diagonally to close and use water to secure edges. Brush filled egg wrappers with olive oil and add to the Instant Crisp Air Fryer. 2 Air Frying. Close air fryer lid. Set temperature to 400°F, and set time to 8 minutes. Cook 8 minutes, flip, and cook another 4 minutes. Served sprinkled with cilantro.

Traditional Beef Taco Soup

Ingredients: Servings: 8 Cooking Time: 20 Mins

2 tbsp. Olive Oil
6 Green Bell pepper, diced
2 medium Yellow Onion, chopped
3 lb Ground Beef, grass fed
Salt and Black Pepper to taste
3 tbsp. Chili Powder
2 tbsp. Cumin Powder
2 tsp. Paprika
1 tsp. Garlic Powder
1 tsp. Cinnamon
1 tsp. Onion Powder
6 C. chopped Tomatoes
½ C. chopped Green Chilies
3 C. Bone Broth
3 C. Milk
Topping:
Chopped Jalapenos, Cilantro and Green Onions, Sliced Avocados, Lime Juice

Next, add the chili powder, cumin powder, black pepper, paprika, cinnamon, garlic powder, onion powder, and green chilies. Give them a good stir.
Top with tomatoes, milk, and bone broth. Close the lid, secure the pressure valve, and select Pressure mode on High for 20 minutes. Press Start. Once the timer has ended, do a quick pressure release.
Adjust the taste with salt and pepper. Dish the taco soup into serving bowls and add the toppings. Serve warm with a side of tortillas.

Directions:

Select Sear/Sauté mode and set High on your cooker. Pour in the oil, once it has heated, add the yellow onion and green peppers. Sauté until they are soft for about 5 minutes. Include the ground beef, stir the

Classic Meatballs with Tomato Sauce

Ingredients: Servings: 6 Cooking Time: 11 Mins

2 lb Ground Beef
1 C. Breadcrumbs
1 Onion, finely chopped
2 cloves Garlic, minced
Salt and Pepper, to taste
1 tsp. dried Oregano
3 tbsp. Milk
1 C. Water
1 C. grated Parmesan Cheese
2 Eggs, cracked into a bowl
4 C. tomato Sauce
1 tbsp. Olive Oil

Directions:

In a bowl, add beef, onion, breadcrumbs, parmesan, eggs, garlic, milk, salt, oregano, and pepper. Mix well with hands and shape bite-size balls. Open the pot, and add the tomato sauce, water and the meatballs. Close the lid, secure the pressure valve, and select Steam mode on High pressure for 6 minutes. Press Start. Once the timer is done, do a natural pressure release for 5 minutes, then do a quick pressure release to let out any extra steam, and open the lid. Dish the meatball sauce over cooked pasta and serve.

Lamb Shanks with Pancetta

Ingredients: Servings: 4 Cooking Time: 60 Mins

2 tbsp. olive oil
One 6-ounce pancetta chunk, chopped
Four 12-ounce lamb shanks
One 28-ounce can diced tomatoes, drained (about 3½ cups)
1 oz. dried mushrooms, preferably porcini, crumbled
1 small yellow onion, chopped
3 tbsp. packed celery leaves, minced
2 tbsp. minced chives
2 C. dry, light white wine, such as Sauvignon Blanc
2 tbsp. all-purpose flour
½ tsp. ground black pepper

Directions:

Preparing the Ingredients. Heat the oil in the Instant Crisp Air Fryer, turned to the "sauté" function. Add the pancetta and brown well, about 6 minutes, stirring often. Use a slotted spoon to transfer the pancetta to a large bowl. Add two of the shanks to the cooker; brown on all sides, turning occasionally, about 8 minutes. Transfer them to the bowl and repeat with the remaining shanks. Add the onion to the pot; cook, often stirring, until softened, about 4 minutes. Stir in the tomatoes, dried mushroom crumbles, celery leaves, and chives. Cook until bubbling, about minutes, stirring often. Whisk the wine, flour, and pepper in a medium bowl until the flour dissolves; stir this mixture into the sauce in the pot. Cook until thickened and bubbling, about 1 minute. Return the shanks, pancetta, and their juices to the cooker. High pressure for 60 minutes. Close the pressure cooking lid and the pressure valve and then cook for 60 minutes. To get 60-minutes cook time, press "Pressure" button and use the Time Adjustment button to adjust the cook time to 60 minutes. Turn off the Instant Crisp Air Fryer or unplug it, so it doesn't jump to its keep-warm setting. Pressure Release. Let its pressure return to normal naturally, 20 to 30 minutes. Finish the dish. Remove the lid from the Instant Crisp Air Fryer. Close air fryer lid. Select AIR FRY, set temperature to 375°F, and set time to 18 minutes. Check after 10 minutes, cooking for an additional 8 minutes if dish needs more browning. Transfer a shank to each serving bowl. Skim any surface fat from the sauce with a flatware spoon. Ladle the sauce and vegetables over the lamb shanks.

Tuscan Pork Chops

Ingredients: Servings: 4 Cooking Time: 10 Mins

1/4 C. all-purpose flour
3/4 tsp. seasoned
1 tsp. salt
3 to 4 garlic cloves
1/3 C. balsamic

pepper
4 (1-inch-thick) boneless pork chops
1 tbsp. olive oil
vinegar
1/3 C. chicken broth
3 plum tomatoes, seeded and diced
1 tbsp. capers

Directions:
Preparing the Ingredients. Combine flour, salt, and pepper Press pork chops into flour mixture on both sides until evenly covered. Air Frying. Lock the air fryer lid. Cook in your Instant Crisp Air Fryer at 360 degrees for 14 minutes, flipping half way through. While the pork chops cook, warm olive oil in a medium skillet. Add garlic and sauté for 1 minute; then mix in vinegar and chicken broth. Add capers and tomatoes and turn to high heat. Bring the sauce to a boil, stirring regularly, then add pork chops, cooking for one minute. Remove from heat and cover for about 5 minutes to allow the pork to absorb some of the sauce; serve hot.

Mini Egg Bake

Ingredients: Servings: 6 Cooking Time: 30 Mins

1 lb. ground turkey sausage
½ C. of half-and-half
½ C. of cheddar cheese, shredded
1 small broccoli head, cut into florets
1 red bell pepper, diced
2 large eggs
1 medium onion, chopped
2 cloves garlic, minced
1 tbsp. olive oil
Salt and pepper to taste
A dash of hot sauce to serve

Directions:
Hit the SAUTE setting and add the oil. Once hot, sauté the sausage and let them brown for about 2-3 minutes. Add the onions and garlic; sauté for another 2 minutes or until the onions are translucent. Next, add the broccoli and red bell peppers. Cook for another 3-4 minutes, occasionally stirring until the broccoli florets are slightly tender. Turn off the SAUTE mode and transfer the sausage-veggie mixture to a large plate. Break the eggs in a large bowl. Add the half-and-half, salt, and pepper then whisk until the mixture is smooth. Grease six 8-ounce ramekins. Add about a quarter C. of the sausage mixture into each ramekin and cover them with egg mixture. Sprinkle about 1½ tbsp. of shredded cheddar cheese on top of each ramekin. Set the tall trivet inside the steel pot of your instant pot and place the fryer basket on top of it. Put three ramekins in the basket (cook in two batches as needed). Attach the air fryer lid and air fry at 320 degrees F for 10 minutes. Repeat step 8 and 9 with the remaining ramekins. Garnish with green onions and drizzle with hot sauce before serving.

Italian Pork Roast with Herb Gravy

Ingredients: Servings: 4 Cooking Time: 20 Mins

2 lb Pork Roast, cut into 2-inch slabs
1 tbsp. Italian Seasoning
1 tsp. Red Wine Vinegar
2 cloves Garlic, minced
Salt and Pepper, to taste
1 tbsp. Ranch Dressing
1 small Onion, chopped
1 tbsp. Olive Oil
2 tsp. Onion Powder
½ tsp. Paprika
2 C. Beef Broth
2 tbsp. Cornstarch
Chopped parsley to garnish

Directions:
Season the pork roast with salt and pepper, and set aside. In a bowl, add Italian seasoning, ranch dressing, red wine vinegar, garlic, onion powder, and paprika. Open the pot, select Sear/Sauté, and heat the oil. Sauté the onion, until translucent. Pour gravy mixture and broth over and add pork. Close the lid, secure the pressure valve, and select Pressure mode on High pressure for 15 minutes. Press Start to start cooking. Once the timer has ended, do a quick pressure release, and open the pot. Remove the pork roast with a slotted spoon onto a serving plate. Mix the cornstarch with the 2 tbsp. water in a bowl and add it to the sauce. Select Sear/Sauté. Stir and cook for 4 minutes, until thickens. Once the gravy is ready, spoon the sauce over the pork. Garnish with parsley and serve.

Pork Tenderloin In the Air Fryer

Ingredients: Servings: 6 Cooking Time: 18 Mins

1½ lb. pork tenderloin
1 tbsp. olive oil
¼ tsp. salt
¼ tsp. ground black pepper
¼ tsp. garlic powder

Directions:
Wash and pat dry the pork tenderloin. In a small bowl, mix the olive oil, black pepper, and garlic powder well and add salt as needed. Rub the seasoning mixture over the tenderloin. Transfer the meat in the air fryer basket. Place the air fryer basket in the inner pot of the Instant Pot Air Fryer. Close the crisp cover. In the ROAST mode, set the timer to 25 minutes. the default heat will show 400°F, which you cannot change in the smart cooking option. Press START to begin the cooking. Flip the tenderloin midway for even cooking. After cooking, allow the meat to cool down before you can slice and serve.

Cheeseburger Egg Rolls

Ingredients: Servings: 6 Cooking Time: 7 Mins

6 egg roll wrappers
6 chopped dill pickle chips
1 tbsp. yellow mustard
3 tbsp. cream cheese
3 tbsp. shredded cheddar cheese
½ C. chopped onion
½ C. chopped bell pepper
¼ tsp. onion powder
¼ tsp. garlic powder
8 oz. of raw lean ground beef

Directions:
1 Preparing the Ingredients. In a skillet, add seasonings, beef, onion, and bell pepper. Stir and crumble beef till fully cooked, and vegetables are soft. Take skillet off the heat and add cream cheese, mustard, and cheddar cheese, stirring till melted. Pour beef mixture into a bowl and fold in pickles. Lay out egg wrappers and place 1/6th of beef mixture into each one. Moisten egg roll wrapper edges with water. Fold sides to the middle and seal with water. Repeat with all other egg rolls. Place rolls into Instant Crisp Air Fryer, one batch at a time. 2 Air Frying. Close air fryer lid. Set temperature to 392°F, and set time to 7 minutes.

Beef with Peas and Mushrooms

Ingredients: Servings: 2 Cooking Time: 22 Mins

Beef steaks – 2, cut into strips
Salt and black pepper to taste
White mushrooms – 8 ounces, halved
Snow peas – 7 ounces
Yellow onion – 1, cut into rings
Soy sauce – 2 tbsps.
Olive oil – 1 tsp.

Directions:
In a bowl, mix soy sauce, and olive oil, and whisk. Add beef strips and coat. In another bowl, mix mushrooms, onion, snow peas with salt, pepper, and the oil. Toss well. Place in pan and cook in the air fryer at 350F for 16 minutes. Add beef strips to the pan as well and cook at 400F for 6 minutes more. Serve.

Rosemary Turkey Breast (air Fryer)

Ingredients: Servings: 6 Cooking Time: 30 Mins

½ tsp. dried rosemary
2 minced garlic cloves
2 tsp. salt
1 tsp. ground black pepper
2½ lb. (1.1 kg) turkey breast
¼ C. olive oil
¼ C. pure maple syrup
1 tbsp. stone-ground brown mustard
1 tbsp. melted vegan butter

Directions:
Combine the rosemary, garlic, salt, ground black pepper, and olive oil in a large bowl. Stir to mix well. Dunk the turkey breast in the mixture and wrap the bowl in plastic. Refrigerate for 2 hours to marinate. Remove the bowl from the refrigerator and let sit for half an hour before cooking. Preheat the air fryer to 400°F (204°C). Spritz the air fryer basket with cooking spray. Remove the turkey from the marinade and place in the preheated air fry and air fry for 20 minutes or until well browned. Flip the breast halfway through. Meanwhile, combine the remaining ingredients in a small bowl. Stir to mix well. Pour half of the butter mixture over the turkey breast in the air fryer and air fry for 10 more minutes. Flip the breast and pour the remaining half of butter mixture over halfway through. Transfer the turkey on a plate and slice to serve.

Pork Fajitas

Ingredients: Servings: 6 Cooking Time: 20 Mins

1 3/4 lbs. pork loin sirloin chops, cut into strips
1 onion, sliced
2 bell pepper, cut into strips
1 1/2 tbsp. Italian seasoning
1/2 C. chicken stock
2 tbsp. fresh lime juice
oz salsa

Directions:
Add all ingredients into the instant pot and stir well. Seal pot with lid and cook on manual high pressure for 1 minute. Once done then allow to release pressure naturally for 10 minutes then release using the quick-release method. Open the lid. Stir and serve.

Crispy Air Fryer Bacon

Ingredients: Servings: 8 Cooking Time: 10 Mins

¾ lb. bacon, thick-cut pieces

Directions:
Place the bacon strips in the air fryer basket, don't overlap them. Put the air fryer basket in the inner pot of the instant pot air fryer. Close the crisp lid. Under the broil mode, set the timer for 10 minutes. the default temperature will read at 400°f. Press start to begin the cooking. Check the air fryer halfway to flip the bacon strips. You can open the crisp lid (this will pause the cooking procedure and close the crisp cover once you have flipped the meat. the cooking will resume as soon as you close the lid. Once the bacon is ready, serve hot.

Crispy Mongolian Beef

Ingredients: Servings: 6 Cooking Time: 10 Mins

Olive oil
½ C. almond flour
2 lb. beef tenderloin or beef chuck, sliced into strips
Sauce:
½ C. chopped green onion
1 tsp. red chili flakes
1 tsp. almond flour
½ C. brown sugar
1 tsp. hoisin sauce
½ C. water
½ C. rice vinegar
½ C. low-sodium soy sauce
1 tbsp. chopped garlic
1 tbsp. finely chopped ginger
2 tbsp. olive oil

Directions:
1 Preparing the Ingredients. Toss strips of beef in almond flour, ensuring they are coated well. Add to the Instant Crisp Air Fryer.
2 Air Frying. Close air fryer lid. Set temperature to 300°F, and set time to 10 minutes, and cook 10 minutes at 300 degrees. Meanwhile, add all sauce ingredients to the pan and bring to a boil. Mix well. Add beef strips to the sauce and cook 2 minutes. Serve over cauliflower rice!

Garlicky Lamb

Ingredients: Servings: 6 Cooking Time: 17 Mins

2 lbs. lamb steak, cut into strips
1 tbsp. olive oil
2 1/2 scallions, chopped
3 tbsp. water
2 tbsp. arrowroot
1/2 C. soy sauce, low-sodium
1/2 C. water
4 garlic cloves, minced

Directions:
Add oil into the instant pot and set the pot on sauté mode. Add meat to the pot and cook for 5 minutes. Add the ginger and garlic and cook for 1-2 minutes. Add remaining ingredients and stir well. Seal pot with lid and cook on manual high for 12 minutes. Once done then release pressure using the quick-release method than open the lid. Serve and enjoy.

Belgian Beef Stew with Beer

Ingredients: Servings: 4 Cooking Time: 50 Mins

2 lb Beef Stewed
3 tbsp. Butter

Meat, cut into pieces	2 cloves Garlic,
Salt and Black Pepper	minced
to taste	1 packet Dry Onion
¼ C. All-purpose	Soup Mix
Flour	2 C. Beef Broth
2 tbsp.	1 medium bottle Beer
Worcestershire Sauce	1 tbsp. Tomato Paste

Directions:
In a zipper bag, add beef, salt, all-purpose flour, and pepper. Close the bag up and shake it to coat the meat well with the mixture. Select Sear/Sauté mode on the cooker. Melt the butter, and brown the beef on both sides, for 5 minutes. Pour the broth to deglaze the bottom of the pot. Stir in tomato paste, beer, Worcestershire sauce, and the onion soup mix. Close the lid, secure the pressure valve, and select Pressure mode on High pressure for 25 minutes. Press Start to start cooking. Once the timer is done, do a natural pressure release for 10 minutes, and then a quick pressure release to let out any remaining steam. Open the pressure lid and close the crisping lid. Cook on Broil mode for 10 minutes. Spoon the beef stew into serving bowls and serve with over a bed of vegetable mash with steamed greens.

Pork Patties

Ingredients: Servings: 6 Cooking Time: 15 Mins

2 lbs ground pork	1 tbsp. dried parsley
1 tsp. red pepper	1 tsp. fennel seed
flakes	1 tsp. paprika
1 1/2 tbsp. Italian	2 tbsp. olive oil
seasoning	2 tsp. salt

Directions:
Line instant pot air fryer basket with parchment paper. In a large bowl, mix together ground pork, fennel seed, paprika, red pepper flakes, parsley, Italian seasoning, olive oil, pepper, and salt. Make small patties from meat mixture and place on place on parchment paper into the air fryer basket. Place basket into the pot. Seal the pot with air fryer basket and select bake mode and cook at 375 F for 15 minutes. Serve and enjoy.

Caramelized Pork Shoulder

Ingredients: Servings: 8 Cooking Time: 20 Mins

1/3 C. soy sauce	2 lb. pork shoulder,
2 tbsp. sugar	cut into 1½-inch
1 tbsp. honey	thick slices

Directions:
1 Preparing the Ingredients. In a bowl, mix together all ingredients except pork. Add pork and coat with marinade generously. Cover and refrigerate o marinate for about 2-8 hours. Preheat the Instant Crisp Air Fryer to 335 degrees F. 2 Air Frying. Place the pork in an Instant Crisp Air Fryer basket. Close the air fryer lid. Cook for about 10 minutes. Now, set the Instant Crisp Air Fryer to 390 degrees F. Cook for about 10 minutes

Pork with Cabbage

Ingredients: Servings: 4 Cooking Time: 10 Mins

1 1/4 lbs pork loin,	1 tsp. dried dill weed
boneless and cut into	1/2 small cabbage,
cubes	cored and cut into
1/2 tsp. pepper	wedges
1/4 tsp. fennel seeds	1 onion, cut into
1 tbsp. vinegar	wedges
1 C. chicken stock	2 tsp. olive oil

Directions:
Add oil into the instant pot and set the pot on sauté mode. Add onion and sauté for 2 minutes. Add meat and cook for 3 minutes. Add cabbage and stir well. In a small bowl, mix dill weed, pepper, and fennel seeds and sprinkle over cabbage. Pour vinegar and stock to the pot. Seal pot with lid and cook on manual high pressure for 5 minutes. Once done then allow to release pressure naturally then open the lid. Serve and enjoy.

Pub Style Corned Beef Egg Rolls

Ingredients: Servings: 10 Cooking Time: 10 Mins

Olive oil	1/16th tsp. pepper
½ C. orange	1 tsp. dry mustard
marmalade	powder
5 slices of Swiss	1 C. heavy cream
cheese	½ C. chicken stock
4 C. corned beef and	¼ C. brandy
cabbage	¾ C. dry white wine
1 egg	¼ tsp. curry powder
10 egg roll wrappers	½ tbsp. cilantro
Brandy Mustard	1 minced shallot
Sauce:	2 tbsp. ghee
2 tbsp. whole grain	
mustard	

Directions:
1 Preparing the Ingredients. To make mustard sauce, add shallots and ghee to skillet, cooking until softened. Then add brandy and wine, heating to a low boil. Cook 5 minutes for liquids to reduce. Add stock and seasonings. Simmer 5 minutes. Turn down heat and add heavy cream. Cook on low till sauce reduces and it covers the back of a spoon. Place sauce in the fridge to chill. Crack the egg in a bowl and set to the side. Lay out an egg wrapper with the corner towards you. Brush the edges with egg wash. Place 1/3 C. of corned beef mixture into the center along with 2 tbsp. of marmalade and ½ a slice of Swiss cheese. Fold the bottom corner over filling. As you are folding the sides, make sure they are stick well to the first flap you made. Place filled rolls into prepared Instant Crisp Air Fryer basket. Spritz rolls with olive oil. 2 Air Frying. Close air fryer lid, set temperature to 390°F, and set time to 10 minutes. Cook 10 minutes at 390 degrees, shaking halfway through cooking. Serve rolls with Brandy Mustard sauce.

The Best Chicken Wild Rice Taco with Wild Rice

Ingredients: Servings: 4 Cooking Time: 25 Mins

4 Chicken Breasts	1 C. Salsa
2 C. Chicken Broth	Salt and Black Pepper
2 ¼ packets Taco	to taste
Seasoning	Sour Cream
1 C. Wild Rice, rinsed	To Serve:
1 Green Bell Pepper,	Grated Cheese, of
seeded and diced	your choice
1 Red Bell Pepper,	Chopped Cilantro

seeded and diced Avocado Slices

Directions:

Pour the chicken broth into the inner pot, add the chicken. Pour the taco seasoning over. Add the salsa and stir lightly with a spoon. Close the pressure lid, secure the pressure valve, and select Pressure on High for 15 minutes. Press Start. Once the timer has ended, do a quick pressure release, and open the lid. Add the wild rice and peppers, and use a spoon to push them into the sauce. Close the pressure lid, secure the pressure valve, and select Pressure mode on High for 8 minutes. Press Start. Once the timer has ended, do a quick pressure release, and open the lid. Gently stir the mixture, adjust the taste with salt and pepper. Stir in sour cream, close the crisping lid and select Broil mode; cook for 2 minutes. Spoon the chicken dish into serving bowls. Top it with avocado slices, sprinkle with chopped cilantro and some cheese. Serve.

Lamb Rack with Pistachio (air Fryer)

Ingredients: Servings: 2 Cooking Time: 20 Mins

½ C. finely chopped pistachios
1 tsp. chopped fresh rosemary
3 tbsp. panko bread crumbs
Salt and freshly ground black pepper, to taste
2 tsp. chopped fresh oregano
1 tbsp. olive oil
1 lamb rack, bones fat trimmed and frenched
1 tbsp. Dijon mustard

Directions:

Preheat the air fryer to 380°F (193°C). Put the pistachios, rosemary, bread crumbs, oregano, olive oil, salt, and black pepper in a food processor. Pulse to combine until smooth. Rub the lamb rack with salt and black pepper on a clean work surface, then place it in the preheated air fryer. Air fry for 12 minutes or until lightly browned. Flip the lamb halfway through the cooking time. Transfer the lamb on a plate and brush with Dijon mustard on the fat side, then sprinkle with the pistachios mixture over the lamb rack to coat well. Put the lamb rack back to the air fryer and air fry for 8 more minutes or until the internal temperature of the rack reaches at least 145°F (63°C). Remove the lamb rack from the air fryer with tongs and allow to cool for 5 minutes before sling to serve.

Taco Meatballs

Ingredients: Servings: 4 Cooking Time: 10 Mins

1 egg
1 lb ground beef
2 tbsp. taco seasoning
1 tbsp. garlic, minced
1/2 C. cheddar cheese, shredded
1/4 C. cilantro, chopped
1/4 C. onion, minced
Pepper
Salt

Directions:

Add all ingredients into the large mixing bowl and mix until well combined. Place the dehydrating tray in a multi-level air fryer basket and place basket in the instant pot. Make meatballs meat mixture and place on dehydrating tray. Seal pot with air fryer lid and select air fry mode then set the temperature to 400 F and timer for 10 minutes. Turn meatballs halfway through. Serve and enjoy.

Chicken Noodle Soup with Bacon

Ingredients: Servings: 8 Cooking Time: 23 Mins

5 oz dry Egg Noodles
4 Chicken Breasts, skinless and boneless
1 large White Onion, chopped
8 Bacon Slices, chopped
4 cloves Garlic, minced
Salt and Black Pepper to taste
2 medium Carrots, sliced
2 C. sliced Celery
½ C. chopped Parsley
1 ½ tsp. Dried Thyme
8 C. Chicken Broth

Directions:

Turn on the cooker, and select Sear/Sauté mode on High. Press Start. Add the chopped bacon and fry for 5 minutes until nicely brown and crispy. Remove to a paper towel to soak up excess oil and set aside. Add the onion and garlic to the pot and cook for 3 minutes until tender. Add the chicken breasts, noodles, carrots, celery, chicken broth, thyme, salt, and pepper. Close the pressure lid, secure the valve to seal, and select Pressure mode on High pressure. Adjust the time to 5 minutes and press Start. Once the timer has ended, do a quick pressure release, and open the lid. Use a wooden spoon to remove the chicken onto a plate. Shred the chicken with two forks and add it back to the soup. Stir in the bacon. Adjust the seasoning as desired. Close the crisping lid and cook on Broil mode for 5 minutes. Adjust the seasoning. Serve.

Chili Chicken Zoodles (pressure Cook)

Ingredients: Servings: 4 Cooking Time: 20 Mins

2 chicken breasts, skinless, boneless and halved
1½ C. chicken stock
3 celery stalks, chopped
1 tbsp. tomato sauce
1 tsp. chili powder
A pinch of salt and black pepper
2 zucchinis, spiralized
1 tbsp. chopped cilantro

Directions:

Mix together all the ingredients except the zucchini noodles and cilantro in the Instant Pot. Secure the lid. Select the Pressure Cook and set the cooking time for 15 minutes at High Pressure. Once cooking is complete, do a natural pressure release for 10 minutes, then release any remaining pressure. Carefully open the lid. Set your Instant Pot to Sauté and add the zucchini noodles. Cook for about 5 minutes, stirring often, or until softened. Sprinkle the cilantro on top for garnish before serving.

Delicious Lamb Chops

Ingredients: Servings: 4 Cooking Time: 8 Mins

1 lb lamb chops
2 tbsp. lemon juice
2 tbsp. olive oil
1 tsp. ground coriander
1 tsp. oregano
1 tsp. thyme
1 tsp. rosemary
1 tsp. salt

Directions:

Add lamb chops and remaining ingredients into the zip-lock bag. Shake well and place it in the refrigerator for 1 hour. Place the dehydrating tray in a multi-level air fryer basket and place basket in the instant pot. Place lamb chops on dehydrating tray. Seal pot with air fryer lid and select air fry mode then set the temperature to 400 F and timer for 8 minutes. Turn lamb chops halfway through. Serve and enjoy.

Roasted Pork Tenderloin

Ingredients: Servings: 4 Cooking Time: 1 Hour

1 (3-pound) pork tenderloin
2 garlic cloves, minced
1 tsp. dried basil
1 tsp. dried oregano
2 tbsp. extra-virgin olive oil
1 tsp. dried thyme
Salt
Pepper

Directions:
1 Preparing the Ingredients. Drizzle the pork tenderloin with the olive oil. Rub the garlic, basil, oregano, thyme, and salt and pepper to taste all over the tenderloin. 2 Air Frying. Place the tenderloin in the Instant Crisp Air Fryer. Close air fryer lid. Cook for 45 minutes. Use a meat thermometer to test for doneness Open the Instant Crisp Air Fryer and flip the pork tenderloin. Cook for an additional 15 minutes. Remove the cooked pork from the Instant Crisp Air Fryer and allow it to rest for 10 minutes before cutting.

Air Fryer Baked Egg Cups Spinach & Cheese

Ingredients: Servings: 1 Cooking Time: 10 Mins

1-2 tsps. grated cheese
1 large egg
1 tbsp. frozen spinach, thawed and sautéed
1 tbsp. milk or half-and-half
Salt and ground pepper to taste
Cooking spray

Directions:
Prepare the ramekins by spraying it with cooking spray. Add all ingredients into the ramekins and add salt and pepper to season. Lightly stir to avoid breaking the egg yolk. Place ramekins inside the air fryer basket and into the instant pot. Attach the air fryer lid and set to Baking. Cook at 330 degrees F for 6-12 minutes. You may cook in batches if preparing more cups. Serve and enjoy.

Lamb with Potatoes

Ingredients: Servings: 6 Cooking Time: 45 Mins

Lamb roast – 4 pounds
Rosemary – 1 spring
Garlic – 3 cloves, minced
Potatoes – 6, halved
Lamb stock – ½ cup
Bay leaves – 4
Salt and pepper to taste

Directions:
Put potatoes in a dish. Add salt, pepper, rosemary spring, garlic, bay leaves, stock, and lamb. Mix and place in the air fryer. Cook at 360F for 45 minutes. Slice lamb, divide among plates, and serve with potatoes and cooking juices.

Herb Garlic Lamb Chops

Ingredients: Servings: 3 Cooking Time: 6 Mins

3 lamb loin chops
1 tbsp. lemon juice
1 tbsp. lemon zest, grated
2 tsp. dried rosemary
1 tsp. dried thyme
1 tbsp. olive oil
2 tsp. garlic, minced

Directions:
Mix together lemon juice, lemon zest, rosemary, thyme, oil, and garlic and rub over lamb chops. Place the dehydrating tray in a multi-level air fryer basket and place basket in the instant pot. Place lamb chops on dehydrating tray. Seal pot with air fryer lid and select air fry mode then set the temperature to 400 F and timer for 6 minutes. Turn lamb chops halfway through. Serve and enjoy.

Rosemary Turkey Scotch Eggs (air Fryer)

Ingredients: Servings: 4 Cooking Time: 12 Mins

1 egg
1 C. panko bread crumbs
½ tsp. rosemary
1 lb. (454 g) ground turkey
4 hard-boiled eggs, peeled
Salt and ground black pepper, to taste
Cooking spray

Directions:
Preheat the air fryer to 400°F (204°C). Spritz the air fryer basket with cooking spray. Whisk the egg with salt in a bowl. Combine the bread crumbs with rosemary in a shallow dish. Stir the ground turkey with salt and ground black pepper in a separate large bowl, then divide the ground turkey into four portions. Wrap each hard-boiled egg with a portion of ground turkey. Dredge in the whisked egg, then roll over the breadcrumb mixture. Place the wrapped eggs in the preheated air fryer and spritz with cooking spray. Air fry for 12 minutes or until golden brown and crunchy. Flip the eggs halfway through. Serve immediately.

Baby Back Ribs

Ingredients: Servings: 4 Cooking Time: 35 Mins

1 tbsp. olive oil
1 rack baby back ribs
1 tbsp. liquid smoke flavoring
1 tbsp. brown sugar
½ tsp. garlic powder
½ tsp. chili powder
1 C. BBQ sauce
½ tsp. ground black pepper
½ tsp. onion powder
½ tsp. salt

Directions:
Cleanse ribs by removing membranes on the back part and run through tap water. Pat dry with a paper towel. Cut ribs into 4 portions. In a mixing bowl, combine liquid smoke with oil and rub ribs on both sides. Add pepper, brown sugar, garlic powder, onion powder, chili powder in a mixing bowl. Also, add salt and pepper. Mix well to combine and rub or brush both sides of the ribs with the seasoning mix. Set aside for 30 minutes to absorb. Place ribs with bone-side down in the air fryer basket. Place the basket back to the instant pot duo crisp and cover with the air fryer lid. Set to cook for 15 minutes at 375 degrees F. Flip over and cook for another 10 minutes. Remove basket from the air fryer and brush ribs with the BBQ sauce. Return the air fryer basket to the instant pot and cook for another 5 minutes or until desired crispness is achieved.

Pork with Couscous

Ingredients: Servings: 6 Cooking Time: 35 Mins

Pork loin – 2 ½ pounds, boneless, and trimmed
Chicken stock – ¾ cup
Olive oil – 2 tbsps.
Sweet paprika – ½ tbsp.
Dried sage – 2 ¼ tsps.
Garlic powder – ½ tsp.
Dried rosemary – ¼ tsp.
Dried marjoram – ¼ tsp.
Dried basil – 1 tsp.
Dried oregano – 1 tsp.
Salt and black pepper to taste
Couscous – 2 cups, cooked

Directions:

In a bowl, mix oil with stock, salt, pepper, oregano, marjoram, thyme, rosemary, sage, garlic powder, and paprika. Whisk well and add pork loin. Mix and marinate for 1 hour. Cook in the air fryer at 370F for 35 minutes. Divide among plates and serve with couscous on the side.

Roasted Stuffed Peppers

Ingredients: Servings: 4 Cooking Time: 20 Mins

4 oz. shredded cheddar cheese
½ tsp. pepper
½ tsp. salt
1 tsp. Worcestershire sauce
½ C. tomato sauce
8 oz. lean ground beef
1 tsp. olive oil
1 minced garlic clove
½ chopped onion
2 green peppers

Directions:

1 Preparing the Ingredients. Ensure your Instant Crisp Air Fryer is preheated to 390 degrees. Spray with olive oil. Cut stems off bell peppers and remove seeds. Cook in boiling salted water for 3 minutes. Sauté garlic and onion together in a skillet until golden in color. Take skillet off the heat. Mix pepper, salt, Worcestershire sauce, ¼ C. of tomato sauce, half of cheese and beef together. Divide meat mixture into pepper halves. Top filled peppers with remaining cheese and tomato sauce. Place filled peppers in the Instant Crisp Air Fryer. 2 Air Frying. Close air fryer lid. Set temperature to 390°F, and set time to 20 minutes, bake 15-20 minutes.

Bbq Meatballs

Ingredients: Servings: 4 Cooking Time: 14 Mins

80/20 ground beef – 1 pound
Ground Italian sausage – ¼ pound
Egg – 1
Garlic powder – ½ tsp.
Dried parsley - 1 tsp.
Onion powder – ¼ tsp.
Bacon – 4 slices, cooked and chopped
Chopped white onion – ¼ cup
Chopped pickled jalapenos – ¼ cup
Barbecue sauce – ½ cup

Directions:

Mix ground beef, sausage and egg in a bowl until fully combined. Mix in all remaining ingredients except barbecue sauce. Make 8 meatballs. Place meatballs into the air fryer basket. Cook at 400F for 14 minutes. Turn once. Remove meatballs from the fryer and toss in barbecue sauce. Serve.

Classic Mini Meatloaf

Ingredients: Servings: 6 Cooking Time: 25 Mins

80/20 ground beef – 1 pound
Yellow onion – ¼, diced
Green bell pepper – ½, diced
Almond flour – 3 tbsps.
Worcestershire sauce – 1 tbsp.
Egg – 1
Garlic powder – ½ tsp.
Dried parsley – 1 tsp.
Tomato paste – 2 tbsps.
Water – ¼ cup
Powdered brown sugar – 1 tbsp.

Directions:

In a bowl, combine almond flour, egg, pepper, onion, and ground beef. Pour in Worcestershire sauce and add the parsley and garlic powder to the bowl. Mix well. Divide the mixture into two and place into two loaf baking pans. In another bowl, mix the sugar, water, and tomato paste. Spoon half the mixture over each loaf. Place loaf pans into the air fryer basket, working in batches. Cook at 350F for 25 minutes. Serve warm.

Pork Cutlet Rolls

Ingredients: Servings: 4 Cooking Time: 15 Mins

4 Sundried Tomatoes in oil
2 Tbsps Parsley, finely chopped
1 Green Onion, finely chopped
4 Pork Cutlets
Black Pepper to taste
2 Tsps Paprika
1/2 Tbsp Olive Oil
* String for Rolled Meat

Directions:

1 Preparing the Ingredients. Preheat the Instant Crisp Air Fryer to 390 degrees Finely chop the tomatoes and mix with the parsley and green onion. Add salt and pepper to taste Spread out the cutlets and coat them with the tomato mixture. Roll up the cutlets and secure intact with the string Rub the rolls with salt, pepper, and paprika powder and thinly coat them with olive oil 2 Air Frying. Put the cutlet rolls in the Instant Crisp Air Fryer tray, close air fryer lid and cook for 15 minutes. Roast until nicely brown and done. Serve with tomato sauce.

Adobo Beef

Ingredients: Servings: 4 Cooking Time: 10 Mins

1 lb. Beef roast, trimmed
1 tbsp. Olive oil
½ tsp. Turmeric powder
¼ tsp. Garlic powder
½ tsp. Oregano; dried
A pinch of salt and black pepper

Directions:

Take a bowl and mix the roast with the rest of the ingredients and rub well. Put the roast in the air fryer's basket and cook at 390°f for 30 minutes. Slice the roast, divide it between plates and serve with a side salad.

Cinnamon-beef Kofta (air Fryer)

Ingredients: Servings: 12 Cooking Time: 13 Mins

1½ lb. (680 g) lean ground beef
1 tsp. onion powder
¾ tsp. ground cinnamon
¾ tsp. ground dried turmeric
1 tsp. ground cumin
¾ tsp. salt
¼ tsp. cayenne
12 (3½- to 4-inch-long) cinnamon sticks
Cooking spray

Directions:
Preheat the air fryer to 375°F (191°C). Spritz the air fryer basket with cooking spray. Combine all the ingredients, except for the cinnamon sticks, in a large bowl. Toss to mix well. Divide and shape the mixture into 12 balls, then wrap each ball around each cinnamon stick and leave a quarter of the length uncovered. Arrange the beef-cinnamon sticks in the preheated air fryer and spritz with cooking spray. Work in batches to avoid overcrowding. Air fry for 13 minutes or until the beef is browned. Flip the sticks halfway through. Serve immediately.

Barbecue Flavored Pork Ribs

Ingredients: Servings: 6 Cooking Time: 15 Mins

¼ C. honey, divided
2 tbsp. tomato ketchup
1 tbsp. Worcestershire sauce
1 tbsp. soy sauce
¾ C. BBQ sauce
½ tsp. garlic powder
Freshly ground white pepper, to taste
1¾ lb. pork ribs

Directions:
Preparing the Ingredients. In a large bowl, mix together 3 tbsp. of honey and remaining ingredients except pork ribs. Refrigerate to marinate for about 20 minutes. Preheat the Instant Crisp Air Fryer to 355 degrees F. Place the ribs in an Instant Crisp Air Fryer basket. Air Frying. Lock the air fryer lid. Cook for about 13 minutes. Remove the ribs from the Instant Crisp Air Fryer and coat with remaining honey. Serve hot.

Air Fried Spicy Lamb Sirloin Steak

Ingredients: Servings: 4 Cooking Time: 15 Mins

½ onion
4 ginger cubes
5 garlic cloves
1 tsp. of garam masala
1 tsp. fennel, ground
1 tsp. cinnamon, ground
½ tsp. cayenne powder
1 tsp. salt
1-pound lamb sirloin, boneless steaks

Directions:
Wash the lamb and pat dry. Add all the ingredients in a blender except for the lamb chops and blend it into a fine paste. Make strips over the lamb chops to ensure the margination reaches within the meat. Rub the paste on to the chops and mix them well. Let the marinade mixture rest for 30 minutes or overnight in the refrigerator, as preferred. Place the lamb steaks in the air fryer basket and put it in the inner pot. Close the crisp lid. Select the smart option roast under air fry mode for 15 minutes. Select the temperature to 380°f. It will automatically select temperature to 380°f by default. Press start to begin the cooking. Halfway through the cooking, open the crisp lid and flip the lamb for even cooking. Close the crisp lid to resume cooking for the remaining period. Serve hot.

Air Fried Sausages

Ingredients: Servings: 6 Cooking Time: 13 Mins

6 sausage
olive oil spray

Directions:
Pour 5 C. of water into Instant Pot Duo Crisp Air Fryer. Place air fryer basket inside the pot, spray inside with nonstick spray and put sausage links inside. Close the Air Fryer lid and steam for about 5 minutes. Remove the lid once done. Spray links with olive oil and close air crisp lid. Set to air crisp at 400°F for 8 min flipping halfway through so both sides get browned.

Beef & Veggie Spring Rolls

Ingredients: Servings: 10 Cooking Time: 12 Mins

2-ounce Asian rice noodles
1 tbsp. sesame oil
7-ounce ground beef
1 small onion, chopped
3 garlic cloves, crushed
1 C. fresh mixed vegetables
1 tsp. soy sauce
1 packet spring roll skins
2 tbsp. water
Olive oil, as required

Directions:
1 Preparing the Ingredients. Soak the noodles in warm water till soft. Drain and cut into small lengths. In a pan heat the oil and add the onion and garlic and sauté for about 4-5 minutes. Add beef and cook for about 4-5 minutes. Add vegetables and cook for about 5-7 minutes or till cooked through. Stir in soy sauce and remove from the heat. Immediately, stir in the noodles and keep aside till all the juices have been absorbed. Preheat the Instant Crisp Air Fryer to 350 degrees F. and preheat the oven to 350 degrees F also. Place the spring rolls skin onto a smooth surface. Add a line of the filling diagonally across. Fold the top point over the filling and then fold in both sides. On the final point brush it with water before rolling to seal. Brush the spring rolls with oil. 2 Air Frying. Arrange the rolls in batches in the Instant Crisp Air Fryer, close air fryer lid and Cook for about 8 minutes. Repeat with remaining rolls. Now, place spring rolls onto a baking sheet. Bake for about 6 minutes per side.

Pork Chops with Bell Peppers (pressure Cook)

Ingredients: Servings: 4 Cooking Time: 35 Mins

2 tbsp. olive oil
4 pork chops
1 red onion, chopped
3 garlic cloves, minced
1 red bell pepper, roughly chopped
1 green bell pepper, roughly chopped
2 C. beef stock
A pinch of salt and black pepper
1 tbsp. parsley, chopped

Directions:
Press the Sauté on your Instant Pot. Add and heat the oil. Brown the pork chops for 2 minutes. Fold in the onion and garlic and brown for an additional 3 minutes. Stir in the bell peppers, stock, salt, and pepper. Lock the lid. Select the

Pressure Cook and cook for 30 minutes at High Pressure. Once cooking is complete, use a natural pressure release for 10 minutes and then release any remaining pressure. Carefully open the lid. Divide the mix among the plates and serve topped with the parsley.

Coconut and Chili Pork

Ingredients: Servings: 4 Cooking Time: 10 Mins

4 pork chops
2 garlic cloves; minced
1 shallot; chopped
3 tbsp. Coconut aminos
1 ½ C. coconut milk
2 tbsp. Olive oil
2 tsp. Chili paste
Salt and black pepper to taste.

Directions:
In a pan that fits your air fryer, mix the pork the rest of the ingredients, toss, introduce the pan in the fryer and cook at 400°f for 25 minutes, shaking the fryer halfway. Divide everything into bowls and serve.

Delightful Pepper Beef Mix

Ingredients: Servings: 4 Cooking Time: 48 Mins

2 lb Beef Chuck Roast
1 tbsp. Onion Powder
1 tbsp. Garlic Powder
1 tbsp. Italian Seasoning
Salt and Black Pepper to taste, cut in 4 pieces
1 C. Beef Broth
1 medium White Onion, sliced
1 Green Bell Pepper, seeded and sliced
1 Red Bell Pepper, seeded and sliced
2 tbsp. Olive Oil

Directions:
Rub the beef with pepper, salt, garlic powder, Italian seasoning, and onion powder. Select Sear/Sauté mode on cooker. Heat 1 tbsp. oil, add the beef pieces and sear them on both sides until brown, for about 5 minutes. Use a pair of tongs to remove them onto a plate after. (You can do this in 2 batches). Pour the beef broth and fish sauce into the pot to deglaze the bottom while you use a spoon to scrape any stuck beef bit at the bottom. Add the meat back to the pot, close the lid, secure the pressure valve, and select Pressure mode on High pressure for 30 minutes. Press Start. Once the timer has stopped, do a quick pressure release, and open the pot. Use two forks to shred the beef, inside the pot. Close the crisping lid and select Broil mode for 10 minutes. When ready, set aside the meat and discard the liquid. Wipe clean the pot. Select Sear/Sauté, heat the remaining oil, add the beef with onions and peppers. Sauté them for 3 minutes and season with salt and pepper. Dish the stir-fried beef into serving plates. Serve.

Spicy Mexican Chicken (pressure Cook)

Ingredients: Servings: 4 Cooking Time: 17 Mins

2 tbsp. avocado oil
1 lb. (454 g) ground chicken
1 (14-ounce / 397-g) can low-sugar fire roasted tomatoes
½ jalapeño, finely chopped
¼ poblano chili pepper, finely chopped
½ C. water
½ tsp. crushed red pepper
½ tsp. coriander
½ tsp. chili powder
½ tsp. curry powder
½ tsp. kosher salt
½ tsp. freshly ground black pepper

Directions:
Press the Sauté button on the Instant Pot and heat the avocado oil. Pour the water into the Instant Pot and stir in the remaining ingredients. Secure the lid. Select the Pressure Cook and set the cooking time for 17 minutes at High Pressure. Once cooking is complete, do a quick pressure release. Carefully open the lid. Let the chicken cool for 5 minutes and serve.

Paprika Beef Chili with Worcestershire Sauce

Ingredients: Servings: 4 Cooking Time: 28 Mins

2 lb Ground Beef
2 tbsp. Olive Oil
1 large Red Bell Pepper, chopped
1 large Yellow Bell Pepper, chopped
1 White Onion, Chopped
2 C. Chopped Tomatoes
2 C. Beef Broth
2 Carrots, cut in little bits
2 tsp. Onion Powder
2 tsp. Garlic Powder
5 tsp. Chili Powder
2 tbsp. Worcestershire Sauce
2 tsp. Paprika
½ tsp. Cumin Powder
2 tbsp. chopped Parsley
Salt and Black Pepper to taste
Once the timer has ended, do a quick pressure release, and open the lid.
Stir the stew and close the crisping lid.
Cook on Broil mode for 10 minutes.
Dish into serving bowls. Serve this beef chili with crackers or potato mash.

Directions:
Select Sear/Sauté mode, and add the olive oil and ground beef. Cook the meat until brown, stirring occasionally, for about 8 minutes. Top with the remaining

Curry Pork Steak (pressure Cook)

Ingredients: Servings: 6 Cooking Time: 15 Mins

1 tsp. cumin seeds
1 tsp. fennel seeds
½ tsp. mustard seeds
2 chili peppers, deseeded and minced
1 tsp. mixed peppercorns
½ tsp. ground bay leaf
1 tbsp. sesame oil
1½ lb. (680 g) pork steak, sliced
3 tbsp. coconut cream
1 C. chicken broth
2 tbsp. balsamic vinegar
2 tbsp. chopped scallions
2 cloves garlic, finely minced
1 tsp. curry powder
1 tsp. grated fresh ginger
¼ tsp. crushed red pepper flakes
¼ tsp. ground black pepper
1 C. vegetable broth
Sea salt, to taste

Directions:
Heat a skillet over medium-high heat and roast the cumin seeds, fennel seeds, mustard seeds, peppers, peppercorns, and ground

bay leaf and until aromatic. Set the Instant Pot to Sauté. Add and heat the sesame oil until sizzling. Sear the pork steak until nicely browned. Stir in the roasted seasonings and the remaining ingredients. Lock the lid. Select the Pressure Cook and set the cooking time for 8 minutes at High Pressure. When the timer beeps, do a quick pressure release. Carefully open the lid. Divide the mix among bowls and serve immediately.

Barbecued Baby Back Ribs

Ingredients: Servings: 4 Cooking Time: 32 Mins

- 1/4 C. canned tomato paste
- 2 tbsp. cider vinegar
- 1 tbsp. sweet paprika
- 1/2 tbsp. coriander seeds
- 1/2 tbsp. fennel seeds
- 1 tsp. onion powder
- 1/2 tsp. salt
- 1 tsp. dried thyme
- 1/2 tsp. ground allspice
- 1/2 tsp. ground black pepper
- 1/4 tsp. celery seeds
- One 4-pound rack baby back ribs, cut into 2 or 3 sections to fit in the cooker

Directions:

Preparing the Ingredients. Whisk the tomato paste, vinegar, paprika, coriander and fennel seeds, onion powder, thyme, allspice, salt, pepper, and celery seeds with 3/4 C. water in an electric Instant Crisp Air Fryer until the tomato paste dissolves. Add the ribs; toss to coat thoroughly and evenly in the sauce. High pressure for 32 minutes. Lock the pressure cooking lid on the Instant Crisp Air Fryer and then cook for 32 minutes. To get 32-minutes cook time, press "Pressure" button and use the Time Adjustment button to adjust the cook time to 32 minutes. Pressure Release. Let the pressure to come down naturally for at least 15 minutes, then quick release any pressure left in the pot. Finish the dish. Remove the lid from the Instant Crisp Air Fryer. Close air fryer lid. Select AIR FRY, set temperature to 400°F, and set time to 15 minutes. Check after 10 minutes, cooking for an additional 5 minutes if dish needs more browning. Transfer the rib rack sections to a large rimmed baking sheet. Set the electric one to its browning function. Bring the sauce to a simmer. Cook, stirring occasionally, until the sauce has thickened, 3 to 5 minutes. Position the oven rack 4 to 6 inches from the broiler; heat the broiler. Brush a light coating of the sauce onto the ribs, then broil until glazed and hot, 6 to 8 minutes, turning once. Slice the racks between the bones to make individual ribs. Serve with the extra sauce on the side.

Pork Cutlets with Creamy Mustard Sauce (pressure Cook)

Ingredients: Servings: 6 Cooking Time: 13 Mins

- 6 pork cutlets
- 1/2 tsp. dried rosemary
- 1/2 tsp. dried marjoram
- 1/4 tsp. paprika
- 1/4 tsp. cayenne pepper
- Kosher salt and ground black pepper, to taste
- 2 tbsp. olive oil
- 1/2 C. water
- 1/2 C. vegetable broth
- 1 tbsp. butter
- 1 C. heavy cream
- 1 tbsp. yellow mustard
- 1/2 C. shredded Cheddar cheese

Directions:

Sprinkle both sides of the pork cutlets with rosemary, marjoram, paprika, cayenne pepper, salt, and black pepper. Press the Sauté button on the Instant Pot and heat the olive oil until sizzling. Add the pork cutlets and sear both sides for about 3 minutes until lightly browned. Pour in the water and vegetable broth. Secure the lid. Select the Pressure Cook and set the cooking time for 8 minutes at High Pressure. When the timer beeps, perform a quick pressure release. Carefully open the lid. Transfer the pork cutlets to a plate and set aside. Press the Sauté button again and melt the butter. Stir in the heavy cream, mustard, and cheese and cook for another 2 minutes until heated through. Add the pork cutlets to the sauce, turning to coat. Remove from the Instant Pot and serve.

Air Fryer Sweet and Sour Pork

Ingredients: Servings: 4 Cooking Time: 12 Mins

- 2 lbs. pork, cut into chunks
- 1 C. potato starch
- 3 tbsps. canola oil
- 2 large eggs
- 1/4 tsp. Chinese Five Spice
- 1 tsp. sesame oil, optional
- Sea salt to taste
- For Sweet and Sour
- 1/2 tsp. garlic powder
- 1 tbsp. ketchup
- 1/2 C. white sugar
- 1 tbsp. low-sodium soy sauce
- 1/2 C. seasoned rice vinegar

Directions:

For Sweet and Sour Sauce To make the sweet and sour sauce, add all sweet and sour sauce ingredients into the instant pot duo and cover with the pressure cooker lid. Set to Sauté mode and cook for about 5 minutes. Transfer to a bowl and reserve for later use. For the Pork Combine all seasonings in a mixing bowl (pepper, Chinese Five Spice and potato starch). Add beaten eggs and sesame oil in a separate bowl. Dredge pork pieces in the potato starch, shaking off any excess starch. Dip one by one into the egg mixture, again shaking to drip off before dipping back to the potato starch mix. Grease instant pot air fryer basket with oil and arrange pork pieces inside. Spray oil on top and attach the air fryer lid for cover. Set to air fry and cook at 340 degrees F for 8-12 minutes until cooked, shaking air fryer basket halfway through cooking. Serve with Sweet and Sour Sauce.

Chinese Braised Pork Belly

Ingredients: Servings: 8 Cooking Time: 20 Mins

- 1 lb Pork Belly, sliced
- 1 Tbsp Oyster Sauce
- 2 Red Fermented Bean Curds
- 1 Tbsp Red Fermented Bean Curd Paste
- 1 Tbsp Sugar
- 1 Tbsp Cooking Wine
- 1/2 Tbsp Soy Sauce
- 1 Tsp Sesame Oil
- 1 Cup All Purpose Flour

Directions:

1 Preparing the Ingredients. Preheat the Instant Crisp Air Fryer to 390 degrees. In a small bowl, mix all ingredients together and rub the pork thoroughly with this mixture Set aside to marinate for at least 30 minutes or preferably overnight for the flavors to permeate the meat Coat each marinated pork belly

slice in flour and place in the Instant Crisp Air Fryer tray 2 Air Frying. Close air fryer lid. Cook for 15 to 20 minutes until crispy and tender.

Air Fryer Steak

Ingredients: Servings: 2 Cooking Time: 14 Mins

2 lbs. bone-in-rib eye
2 cloves garlic
4 tbsps. butter, softened
1 tsp. fresh parsley, chopped
1 tsp. fresh chives
1 tsp. fresh rosemary, chopped
1 tsp. fresh thyme, chopped
Salt and pepper to taste

Directions:
Combine herbs and butter in a bowl. Lay a plastic wrap on a flat surface and place the mixture into its center. Roll up and twist its ends to tighten. Chill in the fridge for about 20 minutes. Rub steaks with salt and pepper on both sides. Place in the air fryer basket and place over the trivet inside the pot. Attach the air fryer lid and cook at 400 degrees F for 12-14 minutes, flipping halfway through. You may have a slice of herb butter for the topping. Garnish with parsley and chives. Serve and enjoy.

Tasty Lamb Chops

Ingredients: Servings: 4 Cooking Time: 10 Mins

1 garlic clove, minced
1/2 tbsp. fresh oregano, chopped
4 lamb chops
1 tbsp. olive oil
Pepper
Salt

Directions:
Coat lamb chops with olive oil and rubs with garlic, oregano, pepper, and salt. Place the dehydrating tray in a multi-level air fryer basket and place basket in the instant pot. Place lamb chops on dehydrating tray. Seal pot with air fryer lid and select air fry mode then set the temperature to 400 F and timer for 10 minutes. Turn lamb chops halfway through. Serve and enjoy.

Swedish Meatballs

Ingredients: Servings: 4 Cooking Time: 14 Mins

For the meatballs
1 lb. 93% lean ground beef
1 (1-ounce) packet Lipton Onion Recipe Soup & Dip Mix
⅓ C. bread crumbs
1 egg, beaten
Salt
Pepper
For the gravy
1 C. beef broth
⅓ C. heavy cream
3 tbsp. all-purpose flour

Directions:
1 Preparing the Ingredients. In a large bowl, combine the ground beef, onion soup mix, bread crumbs, egg, and salt and pepper to taste. Mix thoroughly. Using 2 tbsp. of the meat mixture, create each meatball by rolling the beef mixture around in your hands. This should yield about 10 meatballs. 2 Air Frying. Place the meatballs in the Instant Crisp Air Fryer. It is okay to stack them. Close air fryer lid and cook for 14 minutes. While the meatballs cook, prepare the gravy. Heat a saucepan over medium-high heat. Add the beef broth and heavy cream. Stir for 1 to 2 minutes. Add the flour and stir. Cover and allow the sauce to simmer for 3 to 4 minutes, or until thick. Drizzle the gravy over the meatballs and serve.

Cheesy Frittata

Ingredients: Servings: 6 Cooking Time: 15- 22 Mins

4 large eggs
3 C. spinach
¾ C. onion, diced
⅓ C. tomatoes, diced
⅓ C. Cheddar cheese, shredded
⅓ C. feta cheese
1 tbsp. half-and-half
¾ tsp. Kosher salt
¼ tsp. ground black pepper
2 green onions, sliced

Directions:
Break all the eggs in a bowl and whisk together with the half-and-half, salt, and pepper. Add the onions, spinach, tomatoes, feta cheese, and cheddar cheese, then mix well. Spritz a 6-inch deep round pan with cooking spray. Pour the egg mixture into it. Set the trivet in the inner pot of the instant pot and carefully place the round pan on top of it. Put the air fryer lid on and air fry at 350 degrees F for about 15-22 minutes or until your desired doneness is achieved. Once done, carefully take out the round pan. To serve, top the frittata with sliced green onions.

Lamb Meatballs

Ingredients: Servings: 4 Cooking Time: 20 Mins

1 lb ground lamb
1/4 tsp. red pepper flakes
1 tsp. ground cumin
2 tsp. oregano, chopped
2 tbsp. parsley, chopped
1 tsp. garlic, minced
1 egg, lightly beaten
Pepper
Salt

Directions:
Add all ingredients into the mixing bowl and mix until well combined. Place the dehydrating tray in a multi-level air fryer basket and place basket in the instant pot. Make meatballs meat mixture and place on dehydrating tray. Seal pot with air fryer lid and select bake mode then set the temperature to 380 F and timer for 20 minutes. Turn meatballs halfway through. Serve and enjoy.

Bolognaise Sauce

Ingredients: Servings: 2 Cooking Time: 30 Mins

13 Ozs Ground Beef
1 Carrot
1 Stalk of Celery
10 Ozs Diced Tomatoes
1/2 Onion
Salt and Pepper to taste
Oven safe bowl

Directions:
1 Preparing the Ingredients. Preheat the Instant Crisp Air Fryer to 390 degrees. Finely dice the carrot, celery and onions. Place into the oven safe bowl along with the ground beef and combine well 2 Air Frying. Place the bowl into the Instant Crisp Air Fryer tray, close air fryer lid and cook for 12 minutes until browned. Pour the diced tomatoes into the bowl and replace in the Instant Crisp Air Fryer. Season with salt and pepper,

then cook for another 18 minutes Serve over cooked pasta or freeze for later use.

Air Fryer Pork Chops

Ingredients: Servings: 3 Cooking Time: 15 Mins

3 (6 oz) pork chops
Salt and black pepper to taste
2 tsps. olive oil
A dash of paprika

Directions:
Cleanse pork chops and pat dry. Put in a large mixing bowl and add the olive oil. Add salt and pepper to taste along with paprika and combine to allow the flavor to seep through the pork chops. Leave for a while to marinate. Place the air fryer basket in the instant pot and arrange pork chops inside. You don't need to cook in batches as instant pot duo crisp has a two-layered basket to accommodate your recipe in one sitting. Attach the air fryer lid and set to 380 degrees F and cook for 10-14 minutes, flipping pork chops halfway through cooking. Test for tenderness and cook more if you want it to be crispier. Serve warm.

Greek Chicken & Potatoes

Ingredients: Servings: 6 Cooking Time: 27-30 Mins

12 bone-in chicken thighs
1½ lbs. yellow potatoes
½ C. chicken broth
⅓ C. olive oil
⅓ C. lemon juice
1 tsp. lemon zest
1 tbsp. garlic, minced
2 tsps. dried oregano
1 tsp. dried parsley
1 tsp. black pepper
2 tsps. Kosher salt
2 lemon wedges, for garnish

Directions:
Whisk the lemon juice, olive oil, garlic, parsley, oregano, pepper, lemon zest, and salt in a bowl. If your potatoes are large, cut them into quarters; but if they're small, cut them into halves. Add the chicken broth into your instant pot and arrange the chicken thighs in a single layer. Pour half of the lemon juice mixture over the chicken thighs. Layer the potatoes on top of the thighs and pour the remaining half of the lemon juice mixture over the potatoes. Pressure cook for 15 minutes, and once the time is up, let the pot sit for about 10 minutes. Make sure to move the valve for venting. Once done, remove the lid and transfer the potatoes to a serving dish. Transfer the chicken to a platter and the juices to a container. To brown the chicken, arrange the chicken thighs (in batches as needed) in the fryer basket. Set a tall trivet in the inner steel pot of your cooker and place the basket on top of it. Place the air fryer lid, set the temperature to 500 degrees F and cook for 4 minutes. Put the chicken together with the potatoes in the serving dish. To serve, pour in some of the reserved juices and garnish with lemon wedges.

Tender Beef with Sour Cream Sauce

Ingredients: Servings: 2 Cooking Time: 12 Mins

9 oz. tender beef, chopped
1 C. scallions, chopped
2 cloves garlic, smashed
3/4 C. sour cream
3/4 tsp. salt
1/4 tsp. black pepper, or to taste
1/2 tsp. dried dill weed

Directions:
1 Preparing the Ingredients. Add the beef, scallions, and garlic to the baking dish. 2 Air Frying. Close air fryer lid. Cook for about 5 minutes at 390 degrees F. Once the meat is starting to tender, pour in the sour cream. Stir in the salt, black pepper, and dill. Now, cook 7 minutes longer.

Mexican Beef Shred (pressure Cook)

Ingredients: Servings: 4 Cooking Time: 30 Mins

1 lb. (454 g) tender chuck roast, cut into half
3 tbsp. chipotle sauce
1 (8-ounce / 227-g) can tomato sauce
½ C. chopped cilantro
1 lime, zested and juiced
1 C. beef broth
2 tsp. cumin powder
1 tsp. cayenne pepper
Salt and ground black pepper, to taste
½ tsp. garlic powder
1 tbsp. olive oil

Directions:
In the Instant Pot, add the beef, chipotle sauce, tomato sauce, beef broth, cilantro, lime zest, lime juice, cumin powder, cayenne pepper, salt, pepper, and garlic powder. Seal the lid, then select the Pressure Cook and set the cooking time for 30 minutes at High Pressure. Once cooking is complete, allow a natural pressure release for 10 minutes, then release any remaining pressure. Unlock the lid and using two forks to shred the beef into strands. Stir in the olive oil. Serve warm.

Mustard Pork Chops

Ingredients: Servings: 4 Cooking Time: 10 Mins

4 pork chops
10 oz. Beef stock
2/3 C. cream cheese, soft
1 tbsp. Olive oil
1 tbsp. Parsley; chopped
1 tbsp. Mustard
¼ tsp. Oregano; dried
¼ tsp. Thyme; dried
¼ tsp. Garlic powder
A pinch of salt and black pepper

Directions:
In a baking dish that fits your air fryer, mix all the ingredients, introduce the pan in the fryer and cook at 400°f for 25 minutes Divide everything between plates and serve.

Air Fryer Roast Beef

Ingredients: Servings: 6 Cooking Time: 45 Mins

Roast beef
1 tbsp. olive oil
Seasonings of choice

Directions:
1 Preparing the Ingredients. Ensure your Instant Crisp Air Fryer is preheated to 160 degrees. Place roast in bowl and toss with olive oil and desired seasonings. Put seasoned roast into Instant Crisp Air Fryer. 2 Air Frying. Close air fryer lid. Set temperature to 160°F, and set time to 30 minutes and cook 30 minutes. Turn roast when the timer sounds and cook another 15 minutes.

Tasty Air Fried Pork Chops

Ingredients: Servings: 3 Cooking Time: 10 Mins

3 pork chops
1/4 tsp. garlic powder
1/2 tsp. smoked paprika
2 tsp. avocado oil
Pepper
Salt

Directions:
Coat pork chops with avocado oil and season with garlic powder, paprika, pepper, and salt. Place the dehydrating tray in a multi-level air fryer basket and place basket in the instant pot. Place lamb chops on dehydrating tray. Seal pot with air fryer lid and select air fry mode then set the temperature to 380 F and timer for 10 minutes. Turn lamb chops halfway through. Serve and enjoy.

Easy & Tasty Ribs

Ingredients: Servings: 4 Cooking Time: 40 Mins

2 3/4 lbs. country-style pork ribs
Dry rub:
1 tsp. garlic powder
1 tbsp. brown sugar
1 tsp. cumin
1 tsp. pepper
1 C. chicken stock
1 tsp. cayenne pepper
1 tsp. paprika
1 tsp. onion powder
1 tsp. salt

Directions:
In a small bowl, mix together all rub ingredients and rub over meat. Pour the stock into the instant pot then place ribs into the pot. Seal pot with lid and cook on high pressure for 45 minutes. Once done then allow to release pressure naturally then open the lid. Stir and serve.

Beef Rice Noodles (pressure Cook)

Ingredients: Servings: 4 Cooking Time: 16 Mins

8 oz. (227 g) rice noodles
1 tbsp. sesame oil
1 lb. (454 g) ground beef
2 C. sliced shitake mushrooms
½ C. julienned carrots
1 yellow onion, sliced
1 C. shredded green cabbage
6 C. boiled water
¼ C. sliced scallions, for garnish
Sesame seeds, for garnish
Sauce:
¼ C. tamarind sauce
1 tbsp. hoisin sauce
1 tsp. grated ginger
1 tsp. maple syrup

Directions:
In a medium bowl, whisk together the ingredients for the sauce. Set aside. Pour boiling water into a bowl and add rice noodles. Cover the bowl and allow the noodles to soften for 5 minutes. Drain and set aside. Set the Instant Pot to Sauté mode and heat the sesame oil. Cook the beef in the pot for 5 minutes or until browned. Stir in the mushrooms, carrots, onion, and cabbage. Cook for 5 minutes or until softened. Add the noodles. Top with the sauce and mix well. Cook for 1 more minute. Garnish with scallions and sesame seeds and serve immediately.

Steak and Broccoli

Ingredients: Servings: 4 Cooking Time: 12 Mins

Round steak – ¾ pound, cut into strips
Broccoli florets – 1 pound
Oyster sauce – 1/3 cup
Sesame oil – 2 tsps.
Soy sauce – 1 tsp.
Sugar – 1 tsp.
Sherry – 1/3 cup
Olive oil – 1 tbsp.
Garlic – 1 clove, minced

Directions:
In a bowl, mix sugar, sherry, soy sauce, oyster sauce, and sesame oil. Add beef, toss to coat and marinate for 30 minutes. Transfer to a bowl. Add oil, garlic, and broccoli. Toss to coat. Cook at 380F for 12 minutes. Serve.

Baked Carrot Beef

Ingredients: Servings: 5-6 Cooking Time: 60 Mins

2 carrots, chopped
2 sticks celery, chopped
3 lb. beef
Olive oil to taste
2 medium onions, sliced
Garlic cloves from 1 bunch
1 bunch mixed fresh herbs (thyme, rosemary, bay, sage etc.)

Directions:
Grease a baking pan with some cooking spray. Add the vegetables, beef roast, olive oil, and herbs; combine well. Place Instant Pot Air Fryer Crisp over kitchen platform. Press Air Fry, set the temperature to 400°F and set the timer to 5 minutes to preheat. Press "Start" and allow it to preheat for 5 minutes. In the inner pot, place the Air Fryer basket. In the basket, add the pan. Close the Crisp Lid and press the "Bake" setting. Set temperature to 380°F and set the timer to 60 minutes. Press "Start." Open the Crisp Lid after cooking time is over. Serve warm.

Bruschetta Chicken (air Fryer)

Ingredients: Servings: 4 Cooking Time: 20 Mins

Bruschetta Stuffing:
3 tbsp. balsamic vinegar
1 tsp. Italian seasoning
2 tbsp. chopped fresh basil
3 garlic cloves, minced
2 tbsp. extra-virgin olive oil
1 tomato, diced
Chicken:
4 (4-ounce / 113-g) boneless, skinless chicken breasts, cut 4 slits each
1 tsp. Italian seasoning
Chicken seasoning or rub, to taste
Cooking spray

Directions:
Preheat the air fryer to 370°F (188°C). Spritz the air fryer basket with cooking spray. Combine the ingredients for the bruschetta stuffing in a bowl. Stir to mix well. Set aside. Rub the chicken breasts with Italian seasoning and chicken seasoning on a clean work surface. Arrange the chicken breasts, slits side up, in a single layer in the air fryer basket and spritz with cooking spray. You may need to work in batches to avoid overcrowding. Air fry for 7 minutes, then open the air

fryer and fill the slits in the chicken with the bruschetta stuffing. Cook for another 3 minutes or until the chicken is well browned. Serve immediately.

Garlic Chicken (pressure Cook)

Ingredients: Servings: 4 Cooking Time: 20 Mins

2 chicken breasts, skinless, boneless and halved
1 C. tomato sauce
¼ C. sweet chili sauce
¼ C. chicken stock
4 garlic cloves, minced
1 tbsp. chopped basil

Directions:
Combine all the ingredients in the Instant Pot. Secure the lid. Select the Poultry mode and set the cooking time for 20 minutes at High Pressure. Once cooking is complete, do a natural pressure release for 10 minutes, then release any remaining pressure. Carefully open the lid. Divide the chicken breasts among four plates and serve.

Feta & Spinach Stuffed Chicken Breasts

Ingredients: Servings: 4 Cooking Time: 20 Mins

4 Chicken Breasts, skinless
Salt and Black Pepper to taste
1 C. Baby Spinach, frozen
½ C. crumbled Feta Cheese
½ tsp. dried Oregano
½ tsp. Garlic Powder
2 tbsp. Olive Oil
2 tsp. dried Parsley

Directions:
Wrap the chicken in plastic and put on a cutting board. Use a rolling pin to lb. flat to a quarter inch thickness. Remove the plastic wrap. In a bowl, mix spinach, salt, and feta cheese and scoop the mixture onto the chicken breasts. Wrap the chicken to secure the spinach filling in it. Use toothpicks to secure the wrap firmly from opening. Gently season the chicken pieces with oregano, parsley, garlic powder, and pepper. Select Sear/Sauté mode on the cooker. Heat the oil, add the chicken, and sear to golden brown on each side. Work in 2 batches. Remove the chicken onto a plate and set aside. Pour the 1 C. water into the pot and use a spoon to scrape the bottom of the pot to let loose any chicken pieces or seasoning that is stuck to the bottom of the pot. Fit the reversiblerack into the pot with care as the pot will still be hot. Transfer the chicken onto the rack. Seal the lid and select Pressure mode on High pressure for 10 minutes. Press Start. Once the timer has ended, do a quick pressure release. Close the crisping lid and cook on Bake mode for 5 minutes at 370 F. Serve.

Juicy Pork Tenderloin

Ingredients: Servings: 4 Cooking Time: 20 Mins

2 lb Pork Tenderloin
½ C. Soy Sauce
¼ C. Sugar
½ C. Water + 2 tbsp. Water
2 cloves Garlic, minced
3 tbsp. grated Ginger
2 tbsp. Sesame Oil
2 tsp. Cornstarch
Chopped Scallions to garnish
Sesame Seeds to garnish

Directions:
In the cooker's inner pot, add soy sauce, sugar, half C. of water, ginger, garlic, and sesame oil. Use a spoon to stir them. Then, add the pork. Close the lid, secure the pressure valve, and select Pressure mode on High pressure for 12 minutes. Press Start. Once the timer has ended, do a quick pressure release, and open the pot. Remove the pork and set aside. In a bowl, mix the cornstarch with the remaining water until smooth and pour it into the pot. Bring back the pork. Close the crisping lid and press Broil. Cook for 5 minutes, until the sauce has thickened. Stir the sauce frequently, every 1-2 minutes, to avoid burning. Once the sauce is ready, serve the pork with a side endive salad or steamed veggies. Spoon the sauce all over it.

Smoky Steak

Ingredients: Servings: 2 Cooking Time: 5 Mins

12 oz steaks
1 tsp. liquid smoke
1 tbsp. soy sauce
1/2 tbsp. cocoa powder
1 tbsp. Montreal steak seasoning
Pepper
Salt

Directions:
Add steak, liquid smoke, and soy sauce in a zip-lock bag and shake well. Season steak with seasonings and place in the refrigerator overnight. Place the dehydrating tray in a multi-level air fryer basket and place basket in the instant pot. Place marinated steak on dehydrating tray. Seal pot with air fryer lid and select air fry mode then set the temperature to 375 F and timer for 5 minutes. Serve and enjoy.

Beef Pie

Ingredients: Servings: 4 Cooking Time: 65 Mins

3 tbsp. soy sauce
1 tbsp. Worcestershire sauce
¼ C. plain flour
¼ tsp. salt
½ tsp. pepper
3 bay leaves
2 lbs. lean beef, cubed
3 sprigs thyme
3 garlic cloves
1 carrot, sliced
1 onion, sliced
6 new potatoes, halved
2 celery ribs, sliced
1 C. red wine
1 C. beef stock
2 tbsp. parsley

Directions:
Whisk seasonings with flour, soy, Worcestershire sauce, thyme, and bay leaves in a pot. Stir cook this sauce for 5 minutes then add carrot, garlic, onion, stock, red wine, and beef. Mix well, then spread this beef mixture into the Instant Pot Duo. Put on the Air Fryer lid and seal it. Hit the "Bake Button" and select 60 minutes of cooking time, then press "Start." Once the Instant Pot Duo beeps, remove its lid. Serve

Air Fried Steak Sandwich

Ingredients: Servings: 4 Cooking Time: 16 Mins

Large hoagie bun, sliced in half
6 oz. of sirloin or flank steak, sliced into bite-sized pieces
½ tbsp. of mustard
1 tbsp. of fresh bleu cheese, crumbled
8 medium-sized cherry tomatoes, sliced in half
1 C. of fresh arugula,

powder
½ tbsp. of soy sauce

rinsed and patted dry

Directions:

1 Preparing the Ingredients. In a small mixing bowl, combine the soy sauce and onion powder; stir with a fork until thoroughly combined. Lay the raw steak strips in the soy-mustard mixture, and fully immerse each piece to marinate. Set the Instant Crisp Air Fryer to 320 degrees for 10 minutes. Arrange the soy-mustard marinated steak pieces on a piece of tin foil, flat and not overlapping, and set the tin foil on one side of the Instant Crisp Air Fryer basket. the foil should not take up more than half of the surface. Lay the hoagie-bun halves, crusty-side up and soft-side down, on the other half of the air-fryer. 2 Air Frying. Close air fryer lid. After 10 minutes, the Instant Crisp Air Fryer will shut off; the hoagie buns should be starting to crisp and the steak will have begun to cook. Carefully, flip the hoagie buns so they are now crusty-side down and soft-side up; crumble a layer of the bleu cheese on each hoagie half. with a long spoon, gently stir the marinated steak in the foil to ensure even coverage. Set the Instant Crisp Air Fryer to 360 degrees for 6 minutes. After 6 minutes, when the fryer shuts off, the bleu cheese will be perfectly melted over the toasted bread, and the steak will be juicy on the inside and crispy on the outside. Remove the cheesy hoagie halves first, using tongs, and set on a serving plate; then cover one side with the steak, and top with the cherry-tomato halves and the arugula. Close with the other cheesy hoagie-half, slice into two pieces, and enjoy.

Beefy and Cheesy Spanish Rice Casserole

Ingredients: Servings: 3 Cooking Time: 50 Mins

2 tbsp. chopped green bell pepper
1 tbsp. chopped fresh cilantro
1/2-pound lean ground beef
1/2 C. water
1/2 tsp. brown sugar
1/2 pinch ground black pepper
1/3 C. uncooked long grain rice
1/2 tsp. salt
1/4 C. finely chopped onion
1/4 C. chile sauce
1/4 tsp. ground cumin
1/4 tsp. Worcestershire sauce
1/4 C. shredded Cheddar cheese
1/2 (14.5 ounce) can canned tomatoes

Directions:

1 Preparing the Ingredients. Lightly grease baking pan of Instant Crisp Air Fryer with cooking spray. Add ground beef. 2 Air Frying. Close air fryer lid. For 10 minutes, cook on 360°F. Halfway through cooking time, stir and crumble beef. Discard excess fat, Stir in pepper, Worcestershire sauce, cumin, brown sugar, salt, chile sauce, rice, water, tomatoes, green bell pepper, and onion. Mix well. Cover pan with foil and cook for 25 minutes. Stirring occasionally. Give it one last good stir, press down firmly and sprinkle cheese on top. Cook uncovered for 15 minutes at 390°F until tops are lightly browned. Serve and enjoy with chopped cilantro.

Fall Celeriac Pumpkin Soup

Ingredients: Servings: 4 Cooking Time: 13 Mins

1 Celeriac, peeled and cubed
16 oz Pumpkin Puree
2 C. Vegetable Broth
5 stalks Celery, chopped
1 White Onion, chopped
1 lb Green Beans, cut in 5 to 6 strips each
3 C. Spinach Leaves
1 tbsp. chopped Basil Leaves
¼ tsp. dried Thyme
⅛ tsp. rubbed Sage
Salt to taste

Directions:

Open the cooker and pour in the celeriac, pumpkin puree, celery, onion, green beans, vegetable broth, basil leaves, thyme, sage, and a little salt. Close the lid, secure the pressure valve, and select Steam mode on High pressure for 5 minutes. Press Start. Once the timer has ended, do a quick pressure release and open the lid. Add in the spinach and stir using a spoon. Close the crisping lid and cook for 3 minutes on Broil mode. Use a soup spoon to fetch the soup into serving bowls.

Drunk Whole Roasted Chicken

Ingredients: Servings: 4 Cooking Time: 30 Mins

4-pound whole chicken
½ C. white wine
Juice of 1 lemon
2 limes, juiced
3 tbsp. olive oil
¼ C. coconut aminos
1 tbsp. ground cumin
6 cloves garlic, grated
1 tbsp. salt
3 tbsp. chopped fresh rosemary

Directions:

Rinse the chicken thoroughly with water and tie the legs with butcher's twine. Pour the wine and lemon juice into the pot. Place the chicken in the Cook & Crisp basket and fix the basket in the higher position of the pot. Seal the pressure lid, choose Pressure and set to High. Set the time to 20 minutes, then Choose Start. When ready, perform a quick pressure release. In a bowl, combine the lime juice, the olive oil, coconut aminos, cumin, garlic, and salt; mix until thoroughly combined. Brush the mixture over the chicken. Close the lid, choose Air Fry, set temperature to 390 F, and the time to 15 minutes. Choose Start. After 10 minutes, lift the crisping lid and sprinkle the chicken with rosemary. Continue cooking. When the timer rings, transfer the chicken to a plate. Let the chicken rest for 10 minutes before cutting and serving.

Herbed Lamb Rack

Ingredients: Servings: 2 Cooking Time: 10 Mins

2 tsp. garlic, minced
½ tsp. salt
2 tbsp. rosemary, dried
1 tbsp. thyme, dried
½ tsp. pepper
4 tbsp. olive oil

Directions:

In a mixing bowl, add the olive oil and herbs. Combine the ingredients to mix well with each other. Coat the lamb with the herb mixture. Place Instant Pot Air Fryer Crisp over kitchen platform. Press Air Fry set the temperature to 400°F and set the timer to 5 minutes to preheat. Press "Start" and allow it to preheat for 5 minutes. In the inner pot, place the Air Fryer basket. In the basket, add the lamb rack. Close the Crisp Lid and press the "Air Fry" setting. Set temperature to 360°F and set the timer to 10 minutes. Press "Start." Halfway down, open the Crisp Lid, shake the basket and close the lid to continue cooking for the remaining time. Open the Crisp Lid after cooking time is over. Serve warm.

Homemade Bbq Ribs

Ingredients: Servings: 2 Cooking Time: 35 Mins

½ lb rack Baby Back Ribs
Salt and Pepper to season
¼ C. Beef Broth
½ C. Barbecue Sauce
3 tbsp. Apple Cider Vinegar

Directions:
Select Sear/Sauté mode. Heat the oil into the pot. Meanwhile, season the ribs with salt and pepper. Cook them to brown, for 1 to 2 minutes per side. Pour the barbecue sauce, broth, and apple cider vinegar over the ribs and use tongs to flip so they are well coated. Close the lid and pressure valve and set to Pressure mode on High pressure for 30 minutes. Press Start to start cooking. Once the timer goes off, do a natural pressure release for 12 minutes, then a quick pressure release to let out the remaining steam. Close the crisping lid and set to Air Fry mode for 5 minutes at 350 F. Make sure the sauce is thick enough. Use a knife to slice the ribs and over the sauce all over it. Serve the ribs with a generous side of steamed but crunchy green beans.

Golden Chicken Cutlets (air Fryer)

Ingredients: Servings: 4 Cooking Time: 15 Mins

2 tbsp. panko bread crumbs
¼ C. grated Parmesan cheese
⅛ tbsp. paprika
½ tbsp. garlic powder
2 large eggs
4 chicken cutlets
1 tbsp. parsley
Salt and ground black pepper, to taste
Cooking spray

Directions:
Preheat the air fryer to 400°F (204°C). Spritz the air fryer basket with cooking spray. Combine the bread crumbs, Parmesan, paprika, garlic powder, salt, and ground black pepper in a large bowl. Stir to mix well. Beat the eggs in a separate bowl. Dredge the chicken cutlets in the beaten eggs, then roll over the bread crumbs mixture to coat well. Shake the excess off. Transfer the chicken cutlets in the preheated air fryer and spritz with cooking spray. Air fry for 15 minutes or until crispy and golden brown. Flip the cutlets halfway through. Serve with parsley on top.

Italian-style Air-fried Meatballs

Ingredients: Servings: 12 Cooking Time: 15 Mins

1 medium-size shallot, minced
2 tbsps. olive oil
2 tbsps. whole milk
2 onions, chopped
3 cloves garlic, minced
2/3 lb. lean ground beef
1 large egg, lightly beaten
¼ C. fresh flat-leaf parsley, finely chopped
1 tbsp. Dijon mustard
1 tbsp. fresh thyme, finely chopped
1 tbsp. fresh rosemary, finely chopped
½ tsp. Kosher salt
1 C. panko bread crumbs
⅓ lb. bulk turkey sausage

Directions:
Sauté garlic and onions in the Instant Pot using and cover with the Pressure cooker lid. Set to Sauté function and cook for 1-2 minutes. Remove garlic and shallot from the pot. Combine panko bread crumbs and milk in a large bowl and let them stand for about 5 minutes. Mix the shallot and garlic to the breadcrumb mixture together with the turkey sausage, beef, and the rest of the remaining ingredients. Gently shape the batter into 1½-inch balls using your hands. Place meatballs in the air fryer basket lined with parchment paper over a raised trivet inside the Instant Pot. Cook in batches to avoid overcrowding. Cover the instant pot using the air fryer lid this time and set cooking to 400 degrees F for 10-11 minutes. Remove from the basket to cook the remaining meatballs using the same process.

Italian Meatloaf Sliders

Ingredients: Servings: 8 Cooking Time: 10 Mins

1 lb ground beef
1/4 C. coconut flour
1/2 C. almond flour
1 garlic clove, minced
1/4 C. onion, chopped
2 eggs, lightly beaten
1/2 tsp. dried tarragon
1 tsp. Italian seasoning
1 tbsp. Worcestershire sauce
1/4 C. ketchup
1/4 tsp. pepper
1/2 tsp. sea salt

Directions:
Add all ingredients into the mixing bowl and mix until well combined. Make patties from meat mixture and place them on a plate. Place in refrigerator for 10 minutes. Place the dehydrating tray in a multi-level air fryer basket and place basket in the instant pot. Place patties on dehydrating tray. Seal pot with air fryer lid and select air fry mode then set the temperature to 360 F and timer for 10 minutes. Turn patties halfway through. Serve and enjoy.

Parsley Pork with Coconut Sauce

Ingredients: Servings: 6 Cooking Time: 40 Mins

3 lb Shoulder Roast
1 tbsp. Olive Oil
Salt and Black Pepper to taste
2 C. Coconut Milk
1 tsp. Coriander Powder
1 tsp. Cumin Powder
3 tbsp. grated Ginger
3 tsp. minced Garlic
½ C. Beef Broth
1 Onion, peeled and quartered
Parsley Leaves (unchopped), to garnish

Directions:
In a bowl, add coriander, salt, pepper, and cumin. Use a spoon to mix them. Season the pork with the spice mixture. Rub the spice onto meat, with hands. Open the lid of cooker, add olive oil, pork, onions, ginger, garlic, broth and coconut milk. Close the lid, secure the pressure valve, and select Pressure mode on High for 30 minutes. Press Start to start cooking. Once the timer has stopped, do a quick pressure release. Give it a good stir and close the crisping lid. Cook for 10 minutes on Broil mode, until you perfect texture and creaminess. Dish the meat

with the sauce into a serving bowl, garnish it with the parsley and serve with a side of bread or cooked shrimp.

Greek Meatballs

Ingredients: Servings: 4 Cooking Time: 20 Mins

1 lb ground beef
1 egg, lightly beaten
1/4 C. parsley, chopped
4 oz feta cheese, crumbled
1 tbsp. garlic, minced
1/4 C. breadcrumbs
1/2 onion, chopped
1/2 lb ground lamb
Pepper
Salt

Directions:
Add all ingredients into the mixing bowl and mix until well combined. Place the dehydrating tray in a multi-level air fryer basket and place basket in the instant pot. Make meatballs meat mixture and place on dehydrating tray. Seal pot with air fryer lid and select bake mode then set the temperature to 380 F and timer for 25 minutes. Turn meatballs halfway through. Serve and enjoy.

Curry Pork Roast In Coconut Sauce

Ingredients: Servings: 6 Cooking Time: 60 Mins

½ tsp. curry powder
½ tsp. ground turmeric powder
1 can unsweetened coconut milk
2 tbsp. fish sauce
1 tbsp. sugar
2 tbsp. soy sauce
3 lb. pork shoulder
Salt and pepper to taste

Directions:
1 Preparing the Ingredients. Place all Ingredients in bowl and allow the meat to marinate in the fridge for at least 2 hours. Preheat the Instant Crisp Air Fryer to 390°F. Place the grill pan accessory in the Instant Crisp Air Fryer. 2 Air Frying. Close air fryer lid. Grill the meat for 20 minutes making sure to flip the pork every 10 minutes for even grilling and cook in batches. Meanwhile, pour the marinade in a saucepan and allow to simmer for 10 minutes until the sauce thickens. Baste the pork with the sauce before serving.

Gingered Tofu Noddle Soup

Ingredients: Servings: 4 Cooking Time: 15 Mins

16 oz firm Tofu, water- packed
7 cloves Garlic, minced
2 tbsp. Korean red pepper flakes (gochugaru)
1 tbsp. Sugar
1 tbsp. Olive Oil
2 tbsp. Ginger Paste
¼ C. Soy Sauce
3 C. sliced Bok Choy
6 oz. dry Egg Noodles
4 C. Vegetable Broth
1 C. sliced Shitake Mushrooms
½ C. chopped Cilantro

Directions:
Drain the liquid out of the tofu, pat the tofu dry with paper towels, and use a knife to cut them into 1-inch cubes. Turn your cooker on and select Sear/Sauté mode on Medium. Pour the oil to heat, add the garlic and ginger, and sauté for 2 minutes. Add the sugar, broth, and soy sauce. Stir and cook for 30 seconds. Include the tofu and bok choy, close the lid, secure the pressure valve, and select Pressure mode on High pressure for 10 minutes. Press Start. Once the timer has ended, do a quick pressure release and open the lid. Add the zucchini noodles, give it a good stir using a spoon, and close the crisping lid. Let the soup cook for 4 minutes on Broil mode. Use a soup spoon to fetch the soup into soup bowls, top with cilantro and enjoy.

Lamb Curry with Zucchini (pressure Cook)

Ingredients: Servings: 3 Cooking Time: 25 Mins

1 lb. (454 g) cubed lamb stew meat
2 garlic cloves, minced
½ C. coconut milk
1 tbsp. grated fresh ginger
½ tsp. lime juice
¼ tsp. salt
¼ tsp. black pepper
1 tbsp. olive oil
1½ medium carrots, sliced
½ medium onion, diced
¾ C. diced tomatoes
½ tsp. turmeric powder
½ medium zucchini, diced

Directions:
In a bowl, stir together the garlic, coconut milk, ginger, lime juice, salt and pepper. Add the lamb to the bowl and marinate for 30 minutes. Combine the remaining ingredients, except for the zucchini, in the Instant Pot. Add the meat and the marinade to the pot. Set the lid in place. Select the Pressure Cook and set the cooking time for 20 minutes at High Pressure. Once the timer goes off, use a natural pressure release for 15 minutes, then release any remaining pressure. Open the lid. Add the zucchini to the pot. Select the Sauté mode and cook for 5 minutes. Serve hot.

POULTRY RECIPES

Ranch Chicken Wings

Ingredients: Servings: 6 Cooking Time: 35 Mins

12 chicken wings
1 tbsp. olive oil
1 C. chicken broth
1/4 C. butter
1/2 C. Red Hot Sauce
1/4 tsp. Worcestershire sauce
1 tbsp. white vinegar
1/4 tsp. cayenne pepper
1/8 tsp. garlic powder
Seasoned salt to taste
Ranch dressing for dipping
Celery for garnish

Directions:
Set the Air Fryer Basket in the Instant Pot Duo and pour the broth in it. Spread the chicken wings in the basket and put on the pressure-cooking lid. Hit the "Pressure Button" and select 10 minutes of cooking time, then press "Start." Meanwhile, prepare the sauce and add butter, vinegar, cayenne pepper, garlic powder, Worcestershire sauce, and hot sauce in a small saucepan. Stir cook this sauce for 5 minutes on medium heat until it thickens. Once the Instant Pot Duo beeps, do a quick release and remove its lid. Remove the wings and empty the Instant Pot Duo. Toss the wings with oil, salt, and black pepper. Set the Air Fryer Basket in the Instant Pot Duo and arrange the wings in it. Put on the Air Fryer lid and seal it. Hit the "Air Fryer Button" and select 20 minutes of cooking time, then press "Start." Once the Instant Pot Duo beeps,

remove its lid. Transfer the wings to the sauce and mix well. Serve.

Flavorful Lemon Chicken

Ingredients: Servings: 4 Cooking Time: 4 Hours 5 Mins

20 oz chicken breasts, skinless, boneless, and cut into pieces
1 tsp. dried parsley
2 tbsp. olive oil
2 tbsp. butter
3 tbsp. flour
1/4 C. chicken broth
1/2 C. fresh lemon juice
1/8 tsp. dried thymefla
1/4 tsp. dried basil
1/2 tsp. dried oregano
1 tsp. salt

Directions:

In a bowl, toss chicken with flour. Heat butter and oil in a pan over medium-high heat. Add chicken to the pan and sear until brown. Transfer chicken into the inner pot of instant pot duo crisp. Add remaining ingredients on top of chicken. Seal the pot with pressure cooking lid and select slow cook mode and cook on low for 4 hours. Serve and enjoy.

Cheesy Chicken Fritters

Ingredients: Servings: 17 Cooking Time: 20 Mins

Chicken Fritters:
½ tsp. salt
1/8 tsp. pepper
1 ½ tbsp. fresh dill
1 1/3 C. shredded mozzarella cheese
1/3 C. coconut flour
1/3 C. vegan mayo
2 eggs
1 ½ lb. chicken breasts
Garlic Dip:
1/8 tsp. pepper
¼ tsp. salt
½ tbsp. lemon juice
1 pressed garlic cloves
1/3 C. vegan mayo

Directions:

1 Preparing the Ingredients. Slice chicken breasts into 1/3" pieces and place in a bowl. Add all remaining fritter ingredients to the bowl and stir well. Cover and chill 2 hours or overnight. Ensure your Instant Crisp Air Fryer is preheated to 350 degrees. Spray basket with a bit of olive oil. 2 Air Frying. Add marinated chicken to Instant Crisp Air Fryer. Lock the air fryer lid, set temperature to 350°F, and set time to 20 minutes and cook 20 minutes, making sure to turn halfway through cooking process. To make the dipping sauce, combine all the dip ingredients until smooth.

Ricotta and Parsley Stuffed Turkey Breasts

Ingredients: Servings: 4 Cooking Time: 25 Mins

1 turkey breast, quartered
1 C. Ricotta cheese
1/4 C. fresh Italian parsley, chopped
1 tsp. garlic powder
1/2 tsp. cumin powder
1 egg, beaten
1 tsp. paprika
Salt and ground black pepper, to taste
Crushed tortilla chips
1 ½ tbsp. extra-virgin olive oil

Directions:

1 Preparing the Ingredients. Firstly, flatten out each piece of turkey breast with a rolling pin. Prepare three mixing bowls. In a shallow bowl, combine Ricotta cheese with the parsley, garlic powder, and cumin powder. Place the Ricotta/parsley mixture in the middle of each piece. Repeat with the remaining pieces of the turkey breast and roll them up. In another shallow bowl, whisk the egg together with paprika. In the third shallow bowl, combine the salt, pepper, and crushed tortilla chips. Dip each roll in the whisked egg, then, roll them over the tortilla chips mixture. Transfer prepared rolls to the Instant Crisp Air Fryer basket. Drizzle olive oil over all. 2 Air Frying. Lock the air fryer lid. Cook at 350 degrees F for 25 minutes, working in batches. Serve warm, garnished with some extra parsley, if desired.

Orange Curried Chicken Stir-fry

Ingredients: Servings: 4 Cooking Time: 18 Mins

¾ lb. boneless, skinless chicken thighs, cut into 1-inch pieces
1 yellow bell pepper, cut into 1½-inch pieces
1 small red onion, sliced
Olive oil for misting
¼ C. chicken stock
2 tbsp. honey
¼ C. orange juice
1 tbsp. cornstarch
3 to 3 tsp. curry powder

Directions:

Preparing the Ingredients. Put the chicken thighs, pepper, and red onion in the Instant Crisp Air Fryer basket and mist with olive oil. Air Frying. Lock the air fryer lid. Cook for 12 to 14 minutes or until the chicken is cooked to 165°F, shaking the basket halfway through cooking time. Remove the chicken and vegetables from the Instant Crisp Air Fryer basket and set aside. In a 6-inch metal bowl, combine the stock, honey, orange juice, cornstarch, and curry powder, and mix well. Add the chicken and vegetables, stir, and put the bowl in the basket. Return the basket to the Instant Crisp Air Fryer and cook for 2 minutes. Remove and stir, then cook for 2 to 3 minutes or until the sauce is thickened and bubbly.

Classic Honey Mustard Chicken

Ingredients: Servings: 5-6 Cooking Time: 20 Mins

3 tbsp. honey
6 (6-ounces each) boneless, skinless chicken breasts 2 tbsp. rosemary, minced
2 tbsp. Dijon mustard
¼ tsp. ground black pepper
¾ tsp. salt

Directions:

In a mixing bowl, combine the honey, Dijon mustard, black pepper, rosemary, and salt. Rub the chicken breasts with the mixture. Grease Air Fryer Basket with some cooking spray. Arrange the chicken breasts. Place Instant Pot Air Fryer Crisp over kitchen platform. Press Air Fry, set the temperature to 400°F and set the timer to 5 minutes to preheat. Press "Start" and allow it to preheat for 5 minutes. In the inner pot, place the Air Fryer basket. Close the Crisp Lid and press the "Air Fry" setting. Set temperature to 350°F and set the timer to 20-22 minutes. Press "Start." Halfway down, open the Crisp Lid, shake the basket and close the lid to continue cooking for the remaining time. Open the Crisp Lid after cooking time is over. Serve warm with veggies or cooked rice.

Chicken Mac and Cheese

Ingredients: Servings: 6 Cooking Time: 9 Mins

2 1/2 C. macaroni
2 C. chicken stock
1 C. cooked chicken, shredded
1 1/4 C. heavy cream
8 tbsp. butter
2 2/3 C. cheddar cheese, shredded
1/3 C. parmesan cheese, shredded
1 bag Ritz crackers
1/4 tsp. garlic powder
Salt and pepper to taste

Directions:
Add chicken stock, heavy cream, chicken, 4 tbsp. butter, and macaroni to the Instant Pot Duo. Put on the pressure-cooking lid and seal it. Hit the "Pressure Button" and select 4 minutes of cooking time, then press "Start." Crush the crackers and mix them well with 4 tbsp. melted butter. Once the Instant Pot Duo beeps, do a quick release and remove its lid. Put on the Air Fryer lid and seal it. Hit the "Air Fryer Button" and select 5 minutes of cooking time, then press "Start." Once the Instant Pot Duo beeps, remove its lid. Serve.

Herbed Chicken

Ingredients: Servings: 4 Cooking Time: 40 Mins

Whole chicken – 1
Salt and black pepper to taste
Garlic powder – 1 tsp.
Onion powder – 1 tsp.
Thyme – ½ tsp. dried
Rosemary – 1 tsp. dried
Lemon juice – 1 tbsp.
Olive oil – 2 tbsps.

Directions:
Season chicken with salt and pepper. Rub with onion powder, garlic powder, rosemary, and thyme. Rub with olive oil and lemon juice and marinate for 30 minutes. Cook chicken in the air fryer at 360F for 20 minutes on each side. Carve and serve.

Basil-garlic Breaded Chicken Bake

Ingredients: Servings: 2 Cooking Time: 25 Mins

2 boneless skinless chicken breast halves (4 oz. each)
1 tbsp. butter, melted
1 large tomato, seeded and chopped
2 garlic cloves, minced
1 1/2 tbsp. minced fresh basil
1/2 tsp. salt
1/2 tbsp. olive oil
1/4 C. all-purpose flour
1/4 C. egg substitute
1/4 C. grated Parmesan cheese
1/4 C. dry bread crumbs
1/4 tsp. pepper

Directions:
1 Preparing the Ingredients. In shallow bowl, whisk well egg substitute and place flour in a separate bowl. Dip chicken in flour, then egg, and then flour. In small bowl whisk well butter, bread crumbs and cheese. Sprinkle over chicken. Lightly grease baking pan of Instant Crisp Air Fryer with cooking spray. Place breaded chicken on bottom of pan. Cover with foil. 2 Air Frying. Lock the air fryer lid. For 20 minutes, cook on 390°F. Meanwhile, in a bowl whisk well remaining ingredient. Remove foil from pan and then pour over chicken the remaining Ingredients. Cook for 8 minutes. Serve and enjoy.

Easy Cheesy Chicken

Ingredients: Servings: 6 Cooking Time: 17 Mins

1 1/2 lbs chicken tenders
25 oz tomato sauce
2 tbsp. butter
1/2 C. olive oil
1/2 tsp. garlic powder
1/2 C. parmesan cheese, grated
2 C. mozzarella cheese, shredded

Directions:
Add olive oil into the inner pot of instant pot duo crisp and set pot on sauté mode. Add chicken and sauté until lightly brown from both the sides. Add garlic powder, tomato sauce, butter, and parmesan cheese on top of chicken. Seal the pot with pressure cooking lid and cook on high for 15 minutes. Once done, release pressure using a quick release. Remove lid. Sprinkle mozzarella cheese on top of chicken. Cover pot with air fryer lid and select broil mode and cook for 1-2 minutes. Serve and enjoy.

Air Fryer Garlic Herb Turkey Breast

Ingredients: Servings: 6 Cooking Time: 40 Mins

2 lb. turkey breast with skin.
4 tbsp. melted butter
3 garlic cloves, grated
1 tsp. fresh rosemary, chopped
1 tsp. thyme, finely chopped
1 tsp. ground black pepper
½ tsp. kosher salt
Vegetable cooking spray

Directions:
Clean, wash and pat dry the turkey breasts. Rub salt and pepper on all sides of turkey breasts. Combine rosemary, melted butter, thyme, and garlic in a medium bowl. Brush the mix all over the turkey breast. Spray some cooking oil in the air fryer basket. Place the seasoned turkey in the air fryer basket and put it in the inner pot of the Instant Pot Air fryer. Close the crisp lid and select the temperature to 375°F in AIR FRY mode. Set the timer to 40 minutes and press START to begin the frying. After 20 minutes of frying, open the crisp lid and flip the turkey breast spray some cooking oil. Close the crisp lid to resume cooking. Once the frying is over, allow it to settle down the heat before you want to slice and serve.

Zucchini Tomato Chicken

Ingredients: Servings: 4 Cooking Time: 30 Mins

1 lb chicken tenders
1 tbsp. olive oil
1 dill sprigs
1/2 zucchini, sliced
1/2 C. cherry tomatoes
For topping:
1/2 tbsp. fresh lemon juice
1/2 tbsp. fresh dill, chopped
1 tbsp. feta cheese, crumbled
1/2 tbsp. olive oil

Directions:
In a bowl, toss chicken with oil, dill, zucchini, and cherry tomatoes. Line instant pot multi-level air fryer basket with aluminum foil. Add chicken mixture into the air fryer basket and place basket into the instant pot. Seal pot with air fryer lid

and select bake mode then set the temperature to 380 F and timer for 30 minutes. Stir halfway through. Mix together topping ingredients and sprinkle over chicken and vegetables. Serve and enjoy.

Fried Chicken Tacos

Ingredients: Servings: 4 Cooking Time: 10 Mins

Chicken
1 lb. chicken tenders or breast chopped into 2-inch pieces
1 tsp. garlic powder
½ tsp. onion powder
1 large egg
1 ½ tsp. salt
1 tsp. paprika
3 Tbsp buttermilk
¾ C. All-purpose flour
3 Tbsp corn starch
½ tsp. black pepper
½ tsp. cayenne pepper
oil for spraying
Coleslaw
¼ tsp. red pepper flakes
2 C. coleslaw mix
1 Tbsp brown sugar
½ tsp. salt
2 Tbsp apple cider vinegar
1 Tbsp water
Spicy Mayo
½ tsp. salt
¼ C. mayonnaise
1 tsp. garlic powder
2 Tbsp hot sauce
1 Tbsp buttermilk
Tortilla wrappers

Directions:
Take a large bowl and mix together coleslaw mix, water, brown sugar, salt, apple cider vinegar, and red pepper flakes. Set aside. Take another small bowl and combine mayonnaise, hot sauce, buttermilk, garlic powder, and salt. Set this mixture aside. Select the Instant Pot Duo Crisp Air Fryer option, adjust the temperature to 360°F and push start. Preheating will start. Create a clear station by placing two large flat pans side by side.Whisk together egg and buttermilk with salt and pepper in one of them. In the second, whisk flour, corn starch, black pepper, garlic powder, onion powder, salt, paprika, and cayenne pepper. Cut the chicken tenders into 1-inch pieces. Season all pieces with a little salt and pepper. Once the Instant Pot Duo Crisp Air Fryer is preheated, remove the tray and lightly spray it with oil. Coat your chicken with egg mixture while shaking off any excess egg, followed by the flour mixture, and place it on the tray and tray in the basket, making sure your chicken pieces don't overlap. Close the Air Fryer lid, and cook on 360°F for 10 minutes, while flipping and spraying halfway through cooking. Once the chicken is done, remove and place chicken into warmed tortilla shells. Top with coleslaw and spicy mayonnaise.

Enchilada-braised Chicken Breasts

Ingredients: Servings: 4 Cooking Time: 15 Mins

1 tsp. packed dark brown sugar
1 tsp. ground cumin
1 tsp. smoked paprika
½ tsp. salt
½ tsp. ground black pepper
½ tsp. onion powder
Four 6- to 8-ounce boneless skinless chicken breasts
¼ tsp. garlic powder
2 tbsp. olive oil
One 8-ounce can tomato sauce (1 cup)
½ C. light-colored beer, preferably a Pilsner or an IPA
2 tbsp. chili powder
2 tbsp. fresh lime juice

Directions:
Preparing the Ingredients. Mix the brown sugar, cumin, smoked paprika, salt, pepper, onion powder, and garlic powder in a medium bowl. Massage the spice rub onto the chicken breasts. Heat the oil in the Instant Crisp Air Fryer using the "Sauté" function. Set the breasts in the cooker and brown well, turning once, about 6 minutes. Mix the tomato sauce, beer, chili powder, and lime juice in the bowl the spices were in; pour the sauce over the breasts. High pressure for 15 minutes. Close the pressure cooking lid and Cook for 15 minutes. To get 15-minutes cook time, press the "Pressure" Button and adjust the time. Pressure Release. Use the quick-release method to bring the pot's pressure back to normal. Close the Air Fryer Lid. Select AIR FRY, set temperature to 390°F, and set time to 9 minutes. Check after 6 minutes, cooking for an additional 3 minutes if dish needs more browning. Serve the chicken with the sauce ladled on top.

Chicken Rice

Ingredients: Servings: 6 Cooking Time: 12 Mins

2 lbs. chicken thighs, skinless, boneless, and cut into pieces
18 oz enchilada sauce
15 oz frozen mixed vegetables
1 oz taco seasoning
2 C. rice, uncooked
1 C. chicken stock

Directions:
Spray instant pot duo crisp inner pot with cooking spray and set the pot on sauté mode. Season chicken with taco seasoning and place in the pot. Sear chicken until brown from all the sides, about 10 minutes. Add rice, stock, enchilada sauce, and vegetables and stir well. Seal the pot with pressure cooking lid and cook on high for 2 minutes. Once done, allow to release pressure naturally for 10 minutes then release remaining pressure using a quick release. Remove lid. Stir well and serve.

Asian Style Chicken Meal

Ingredients: Servings: 2-3 Cooking Time: 30 Mins

½ C. rice vinegar
1 lb. chicken wings
2 cloves garlic, minced
1 tsp. ginger, grated
1 tsp. sea salt
1 small orange, zest, and juice
2 tsp. red chili pepper paste

Directions:
Place Instant Pot Air Fryer Crisp over kitchen platform. In the inner pot, add 2 C. water and arrange trivet and place the chicken wings over. Close the Pressure Lid and press the "Pressure" setting. Set the "Hi" pressure level and set the timer to 2 minutes. Press "Start." Instant Pot will start building pressure. Quick-release pressure after cooking time is over (just press the button on the lid), and open the lid. Take out the wings and empty water. In a mixing bowl, combine the orange zest, orange juice, rice vinegar, honey, red pepper paste, ginger, garlic, and salt. Add the sauce in the pot and place trivet; place the chicken over the trivet. Close the Crisp Lid and press the "Air Fry" setting. Set temperature to 390°F and set the timer to 30 minutes. Press "Start." Halfway down, open the Crisp Lid, shake the basket and close the lid to continue cooking for the remaining time. Open the Crisp Lid after cooking time is over. Serve the chicken with the honey sauce.

Chicken Bbq with Sweet and Sour Sauce

Ingredients: Servings: 6 Cooking Time: 40 Mins

¼ C. minced garlic
¼ C. tomato paste
¾ C. minced onion
¾ C. sugar
1 C. soy sauce
1 C. water
1 C. white vinegar
6 chicken drumsticks
Salt and pepper to taste

Directions:
1 Preparing the Ingredients. Place all Ingredients in a Ziploc bag Allow to marinate for at least 2 hours in the fridge. Preheat the Instant Crisp Air Fryer to 390°F. Place the grill pan accessory in the Instant Crisp Air Fryer. 2 Air Frying. Lock the air fryer lid. Grill the chicken for 40 minutes. Flip the chicken every 10 minutes for even grilling. Meanwhile, pour the marinade in a saucepan and heat over medium flame until the sauce thickens. Before serving the chicken, brush with the glaze.

Spicy Chicken Breast

Ingredients: Servings: 2 Cooking Time: 35 Mins

2 chicken breasts, bone-in, and skin-on
1 tbsp. ground fennel
1 tbsp. chili powder
1 tbsp. olive oil
1 tsp. ground cumin
1 tsp. garlic powder
1 tsp. onion powder
1 tbsp. paprika
1/2 tsp. black pepper
1 tsp. sea salt

Directions:
In a small bowl, mix together all dried spices. Brush chicken with olive oil and rub with spice mixture. Place chicken in the instant pot air fryer basket and place basket in the pot. Seal the pot with air fryer lid and select air fry mode and cook at 375 f for 35 minutes. Serve and enjoy.

Honey-chipotle Chicken Wings

Ingredients: Servings: 2 Cooking Time: 10 Mins

1 C. water, for steaming
3 tbsp. Mexican hot sauce (such as Valentina brand)
2 tbsp. honey
1 tsp. minced canned chipotle in adobo sauce

Directions:
Preparing the Ingredients. If using whole wings, cut off the tips and discard. Cut the wings at the joint into two pieces each, the "drumette" and the "flat." Add the water and insert the steamer basket or trivet. Place the wings on the steamer insert. High pressure for 10 minutes. Close the pressure cooking lid and the pressure valve and then cook for 10 minutes. To get 10-minutes cook time, press "Pressure" button and the time selector. Pressure Release. Use the quick-release method. Finish the dish. While the wings are cooking, make the sauce. In a large bowl, whisk together the hot sauce, honey, and minced chipotle. Close the Air Fryer lid. Select AIR FRY, set temperature to 390°F, and set time to 10 minutes. Select START to begin.

Flavorful Herb Chicken

Ingredients: Servings: 6 Cooking Time: 4 Hours

6 chicken breasts, skinless and boneless
1 onion, sliced
14 oz can tomato, diced
1 tsp. dried basil
1 tsp. dried rosemary
1 tbsp. olive oil
1/2 C. balsamic vinegar
1/2 tsp. thyme
1 tsp. dried oregano
4 garlic cloves
Pepper
Salt

Directions:
Add all ingredients into the inner pot of instant pot duo crisp and stir well. Seal the pot with pressure cooking lid and select slow cook mode and cook on high for 4 hours. Stir well and serve.

Jamaican Chicken

Ingredients: Servings: 6 Cooking Time: 15 Mins

6 chicken drumsticks
1 tbsp. jerk seasoning
1/4 C. red wine vinegar
3 tbsp. soy sauce
1/4 C. brown sugar
1/2 C. ketchup
1 tsp. salt

Directions:
Add all ingredients except chicken into the inner pot of instant pot duo crisp and stir well. Add chicken and stir to coat. Seal the pot with pressure cooking lid and cook on high for 10 minutes. Once done, release pressure using a quick release. Remove lid. Remove chicken from pot. Set pot on sauté mode and cook sauce for 5 minutes. Pour sauce over chicken and serve.

Dijon Chicken

Ingredients: Servings: 4 Cooking Time: 50 Mins

1 1/2 lbs. chicken thighs, skinless and boneless
2 tbsp. dijon mustard
1/4 C. French mustard
4 tbsp. maple syrup
2 tsp. olive oil

Directions:
In a large bowl, mix together maple syrup, olive oil, dijon mustard, and french mustard. Add chicken to the bowl and mix until chicken is well coated. Transfer chicken into the instant pot air fryer basket and place basket in the pot. Seal the pot with air fryer lid and select bake mode and cook at 375 f for 45-50 minutes. Serve and enjoy.

Caesar Marinated Grilled Chicken

Ingredients: Servings: 3 Cooking Time: 24 Mins

¼ C. crouton
1 tsp. lemon zest.
Form into ovals, skewer and grill.
1/2 C. Parmesan
1/4 C. breadcrumbs
1-pound ground chicken
2 tbsp. Caesar dressing and more for drizzling
2-4 romaine leaves

Directions:
Preparing the Ingredients. In a shallow dish, mix well chicken, 2 tbsp. Caesar dressing, parmesan, and breadcrumbs. Mix well

with hands. Form into 1-inch oval patties. Thread chicken pieces in skewers. Place on skewer rack in Instant Crisp Air Fryer. Air Frying. Lock the air fryer lid. For 12 minutes, cook on 360°F. Halfway through cooking time, turnover skewers. If needed, cook in batches. Serve and enjoy on a bed of lettuce and sprinkle with croutons and extra dressing.

Korean Chicken Wings

Ingredients: Servings: 8 Cooking Time: 10 Mins

Wings:
1 tsp. pepper
1 tsp. salt
2 lb. chicken wings
Sauce:
2 packets Splenda
1 tbsp. minced garlic
1 tbsp. minced ginger
1 tbsp. sesame oil
1 tsp. agave nectar
1 tbsp. mayo
2 tbsp. gochujang
Finishing:
¼ C. chopped green onions
2 tsp. sesame seeds

Directions:

1 Preparing the Ingredients. Ensure Instant Crisp Air Fryer is preheated to 400 degrees. Line a small pan with foil and place a rack onto the pan, then place into Instant Crisp Air Fryer. Season wings with pepper and salt and place onto the rack. 2 Air Frying. Lock the air fryer lid. Set temperature to 160°F, and set time to 20 minutes and air fry 20 minutes, turning at 10 minutes. As chicken air fries, mix together all the sauce components. Once a thermometer says that the chicken has reached 160 degrees, take out wings and place into a bowl. Pour half of the sauce mixture over wings, tossing well to coat. Put coated wings back into Instant Crisp Air Fryer for 5 minutes or till they reach 165 degrees. Remove and sprinkle with green onions and sesame seeds. Dip into extra sauce.

Garlic Ranch Chicken Wings

Ingredients: Servings: 4 Cooking Time: 25 Mins

1 lb chicken wings
3 garlic cloves, minced
2 tbsp. butter, melted
1 1/2 tbsp. ranch seasoning

Directions:

Add chicken wings into the large bowl. Mix together butter, ranch seasoning, and garlic and pour over chicken wings and toss well. Cover bowl and place in the refrigerator overnight. Place marinated chicken wings into the air fryer basket and place basket in the pot. Seal pot with air fryer lid and select air fry mode then set the temperature to 360 F and timer for 20 minutes. Mix halfway through. Turn temperature to 390 F and air fry for 5 minutes more. Serve and enjoy.

Turkey Sausage Bake

Ingredients: Servings: 6 Cooking Time: 30 Mins

Ground turkey sausage – 1 lb.
Eggs - 6
Half-and-half – ½ cup
Cheddar cheese – ½ cup, shredded
Broccoli – 1 small head, chopped into florets
Red bell pepper – 1, diced
Onion – 1, chopped
Garlic – 2 cloves, chopped
Olive oil – 1 tbsp.
Salt and pepper to taste

Directions:

Heat the oil on Sauté. Sauté the sausage for 3 minutes. Add the onions and garlic and sauté for 2 minutes. Add the broccoli and red pepper and cook for 4 minutes. Then remove the mixture to a bowl. Crack the eggs in another bowl. add half-and-half, salt, and pepper then whisk to make it smooth. Grease ramekins and add about a quarter C. of the sausage mixture into each ramekin and cover with egg mixture. Sprinkle about 1 ½ tbsps. shredded cheddar cheese on top. Cook at 320F for 10 minutes. Cook in batches if necessary. Serve.

Buffalo Chicken Wings

Ingredients: Servings: 8 Cooking Time: 30 Mins

1 tsp. salt
1-2 tbsp. brown sugar
1 tbsp. Worcestershire sauce
½ C. vegan butter
½ C. cayenne pepper sauce
4 lb. chicken wings

Directions:

1 Preparing the Ingredients. Whisk salt, brown sugar, Worcestershire sauce, butter, and hot sauce together and set to the side. Dry wings and add to Instant Crisp Air Fryer basket. 2 Air Frying. Lock the air fryer lid. Set temperature to 380°F, and set time to 25 minutes. Cook tossing halfway through. When timer sounds, shake wings and bump up the temperature to 400 degrees and cook another 5 minutes. Take out wings and place into a big bowl. Add sauce and toss well. Serve alongside celery sticks!

Asian Wings

Ingredients: Servings: 4 Cooking Time: 25 Mins

1 lb chicken wings
1/4 tsp. pepper
1/2 tsp. salt
For sauce:
1 tbsp. sugar
1/2 tbsp. garlic, minced
1/2 tbsp. mayonnaise
1 tbsp. gochujang
1/2 tbsp. ginger, minced
1/2 tbsp. sesame oil
1/2 tsp. honey

Directions:

Season chicken wings with pepper and salt. Spray instant pot multi-level air fryer basket with cooking spray. Add chicken wings into the air fryer basket and place basket into the instant pot. Seal pot with air fryer lid and select air fry mode then set the temperature to 400 F and timer for 25 minutes. Turn chicken wings halfway through. Meanwhile, in a bowl, mix together all sauce ingredients. Add chicken wings to the sauce bowl and toss well. Serve and enjoy.

Creamy Italian Chicken

Ingredients: Servings: 8 Cooking Time: 10 Mins

2 lbs chicken breasts, skinless and boneless
1 C. chicken stock
1/4 C. butter
14 oz can cream of chicken soup
8 oz cream cheese
1 tbsp. Italian seasoning

Directions:

Add the chicken stock into the inner pot of instant pot duo crisp. Add cream of chicken soup, Italian seasoning, and butter into the pot and stir well. Seal the pot with pressure cooking lid and cook on high for 10 minutes. Once done, release pressure using a quick release. Remove lid. Add cream cheese and stir until cheese is melted Serve and enjoy.

Garlicky Chicken

Ingredients: Servings: 4 Cooking Time: 30 Mins

1 lb chicken drumsticks
1 tbsp. parsley, minced
1/2 fresh lemon juice
4 garlic cloves, minced
1 tbsp. olive oil
Pepper
Salt

Directions:
Season chicken with pepper and salt. Mix together parsley, lemon juice, garlic, and oil and rub over chicken. Place the dehydrating tray in a multi-level air fryer basket and place basket in the instant pot. Place chicken drumsticks on dehydrating tray. Seal pot with air fryer lid and select bake mode then set the temperature to 380 F and timer for 30 minutes. Turn chicken halfway through. Serve and enjoy.

Chicken Vegetable Fajitas

Ingredients: Servings: 4 Cooking Time: 20 Mins

8 oz chicken thighs, boneless, skinless, and cut into strips
1 jalapeno pepper, sliced
1 tbsp. olive oil
1/2 C. onion, sliced
1 1/2 C. bell peppers, sliced
1 tbsp. taco seasoning

Directions:
Add chicken and remaining ingredients into the mixing bowl and toss well. Spray instant pot multi-level air fryer basket with cooking spray. Add chicken vegetable mixture into the air fryer basket and place basket into the instant pot. Seal pot with air fryer lid and select bake mode then set the temperature to 380 F and timer for 20 minutes. Mix halfway through. Serve and enjoy.

Chicken Pasta

Ingredients: Servings: 4 Cooking Time: 15 Mins

1 lb. chicken breasts, boneless and skinless, cut into bite-size pieces
1 tbsp. garlic, minced
2 bell peppers, seeded and diced
2 tbsp. olive oil
1 onion, diced
1 C. chicken stock
3 tbsp. fajita seasoning
8 oz penne pasta, dry
7 oz can tomato

Directions:
Add olive oil in the inner pot of instant pot duo crisp and set pot on sauté mode. Add chicken and half fajita seasoning in the pot and sauté chicken for 3-5 minutes. Add garlic, bell pepper, onions, and remaining fajitas seasoning and sauté for 2 minutes. Add tomatoes, stock, and pasta and stir well. Seal the pot with pressure cooking lid and cook on high for 6 minutes. Once done, release pressure using a quick release. Remove lid. Set pot on sauté mode and cook for 1-2 minutes. Serve and enjoy.

Juicy Turkey Burgers

Ingredients: Servings: 8 Cooking Time: 25 Mins

1 lb ground turkey 85% lean / 15% fat
¼ C. unsweetened apple sauce
½ onion grated
1 Tbsp ranch seasoning
2 tsp. Worcestershire Sauce
1 tsp. minced garlic
¼ C. plain breadcrumbs
Salt and pepper to taste

Directions:
Combine the onion, ground turkey, unsweetened apple sauce, minced garlic, breadcrumbs, ranch seasoning, Worchestire sauce, and salt and pepper. Mix them with your hands until well combined. Form 4 equally sized hamburger patties with them. Place these burgers in the refrigerator for about 30 minutes to have them firm up a bit. While preparing for cooking, select the Air Fry option. Set the temperature of 360°F and the cook time as required. Press start to begin preheating. Once the preheating temperature is reached, place the burgers on the tray in the Air fryer basket, making sure they don't overlap or touch. Cook on for 15 minutes, flipping halfway through.

Chicken Fajitas

Ingredients: Servings: 4 Cooking Time: 10 Mins

4 boneless, skinless chicken breasts, sliced
1 small red onion, sliced
2 red bell peppers, sliced
½ tsp. dried oregano
½ C. spicy ranch salad dressing, divided
8 corn tortillas
2 C. torn butter lettuce
2 avocados, peeled and chopped

Directions:
Preparing the Ingredients. Place the chicken, onion, and pepper in the Instant Crisp Air Fryer basket. Drizzle with 1 tbsp. of the salad dressing and add the oregano. Toss to combine. Air Frying. Grill for 10 to 14 minutes or until the chicken is 165°F on a food thermometer. Transfer the chicken and vegetables to a bowl and toss with the remaining salad dressing. Serve the chicken mixture with the tortillas, lettuce, and avocados and let everyone make their own creations.

Balsamic Chicken

Ingredients: Servings: 6 Cooking Time: 17 Mins

2 lbs chicken breasts
1/3 C. balsamic vinegar
1 onion, chopped
1/2 C. chicken broth
1 tbsp. Dijon mustard
1/2 tsp. dried thyme
1 tsp. garlic, chopped

Directions:
Mix together Dijon, chicken broth, and vinegar and pour into the inner pot of instant pot duo crisp. Add chicken, thyme, garlic, and onion and stir well. Seal the pot with pressure cooking lid and cook on high pressure for 12 minutes. Once done, release pressure using a quick release. Remove lid. Remove chicken from pot and shred using a fork. Pour the leftover liquid of pot over shredded chicken. Line air fryer basket with foil. Add shredded chicken to the air fryer basket

and place basket in the pot. Seal the pot with air fryer lid and select broil mode and cook for 5 minutes. Serve and enjoy.

Duck Breasts with Endives

Ingredients: Servings: 4 Cooking Time: 25 Mins

Duck breasts – 2
Salt and black pepper to taste
Sugar – 1 tbsp.
Olive oil – 1 tbsp.
Endives – 6, julienned
Cranberries – 2 tbsps.
White wine – 8 ounces
Garlic – 1 tbsp. minced
Heavy cream – 2 tbsps.

Directions:
Score duck breasts and season with salt and pepper. Cook in the air fryer at 350F for 20 minutes. Flip once. Meanwhile, heat up a pan with oil over medium heat. Add endives, and sugar. Stir and cook for 2 minutes. Add salt, pepper, wine, garlic, cream, and cranberries — Stir-Fry for 3 minutes. Divide duck breasts on plates. Drizzle with the endives sauce and serve.

Creamy Coconut Chicken

Ingredients: Servings: 4 Cooking Time: 25 Mins

Big chicken legs – 4
Turmeric powder – 5 tsps.
Ginger – 2 tbsps. grated
Salt and black pepper to taste
Coconut cream – 4 tbsps.

Directions:
In a bowl, mix salt, pepper, ginger, turmeric, and cream. Whisk. Add chicken pieces, coat and marinate for 2 hours. Transfer chicken to the preheated air fryer and cook at 370F for 25 minutes. Serve.

Turkey Legs

Ingredients: Servings: 2 Cooking Time: 40 Mins

2 large turkey legs
1 1/2 tsp. smoked paprika
1 tsp. brown sugar
1 tsp. season salt
½ tsp. garlic powder
oil for spraying avocado, canola, etc.

Directions:
Mix the smoked paprika, brown sugar, seasoned salt, garlic powder thoroughly. Wash and pat dry the turkey legs. Rub the made seasoning mixture all over the turkey legs making sure to get under the skin also. While preparing for cooking, select the Air Fry option. Press start to begin preheating. Once the preheating temperature is reached, place the turkey legs on the tray in the Instant Pot Duo Crisp Air Fryer basket. Lightly spray them with oil. Air Fry the turkey legs on 400°F for 20 minutes. Then, open the Air Fryer lid and flip the turkey legs and lightly spray with oil. Close the Instant Pot Duo Crisp Air Fryer lid and cook for 20 more minutes. Remove and Enjoy.

Chinese Duck Legs

Ingredients: Servings: 2 Cooking Time: 36 Mins

Duck legs – 2
Ginger – 4 slices
Dried chilies – 2, chopped
Olive oil – 1 tbsp.
Star anise – 2
Spring onions – 1 bunch, chopped
Oyster sauce – 1 tbsp.
Soy sauce – 1 tbsp.
Sesame oil – 1 tsp.
Water – 14 ounces
Rice wine – 1 tbsp.

Directions:
Heat oil in a pan. Add water, soy sauce, oyster sauce, ginger, rice wine, sesame oil, star anise, and chili. Stir and cook for 6 minutes. Add spring onions and duck legs, toss to coat and transfer to a pan. Place the pan in the air fryer and cook at 370F for 30 minutes. Serve.

Perfect Chicken Parmesan

Ingredients: Servings: 2 Cooking Time: 25 Mins

2 large white meat chicken breasts, approximately 5-6 ounces
1 C. of breadcrumbs (Panko brand works well)
2 medium-sized eggs
Pinch of salt and pepper
1 tbsp. of dried oregano
1 C. of marinara sauce (store-bought or homemade will do equally well)
2 slices of provolone cheese
1 tbsp. of parmesan cheese

Directions:
Preparing the Ingredients. Cover the basket of the Instant Crisp Air Fryer with a lining of tin foil, leaving the edges uncovered to allow air to circulate through the basket. Preheat the Instant Crisp Air Fryer to 350 degrees. In a mixing bowl, beat the eggs until fluffy and until the yolks and whites are fully combined, and set aside. In a separate mixing bowl, combine the breadcrumbs, oregano, salt and pepper, and set aside. One by one, dip the raw chicken breasts into the bowl with dry ingredients, coating both sides; then submerge into the bowl with wet ingredients, then dip again into the dry ingredients. This double coating will ensure an extra crisp-and-delicious air-fry! Lay the coated chicken breasts on the foil covering the Instant Crisp Air Fryer basket, in a single flat layer. Air Frying. Lock the air fryer lid. Set the Instant Crisp Air Fryer timer for 10 minutes. After 10 minutes, the Instant Crisp Air Fryer will turn off and the chicken should be mid-way cooked and the breaded coating starting to brown. Using tongs, turn each piece of chicken over to ensure a full all-over fry. Reset the Instant Crisp Air Fryer to 320 degrees for another 10 minutes. While the chicken is cooking, pour half the marinara sauce into a 7-inch heat-safe pan. After 15 minutes, when the Instant Crisp Air Fryer shuts off, remove the fried chicken breasts using tongs and set in the marinara-covered pan. Drizzle the rest of the marinara sauce over the fried chicken, then place the slices of provolone cheese atop both of them and sprinkle the parmesan cheese over the entire pan. Reset the Instant Crisp Air Fryer to 350 degrees for 5 minutes. After 5 minutes, when the Instant Crisp Air Fryer shuts off, remove the dish from the Instant Crisp Air Fryer using tongs or oven mitts. the chicken will be perfectly crisped and the cheese melted and lightly toasted. Serve while hot!

Spiced Chicken Legs

Ingredients: Servings: 6 Cooking Time: 50 Mins

Chicken drumsticks – 2.5 lbs.
Olive oil – 2 tbsps.
Salt and pepper to taste
Garlic powder – 1 tsp.
Smoked paprika – 1 tsp.
Cumin – ½ tsp.

Directions:

In a bowl, add drumsticks with oil and mix. In another bowl, mix the other ingredients then coat the drumsticks with the mixture. Cook the chicken at 400F for 25 minutes in batches. Shake the basket at the halfway mark. Chicken is cooked when it reaches 165F. Serve.

Teriyaki Wings

Ingredients: Servings: 4 Cooking Time: 25 Mins

Chicken wings – 2 pounds
Teriyaki sauce – ½ cup
Minced garlic – 2 tsp.
Ground ginger - ¼ tsp.
Baking powder – 2 tsp.

Directions:

Except for the baking powder, place all ingredients in a bowl and marinate for 1 hour in the refrigerator. Place wings into the air fryer basket and sprinkle with baking powder. Gently rub into wings. Cook at 400F for 25 minutes. Shake the basket two or three times during cooking. Serve.

Chicken Kabab

Ingredients: Servings: 4 Cooking Time: 15 Mins

1 lb chicken thighs, skinless, boneless & cut into 1/2-inch cubes
1 C. bell pepper, cut into 2-inch cubes
1/2 C. onion, cut into 2-inch cubes
1 tbsp. olive oil
For marinade:
1/2 tbsp. dried fenugreek leaves
1 tsp. coriander powder
1 tsp. garam masala
1/2 tsp. turmeric
2 tsp. chili powder
1 tbsp. fresh lime juice
1 tbsp. ginger garlic paste
1/2 C. yogurt
1 tsp. salt

Directions:

In a bowl, mix together all marinade ingredients. Add chicken mix well and marinate for 30 minutes. Add bell pepper, onion, and oil into the chicken marinade and mix well. Thread marinated chicken, onion, and peppers in the wooden skewers. Spray instant pot air fryer basket with cooking spray and place skewers in the basket. Do not overcrowd. Place basket in the instant pot. Seal pot with air fryer lid and select air fry mode and set the temperature of 400 F and timer for 8 minutes. Turn skewers to the other side and air fry for 7 minutes more. Serve and enjoy.

Honey and Wine Chicken Breasts

Ingredients: Servings: 4 Cooking Time: 15 Mins

2 chicken breasts, rinsed and halved
1 tbsp. melted butter
1/2 tsp. freshly ground pepper, or to taste
1 tsp. paprika
3/4 tsp. sea salt, or to taste
1 tsp. dried rosemary
2 tbsp. dry white wine
1 tbsp. honey

Directions:

Preparing the Ingredients. Firstly, pat the chicken breasts dry. Lightly coat them with the melted butter. Then, add the remaining ingredients. Air Frying. Transfer them to the Instant Crisp Air Fryer basket; Lock the air fryer lid, bake about 15 minutes at 330 degrees F. Serve warm and enjoy!

Chicken Nuggets

Ingredients: Servings: 4 Cooking Time: 20 Mins

1 lb. boneless, skinless chicken breasts
Chicken seasoning or rub
Salt
Pepper
2 eggs
6 tbsp. bread crumbs
2 tbsp. panko bread crumbs
Cooking oil

Directions:

Preparing the Ingredients. Cut the chicken breasts into 1-inch pieces. In a large bowl, combine the chicken pieces with chicken seasoning, salt, and pepper to taste. In a small bowl, beat the eggs. In another bowl, combine the bread crumbs and panko. Dip the chicken pieces in the eggs and then the bread crumbs. Place the nuggets in the Instant Crisp Air Fryer. Do not overcrowd the basket. Cook in batches. Spray the nuggets with cooking oil. Air Frying. Lock the air fryer lid. Cook for 4 minutes. Open the Instant Crisp Air Fryer and shake the basket. Cook for an additional 4 minutes. Remove the cooked nuggets from the Instant Crisp Air Fryer, then repeat for the remaining chicken nuggets. Cool before serving.

Herbed Turkey Breast

Ingredients: Servings: 8 Cooking Time: 1 Hour

Turkey breast – 3 lbs.
Rub ingredients
Olive oil – 2 tbsps.
Lemon juice – 2 tbsps.
Minced garlic – 1 tbsp.
Ground mustard – 2 tsps.
Salt and pepper to taste
Dried rosemary – 1 tsp.
Dried thyme – 1 tsp.
Ground sage – 1 tsp.

Directions:

Combine the rub ingredients in a bowl and rub the turkey with it. Rub under any loose skin. Place the turkey on a cooking tray, skin side up. Cook in the air fryer at 360F for 1 hour. the turkey is done when it reaches 160F. Rest, slice and serve.

Chicken Fillets, Brie & Ham

Ingredients: Servings: 4 Cooking Time: 15 Mins

2 Large Chicken Fillets
4 Small Slices of Brie (Or your cheese of choice)
Freshly Ground Black Pepper
1 Tbsp Freshly Chopped Chives
4 Slices Cured Ham

Directions:

Preparing the Ingredients. Slice the fillets into four and make incisions as you would for a hamburger bun. Leave a little "hinge" uncut at the back. Season the inside and pop some brie and chives in there. Close them, and wrap them each in a slice of ham. Brush with oil and pop them into the basket. Air Frying. Heat the Instant Crisp Air Fryer to 350° F. Lock the air fryer lid. Roast the little parcels until they look tasty (15 min)

Air Fryer Turkey Breast

Ingredients: Servings: 6 Cooking Time: 60 Mins

Pepper and salt
1 oven-ready turkey breast
Turkey seasonings of choice

Directions:
1 Preparing the Ingredients. Preheat the Instant Crisp Air Fryer to 350 degrees. Season turkey with pepper, salt, and other desired seasonings. Place turkey in Instant Crisp Air Fryer basket. 2 Air Frying. Lock the air fryer lid. Set temperature to 350°F, and set time to 60 minutes. Cook 60 minutes. the meat should be at 165 degrees when done. Allow to rest 10-15 minutes before slicing. Enjoy!

Italian Chicken Wings

Ingredients: Servings: 4 Cooking Time: 15 Mins

12 chicken wings
1 tbsp. chicken seasoning
3 tbsp. olive oil
1 tbsp. garlic powder
1 tbsp. basil
1/2 tbsp. oregano
3 tbsp. tarragon
Pepper
Salt

Directions:
Add all ingredients into the mixing bowl and toss well. Pour 1 C. water into the inner pot of instant pot duo crisp then place steamer rack in the pot. Arrange chicken wings on top of the steamer rack. Seal the pot with pressure cooking lid and cook on high pressure for 10 minutes. Once done, release pressure using a quick release. Remove lid. Remove chicken wings from the pot. Dump leftover liquid from the pot. Add chicken wings into the air fryer basket then place a basket in the pot. Seal the pot with air fryer lid and select broil mode and cook for 5 minutes. Serve and enjoy.

Bbq Chicken Breasts

Ingredients: Servings: 4 Cooking Time: 15 Mins

4 boneless skinless chicken breast about 6 oz each
1-2 Tbsp bbq seasoning

Directions:
Cover both sides of chicken breast with the BBQ seasoning. Cover and marinate the in the refrigerator for 45 minutes. Choose the Air Fry option and set the temperature to 400°F. Push start and let it preheat for 5 minutes. Upon preheating, place the chicken breast in the Instant Pot Duo Crisp Air Fryer basket, making sure they do not overlap. Spray with oil. Cook for 13-14 minutes, flipping halfway. Remove chicken when the chicken reaches an internal temperature of 160°F. Place on a plate and allow to rest for 5 minutes before slicing.

Easy Turkey Breast

Ingredients: Servings: 4 Cooking Time: 60 Mins

1 frozen turkey breast with frozen gravy packet
1 whole onion

Directions:
Preparing the Ingredients. Place frozen turkey breast, frozen gravy packet and whole onion in the Instant Crisp Air Fryer. High pressure for 30 minutes. Lock the pressure cooking lid on the Instant Crisp Air Fryer and then cook for 30 minutes. To get 30-minutes cook time, press "Pressure" button and use the Time Adjustment button to adjust the cook time to 30 minutes. Pressure Release. Use natural-release method. Remove lid, turn turkey breast over High pressure for 30 minutes. Replace pressure cooking lid on the Instant Crisp Air Fryer and then cook for 30 minutes. To get 30-minutes cook time, press "Pressure" button and use the Time Adjustment button to adjust the cook time to 30 minutes. Pressure Release. Use natural-release method, again. Finish the dish. Close Air fryer lid. Select AIR FRY, set temperature to 360°F, and set time to 10 minutes. Check after 5 minutes, cooking for an additional 5 minutes if dish needs more browning. Remove mesh. Remove turkey and slice. Places slices and turkey gravy into serving dish.

Honey Cashew Butter Chicken

Ingredients: Servings: 3 Cooking Time: 7 Mins

1 lb chicken breast, cut into chunks
2 tbsp. rice vinegar
2 tbsp. honey
2 tbsp. coconut aminos
1/4 C. cashew butter
2 garlic cloves, minced
1/4 C. chicken broth
1/2 tbsp. sriracha

Directions:
Add chicken into the inner pot of instant pot duo crisp. In a small bowl, mix together cashew butter, garlic, broth, sriracha, vinegar, honey, and coconut aminos and pour over chicken. Seal the pot with pressure cooking lid and cook on high for 7 minutes. Once done, release pressure using a quick release. Remove lid. Stir well and serve.

Buffalo Chicken Tenders

Ingredients: Servings: 4 Cooking Time: 20 Mins

Boneless, skinless chicken tenders – 1 pound
Pork rinds – 1 ½ ounces, finely ground
Hot sauce – ¼ cup
Chili powder – 1 tsp.
Garlic powder – 1 tsp.

Directions:
Place chicken breasts in a bowl and pour hot sauce over them. Toss to coat. Mix ground pork rinds, chili powder and garlic powder in another bowl. Place each tender in the ground pork rinds, and coat well. with wet hands, press down the pork rinds into the chicken. Place the tender in a single layer into the air fryer basket. Cook at 375F for 20 minutes. Flip once. Serve.

Air Fryer Spicy Chicken Thighs

Ingredients: Servings: 4 Cooking Time: 15 Mins

2 lb. (4 Nos.) chicken thighs with bone and skin.
⅓ C. soy sauce, low sodium
2 tbsp. chili garlic sauce
1 tbsp. lime zest
2 garlic cloves, finely grated
2 tsp. minced ginger
2 tbsp. honey
½ C. green onions, finely chopped
4 tbsp. sesame seeds, toasted
¼ C. virgin olive oil
¼ tsp. kosher salt

Directions:
Clean, wash, and pat dry the chicken thighs. Combine olive oil, chili garlic sauce, honey soy sauce, lime juice, minced ginger, grated garlic, and salt thoroughly. Keep half a C. of the marinade for later use. Put the chicken thighs into the bowl and coat the marinade well. Transfer it into a container, cover, and refrigerate for 30 minutes. For making the dish juicier, it would be better to broil the chicken. For broiling, use the separator available with the Instant Pot Air Fryer. Place the air fryer basket in the inner pot and place the separator in the air fryer basket. Now place the marinated chicken thighs on the separator. Close the crisp cover. In the AIR FRYER section, select the BROIL option. You don't need to select the temperature, because by default the heat will set to 400°F. Set the timer for 20 minutes. Press START to begin cooking. While the frying is on, you can make the sauce. Put the reserved marinade in a saucepan and bring to boiling. Simmer for about 5 minutes and allow the sauce to becomes thick. When the sauce becomes thick, remove it from the heat. Now take out the broiled chicken thighs and brush the marinade sauce over the thighs. Serve by garnishing with toasted sesame seeds and chopped green onions. Enjoy your juicy, chicken thighs.

Jerk Chicken Wings

Ingredients: Servings: 6 Cooking Time: 16 Mins

1 tsp. salt
½ C. red wine vinegar
5 tbsp. lime juice
4 chopped scallions
1 tbsp. grated ginger
2 tbsp. brown sugar
1 tbsp. chopped thyme
1 tsp. white pepper
1 tsp. cayenne pepper
1 tsp. cinnamon
1 tbsp. allspice
1 Habanero pepper (seeds/ribs removed and chopped finely)
6 chopped garlic cloves
2 tbsp. low-sodium soy sauce
2 tbsp. olive oil
4 lb. of chicken wings

Directions:
Preparing the Ingredients. Combine all ingredients except wings in a bowl. Pour into a gallon bag and add chicken wings. Chill 2-24 hours to marinate. Ensure your Instant Crisp Air Fryer is preheated to 390 degrees. Place chicken wings into a strainer to drain excess liquids. Air Frying. Pour half of the wings into your Instant Crisp Air Fryer. Lock the air fryer lid. Set temperature to 390°F, and set time to 16 minutes and cook 14-16 minutes, making sure to shake halfway through the cooking process. Remove and repeat the process with remaining wings.

Garlic Parmesan Chicken

Ingredients: Servings: 4 Cooking Time: 20 Mins

Chicken thighs – 2 pounds, with bone and skin
Eggs – 2
Shredded parmesan - ¾ cup
Panko breadcrumbs – 1 cup
Italian seasoning – tsp.
Garlic powder – 1 tsp.
Salt and pepper to taste
Cooking spray

Directions:
Rub chicken with salt and pepper. Combine panko breadcrumbs, Italian seasoning, garlic powder, grated parmesan in a bowl. Beats eggs in a bowl. Dip the chicken in the egg and then in the bread mixture. Cook in the air fryer at 400F for 20 minutes. Flip at the halfway mark. Serve.

Herb Turkey Breast

Ingredients: Servings: 6 Cooking Time: 40 Mins

Turkey breast with skin – 2 pounds
Melted butter – 4 tbsps.
Garlic – 3 cloves, grated
Salt to taste
Fresh rosemary – 1 tsp. chopped
Thyme – 1 tsp. chopped
Ground black pepper – 1 tsp.
Cooking spray

Directions:
Rub the turkey with salt and pepper. Combine rosemary, butter, thyme, and garlic in a bowl. Rub the turkey with this mixture. Grease the air fryer with cooking spray. Cook the turkey for 40 minutes at 375F. After 20 minutes, flip the turkey breast and spray with cooking oil. Finish cooking. Serve.

Minty Chicken-fried Pork Chops

Ingredients: Servings: 6 Cooking Time: 30 Mins

4 medium-sized pork chops, approximately 3.5 oz. each
1 C. of breadcrumbs (Panko brand works well)
2 medium-sized eggs
Pinch of salt and pepper
½ tbsp. of mint, either dried and ground; or fresh, rinsed, and finely chopped

Directions:
Preparing the Ingredients. Cover the basket of the Instant Crisp Air Fryer with a lining of tin foil, leaving the edges uncovered to allow air to circulate through the basket. Preheat the Instant Crisp Air Fryer to 350 degrees. In a mixing bowl, beat the eggs until fluffy and until the yolks and whites are fully combined, and set aside. In a separate mixing bowl, combine the breadcrumbs, mint, salt and pepper, and set aside. One by one, dip each raw pork chop into the bowl with dry ingredients, coating all sides; then submerge into the bowl with wet ingredients, then dip again into the dry ingredients. This double coating will ensure an extra crisp air-fry. Lay the coated pork chops on the foil covering the Instant Crisp Air Fryer basket, in

a single flat layer. Air Frying. Lock the air fryer lid. Set the Instant Crisp Air Fryer timer for 15 minutes. After 15 minutes, the Instant Crisp Air Fryer will turn off and the pork should be mid-way cooked and the breaded coating starting to brown. Using tongs, turn each piece of steak over to ensure a full all-over fry. Reset the Instant Crisp Air Fryer to 320 degrees for 15 minutes. After 15 minutes, when the Instant Crisp Air Fryer shuts off, remove the fried pork chops using tongs and set on a serving plate. Eat as soon as cool enough to handle – and enjoy!

Chicken Pot Pie with Coconut Milk

Ingredients: Servings: 8 Cooking Time: 30 Mins

¼ small onion, chopped
½ C. broccoli, chopped
¾ C. coconut milk
1 C. chicken broth
1/3 C. coconut flour
1-pound ground chicken
2 cloves of garlic, minced
2 tbsp. butter
4 ½ tbsp. butter, melted
4 eggs
Salt and pepper to taste

Directions:
1 Preparing the Ingredients. Preheat the Instant Crisp Air Fryer for 5 minutes. Place 2 tbsp. butter, broccoli, onion, garlic, coconut milk, chicken broth, and ground chicken in a baking dish that will fit in the Instant Crisp Air Fryer. Season with salt and pepper to taste. In a mixing bowl, combine the butter, coconut flour, and eggs. Sprinkle evenly the top of the chicken and broccoli mixture with the coconut flour dough. Place the dish in the Instant Crisp Air Fryer. 2 Air Frying. Lock the air fryer lid. Cook for 30 minutes at 325°F.

Bbq Chicken Wings

Ingredients: Servings: 4 Cooking Time: 35 Mins

1 lb chicken wings
1/2 C. BBQ sauce
1 tbsp. olive oil
1/2 C. hot sauce
Pepper
Salt

Directions:
Toss chicken wings with olive oil and season with pepper and salt. Spray instant pot multi-level air fryer basket with cooking spray. Add chicken wings into the air fryer basket and place basket into the instant pot. Seal pot with air fryer lid and select air fry mode then set the temperature to 400 F and timer for 30 minutes. Stir halfway through. In a large bowl, mix together hot sauce and BBQ sauce. Add chicken wings in sauce mixture and toss until well coated. Serve and enjoy.

Chicken Roast with Pineapple Salsa

Ingredients: Servings: 2 Cooking Time: 45 Mins

¼ C. extra virgin olive oil
¼ C. freshly chopped cilantro
1 avocado, diced
1-pound boneless chicken breasts
2 C. canned pineapples
2 tsp. honey
Juice from 1 lime
Salt and pepper to taste

Directions:
1 Preparing the Ingredients. Preheat the Instant Crisp Air Fryer to 390°F. Place the grill pan accessory in the Instant Crisp Air Fryer. Season the chicken breasts with lime juice, olive oil, honey, salt, and pepper. 2 Air Frying. Place on the grill pan, lock the air fryer lid and cook for 45 minutes. Flip the chicken every 10 minutes to grill all sides evenly. Once the chicken is cooked, serve with pineapples, cilantro, and avocado.

Yummy Hawaiian Chicken

Ingredients: Servings: 6 Cooking Time: 12 Mins

2 lbs chicken breasts, skinless, boneless, and cut into chunks
2 tbsp. cornstarch
20 oz can pineapple tidbits
1 C. chicken broth
1 tbsp. garlic, crushed
2 tbsp. brown sugar
6 tbsp. soy sauce
1/2 tsp. ground ginger
1/2 tsp. salt

Directions:
Add all ingredients except cornstarch into the inner pot of instant pot duo crisp and stir well. Seal the pot with pressure cooking lid and cook on high pressure for 10 minutes. Once done, release pressure using a quick release. Remove lid. In a small bowl, whisk together 1/4 C. water and cornstarch and pour into the pot. Set pot on sauté mode. Cook chicken on sauce mode until sauce thickens. Serve over rice and enjoy.

Crispy Honey Garlic Chicken Wings

Ingredients: Servings: 8 Cooking Time: 25 Mins

1/8 C. water
½ tsp. salt
4 tbsp. minced garlic
¼ C. vegan butter
¼ C. raw honey
¾ C. almond flour
16 chicken wings

Directions:
1 Preparing the Ingredients. Rinse off and dry chicken wings well. Spray Instant Crisp Air Fryer basket with olive oil. Coat chicken wings with almond flour and add coated wings to Instant Crisp Air Fryer. 2 Air Frying. Set temperature to 380°F, and set time to 25 minutes. Cook shaking every 5 minutes. When the timer goes off, cook 5-10 minutes at 400 degrees till skin becomes crispy and dry. As chicken cooks, melt butter in a saucepan and add garlic. Sauté garlic 5 minutes. Add salt and honey, simmering 20 minutes. Make sure to stir every so often, so the sauce does not burn. Add a bit of water after 15 minutes to ensure sauce does not harden. Take out chicken wings from Instant Crisp Air Fryer and coat in sauce. Enjoy!

Cheesy Chicken Wings

Ingredients: Servings: 4 Cooking Time: 18 Mins

2 lbs chicken wings
1/2 C. chicken stock
1 tsp. season salt
1/2 C. parmesan cheese, grated
1 tbsp. garlic, crushed
For sauce:
1 stick butter, melted
1/2 tsp. black pepper
1/2 tsp. dried parsley flakes
1 tsp. garlic powder

Directions:
Season chicken wings with seasoned salt. Add chicken wings to the inner pot of instant pot duo crisp along with the chicken

stock. Seal the pot with pressure cooking lid and cook on high for 8 minutes. Meanwhile, mix together butter, pepper, parmesan cheese, parsley flakes, garlic powder, and garlic. Set aside. Once chicken wings done then release pressures using a quick release. Remove lid. Remove chicken wings from the pot and clean the pot. Spray instant pot air fryer basket with cooking spray and place in the pot. Toss chicken wings with melted butter and add into the air fryer basket. Seal the pot with air fryer lid and select broil mode and cook for 10 minutes. Serve and enjoy.

Cheesy Chicken Tenders

Ingredients: Servings: 4 Cooking Time: 30 Mins

- 1 large white meat chicken breast, approximately 5-6 ounces, sliced into strips
- Pinch of salt and pepper
- 1 C. of breadcrumbs (Panko brand works well)
- 2 medium-sized eggs
- 1 tbsp. of grated or powdered parmesan cheese

Directions:

Preparing the Ingredients. Cover the basket of the Instant Crisp Air Fryer with a lining of tin foil, leaving the edges uncovered to allow air to circulate through the basket. Preheat the Instant Crisp Air Fryer to 350 degrees. In a mixing bowl, beat the eggs until fluffy and until the yolks and whites are fully combined, and set aside. In a separate mixing bowl, combine the breadcrumbs, parmesan, salt and pepper, and set aside. One by one, dip each piece of raw chicken into the bowl with dry ingredients, coating all sides; then submerge into the bowl with wet ingredients, then dip again into the dry ingredients. Lay the coated chicken pieces on the foil covering the Instant Crisp Air Fryer basket, in a single flat layer. Air Frying. Set the Instant Crisp Air Fryer timer for 15 minutes. After 15 minutes, the Instant Crisp Air Fryer will turn off and the chicken should be mid-way cooked and the breaded coating starting to brown. Using tongs turn each piece of chicken over to ensure a full all over fry. Reset the Instant Crisp Air Fryer to 320 degrees for another 15 minutes. After 15 minutes, when the Instant Crisp Air Fryer shuts off, remove the fried chicken strips using tongs and set on a serving plate. Eat as soon as cool enough to handle, and enjoy!

Lemony Drumsticks

Ingredients: Servings: 2 Cooking Time: 25 Mins

- Baking powder – 2 tsps.
- Garlic powder – ½ tsp.
- Chicken drumsticks – 8
- Salted butter – 4 tbsps. melted
- Lemon pepper seasoning – 1 tbsp.

Directions:

Sprinkle garlic powder and baking powder over drumsticks and rub into chicken skin. Place drumsticks into the air fryer basket. Cook at 375F for 25 minutes. Flip the drumsticks once halfway through the cooking time. Remove when cooked. Mix seasoning and butter in a bowl. Add drumsticks to the bowl and toss to coat. Serve.

Spicy Chicken Wings

Ingredients: Servings: 4 Cooking Time: 20 Mins

- 2 lbs. frozen chicken wings
- 2 tbsp. apple cider vinegar
- 2 tbsp. butter, melted
- 1/2 C. hot pepper sauce
- 1/2 C. water
- 1/2 tsp. paprika
- 1 oz ranch seasoning

Directions:

Add water, vinegar, butter, and hot pepper sauce into instant pot air fryer crisp. Add chicken wings and stir well. Seal the pot with pressure cooking lid and cook on high for 5 minutes. Once done, release pressure using a quick release. Remove lid. Sprinkle paprika and ranch seasoning over the chicken. Seal the pot with air fryer lid and select air fry mode and cook at 375 f for 15 minutes. Toss wings in sauce and serve.

Chicken Salad

Ingredients: Servings: 4 Cooking Time: 10 Mins

- Chicken breast – 1 pound, boneless, skinless and halved
- Cooking spray
- Salt and black pepper to taste
- Feta cheese – ½ cup, cubed
- Lemon juice – 2 tbsps.
- Mustard – 1 ½ tsps.
- Olive oil – 1 tbsp.
- Red wine vinegar – 1 ½ tsps.
- Anchovies – ½ tsp. minced
- Garlic – ¾ tsp. minced
- Water – 1 tbsp.
- Lettuce leaves – 8 cups, cut into strips
- Parmesan – 4 tbsps. grated

Directions:

Spray chicken breasts with cooking oil. Season with salt and pepper. Place in the air fryer and cook at 370F for 10 minutes. Flip once. Shred the chicken with 2 forks. Put in a salad bowl and mix with lettuce leaves. In the blender, mix feta cheese with lemon juice, olive oil, mustard, vinegar, garlic, anchovies, water and half of the parmesan and blend very well. Add this over the chicken mix. Toss and sprinkle the rest of the parmesan and serve.

Mexican Chicken

Ingredients: Servings: 4 Cooking Time: 22 Mins

- Salsa verde – 16 ounces
- Salt and black pepper to taste
- Chicken breast – 1 pound, boneless, and skinless
- Olive oil – 1 tbsp.
- Monetary Jack cheese – 1 ½ cups, grated
- Cilantro – ¼ cup, chopped
- Garlic powder – 1 tsp.

Directions:

Pour salsa verde in a baking dish. Season chicken with garlic powder, salt, pepper, and brush with olive oil. Place over the salsa verde. Place in the air fryer and cook at 380F for 20 minutes. Sprinkle cheese on top and cook 2 minutes more. Serve.

Chinese Chicken Wings

Ingredients: Servings: 6 Cooking Time: 15 Mins

Chicken wings – 16
Honey – 2 tbsps.
Salt and black pepper to taste
Soy sauce – 2 tbsps.
White pepper – ¼ tsp.
Lime juice – 3 tbsps.

Directions:
In a bowl, mix soy sauce, honey, salt, black pepper, lime juice, and white pepper. Whisk well. Add chicken pieces and coat well. Marinate in the refrigerator for 2 hours. Then cook in the air fryer at 370F for 6 minutes on each side. Then increase heat to 400F and cook for 3 minutes more. Serve.

Mustard Chicken

Ingredients: Servings: 4 Cooking Time: 20 Mins

1 garlic clove, minced
1/2 oz fresh lemon juice
2 tbsp. fresh tarragon, chopped
1 lbs chicken tenders
1/2 C. whole grain mustard
1/2 tsp. paprika
1/2 tsp. pepper
1/4 tsp. kosher salt

Directions:
Add all ingredients except chicken to the large bowl and mix well. Add chicken to the bowl and stir until well coated. Place the dehydrating tray in a multi-level air fryer basket and place basket in the instant pot. Place chicken tenders on dehydrating tray. Seal pot with air fryer lid and select bake mode then set the temperature to 380 F and timer for 20 minutes. Turn chicken halfway through. Serve and enjoy.

Garlic Lemon Chicken

Ingredients: Servings: 4 Cooking Time: 40 Mins

2 lbs. chicken drumsticks
4 tbsp. butter
2 tbsp. parsley, chopped
1 fresh lemon juice
10 garlic cloves, minced
2 tbsp. olive oil
Pepper
Salt

Directions:
Add butter, parsley, lemon juice, garlic, oil, pepper, and salt into the mixing bowl and mix well. Add chicken to the bowl and toss until well coated. Transfer chicken into the instant pot air fryer basket and place basket in the pot. Seal the pot with air fryer lid and select bake mode and cook at 400 f for 40 minutes. Serve and enjoy.

Crispy Crust Whole Chicken

Ingredients: Servings: 4 Cooking Time: 45 Mins

1 1/2 C. chicken broth
2 tbsp. Montreal steak seasoning
1 tsp. Italian seasoning
1 whole chicken
1 tsp. paprika
1 tsp. onion powder
1 tsp. garlic powder
2 tbsp. olive oil

Directions:
Pour broth into the instant pot. Mix together Montreal steak seasoning, Italian seasoning, paprika, onion powder, and garlic powder. Brush chicken with olive oil and rub with seasoning. Place chicken in the air fryer basket and place basket in the instant pot. Seal the pot with pressure cooking lid and cook on high pressure for 25 minutes. Once done, allow to release pressure naturally for 15 minutes then release remaining pressure using quick release. Remove lid. Remove liquid from the instant pot. Seal pot with air fryer lid and select air fry mode and set the temperature to 400 F and timer for 10 minutes. Turn chicken to the other side and air fry for 10 minutes more. Serve and enjoy.

Crusted Chicken Tenders

Ingredients: Servings: 3 Cooking Time: 15 Mins

½ C. all-purpose flour
2 eggs, beaten
Salt and freshly ground black pepper, to taste
½ C. seasoned breadcrumbs
2 tbsp. olive oil
¾ lb. chicken tenders

Directions:
1 Preparing the Ingredients. In a bowl, place the flour. In a second bowl, place the eggs. In a third bowl, mix together breadcrumbs, salt, black pepper and oil. Coat the chicken tenders in the flour, Then dip into the eggs and finally coat with the breadcrumbs mixture evenly. 2 Air Frying. Preheat the Instant Crisp Air Fryer to 330 degrees F. Arrange the chicken tenderloins in Instant Crisp Air Fryer basket. Lock the air fryer lid. Cook for about 10 minutes. Now, set the Instant Crisp Air Fryer to 390 degrees F. Cook for about 5 minutes further.

Barbecue Air Fried Chicken

Ingredients: Servings: 10 Cooking Time: 26 Mins

1 tsp. Liquid Smoke
2 cloves Fresh Garlic smashed
1/2 C. Apple Cider Vinegar
1 Tablespoon Kosher Salt
1 Tablespoon Freshly Ground Black Pepper
2 tsp. Garlic Powder
3 lb. Chuck Roast well-marbled with intramuscular fat
1.5 C. Barbecue Sauce
1/4 C. Light Brown Sugar + more for sprinkling
2 Tablespoons Honey optional and in place of 2 TBL sugar

Directions:
Add meat to the Instant Pot Duo Crisp Air Fryer Basket, spreading out the meat. Select the option Air Fry. Close the Air Fryer lid and cook at 300 degrees F for 8 minutes. Pause the Air Fryer and flip meat over after 4 minutes. Remove the lid and baste with more barbecue sauce and sprinkle with a little brown sugar. Again Close the Air Fryer lid and set the temperature at 400°F for 9 minutes. Watch meat though the lid and flip it over after 5 minutes.

Parmesan Chicken Wings

Ingredients: Servings: 4 Cooking Time: 25 Mins

1 lb chicken wings
1/4 C. parmesan cheese, grated
2 tbsp. cornstarch
1/2 tsp. onion powder
1/2 tsp. paprika

1/2 tbsp. garlic powder
Pepper
Salt

Directions:
In a bowl, mix together cornstarch, garlic powder, onion powder, paprika, parmesan cheese, pepper, and salt. Add chicken wings in cornstarch mixture and toss until well coated. Place the dehydrating tray in a multi-level air fryer basket and place basket in the instant pot. Place chicken wings on dehydrating tray. Seal pot with air fryer lid and select air fry mode then set the temperature to 380 F and timer for 25 minutes. Turn chicken halfway through. Serve and enjoy.

Honey Duck Breasts

Ingredients: Servings: 2 Cooking Time: 22 Mins

Smoked duck breast – 1, halved
Honey – 1 tsp.
Tomato paste – 1 tsp.
Mustard – 1 tbsp.
Apple vinegar – ½ tsp.

Directions:
Mix tomato paste, honey, mustard, and vinegar in a bowl. Whisk well. Add duck breast pieces and coat well. Cook in the air fryer at 370F for 15 minutes. Remove the duck breast from the air fryer and add to the honey mixture. Coat again. Cook again at 370F for 6 minutes. Serve.

Tex-mex Turkey Burgers

Ingredients: Servings: 4 Cooking Time: 15 Mins

⅓ C. finely crushed corn tortilla chips
1 egg, beaten
¼ C. salsa
⅓ C. shredded pepper Jack cheese
Pinch salt
Freshly ground black pepper
1 lb. ground turkey
1 tbsp. olive oil
1 tsp. paprika

Directions:
Preparing the Ingredients. In a medium bowl, combine the tortilla chips, egg, salsa, cheese, salt, and pepper, and mix well. Add the turkey and mix gently but thoroughly with clean hands. Form the meat mixture into patties about ½ inch thick. Make an indentation in the center of each patty with your thumb so the burgers don't puff up while cooking. Brush the patties on both sides with the olive oil and sprinkle with paprika. Air Frying. Put in the Instant Crisp Air Fryer basket, lock the air fryer lid and Grill for 14 to 16 minutes or until the meat registers at least 165°F.

Chicken Bbq Recipe From Peru

Ingredients: Servings: 4 Cooking Time: 40 Mins

½ tsp. dried oregano
1 tsp. paprika
1/3 C. soy sauce
2 ½ lb. chicken, quartered
2 tbsp. fresh lime juice
2 tsp. ground cumin
5 cloves of garlic, minced

Directions:
1 Preparing the Ingredients. Place all Ingredients in a Ziploc bag and shake to mix everything. Allow to marinate for at least 2 hours in the fridge. Preheat the Instant Crisp Air Fryer to 390°F. Place the grill pan accessory in the Instant Crisp Air Fryer. 2 Air Frying. Lock the air fryer lid. Grill the chicken for 40 minutes making sure to flip the chicken every 10 minutes for even grilling.

Crisp Chicken Casserole

Ingredients: Servings: 4 Cooking Time: 15 Mins

3 C. chicken, shredded
12 oz bag egg noodles
1/2 large onion
1/2 C. chopped carrots
1/4 C. frozen peas
1/4 C. frozen broccoli pieces
2 stalks celery chopped
5 C. chicken broth
1 tsp. garlic powder
salt and pepper to taste
1 C. cheddar cheese, shredded
1 package French's onions
1/4 C. sour cream
1 can cream of chicken and mushroom soup

Directions:
Place the chicken, vegetables, garlic powder, salt and pepper, and broth and stir. Then place it into the Instant Pot Duo Crisp Air Fryer Basket. Press or lightly stir the egg noodles into the mix until damp/wet. Select the option Air Fryer and cook for 4 minutes. Stir in the sour cream, can of soup, cheese, and 1/3 of the French's onions. Top with the remaining French's onions and close the Air Fryer lid and cook for about 10 more minutes.

Cheesy Turkey-rice with Broccoli

Ingredients: Servings: 4 Cooking Time: 40 Mins

1 C. cooked, chopped turkey meat
1 tbsp. and 1-1/2 tsp. butter, melted
1/2 (10 ounce) package frozen broccoli, thawed
1/2 (7 ounce) package whole wheat crackers, crushed
1/2 C. shredded Cheddar cheese
1/2 C. uncooked white rice

Directions:
1 Preparing the Ingredients. Bring to a boil 2 C. of water in a saucepan. Stir in rice and simmer for 20 minutes. Turn off fire and set aside. Lightly grease baking pan of Instant Crisp Air Fryer with cooking spray. Mix in cooked rice, cheese, broccoli, and turkey. Toss well to mix. Mix well melted butter and crushed crackers in a small bowl. Evenly spread on top of rice. 2 Air Frying. Lock the air fryer lid. For 20 minutes, cook on 360°F until tops are lightly browned. Serve and enjoy.

Lemon Chicken Potatoes

Ingredients: Servings: 5-6 Cooking Time: 20 Mins

12 chicken thighs, bone-in
1 ½ lb. yellow potatoes, quartered
⅓ C. olive oil
⅓ C. lemon juice
1 tsp. lemon zest
1 tsp. dried parsley
1 tsp. black pepper
1 tbsp. garlic, minced
2 tsp. dried oregano
2 tsp. kosher salt
Lemon wedges to serve

Directions:
In a mixing bowl, whisk the lemon juice, olive oil, garlic, parsley, oregano, pepper, lemon zest, and salt. Place Instant Pot Air Fryer Crisp over kitchen platform. In the inner pot, add the broth and chicken. Arrange the potatoes on top and pour the lemon mixture. Close the Pressure Lid and press the "Pressure" setting. Set the "Hi" pressure level and set the timer to 15 minutes. Press "Start." Instant Pot will start building pressure. Quick-release pressure after cooking time is over (just press the button on the lid), and open the lid. Add the chicken mixture to a serving plate along with the lemon sauce. Add back the chicken to the pot. Close the Crisp Lid and press the "Air Fry" setting. Set temperature to 400°F and set the timer to 4 minutes. Press "Start." Halfway down, open the Crisp Lid, shake the basket and close the lid to continue cooking for the remaining time. Open the Crisp Lid after cooking time is over. Add the chicken to the potato mixture and serve warm.

Zingy & Nutty Chicken Wings

Ingredients: Servings: 4 Cooking Time: 18 Mins

1 tbsp. fish sauce
1 tbsp. fresh lemon juice
12 chicken middle wings, cut into half
1 tsp. sugar
2 fresh lemongrass stalks, chopped finely
¼ C. unsalted cashews, crushed

Directions:
Preparing the Ingredients. In a bowl, mix together fish sauce, lime juice and sugar. Add wings ad coat with mixture generously. Refrigerate to marinate for about 1-2 hours. Preheat the Instant Crisp Air Fryer to 355 degrees F. Air Frying. In the Instant Crisp Air Fryer pan, place lemongrass stalks. Lock the air fryer lid. Cook for about 2-3 minutes. Remove the cashew mixture from Instant Crisp Air Fryer and transfer into a bowl. Now, set the Instant Crisp Air Fryer to 390 degrees F. Place the chicken wings in Instant Crisp Air Fryer pan. Cook for about 13-15 minutes further. Transfer the wings into serving plates. Sprinkle with cashew mixture and serve.

Simple Spiced Chicken Legs

Ingredients: Servings: 6 Cooking Time: 25 Mins

2-2.5 lbs chicken drumsticks 6-8 legs
2 tbsp. olive oil
1 tsp. kosher salt
1 tsp. pepper
1 tsp. garlic powder
1 tsp. smoked paprika
1/2 tsp. cumin

Directions:
Take a large bowl and drizzle the drumsticks with olive oil and toss them to coat. Take a small bowl, stir together the remaining ingredients followed by sprinkling over drumsticks and toss to coat evenly. Divide the coated chicken onto cooking trays of the Instant Pot Duo Crisp Air Fryer. Select Air Fry from the display panel, then adjust the temperature to 400°F and the time to 25 minutes, touch the start button. Once preheated,insert two cooking trays in the top-most position and in the bottom-most position one in each. After half time, turn the food over and switch the cooking trays between the top and bottom positions. When the Air Fryer program is complete, check to make sure the thickest portion of the meat reads at least 165°F. Remove and serve hot.

Chicken Parmesan Wings

Ingredients: Servings: 4 Cooking Time: 15 Mins

Chicken wings – 2 lbs. cut into drumettes, pat dried
Parmesan – ½ cup, plus 6 tbsps. grated
Herbs de Provence – 1 tsp.
Paprika – 1 tsp.
Salt to taste

Directions:
Combine the parmesan, herbs, paprika, and salt in a bowl and rub the chicken with this mixture. Preheat the air fryer at 350F. Grease the basket with cooking spray. Cook for 15 minutes. Flip once at the halfway mark. Garnish with parmesan and serve.

Tasty Butter Chicken

Ingredients: Servings: 6 Cooking Time: 8 Mins

3 lbs. chicken breasts, boneless, skinless, and cut into cubes
1/2 C. butter, cut into cubes
2 tbsp. tomato paste
1 tsp. turmeric powder
2 tbsp. garam masala
1 tbsp. ginger paste
1 tbsp. garlic paste
1 onion, diced
1/4 C. fresh cilantro, chopped
1/2 C. heavy cream
1 1/4 C. tomato sauce
2/3 C. chicken stock
1 1/2 tsp. olive oil
1 tsp. kosher salt

Directions:
Add 3 tbsp. butter and oil in the inner pot of instant pot duo crisp and set pot on sauté mode. Add garlic paste and onion and sauté for a minute. Add chicken, tomato sauce, stock, tomato paste, turmeric, garam masala, ginger paste, and salt and stir to combine. Seal the pot with pressure cooking lid and cook on high for 5 minutes. Once done, release pressure using a quick release. Remove lid. Set pot on sauté mode. Add remaining butter and heavy cream and cook for 2 minutes. Stir well and serve.

Chicken Fritters

Ingredients: Servings: 4 Cooking Time: 25 Mins

1 lb ground chicken
1 1/2 C. mozzarella cheese, shredded
1/2 C. shallots, chopped
2 C. broccoli, chopped
3/4 C. breadcrumbs
1 garlic clove, minced
1 egg, lightly beaten
Pepper
Salt

Directions:
Add all ingredients into the large bowl and mix until well combined. Place the dehydrating tray in a multi-level air fryer basket and place basket in the instant pot. Make small patties from meat mixture and place on dehydrating tray. Seal pot with air fryer lid and select bake mode then set the temperature to 380 F and timer for 25 minutes. Turn patties halfway through. Serve and enjoy.

Boneless Air Fryer Turkey Breasts

Ingredients: Servings: 4 Cooking Time: 50 Mins

3 lb boneless breast	1 tsp. salt
1/4 C. mayonnaise	1/2 tsp. garlic powder
2 tsp. poultry seasoning	1/4 tsp. black pepper

Directions:
Choose the Air Fry option on the Instant Pot Duo Crisp Air fryer. Set the temperature to 360°F and push start. the preheating will start. Season your boneless turkey breast with mayonnaise, poultry seasoning, salt, garlic powder, and black pepper. Once preheated, Air Fry the turkey breasts on 360°F for 1 hour, turning every 15 minutes or until internal temperature has reached a temperature of 165°F.

Turkey Burgers

Ingredients: Servings: 4 Cooking Time: 16 Mins

Turkey meat – 1 pound, ground	Zest from 1 lime, grated
Shallot – 1 minced	Salt and black pepper to taste
A drizzle of olive oil	Cumin – 1 tsp. ground
Small jalapeno pepper – 1, minced	Sweet paprika – 1 tsp.
Lime juice – 2 tsps.	Guacamole for serving

Directions:
In a bowl, mix turkey meat with lime juice, zest, jalapeno, shallot, paprika, cumin, salt, and pepper. Mix well. Shape burgers from this mix and drizzle the oil over them. Cook in the preheated air fryer at 370F for 8 minutes on each side. Divide among plates and serve with guacamole on top.

Fennel Chicken

Ingredients: Servings: 4 Cooking Time: 15 Mins

1 lb chicken thighs, boneless and cut into three pieces	1 tsp. paprika
1 tsp. cayenne	2 tsp. garlic, minced
1 tsp. turmeric	2 tsp. ginger, minced
1 tsp. garam masala	1 tbsp. olive oil
1 tsp. ground fennel seeds	1 onion, sliced
	Pepper
	Salt

Directions:
Add chicken and remaining ingredients into the mixing bowl and toss well and place it in the refrigerator overnight. Spray instant pot multi-level air fryer basket with cooking spray. Add marinated chicken mixture into the air fryer basket and place basket into the instant pot. Seal pot with air fryer lid and select air fry mode then set the temperature to 360 F and timer for 15 minutes. Mix halfway through. Serve and enjoy.

Sweet and Sour Chicken

Ingredients: Servings: 6 Cooking Time: 20 Mins

3 Chicken Breasts, cubed	3/4 Cup Sugar
	2 Tbsps Cornstarch
1/2 Cup Flour	1/3 Cup Vinegar
1/2 Cup Cornstarch	2/3 Cup Water
2 Red Peppers, sliced	1/4 C. Soy sauce
1Onion,chopped	1 Tbsp Ketchup
2 Carrots, julienned	

Directions:
Preparing the Ingredients. Preheat the Instant Crisp Air Fryer to 375 degrees. Combine the flour, cornstarch and chicken in an air tight container and shake to combine Remove chicken from the container and shake off any excess flour. Air Frying. Add chicken to the Instant Crisp Air Fryer tray and cook for 20 minutes. In a saucepan, whisk together sugar, water, vinegar, soy sauce and ketchup. Bring to a boil over medium heat, reduce the heat then simmer for 2 minutes After cooking the chicken for 20 minutes, add the vegetables and sauce mixture to the Instant Crisp Air Fryer and cook for another 5 minutes Serve over hot rice

Mustard Chicken Tenders

Ingredients: Servings: 4 Cooking Time: 20 Mins

1/2 C. coconut flour	2 beaten eggs
1 tbsp. spicy brown mustard	1 lb. of chicken tenders

Directions:
1 Preparing the Ingredients. Season tenders with pepper and salt. Place a thin layer of mustard onto tenders and then dredge in flour and dip in egg. 2 Air Frying. Add to the Instant Crisp Air Fryer,lock the air fryer lid, set temperature to 390°F, and set time to 20 minutes.

Cheese Stuffed Chicken

Ingredients: Servings: 4 Cooking Time: 30 Mins

1 tbsp. creole seasoning	1 tsp. garlic powder
	1 tsp. onion powder
1 tbsp. olive oil	4 slices Colby cheese
4 chicken breasts, butterflied and pounded	4 slices pepper jack cheese

Directions:
1 Preparing the Ingredients. Preheat the Instant Crisp Air Fryer to 390°F. Place the grill pan accessory in the Instant Crisp Air Fryer. Create the dry rub by mixing in a bowl the creole seasoning, garlic powder, and onion powder. Season with salt and pepper if desired. Rub the seasoning on to the chicken. Place the chicken on a working surface and place a slice each of pepper jack and Colby cheese. Fold the chicken and secure the edges with toothpicks. Brush chicken with olive oil. 2 Air Frying. Lock the air fryer lid. Grill for 30 minutes and make sure to flip the meat every 10 minutes.

Fried Whole Chicken

Ingredients: Servings: 4 Cooking Time: 70 Mins

1 Whole chicken	1 tsp. Italian seasoning
2 Tbsp or spray of oil of choice	2 Tbsp Montreal Steak Seasoning (or salt and pepper to taste)
1 tsp. garlic powder	1.5 C. chicken broth
1 tsp. onion powder	
1 tsp. paprika	

Directions:

Truss and wash the chicken. Mix the seasoning and rub a little amount on the chicken. Pour the broth inside the Instant Pot Duo Crisp Air Fryer. Place the chicken in the air fryer basket. Select the option Air Fry and Close the Air Fryer lid and cook for 25 minutes. Spray or rub the top of the chicken with oil and rub it with half of the seasoning. Close the air fryer lid and air fry again at 400°F for 10 minutes. Flip the chicken, spray it with oil, and rub with the remaining seasoning. Again air fry it for another ten minutes. Allow the chicken to rest for 10 minutes.

Whole Chicken

Ingredients: Servings: 6 Cooking Time: 45 Mins

Whole chicken – 1 (2 ½ pounds) washed and pat dried

Dry rub – 2 tbsps.

Salt – 1 tsp.

Cooking spray

Directions:

Preheat the air fryer at 350F. Rub the dry rub on the chicken. Then rub with salt. Cook in the air fryer at 350F for 45 minutes. After 30 minutes, flip the chicken and finish cooking. Chicken is done when it reaches 165F.

Herbed Turkey Dinner

Ingredients: Servings: 5-6 Cooking Time: 40 Mins

2 lb. turkey breast with skin

1 tsp. rosemary, chopped

1 tsp. thyme, finely chopped

4 tbsp. melted butter

3 garlic cloves, grated

½ tsp. kosher salt

1 tsp. ground black pepper

Directions:

Rub the salt and black pepper over the turkey breasts. In a bowl, combine the rosemary, melted butter, thyme, and garlic in a medium bowl. Add the turkey and coat well. Place Instant Pot Air Fryer Crisp over kitchen platform. Press Air Fry, set the temperature to 400°F and set the timer to 5 minutes to preheat. Press "Start" and allow it to preheat for 5 minutes. In the inner pot, place the Air Fryer basket. In the basket, add the turkey. Close the Crisp Lid and press the "Air Fry" setting. Set temperature to 375°F and set the timer to 40 minutes. Press "Start." Halfway down, open the Crisp Lid, shake the basket and close the lid to continue cooking for the remaining time. Open the Crisp Lid after cooking time is over. Slice and serve warm.

Turkey Breasts

Ingredients: Servings: 4 Cooking Time: 50 Mins

Boneless turkey breast – 3 lbs.

Mayonnaise – ¼ cup

Poultry seasoning – 2 tsps.

Salt and pepper to taste

Garlic powder – ½ tsp.

Directions:

Preheat the air fryer to 360F. Season the turkey with mayonnaise, seasoning, salt, garlic powder, and black pepper. Cook the turkey in the air fryer for 1 hour at 360F. Turning after every 15 minutes. the turkey is done when it reaches 165F.

Rotisserie Chicken

Ingredients: Servings: 4 Cooking Time: 60 Mins

Whole chicken – 1, cleaned and patted dry

Olive oil – 2 tbsps.

Seasoned salt – 1 tbsp.

Directions:

Remove the giblet packet from the cavity. Rub the chicken with oil and salt. Place in the air fryer basket, breast-side down. Cook at 350F for 30 minutes. Then flip and cook another 30 minutes. Chicken is done when it reaches 165F.

Air Fryer Chicken Parmesan

Ingredients: Servings: 4 Cooking Time: 9 Mins

½ C. keto marinara

6 tbsp. mozzarella cheese

2 tbsp. grated parmesan cheese

1 tbsp. melted ghee

6 tbsp. gluten-free seasoned breadcrumbs

1 8-ounce chicken breasts

Directions:

1 Preparing the Ingredients. Ensure Instant Crisp Air Fryer is preheated to 360 degrees. Spray the basket with olive oil. Mix parmesan cheese and breadcrumbs together. Melt ghee. Brush melted ghee onto the chicken and dip into breadcrumb mixture. Place coated chicken in the Instant Crisp Air Fryer and top with olive oil. 2 Air Frying. Lock the air fryer lid. Set temperature to 360°F, and set time to 6 minutes. Cook 2 breasts for 6 minutes and top each breast with a tbsp. of sauce and 1½ tbsp. of mozzarella cheese. Cook another 3 minutes to melt cheese. Keep cooked pieces warm as you repeat the process with remaining breasts.

Chicken Parmesan

Ingredients: Servings: 4 Cooking Time: 15 Mins

Panko bread crumbs – 2 cups

Parmesan – ¼ cup, grated

Garlic powder – ½ tsp.

Chicken cutlets – 1 ½ pounds, skinless, and boneless

White flour – 2 cups

Egg – 1, whisked

Salt and pepper to taste

Mozzarella - 1 cup, grated

Tomato sauce – 2 cups

Basil – 3 tbsps. chopped

Directions:

In a bowl, mix garlic powder, and parmesan and stir. Put flour in a second bowl and the egg in a third. Season chicken with salt, and pepper. Dip in flour, then in the egg mix and in panko. Cook chicken pieces in the air fryer at 360F for 3 minutes on each side. Transfer chicken to a baking dish. Add tomato sauce, and top with mozzarella. Cook in the air fryer at 375F for 7 minutes. Divide among plates, sprinkle basil on top and serve.

Italian Chicken

Ingredients: Servings: 4 Cooking Time: 16 Mins

Chicken thighs – 8

Chicken stock - ¾

Olive oil – 1 tbsp.
Garlic – 2 cloves, minced
Thyme - 1 tbsp. chopped
Heavy cream – ½ cup
Red pepper flakes – 1 tsp. crushed
cup
Parmesan – ¼ cup, grated
Sun-dried tomatoes – ½ cup
Basil – 2 tbsps. chopped
Salt and black pepper to taste

Directions:
Season chicken with salt and pepper, and rub with half of the oil. Place in the preheated air fryer at 350F and cook for 4 minutes. Meanwhile, heat the rest of the oil in a pan and add garlic, thyme, pepper flakes, tomatoes, stock, heavy cream, salt, parmesan, and pepper. Bring to a simmer and remove from the heat. Place the mixture in a dish. Add chicken thighs on top and cook in the air fryer at 320F for 12 minutes. Serve with basil sprinkled on top.

Air Fryer Chicken

Ingredients: Servings: 4 Cooking Time: 30 Mins

Chicken wings – 2 lbs.
Cooking spray
Salt and pepper to taste

Directions:
Season the chicken wings with salt and pepper. Spray the air fryer basket with cooking spray. Add chicken wings and cook at 400F for 35 minutes. Flip 3 times during cooking for even cooking. Serve.

Paprika Chicken

Ingredients: Servings: 4 Cooking Time: 30 Mins

4 chicken breasts, skinless and boneless, cut into chunks
2 tsp. garlic, minced
2 tbsp. smoked paprika
3 tbsp. olive oil
2 tbsp. lemon juice
Pepper
Salt

Directions:
In a small bowl, mix together garlic, lemon juice, paprika, oil, pepper, and salt. Rub chicken with garlic mixture. Add chicken into the instant pot air fryer basket and place basket in the pot. Seal the pot with air fryer lid and select bake mode and cook at 350 f for 30 minutes. Serve and enjoy.

Crispy Southern Fried Chicken

Ingredients: Servings: 4 Cooking Time: 25 Mins

1 tsp. cayenne pepper
2 tbsp. mustard powder
2 tbsp. oregano
2 tbsp. thyme
3 tbsp. coconut milk
1 beaten egg
¼ C. cauliflower
¼ C. gluten-free oats
8 chicken drumsticks

Directions:
1 Preparing the Ingredients. Ensure the Instant Crisp Air Fryer is preheated to 350 degrees. Lay out chicken and season with pepper and salt on all sides. Add all other ingredients to a blender, blending till a smooth-like breadcrumb mixture is created. Place in a bowl and add a beaten egg to another bowl. Dip chicken into breadcrumbs, then into egg, and breadcrumbs once more. 2 Air Frying. Place coated drumsticks into the Instant Crisp Air Fryer. Lock the air fryer lid. Set temperature to 350°F, and set time to 20 minutes and cook 20 minutes. Bump up the temperature to 390 degrees and cook another 5 minutes till crispy.

Mango Chicken

Ingredients: Servings: 2 Cooking Time: 15 Mins

2 chicken breasts, skinless and boneless
1 ripe mango, peeled and diced
1/2 tbsp. turmeric
2 garlic cloves, minced
1/2 C. chicken broth
1/2 tsp. ginger, grated
1 fresh lime juice
1/2 tsp. pepper
1/2 tsp. salt

Directions:
Add chicken into the inner pot of instant pot duo crisp and top with mango. Add lime juice, broth, turmeric, pepper, and salt. Seal the pot with pressure cooking lid and cook on high for 15 minutes. Once done, allow to release pressure naturally. Remove lid. Shred chicken using a fork and stir well. Serve and enjoy.

Lemon-pepper Chicken Wings

Ingredients: Servings: 4 Cooking Time: 20 Mins

8 whole chicken wings
Juice of ½ lemon
½ tsp. garlic powder
1 tsp. onion powder
Salt
Pepper
¼ C. low-fat buttermilk
½ C. all-purpose flour
Cooking oil

Directions:
Preparing the Ingredients. Place the wings in a sealable plastic bag. Drizzle the wings with the lemon juice. Season the wings with the garlic powder, onion powder, and salt and pepper to taste. Seal the bag. Shake thoroughly to combine the seasonings and coat the wings. Pour the buttermilk and the flour into separate bowls large enough to dip the wings. Spray the Instant Crisp Air Fryer basket with cooking oil. One at a time, dip the wings in the buttermilk and then the flour. Air Frying. Place the wings in the Instant Crisp Air Fryer basket. It is okay to stack them on top of each other. Spray the wings with cooking oil, being sure to spray the bottom layer. Lock the air fryer lid. Cook for 5 minutes. Remove the basket and shake it to ensure all of the pieces will cook fully. Return the basket to the Instant Crisp Air Fryer and continue to cook the chicken. Repeat shaking every 5 minutes until a total of 20 minutes has passed. Cool before serving.

Herb-roasted Turkey Breast

Ingredients: Servings: 8 Cooking Time: 60 Mins

3 lb turkey breast
Rub Ingredients
2 tbsp. olive oil
2 tbsp. lemon juice
1 tbsp. minced Garlic
2 tsp. kosher salt
1 tsp. pepper
1 tsp. dried rosemary
1 tsp. dried thyme
1 tsp. ground sage

2 tsp. ground
mustard

Directions:
Take a small bowl and thoroughly combine the Rub Ingredients in it. Rub this on the outside of the turkey breast and under any loose skin. Place the coated turkey breast keeping skin side up on a cooking tray. Place the drip pan at the bottom of the cooking chamber of the Instant Pot Duo Crisp Air Fryer. Select Air Fry option, post this, adjust the temperature to 360°F and the time to one hour, then touch start. When preheated, add the food to the cooking tray in the lowest position. Close the lid for cooking. When the Air Fry program is complete, check to make sure that the thickest portion of the meat reads at least 160°F, remove the turkey and let it rest for 10 minutes before slicing and serving.

Sweet & Tangy Tamarind Chicken

Ingredients: Servings: 4 Cooking Time: 15 Mins

2 lbs chicken breasts, skinless, boneless, and cut into pieces
1 tbsp. ketchup
1 tbsp. vinegar
1 garlic clove, minced
2 tbsp. ginger, grated
3 tbsp. olive oil
1 tbsp. arrowroot powder
1/2 C. tamarind paste
2 tbsp. brown sugar
1 tsp. salt

Directions:
Add oil into the inner pot of instant pot duo crisp and set the pot on sauté mode. Add ginger and garlic and sauté for 30 seconds. Add chicken and sauté for 3-4 minutes. In a small bowl, mix together the tamarind paste, brown sugar, ketchup, vinegar, and salt and pour over chicken and stir well. Seal the pot with pressure cooking lid and cook on high for 8 minutes. Once done, release pressure using a quick release. Remove lid. In a small bowl, whisk arrowroot powder with 2 tbsp. water and pour it into the pot. Set pot on sauté mode and cook chicken for 1-2 minutes. Serve and enjoy.

Roasted Chicken

Ingredients: Servings: 4 Cooking Time: 15 Mins

4 chicken thighs
5 oz jar roasted red peppers, drained and sliced
1 C. grape tomatoes
1/2 lb potatoes, cut into small chunks
2 tbsp. fresh parsley, chopped
2 tbsp. olive oil
1/2 tsp. dried oregano
3 garlic cloves, crushed
2 tbsp. capers, drained
Pepper
Salt

Directions:
Line instant pot multi-level air fryer basket with aluminum foil. Season chicken with pepper and salt and place into the air fryer basket and place basket into the instant pot. Mix together remaining ingredients and pour over chicken and mix well. Seal pot with air fryer lid and select roast mode then set the temperature to 380 F and timer for 40-45 minutes. Stir halfway through. Serve and enjoy.

Chicken Casserole

Ingredients: Servings: 4 Cooking Time: 15 Mins

Chicken - 3 cups, shredded
Egg noodles – 1(12 oz.) bag (boiled in hot water for 2 to 3 minutes then drain)
Onion – ½, chopped
Chopped carrots – ½ cup
Frozen peas – ¼ cup
Frozen broccoli pieces – ¼ cup
Celery -2 stalks, chopped
Chicken broth – 5 cups
Garlic powder – 1 tsp.
Salt and pepper to taste
Cheddar cheese – 1 cup, shredded
French onions – 1 package
Sour cream – ¼ cup
Cream of chicken and mushroom soup – 1 can

Directions:
Place the chicken, vegetables, garlic powder, salt, and pepper and broth in a bowl and mix. Then place in the air fryer basket. Lightly stir the egg noodles into the mix until damp. Cook for 4 minutes at 350F. Then stir in the can of soup, sour cream, cheese and 1/3 of the French onions. Top with the remaining French onion and close. Cook for 10 minutes more. Serve.

FISH AND SEAFOOD RECIPES

Cheddar Cheese Dip

Ingredients: Servings: 16 Cooking Time: 9 Mins

1 lb bacon slices, cooked and crumbled
1 green onion, sliced
2 C. cheddar cheese, shredded
1 C. non-alcoholic beer
1/4 C. heavy cream
1 tsp. garlic powder
1 1/2 tbsp. dijon mustard
1/4 C. sour cream
18 oz cream cheese, softened

Directions:
Add cream cheese, bacon, beer, garlic powder, mustard, and sour cream into the instant pot and stir well. Seal pot with lid and cook on manual high pressure for 5 minutes. Once done then release pressure using the quick-release method than open the lid. Stir in heavy cream and cheese and cook on sauté mode for 3-4 minutes. Garnish with green onion and serve.

Old Bay Seasoned Haddock

Ingredients: Servings: 2 Cooking Time: 7 Mins

1/2 lb haddock
1 tbsp. fresh lemon juice
1/4 C. water
1 tbsp. mayonnaise
1/4 tsp. old bay seasoning
1/2 tsp. olive oil
1/4 tsp. dill, chopped

Directions:
Add water, mayonnaise, seasoning, olive oil, dill, and lemon juice in instant pot and stir well. Place fish fillets in the pot. Seal pot with lid and cook on manual high pressure for 7 minutes. Once done then release pressure using the quick-release method than open the lid. Serve and enjoy.

Bacon Wrapped Shrimp

Ingredients: Servings: 4 Cooking Time: 5 Mins

1¼ lb. tiger shrimp, peeled and deveined
1 lb. bacon

Directions:

1 Preparing the Ingredients. Wrap each shrimp with a slice of bacon. Refrigerate for about 20 minutes. Preheat the Instant Crisp Air Fryer to 390 degrees F. 2 Air Frying. Arrange the shrimp in the Instant Crisp Air Fryer basket. Close air fryer lid, cook for about 5-7 minutes.

Garlic-lemon Shrimp

Ingredients: Servings: 2 Cooking Time: 15 Mins

Raw shrimp – 1 lb. peeled and deveined
Garlic powder – ¼ tsp.
Lemon wedges to taste
Cooking spray
Salt and pepper to taste
Parsley – 1 tbsp. minced
Chili flakes to taste

Directions:

Add shrimp in a bowl. Add oil and mix. Add garlic powder, and season with salt and pepper. Mix well. Cook in the air fryer at 400F for 10 to 14 minutes. Flip once at the halfway mark. Then remove and squeeze over lemon juice. Sprinkle with chili flakes and parsley and serve.

Monk Fish with Power Greens

Ingredients: Servings: 4 Cooking Time: 15 Mins

2 tbsp. Olive Oil
4 (8 oz) Monk Fish Fillets, cut in 2 pieces each
½ C. chopped Green Beans
2 cloves Garlic, sliced
1 C. Kale Leaves
½ lb Baby Bok Choy, stems removed and chopped largely
1 Lemon, zested and juiced
Lemon Wedges to serve
Salt and White Pepper to taste

Directions:

Pour in the coconut oil, garlic, red chili, and green beans. Stir fry for 5 minutes on Sear/Sauté mode. Add the kale leaves, and cook them to wilt, about 3 minutes. Meanwhile, place the fish on a plate and season with salt, white pepper, and lemon zest. After, remove the green beans and kale into a plate and set aside. Back to the pot, add the olive oil and fish. Brown the fillets on each side for about 2 minutes and then add the bok choy in. Pour the lemon juice over the fish and gently stir. Cook for 2 minutes and then press Cancel to stop cooking. Spoon the fish with bok choy over the green beans and kale. Serve with a side of lemon wedges and there, you have a complete meal.

Baba Ghanoush

Ingredients: Servings: 6 Cooking Time: 13 Mins

1 eggplant, pierce with a fork
2 tbsp. sesame seeds
2 tbsp. sesame oil
2 tsp. lemon juice
1/2 tsp. ground cumin
1 garlic clove, minced
1/2 onion, chopped
1 tsp. sea salt

Directions:

Pour 1 C. of water into the inner pot of instant pot duo crisp. Place steamer rack in the pot. Place eggplant on top of the steamer rack. Seal the pot with pressure cooking lid and cook on high pressure for 8 minutes. Once done, release pressure using a quick release. Remove lid. Remove eggplant from pot and clean the pot. Peel and slice cooked eggplant. Add oil into the pot and set a pot on sauté mode. Add onion and eggplant and sauté for 3-5 minutes. Add remaining ingredients and stir everything well to combine. Turn off the instant pot. Blend eggplant mixture using blender until smooth. Serve and enjoy.

Creamy Eggplant Dip

Ingredients: Servings: 8 Cooking Time: 8 Mins

2 eggplants, cut into wedges
1 tsp. dried oregano
1 tbsp. garlic, crushed
1/2 lemon juice
2 tbsp. olive oil
1 C. of water
1/2 tsp. Italian seasoning
1/4 tsp. pepper
1 tsp. salt

Directions:

Pour 1 C. of water into the inner pot of instant pot duo crisp. Place steamer rack in the pot. Arrange eggplant on top of the steamer rack. Seal the pot with a lid and cook on high for 8 minutes. Once done, release pressure using a quick release. Remove lid. Remove eggplant wedges from pot and peel. Transfer eggplant and remaining ingredients into the blender and blend until smooth. Serve and enjoy.

Air Fried Shrimps

Ingredients: Servings: 4 Cooking Time: 8 Mins

1 lb. large shrimps, peeled and deveined
1 tbsp. butter
½ tsp. garlic granules
1 tsp. lemon juice
1/8 C. Parmesan cheese, freshly grated
1/8 tsp. salt

Directions:

Remove shrimps' tails. Mix in garlic granules, lemon, and salt to a bowl with the melted butter. Add the shrimps and toss to coat evenly on all sides. Line the air fryer basket with parchment paper and place shrimps inside. Sprinkle Parmesan cheese over shrimps. Place the air fryer basket inside the instant pot duo crisp and attach the air fryer lid. Set to air fry at 400 degrees F for 8 minutes. Cook until shrimps become bright red and the meat is opaque.

Louisiana Shrimp Po Boy

Ingredients: Servings: 6 Cooking Time: 10 Mins

1 tsp. creole seasoning
8 slices of tomato
Lettuce leaves
¼ C. buttermilk
½ C. Louisiana Fish Fry
1 lb. deveined shrimp
1 chopped green onion
1 tsp. hot sauce
1 tsp. Dijon mustard
½ tsp. creole seasoning
1 tsp. Worcestershire sauce

Remoulade sauce:	Juice of ½ a lemon ½ C. vegan mayo

Directions:

1 Preparing the Ingredients. To make the sauce, combine all sauce ingredients until well incorporated. Chill while you cook shrimp. Mix seasonings together and liberally season shrimp. Add buttermilk to a bowl. Dip each shrimp into milk and place in a Ziploc bag. Chill half an hour to marinate. Add fish fry to a bowl. Take shrimp from marinating bag and dip into fish fry, then add to Instant Crisp Air Fryer. Ensure your Instant Crisp Air Fryer is preheated to 400 degrees. Spray shrimp with olive oil. 2 Air Frying. Close air fryer lid. Set temperature to 400°F, and set time to 5 minutes. Cook 5 minutes, flip and then cook another 5 minutes. Assemble "Keto" Po Boy by adding sauce to lettuce leaves, along with shrimp and tomato.

Maple & Ginger Mahi-mahi

Ingredients: Servings: 4 Cooking Time: 5 Mins

- 4 Mahi Mahi Fillets, fresh
- 4 cloves Garlic, minced
- 1 ¼ -inch Ginger, grated
- Salt and Black Pepper
- 2 tbsp. Chili Powder
- 1 tbsp. Sriracha Sauce
- 1 ½ tbsp. Maple Syrup
- 1 Lime, juiced
- 1 C. Water

Directions:

Place mahi mahi on a plate and season with salt and pepper on both sides. In a bowl, add garlic, ginger, chili powder, sriracha sauce, maple syrup, and lime juice. Use a spoon to mix it. with a brush, apply the hot sauce mixture on the fillet. Then, open the cooker's lid, pour the water it and fit the rack at the bottom of the pot. Put the fillets on the trivet. Close the lid, secure the pressure valve, and select Steam mode on High pressure for 5 minutes. Press Start to start cooking. Once the timer has ended, do a quick pressure release, and open the lid. Use a set of tongs to remove the mahi mahi onto serving plates. Serve with steamed or braised asparagus. For a crispier taste, cook them for 2 minutes on Air Fry mode, at 300 F.

Spicy Prawns

Ingredients: Servings: 4 Cooking Time: 6 Mins

- 12 king prawns
- 1/4 tsp. black pepper
- 1 tsp. chili powder
- 1 tsp. red chili flakes
- 1 tbsp. vinegar
- 1 tbsp. ketchup
- 3 tbsp. mayonnaise
- 1/2 tsp. sea salt

Directions:

Add prawns, chili flakes, chili powder, black pepper, and salt to the bowl and toss well. Spray instant pot multi-level air fryer basket with cooking spray. Add shrimp into the air fryer basket and place basket into the instant pot. Seal pot with air fryer lid and select air fry mode then set the temperature to 350 F and timer for 6 minutes. Stir halfway through. In a small bowl, mix together mayonnaise, ketchup, and vinegar. Serve shrimp with mayo mixture.

Pesto Shrimp

Ingredients: Servings: 6 Cooking Time: 5 Mins

- 1 lb shrimp, defrosted
- 14 oz basil pesto

Directions:

Add shrimp and pesto into the mixing bowl and toss well. Spray instant pot multi-level air fryer basket with cooking spray. Add shrimp into the air fryer basket and place basket into the instant pot. Seal pot with air fryer lid and select air fry mode then set the temperature to 400 F and timer for 5 minutes. Serve and enjoy.

Seafood Casserole

Ingredients: Servings: 6 Cooking Time: 40 Mins

- Butter – 6 tbsps.
- Mushrooms – 2 ounces, chopped
- Green bell pepper – 1 small, chopped
- Celery – 1 stalk, chopped
- Garlic – 2 cloves, minced
- Small yellow onion – 1, chopped
- Salt and black pepper to taste
- Flour – 4 tbsps.
- White wine – ½ cup
- Milk – 1 ½ cups
- Haddock – 4 ounces, skinless, boneless and cut into small pieces
- Heavy cream – ½ cup
- Sea scallops – 4, sliced
- Lobster meat – 4 ounces, cooked and cut into small pieces
- Mustard powder – ½ tsp.
- Lemon juice – 1 tbsp.
- Bread crumbs – 1/3 cup
- Salt and black pepper to taste
- Cheddar cheese – 3 tbsps. grated
- Handful parsley, chopped
- Sweet paprika – 1 tsp.

Directions:

Heat 4 tbsps. of butter in a pan over a medium-high heat. Add wine, onion, garlic, celery, mushrooms, and bell pepper and cook for 10 minutes. Add milk, cream, and flour, stir well and cook for 6 minutes. Add haddock, lobster meat, scallops, mustard powder, salt, pepper, and lemon juice and stir well. Remove from heat and place in a pan. In a bowl, mix the rest of the butter with cheese, paprika, and bread crumbs and sprinkle over seafood mix. Transfer the pan to the air fryer and cook at 360F for 16 minutes. Serve garnish with parsley.

Lime Tilapia Fillets (pressure Cook)

Ingredients: Servings: 4 Cooking Time: 2 Mins

- 4 tbsp. lime juice
- 3 tbsp. chili powder
- 1 C. water
- ½ tsp. salt
- 1 lb. (454 g) tilapia fillets

Directions:

Pour the water into Instant Pot and insert a trivet. Whisk together the lime juice, chili powder, and salt in a small bowl until combined. Brush both sides of the tilapia fillets generously with the sauce. Put the tilapia fillets on top of the trivet. Secure the lid. Select the Pressure Cook and set the cooking time for 2 minutes at High Pressure. Once cooking is complete, do a quick pressure release. Carefully open the lid. Remove the tilapia fillets from the Instant Pot to a plate and serve.

Spiced Cauliflower

Ingredients: Servings: 4 Cooking Time: 10 Mins

1 cauliflower head, florets separated
1 tbsp. Olive oil
1 tbsp. Butter; melted
¼ tsp. Cinnamon powder
¼ tsp. Cloves, ground
¼ tsp. Turmeric powder
½ tsp. Cumin, ground
A pinch of salt and black pepper

Directions:
Take a bowl and mix cauliflower florets with the rest of the ingredients and toss. Put the cauliflower in your air fryer's basket and cook at 390°f for 15 minutes Divide between plates and serve as a side dish.

Easy Garlic Lemon Shrimp

Ingredients: Servings: 3 Cooking Time: 5 Mins

1 lb large shrimp
2 garlic cloves, minced
3 tbsp. butter
1/2 tsp. paprika
2 lemons, sliced

Directions:
Add butter into the pot and set the pot on sauté mode. Add garlic and sauté for 1 minute. Add shrimp, paprika, and lemon slices, and stirs well. Seal pot with lid and cook on manual high pressure for 4 minutes. Once done then allow to release pressure naturally then open the lid. Serve and enjoy.

Buffalo Chicken Dip

Ingredients: Servings: 10 Cooking Time: 12 Mins

2 lbs chicken breast, skinless, boneless and halves
1/4 C. hot sauce
8 oz cream cheese
1 C. chicken broth

Directions:
Add chicken and broth into the inner pot of instant pot duo crisp. Seal the pot with pressure cooking lid and cook on high for 10 minutes. Once done, allow to release pressure naturally for 10 minutes then release remaining pressure using a quick release. Remove lid. Remove chicken from pot and shred using a fork. Clean the instant pot. Add shredded chicken, hot sauce, and cream cheese into the instant pot and cook on sauté mode until cheese is melted. Serve and enjoy.

Minty Summer Squash

Ingredients: Servings: 4 Cooking Time: 15 Mins

4 summer squash; cut into wedges
½ C. mint; chopped.
1 C. mozzarella; shredded
¼ C. olive oil
¼ C. lemon juice
Salt and black pepper to taste.

Directions:
In a pan that fits your air fryer, mix the squash with the rest of the ingredients, toss, introduce the pan in the air fryer and cook at 370°f for 25 minutes Divide between plates and serve as a side dish.

Firecracker Shrimp

Ingredients: Servings: 4 Cooking Time: 8 Mins

For the shrimp
1 lb. raw shrimp, peeled and deveined
Salt
Pepper
½ C. all-purpose flour
¾ C. panko bread crumbs
1 egg
Cooking oil
For the firecracker sauce
⅓ C. sour cream
2 tbsp. Sriracha
¼ C. sweet chili sauce

Directions:
1 Preparing the Ingredients. Season the shrimp with salt and pepper to taste. In a small bowl, beat the egg. In another small bowl, place the flour. In a third small bowl, add the panko bread crumbs. Spray the Instant Crisp Air Fryer basket with cooking oil. Dip the shrimp in the flour, then the egg, and then the bread crumbs. Place the shrimp in the Instant Crisp Air Fryer basket. It is okay to stack them. Spray the shrimp with cooking oil. 2 Air Frying. Close air fryer lid and cook for 4 minutes. Open the Instant Crisp Air Fryer and flip the shrimp. I recommend flipping individually instead of shaking to keep the breading intact. Cook for an additional 4 minutes or until crisp. While the shrimp is cooking, make the firecracker sauce: In a small bowl, combine the sour cream, Sriracha, and sweet chili sauce. Mix well. Serve with the shrimp.

Cod with Orange Sauce (pressure Cook)

Ingredients: Servings: 4 Cooking Time: 7 Mins

4 cod fillets, boneless
1 C. white wine
A small grated ginger piece
Juice from 1 orange
Salt and ground black pepper, to taste
4 spring onions, chopped

Directions:
Combine the wine, orange juice, and ginger in your Instant Pot and stir well. Insert a steamer basket. Arrange the cod fillets on the basket. Sprinkle with the salt and pepper. Secure the lid. Press the Pressure Cook on your Instant Pot and set the cooking time for 7 minutes at High Pressure. Once the timer beeps, do a quick pressure release. Carefully remove the lid. Drizzle the sauce all over the fish and sprinkle with the green onions. Transfer to a serving plate and serve immediately.

Healthy Catfish

Ingredients: Servings: 3 Cooking Time: 20 Mins

3 catfish fillets
1/4 C. fish seasoning
1 tbsp. fresh parsley, chopped
1 tbsp. olive oil

Directions:
Place the dehydrating tray in a multi-level air fryer basket and place basket in the instant pot. Seasoned fish with seasoning and place on dehydrating tray. Brush with olive oil. Seal pot with air fryer lid and select air fry mode then set the temperature to 400 F and timer for 20 minutes. Turn fish fillets halfway through. Garnish with parsley and serve.

Shrimp with Garlic Sauce

Ingredients: Servings: 4 Cooking Time: 13 Mins

1 1/4 lbs. Shrimp, peeled and deveined
1 tbsp. minced garlic
2 tbsp. fresh lemon juice
1/4 C. butter
Salt and pepper
1/8 tsp. red pepper flakes
2 tbsp. minced fresh parsley

Directions:

Toss the shrimp with oil and all other ingredients in a bowl. Spread the seasoned shrimp in the baking pan. Press "power button" of air fry oven and turn the dial to select the "bake" mode. Press the time button and again turn the dial to set the cooking time to 13 minutes. Now push the temp button and rotate the dial to set the temperature at 350 degrees f. Once preheated, place the baking pan in the oven and close its lid. Serve warm.

Tha Fish Cakes with Mango Relish

Ingredients: Servings: 4 Cooking Time: 10 Mins

1 lb White Fish Fillets
3 Tbsps Ground Coconut
1 Ripened Mango
½ Tsps Chili Paste
Tbsps Fresh Parsley
1 Green Onion
1 Lime
1 Tsp Salt
1 Egg

Directions:

1 Preparing the Ingredients. To make the relish, peel and dice the mango into cubes. Combine with a half tsp. of chili paste, a tbsp. of parsley, and the zest and juice of half a lime. In a food processor, pulse the fish until it forms a smooth texture. Place into a bowl and add the salt, egg, chopped green onion, parsley, two tbsp. of the coconut, and the remainder of the chili paste and lime zest and juice. Combine well Portion the mixture into 10 equal balls and flatten them into small patties. Pour the reserved tbsp. of coconut onto a dish and roll the patties over to coat. Preheat the Instant Crisp Air Fryer to 390 degrees 2 Air Frying. Place the fish cakes into the Instant Crisp Air Fryer, close air fryer lid and cook for 8 minutes. They should be crisp and lightly browned when ready Serve hot with mango relish

Beer-battered Fish and Chips

Ingredients: Servings: 4 Cooking Time: 30 Mins

2 eggs
1 C. malty beer, such as Pabst Blue Ribbon
1 C. all-purpose flour
½ C. cornstarch
1 tsp. garlic powder
Salt
Pepper
Cooking oil
(4-ounce) cod fillets

Directions:

1 Preparing the Ingredients. In a medium bowl, beat the eggs with the beer. In another medium bowl, combine the flour and cornstarch, and season with the garlic powder and salt and pepper to taste. Spray the Instant Crisp Air Fryer basket with cooking oil. Dip each cod fillet in the flour and cornstarch mixture and then in the egg and beer mixture. Dip the cod in the flour and cornstarch a second time. 2 Air Frying. Place the cod in the Instant Crisp Air Fryer. Do not stack. Cook in batches. Spray with cooking oil. Close air fryer lid and cook for 8 minutes. Open the Instant Crisp Air Fryer and flip the cod. Cook for an additional 7 minutes. Remove the cooked cod from the Instant Crisp Air Fryer, then repeat steps 4 and 5 for the remaining fillets. Serve with prepared air fried frozen fries. Frozen fries will need to be cooked for 18 to 20 minutes at 400°F. Cool before serving.

Instant Pot Salsa

Ingredients: Servings: 10 Cooking Time: 10 Mins

4 C. tomatoes, peel, core, and dice
15 oz can tomato sauce
1/2 C. apple cider vinegar
1 tbsp. cayenne pepper sauce
6 oz can tomato paste
1 tbsp. cumin
1 tbsp. garlic, minced
2 jalapeno pepper, diced
2 bell peppers, diced
1 onion, diced
2 tbsp. kosher salt

Directions:

Add all ingredients into the inner pot of instant pot duo crisp and stir well. Seal the pot with a lid and cook on high for 10 minutes. Once done, allow to release pressure naturally. Remove lid. Allow to cool completely then store or serve.

Steam Shrimp

Ingredients: Servings: 4 Cooking Time: 6 Mins

2 lbs shrimp, cleaned
1 1/2 tsp. old bay seasoning
1 tsp. Cajun seasoning
Pepper
Salt

Directions:

Add all ingredients into the inner pot of instant pot duo crisp and stir well. Seal the pot with pressure cooking lid and select steam mode and cook for 6 minutes. Once done, release pressure using a quick release. Remove lid. Stir well and serve.

Old Bay Crab Cakes

Ingredients: Servings: 4 Cooking Time: 20 Mins

slices dried bread, crusts removed
1 tbsp. mayonnaise
1 tbsp. Worcestershire sauce
1 tbsp. baking powder
Small amount of milk
1 tbsp. parsley flakes
1 tsp. Old Bay® Seasoning
1/4 tsp. salt
1 egg
1 lb. lump crabmeat

Directions:

1 Preparing the Ingredients. Crush your bread over a large bowl until it is broken down into small pieces. Add milk and stir until bread crumbs are moistened. Mix in mayo and Worcestershire sauce. Add remaining ingredients and mix well. Shape into 4 patties. 2 Air Frying. Close air fryer lid. Cook at 360 degrees for 20 minutes, flip half way through.

Bacon-wrapped Shrimp

Ingredients: Servings: 6 Cooking Time: 10 Mins

1-pound shrimp
1 package bacon
1/2 tsp. lemon zest
1 tsp. garlic powder

1/2 tsp. cayenne pepper	1 tbsp. Worcestershire sauce
1/2 tsp. ground cumin	1 tbsp. lemon juice
1/2 tsp. onion powder	

Directions:

Whisk Worcestershire sauce with cayenne pepper, onion powder, cumin, lemon zest, and garlic powder in a large bowl. Toss in shrimp and mix well to coat then cover them to refrigerate for 1 hour. Cut the bacon in half and wrap each half around each shrimp. Place the wrapped shrimp in the Air Fryer Basket and set it in the Instant Pot Duo. Put on the Air Fryer lid and seal it. Hit the "Air fry Button" and select 10 minutes of cooking time, then press "Start." Once the Instant Pot Duo beeps, remove its lid. Serve.

Coconut Chili Shrimp

Ingredients: Servings: 5-6 Cooking Time: 6 Mins

3 C. panko breadcrumbs	½ tsp. kosher salt
½ C. all-purpose flour	2 tsp. fresh cilantro, chopped
2 large eggs	3 C. flaked coconut, unsweetened
½ tsp. ground black pepper	12 oz. medium-size raw shrimps, peeled, and deveined) ¼ C. lime juice
¼ C. honey	
1 serrano chili, thinly sliced	

Directions:

In a mixing bowl, combine honey, Serrano chili with lime juice. In a mixing bowl, combine the pepper and flour. In a mixing bowl, beat the eggs. In another bowl, combine the coconut and breadcrumbs. Coat the shrimps with the eggs, then with the flour, and then with the crumbs. Coat with some cooking spray. Place Instant Pot Air Fryer Crisp over kitchen platform. Press Air Fry, set the temperature to 400°F and set the timer to 5 minutes to preheat. Press "Start" and allow it to preheat for 5 minutes. In the inner pot, place the Air Fryer basket. Line with a parchment paper, add the shrimps. Close the Crisp Lid and press the "Air Fry" setting. Set temperature to 200°F and set the timer to 6 minutes. Press "Start." Halfway down, open the Crisp Lid, shake the basket and close the lid to continue cooking for the remaining time. Open the Crisp Lid after cooking time is over. Serve the shrimps warm with the chili sauce.

Tasty Spicy Shrimp

Ingredients: Servings: 2 Cooking Time: 6 Mins

1/2 lb shrimp, peeled and deveined	1/4 tsp. cayenne pepper
1/2 tsp. old bay seasoning	1/4 tsp. paprika
1 tbsp. olive oil	1/8 tsp. salt

Directions:

Add all ingredients into the mixing bowl and toss well. Spray instant pot multi-level air fryer basket with cooking spray. Add shrimp into the air fryer basket and place basket into the instant pot. Seal pot with air fryer lid and select air fry mode then set the temperature to 390 F and timer for 6 minutes. Serve and enjoy.

Honey Mustard Salmon

Ingredients: Servings: 2 Cooking Time: 9 Mins

2 salmon fillets	1/4 C. mayonnaise
2 tbsp. Dijon mustard	Pepper
2 tbsp. honey	Salt

Directions:

In a small bowl, mix together mustard, honey, mayonnaise, pepper, and salt and brush over salmon. Place the dehydrating tray in a multi-level air fryer basket and place basket in the instant pot. Place salmon fillets on dehydrating tray. Seal pot with air fryer lid and select air fry mode then set the temperature to 350 F and timer for 9 minutes. Serve and enjoy.

Meaditerranean Scallops with Butter-caper Sauce

Ingredients: Servings: 6 Cooking Time: 12 Mins

2 lb Sea Scallops, foot removed	4 tbsp. Capers, drained
10 tbsp. Butter, unsalted	1 C. Dry White Wine
4 tbsp. Olive Oil	3 tsp. lemon Zest

Directions:

Melt the butter to caramel brown on Sear/Sauté. Use a soup spook to fetch the butter out into a bowl. Next, heat the oil in the pot, once heated add the scallops and sear them on both sides to golden brown which is about 5 minutes. Remove to a plate and set aside. Pour the white wine in the pot to deglaze the bottom while using a spoon to scrape the bottom of the pot of any scallop bits. Add the capers, butter, and lemon zest. Use a spoon to stir the mixture once gently. After 40 seconds, spoon the sauce with capers over the scallops. Serve.

Air Fryer Fish Sticks

Ingredients: Servings: 4 Cooking Time: 10 Mins

½ C. all-purpose flour	½ C. panko bread crumbs
1 lb. white fish fillet, tilapia or cod	1 tsp. paprika
1 large egg	1 tbsp. parsley flakes
½ C. Parmesan cheese, grated	1 tsp. black pepper
	Cooking spray

Directions:

Cleanse fish and pat dry with paper towels. Cut into 1"x3" sticks. Prepare 3 shallow dishes. Put flour in the first dish. Beat egg in the second dish and mix Parmesan cheese, panko bread crumbs and seasonings in the third dish. Coat fish sticks evenly with flour and then dip to the dish with beaten eggs. Shake off excess liquid. Dip in the seasoned bread crumbs to coat and shake off excess bread crumbs. Line air fryer basket with parchment paper and spray cooking oil. Arrange fish sticks on the air fryer basket and spray cooking oil on top before putting inside the instant pot. Cover with the air fryer lid and air fry at 400 degrees F for 5 minutes. Flip fish sticks after the timer ended and cook for an additional 5 minutes. Serve in a platter.

Crumbled Fish

Ingredients: Servings: 4 Cooking Time: 12 Mins

Oil – ¼ cup
Egg – 1, beaten
Flounder fillets – 4
Dry bread crumbs – 1 cup
Lemon – 1 sliced

Directions:
In a bowl, mix oil and bread crumbs. Dredge fillets into the egg, then into the bread crumbs to coat well. Cook in the air fryer at 350F for 12 minutes. Flip at the halfway mark of the cooking. Garnish with lemon slices and serve.

Tasty Eggplant Slices

Ingredients: Servings: 4 Cooking Time: 4 Hours

1 eggplant, cut into 1/4-inch thick slices
1/4 tsp. garlic powder
1 tsp. paprika
1/4 tsp. onion powder

Directions:
Add all ingredients into the mixing bowl and toss until well coated. Spray the dehydrating tray with cooking spray and place in instant pot duo crisp air fryer basket. Arrange eggplant slices on the dehydrating tray. Place air fryer basket into the pot. Seal the pot with air fryer lid and select dehydrate mode and cook at 145 F for 4 hours. Serve or store.

Tuna Noodles

Ingredients: Servings: 4 Cooking Time: 4 Mins

1 can tuna, drained
15 oz egg noodles
3 C. of water
3/4 C. frozen peas
4 oz cheddar cheese, shredded
28 oz can cream of mushroom soup

Directions:
Add noodles and water into the inner pot of instant pot duo crisp and stir well. Add cream of mushroom soup, peas, and tuna on top of noodles. Seal the pot with pressure cooking lid and cook on high for 4 minutes. Once done, release pressure using a quick release. Remove lid. Add cheese and stir well and serve.

Honey Glazed Salmon

Ingredients: Servings: 2 Cooking Time: 8 Mins

3 tsp. rice wine vinegar
6 tbsp. low-sodium soy sauce
1 tsp. water
6 tbsp. raw honey
2 salmon fillets

Directions:
1 Preparing the Ingredients. Combine water, vinegar, honey, and soy sauce together. Pour half of this mixture into a bowl. Place salmon in one bowl of marinade and let chill 2 hours. 2 Air Frying. Ensure your Instant Crisp Air Fryer is preheated to 356 degrees and add salmon. Close air fryer lid and cook 8 minutes, flipping halfway through. Baste salmon with some of the remaining marinade mixture and cook another 5 minutes. To make a sauce to serve salmon with, pour remaining marinade mixture into a saucepan, heating till simmering. Let simmer 2 minutes. Serve drizzled over salmon!

Sesame Seeds Coated Fish

Ingredients: Servings: 5 Cooking Time: 8 Mins

3 tbsp. plain flour
2 eggs
½ C. sesame seeds, toasted
½ C. breadcrumbs
1/8 tsp. dried rosemary, crushed
Pinch of salt
Pinch of black pepper
3 tbsp. olive oil
5 frozen fish fillets (white fish of your choice)

Directions:
1 Preparing the Ingredients. In a shallow dish, place flour. In a second shallow dish, beat the eggs. In a third shallow dish, add remaining ingredients except fish fillets and mix till a crumbly mixture forms. Coat the fillets with flour and shake off the excess flour. Next, dip the fillets in egg. Then coat the fillets with sesame seeds mixture generously. Preheat the Instant Crisp Air Fryer to 390 degrees F. 2 Air Frying. Line an Instant Crisp Air Fryer basket with a piece of foil. Arrange the fillets into prepared basket. Close air fryer lid and cook for about 14 minutes, flipping once after 10 minutes.

Fish Sticks

Ingredients: Servings: 4 Cooking Time: 10 Mins

All-purpose flour – ½ cup
Whitefish fillet – 1 lb. cut into 1x3 inch sticks
Egg – 1, beaten
Parmesan cheese – ½ cup, grated
Panko bread crumbs – ½ cup
Paprika – 1 tsp.
Parsley flakes – 1 tbsp.
Black pepper -1 tsp.
Cooking spray

Directions:
Take 3 bowls. Put flour in the first bowl. Beaten egg in the second bowl and mix parmesan, panko bread crumbs, and seasoning in the third bowl. Coat fish sticks with flour, then dip in the egg and lastly dip in the seasoned bread crumbs. Coat well. Line the air fryer basket with parchment and spray with cooking oil. Cook the fish sticks at 400F for 5 minutes. Then flip the fish stick and cook for 5 minutes more. Serve.

Paprika Shrimp (air Fryer)

Ingredients: Servings: 4 Cooking Time: 10 Mins

1 lb. (454 g) tiger shrimp
2 tbsp. olive oil
½ tbsp. old bay seasoning
¼ tbsp. smoked paprika
¼ tsp. cayenne pepper
A pinch of sea salt

Directions:
Preheat the air fryer to 380°F (193°C). Toss all the ingredients in a large bowl until the shrimp are evenly coated. Arrange the shrimp in the air fryer basket and air fry for 10 minutes, shaking the basket halfway through, or until the shrimp are pink and cooked through. Serve hot.

Dill Red Cabbage

Ingredients: Servings: 4 Cooking Time: 15 Mins

30 oz. Red cabbage; shredded	4 oz. Butter; melted
1 tbsp. Red wine vinegar	1 tsp. Cinnamon powder
2 tbsp. Dill; chopped.	A pinch of salt and black pepper

Directions:
In a pan that fits your air fryer, mix the cabbage with the rest of the ingredients, toss, put the pan in the machine and cook at 390°f for 20 minutes Divide between plates and serve as a side dish.

Spicy Spinach Dip

Ingredients: Servings: 8 Cooking Time: 8 Mins

1 lb fresh spinach	1 tsp. onion powder
1 tbsp. hot sauce	4 oz cream cheese, cubed
1 tsp. cumin	1/4 C. half and half
1 tsp. chili powder	1/4 C. sour cream
1/2 C. olives, sliced	1 tbsp. olive oil
2 jalapeno pepper, minced	2 large tomatoes, chopped
1 C. cheddar cheese, shredded	4 garlic cloves, minced
1 C. mozzarella cheese, shredded	1/4 tsp. pepper
	1/2 tsp. salt

Directions:
Add oil into the instant pot duo crisp and set pot on sauté mode. Add tomatoes, spinach, and garlic and sauté until spinach is cooked. Turn off the sauté mode. Add remaining ingredients and stir well. Seal the pot with pressure cooking lid and cook on high pressure for 4 minutes. Once done, release pressure using a quick release. Remove lid. Serve and enjoy.

Air Fried Salmon

Ingredients: Servings: 2 Cooking Time: 8 Mins

Salmon fillets – 2	Water – 1/3 cup
Lemon juice – 2 tbsps.	Soy sauce – 1/3 cup
Salt and black pepper to taste	Scallions – 3, chopped
Garlic powder – ½ tsp.	Brown sugar – 1/3 cup
	Olive oil – 2 tbsps.

Directions:
In a bowl, mix water, sugar, garlic powder, soy sauce, salt, pepper, oil, and lemon juice. Whisk well and add salmon fillets. Coat well and marinate in the refrigerator for 1 hour. Cook salmon in the air-fryer at 360F for 8 minutes. Flip once. Divide salmon on plates. Sprinkle scallions to the top and serve.

Cajun and Lemon Pepper Cod (air Fryer)

Ingredients: Servings: 2 Cooking Time: 12 Mins

1 tbsp. Cajun seasoning	½ tsp. freshly ground black pepper
1 tsp. salt	Cooking spray
½ tsp. lemon pepper	2 tbsp. unsalted butter, melted
2 (8-ounce / 227-g) cod fillets, cut to fit into the air fryer basket	1 lemon, cut into 4 wedges

Directions:
Preheat the air fryer to 360°F (182°C). Spritz the air fryer basket with cooking spray. Thoroughly combine the Cajun seasoning, salt, lemon pepper, and black pepper in a small bowl. Rub this mixture all over the cod fillets until completely coated. Put the fillets in the air fryer basket and brush the melted butter over both sides of each fillet. Bake in the preheated air fryer for 12 minutes, flipping the fillets halfway through, or until the fish flakes easily with a fork. Remove the fillets from the basket and serve with fresh lemon wedges.

Air-fryer Cajun Salmon

Ingredients: Servings: 2 Cooking Time: 10 Mins

2 (6 oz.) salmon fillets, skin included	1 tbsp. Cajun seasoning
1 tsp. brown sugar	Cooking spray

Directions:
Rinse salmon fillets and pat dry with paper towels. In a small mixing bowl, combine Cajun seasoning and brown sugar. Dip fillets into the mixture, coating evenly all sides. Lay coated fillets on the air frying basket with skin-side down and mist with cooking spray. Place air frying basket inside the instant pot duo crisp and attach the air fryer lid. Set to air fry at 390 degrees F and cook for 8 minutes. Remove from the air fryer and set aside for 2 minutes before serving.

Lobster Tails

Ingredients: Servings: 2 Cooking Time: 8 Mins

2 6oz lobster tails	1 tsp. chopped chives
1 tsp. salt	1 Tbsp minced garlic
2 Tbsp unsalted butter melted	1 tsp. lemon juice

Directions:
Combine butter, garlic, salt, chives, and lemon juice to prepare butter mixture. Butterfly lobster tails by cutting through shell followed by removing the meat and resting it on top of the shell. Place them on the tray in the Instant Pot Duo Crisp Air Fryer basket and spread butter over the top of lobster meat. Close the Air Fryer lid, select the Air Fry option and cook on 380°F for 4 minutes. Open the Air Fryer lid and spread more butter on top, cook for extra 2-4 minutes until done.

Garlic Mussels

Ingredients: Servings: 4 Cooking Time: 6 Mins

1 lb. Mussels	1 C. of water
1 tbsp. butter	1 tsp. chives
2 tsp. minced garlic	1 tsp. basil
	1 tsp. parsley

Directions:
Toss the mussels with oil and all other ingredients in a bowl. Spread the seasoned shrimp in the oven baking tray. Press "power button" of air fry oven and turn the dial to select the "air roast" mode. Press the time button and again turn the dial to set the cooking time to 6 minutes. Now push the temp button and rotate the dial to set the temperature at 390 degrees f.

Once preheated, place the mussel's tray in the oven and close its lid. Serve warm.

Asian Salmon

Ingredients: Servings: 2 Cooking Time: 15 Mins

Salmon fillets – 2 medium
Light soy sauce – 6 tbsps.
Mirin – 3 tbsps.
Water – 1 tsp.
Honey – 6 tbsps.

Directions:

Mix soy sauce with water, honey, mirin and whisk well. Add salmon, rub well and marinate in the fridge for 1 hour. Cook at 360F for 15 minutes in the air-fryer. Flip once after 7 minutes. Meanwhile, put the soy marinade in a pan, and simmer and whisk on medium heat for 2 minutes. Divide salmon on plates. Drizzle marinade all over and serve.

Steamed Salmon & Sauce

Ingredients: Servings: 2 Cooking Time: 10 Mins

1 C. Water
2 x 6 oz Fresh Salmon
2 Tsp Vegetable Oil
A Pinch of Salt for Each Fish
½ C. Plain Greek Yogurt
½ C. Sour Cream
2 Tbsp Finely Chopped Dill (Keep a bit for garnishing)
A Pinch of Salt to Taste

Directions:

1 Preparing the Ingredients. Pour the water into the bottom of the fryer and start heating to 285° F. Drizzle oil over the fish and spread it. Salt the fish to taste. 2 Air Frying. Close air fryer lid, now pop it into the fryer for 10 min. In the meantime, mix the yogurt, cream, dill and a bit of salt to make the sauce. When the fish is done, serve with the sauce and garnish with sprigs of dill.

Creamy Parmesan Shrimp

Ingredients: Servings: 4 Cooking Time: 5 Mins

1 lb shrimp, deveined and cleaned
1 oz parmesan cheese, grated
1 tbsp. garlic, minced
1 tbsp. lemon juice
1/4 C. salad dressing

Directions:

Spray instant pot multi-level air fryer basket with cooking spray. Add shrimp into the air fryer basket and place basket into the instant pot. Seal pot with air fryer lid and select air fry mode then set the temperature to 400 F and timer for 5 minutes. Transfer shrimp into the mixing bowl. Add remaining ingredients over shrimp and stir for 1 minute. Serve and enjoy.

Creamy Tuna and Eggs (pressure Cook)

Ingredients: Servings: 4 Cooking Time: 15 Mins

2 cans tuna, drained
2 eggs, beaten
1 can cream of celery soup
½ C. water
¾ C. milk
¼ C. diced onions
2 tbsp. butter
2 carrots, peeled and chopped
1 C. frozen peas
Salt and ground black pepper, to taste

Directions:

Combine all the ingredients in the Instant Pot and stir to mix well. Secure the lid. Select the Pressure Cook and set the cooking time for 15 minutes at High Pressure. Once cooking is complete, do a quick pressure release. Carefully open the lid. Divide the mix into bowls and serve.

Ranch Mushrooms

Ingredients: Servings: 4 Cooking Time: 11 Mins

16 oz mushrooms, rinsed
1 C. chicken broth
1 oz dry ranch dressing mix
1/4 C. parmesan cheese
1 tbsp. garlic, minced
1/4 C. butter

Directions:

Add butter into the inner pot of instant pot duo crisp and set pot on sauté mode. Add garlic and sauté for 1 minute. Add mushrooms and sauté for 5 minutes. Add remaining ingredients and stir well. Seal the pot with pressure cooking lid and cook on high for 5 minutes. Once done, release pressure using a quick release. Remove lid. Stir well and serve.

Cilantro-lime Fried Shrimp

Ingredients: Servings: 4 Cooking Time: 10 Mins

1 lb. raw shrimp, peeled and deveined with tails on or off (see Prep tip)
½ C. chopped fresh cilantro
Juice of 1 lime
1 egg
½ C. all-purpose flour
¾ C. bread crumbs
Salt
Pepper
Cooking oil
½ C. cocktail sauce (optional)

Directions:

1 Preparing the Ingredients. Place the shrimp in a plastic bag and add the cilantro and lime juice. Seal the bag. Shake to combine. Marinate in the refrigerator for 30 minutes. In a small bowl, beat the egg. In another small bowl, place the flour. Place the bread crumbs in a third small bowl, and season with salt and pepper to taste. Spray the Instant Crisp Air Fryer basket with cooking oil. Remove the shrimp from the plastic bag. Dip each in the flour, then the egg, and then the bread crumbs. 2 Air Frying. Place the shrimp in the Instant Crisp Air Fryer. It is okay to stack them. Spray the shrimp with cooking oil. Close air fryer lid and cook for 4 minutes. Open the Instant Crisp Air Fryer and flip the shrimp. I recommend flipping individually instead of shaking to keep the breading intact. Cook for an additional 4 minutes, or until crisp. Cool before serving. Serve with cocktail sauce if desired.

Easy Salmon Patties (air Fryer)

Ingredients: Servings: 6 Cooking Time: 10 To 11 Mins

1 (14.75-ounce / 418-g) can Alaskan pink salmon, drained
2 scallions, diced
1 tsp. garlic powder
Salt and pepper, to

and bones removed
½ C. bread crumbs
1 egg, whisked
taste
Cooking spray

Directions:
Preheat the air fryer to 400°F (204°C). Stir together the salmon, bread crumbs, whisked egg, scallions, garlic powder, salt, and pepper in a large bowl until well incorporated. Divide the salmon mixture into six equal portions and form each into a patty with your hands. Arrange the salmon patties in the air fryer basket and spritz them with cooking spray. Air fry for 10 to 11 minutes, flipping the patties once during cooking, or until the patties are golden brown and cooked through. Remove the patties from the basket and serve on a plate.

Alaskan Cod with Pinto Beans & Fennel

Ingredients: Servings: 4 Cooking Time: 21 Mins

2 (18 oz) Alaskan Cod, cut into 4 pieces each
4 tbsp. Olive Oil
2 cloves Garlic, minced
2 small Onions, chopped
½ C. Olive Brine
3 C. Chicken Broth
Salt and Black Pepper to taste
½ C. Tomato Puree
1 head Fennel, quartered
1 C. Pinto Beans, soaked, drained and rinsed
1 C. Green Olives, pitted and crushed
½ C. Basil Leaves
Lemon Slices to garnish

Directions:
Select Sear/Sauté and heat olive oil. Stir-fry garlic and onion for 3 minutes. Pour in chicken broth, tomato puree, fennel, olives, beans, salt, and pepper. Seal the lid and select Steam on High pressure for 10 minutes. Press Start. Once the timer has stopped, do a quick pressure release, and open the lid. Transfer the beans to a plate with a slotted spoon. Adjust broth's taste with salt and pepper and add the cod pieces to the cooker. Close the lid again, secure the pressure valve, and select Steam mode on Low pressure for 3 minutes. Press Start. Once the timer has ended, do a quick pressure release, and open the lid. Remove the cod into soup plates, top with the beans and basil leaves, and spoon the broth over them. Serve with a side of crusted bread.

Crispy Air Fried Sushi Roll

Ingredients: Servings: 12 Cooking Time: 5 Mins

Kale Salad:
1 tbsp. sesame seeds
¾ tsp. soy sauce
¼ tsp. ginger
1/8 tsp. garlic powder
¾ tsp. toasted sesame oil
½ tsp. rice vinegar
1 ½ C. chopped kale
Sushi Rolls:
½ of a sliced avocado
3 sheets of sushi nori
1 batch cauliflower rice
Sriracha Mayo:
Sriracha sauce
¼ C. vegan mayo
Coating:
½ C. panko breadcrumbs

Directions:
1 Preparing the Ingredients. Combine all of kale salad ingredients together, tossing well. Set to the side. Lay out a sheet of nori and spread a handful of rice on. Then place 2-3 tbsp. of kale salad over rice, followed by avocado. Roll up sushi. To make mayo, whisk mayo ingredients together until smooth. Add breadcrumbs to a bowl. 2 Air Frying. Coat sushi rolls in crumbs till coated and add to the Instant Crisp Air Fryer. Close air fryer lid and cook rolls 10 minutes at 390 degrees, shaking gently at 5 minutes. Slice each roll into 6-8 pieces and enjoy!

Marinated Salmon

Ingredients: Servings: 4 Cooking Time: 12 Mins

Salmon – 4 fillets
Brown sugar – 1 tbsp.
Minced garlic – ½ tbsp.
Soy sauce – 6 tbsps.
Dijon mustard – ¼ cup
Chopped green onion – 1

Directions:
In a bowl, mix mustard, soy sauce, brown sugar, and minced garlic. Pour this mixture over salmon fillets and coat well. Marinate for 30 minutes in the refrigerator. Then cook in the air fryer at 400F for 12 minutes. Garnish with green onions and serve.

Mackerel with Pernod & Vegetables En Papillote

Ingredients: Servings: 6 Cooking Time: 5 Mins

3 large Whole Mackerel, cut into 2 pieces
1 lb. Asparagus, trimmed
1 Carrot, cut into sticks
1 Celery stalk, cut into sticks
½ C. Butter, at room temperature
6 medium Tomatoes, quartered
1 large Brown Onion, sliced thinly
1 Orange Bell Pepper, seeded and cut into sticks
Salt and Black Pepper to taste
2 ½ tbsp. Pernod
3 cloves Garlic, minced
2 Lemons, cut into wedges
1 ½ C. Water

Directions:
Cut out 6 pieces of parchment paper a little longer and wider than a piece of fish with kitchen scissors. Then, cut out 6 pieces of foil slightly longer than the parchment papers. Lay the foil wraps on a flat surface and place each parchment paper on each aluminium foil. In a bowl, add tomatoes, onions, garlic, bell pepper, pernod, butter, asparagus, carrot, celery, salt, and pepper. Use a spoon to mix them. Place each fish piece on the layer of parchment and foil wraps. Spoon the vegetable mixture on each fish. Then, wrap the fish and place the fish packets in the refrigerator to marinate for 2 hours. Remove the fish to a flat surface. Open the cooker, pour the water in, and fit the reversible rack at the bottom of the pot. Put the packets on the trivet. Seal the lid and select Steam mode on High pressure for 3 minutes. Press Start to start cooking. Once the timer has ended, do a quick pressure release, and open the lid. Remove the trivet with the fish packets onto a flat surface. Carefully open the foil and using a spatula. Return the packets to the pot, on top of the rack. Close the crisping lid and cook on Air Fry for 3 minutes at 300 F. Then, remove to serving plates. Serve with lemon wedges.

Soy and Ginger Shrimp

Ingredients: Servings: 4 Cooking Time: 10 Mins

2 tbsp. olive oil
2 tbsp. scallions, finely chopped
2 cloves garlic, chopped
1 tsp. fresh ginger, grated
1 tbsp. dry white wine
1 tbsp. balsamic vinegar
1/4 C. soy sauce
1 tbsp. sugar
1 lb. shrimp
Salt and ground black pepper, to taste

Directions:
1 Preparing the Ingredients. To make the marinade, warm the oil in a saucepan; cook all ingredients, except the shrimp, salt, and black pepper. Now, let it cool. Marinate the shrimp, covered, at least an hour, in the refrigerator. 2 Air Frying. After that, close air fryer lid and bake the shrimp at 350 degrees F for 8 to 10 minutes (depending on the size), turning once or twice. Season prepared shrimp with salt and black pepper and serve right away!

Parmesan Fish Fillets (air Fryer)

Ingredients: Servings: 4 Cooking Time: 17 Mins

⅓ C. grated Parmesan cheese
½ tsp. fennel seed
½ tsp. tarragon
⅓ tsp. mixed peppercorns
2 eggs, beaten
4 (4-ounce / 113-g) fish fillets, halved
2 tbsp. dry white wine
1 tsp. seasoned salt

Directions:
Preheat the air fryer to 345°F (174°C). Place the grated Parmesan cheese, fennel seed, tarragon, and mixed peppercorns in a food processor and pulse for about 20 seconds until well combined. Transfer the cheese mixture to a shallow dish. Place the beaten eggs in another shallow dish. Drizzle the dry white wine over the top of fish fillets. Dredge each fillet in the beaten eggs on both sides, shaking off any excess, then roll them in the cheese mixture until fully coated. Season with the salt. Arrange the fillets in the air fryer basket and air fry for about 17 minutes, or until the fish is cooked through and no longer translucent. Flip the fillets once halfway through the cooking time. Cool for 5 minutes before serving.

Quick Fried Catfish

Ingredients: Servings: 4 Cooking Time: 15 Mins

3/4 C. Original Bisquick™ mix
1/2 C. yellow cornmeal
1 tbsp. seafood seasoning
4 catfish fillets (4 to 6 oz. each)
1/2 C. ranch dressing
Lemon wedges

Directions:
1 Preparing the Ingredients. In a shallow bowl mix together the Bisquick mix, cornmeal, and seafood seasoning. Pat the filets dry, then brush them with ranch dressing. Press the filets into the Bisquick mix on both sides until the filet is evenly coated. 2 Air Frying. Close air fryer lid and cook in your Instant Crisp Air Fryer at 360 degrees for 15 minutes, flip the filets halfway through. Serve with a lemon garnish.

Kale and Cauliflower Mash

Ingredients: Servings: 4 Cooking Time: 10 Mins

1 cauliflower head, florets separated
4 garlic cloves; minced
3 C. kale; chopped.
2 scallions; chopped.
1/3 C. coconut cream
1 tbsp. Parsley; chopped.
4 tsp. Butter; melted
A pinch of salt and black pepper

Directions:
In a pan that fits the air fryer, combine the cauliflower with the butter, garlic, scallions, salt, pepper and the cream, toss, introduce the pan in the machine and cook at 380°f for 20 minutes Mash the mix well, add the remaining ingredients, whisk, divide between plates and serve.

Roasted Tomatoes

Ingredients: Servings: 4 Cooking Time: 10 Mins

4 tomatoes; halved
½ C. parmesan; grated
1 tbsp. Basil; chopped.
½ tsp. Onion powder
½ tsp. Oregano; dried
½ tsp. Smoked paprika
½ tsp. Garlic powder
Cooking spray

Directions:
Take a bowl and mix all the ingredients except the cooking spray and the parmesan. Arrange the tomatoes in your air fryer's pan, sprinkle the parmesan on top and grease with cooking spray Cook at 370°f for 15 minutes, divide between plates and serve.

Browned Shrimp Patties (air Fryer)

Ingredients: Servings: 4 Cooking Time: 10 To 12 Mins

½ lb. (227 g) raw shrimp, shelled, deveined, and chopped finely
2 C. cooked sushi rice
¼ C. chopped red bell pepper
¼ C. chopped celery
¼ C. chopped green onion
2 tsp. Worcestershire sauce
½ tsp. salt
½ tsp. garlic powder
½ tsp. Old Bay seasoning
½ C. plain bread crumbs
Cooking spray

Directions:
Preheat the air fryer to 390°F (199°C). Put all the ingredients except the bread crumbs and oil in a large bowl and stir to incorporate. Scoop out the shrimp mixture and shape into 8 equal-sized patties with your hands, no more than ½-inch thick. Roll the patties in the bread crumbs on a plate and spray both sides with cooking spray. Place the patties in the air fryer basket. You may need to work in batches to avoid overcrowding. Air fry for 10 to 12 minutes, flipping the patties halfway through, or until the outside is crispy brown. Divide the patties among four plates and serve warm.

Scottish Seafood Curry

Ingredients: Servings: 8 Cooking Time: 33 Mins

Seafood:
½ lb Squid, trimmed and cut into 1-inch rings
½ lb Langoustine Tall Meat
½ lb Scallop Meat
½ lb Mussel Meat
Curry:
4 tbsp. Olive Oil
2 C. Shellfish Stock
2 Curry Leaves
2 tbsp. Shallot Puree
3 tbsp. Yellow Curry Paste
2 tbsp. Ginger Paste
2 tbsp. Garlic Paste
1 ½ tbsp. Chili Powder
1 ½ tbsp. Chili Paste
2 tbsp. Lemongrass Paste
½ tsp. Turmeric Powder
2 tsp. Shrimp Powder
1 tsp. Shrimp Paste
1 ½ C. Coconut Milk
1 C. Milk
1 tbsp. Grants Scotch Whiskey
2 tbsp. Fish Curry Powder
Salt to taste
Vegetables:
¼ C. diced Tomatoes
¼ C. chopped Onion
¼ C. chopped Okra
¼ C. chopped Eggplants

Directions:
Add olive oil, shallot paste, yellow curry paste, ginger puree, garlic paste, lemongrass paste, chili paste, shrimp paste, and curry leaves. Stir-fry for 10 minutes on Sear/Sauté mode, until well combined and aromatic. Next, add turmeric powder, fish curry powder, and shrimp powder. Stir-fry for another minute. Pour in the shellfish stock and close the crisping lid. Cook on Broil mode for 15 minutes. Open the lid, and add the scallops, squid, chopped onion, okra, tomatoes, and aubergine. Stir lightly.Close the pressure lid, secure the pressure valve, and select Steam mode on High pressure for 5 minutes. Press Start to start cooking. Once the timer has ended, do a quick pressure release, and open the lid. Add milk, coconut milk, scotch whiskey, and salt. Stir carefully not to mash the aubergine. Select Sear/Sauté and add mussel meat and langoustine. Stir carefully. Simmer the sauce for 3 minutes, press Stop, and turn off the cooker. Dish the seafood with sauce and veggies into serving bowls. Serve with broccoli mash.

Chicken Jalapeno Popper Dip

Ingredients: Servings: 10 Cooking Time: 14 Mins

1 lb chicken breast, boneless
1/2 C. water
1/2 C. breadcrumbs
3/4 C. sour cream
3 jalapeno pepper, sliced
8 oz cream cheese
8 oz cheddar cheese

Directions:
Add chicken, jalapeno, water, and cream cheese into the instant pot. Seal pot with lid and cook on manual high pressure for 12 minutes. Once done then release pressure using the quick-release method than open the lid. Stir in cream and cheddar cheese. Transfer instant pot mixture to the baking dish and top with breadcrumbs and broil for 2 minutes. Serve and enjoy.

Asian Halibut

Ingredients: Servings: 3 Cooking Time: 10 Mins

Halibut steaks – 1 pound
Soy sauce – 2/3 cup
Sugar – ¼ cup
Lime juice – 2 tbsps.
Red pepper flakes – ¼ tsp. crushed
Mirin – ½ cup
Orange juice – ¼ cup
Ginger – ¼ tsp. grated
Garlic – 1 clove, minced

Directions:
Pour soy sauce in a pan and heat over medium heat. Add garlic, ginger, pepper flakes, orange juice, lime, sugar, and mirin. Stir well, bring to a boil and take off the heat. Transfer half of the marinade to a bowl, add halibut, toss to coat and marinate in the refrigerator for 30 minutes. Cook halibut in the air fryer at 390F for 10 minutes. Flipping once. Divide halibut steaks on plates, drizzle the rest of the marinade all over and serve.

White Fish with Cilantro Sauce

Ingredients: Servings: 4 Cooking Time: 30 Mins

1 large bunch of cilantros, chopped
1 small onion, chopped
3 cloves of fresh garlic, peeled and chopped
3 tbsp. butter
2 C. sour cream
2 tsp. salt
4 tbsp. lime juice
2 1/2 lb. white fish fillets

Directions:
Add butter to a suitably sized skillet to melt over medium heat. Stir in garlic and onion, then sauté for 5 minutes, then transfer to a blender. Add cream, cilantro, salt, and lime juice, then puree this sauce until smooth. Place the fish fillets in the Instant Pot Duo basket. Put on the Air Fryer lid and seal it. Hit the "Bake Button" and select 25 minutes of cooking time, then press "Start." Once the Instant Pot Duo beeps, do a quick release and remove its lid. Serve.

Balsamic Asparagus

Ingredients: Servings: 4 Cooking Time: 10 Mins

1 lb. Asparagus stalks
¼ C. olive oil+ 1 tsp.
2 tbsp. Balsamic vinegar
1 tbsp. Lime juice
1 tbsp. Smoked paprika
Salt and black pepper to taste.

Directions:
Take a bowl and mix the asparagus with salt, pepper and 1 tsp. Oil, toss, transfer to your air fryer's basket and cook at 370°f for 20 minutes. Meanwhile, in a bowl, mix all the other ingredients and whisk them well Divide the asparagus between plates, drizzle the balsamic vinaigrette all over and serve as a side dish.

Delicious Shrimp Risotto

Ingredients: Servings: 4 Cooking Time: 17 Mins

1 lb. shrimp, peeled, deveined, and
1 onion, chopped
1/2 C. parmesan

chopped	cheese, grated
1 1/2 C. arborio rice	1 C. clam juice
1/2 tbsp. paprika	3 C. chicken stock
1/2 tbsp. oregano, minced	1/4 C. dry sherry
1 red pepper, chopped	2 tbsp. butter
	1/4 tsp. pepper
	1/2 tsp. salt

Directions:
Add butter into the instant pot and set the pot on sauté mode. Add onion and pepper and sauté until onion is softened. Add paprika, oregano, pepper, and salt. Stir for minute. Add rice and stir for a minute. Add sherry, clam juice, and stock. Stir well. Seal pot with lid and cook on manual high pressure for 10 minutes. Once done then release pressure using the quick-release method than open the lid. Add shrimp and cook on sauté mode for 2 minutes. Stir in cheese and serve.

Asparagus Shrimp Risotto

Ingredients: Servings: 6 Cooking Time: 16 Mins

1 1/2 C. arborio rice	1/2 C. white wine
1 tbsp. butter	1 lb shrimp, cooked
3 1/2 C. chicken stock	1 C. asparagus, chopped
1 C. mushrooms, sliced	1/2 onion, diced
1/4 C. parmesan cheese, grated	2 tsp. olive oil
	1/2 tsp. pepper
	Salt

Directions:
Add oil into the instant pot and set the pot on sauté mode. Add onion to the pot and sauté for 2-3 minutes. Add mushrooms and cook for 5 minutes. Add rice and cook until lightly brown. Add stock and wine and stir well. Seal pot with lid and cook on manual high pressure for 6 minutes, Once done then release pressure using the quick-release method than open the lid. Add asparagus and butter and cook on sauté mode for 1 minute. Add shrimp and cook for 1 minute. Stir in cheese and serve.

Salmon Rice Pilaf

Ingredients: Servings: 2 Cooking Time: 5 Mins

2 salmon fillets	1/4 C. vegetable soup mix
1 C. chicken stock	1/4 tsp. sea salt
1 tbsp. butter	
1/2 C. of rice	

Directions:
Add all ingredients except fish fillets into the instant pot and stir well. Place steamer rack on top of rice mixture. Place fish fillets on top of rack and season with pepper and salt. Seal pot with lid and cook on manual high pressure for 5 minutes. Once done then release pressure using the quick-release method than open the lid. Serve and enjoy.

Jalapeno Hummus

Ingredients: Servings: 4 Cooking Time: 25 Mins

1 C. chickpeas	1/2 C. fresh cilantro
1 tsp. dried onion, minced	1 tbsp. tahini
1 tsp. ground cumin	1/2 C. avocado oil
	1/2 tsp. sea salt
	1/4 C. jalapeno, diced

Directions:
Add chickpeas and 2 C. water into the instant pot. Seal pot with lid and cook on manual high pressure for 25 minutes. Once done then allow to release pressure naturally then open the lid. Transfer chickpeas to the food processor along with remaining ingredients and process until smooth. Serve and enjoy.

Grilled Cod with Sauce

Ingredients: Servings: 2 Cooking Time: 10 Mins

Cod fillets – 1 pound	Heavy cream – ½ cup
Olive oil – 2 tbsps.	Ground mustard – 3 tbsps.
Lemon juice – 1 tbsp.	Butter – 1 tbsp.
Salt and pepper to taste	Salt to taste
Sauce	

Directions:
Spread some oil on the fillets. Rub salt, pepper, and lemon juice on the fillets. Grease the air fryer basket and cook the fillets at 350F for 5 minutes. Then flip the fish and increase the temperature to 400F and cook for 5 minutes more. Meanwhile, add all the sauce ingredients in a saucepan and cook for 4 minutes or until thick. Serve cod with sauce.

Buttered Shrimp Skewers

Ingredients: Servings: 2 Cooking Time: 6 Mins

Shrimps – 8, peeled and deveined	Green bell pepper slices – 8
Garlic – 4 cloves, minced	Rosemary – 1 tbsp. chopped
Salt and black pepper to taste	Butter – 1 tbsp. melted

Directions:
In a bowl, mix bell pepper slices, rosemary, pepper, salt, butter, garlic, and shrimp. Toss to coat and marinate for 10 minutes. Arrange 2 bell pepper slices and 2 shrimp on a skewer and repeat with the rest of the shrimp and bell pepper pieces. Cook them at 360F for 6 minutes. Serve.

Roasted Red Pepper Hummus

Ingredients: Servings: 4 Cooking Time: 40 Mins

1 C. chickpeas, dry and rinsed	3 tbsp. fresh lemon juice
2 tbsp. olive oil	1/2 C. roasted red peppers
1/4 tsp. cumin	3 C. chicken broth
2 garlic cloves	1/2 tsp. salt
2 1/2 tbsp. tahini	

Directions:
Add chickpeas and broth into the inner pot of instant pot duo crisp and stir well. Seal the pot with pressure cooking lid and cook on high for 40 minutes. Once done, allow to release pressure naturally. Remove lid. Drain chickpeas well and reserved half C. broth. Transfer chickpeas, reserved broth, and remaining ingredients into the food processor and process until smooth. Serve and enjoy.

Tuna Patties

Ingredients: Servings: 4 Cooking Time: 6 Mins

Canned tuna – 7 ounces
Egg – 1
Breadcrumbs – ¼ cup
Mustard – 1 tbsp.
Salt and pepper to taste
Cooking spray

Directions:
Combine egg, tuna, bread crumbs, salt, pepper and mustard in a bowl. Make four patties with this mixture. Grease the air fryer basket with cooking oil. Cook the patties in Broil setting for 6 minutes. Flip the patties after 3 minutes. Serve.

Fish Finger Sandwich In Instant Pot Air Fryer

Ingredients: Servings: 4 Cooking Time: 15 Mins

13 oz. (4 Nos.) cod fillet, skin removed
2 tbsp. flour
1½ oz. breadcrumbs
10 oz. of frozen peas
1 tbsp. Greek yogurt
12 capers
1 tbsp. lemon juice
8 small slices of bread
¼ tsp. salt
½ tsp. ground black pepper
Cooking oil spray

Directions:
Wash the fillets and pat dry. Close the crisp cover of the Instant Pot Air Fryer and set the temperature to 390°F. Set the timer 5 minutes and press start for preheating in AIR FRY mode. Rub salt and pepper on all sides of the fillets. Place the flour in a medium shallow bowl. Similarly, place the breadcrumbs in a shallow bowl. Now dredge the cod fillets in the flour and then dredge in the breadcrumbs. Spray some cooking in the instant fryer basket and place the cod fillets in it. Place the basket in the inner pot of the Instant Pot. Close the crisp cover and keep the temperature at 390°F in AIR FRY mode. Set the timer to 15 minutes and press START for air frying. When the cooking is under process, boil the peas for 5 minutes until it becomes tender. Once it becomes tender, drain it and put it in a blender. Add capers, Greek yogurt, and lemon juice. Blitz the ingredients until it blends thoroughly. After finish cooking, remove the fillets from the Instant Pot Air Fryer and layer it for making the sandwich. Over the bread slice, layer fish fillet and spread the pea puree. Serve warm.

Tomatillo Salsa

Ingredients: Servings: 12 Cooking Time: 15 Mins

2 lbs tomatillos, husk removed
2 C. of water
2 garlic cloves, peeled
35 dried arbol chilies, stems removed
1 tbsp. olive oil
Salt

Directions:
Add oil into the inner pot of instant pot duo crisp and set pot on sauté mode. Add garlic and chilies to the pot and sauté for 2-3 minutes. Add remaining ingredients and stir well. Seal the pot with pressure cooking lid and cook on high for 12 minutes. Once done, release pressure using a quick release. Remove lid. Blend tomatillo mixture using blender until smooth. Season with salt and serve.

Buffalo Cauliflower

Ingredients: Servings: 4 Cooking Time: 15 Mins

½ (1-oz.dry ranch seasoning packet
4 C. cauliflower florets
¼ C. buffalo sauce
2 tbsp. Salted butter; melted.

Directions:
Take a large bowl, toss cauliflower with butter and dry ranch. Place into the air fryer basket. Adjust the temperature to 400 degrees f and set the timer for 5 minutes. Shake the basket two-or three-times during cooking. When tender, remove cauliflower from fryer basket and toss in buffalo sauce. Serve warm.

Whitefish with Garlic and Lemon

Ingredients: Servings: 2 Cooking Time: 10 Mins

Salt and pepper to taste
Lemon pepper seasoning – ½ tsp.
Whitefish fillets – 12 oz.
Chopped parsley to taste
Garlic powder – ½ tsp.
Lemon wedges to taste
Onion powder – ½ tsp.

Directions:
Coat the fish with oil. Season with onion powder, garlic powder, and lemon pepper. Then season with salt and pepper. Coat well. Line the air fryer basket with parchment and spray with oil. Arrange fish and add a few lemon wedges. Cook at 360F for 6 to 12 minutes or until fish is cooked. Flip once at the halfway mark. Serve.

Scallops Curry

Ingredients: Servings: 4 Cooking Time: 9 Mins

1 lb. scallops
1 C. of coconut milk
1/2 tsp. soy sauce
1/4 tsp. nutmeg powder
1/2 C. red curry paste
1 1/2 C. chicken broth
1/2 tsp. curry powder
1 tsp. vinegar
1 tbsp. olive oil
1/2 tsp. salt

Directions:
Add oil into the instant pot and set the pot on sauté mode. Add scallops and sauté for 3 minutes. Add remaining ingredients and stir well. Seal pot with lid and cook on manual high pressure for 6 minutes. Once done then release pressure using the quick-release method than open the lid. Serve and enjoy.

Perfect Salmon Dinner

Ingredients: Servings: 3 Cooking Time: 2 Mins

1 lb. salmon fillet, cut into three pieces
2 garlic cloves, minced
1/2 tsp. ground cumin
1 tsp. red chili powder
Pepper
Salt

Directions:
Pour 1 1/2 C. water into the instant pot then place trivet into the pot. In a small bowl, mix together garlic, cumin, chili powder, pepper, and salt. Rub salmon with spice mixture and place on top of the trivet. Seal pot with lid and cook on steam mode for 2 minutes. Once done then release pressure using the quick-release method than open the lid. Serve and enjoy.

Easy Shrimp and Vegetable Paella (air Fryer)

Ingredients: Servings: 4 Cooking Time: 14 To 17 Mins

1 (10-ounce / 284-g) package frozen cooked rice, thawed
1 (6-ounce / 170-g) jar artichoke hearts, drained and chopped
½ tsp. dried thyme
¼ C. vegetable broth
½ tsp. turmeric
1 C. frozen cooked small shrimp
½ C. frozen baby peas
1 tomato, diced

Directions:
Preheat the air fryer to 340°F (171°C). Mix together the cooked rice, chopped artichoke hearts, vegetable broth, thyme, and turmeric in a baking pan and stir to combine. Put the baking pan in the preheated air fryer and bake for about 9 minutes, or until the rice is heated through. Remove the pan from the air fryer and fold in the shrimp, baby peas, and diced tomato and mix well. Return to the air fryer and continue cooking for 5 to 8 minutes, or until the shrimp are done and the paella is bubbling. Cool for 5 minutes before serving.

Fish Finger Sandwich

Ingredients: Servings: 4 Cooking Time: 15 Mins

Cod fillet – 13 ounces, skin removed
Flour – 2 tbsps.
Breadcrumbs -1 ½ ounces
Capers – 12
Frozen peas – 10 ounces
Greek yogurt -1 tbsp.
Lemon juice – 1 tbsp.
Bread – 8 small slices
Salt and pepper to taste
Cooking oil spray

Directions:
Preheat the air fryer to 390F. Rub the fillet with salt and pepper. Place flour and breadcrumbs in separate bowls. Then coat the fillets in flour and in breadcrumbs. Spray with cooking oil and place in the air fryer. Cook at 390F for 15 minutes. Flip once at the halfway mark. Meanwhile. Boil the peas for 5 minutes or until tender. Then drain and put them in a blender. Add capers, yogurt, and lemon juice. Mix. Arrange the sandwich with bread, fish and pea puree. Serve.

Air Fryer Salmon

Ingredients: Servings: 2 Cooking Time: 10 Mins

½ tsp. salt
½ tsp. garlic powder
½ tsp. smoked paprika
Salmon

Directions:
Preparing the Ingredients. Mix spices together and sprinkle onto salmon. Place seasoned salmon into the Instant Crisp -Pot. Air Frying. Close air fryer lid. Set temperature to 400°F, and set time to 10 minutes.

Jalapeno Chicken Dip

Ingredients: Servings: 10 Cooking Time: 14 Mins

1 lb chicken breast, skinless and boneless
1/2 C. water
1/2 C. breadcrumbs
1/2 C. sour cream
8 oz cheddar cheese, shredded
2 jalapeno pepper, sliced
8 oz cream cheese

Directions:
Add chicken, water, cream cheese, and jalapenos into the inner pot of instant pot duo crisp. Seal the pot with pressure cooking lid and cook on high for 12 minutes. Once done, release pressure using a quick release. Remove lid. Remove chicken from pot and shred using a fork. Return shredded chicken to the pot. Add sour cream and cheddar cheese and stir well. Sprinkle breadcrumbs on top. Seal the pot with air fryer lid and select broil mode and cook for 2 minutes. Serve and enjoy.

Lobster Tails with Lemon-garlic Butter

Ingredients: Servings: 2 Cooking Time: 10 Mins

4 tbsps. butter
2 (4 oz.) lobster tails
1 tsp. lemon zest
1 tsp. fresh parsley, chopped
1 clove of garlic, minced and grated
2 lemon wedges
Salt and ground black pepper to taste

Directions:
Use kitchen shears to cut the lobster tails lengthwise through the center hard shell and flesh but not through the other side of the shell. Spread tails apart and place them in the air fryer basket with the lobster's meat facing upward. Add butter, lemon zest and garlic to the instant pot duo and attach the pressure cooker lid. Set to sauté function for 30 seconds. Once the butter has melted and garlic is tender, transfer 2 tbsp. of butter mixture to the small bowl and brush onto the lobster. Season lobster with salt and pepper. Place the air fryer into the instant pot. Detach the pressure cooker lid and attach the air fryer lid and air fry at 380 degrees F for 5-7 minutes. Once done, remove the lobster tails from the air fryer and transfer to a platter. Spoon some melted butter from the inner pot over the dish and top with lemon wedges and parsley.

Panko-crusted Tilapia

Ingredients: Servings: 3 Cooking Time: 10 Mins

2 tsp. Italian seasoning
2 tsp. lemon pepper
1/3 C. panko breadcrumbs
1/3 C. egg whites
1/3 C. almond flour
3 tilapia fillets
Olive oil

Directions:
Preparing the Ingredients. Place panko, egg whites, and flour into separate bowls. Mix lemon pepper and Italian seasoning in with breadcrumbs. Pat tilapia fillets dry. Dredge in flour, then egg, then breadcrumb mixture. Air Frying. Add to the Instant Crisp Air Fryer basket and spray lightly with olive oil. Close air fryer lid. Cook 10-11 minutes at 400 degrees, making sure to flip halfway through cooking.

Horseradish Salmon

Ingredients: Servings: 2 Cooking Time: 7 Mins

2 salmon fillets
1/4 C. breadcrumbs
2 tbsp. olive oil
1 tbsp. horseradish
Pepper
Salt

Directions:

Place the dehydrating tray in a multi-level air fryer basket and place basket in the instant pot. Place salmon fillets on dehydrating tray. In a small bowl, mix together breadcrumbs, oil, horseradish, pepper, and salt and spread over salmon fillets. Seal pot with air fryer lid and select air fry mode then set the temperature to 400 F and timer for 7 minutes. Serve and enjoy.

Beer Potato Fish

Ingredients: Servings: 6 Cooking Time: 40 Mins

1 lb. fish fillet
4 medium size potatoes, peeled and diced
1 C. beer
1 red pepper sliced
1 tbsp. oil
1 tbsp. oyster flavored sauce
1 tbsp. rock candy
1 tsp. salt

Directions:

Preparing the Ingredients. Put all ingredients into your Instant Crisp Air Fryer. High pressure for 40 minutes. Lock the pressure cooking lid on the Instant Crisp Air Fryer and then cook for 40 minutes. To get 40-minutes cook time, press "Pressure" button and use the Time Adjustment button to adjust the cook time to 40 minutes. Pressure Release. Release the pressure using natural release method. Finish the dish. Close the air fryer lid. Select BROIL, and set the time to 5 minutes. Select START to begin. Cook until top is browned. Then that is it! Simple, fast, delicious, retaining flavour and nutrition, consistent results all the time. Serve and Enjoy!

Cajuned Salmon Meal

Ingredients: Servings: 2 Cooking Time: 8 Mins

1 tbsp. Cajun seasoning
1 tsp. brown sugar
2 salmon fillets (6 oz. each and with skin)

Directions:

In a mixing bowl, combine Cajun seasoning and brown sugar. Add the fillets and coat well. Place Instant Pot Air Fryer Crisp over kitchen platform. Press Air Fry, set the temperature to 400°F and set the timer to 5 minutes to preheat. Press "Start" and allow it to preheat for 5 minutes. In the inner pot, place the Air Fryer basket. Spray it with some cooking oil, and in the basket, add the fillets. Close the Crisp Lid and press the "Air Fry" setting. Set temperature to 390°F and set the timer to 8 minutes. Press "Start." Halfway down, open the Crisp Lid, flip the fillets, and close the lid to continue cooking for the remaining time. Open the Crisp Lid after cooking time is over. Serve warm.

Delicious Catfish

Ingredients: Servings: 4 Cooking Time: 20 Mins

Catfish fillets – 4
Salt and black pepper to taste
A pinch of sweet paprika
Parsley – 1 tbsp. chopped
Lemon juice – 1 tbsp.
Olive oil – 1 tbsp.

Directions:

Season catfish fillets with oil, paprika, pepper, and salt. Rub well. Cook in the air-fryer at 400F for 20 minutes. Flip the fish after 10 minutes. Divide fish on plates, drizzle lemon juice all over, sprinkle parsley and serve.

Fish Sandwiches

Ingredients: Servings: 4 Cooking Time: 20 Mins

lbs White Fish Fillets
1/4 Cup Yellow Cornmeal
1 Tsp Greek Seasoning
Salt and Pepper to taste
2 ½ Cups Plain Flour
2 Tsps Baking Powder
2 Cups Beer
4 Hamburger Buns
Mayonnaise
Lettuce Leaves
1 Tomato, sliced
1 Egg

Directions:

1 Preparing the Ingredients. Cut the fish fillets into burger patty sized strips. Season with salt and pepper to desired taste. In a medium bowl, mix together the beer, egg, baking powder, plain flour, cornmeal, Greek seasoning and additional salt and pepper Heat the Instant Crisp Air Fryer to 340 degrees Place each seasoned fish strip into the batter, ensuring that it is well coated 2 Air Frying. Place battered fish into the Instant Crisp Air Fryer tray, close air fryer lid and cook in batches for 6 minutes or until crispy Compile the sandwich by topping each bun with mayonnaise, then a lettuce leaf, tomato slices, and finally the cooked fish strip

3-ingredient Air Fryer Catfish

Ingredients: Servings: 4 Cooking Time: 13 Mins

1 tbsp. chopped parsley
1 tbsp. olive oil
¼ C. seasoned fish fry
4 catfish fillets

Directions:

1 Preparing the Ingredients. Ensure your Instant Crisp Air Fryer is preheated to 400 degrees. Rinse off catfish fillets and pat dry. Add fish fry seasoning to Ziploc baggie, then catfish. Shake bag and ensure fish gets well coated. Spray each fillet with olive oil. Add fillets to Instant Crisp Air Fryer basket. 2 Air Frying. Close air fryer lid. Set temperature to 400°F, and set time to 10 minutes. Cook 10 minutes. Then flip and cook another 2-3 minutes.

Cauliflower Chicken Dip

Ingredients: Servings: 8 Cooking Time: 5 Mins

1 medium cauliflower head, chopped
2 C. cheddar cheese, shredded
4 oz cream cheese, cubed
1 tsp. paprika
1/4 C. ranch dressing
1/2 C. buffalo sauce
2 C. cooked chicken, shredded
Pepper
Salt

Directions:

Add cauliflower, ranch dressing, buffalo sauce, seasonings, and chicken into the inner pot of instant pot duo crisp. Mix well. Seal the pot with pressure cooking lid and cook on high pressure for 5 minutes. Once done, release pressure using a quick release. Remove lid. Add cream cheese and cheddar cheese and stir until combined. Serve and enjoy.

Shrimp Mac N Cheese

Ingredients: Servings: 2 Cooking Time: 10 Mins

1 1/4 C. elbow macaroni
1 tbsp. butter
2/3 C. milk
1 bell pepper, chopped
15 shrimp
1 tbsp. cajun spice
1/2 C. flour
1 C. cheddar cheese, shredded

Directions:

Add butter in instant pot and set the pot on sauté mode. Add bell pepper and sauté for minutes. Add water and pasta and stir well. Seal pot with lid and cook on manual high pressure for 3 minutes. Once done then release pressure using the quick-release method than open the lid. Add cajun spices and flour and stir well. Set pot on sauté mode. Add shrimp and cook for 2 minutes. Add cheese and milk and stir well. Serve and enjoy.

Kale and Walnuts

Ingredients: Servings: 4 Cooking Time: 10 Mins

3 garlic cloves
10 C. kale; roughly chopped.
1/3 C. parmesan; grated
¼ C. walnuts; chopped.
½ C. almond milk s
1 tbsp. Butter; melted
¼ tsp. Nutmeg, ground
Salt and black pepper to taste.

Directions:

In a pan that fits the air fryer, combine all the ingredients, toss, introduce the pan in the machine and cook at 360°f for 15 minutes Divide between plates and serve.

Lemon Garlicky Shrimp

Ingredients: Servings: 4 Cooking Time: 5 Mins

1 lb shrimp, peeled
1 tbsp. olive oil
1 lemon juice
1 lemon zest
1/4 C. fresh parsley, chopped
4 garlic cloves, minced
1/4 tsp. red pepper flakes
1/4 tsp. sea salt

Directions:

Add all ingredients except parsley and lemon juice into the mixing bowl and toss well. Spray instant pot multi-level air fryer basket with cooking spray. Add shrimp into the air fryer basket and place basket into the instant pot. Seal pot with air fryer lid and select air fry mode then set the temperature to 400 F and timer for 5 minutes. Garnish shrimp with parsley and drizzle with lemon juice. Serve and enjoy.

Zucchinis and Walnuts

Ingredients: Servings: 4 Cooking Time: 10 Mins

1 lb. Zucchinis; sliced
¼ C. chives; chopped.
4 oz. Arugula leaves
1 C. walnuts; chopped.
1 tbsp. Olive oil
Salt and white pepper to the taste

Directions:

In a pan that fits the air fryer, combine all the ingredients except the arugula and walnuts, toss, put the pan in the machine and cook at 360°f for 20 minutes Transfer this to a salad bowl, add the arugula and the walnuts, toss and serve as a side salad.

Fish and Chips

Ingredients: Servings: 4 Cooking Time: 20 Mins

4 (4-ounce) fish fillets
Pinch salt
Freshly ground black pepper
½ tsp. dried thyme
1 egg white
¾ C. crushed potato chips
2 tbsp. olive oil, divided
3 russet potatoes, peeled and cut into strips

Directions:

1 Preparing the Ingredients. Pat the fish fillets dry and sprinkle with salt, pepper, and thyme. Set aside. In a shallow bowl, beat the egg white until foamy. In another bowl, combine the potato chips and 1 tbsp. of olive oil and mix until combined. Dip the fish fillets into the egg white, then into the crushed potato chip mixture to coat. Toss the fresh potato strips with the remaining 1 tbsp. olive oil. 2 Air Frying. Use your separator to divide the Instant Crisp Air Fryer basket in half, close air fryer lid and fry the chips and fish. the chips will take about 20 minutes; the fish will take about 10 to 12 minutes to cook.

Snapper Scampi

Ingredients: Servings: 4 Cooking Time: 10 Mins

4 (6-ounce) skinless snapper or arctic char fillets
1 tbsp. olive oil
3 tbsp. lemon juice, divided
½ tsp. dried basil
Pinch salt
Freshly ground black pepper
2 tbsp. butter
cloves garlic, minced

Directions:

1 Preparing the Ingredients. Rub the fish fillets with olive oil and 1 tbsp. of the lemon juice. Sprinkle with the basil, salt, and pepper, and place in the Instant Crisp Air Fryer basket. 2 Air Frying. Close air fryer lid and grill the fish for 7 to 8 minutes or until the fish just flakes when tested with a fork. Remove the fish from the basket and put on a serving plate. Cover to keep warm. In a 6-by-6-by-2-inch pan, combine the butter, remaining 2 tbsp. lemon juice, and garlic. Cook in the Instant Crisp Air Fryer for 1 to 2 minutes or until the garlic is sizzling. Pour this mixture over the fish and serve.

Radishes and Sesame Seeds

Ingredients: Servings: 4 Cooking Time: 15 Mins

20 radishes; halved
2 spring onions; chopped.
3 green onions; chopped.
2 tbsp. Olive oil
1 tbsp. Olive oil
3 tsp. Black sesame seeds
Salt and black pepper to taste.

Directions:
Take a bowl and mix all the ingredients and toss well. Put the radishes in your air fryer's basket, cook at 400°f for 15 minutes, divide between plates and serve as a side dish

Delicious Tilapia

Ingredients: Servings: 4 Cooking Time: 8 Mins

2 tilapia fillets
1/4 tsp. cayenne
1/2 tsp. cumin
1 tsp. garlic powder
1 tsp. dried oregano
2 tsp. brown sugar
2 tbsp. paprika
Salt

Directions:
In a small bowl, mix together cayenne, cumin, garlic powder, oregano, sugar, paprika, and salt and rub over tilapia fillets. Place the dehydrating tray in a multi-level air fryer basket and place basket in the instant pot. Place tilapia fillets on dehydrating tray. Seal pot with air fryer lid and select air fry mode then set the temperature to 400 F and timer for 8 minutes. Turn tilapia fillets halfway through. Serve and enjoy.

Air Fried, Instant Pot Homemade Tuna Patties

Ingredients: Servings: 4 Cooking Time: 6 Mins

7 oz. of canned tuna
1 egg, large
¼ C. breadcrumbs
1 tbsp. mustard
½ tsp. ground black pepper
¼ tsp. salt
Cooking oil spray

Directions:
In a medium bowl, combine egg, tuna, breadcrumbs, pepper, salt, and mustard with your hand. Spray some cooking oil in the inner pot of the Instant Pot Air Fryer. Make the tuna egg mix into four patties and place it in the inner pot. Close the crisp cover. In the AIR FRYER mode, select BROIL, which comes with a default temperature of 400°F Set the timer for 6 minutes and press START to air fry. After 3 minutes, open the crisp cover, flip the patties. Close the crisp cover to resume cooking for the remaining period. Serve along with ketchup.

Ranch Air Fryer Fish Fillets

Ingredients: Servings: 4 Cooking Time: 12 Mins

Tilapia fillets – 24 ounces
Dry ranch-style dressing mix – 5 ounces
Panko breadcrumbs – ¾ cup
Eggs - 2
Oil – 2 ½ tbsps.
Lemon wedges- 4

Directions:
Mix the ranch dressing and breadcrumbs in a bowl. Add oil and mix again. Preheat the air fryer. Beat the eggs in a bowl. Dip the fillet in the egg mix then in the breadcrumbs. Coat well. Cook the fish in the air fryer at 360F for 12 minutes. Flip the fish at the halfway mark. Serve with lemon wedges.

Steamed Cod and Veggies (pressure Cook)

Ingredients: Servings: 2 Cooking Time: 2 To 4 Mins

½ C. water
Kosher salt and freshly ground black pepper, to taste
2 tbsp. freshly squeezed lemon juice, divided
2 tbsp. melted butter
1 zucchini or yellow summer squash, cut into thick slices
1 garlic clove, minced
1 C. cherry tomatoes
1 C. whole Brussels sprouts
2 (6-ounce / 170-g) cod fillets
2 thyme sprigs or ½ tsp. dried thyme
Hot cooked rice, for serving

Directions:
Pour the water into your Instant Pot and insert a steamer basket. Sprinkle the fish with the salt and pepper. Mix together 1 tbsp. of the lemon juice, the butter, and garlic in a small bowl. Set aside. Add the zucchini, tomatoes, and Brussels sprouts to the basket. Sprinkle with the salt and pepper and drizzle the remaining 1 tbsp. of lemon juice over the top. Place the fish fillets on top of the veggies. Brush with the mixture and then turn the fish and repeat on the other side. Drizzle any remaining mixture all over the veggies. Place the thyme sprigs on top. Lock the lid. Select the Steam mode and set the cooking time for 2 to 4 minutes at High Pressure, depending on the thickness of the fish. Once cooking is complete, use a quick pressure release. Carefully open the lid. Serve the cod and veggies over the cooked rice.

Fast Salmon with Broccoli (pressure Cook)

Ingredients: Servings: 2 Cooking Time: 5 Mins

1 C. water
8 oz. (227 g) broccoli, cut into florets
8 oz. (227 g) salmon fillets
Salt and ground black pepper, to taste

Directions:
Pour the water into the Instant Pot and insert a trivet. Season the salmon and broccoli florets with salt and pepper. Put them on the trivet. Secure the lid. Select the Steam mode and set the cooking time for 5 minutes at High Pressure. Once cooking is complete, do a natural pressure release for 10 minutes, then release any remaining pressure. Carefully open the lid. Serve hot.

Lemony Tuna

Ingredients: Servings: 4 Cooking Time: 10 Mins

2 (6-ounce) cans water packed plain tuna
2 tsp. Dijon mustard
1 tbsp. fresh lime juice
2 tbsp. fresh parsley, chopped
½ C. breadcrumbs
1 egg
Instant Crisp Air Fryer of hot sauce
3 tbsp. canola oil
Salt and freshly ground black pepper, to taste

Directions:

1 Preparing the Ingredients. Drain most of the liquid from the canned tuna. In a bowl, add the fish, mustard, crumbs, citrus juice, parsley and hot sauce and mix till well combined. Add a little canola oil if it seems too dry. Add egg, salt and stir to combine. Make the patties from tuna mixture. Refrigerate the tuna patties for about 2 hours. 2 Air Frying. Preheat the Instant Crisp Air Fryer to 355 degrees F. Close air fryer lid and cook for about 10-12 minutes

Salmon Noodles

Ingredients: Servings: 4 Cooking Time: 16 Mins

1 Salmon Fillet
1 Tbsp Teriyaki Marinade
3 ½ Ozs Soba Noodles, cooked and drained
10 Ozs Firm Tofu
7 Ozs Mixed Salad
1 Cup Broccoli
Olive Oil
Salt and Pepper to taste

Directions:
1 Preparing the Ingredients. Season the salmon with salt and pepper to taste, then coat with the teriyaki marinate. Set aside for 15 minutes 2 Air Frying. Preheat the Instant Crisp Air Fryer at 350 degrees, close air fryer lid and cook the salmon for 8 minutes. Whilst the Instant Crisp Air Fryer is cooking the salmon, start slicing the tofu into small cubes. Next, slice the broccoli into smaller chunks. Drizzle with olive oil. Once the salmon is cooked, put the broccoli and tofu into the Instant Crisp Air Fryer tray for 8 minutes. Plate the salmon and broccoli tofu mixture over the soba noodles. Add the mixed salad to the side and serve

Tuna Stuffed Potatoes

Ingredients: Servings: 4 Cooking Time: 30 Mins

½ tbsp. olive oil
1 (6-ounce) can tuna, drained
2 tbsp. plain Greek yogurt
1 tsp. red chili powder
4 starchy potatoes
Salt and freshly ground black pepper, to taste
1 scallion, chopped and divided
1 tbsp. capers

Directions:
1 Preparing the Ingredients. In a large bowl of water, soak the potatoes for about 30 minutes. Drain well and pat dry with paper towel. Preheat the Instant Crisp Air Fryer to 355 degrees F. Place the potatoes in a fryer basket. 2 Air Frying. Close air fryer lid and cook for about 30 minutes. Meanwhile in a bowl, add tuna, yogurt, red chili powder, salt, black pepper and half of scallion and with a potato masher, mash the mixture completely. Remove the potatoes from the Instant Crisp Air Fryer and place onto a smooth surface. Carefully, cut each potato from top side lengthwise. with your fingers, press the open side of potato halves slightly. Stuff the potato open portion with tuna mixture evenly. Sprinkle with the capers and remaining scallion. Serve immediately.

Pesto Zucchini Pasta

Ingredients: Servings: 4 Cooking Time: 10 Mins

4 oz. Mozzarella; shredded
2 C. zucchinis, cut with a spiralizer
½ C. coconut cream
¼ C. basil pesto
1 tbsp. Olive oil
Salt and black pepper to taste.

Directions:
In a pan that fits your air fryer, mix the zucchini noodles with the pesto and the rest of the ingredients, toss, introduce the pan in the fryer and cook at 370°f for 15 minutes Divide between plates and serve as a side dish.

Lemon Garlic Shrimp

Ingredients: Servings: 4 Cooking Time: 5 Mins

Shrimp – 1 pound
Garlic – 4 cloves, chopped
Crushed red pepper flakes – ¼ tsp.
Oil – 1 tbsp.
Juice and zest of 1 lemon
Parsley – ¼ cup, chopped
Salt to taste

Directions:
Peel, devein, and remove the tails of the shrimps. Place minced garlic, lemon zest, shrimps, red pepper flakes, salt, and oil in a bowl. Mix. Preheat the air fryer at 400F. Coat the shrimps in the garlic mixture. Cook in the air fryer for 5 minutes at 400F. Flip the shrimp at the halfway mark. Finish cooking. Drizzle with lemon juice and garnish with chopped parsley.

Pesto Shrimp Kebobs

Ingredients: Servings: 12 Cooking Time: 5 Mins

1-pound shrimp
16 oz. basil pesto

Directions:
Toss the shrimp with pesto and coat them well. Thread these pesto shrimp on the skewers. Place the skewers in the Air Fryer Basket and set it in the Instant Pot Duo. Put on the Air Fryer lid and seal it. Hit the "Air fry Button" and select 5 minutes of cooking time, then press "Start." Once the Instant Pot Duo beeps, remove its lid. Serve.

Coriander Artichokes

Ingredients: Servings: 4 Cooking Time: 10 Mins

12 oz. Artichoke hearts
1 tbsp. Lemon juice
1 tsp. Coriander, ground
½ tsp. Cumin seeds
½ tsp. Olive oil
Salt and black pepper to taste.

Directions:
In a pan that fits your air fryer, mix all the ingredients, toss, introduce the pan in the fryer and cook at 370°f for 15 minutes Divide the mix between plates and serve as a side dish.

Healthy Beet Hummus

Ingredients: Servings: 16 Cooking Time: 40 Mins

1 C. chickpeas
1/3 C. water
1/4 C. fresh lemon juice
3 beets, peeled and
1/4 C. olive oil
2 garlic cloves, peeled
1/4 C. sunflower seeds
1 1/2 tsp. kosher salt

diced

Directions:

Add beets, chickpeas, 1 tsp. salt, 3 C. water, garlic, and sunflower seeds into the instant pot. Seal pot with lid and cook on manual high pressure for 40 minutes. Strain beet, chickpeas, garlic, and sunflower seeds and place in a food processor along with lemon juice and remaining salt and process until smooth. Add oil and 1/3 C. water and process until smooth. Serve and enjoy.

Grilled Salmon

Ingredients: Servings: 3 Cooking Time: 10 Mins

2 Salmon Fillets
1/2 Tsp Lemon Pepper
1/2 Tsp Garlic Powder
Salt and Pepper
1/3 Cup Soy Sauce
1/3 Cup Sugar
1 Tbsp Olive Oil

Directions:

1 Preparing the Ingredients. Season salmon fillets with lemon pepper, garlic powder and salt. In a shallow bowl, add a third C. of water and combine the olive oil, soy sauce and sugar. Place salmon the bowl and immerse in the sauce. Cover with cling film and allow to marinate in the refrigerator for at least an hour 2 Air Frying. Preheat the Instant Crisp Air Fryer at 350 degrees. Place salmon into the Instant Crisp Air Fryer, close air fryer lid and cook for 10 minutes or more until the fish is tender. Serve with lemon wedges

Shrimp Macaroni

Ingredients: Servings: 6 Cooking Time: 8 Mins

1 lb frozen shrimp, cooked
1 C. shredded gouda cheese
2 C. cheddar cheese, shredded
1 1/2 C. elbow macaroni, uncooked
1/4 tsp. ground nutmeg
2 tbsp. parsley, chopped
1/4 tsp. white pepper
2 tbsp. chives, minced
1 1/2 tbsp. hot sauce
1 C. blue cheese, crumbled
1/2 tsp. onion powder
1 tsp. ground mustard
1 tbsp. butter
1 C. half and half
2 C. of milk

Directions:

Add milk, butter, mustard, onion powder, white pepper, half and half, and ground nutmeg into the inner pot of instant pot duo crisp and stir well. Seal the pot with pressure cooking lid and cook on high for 3 minutes. Once done, allow to release pressure naturally. Remove lid. Add remaining ingredients and stir well and cook on sauté mode for 5 minutes. Serve and enjoy.

Air Fried White Fish with Garlic & Lemon

Ingredients: Servings: 2 Cooking Time: 10 Mins

Freshly cracked black pepper to taste
12 oz. tilapia fillets or white fish
½ tsp. lemon powder
½ tsp. garlic powder
4 lemon wedges
½ tsp. onion powder, optional
1 tbsp. freshly chopped parsley
Salt to taste

Directions:

Cleanse and pat dry fish fillets. Coat with olive oil and season with onion powder, garlic powder and lemon powder. Season with salt and pepper. Make sure fillets are evenly coated. Line air fryer basket with parchment paper and lightly grease with cooking spray. Arrange fish on top, adding few lemon wedges. Insert the air fryer basket to the instant pot duo crisp and attach the air fryer lid. Secure lock and air-fry at 360 degrees F for about 6-12 minutes or until fish can be flaked. Expect thicker fillets to take longer time to cook so adjust cooking time. Sprinkle chopped parsley on the cooked dish and serve immediately with roasted lemon wedges.

Tabasco Shrimp

Ingredients: Servings: 4 Cooking Time: 10 Mins

Shrimp – 1 pound, peeled and deveined
Red pepper flakes – 1 tsp.
Olive oil – 2 tbsps.
Tabasco sauce – 1 tsp.
Water – 2 tbsps.
Oregano – 1 tsp. dried
Salt and black pepper to taste
Dried parsley – ½ tsp.
Smoked paprika – ½ tsp.

Directions:

In a bowl, mix water, oil, Tabasco sauce, shrimp, paprika, pepper, salt, parsley, oregano, and pepper flakes. Coat well. Transfer shrimp to preheated air fryer at 370F and cook for 10 minutes. Shake once. Serve.

Homemade Fish Sticks (air Fryer)

Ingredients: Servings: 8 Cooking Time: 6 To 8 Min

8 oz. (227 g) fish fillets (pollock or cod), cut into ½×3-inch strips
Cooking spray
Salt, to taste (optional)
½ C. plain bread crumbs

Directions:

Preheat the air fryer to 390°F (199°C). Season the fish strips with salt to taste, if desired. Place the bread crumbs on a plate. Roll the fish strips in the bread crumbs to coat. Spritz the fish strips with cooking spray. Arrange the fish strips in the air fryer basket in a single layer and air fry for 6 to 8 minutes or until golden brown. Cool for 5 minutes before serving.

Shrimp Parmesan Bake

Ingredients: Servings: 4 Cooking Time: 8 Mins

1 1/2 lb. Large raw shrimp, peeled and deveined
1 tsp. coarse salt
1/4 tsp. black pepper
1/4 C. melted butter
1 tsp. garlic powder
1/2 tsp. crushed red pepper
1/4 C. parmesan cheese, grated

Directions:

Toss the shrimp with oil and all other ingredients in a bowl. Spread the seasoned shrimp in the baking tray. Press "power button" of air fry oven and turn the dial to select the "bake" mode. Press the time button and again turn the dial to set the cooking time to 8 minutes. Now push the temp button and rotate the dial to set the temperature at 400 degrees f. Once preheated, place the lobster's baking tray in the oven and close its lid. Switch the air fryer oven to broil mode and cook for 1 minute. Serve warm.

Sole with Mint and Ginger

Ingredients: Servings: 4 Cooking Time: 15 Mins

1 2-inch piece ginger, peeled and chopped
1 tbsp. vegetable or canola oil
2 lb. sole fillets
1 bunch mint
1/2 tsp. salt
1/4 tsp. freshly ground black pepper

Directions:
Add mint, salt, black pepper, ginger, and oil to a blender and blend until smooth. Stir in 2 tsp. water if the sauce is too thick then mix well. Rub the fish with the mint sauce to coat it liberally. Place the coated fish in the Instant Pot Duo. Put on the Air Fryer lid and seal it. Hit the "Air fry Button" and select 15 minutes of cooking time, then press "Start." Once the Instant Pot Duo beeps, remove its lid. Serve warm.

Simple & Perfect Salmon

Ingredients: Servings: 2 Cooking Time: 7 Mins

2 salmon fillets, remove any bones
2 tsp. olive oil
2 tsp. paprika
Pepper
Salt

Directions:
Coat salmon with oil and season with paprika, pepper, and salt. Place the dehydrating tray in a multi-level air fryer basket and place basket in the instant pot. Place salmon fillets on dehydrating tray. Seal pot with air fryer lid and select air fry mode then set the temperature to 390 F and timer for 7 minutes. Serve and enjoy.

Chili Dip

Ingredients: Servings: 8 Cooking Time: 15 Mins

1 (8-oz. package cream cheese, softened
1 (16-oz.can hormel chili without beans
1 (16-oz. package mild cheddar cheese, shredded

Directions:
In a baking pan, place the cream cheese and spread in an even layer. Top with chili evenly, followed by the cheese. Press "power button" of air fry oven and turn the dial to select the "air bake" mode. Press the time button and again turn the dial to set the cooking time to 15 minutes. Now push the temp button and rotate the dial to set the temperature at 375 degrees f. Press "start/pause" button to start. When the unit beeps to show that it is preheated, open the lid. Arrange pan over the "wire rack" and insert in the oven. Serve hot.

Shrimp with Bang Bang Sauce

Ingredients: Servings: 4 Cooking Time: 24 Mins

Raw shrimp – 1 lb. peeled and deveined
Mayonnaise – ½ cup
Sriracha sauce – 1 tbsp.
Sweet chili sauce – ¼ cup
Lettuce – 1 head
All-purpose flour – ¼ cup
Green onions – 2 chopped
Panko bread crumbs – 1 cup

Directions:
To make the sauce, add chili sauce, mayonnaise, and sriracha sauce in a bowl and whisk until smooth. Place flour in a bowl and panko breadcrumbs on another dish. Coat shrimp with flour then with the breadcrumbs. Line air fryer basket with parchment and grease with cooking spray. Cook shrimp for 12 minutes at 500F. Flip at the halfway mark spray cooking oil. Finish cooking. Serve with lettuce and green onions.

Golden Beer-battered Cod (air Fryer)

Ingredients: Servings: 4 Cooking Time: 15 Mins

2 eggs
1 C. malty beer
1 C. all-purpose flour
1 tsp. garlic powder
½ C. cornstarch
Salt and pepper, to taste
4 (4-ounce / 113-g) cod fillets
Cooking spray

Directions:
Preheat the air fryer to 400°F (204°C). In a shallow bowl, beat together the eggs with the beer. In another shallow bowl, thoroughly combine the flour and cornstarch. Sprinkle with the garlic powder, salt, and pepper. Dredge each cod fillet in the flour mixture, then in the egg mixture. Dip each piece of fish in the flour mixture a second time. Spritz the air fryer basket with cooking spray. Arrange the cod fillets in the basket in a single layer. Air fry in batches for 15 minutes until the cod reaches an internal temperature of 145°F (63°C) on a meat thermometer and the outside is crispy. Flip the fillets halfway through the cooking time. Let the fish cool for 5 minutes and serve.

Asian Shrimp

Ingredients: Servings: 4 Cooking Time: 10 Mins

1 lb shrimp, peeled and deveined
1 tbsp. cornstarch
1/8 tsp. ginger, minced
2 garlic cloves, minced
2 tbsp. soy sauce
1 tsp. sesame seeds
1 tbsp. green onion, sliced
2 tbsp. Thai chili sauce

Directions:
Spray instant pot multi-level air fryer basket with cooking spray. Toss shrimp with cornstarch and place into the air fryer basket and place basket into the instant pot. Seal pot with air fryer lid and select air fry mode then set the temperature to 400 F and timer for 10 minutes. Turn shrimp halfway through. Meanwhile, in a bowl, mix together soy sauce, ginger, garlic, and chili sauce. Add shrimp to the bowl and mix well. Sprinkle with green onions and sesame seeds.

Crispy-fried Salmon

Ingredients: Servings: 2 Cooking Time:10 Mins

Thyme – ½ tsp.
Brown sugar – 1 tsp.
Whole grain mustard – 2 tbsps.
Black pepper to taste
Salmon fillets – 2 (6 oz. each)
Olive oil – 2 tsps.
Garlic – 1 clove, minced

Directions:
Rub the salmon with salt and pepper. In a bowl, mix the garlic, mustard, sugar, thyme, and oil. Whisk to blend. Spread the mixture on top of the salmon. Cook in the air fryer at 400F for 10 minutes. Flip once at the halfway mark. Serve.

Horseradish Crusted Salmon

Ingredients: Servings: 2 Cooking Time: 5 Mins

2 pieces of salmon fillet
1 tsp. salt
1 tsp. black pepper
1 tbsp. horseradish
2 tbsp. olive oil
1/4 C. bread crumbs

Directions:
Whisk bread crumbs with salt, olive oil, horseradish and black pepper in a bowl. Coat the salmon with this crumbly mixture liberally. Place the breaded salmon in the Air Fryer Basket and set it inside the Instant Pot Duo. Put on the Air Fryer lid and seal it. Hit the "Air fry Button" and select 5 minutes of cooking time, then press "Start." Once the Instant Pot Duo beeps, remove its lid. Serve.

Air Fried Shrimp

Ingredients: Servings: 4 Cooking Time: 5 Mins

1 1/4 lbs shrimp, peeled and deveined
1 tbsp. olive oil
1/2 tsp. old bay seasoning
1/2 tsp. paprika
1/4 tsp. cayenne pepper
1/4 tsp. salt

Directions:
Add all ingredients into the mixing bowl and toss well. Place seasoned shrimp in instant pot air fryer basket and place basket in the pot. Seal the pot with air fryer lid and select air fry mode and cook at 400 F for 5 minutes. Serve and enjoy.

Saucy Salmon with Lime

Ingredients: Servings: 4 Cooking Time: 5 Mins

4 (5 oz) Salmon Filets
1 C. Water
Salt and Black Pepper to taste
2 tsp. Cumin Powder
2 tbsp. chopped Parsley
1 ½ tsp. Paprika
2 tbsp. Olive Oil
2 tbsp. Hot Water
1 tbsp. Maple Syrup
2 cloves Garlic, minced
1 Lime, juiced

Directions:
In a bowl, add cumin, paprika, parsley, olive oil, hot water, maple syrup, garlic, and lime juice. Mix with a whisk. Set aside. Open the cooker and pour the water in. Then, fit the rack. Season the salmon with pepper and salt; and place them on the rack. Close the lid, secure the pressure valve, and select Steam mode on High pressure for 3 minutes. Press Start. Once the timer has ended, do a quick pressure release, and open the pot. Close the crisping lid and cook on Air Fry mode for 3 minutes at 300 F. Use a set of tongs to transfer the salmon to a serving plate and drizzle the lime sauce all over it. Serve with steamed swiss chard.

Air Fryer Garlic-lemon Shrimp

Ingredients: Servings: 2-3 Cooking Time: 15 Mins

1 lb. raw shrimp, peeled and deveined
2 lemon wedges, juiced
1 tbsp. vegetable oil or spray for coating
¼ tsp. garlic powder
Salt and black pepper to taste
A pinch of parsley, minced
Optional: a dash of chili flakes

Directions:
Add shrimp in a bowl. Pour oil and toss to combine. Add garlic powder and season with salt and pepper. Toss to coat evenly. Place shrimp in a single-layered instant pot air fryer basket. Attach to the instant pot duo crisp air fryer lid and securely cover the pot. Set to air frying mode and cook at 400 degrees F for 10-14 minutes, flipping halfway for even cooking. Once the timer is off or when the shrimp is cooked, transfer to a plate and squeeze lemon juice over it. Sprinkle with parsley or chili flakes or both. Serve while hot.

Cheese Crust Salmon

Ingredients: Servings: 2 Cooking Time: 10 Mins

2 salmon fillets
2 tbsp. fresh parsley, chopped
1 garlic clove, minced
1/4 C. parmesan cheese, shredded
1/2 tsp. McCormick's BBQ seasoning
1/2 tsp. paprika
1 tbsp. olive oil
Pepper
Salt

Directions:
Add salmon, seasoning, and olive oil to the bowl and mix well. Mix together cheese, garlic, and parsley. Sprinkle cheese mixture on top of salmon. Place the dehydrating tray in a multi-level air fryer basket and place basket in the instant pot. Place salmon fillets on dehydrating tray. Seal pot with air fryer lid and select air fry mode then set the temperature to 400 F and timer for 10 minutes. Serve and enjoy.

Bacon Wrapped Scallops

Ingredients: Servings: 4 Cooking Time: 5 Mins

1 tsp. paprika
5 slices of center-cut bacon
1 tsp. lemon pepper
20 raw sea scallops

Directions:
Preparing the Ingredients. Rinse and drain scallops, placing on paper towels to soak up excess moisture. Cut slices of bacon into 4 pieces. Wrap each scallop with a piece of bacon, using toothpicks to secure. Sprinkle wrapped scallops with paprika and lemon pepper. Air Frying. Spray Instant Crisp Air Fryer basket with olive oil and add scallops. Close air fryer lid and cook 5-6 minutes at 400 degrees, making sure to flip halfway through.

Bok Choy and Butter Sauce

Ingredients: Servings: 4 Cooking Time: 15 Mins

2 bok choy heads; trimmed and cut into strips
1 tbsp. Butter; melted
2 tbsp. Chicken stock
1 tsp. Lemon juice
1 tbsp. Olive oil
A pinch of salt and black pepper

Directions:
In a pan that fits your air fryer, mix all the ingredients, toss, introduce the pan in the air fryer and cook at 380°f for 15 minutes. Divide between plates and serve as a side dish

Flying Fish

Ingredients: Servings: 6 Cooking Time: 12 Mins

4 Tbsp Oil
1 Whisked Whole Egg in a Saucer/Soup Plate
3–4 oz Breadcrumbs
4 Fresh Fish Fillets
Fresh Lemon (For serving)

Directions:
1 Preparing the Ingredients. Preheat the Instant Crisp Air Fryer (if necessary) to 350° F. Mix the crumbs and oil until it looks nice and loose. Dip the fish in the egg and coat lightly, then move on to the crumbs. Make sure the fillet is covered evenly. 2 Air Frying. Close air fryer lid. Cook in the Instant Crisp Air Fryer basket for roughly 12 minutes – depending on the size of the fillets you are using. Serve with fresh lemon & chips to complete the duo.

Crispy Cheesy Fish Fingers

Ingredients: Servings: 4 Cooking Time: 20 Mins

Large cod fish filet, approximately 6-8 ounces, fresh or frozen and thawed, cut into 1 ½-inch strips
½ C. of breadcrumbs (we like Panko, but any brand or home recipe will do)
2 raw eggs
2 tbsp. of shredded or powdered parmesan cheese
1 tbsp. of shredded cheddar cheese
Pinch of salt and pepper

Directions:
1 Preparing the Ingredients. Cover the basket of the Instant Crisp Air Fryer with a lining of tin foil, leaving the edges uncovered to allow air to circulate through the basket. Preheat the Instant Crisp Air Fryer to 350 degrees. In a large mixing bowl, beat the eggs until fluffy and until the yolks and whites are fully combined. Dunk all the fish strips in the beaten eggs, fully submerging. In a separate mixing bowl, combine the bread crumbs with the parmesan, cheddar, and salt and pepper, until evenly mixed. One by one, coat the egg-covered fish strips in the mixed dry ingredients so that they're fully covered, and place on the foil-lined Instant Crisp Air Fryer basket. 2 Air Frying. Close air fryer lid. Set the air-fryer timer to 20 minutes. Halfway through the cooking time, shake the handle of the air-fryer so that the breaded fish jostles inside and fry-coverage is even. After 20 minutes, when the fryer shuts off, the fish strips will be perfectly cooked and their breaded crust golden-brown and delicious! Using tongs, remove from the Instant Crisp Air Fryer and set on a serving dish to cool.

Crisp & Delicious Catfish

Ingredients: Servings: 2 Cooking Time: 20 Mins

2 catfish fillets
1/4 C. cornmeal
1/2 tsp. garlic powder
1/2 tsp. onion powder
1/2 tsp. salt

Directions:
Add cornmeal, garlic powder, onion powder, and salt into a zip-lock bag. Add fish fillets to the zip-lock bag. Seal bag and shake gently to coat fish fillet. Line instant pot air fryer basket with parchment paper. Place coated fish fillets on parchment paper in the air fryer basket. Place basket in the pot. Seal the pot with air fryer lid and select air fry mode and cook at 400 F for 20 minutes. Turn fish fillets halfway through. Serve and enjoy.

Salmon Quiche

Ingredients: Servings: 4 Cooking Time: 12 Mins

5 Ozs Salmon Fillet
1/2 Tbsp Lemon Juice
1/2 Cup Flour
1/4 Cup Butter, melted
2 Eggs and 1 Egg Yolk
3 Tbsps Whipped Cream
Tsps Mustard
Black Pepper to taste
Salt and Pepper
* Quiche Pan

Directions:
1 Preparing the Ingredients. Clean and cut the salmon into small cubes. Heat the Instant Crisp Air Fryer to 375 degrees Pour the lemon juice over the salmon cubes and allow to marinate for an hour. Combine a tbsp. of water with the butter, flour and yolk in a large bowl. Using your hands, knead the mixture until smooth On a clean surface, use a rolling pin to form a circle of dough. Place this into the quiche pan, using your fingers to adhere the pastry to the edges Whisk the cream, mustard and eggs together. Season with salt and pepper. Add the marinated salmon into the bowl and combine. Pour the content of the bowl into the dough lined quiche pan 2 Air Frying. Put the pan in the Instant Crisp Air Fryer tray, close air fryer lid and cook for 25 minutes until browned and crispy.

Crispy Coconut Shrimp

Ingredients: Servings: 2 Cooking Time: 10 Mins

12 large shrimp
1 C. coconut, dried
1 C. flour
1 C. breadcrumbs
1 C. egg white
1 tbsp. cornstarch

Directions:
In a shallow dish, mix together coconut and breadcrumbs and set aside. In another dish, mix together flour and cornstarch and set aside. Add egg white in a small bowl. Line instant pot multi-level air fryer basket with aluminum foil. Dip shrimp in egg white then roll in flour and coat with breadcrumb. Place coated shrimp into the air fryer basket and place basket into the instant pot. Seal pot with air fryer lid and select air fry mode then set the temperature to 350 F and timer for 10 minutes. Turn shrimp halfway through. Serve and enjoy.

Air Fryer Coconut Shrimp

Ingredients: Servings: 6 Cooking Time: 10 Mins

2 large eggs
½ tsp. ground black pepper
3 C. panko bread crumbs
½ C. all-purpose flour
¼ C. honey
3 C. flaked coconut, unsweetened
12 oz. medium-sized raw shrimps, peeled and deveined
1 Serrano chili, thinly sliced
½ tsp. Kosher salt, divided
2 tsps. fresh cilantro, chopped
¼ C. lime juice

Directions:
Combine pepper and flour in a shallow dish. Stir to combine. In another shallow dish, add the lightly beaten eggs. Add coconut and bread crumbs in another shallow dish. Dredge shrimps in the shallow dish with flour. Shake lightly to remove excess flour. One by one, dip shrimp to the dish with the egg mixture. Allow excess liquid to drip off. Transfer to the third dish with coconut-bread crumbs mixture. Coat shrimps evenly on all sides and lay them inside the 2-layered air fryer basket of the instant pot duo crisp lined with parchment paper. Coat shrimps with cooking spray, avoiding overcrowding. Place the air fryer inside the instant pot and cover with air fryer lid. Lock in place and air fry at 200 degrees F for about 3 minutes, flip and cook for another 3 minutes. Season with salt to taste. In a small bowl, combine honey, Serrano chili and lime juice. Whisk together for the dip. Serve crisp shrimps sprinkled with cilantro and the sauce for dipping.

Lemony Saba Fish

Ingredients: Servings: 2 Cooking Time: 8 Mins

Saba fish fillet – 4, boneless
Salt and black pepper to taste
Red chili pepper – 3, chopped
Lemon juice – 2 tbsps.
Olive oil – 2 tbsps.
Garlic – 2 tbsps. minced

Directions:
Season fish fillets with salt and pepper and place in a bowl. Add garlic, chili, oil, and lemon juice and toss to coat. Transfer fish to the air fryer and cook at 360F for 8 minutes. Flipping halfway. Serve.

Curry-flavored Shrimp (pressure Cook)

Ingredients: Servings: 2 To 4 Cooking Time: 4 Mins

2 C. water
1 lb. (454 g) shrimp, peeled and deveined
8 oz. (227 g) unsweetened coconut milk
1 tsp. curry powder
1 tbsp. garlic, minced
Salt and ground black pepper, to taste

Directions:
Pour the water into the Instant Pot and insert a trivet. Mix together the shrimp, coconut milk, curry powder, and garlic in a large bowl. Sprinkle with the salt and pepper. Add the mixture to the pan and place the dish onto the trivet, uncovered. Secure the lid. Press the Pressure Cook on the Instant Pot and cook for 4 minutes at Low Pressure. Once cooking is complete, use a quick pressure release. Carefully open the lid. Stir well and serve.

Cajun Shrimp

Ingredients: Servings: 4 Cooking Time: 2 Mins

1 lb. shrimp, peeled and deveined
15 asparagus spears
1 tbsp. cajun seasoning
1 tsp. olive oil

Directions:
Pour 1 C. of water in instant pot then place the steam rack inside the pot. Arrange asparagus on a steam rack in a layer. Place shrimp on the top of asparagus. Sprinkle cajun seasoning over shrimp and drizzle with olive oil. Seal pot with lid and cook on steam mode for 2 minutes. Once done then release pressure using the quick-release method than open the lid. Serve and enjoy.

Shrimp Spaghetti with Parmesan (pressure Cook)

Ingredients: Servings: 4 Cooking Time: 10 Mins

6 tbsp. butter, divided
12 oz. (340 g) small shrimp, peeled and deveined
½ tsp. salt
1 lb. (454 g) spaghetti
4 C. chicken broth
1 C. grated Parmesan cheese
1 C. heavy whipping cream
1 tsp. lemon pepper

Directions:
Set your Instant Pot to Sauté and add 2 tbsp. of butter. Add the shrimp and salt to the Instant Pot and sauté for 4 minutes, or until the flesh is pink and opaque. Remove the shrimp and set aside. Add the broth and scrape up any bits on the bottom of the pot. Break the spaghetti in half and add to the pot. Place the remaining 4 tbsp. of butter on top. Secure the lid. Press the Pressure Cook on the Instant Pot and cook for 5 minutes at High Pressure. Once the timer goes off, use a quick pressure release. Carefully open the lid. Fold in the cooked shrimp, Parmesan, cream, and lemon pepper. Stir until thoroughly combined. Transfer to a serving plate and serve hot.

Healthy Salmon Patties

Ingredients: Servings: 4 Cooking Time: 10 Mins

14 oz can salmon, drained and remove bones
2 eggs, lightly beaten
1/2 C. almond flour
1/2 onion, minced
1/4 C. butter
1/2 tsp. pepper
1 avocado, diced
1 tsp. salt

Directions:
Add all ingredients into the mixing bowl and mix until well combined. Place the dehydrating tray in a multi-level air fryer basket and place basket in the instant pot. Make patties from mixture and place on dehydrating tray. Seal pot with air fryer lid and select air fry mode then set the temperature to 400 F and timer for 10 minutes. Turn patties halfway through. Serve and enjoy.

Zucchini Spaghetti

Ingredients: Servings: 4 Cooking Time: 10 Mins

1 lb. Zucchinis, cut with a spiralizer	6 garlic cloves; minced
1 C. parmesan; grated	½ tsp. Red pepper flakes
¼ C. parsley; chopped.	Salt and black pepper to taste.
¼ C. olive oil	

Directions:

In a pan that fits your air fryer, mix all the ingredients, toss, introduce in the fryer and cook at 370°f for 15 minutes Divide between plates and serve as a side dish.

Delicious Shrimp Paella

Ingredients: Servings: 4 Cooking Time: 5 Mins

1 lb jumbo shrimp, frozen	1 C. of rice
1/2 C. white wine	1/4 C. cilantro, chopped
1 C. fish broth	1/4 tsp. red pepper flakes
1 red pepper, chopped	1 tsp. turmeric
4 garlic cloves, chopped	1 tsp. paprika
1 onion, chopped	1/4 tsp. pepper
1/4 butter	1/2 tsp. salt

Directions:

Add butter into the inner pot of instant pot duo crisp and set pot on sauté mode. Add garlic and onion and cook for a minute. Add remaining ingredients and stir well. Seal the pot with pressure cooking lid and cook on high for 5 minutes. Once done, release pressure using a quick release. Remove lid. Serve and enjoy.

Lemony Shrimp (pressure Cook)

Ingredients: Servings: 4 To 6 Cooking Time: 3 Mins

2 tbsp. butter	2 lb. (907 g) shrimp
1 tbsp. lemon juice	Salt and ground black pepper, to taste
1 tbsp. garlic, minced	1 tbsp. parsley, for garnish
½ C. chicken stock	
½ C. white wine	

Directions:

Place the butter, lemon juice, and garlic in your Instant Pot. Stir in the stock and wine. Add the shrimp and sprinkle with the salt and pepper. Stir well. Secure the lid. Press the Pressure Cook on your Instant Pot and set the cooking time for 3 minutes at High Pressure. Once the timer beeps, do a quick pressure release. Carefully remove the lid. Serve topped with the parsley.

Healthy Shrimp Pasta

Ingredients: Servings: 6 Cooking Time: 4 Mins

1 lb jumbo shrimp, peeled and deveined	1 lime juice
1/2 C. green onion, chopped	1/4 C. honey
1 tbsp. sriracha sauce	1 tsp. coconut oil
1 1/2 C. yogurt	1 tsp. garlic, minced
1 tbsp. vinegar	4 C. of water
1/4 C. Fresno pepper, diced	13 oz spaghetti noodles, break in half
	1/4 tsp. pepper

Directions:

Add oil into the inner pot of instant pot duo crisp and set pot on sauté mode. Add Fresno peppers and garlic and sauté for 30 seconds. Add noodles then pour water over noodles. Add shrimp, lime juice, honey, vinegar, and pepper on top of noodles. Seal the pot with pressure cooking lid and cook on high for 3 minutes. Once done, release pressure using a quick release. Remove lid. Add sriracha, yogurt, and green onions and stir well. Serve and enjoy.

Fried Calamari

Ingredients: Servings: 6-8 Cooking Time: 7 Mins

½ tsp. salt	½ C. semolina flour
½ tsp. Old Bay seasoning	½ C. almond flour
1/3 C. plain cornmeal	5-6 C. olive oil
	1 ½ lb. baby squid

Directions:

Preparing the Ingredients. Rinse squid in cold water and slice tentacles, keeping just ¼-inch of the hood in one piece. Combine 1-2 pinches of pepper, salt, Old Bay seasoning, cornmeal, and both flours together. Dredge squid pieces into flour mixture and place into the Instant Crisp Air Fryer. Air Frying. Spray liberally with olive oil. Close air fryer lid and cook 15 minutes at 345 degrees till coating turns a golden brown.

Teriyaki Beef Jerky

Ingredients: Servings: 4 Cooking Time: 6 Hours

3/4 lbs beef bottom round thin meat	1/2 tsp. liquid smoke
2 1/2 tbsp. soy sauce	1/2 tsp. onion powder
3 tbsp. Worcestershire sauce	1/2 tsp. garlic, minced
1/4 C. teriyaki sauce	1/2 tsp. red pepper flakes

Directions:

Cut meat into the thin slices. Add teriyaki sauce, soy sauce, Worcestershire sauce, onion powder, garlic, red pepper flakes, and liquid smoke in the large bowl. Add meat slices in the bowl and mix until coated. Cover bowl and place in the refrigerator for overnight. Spray the dehydrating tray with cooking spray and place in instant pot duo crisp air fryer basket. Arrange marinated meat slices on dehydrating tray. Place air fryer basket into the pot. Seal the pot with air fryer lid and select dehydrate mode and cook at 160 F for 6 hours. Store or serve.

Bang Bang Breaded Shrimp

Ingredients: Servings: 4 Cooking Time: 14 Mins

1 lb. Raw shrimp peeled and deveined	Salt and pepper to taste
1 egg white	Cooking spray
1/2 C. flour	Bang bang sauce
3/4 C. panko bread crumbs	1/3 C. greek yogurt
1 tsp. paprika	2 tbsp. sriracha
	1/4 C. sweet chili

Montreal seasoning to taste

sauce

Directions:

Mix flour with salt, black pepper, paprika, and Montreal seasoning in a bowl. Dredge the shrimp the flour then dips in the egg. Coat the shrimp with the breadcrumbs and place them in an air fryer basket. Press "power button" of air fry oven and turn the dial to select the "air roast" mode. Press the time button and again turn the dial to set the cooking time to 14 minutes. Now push the temp button and rotate the dial to set the temperature at 400 degrees f. Once preheated, place the air fryer basket in the oven and close its lid. Toss and flip the shrimp when cooked halfway through. Serve warm.

Garlic Shrimp

Ingredients: Servings: 4 Cooking Time: 8 Mins

1 lb shrimp, peeled and deveined
2 tsp. olive oil
For sauce:
1/4 C. honey
1/4 C. soy sauce
1 tbsp. ginger, minced
1 tbsp. garlic, minced

Directions:

In a mixing bowl, mix together all sauce ingredients. Add shrimp into the bowl and toss well. Add oil, shrimp with sauce mixture into the inner pot of instant pot duo crisp and cook on sauté mode for 3 minutes. Seal the pot with pressure cooking lid and cook on high for 5 minutes. Once done, release pressure using a quick release. Remove lid. Stir well and serve.

White Wine Black Mussels

Ingredients: Servings: 4 Cooking Time: 30 Mins

1 ½ lb Black Mussels, cleaned and de-bearded
3 tbsp. Olive Oil
3 large Chilies, seeded and chopped
3 cloves Garlic, peeled and crushed
1 White Onion, chopped finely
10 Tomatoes, skin removed and chopped
4 tbsp. Tomato Paste
1 C. Dry White Wine
3 C. Vegetable Broth
⅓ C. fresh Basil Leaves
1 C. fresh Parsley Leaves

Directions:

Heat the olive oil on Sear/Sauté mode, and stir-fry the onion, until soft. Add the chilies and garlic, and cook for 2 minutes, stirring frequently. Stir in the tomatoes and tomato paste, and cook for 2 more minutes. Then, pour in the wine and vegetable broth. Let simmer for 5 minutes. Add the mussels, close the lid, secure the pressure valve, and press Steam mode on High pressure for 3 minutes. Press Start to start cooking. Once the timer has ended, do a natural pressure release for 15 minutes, then a quick pressure release, and open the lid. Remove and discard any unopened mussels. Then, add half of the basil and parsley, and stir. Close the crisping lid and cook on Broil mode for 5 minutes. Dish the mussels with sauce in serving bowls and garnish it with the remaining basil and parsley. Serve with a side of crusted bread.

Shrimp and Crab Mix

Ingredients: Servings: 4 Cooking Time: 25 Mins

Yellow onion – ½ cup, chopped
Green bell pepper – 1 cup, chopped
Celery – 1 cup, chopped
Shrimp – 1 cup, peeled and deveined
Crabmeat – 1 cup, flaked
Mayonnaise – 1 cup
Worcestershire sauce – 1 tsp.
Salt and black pepper to taste
Breadcrumbs – 2 tbsps.
Butter – 1 tbsp. melted
Sweet paprika -1 tsp.

Directions:

In a bowl, mix crab meat, shrimp, onion, bell pepper, celery, mayo, salt, pepper and Worcestershire sauce. Transfer to a pan. Add melted butter, paprika, and bread crumbs. Coat well and place in the air fryer. Cook at 320F for 25 minutes. Shake once at the halfway mark. Serve.

Steam Clams

Ingredients: Servings: 3 Cooking Time: 3 Mins

1 lb mushy shell clams
2 tbsp. butter, melted
1/4 C. white wine
1/2 tsp. garlic powder
1/4 C. fresh lemon juice

Directions:

Add white wine, lemon juice, garlic powder, and butter into the instant pot. Place trivet into the pot. Arrange clams on top of the trivet. Seal pot with lid and cook on manual high pressure for 3 minutes. Once done then allow to release pressure naturally then open the lid. Serve and enjoy.

Coconut Shrimp with Dip

Ingredients: Servings: 4 Cooking Time: 9 Mins

1 lb large raw shrimp peeled and deveined with tail on
2 eggs beaten
¼ C. Panko Breadcrumbs
1 tsp. salt
¼ tsp. black pepper
½ C. All-Purpose Flour
½ C. unsweetened shredded coconut
Oil for spraying

Directions:

Clean and dry the shrimp. Set it aside. Take 3 bowls. Put flour in the first bowl. Beat eggs in the second bowl. Mix coconut, breadcrumbs, salt, and black pepper in the third bowl. Select the Air Fry option and adjust the temperature to 390°F. Push start and preheating will start. Dip each shrimp in flour followed by the egg and then coconut mixture, ensuring shrimp is covered on all sides during each dip. Once the preheating is done, place shrimp in a single layer on greased tray in the basket of the Instant Pot Duo Crisp Air Fryer. Spray the shrimp with oil lightly, and then close the Air Fryer basket lid. Cook for around 4 minutes. After 4 minutes, open the Air Fryer basket lid and flip the shrimp over. Respray the shrimp with oil, close the Air Fryer basket lid, and cook for five more minutes. Remove shrimp from the basket and serve with Thai Sweet Chili Sauce.

Cheesy Shrimp Grits

Ingredients: Servings: 6 Cooking Time: 7 Mins

1 lb shrimp, thawed
1/2 C. cheddar cheese, shredded
1/2 C. quick grits
1 tbsp. butter
1 1/2 C. chicken broth
1/4 tsp. red pepper flakes
1/2 tsp. paprika
2 tbsp. cilantro, chopped
1 tbsp. coconut oil
1/2 tsp. kosher salt

Directions:
Add oil into the instant pot and set the pot on sauté mode. Add shrimp and cook until shrimp is no longer pink. Season with red pepper flakes and salt. Remove shrimp from the pot and set aside. Add remaining ingredients into the pot and stir well. Seal pot with lid and cook on manual high pressure for 7 minutes. Once done then allow to release pressure naturally then open the lid. Stir in cheese and top with shrimp.

VEGETARIAN AND VEGAN RECIPES

Toasted Coco Flakes

Ingredients: Servings: 4 Cooking Time: 20 Mins

1 C. unsweetened coconut flakes
2 tsp. Coconut oil
¼ C. granular erythritol.
⅛ tsp. Salt

Directions:
Toss coconut flakes and oil in a large bowl until coated. Sprinkle with erythritol and salt. Place coconut flakes into the air fryer basket. Adjust the temperature to 300 degrees f and set the timer for 3 minutes. Toss the flakes when 1-minute remains. Add an extra minute if you would like a more golden coconut flake. Store in an airtight container up to 3 days.

Mediterranean Veggies

Ingredients: Servings: 4 Cooking Time: 20 Mins

1 large courgette
2 oz. cherry tomatoes
1 green pepper
1 medium carrot
1 large parsnip
1 tsp. mixed herbs
2 tbsps. honey
3 tbsps. olive oil
2 tsps. garlic puree
1 tsp. mustard
Salt and pepper to taste

Directions:
Slice up the courgette and the green pepper. Peel and dice the carrot and the parsnip. Add them all altogether in the air fryer basket of the instant pot duo along with raw cherry tomatoes, herbs, garlic puree, mustard, salt and pepper. Drizzle with three tbsp. of olive oil. Place the air fryer in the pot and air fry for 15 minutes at 356 degrees F using the instant pot duo crisp air fryer. Sprinkle with more salt if needed and serve.

Winter Vegetarian Frittata

Ingredients: Servings: 4 Cooking Time: 30 Mins

1 leek, peeled and thinly sliced into rings
2 cloves garlic, finely minced
3 medium-sized carrots, finely chopped
2 tbsp. olive oil
6 large-sized eggs
Sea salt and ground black pepper, to taste
1/2 tsp. dried marjoram, finely minced
1/2 C. yellow cheese of choice

Directions:
1 Preparing the Ingredients. Sauté the leek, garlic, and carrot in hot olive oil until they are tender and fragrant; reserve. In the meantime, preheat your Instant Crisp Air Fryer to 330 degrees F. In a bowl, whisk the eggs along with the salt, ground black pepper, and marjoram. Then, grease the inside of your baking dish with a nonstick cooking spray. Pour the whisked eggs into the baking dish. Stir in the sautéed carrot mixture. Top with the cheese shreds. 2 Air Frying. Place the baking dish in the Instant Crisp Air Fryer cooking basket. Lock the air fryer lid. Cook about 30 minutes and serve warm.

Crispy Ratatouille

Ingredients: Servings: 4 Cooking Time: 4 Mins

Kosher salt, for salting and seasoning
1 small eggplant, peeled and sliced ½ inch thick
1 medium zucchini, sliced ½ inch thick
2 tbsp. olive oil
1 C. chopped onion
1 small green bell pepper, cut into ½-inch chunks (about 1 cup)
1 small red bell pepper, cut into ½-inch chunks (about 1 cup)
3 garlic cloves, minced or pressed
1 rib celery, sliced (about 1 cup)
1 (14.5-ounce) can diced tomatoes, undrained
¼ C. water
½ tsp. dried oregano
¼ tsp. freshly ground black pepper
2 tbsp. minced fresh basil
¼ C. pitted green or black olives (optional)

Directions:
Preparing the Ingredients. Place a rack on a baking sheet. with kosher salt, very liberally salt one side of the eggplant and zucchini slices, and place them, salted-side down, on the rack. Salt the other side. Let the slices sit for 15 to 20 minutes, or until they start to exude water (you'll see it beading up on the surface of the slices and dripping into the sheet pan). Rinse the slices, and blot them dry. Cut the zucchini slices into quarters and the eggplant slices into eighths. Turn the Instant Crisp Air Fryer to "Sauté", heat the olive oil until it shimmers and flows like water. Add the onion and garlic, and sprinkle with a pinch or two of kosher salt. Cook for about 3 minutes, stirring until the onions just begin to brown. Add the eggplant, zucchini, green bell pepper, red bell pepper, celery, and tomatoes with their juice, water, and oregano. High pressure for 4 minutes. Lock the pressure cooking lid on the Instant Crisp Air Fryer and then cook for 4 minutes. To get 4-minutes cook time, press "Pressure" button and use the Time Adjustment button to adjust the cook time to 4 minutes. Pressure Release. Use the quick-release method. Finish the dish. Unlock and remove the lid. Close the Air Fryer Lid, select BROIL, and set the time to 5 minutes. Select START to begin. Cook until top is browned. Stir in the pepper, basil, and olives (if using). Taste, adjust the seasoning as needed, and serve. While this vegetable dish is

usually served on its own, it's great tossed with cooked pasta or served over polenta.

Italian Seasoned Cauliflower

Ingredients: Servings: 4 Cooking Time: 12 Mins

1 cauliflower head, cut into florets
1/2 tsp. Italian seasoning
1/2 tsp. garlic powder
1 lemon zest
3 tbsp. olive oil
2 tsp. lemon juice
1/4 tsp. pepper
1/4 tsp. salt

Directions:
In a bowl, mix together olive oil, lemon juice, Italian seasoning, garlic powder, lemon zest, pepper, and salt. Add cauliflower florets into the bowl and toss well. Spray instant pot multi-level air fryer basket with cooking spray. Add cauliflower florets into the air fryer basket and place basket into the instant pot. Seal pot with air fryer lid and select air fry mode then set the temperature to 400 F and timer for 12 minutes. Stir halfway through. Serve and enjoy.

Buttery Carrots with Pancetta

Ingredients: Servings: 4 - 6 Cooking Time: 7 Mins

1 medium leek, white and pale green parts only, sliced lengthwise, washed, and thinly sliced
¼ C. moderately sweet white wine, such as a dry Riesling
4 oz. pancetta, diced
1 lb. baby carrots
½ tsp. ground black pepper
2 tbsp. unsalted butter, cut into small bits

Directions:
Preparing the Ingredients. Put the pancetta in the Instant Crisp Air Fryer turned to the "Air Fry" function and use the Time Adjustment button to adjust the cook time to 5 minutes. Add the leek; cook, often stirring, until softened. Pour in the wine and scrape up any browned bits at the bottom of the pot as it comes to a simmer. Add the carrots and pepper; stir well. Scrape and pour the contents of the Instant Crisp Air Fryer into a 1-quart, round, high-sided soufflé or baking dish. Dot with the bits of butter. Lay a piece of parchment paper on top of the dish, then a piece of aluminum foil. Seal the foil tightly over the baking dish. Set the Instant Crisp Air Fryer rack inside, and pour in 2 C. water. Use aluminum foil to build a sling for the baking dish; lower the baking dish into the cooker. High pressure for 7 minutes. Lock the Pressure cooking lid on the Instant Crisp Air Fryer and then cook for 7 minutes. To get 7-minutes cook time, press "Pressure" button and use the Time Adjustment button to adjust the cook time to 7 minutes. Pressure Release. Use the quick-release method to return the pot's pressure to normal. Finish the dish. Close the Air Fryer Lid. Select BROIL, and set the time to 5 minutes. Select START to begin. Cook until top is browned. Unlock and open the pot. Use the foil sling to lift the baking dish out of the cooker. Uncover, stir well, and serve.

Jumbo Stuffed Mushrooms

Ingredients: Servings: 4 Cooking Time: 20 Mins

4 jumbo portobello mushrooms
1 tbsp. olive oil
5 tbsp. Parmesan cheese, divided
¼ C. ricotta cheese
1 C. frozen chopped spinach, thawed and drained
⅓ C. bread crumbs
¼ tsp. minced fresh rosemary

Directions:
1 Preparing the Ingredients. Wipe the mushrooms with a damp cloth. Remove the stems and discard. Using a spoon, gently scrape out most of the gills. Rub the mushrooms with the olive oil. 2 Air Frying Put in the Instant Crisp Air Fryer basket, hollow side up, lock the air fryer lid and bake for 3 minutes. Carefully remove the mushroom caps, because they will contain liquid. Drain the liquid out of the caps. In a medium bowl, combine the ricotta, 3 tbsp. of Parmesan cheese, spinach, bread crumbs, and rosemary, and mix well. Stuff this mixture into the drained mushroom caps. Sprinkle with the remaining 2 tbsp. of Parmesan cheese. Put the mushroom caps back into the basket and bake for 4 to 6 minutes or until the filling is hot and the mushroom caps are tender.

Eggplant Mousaka

Ingredients: Servings: 4 Cooking Time: 18 Mins

3 large Eggplants, sliced in uniform ¼ inches
4 ¼ C. Marinara Sauce
1 ½ C. shredded Mozzarella Cheese
Cooking Spray
Chopped Fresh Basil to garnish
Lightly spray the eggplant with cooking spray and pour the marinara sauce all over it.
Close the lid and pressure valve, and select Pressure mode on High pressure for 8 minutes. Press Start.
¼ C. Parmesan Cheese, grated
Once the timer has stopped, do a quick pressure release, and open the lid. Sprinkle with grated parmesan cheese, close the crisping lid and cook for 10 minutes on Bake mode on 380 F.
With two napkins in hand, gently remove the inner pot. Allow cooling for 10 minutes before serving.
Garnish the lasagna with basil and serve warm as a side dish.

Directions:
Open the pot and grease it with cooking spray. Arrange the eggplant slices in a single layer on the bottom of the pot and sprinkle some cheese all over it. Arrange another layer of eggplant slices on the cheese, sprinkle this layer with cheese also, and repeat the layering of eggplant and cheese until both

Steamed Lemony Cabbage (pressure Cook)

Ingredients: Servings: 2 To 4 Cooking Time: 2 Mins

1 C. water
1 large cabbage, cut into wedges
2 tbsp. melted butter
Juice of 1 lemon
Salt and black pepper, to taste
¼ tsp. red chili flakes

Directions:

Pour the water in the Instant Pot, then fit in a trivet. Place the cabbage in the trivet. Seal the lid. Select the Pressure Cook and set the time for 2 minutes at High Pressure. Once cooking is complete, do a quick pressure release, then unlock the lid. Transfer the cabbage on a plate. In a bowl, whisk together the lemon juice, butter, salt, pepper, and chili flakes. Drizzle the mixture all over the cabbage and serve.

Cheesy Asparagus (pressure Cook)

Ingredients: Servings: 4 Cooking Time: 8 Mins

1 C. water
1 lb. (454 g) asparagus, chopped
2 garlic cloves, minced
2 tbsp. butter, softened
Salt and black pepper, to taste
1 tbsp. olive oil
½ lemon, juiced
2 tbsp. grated Parmesan cheese

Directions:
In the Instant pot, pour the water and fit in a trivet. Cut out a foil sheet, place the asparagus on top with garlic and butter. Season with salt and black pepper. Wrap the foil and place on the trivet. Seal the lid. Select the Pressure Cook and set to 8 minutes at High Pressure. Once cooking is complete, do a quick pressure release. Carefully open the lid. Remove the foil, then transfer the asparagus onto a platter. Drizzle with lemon juice, and top with Parmesan cheese to serve.

Veggie Kabobs

Ingredients: Servings: 6 Cooking Time: 10 Mins

¼ C. carrots, peeled and chopped
¼ C. French beans
½ C. green peas
1 tsp. ginger
3 garlic cloves, peeled
3 green chilies
¼ C. fresh mint leaves
½ C. cottage cheese
2 medium boiled potatoes, mashed
½ tsp. five spice powder
Salt, to taste
2 tbsp. corn flour
Olive oil cooking spray

Directions:
In a food processor, add the carrot, beans, peas, ginger, garlic, mint, cheese and pulse until smooth. Transfer the mixture into a bowl. Add the potato, five spice powder, salt and corn flour and mix until well combined. Divide the mixture into equal sized small balls. Press each ball around a skewer in a sausage shape. Spray the skewers with cooking spray. Press "power button" of air fry oven and turn the dial to select the "air fry" mode. Press the time button and again turn the dial to set the cooking time to 10 minutes. Now push the temp button and rotate the dial to set the temperature at 390 degrees f. Press "start/pause" button to start. When the unit beeps to show that it is preheated, open the lid. Arrange the skewers in greased "air fry basket" and insert in the oven. Serve warm.

Stuffed Garlic Mushrooms

Ingredients: Servings: 4 Cooking Time: 25 Mins

6 Small Mushrooms
0.7oz Onion peeled and diced
1 Tsp Garlic Puree
1 Tbsp Olive Oil
1 Tsp Parsley
1 Tbsp Breadcrumbs
Salt & Pepper

Directions:
In a bowl, mix together garlic, breadcrumbs, olive oil, onion, parsley, salt, and pepper. Make sure they are mixed thoroughly. Clean the mushrooms and remove the middle stalks. Fill the middle area with your breadcrumb mixture. Place them into the Instant Pot Duo Crisp Air Fryer Basket. Close the Air Fryer lid and cook the mushrooms on a 350°F heat for 10 minutes and then serve.

Air-fried Green Beans

Ingredients: Servings: 4 Cooking Time: 15 Mins

1 lb. fresh green beans (with ends trimmed and cut into halves)
½ tsp. garlic powder
1 tbsp. olive oil or cooking spray
Salt and pepper to taste
2 fresh lemon slices

Directions:
Combine the green beans with garlic powder in a bowl and season with salt and pepper. Arrange the seasoned green beans in the air fryer basket. Place the basket inside the instant pot duo crisp and attach the air fryer lid. Make sure it locks before setting it to air frying mode. Cook at 360 degrees F for 10-14 minutes. Toss and shake two times while cooking. Adjust the seasonings to taste if needed. Garnish with lemon slices and serve.

Garlic Broccoli Mash

Ingredients: Servings: 4 Cooking Time: 7 Mins

3 heads Broccoli, chopped
6 oz Cream Cheese
2 cloves Garlic, crushed
2 tbsp. Butter, unsalted
Salt and Black Pepper to taste
2 C. Water
Stir in Cream cheese. Adjust the taste with salt and pepper. Close the crisping lid and cook for 2 minutes on Broil mode. Serve warm.

Directions:
Turn on the cooker and select Sear/Sauté mode, adjust to High. Drop in the butter, once it melts add the garlic and cook for 30 seconds while stirring frequently to prevent the garlic from burning. Then, add the broccoli, water, salt, and pepper. Close the lid, secure the pressure valve, and select Pressure mode on High pressure for 5 minutes. Press Start. Once the timer has ended, do a quick pressure release and use a stick blender to mash the

Haloumi Baked Rusti

Ingredients: Servings: 4 Cooking Time: 35 Mins

Olive oil, to brush
7 oz. sweet potato, coarsely grated
10 oz. potatoes, coarsely grated
10 oz. carrots, coarsely grated
9 oz. halloumi,
Fennel Salad
2 celery stalks, thinly sliced
1 fennel, thinly sliced
1/2 C. olives, chopped
Juice of 1 lemon
1 lemon quarter, chopped

coarsely grated
1/2 onion, coarsely grated
2 tbsp. thyme leaves
2 eggs
1/3 C. plain flour
1/2 C. sour cream, to serve
1 tsp. toasted coriander seeds, ground
Serve the sweet potato rosti with the prepared salad.

Directions:
Toss sweet potato, carrot, potato, onion, halloumi, thyme, flour, and eggs in a bowl. Spread this mixture in the Instant Pot Duo insert. Put on the Air Fryer lid and seal it. Hit the "Bake Button" and select 35 minutes of cooking time, then press "Start." Once the Instant Pot Duo beeps, remove its lid. Prepare the salad by mixing its

Tofu In Sweet & Sour Sauce

Ingredients: Servings: 4 Cooking Time: 20 Mins

For tofu:
1 (14-oz. block firm tofu, pressed and cubed
½ C. arrowroot flour
½ tsp. sesame oil
For sauce:
4 tbsp. low-sodium soy sauce
1½ tbsp. rice vinegar
1½ tbsp. chili sauce
1 tbsp. agave nectar
2 large garlic cloves, minced
1 tsp. fresh ginger, peeled and grated
2 scallions (green part), chopped

Directions:
In a bowl, mix together the tofu, arrowroot flour, and sesame oil. Press "power button" of air fry oven and turn the dial to select the "air fry" mode. Press the time button and again turn the dial to set the cooking time to 20 minutes. Now push the temp button and rotate the dial to set the temperature at 360 degrees f. Press "start/pause" button to start. When the unit beeps to show that it is preheated, open the lid. Arrange the tofu cubes in greased "air fry basket" and insert in the oven. Flip the tofu cubes once halfway through. Meanwhile, for the sauce: in a bowl, add all the ingredients except scallions and beat until well combined. Transfer the tofu into a skillet with sauce over medium heat and cook for about 3 minutes, stirring occasionally. Garnish with scallions and serve hot.

Garlic Lemon Green Beans

Ingredients: Servings: 4 Cooking Time: 10 Mins

1 lb green beans, Trimmed ends and cut into pieces
2 tbsp. butter
1 tbsp. parmesan cheese, grated
1/4 C. lemon juice
2 garlic cloves, minced
2 tbsp. olive oil
Pepper
Salt

Directions:
Add beans, oil, pepper, and salt into the mixing bowl and toss well. Spray instant pot multi-level air fryer basket with cooking spray. Add green beans into the air fryer basket and place basket into the instant pot. Seal pot with air fryer lid and select air fry mode then set the temperature to 390 F and timer for 10 minutes. Stir beans halfway through. Meanwhile, in a pan, melt butter. Add garlic and saute for 30 seconds. Add lemon juice and cook for 2 minutes. Transfer green beans into the mixing bowl. Pour melted butter mixture over green beans and toss well. Sprinkle with parmesan cheese and serve.

Parmesan Zucchini Chips (air Fryer)

Ingredients: Servings: 4 Cooking Time: 14 Mins

Salt and black pepper, to taste
½ C. seasoned bread crumbs
2 tbsp. grated Parmesan cheese
2 egg whites
¼ tsp. garlic powder
2 medium zucchinis, sliced
Cooking spray

Directions:
Preheat the air fryer to 400°F (204°C). Spritz the air fryer basket with cooking spray. In a bowl, beat the egg whites with salt and pepper. In a separate bowl, thoroughly combine the bread crumbs, Parmesan cheese, and garlic powder. Dredge the zucchini slices in the egg white, then coat in the bread crumb mixture. Arrange the zucchini slices in the air fryer basket and air fry for 14 minutes, flipping the zucchini halfway through. Remove from the basket to a plate and serve.

Cheesy Cauliflower Fritters

Ingredients: Servings: 8 Cooking Time: 7 Mins

1 C. Italian breadcrumbs
1/3 C. shredded mozzarella cheese
1/3 C. shredded sharp cheddar cheese
½ C. chopped parsley
1 egg
2 minced garlic cloves
3 chopped scallions
1 head of cauliflower

Directions:
1 Preparing the Ingredients. Cut cauliflower up into florets. Wash well and pat dry. Place into a food processor and pulse 20-30 seconds till it looks like rice. Place cauliflower rice in a bowl and mix with pepper, salt, egg, cheeses, breadcrumbs, garlic, and scallions. with hands, form 15 patties of the mixture. Add more breadcrumbs if needed. 2 Air Frying. with olive oil, spritz patties, and place into your Instant Crisp Air Fryer in a single layer. Lock the air fryer lid. Set temperature to 390°F, and set time to 7 minutes, flipping after 7 minutes.

Charred Green Beans with Sesame Seeds (air Fryer)

Ingredients: Servings: 4 Cooking Time: 8 Mins

½ tbsp. Sriracha sauce
4 tsp. toasted sesame oil, divided
12 oz. (340 g) trimmed green beans
1 tbsp. reduced-sodium soy sauce or tamari
½ tbsp. toasted sesame seeds

Directions:
Preheat the air fryer to 375°F (191°C). Whisk together the soy sauce, Sriracha sauce, and 1 tsp. of sesame oil in a small bowl until smooth. Toss the green beans with the remaining sesame oil in a large bowl until evenly coated. Place the green beans in the air fryer basket in a single layer. You may need to work in batches to avoid overcrowding. Air fry for about 8 minutes until the green beans are lightly charred and tender. Shake the

basket halfway through the cooking time. Remove from the basket to a platter. Repeat with the remaining green beans. Pour the prepared sauce over the top of green beans and toss well. Serve sprinkled with the toasted sesame seeds.

Glazed Veggies

Ingredients: Servings: 4 Cooking Time: 20 Mins

2 oz. Cherry tomatoes
2 large zucchinis, chopped
2 green bell peppers, seeded and chopped
6 tbsp. olive oil, divided
2 tbsp. honey
1 tsp. dijon mustard
1 tsp. dried herbs
1 tsp. garlic paste
Salt, as required

Directions:
In a parchment paper-lined baking pan, place the vegetables and drizzle with 3 tbsp. of oil. Press "power button" of air fry oven and turn the dial to select the "air fry" mode. Press the time button and again turn the dial to set the cooking time to 15 minutes. Now push the temp button and rotate the dial to set the temperature at 355 degrees f. Press "start/pause" button to start. When the unit beeps to show that it is preheated, open the lid. Arrange the pan over the "wire rack" and insert in the oven. Meanwhile, in a bowl, add the remaining oil, honey, mustard, herbs, garlic, salt, and black pepper and mix well. After 15 minutes of cooking, add the honey mixture into vegetable mixture and mix well. Now, set the temperature to 392 degrees f for 5 minutes. Serve immediately.

Beans & Veggie Burgers

Ingredients: Servings: 4 Cooking Time: 22 Mins

1 C. cooked black beans
2 C. boiled potatoes, peeled and mashed
1 C. fresh spinach, chopped
1 C. fresh mushrooms, chopped
2 tsp. chile lime seasoning
Olive oil cooking spray

Directions:
In a large bowl, add the beans, potatoes, spinach, mushrooms, and seasoning and with your hands, mix until well combined. Make 4 equal-sized patties from the mixture. Spray the patties with cooking spray evenly. Press "power button" of air fry oven and turn the dial to select the "air fry" mode. Press the time button and again turn the dial to set the cooking time to 22 minutes. Now push the temp button and rotate the dial to set the temperature at 370 degrees f. Press "start/pause" button to start. When the unit beeps to show that it is preheated, open the lid. Arrange the skewers in greased "air fry basket" and insert in the oven. Flip the patties once after 12 minutes.

Fried Cauliflower

Ingredients: Servings: 4 Cooking Time: 15 Mins

Chickpeas – 15 oz.
Olive oil – 1 tsp.
Cauliflower – 1 lb. cut into florets
Salt – ½ tsp.
Olive oil – ¼ cup
Grated Parmesan cheese – ¼ cup
Finely chopped parsley – 1 tbsp.
Ground pepper – ¼ tsp.
Lemon slices for garnish
Sauce mixture
Lemon juice – 1 tbsp.
Lemon zest – 1 tsp.
Salt and ground pepper to taste

Directions:
In a bowl, combine the cauliflower, oil, salt, and pepper. Mix. Cook in the air fryer for 15 minutes at 400F. Stir. Meanwhile, mix the sauce ingredients in a bowl. Serve.

Creamy Endives

Ingredients: Servings: 6 Cooking Time: 10 Mins

Endives – 6, trimmed and halved
Garlic powder – 1 tsp.
Greek yogurt – ½ cup
Curry powder – ½ tsp.
Salt and black pepper to taste
Lemon juice – 3 tbsps.

Directions:
In a bowl, mix endives with lemon juice, salt, pepper, curry powder, yogurt, and garlic powder. Coat well and set aside for 10 minutes. Cook in the preheated 350F air fryer for 10 minutes. Serve.

Air Fryer Chickpeas

Ingredients: Servings: 4 Cooking Time: 20 Mins

Canned chickpeas – 15 ½ ounces, rinsed and drained
Cumin powder – ¼ tsp.
Cayenne pepper powder – ¼ tsp.
Salt – 1 tsp.
Cooking spray

Directions:
Cook the chickpeas in the air fryer at 390F for 20 minutes. Meantime, combine cumin powder, cayenne pepper, and salt in a bowl. After 5 minutes, open the lid and spray some oil on the chickpeas. Sprinkle a quarter of the seasoning and stir the chickpeas with a spoon. Close and continue to cook. Shake the basket after every 5 minutes. Remove from the air fryer and add the remaining seasoning. Mix and serve.

Veggie Bake Cakes

Ingredients: Servings: 2 Cooking Time: 12 Mins

Leftover Vegetable Bake
1 Tbsp Plain Flour

Directions:
Preheat the Instant Pot Duo Crisp Air Fryer at 350°F. Mix the flour with the leftover vegetable bake. It will now become a thick dough. Place them into the Instant Pot Duo Crisp Air Fryer Basket. Close the Air Fryer lid and cook for 12 minutes on 350°F. Serve hot.

Rosemary Air-fried Potatoes

Ingredients: Servings: 4 Cooking Time: 15 Mins

3 tbsps. vegetable oil
4 yellow baby potatoes, quartered
1 tsp. ground black pepper
¼ C. chopped parsley

2 tsps. dried rosemary, minced	1 tbsp. fresh lime or lemon juice
1 tbsp. minced garlic	1 tsp. salt

Directions:
Add potatoes, garlic, rosemary, oil, pepper, and salt in a large bowl. Mix thoroughly. Arrange seasoned potatoes in the air fryer basket and place inside the instant pot duo. Cover with the air fryer lid and air-fry at 400 degrees F for about 15 minutes. Check to see if potatoes are cooked through. Once cooked, take it out of the air fryer and place in a platter. Sprinkle with lemon juice and parsley. Serve warm.

Bulgur Wheat Bowl with Shallots (pressure Cook)

Ingredients: Servings: 2 Cooking Time: 14 Mins

1 tbsp. butter	½ C. bulgur wheat
2 shallots, chopped	¼ tsp. sea salt
1 tsp. minced fresh garlic	¼ tsp. ground black pepper
1 C. vegetable broth	

Directions:
Set the Instant Pot to the Sauté mode and melt the butter. Add the shallots to the pot and sauté for 3 minutes, or until just tender and fragrant. Add the garlic and sauté for 1 minute, or until fragrant. Stir together the remaining ingredients in the pot. Lock the lid. Select the Pressure Cook and set the cooking time for 10 minutes at High Pressure. When the timer beeps, perform a natural pressure release for 10 minutes, then release any remaining pressure. Carefully open the lid. Fluff the bulgur wheat with a fork and serve immediately.

Veggie Cake

Ingredients: Servings: 2 Cooking Time: 12 Mins

Leftover vegetable bake – 1 cup	Plain flour – 1 tbsp.

Directions:
Preheat the air fryer at 350F. Mix the flour and veggies. Make a thick dough. Grease the basket with cooking spray. Cook at 350F for 12 minutes. Flip at the halfway mark. Slice and serve.

Creamy Spinach Quiche

Ingredients: Servings: 4 Cooking Time: 20 Mins

Premade quiche crust, chilled and rolled flat to a 7-inch round	Pinch of salt and pepper
eggs	½ C. of cooked spinach, drained and coarsely chopped
¼ C. of milk	¼ C. of shredded mozzarella cheese
1 clove of garlic, peeled and finely minced	¼ C. of shredded cheddar cheese

Directions:
Preparing the Ingredients. Preheat the Instant Crisp Air Fryer to 360 degrees. Press the premade crust into a 7-inch pie tin, or any appropriately sized glass or ceramic heat-safe dish. Press and trim at the edges if necessary. with a fork, pierce several holes in the dough to allow air circulation and prevent cracking of the crust while cooking. In a mixing bowl, beat the eggs until fluffy and until the yolks and white are evenly combined. Add milk, garlic, spinach, salt and pepper, and half the cheddar and mozzarella cheese to the eggs. Set the rest of the cheese aside for now, and stir the mixture until completely blended. Make sure the spinach is not clumped together, but rather spread among the other ingredients. Pour the mixture into the pie crust, slowly and carefully to avoid splashing. the mixture should almost fill the crust, but not completely – leaving a ¼ inch of crust at the edges. Air Frying. Lock the air fryer lid. Set the air-fryer timer for 15 minutes. After15 minutes, the Instant Crisp Air Fryer will shut off, and the quiche will already be firm and the crust beginning to brown. Sprinkle the rest of the cheddar and mozzarella cheese on top of the quiche filling. Reset the Instant Crisp Air Fryer at 360 degrees for 5 minutes. After 5 minutes, when the Instant Crisp Air Fryer shuts off, the cheese will have formed an exquisite crust on top and the quiche will be golden brown and perfect. Remove from the Instant Crisp Air Fryer using oven mitts or tongs, and set on a heat-safe surface to cool for a few minutes before cutting.

Cauliflower Bites

Ingredients: Servings: 4 Cooking Time: 18 Mins

1 Head Cauliflower, cut into small florets	Tsps Garlic Powder
	1 Tbsp Butter, melted
Pinch of Salt and Pepper	1/2 Cup Chili Sauce
	Olive Oil

Directions:
1 Preparing the Ingredients. Place cauliflower into a bowl and pour oil over florets to lightly cover. Season florets with salt, pepper and the garlic powder and toss well. 2 Air Frying. Place florets into the Instant Crisp Air Fryer, lock the air fryer lid and set at 350 degrees for 14 minutes. Remove cauliflower from the Instant Crisp Air Fryer. Combine the melted butter with the chili sauce Pour over the florets so that they are well coated. Return to the Instant Crisp Air Fryer and cook for additional 3 to 4 minutes Serve as a side or with ranch or cheese dip as a snack

Roasted Squash

Ingredients: Servings: 4 Cooking Time: 12 Mins

1 lb butternut squash, peeled and cut into chunks	1 tbsp. sage
	1 tbsp. olive oil
	Pepper
1 tsp. thyme	Salt

Directions:
Add squash and remaining ingredients into the large bowl and toss well. Line instant pot multi-level air fryer basket with foil. Add squash mixture into the air fryer basket and place basket into the instant pot. Seal pot with air fryer lid and select air fry mode then set the temperature to 390 F and timer for 12 minutes. Stir after 10 minutes. Serve and enjoy.

Falafel Balls

Ingredients: Servings: 3 Cooking Time: 12 Mins

Sweet onion – ½ cup, diced	Cooked chickpeas – 2 cups, drained and rinsed
Oil – 2 tbsps.	

Turmeric – ½ tsp.	Juice of 1 lemon
Carrots – ½ cup, minced	Soy sauce – 2 tbsps.
Rolled oats -1 cup	Flax meal – 1 tbsp.
Roasted, salted cashews – ½ cup	Garlic powder – ½ tsp.
	Ground cumin – ½

Directions:
Heat a little oil and sauté onions and carrots in the Instant Pot Duo. Cook for 7 minutes, then transfer to a bowl. Place cashew and oats in a food processor and process until you get a coarse meal consistency. Add this mixture to the bowl with vegetables. Place the chickpeas, lemon juice and soy sauce into the food processor and puree until a semi-smooth consistency. Transfer it to the bowl and add in the flax and spices. Mix well. Form falafel balls. Line the air fryer with parchment paper. Cook the balls in the air fryer at 370F for 12 minutes. Shake the basket after 8 minutes of cooking. Serve.

Roasted Vegetables Salad

Ingredients: Servings: 5 Cooking Time: 85 Mins

- 3 eggplants
- 1 tbsp. of olive oil
- 3 medium zucchini
- 1 tbsp. of olive oil
- 4 large tomatoes, cut them in eighths
- 4 C. of one shaped pasta
- 2 peppers of any color
- 1 C. of sliced tomatoes cut into small cubes
- 2 tsp. of salt substitute
- 8 tbsp. of grated parmesan cheese
- ½ C. of Italian dressing
- Leaves of fresh basil

Directions:
1 Preparing the Ingredients. Wash your eggplant and slice it off then discard the green end. Make sure not to peel. Slice your eggplant into1/2 inch of thick rounds. 1/2 inch) Pour 1tbsp of olive oil on the eggplant round. 2 Air Frying. Put the eggplants in the basket of the Instant Crisp Air Fryer, lock the air fryer lid and then toss it in the Instant Crisp Air Fryer. Cook the eggplants for 40 minutes. Set the heat to 360 ° F Meanwhile, wash your zucchini and slice it then discard the green end. But do not peel it. Slice the Zucchini into thick rounds of ½ inch each. In the basket of the Instant Crisp Air Fryer, toss your ingredients Add 1 tbsp. of olive oil. 3 Air Frying. Cook the zucchini for 25 minutes on a heat of 360° F and when the time is off set it aside. Wash and cut the tomatoes. 4 Air Frying. Arrange your tomatoes in the basket of the Instant Crisp Air Fryer. Set the timer to 30 minutes. Set the heat to 350° F When the time is off, cook your pasta according to the pasta guiding directions, empty it into a colander. Run the cold water on it and wash it and drain the pasta and put it aside. Meanwhile, wash and chop your peppers and place it in a bow Wash and thinly slice your cherry tomatoes and add it to the bowl. Add your roasted veggies. Add the pasta, a pinch of salt, the topping dressing, add the basil and the parm and toss everything together. (It is better to mix with your hands). Set the ingredients together in the refrigerator, and let it chill Serve your salad and enjoy it!

Gold Potato and Boiled Egg Salad (pressure Cook)

Ingredients: Servings: 4 Cooking Time: 12 Mins

- 1 C. water
- 1 lb. (454 g) small Yukon Gold potatoes
- 2 boiled eggs, peeled and chopped
- 1 celery rib, diced
- ¼ C. pickle relish
- ½ yellow onion, sliced
- 1 garlic clove, minced
- ⅓ C. mayonnaise
- ½ tsp. fresh rosemary, chopped
- ½ tbsp. yellow mustard
- ⅓ tsp. cayenne pepper
- Sea salt and ground black pepper, to taste

Directions:
Pour the water in the Instant Pot and fit in a steamer basket. Place the potatoes in the steamer basket. Secure the lid. Choose the Pressure Cook and set the cooking time for 12 minutes at High pressure. Once cooking is complete, do a quick pressure release. Carefully remove the lid. Allow to cool for a few minutes until cool enough to handle. Peel and slice the potatoes, then place them in a large bowl and toss with the remaining ingredients. Stir to combine. Serve immediately.

Coconut Battered Cauliflower Bites

Ingredients: Servings: 4 Cooking Time: 20 Mins

- salt and pepper to taste
- 1 flax egg (1 tbsp. flaxseed meal + 3 tbsp. water)
- 1 small cauliflower, cut into florets
- 1 tsp. mixed spice
- 1/3 C. oats flour
- ½ tsp. mustard powder
- 2 tbsp. maple syrup
- 1 clove of garlic, minced
- 2 tbsp. soy sauce
- 1/3 C. plain flour
- 1/3 C. desiccated coconut

Directions:
1 Preparing the Ingredients.. In a mixing bowl, mix together oats, flour, and desiccated coconut. Season with salt and pepper to taste. Set aside. In another bowl, place the flax egg and add a pinch of salt to taste. Set aside. Season the cauliflower with mixed spice and mustard powder. Dredge the florets in the flax egg first then in the flour mixture. 2 Air Frying. Place inside the Instant Crisp Air Fryer, lock the air fryer lid and cook at 400°F or 15 minutes. Meanwhile, place the maple syrup, garlic, and soy sauce in a sauce pan and heat over medium flame. Bring to a boil and adjust the heat to low until the sauce thickens. After 15 minutes, take out the florets from the Instant Crisp Air Fryer and place them in the saucepan. Toss to coat the florets and place inside the Instant Crisp Air Fryer and cook for another 5 minutes.

Parsley Portobello Mushroom Pilaf

Ingredients: Servings: 4 Cooking Time: 10 Mins

- 2 C. Brown Rice, rinsed
- 4 C. Vegetable Broth
- 1 C. Portobello Mushrooms, thinly sliced
- 3 tsps Olive oil
- ¼ C. Romano Cheese, grated
- Salt to taste
- 2 sprigs Parsley, to garnish

Directions:
Heat the oil on Sear/Sauté on Medium, and stir-fry the mushrooms for 3 minutes until golden. Season with salt, and add rice and broth. Close the lid, secure the pressure valve,

and select Pressure mode on High pressure for 5 minutes. Press Start to start cooking. Once the timer has ended, do a quick pressure release and open the lid. Spread the cheese over and close the crisping lid. Select Bake, adjust to 375 F and the timer to 2 minutes. Press Start to start cooking. To serve, plate the pilaf and top with freshly chopped parsley.

Air Fried Acorn Squash

Ingredients: Servings: 4 Cooking Time: 20 Mins

1 acorn squash
3 tbsps. butter, melted
2 tsps. brown sugar
½ tsp. Kosher salt
Black pepper to taste
Optional toppings: melted butter, roasted nuts (chopped), pomegranate seeds

Directions:
Cleanse the squash and trim the ends. Cut in half and core to remove seeds. Cut into about half an inch thick. Combine brown sugar and melted butter in a bowl. Season with salt and pepper. Add in the acorn squash and toss to coat. Place the coated squash into the air fryer basket and attach the air fryer lid to the instant pot. Set to air fry at 375 degrees F for 15-20 minutes or until tender, flipping after 10 minutes of cooking. Once done, serve in a platter drizzled with melted butter, pomegranate seeds and chopped nuts. Taste for seasoning and adjust flavor if needed.

Cheesy Cabbage Wedges (air Fryer)

Ingredients: Servings: 4 Cooking Time: 20 Mins

4 tbsp. melted butter
1 head cabbage, cut into wedges
1 C. shredded Parmesan cheese
Salt and black pepper, to taste
½ C. shredded Mozzarella cheese

Directions:
Preheat the air fryer to 380°F (193°C). Brush the melted butter over the cut sides of cabbage wedges and sprinkle both sides with the Parmesan cheese. Season with salt and pepper to taste. Place the cabbage wedges in the air fryer basket and air fry for 20 minutes, flipping the cabbage halfway through, or until the cabbage wedges are lightly browned. Transfer the cabbage wedges to a plate and serve with the Mozzarella cheese sprinkled on top.

Crispy Chickpeas

Ingredients: Servings: 2 Cooking Time: 20 Mins

Chickpeas – 1(15 oz.) can, drained and rinsed
Olive oil – 1 tsp.
Dry ranch seasoning mix – 1 tbsp.

Directions:
Mix oil and chickpeas in a bowl. Spread the mixture in the air fryer basket and cook at 390F for 17 minutes. Shake once at the halfway mark. Remove and toss with seasoning. Serve.

Air Fryer Carrots

Ingredients: Servings: 4 Cooking Time: 20 Mins

Carrots – 1 lb. peeled
Grated parmesan cheese – ¼ cup
Salt and pepper to taste
Olive oil – 2 tbsps.
Garlic powder – ½ tsp.
Paprika – ½ tsp.
Fresh chopped parsley to taste

Directions:
In a bowl, place the carrots and toss them with oil, garlic powder, and paprika. Cook in the air fryer at 380F for 20 minutes. Shake the basket at the halfway mark. Top with parmesan cheese and parsley. Season with salt and pepper and serve.

Mediterranean Herbed Cabbage (pressure Cook)

Ingredients: Servings: 4 Cooking Time: 6 Mins

1 (1-pound / 454-g) head cabbage, cut into wedges
1 bell pepper, chopped
1 carrot, chopped
1 bay leaf
1 sprig thyme
1 sprig rosemary
1 C. roasted vegetable broth
½ tsp. cayenne pepper
2 tbsp. olive oil
Sea salt and ground black pepper, to taste

Directions:
Add all ingredients to the Instant Pot. Stir to combine. Secure the lid. Choose the Pressure Cook and set the cooking time for 6 minutes at High pressure. Once cooking is complete, perform a quick pressure release. Carefully open the lid. Discard the bay leaf, thyme, and rosemary. Divide them into bowls and serve warm.

Kale and Mushrooms

Ingredients: Servings: 4 Cooking Time: 10 Mins

1 lb. Brown mushrooms; sliced
1 lb. Kale, torn
14 oz. Coconut milk
2 tbsp. Olive oil
Salt and black pepper to taste.

Directions:
In a pan that fits your air fryer, mix the kale with the rest of the ingredients and toss Put the pan in the fryer, cook at 380°f for 15 minutes, divide between plates and serve

Parmesan Broccoli and Asparagus

Ingredients: Servings: 4 Cooking Time: 15 Mins

½ lb. Asparagus, trimmed
1 broccoli head, florets separated
Juice of 1 lime
3 tbsp. Parmesan, grated
2 tbsp. Olive oil
Salt and black pepper to taste.

Directions:
Take a bowl and mix the asparagus with the broccoli and all the other ingredients except the parmesan, toss, transfer to your air fryer's basket and cook at 400°f for 15 minutes Divide between plates, sprinkle the parmesan on top and serve.

Parmesan Zucchini & Eggplant

Ingredients: Servings: 6 Cooking Time: 35 Mins

1 eggplant, sliced
1 tbsp. olive oil
1 C. cherry tomatoes, halved
3 medium zucchinis, sliced
1/4 C. basil, chopped
1 tbsp. garlic, minced
3 oz parmesan cheese, grated
1/4 C. parsley, chopped
1/4 tsp. pepper
1/4 tsp. salt

Directions:
Line instant pot air fryer basket with parchment paper or foil. In a mixing bowl, add cherry tomatoes, eggplant, zucchini, olive oil, garlic, cheese, basil, pepper, and salt toss well. Transfer vegetable mixture into the air fryer basket and place basket in the pot. Seal the pot with air fryer basket and select bake mode and cook at 350 f for 35 minutes. Garnish with parsley and serve.

Baked Cheesy Eggplant with Marinara

Ingredients: Servings: 3 Cooking Time: 45 Mins

1 clove garlic, sliced
1 large eggplants
1 tbsp. olive oil
1 tbsp. olive oil
1/2 pinch salt, or as needed
1/4 C. and 2 tbsp. dry bread crumbs
1/4 C. and 2 tbsp. ricotta cheese
1/4 C. grated Parmesan cheese
1/4 C. grated Parmesan cheese
1/4 C. water, plus more as needed
1/4 tsp. red pepper flakes
1-1/2 C. prepared marinara sauce
1-1/2 tsp. olive oil
2 tbsp. shredded pepper jack cheese
salt and freshly ground black pepper to taste

Directions:
Preparing the Ingredients. Cut eggplant crosswise in 5 pieces. Peel and chop two pieces into ½-inch cubes. Lightly grease baking pan of Instant Crisp Air Fryer with 1 tbsp. olive oil for 5 minutes, heat oil at 390°F. Add half eggplant strips and cook for 2 minutes per side. Transfer to a plate. Add 1 ½ tsp. olive oil and add garlic. Cook for a minute. Add chopped eggplants. Season with pepper flakes and salt. Cook for 4 minutes. Lower heat to 330°F. and continue cooking eggplants until soft, around 8 minutes more. Stir in water and marinara sauce. Cook for 7 minutes until heated through. Stirring every now and then. Transfer to a bowl. In a bowl, whisk well pepper, salt, pepper jack cheese, Parmesan cheese, and ricotta. Evenly spread cheeses over eggplant strips and then fold in half. Lay folded eggplant in baking pan. Pour marinara sauce on top. In a small bowl whisk well olive oil, and bread crumbs. Sprinkle all over sauce. Air Frying. Lock the air fryer lid. Cook for 15 minutes at 390°F until tops are lightly browned. Serve and enjoy.

Wheat Berry Pilaf

Ingredients: Servings: 6 Cooking Time: 35 Mins

1 1/2 C. wheat berries, rinsed and drained
1/2 C. onion, minced
1 tsp. coriander seeds
2 tsp. cumin seeds
1 tbsp. olive oil
3 C. of water
1 1/2 tsp. turmeric
1 tbsp. garlic, minced
Salt

Directions:
Add oil into the inner pot of instant pot duo crisp and set pot on sauté mode. Add onion and cook until softened. Add turmeric, garlic, coriander, and cumin and sauté for 2 minutes. Add wheat berries and sauté for 2 minutes. Add water and stir everything well. Seal the pot with pressure cooking lid and cook on high for 30 minutes. Once done, allow to release pressure naturally. Remove lid. Stir well and serve.

Roasted Carrots

Ingredients: Servings: 4 Cooking Time: 30 Mins

Carrots – 2 pounds, quartered
Black pepper and salt to taste
Olive oil – 3 tbsps.
Chopped parsley – ¼ cup, fresh for garnish

Directions:
Combine everything in a bowl, except for the parsley. Mix well. Cook in the air fryer at 400F for 30 minutes. Shake the basket at the halfway mark. Serve with chopped parsley.

Roasted Asparagus

Ingredients: Servings: 4 Cooking Time: 10 Mins

1 lb. asparagus with ends trimmed and cut into pieces
1-2 tsps. olive oil
Salt and black pepper to taste

Directions:
Place the asparagus pieces in a shallow dish and coat them with olive oil. Season with salt and pepper. Make sure to properly coat the asparagus ends to prevent them from burning or drying out quickly. Place asparagus inside the air fryer basket and put inside the instant pot duo crisp. Choose the air fryer lift for cover, secure, and set to air frying at 380 degrees F for 7-10 minutes. Shake basket halfway through cooking to cook asparagus evenly. Taste for seasoning and tenderness. Adjust if needed. Serve warm.

Asian Cauliflower

Ingredients: Servings: 2 Cooking Time: 10 Mins

1/2 cauliflower head, cut into florets
1/2 tbsp. vinegar
2 garlic cloves, sliced
3/4 tbsp. tamari
1/4 C. onion, sliced
1 green onion, sliced
1/2 tbsp. hot sauce
1/4 tsp. coconut sugar

Directions:
Line instant pot multi-level air fryer basket with foil. Add cauliflower florets into the air fryer basket and place basket into the instant pot. Seal pot with air fryer lid and select air fry mode then set the temperature to 400 F and timer for 10 minutes. Stir halfway through. Transfer cauliflower into the mixing bowl. Add remaining ingredients and toss well. Serve and enjoy.

Spicy Tomato Chutney

Ingredients: Servings: 4 Cooking Time: 6 Mins

4 green tomatoes, chopped
1/2 tsp. mustard seeds
2 jalapeno pepper, chopped
1 tbsp. brown sugar
1/2 tsp. turmeric
1 tbsp. olive oil
1 tsp. salt

Directions:
Add oil into the inner pot of instant pot duo crisp and set pot on sauté mode. Once the oil is hot then add mustard seeds and let them pop. Add remaining ingredients and stir well. Seal the pot with pressure cooking lid and cook on high for 5 minutes. Once done, release pressure using a quick release. Remove lid. Mash tomatoes mixture using a potato masher until getting the desired consistency. Serve and enjoy.

Delicious Pigeon Pea

Ingredients: Servings: 4 Cooking Time: 7 Mins

1 C. split pigeon pea, rinsed and drained
1 tbsp. ginger, chopped
1 green chili, sliced
1/4 tsp. cumin seeds
1 tbsp. olive oil
2 C. spinach
1/2 tsp. garam masala
3 C. of water
1 large tomato, chopped
1 tbsp. garlic, chopped
Spices:
1/4 tsp. turmeric
1/2 tsp. chili powder
1 tsp. salt

Directions:
Add oil into the inner pot of instant pot duo crisp and set pot on sauté mode. Add cumin seeds, garlic, ginger, and green chili and sauté for 30 seconds. Add tomatoes and spices and sauté for 1 minute. Add lentils and water. Stir well. Seal the pot with pressure cooking lid and cook on high for 3 minutes. Once done, release pressure using a quick release. Remove lid. Set pot on sauté mode. Add spinach and garam masala and stir until spinach is wilted. Serve and enjoy.

Air Fryer Brussels Sprouts

Ingredients: Servings: 8 Cooking Time: 10 Mins

¼ tsp. salt
1 tbsp. balsamic vinegar
1 tbsp. olive oil
2 C. Brussels sprouts

Directions:
1 Preparing the Ingredients. Cut Brussels sprouts in half lengthwise. Toss with salt, vinegar, and olive oil till coated thoroughly. 2 Air Frying. Add coated sprouts to the Instant Crisp Air Fryer, close air fryer lid, set temperature to 400°F, and set time to 10 minutes. Shake after 5 minutes of cooking. Brussels sprouts are ready to devour when brown and crisp!

Garlic Rosemary Brussels Sprouts

Ingredients: Servings: 4 Cooking Time: 13 Mins

Brussels sprouts – 1 pound, halved
Olive oil - 3 tbsps.
Salt and pepper to taste
Panko breadcrumbs – ½ cup
Garlic – 2 cloves, chopped
Chopped fresh rosemary -1 ½ tsps.

Directions:
In a bowl, put pepper, salt, garlic, and oil and microwave for 30 seconds. Preheat the air fryer for 5 minutes at 350F. Mix the Brussels sprouts in the heated oil mixture. Cook in the air fryer for 8 minutes. Shake the basket after 5 minutes and then finish cooking. In a bowl combine breadcrumbs, remaining oil mixture and rosemary. When the cooking is over, open the air fryer and sprinkle the breadcrumb mixture over the sprouts. Close and cook for 5 minutes more. Serve.

Bell Pepper-corn Wrapped In Tortilla

Ingredients: Servings: 4 Cooking Time: 15 Mins

1 small red bell pepper, chopped
1 small yellow onion, diced
1 tbsp. water
2 cobs grilled corn kernels
4 large tortillas
4 pieces commercial vegan nuggets, chopped
mixed greens for garnish

Directions:
Preparing the Ingredients. Preheat the Instant Crisp Air Fryer to 400°F. In a skillet heated over medium heat, water sauté the vegan nuggets together with the onions, bell peppers, and corn kernels. Set aside. Place filling inside the corn tortillas. Air Frying. Lock the air fryer lid. Fold the tortillas and place inside the Instant Crisp Air Fryer and cook for 15 minutes until the tortilla wraps are crispy. Serve with mix greens on top.

Rosemary Potatoes

Ingredients: Servings: 2 Cooking Time: 15 Mins

Vegetable oil – 3 tbsps.
Yellow baby potatoes – 4, quartered
Dried rosemary minced – 2 tsps.
Minced garlic – 1 tbsp.
Ground black pepper – 1 tsp.
Chopped parsley – ¼ cup
Fresh lime juice – 1 tbsp.
Salt -1 tsp.

Directions:
In a bowl, add potatoes, garlic, rosemary, pepper, and salt. Mix well. Bake in the air fryer at 400F for 15 minutes. Flip the potatoes at the halfway mark. Then sprinkle with lemon juice and parsley and serve.

Jalapeño Cheese Balls

Ingredients: Servings: 12 Cooking Time: 8 Mins

4 oz. cream cheese
⅓ C. shredded mozzarella cheese
⅓ C. shredded Cheddar cheese
2 jalapeños, finely chopped
½ C. bread crumbs
2 eggs
½ C. all-purpose flour
Salt
Pepper
Cooking oil

Directions:

1 Preparing the Ingredients. In a medium bowl, combine the cream cheese, mozzarella, Cheddar, and jalapeños. Mix well. Form the cheese mixture into balls about an inch thick. Using a small ice cream scoop works well. Arrange the cheese balls on a sheet pan and place in the freezer for 15 minutes. This will help the cheese balls maintain their shape while frying. Spray the Instant Crisp Air Fryer basket with cooking oil. Place the bread crumbs in a small bowl. In another small bowl, beat the eggs. In a third small bowl, combine the flour with salt and pepper to taste, and mix well. Remove the cheese balls from the freezer. Dip the cheese balls in the flour, then the eggs, and then the bread crumbs. 2 Air Frying. Place the cheese balls in the Instant Crisp Air Fryer. Spray with cooking oil. Lock the air fryer lid. Cook for 8 minutes. Open the Instant Crisp Air Fryer and flip the cheese balls. I recommend flipping them instead of shaking so the balls maintain their form. Cook an additional 4 minutes. Cool before serving.

Air Fried Bell Peppers

Ingredients: Servings: 3 Cooking Time: 8 Mins

3 C. bell peppers, cut into chunks
1/4 tsp. garlic powder
1 tsp. olive oil
Pepper
Salt

Directions:

Add all ingredients into the mixing bowl and toss well. Spray instant pot multi-level air fryer basket with cooking spray. Transfer bell peppers into the air fryer basket and place basket into the instant pot. Seal pot with air fryer lid and select air fry mode then set the temperature to 360 F and timer for 8 minutes. Stir halfway through. Serve and enjoy.

Braised Red Cabbage with Apples

Ingredients: Servings: 4 Cooking Time: 13 Mins

4 thin bacon slices, chopped
1 small red onion, chopped
1 medium tart green apple, such as Granny Smith, peeled, cored, and chopped
1 tsp. dried thyme
¼ tsp. ground allspice
¼ tsp. ground mace
1 tbsp. packed dark brown sugar
1 tbsp. balsamic vinegar
1 medium red cabbage (about 2 pounds), cored and thinly sliced
½ C. chicken broth

Directions:

Preparing the Ingredients. Lock the air fryer lid. Fry the bacon in the Instant Crisp Air Fryer turned to the "Air Fry" function, until crisp, about 4 minutes. Add the onion to the pot; cook, often stirring, until soft, about 4 minutes. Add the apple, thyme, allspice, and mace. Cook about 1 minute, stirring all the while, until fragrant. Stir in the brown sugar and vinegar; keep stirring until bubbling, about 1 minute. Add the cabbage; toss well to mix evenly with the other ingredients. Drizzle the broth over the cabbage mixture. High pressure for 13 minutes. Lock the Pressure cooking Lid on the Instant Crisp Air Fryer and then cook for 13 minutes. To get 13-minutes cook time, press "Pressure" button, and use the Time Adjustment button to adjust the cook time to 13 minutes. Pressure Release. Use the quick-release method to return the pot to normal pressure. Unlock and open the pot. Close the Air Fryer Lid. Select BROIL, and set the time to 5 minutes. Select START to begin. Cook until top is browned. Serve.

Zucchini Fries

Ingredients: Servings: 4 Cooking Time: 12 Mins

Zucchini – 1, cut into medium sticks
Salt and black pepper to taste
Olive oil – 1 drizzle
Eggs – 2, whisked
Bread crumbs – 1 cup
Flour – ½ cup

Directions:

In a bowl, add flour and mix with salt and pepper. Put breadcrumbs in another bowl. In a third bowl, mix the egg with salt and pepper. Dredge zucchini fries in flour, then in eggs and in bread crumbs. Grease the air fryer with olive oil. Heat up at 400F. Add zucchini fries and cook them for 12 minutes. Serve.

Sage-butter Spaghetti Squash

Ingredients: Servings: 6 Cooking Time: 12 Mins

One 3- to 3½-pound spaghetti squash, halved lengthwise and seeded
2 tbsp. packed fresh sage leaves, minced
½ tsp. salt
6 tbsp. unsalted butter
½ tsp. ground black pepper
½ C. finely grated Parmesan cheese (about 1 ounce)

Directions:

Preparing the Ingredients. Put the squash cut side up in the cooker; add 1 C. water. High pressure for 12 minutes. Lock the lid on the Instant Crisp Air Fryer and then cook for 12 minutes. To get 12-minutes cook time, press "Pressure" button, and use the Time Adjustment button to adjust the cook time to 12 minutes. Pressure Release. Use the quick-release method to bring the pot's pressure back to normal. Finish the dish. Unlock and open the cooker. Transfer the squash halves to a cutting board; cool for 10 minutes. Discard the liquid in the cooker. Use a fork to scrape the spaghetti-like flesh off the skin and onto the cutting board; discard the skins. Melt the butter in the electric cooker turned to its browning function. Stir in the sage, salt, and pepper, then add all of the squash. Stir and toss over the heat until well combined and heated through about 2 minutes. Add the cheese, toss well. Close the Air Fryer Lid. Select BROIL, and set the time to 5 minutes. Select START to begin. Cook until top is browned. Serve.

Brussels Pancetta Pizza

Ingredients: Servings: 4-6 Cooking Time: 20 Mins

Brussels sprouts, trimmed and thinly sliced, to taste 1 (1 1/2-inch thick) medium-size pizza crust
9 slices pancetta
2 cloves garlic, minced
2 tsp. extra-virgin olive oil
1/2 tsp. fennel seeds

Directions:

Place Instant Pot Air Fryer Crisp over kitchen platform. Press "Sauté," select "Hi" setting and press "Start." In the inner pot, add 1 tbsp. oil and allow it to heat. Add the pancetta and stir-cook until it becomes softened for 4-5 minutes. Drain over paper towels. Add remaining oil and garlic and stir-cook until it becomes fragrant for 20-30 seconds. Mix in the sprouts and stir-cook until softened 5-10 minutes. Add the sprouts and garlic to a bowl; add the pancetta, cheese, and fennel seed. Toss well. Place Instant Pot Air Fryer Crisp over kitchen platform. Press Air Fry, set the temperature to 400°F and set the timer to 5 minutes to preheat. Press "Start" and allow it to preheat for 5 minutes. In the inner pot, place the Air Fryer basket. Line it with a parchment paper and arrange the pizza crust over. On top, add the prepared mixture. Close the Crisp Lid and press the "Bake" setting. Set temperature to 450°F and set the timer to 12-15 minutes. Press "Start." Cook until the crust becomes golden brown. Open the Crisp Lid after cooking time is over. Slice and serve warm.

Rice Bowl with Raisins and Almonds (pressure Cook)

Ingredients: Servings: 4 Cooking Time: 20 Mins

1 C. brown rice
1 C. water
1 C. coconut milk
½ C. coconut chips
½ C. maple syrup
¼ C. raisins
¼ C. almonds
A pinch of cinnamon powder
Salt, to taste

Directions:
Place the rice and water into the Instant Pot and give a stir. Secure the lid. Select the Pressure Cook and set the cooking time for 15 minutes at High Pressure. When the timer beeps, perform a quick pressure release. Carefully remove the lid. Stir in the coconut milk, coconut chips, maple syrup, raisins, almonds, cinnamon powder, and salt. Lock the lid. Select the Pressure Cook and set the cooking time for 5 minutes at High Pressure. Once cooking is complete, do a quick pressure release. Open the lid. Serve warm.

Cannellini Beans with Bacon (pressure Cook)

Ingredients: Servings: 4 Cooking Time: 14 Mins

3 bacon slices, chopped
2 (15-ounce / 425-g) cans cannel in beans, rinsed and drained
1 C. water
½ C. canned tomatoes
1 tbsp. ground mustard
1 tsp. chili powder
1 C. cooked white rice
¼ C. chopped mint

Directions:
Set the Instant Pot on the Sauté mode. Add the bacon to the pot and cook for 6 minutes, or until crispy and browned. Transfer the bacon to a plate with paper towels to soak up excess fat. Add the cannellini beans, water, tomatoes, mustard and chili powder to the pot. Place the bacon back in the pot. Lock the lid. Select the Pressure Cook and set the cooking time for 8 minutes at High Pressure. When the timer goes off, use a natural pressure release for 10 minutes, then release any remaining pressure. Carefully open the lid. Stir in the cooked white rice and serve garnished with the chopped mint.

Creamy and Cheese Broccoli Bake

Ingredients: Servings: 2 Cooking Time: 30 Mins

1-pound fresh broccoli, coarsely chopped
2 tbsp. all-purpose flour
1 tbsp. dry bread crumbs, or to taste
1/2 large onion, coarsely chopped
salt to taste
1/2 (14 ounce) can evaporated milk, divided
1/2 C. cubed sharp Cheddar cheese
1-1/2 tsp. butter, or to taste
1/4 C. water

Directions:
1 Preparing the Ingredients. Lightly grease baking pan of Instant Crisp Air Fryer with cooking spray. Mix in half of the milk and flour in pan and for 5 minutes, cook on 360°F. Halfway through cooking time, mix well. Add broccoli and remaining milk. Mix well and cook for another 5 minutes. Stir in cheese and mix well until melted. In a small bowl mix well, butter and bread crumbs. Sprinkle on top of broccoli. 2 Air Frying. Lock the air fryer lid. Cook for 20 minutes at 360°F until tops are lightly browned. Serve and enjoy.

Cheesy Black Beans (pressure Cook)

Ingredients: Servings: 2 Cooking Time: 15 Mins

1 large white onion, chopped
1 tsp. grated garlic
3 C. vegetable broth
1 C. dried black beans, soaked
1 tsp. olive oil
1 tsp. Mexican seasoning
Salt, to taste
½ C. Cotija cheese
¼ C. chopped cilantro

Directions:
Set the Instant Pot to the Sauté mode and heat the olive oil. Add the onion and garlic to the pot and sauté for 3 minutes, or until tender. Stir in the vegetable broth, black beans, Mexican seasoning and salt. Set the lid in place. Select the Pressure Cook and set the cooking time for 12 minutes at High Pressure. When the timer goes off, perform a quick pressure release. Carefully open the lid. Divide the beans between 2 plates and serve topped with the Cotija cheese and cilantro.

Broccoli Salad

Ingredients: Servings: 4 Cooking Time: 8 Mins

Broccoli – 1 head, florets separated
Peanut oil – 1 tbsp.
Garlic – 6 cloves, minced
Chinese rice wine vinegar – 1 tbsp.
Salt and black pepper to taste

Directions:
In a bowl, mix broccoli with half of the oil, salt, and pepper and toss. Cook in the air fryer at 350F for 8 minutes. Shake once. Transfer broccoli to a bowl. Add the rest of the peanut oil, rice vinegar, and garlic, and toss well. Serve.

Jeweled Quinoa-stuffed Red Peppers

Ingredients: Servings: 4 Cooking Time: 25 Mins

4 Red Bell Peppers
2 large Tomatoes, chopped
1 small Onion, chopped
2 cloves Garlic, minced
1 tbsp. Olive Oil
1 C. Quinoa, rinsed
2 C. Chicken Broth
1 small Zucchini, chopped
1 ½ C. Water
½ tsp. Smoked Paprika
½ C. chopped Mushrooms
Salt and Black Pepper to taste
1 C. grated Gouda Cheese

Directions:
Select Sear/Sauté mode on High. Once it is ready, add the olive oil to heat and then add the onion and garlic. Sauté for 3 minutes to soften, stirring occasionally. Include the tomatoes, cook for 3 minutes and then add the quinoa, zucchinis, and mushrooms. Season with paprika, salt, and black pepper and stir with a spoon. Cook for 5 to 7 minutes, then, turn the pot off. Use a knife to cut the bell peppers in halves (lengthwise) and remove their seeds and stems. Spoon the quinoa mixture into the bell peppers. Put the peppers in a greased baking dish and pour the broth over. Wipe the pot clean with some paper towels, and pour the water into it. After, fit the steamer rack at the bottom of the pot. Place the baking dish on top of the reversible rack, cover with aluminum foil, close the lid, secure the pressure valve, and select Pressure mode on High pressure for 15 minutes. Press Start. Once the timer has ended, do a quick pressure release and open the lid. Remove the aluminum foil and sprinkle with the gouda cheese. Close the crisping lid, select Roast mode and cook for 10 minutes on 375 F. Arrange the stuffed peppers on a serving platter and serve right away or as a side to a meat dish.

Spicy Sweet Potato Fries

Ingredients: Servings: 4 Cooking Time: 37 Mins

2 tbsp. sweet potato fry seasoning mix
2 tbsp. olive oil
2 sweet potatoes
Seasoning Mix:
2 tbsp. salt
1 tbsp. cayenne pepper
1 tbsp. dried oregano
1 tbsp. fennel
2 tbsp. coriander

Directions:
Preparing the Ingredients. Slice both ends off sweet potatoes and peel. Slice lengthwise in half and again crosswise to make four pieces from each potato. Slice each potato piece into 2-3 slices, then slice into fries. Grind together all of seasoning mix ingredients and mix in the salt. Ensure the Instant Crisp Air Fryer is preheated to 350 degrees. Toss potato pieces in olive oil, sprinkling with seasoning mix and tossing well to coat thoroughly. Air Frying. Add fries to Instant Crisp Air Fryer basket. Lock the air fryer lid. Set temperature to 350°F, and set time to 27 minutes. Select START to begin. Take out the basket and turn fries. Turn off Instant Crisp Air Fryer and let cook 10-12 minutes till fries are golden.

Broccoli, Spinach, and Avocado Mash (pressure Cook)

Ingredients: Servings: 4 Cooking Time: 3 Mins

1 medium broccoli, cut into florets
2 C. spinach
1 C. vegetable broth
2 avocados, halved, pitted, and peeled
2 tbsp. chopped parsley
2 tbsp. butter
Salt and black pepper, to taste
3 tbsp. Greek yogurt
2 tbsp. toasted pine nuts, for topping

Directions:
Add the broccoli, spinach, and broth to the Instant Pot. Stir to mix well. Seal the lid. Select the Pressure Cook and set the cooking time for 3 minutes at High Pressure. Once cooking is complete, do a quick pressure release. Carefully open the lid. Stir in the avocado, parsley, butter, salt, pepper, and Greek yogurt. Pour the mixture in a food processor and pulse until smooth. Spoon into serving bowls and top with pine nuts. Serve immediately.

Acorn Squash

Ingredients: Servings: 4 Cooking Time: 20 Mins

Acorn squash – 1, cut into half an inch thick cubes
Butter – 3 tbsps. melted
Brown sugar – 2 tsps.
Kosher salt and black pepper to taste
Chopped nuts and melted butter for topping

Directions:
In a bowl, combine melted butter, brown sugar, season with salt and pepper. Add in the acorn squash and mix. Cook in the air fryer at 375F for 15 to 20 minutes. Flip after 10 minutes of cooking. Serve with toppings.

Onion-artichoke Corn Risotto (pressure Cook)

Ingredients: Servings: 4 Cooking Time: 13 Mins

2 tbsp. olive oil
2 large white onions, chopped
1 medium zucchini, chopped
4 garlic cloves, minced
Salt and black pepper, to taste
1 C. Arborio rice
½ C. white wine
2½ C. chicken stock
2 C. corn kernels
1 (6-ounce / 170-g) can artichokes, drained and chopped
1 C. grated Parmesan cheese
3 tbsp. lemon juice
1 tbsp. lemon zest
¼ C. chopped basil, plus more for garnish

Directions:
Set the Instant Pot on the Sauté function and heat the olive oil. Add the onions, zucchini and garlic to the pot and sauté for 5 minutes, or until tender. Season with salt and pepper. Stir in the rice and cook for 2 minutes, or until translucent. Pour in the white wine and keep cooking until it has a thick consistency and reduces about one-third. Stir in the chicken stock, corn, salt and pepper. Lock the lid. Select the Pressure Cook and set the cooking time for 6 minutes at High Pressure. When the timer goes off, use a natural pressure release for 15 minutes, then release any remaining pressure. Carefully open the lid. Add the artichokes, cheese, lemon juice and zest and whisk until risotto is sticky. Stir in the chopped basil and transfer the risotto into bowls. Serve garnished with the basil.

Air Fryer Crispy Broccoli

Ingredients: Servings: 4 Cooking Time: 15 Mins

2 tbsps. cooking oil
1 lb. broccoli, cut into bite-sized pieces
½ tsp. garlic powder
Salt and pepper to taste
2 fresh lemon wedges

Directions:
Add broccoli to a large bowl and drizzle evenly with olive oil. Season broccoli with garlic powder, salt and pepper. Put in the instant pot duo crisp air fryer basket and cover with the air fryer lid. Air Fry at 380 degrees F for 12-15 minutes, flipping and shaking 3 times through cooking and cook until crispy. Serve with lemon wedges.

Crispy and Healthy Avocado Fingers

Ingredients: Servings: 4 Cooking Time: 10 Mins

½ C. panko breadcrumbs
1 pitted Haas avocado, peeled and sliced
½ tsp. salt
liquid from 1 can white beans or aquafaba

Directions:
1 Preparing the Ingredients. Preheat the Instant Crisp Air Fryer at 350°F. In a shallow bowl, toss the breadcrumbs and salt until well combined. Dredge the avocado slices first with the aquafaba then in the breadcrumb mixture. Place the avocado slices in a single layer inside the Instant Crisp Air Fryer basket. 2 Air Frying. Lock the air fryer lid. Cook for 10 minutes and shake halfway through the cooking time.

Eggplant and Zucchini Mix

Ingredients: Servings: 4 Cooking Time: 8 Mins

Zucchinis – 3, roughly cubed
Lemon juice - 2 tbsps.
Salt and black pepper to taste
Eggplant – 1, cubed
Thyme – 1 tsp. dried
Oregano – 1 tsp. dried
Olive oil – 3 tbsps.

Directions:
Put eggplant in a dish. Add olive oil, oregano, thyme, salt, pepper, lemon juice, and zucchinis. Toss to mix. Place the dish in the air fryer and at 360F for 8 minutes. Serve.

Cinnamon Butternut Squash Fries

Ingredients: Servings: 8 Cooking Time: 10 Mins

1 pinch of salt
1 tbsp. powdered unprocessed sugar
½ tsp. nutmeg
2 tsp. cinnamon
1 tbsp. coconut oil
10 oz. pre-cut butternut squash fries

Directions:
1 Preparing the Ingredients. In a plastic bag, pour in all ingredients. Coat fries with other components till coated and sugar is dissolved. 2 Air Frying. Spread coated fries into a single layer in the Instant Crisp Air Fryer. Lock the air fryer lid. Set temperature to 390°F, and set time to 10 minutes. Cook until crispy.

Cheddar, Squash, and Zucchini Casserole

Ingredients: Servings: 4 Cooking Time: 30 Mins

1 egg
5 saltine crackers, or as needed, crushed
2 tbsp. bread crumbs
1/2-pound yellow squash, sliced
1/2-pound zucchini, sliced
1/2 C. shredded Cheddar cheese
1-1/2 tsp. white sugar
1/2 tsp. salt
1/4 onion, diced
1/4 C. biscuit baking mix
1/4 C. butter

Directions:
1 Preparing the Ingredients. Lightly grease baking pan of Instant Crisp Air Fryer with cooking spray. Add onion, zucchini, and yellow squash. Cover pan with foil and for 15 minutes, cook on 360° F or until tender. Stir in salt, sugar, egg, butter, baking mix, and cheddar cheese. Mix well. Fold in crushed crackers. Top with bread crumbs. 2 Air Frying Lock the air fryer lid. Cook for 15 minutes at 390° F until tops are lightly browned. Serve and enjoy.

Scalloped Potatoes (air Fryer)

Ingredients: Servings: 4 Cooking Time: 20 Mins

2 C. sliced frozen potatoes, thawed
3 cloves garlic, minced
Pinch salt
Freshly ground black pepper, to taste
¾ C. heavy cream

Directions:
Preheat the air fryer to 380°F (193°C). Toss the potatoes with the garlic, salt, and black pepper in a baking pan until evenly coated. Pour the heavy cream over the top. Place the baking pan in the air fryer basket and bake for 15 minutes, or until the potatoes are tender and top is golden brown. Check for doneness and bake for another 5 minutes as needed. Serve hot.

Parmesan Breaded Zucchini Chips

Ingredients: Servings: 5 Cooking Time: 20 Mins

For the zucchini chips:
2 medium zucchini
2 eggs
⅓ C. bread crumbs
⅓ C. grated Parmesan cheese
Salt
Pepper
Cooking oil

For the lemon aioli:
½ C. mayonnaise
½ tbsp. olive oil
Juice of ½ lemon
1 tsp. minced garlic
Salt
Pepper

Directions:
1 Preparing the Ingredients. To make the zucchini chips: Slice the zucchini into thin chips (about ⅛ inch thick) using a knife or mandoline. In a small bowl, beat the eggs. In another small bowl, combine the bread crumbs, Parmesan cheese, and salt and pepper to taste. Spray the Instant Crisp basket with cooking oil. Dip the zucchini slices one at a time in the eggs and then the bread crumb mixture. You can also sprinkle the bread crumbs onto the zucchini slices with a spoon. Place the zucchini chips in the Instant Crisp Air Fryer basket, but do not stack. 2 Air Frying. Lock the air fryer lid. Cook in batches.

Spray the chips with cooking oil from a distance (otherwise, the breading may fly off). Cook for 10 minutes. Remove the cooked zucchini chips from the Instant Crisp Air Fryer, then repeat step 5 with the remaining zucchini. To make the lemon aioli: While the zucchini is cooking, combine the mayonnaise, olive oil, lemon juice, and garlic in a small bowl, adding salt and pepper to taste. Mix well until fully combined. Cool the zucchini and serve alongside the aioli.

Marinated Tofu

Ingredients: Servings: 4 Cooking Time: 25 Mins

2 tbsp. low-sodium soy sauce
12 oz. Extra-firm tofu, drained and cubed into 1-inch size
2 tbsp. fish sauce
1 tsp. olive oil
1 tsp. butter, melted

Directions:
In a large bowl, add the soy sauce, fish sauce and oil and mix until well combined. Add the tofu cubes and toss to coat well. Set aside to marinate for about 30 minutes, tossing occasionally. Press "power button" of air fry oven and turn the dial to select the "air fry" mode. Press the time button and again turn the dial to set the cooking time to 25 minutes. Now push the temp button and rotate the dial to set the temperature at 355 degrees f. Press "start/pause" button to start. When the unit beeps to show that it is preheated, open the lid. Arrange the tofu cubes in greased "air fry basket" and insert in the oven. Flip the tofu after every 10 minutes during the cooking. Serve hot.

Parmesan Mixed Veggies

Ingredients: Servings: 5 Cooking Time: 18 Mins

1 tbsp. olive oil
1 tbsp. garlic, minced
1 C. cauliflower florets
1 C. broccoli florets
1 C. zucchini, sliced
½ C. yellow squash, sliced
½ C. fresh mushrooms, sliced
1 small onion, sliced
¼ C. balsamic vinegar
1 tsp. red pepper flakes
Salt and ground black pepper, as required
¼ C. parmesan cheese, grated

Directions:
In a large bowl, add all the ingredients except cheese and toss to coat well. Press "power button" of air fry oven and turn the dial to select the "air fry" mode. Press the time button and again turn the dial to set the cooking time to 18 minutes. Now push the temp button and rotate the dial to set the temperature at 400 degrees f. Press "start/pause" button to start. When the unit beeps to show that it is preheated, open the lid. Arrange the vegetables in greased "air fry basket" and insert in the oven. After 8 minutes of cooking, flip the vegetables. After 16 minutes of cooking, sprinkle the vegetables with cheese evenly. Serve hot.

Tofu with Capers

Ingredients: Servings: 4 Cooking Time: 20 Mins

For marinade:
¼ C. fresh lemon juice
2 tbsp. fresh parsley
1 garlic clove, peeled
Salt and ground black pepper, as required
For tofu:
1 (14-oz. block extra-firm tofu, pressed and cut into 8 rectangular cutlets
½ C. mayonnaise
1 C. panko breadcrumbs
For sauce:
1 C. vegetable broth
¼ C. lemon juice
1 garlic clove, peeled
2 tbsp. fresh parsley
2 tsp. cornstarch
Salt and ground black pepper, as required
2 tbsp. capers

Directions:
For marinade: in a food processor, add all the ingredients and pulse until smooth. In a bowl, mix together the marinade and tofu. Set aside for about 15-30 minutes. In 2 shallow bowls, place the mayonnaise and panko breadcrumbs respectively. Coat the tofu pieces with mayonnaise and then, roll into the panko. Press "power button" of air fry oven and turn the dial to select the "air fry" mode. Press the time button and again turn the dial to set the cooking time to 20 minutes. Now push the temp button and rotate the dial to set the temperature at 375 degrees f. Press "start/pause" button to start. When the unit beeps to show that it is preheated, open the lid. Arrange the tofu cubes in greased "air fry basket" and insert in the oven. Flip the tofu cubes once halfway through. Meanwhile, for the sauce: add broth, lemon juice, garlic, parsley, cornstarch, salt and black pepper in a food processor and pulse until smooth. Transfer the sauce into a small pan and stir in the capers. Place the pan over medium heat and bring to a boil. Reduce the heat to low and simmer for about 5-7 minutes, stirring continuously. Transfer the tofu cubes onto serving plates. Top with the sauce and serve.

Vegetable Basmati Rice (pressure Cook)

Ingredients: Servings: 6 To 8 Cooking Time: 9 To 10 Mins

3 tbsp. olive oil
3 cloves garlic, minced
1 large onion, finely chopped
3 tbsp. chopped cilantro stalks
1 C. garden peas, frozen
1 C. sweet corn, frozen
2 C. basmati rice, rinsed
1 tsp. turmeric powder
¼ tsp. salt
3 C. chicken stock
2 tbsp. butter (optional)

Directions:
Press the Sauté button on the Instant Pot and heat the olive oil. Add the garlic, onion, and cilantro and sauté for 5 to 6 minutes, stirring occasionally, or until the garlic is fragrant. Stir in the peas, sweet corn, and rice. Scatter with the turmeric and salt. Pour in the chicken stock and stir to combine. Lock the lid. Select the Pressure Cook and set the cooking time for 4 minutes at High Pressure. Once cooking is complete, do a quick pressure release. Carefully open the lid. You can add the butter, if desired. Serve warm.

Air-fried Avocado

Ingredients: Servings: 2 Cooking Time: 10 Mins

½ C. all-purpose
2 large eggs

flour	1½ tsps. black pepper
2 avocados	¼ tsp. Kosher salt
2 tbsps. canola mayonnaise	½ C. Panko bread crumbs
1 tbsp. apple cider vinegar	¼ C. no-salt-added ketchup
1 tbsp. Sriracha chili sauce	1 tbsp. water
	Cooking spray

Directions:

Cut avocados into 4 wedges each. Prepare 3 shallow dishes. In the first shallow dish, combine avocado wedges with flour and pepper. In another dish, lightly beat eggs. Place bread crumbs in the third dish. First, dredge avocado wedges in the flour mixture, one after the other. After coating with flour, shake lightly to remove excess flour and dip the avocado to the egg mixture, likewise shaking lightly to drip off excess liquid. Finally, dip each wedge to the bread crumbs coating them evenly on all sides and spray with cooking oil. Arrange avocado wedges in the instant pot duo air fryer basket, place inside the pot, and cover with the air fryer lid. Set to air fry at 400 degrees F until wedges turn golden brown, turning them over halfway through cooking. Remove avocado wedges from the fryer and sprinkle them with salt. Meanwhile, while waiting for the avocado wedges to get cooked, mix mayonnaise, ketchup, apple cider vinegar, water and Sriracha sauce in a small bowl. Serve the prepared sauce with the avocado wedges while still warm.

Air Fried Ratatouille

Ingredients: Servings: 6 Cooking Time: 15 Mins

1 eggplant, diced	3 garlic cloves, chopped
2 bell peppers, diced	1 onion, diced
1 tbsp. vinegar	3 tomatoes, diced
1 1/2 tbsp. olive oil	Pepper
2 tbsp. herb de Provence	Salt

Directions:

Line instant pot multi-level air fryer basket with foil. Add all ingredients into the bowl and toss well and transfer into the air fryer basket and place basket into the instant pot. Seal pot with air fryer lid and select air fry mode then set the temperature to 400 F and timer for 15 minutes. Stir halfway through. Serve and enjoy.

Air Fried Cauliflower Rice

Ingredients: Servings: 2 Cooking Time: 15 Mins

2 C. cauliflower florets	½ tsp. smoked paprika
3 cloves of garlic	1 tbsp. peanut oil

Directions:

Smash garlic using the blade of a knife. Place all ingredients in a mixing bowl and mix to coat cauliflower florets with the seasoning. Line the air fryer basket with parchment paper and place coated florets in it. Insert the basket inside the instant pot duo crisp and attach the Air Fryer Lid. Air fry for 15 minutes at 400 degrees F, shaking the air fryer basket every 5 minutes. If you want it crispier, cook for an additional 5 minutes. Serve and enjoy!

Air Fried Mushrooms

Ingredients: Servings: 2 Cooking Time: 8 Mins

12 button mushrooms, cleaned	1/4 tsp. Pepper
1 tsp. olive oil	1/4 tsp. garlic salt

Directions:

Add all ingredients into the bowl and toss well. Spray instant pot multi-level air fryer basket with cooking spray. Transfer mushrooms into the air fryer basket and place basket into the instant pot. Seal pot with air fryer lid and select air fry mode then set the temperature to 380 F and timer for 8 minutes. Stir halfway through. Serve and enjoy.

Collard Greens Mix

Ingredients: Servings: 4 Cooking Time: 10 Mins

Collard greens – 1 bunch, trimmed	Garlic – 3 cloves, minced
Olive oil – 2 tbsps.	Salt and black pepper to taste
Tomato paste – 2 tbsps.	Balsamic vinegar – 1 tbsp.
Yellow onion – 1, chopped	Sugar – 1 tsp.

Directions:

In a bowl, mix tomato puree, onion, vinegar, garlic, and oil. Whisk. Add sugar, salt, pepper, and collard greens. Mix. Place the bowl in the air fryer and cook at 320F for 10 minutes. Serve.

Teriyaki Cauliflower (air Fryer)

Ingredients: Servings: 4 Cooking Time: 14 Mins

½ C. soy sauce	1 tsp. cornstarch
⅓ C. water	½ tsp. chili powder
1 tbsp. brown sugar	1 big cauliflower head, cut into florets
1 tsp. sesame oil	
2 cloves garlic, chopped	

Directions:

Preheat the air fryer to 340°F (171°C). Make the teriyaki sauce: In a small bowl, whisk together the soy sauce, water, brown sugar, sesame oil, cornstarch, garlic, and chili powder until well combined. Place the cauliflower florets in a large bowl and drizzle the top with the prepared teriyaki sauce and toss to coat well. Put the cauliflower florets in the air fryer basket and air fry for 14 minutes, shaking the basket halfway through, or until the cauliflower is crisp-tender. Let the cauliflower cool for 5 minutes before serving.

Balsamic Artichokes

Ingredients: Servings: 4 Cooking Time: 7 Mins

Big artichokes – 4, trimmed	Balsamic vinegar – 2 tsps.
Salt and black pepper to taste	Oregano – 1 tsp. dried
Lemon juice – 2 tbsps.	Garlic – 2 cloves, minced
Extra-virgin olive oil – ¼ cup	

Directions:
Season artichokes with salt and pepper. Rub with half of the lemon juice and half of the oil. Cook in the air fryer at 360F for 7 minutes. Meanwhile, in a bowl, mix the remaining oil, and lemon juice with vinegar, salt, pepper, garlic, and oregano. Mix well. Arrange artichokes on a platter. Drizzle the balsamic vinaigrette over them and serve.

Honey-glazed Carrots

Ingredients: Servings: 6 Cooking Time: 35 Mins

Carrots – 2 pounds, peeled and cut lengthwise
Honey – 2 tbsps.
Butter – ¼ cup
Garlic powder – ½ tsp.
Rosemary – ½ tsp. dried
Salt and pepper to taste
Fresh thyme – 4 tbsps. chopped

Directions:
Melt butter in a saucepan. Add garlic powder, rosemary, honey, pepper, and salt and mix well. Remove and set aside. Add the carrots and mix. Preheat the air fryer at 400F. Line the air fryer basket with a baking sheet and cook the carrots at 400F for 35 minutes. Garnish and serve.

Squash and Carrot Curry with Tofu (pressure Cook)

Ingredients: Servings: 4 Cooking Time: 12 Mins

1 large onion, sliced
4 cubes (about 2⅝ oz. / 74 g in total) mild Japanese curry sauce mix
1 lb. (454 g) winter squash, peeled and cut into 1-inch chunks
1 tbsp. canola oil
1½ C. water
2 large carrots, peeled and cut into 1-inch-thick slices
1 lb. (454 g) extra-firm tofu, cut into 1-inch cubes

Directions:
Select the Sauté mode of the Instant Pot. Heat the canola oil until shimmering. Add the onions and sauté for 4 minutes or until translucent. Add the curry mix and water in the pot. Break up the curry cubes with a wooden spoon. Add the squash and carrots and stir to combine. Arrange the tofu cubes on top. Lock the lid. Select the Manual function, and set the cooking time for 8 minutes at High Pressure. When the cooking time is up, quick release the pressure. Carefully open the lid. Stir gently to combine the tofu and other ingredients. Serve immediately.

Buttered Carrot-zucchini with Mayo

Ingredients: Servings: 4 Cooking Time: 25 Mins

1 tbsp. grated onion
2 tbsp. butter, melted
1/2-pound carrots, sliced
1-1/2 zucchinis, sliced
1/4 C. water
1/4 C. mayonnaise
1/4 tsp. prepared horseradish
1/4 tsp. salt
1/4 tsp. ground black pepper
1/4 C. Italian bread crumbs

Directions:
1 Preparing the Ingredients. Lightly grease baking pan of Instant Crisp Air Fryer with cooking spray. Add carrots. For 8 minutes, cook on 360°F. Add zucchini and continue cooking for another 5 minutes. Meanwhile, in a bowl whisk well pepper, salt, horseradish, onion, mayonnaise, and water. Pour into pan of veggies. Toss well to coat. In a small bowl mix melted butter and bread crumbs. Sprinkle over veggies. 2 Air Frying. Lock the air fryer lid. Cook for 10 minutes at 390°F, until tops are lightly browned. Serve and enjoy.

Celeriac Potato Gratin

Ingredients: Servings: 6 Cooking Time: 63 Mins

2 C. cream
1 tsp. caraway seeds, toasted
1 garlic clove, crushed
1 tsp. fennel seeds, toasted
2 bay leaves
1/4 tsp. ground cloves
Zest of 1/2 a lemon
2 tsp. melted butter
1kg potatoes, peeled
1 C. celeriac, peeled and minced
6 slices prosciutto, torn
3/4 C. fresh ricotta
¼ C. fontina cheese, grated

Directions:
Add cream, garlic, caraway seeds, cloves, bay leaves, fennel, zest, and cloves to a saucepan. Stir cook this mixture for 3 minutes then remove from the heat. Thinly slices potato by passing through the mandolin and spread the potatoes in the insert of Instant Pot Duo. Top the potato with celeriac, prepared white sauce, prosciutto, and ricotta. Put on the Air Fryer lid and seal it. Hit the "Bake Button" and select 60 minutes of cooking time, then press "Start." Once the Instant Pot Duo beeps, remove its lid. Serve.

Roasted Veggie Casserole

Ingredients: Servings: 6 Cooking Time: 50 Mins

½ head cauliflower, cut into chunks
1 sweet potato, peeled and cubed
2 red bell peppers, cubed
1 yellow onion, sliced
3 tbsp. olive oil
1 tsp. ground cumin
Freshly ground black pepper
Salt
2 ¼ C. red salsa
½ C. chopped fresh cilantro
9 corn tortillas cut in half
1 can (15 oz.) black beans, drained
2 big handfuls (about 2 oz.) baby spinach leaves
2 C. Monterey Jack cheese, shredded

Directions:
Toss the vegetables with olive oil, salt, black pepper, and cumin in a large bowl. Add these vegetables to the Air Fryer Basket and set it inside the Instant Pot Duo. Put on the Air Fryer lid and seal it. Hit the "Bake Button" and select 30 minutes of cooking time, then press "Start." Once the Instant Pot Duo beeps, remove its lid. Transfer the veggies to a baking pan and top it with salsa, tortilla, beans, spinach, and cheese. Place this pan in the Instant Pot Duo. Put on the Air Fryer lid and seal it. Hit the "Bake Button" and select 20 minutes of cooking time, then press "Start." Once the Instant Pot Duo beeps, remove its lid. Serve.

Healthy Quinoa Black Bean Chili

Ingredients: Servings: 6 Cooking Time: 12 Mins

1/2 C. quinoa, rinsed and drained
14 oz can black beans, rinsed and drained
14 oz can tomato, diced
2 tbsp. tomato paste
4 C. vegetable broth
2 celery stalks, diced
1 tsp. garlic, minced
1 onion, chopped
1 tsp. chili powder
1 tsp. ground coriander
2 tsp. ground cumin
2 tsp. paprika
3 sweet potatoes, peeled and diced
1 bell pepper, diced
1 tsp. salt

Directions:
Add all ingredients into the inner pot of instant pot duo crisp and stir well. Seal the pot with pressure cooking lid and cook on high for 12 minutes. Once done, release pressure using a quick release. Remove lid. Stir and serve.

Vegetable Pasta (pressure Cook)

Ingredients: Servings: 4 To 6 Cooking Time: 7 Mins

2 C. dried pasta
1 C. water
½ jar spaghetti sauce
½ can chickpeas, rinsed and drained
½ can black olives, rinsed and drained
½ C. frozen lima beans
½ C. frozen spinach
½ squash, shredded
½ zucchini, sliced
½ tbsp. Italian seasoning
½ tsp. cumin
½ tsp. garlic powder

Directions:
Add all the ingredients to the Instant Pot and stir to combine. Press the Pressure Cook on the Instant Pot and set the cooking time for 7 minutes at High Pressure. Once cooking is complete, perform a natural pressure release for 10 minutes and then release any remaining pressure. Carefully open the lid. Transfer to a serving dish and serve immediately.

Crispy Tofu Sticks (air Fryer)

Ingredients: Servings: 4 Cooking Time: 14 Mins

2 tbsp. olive oil, divided
½ C. flour
½ C. crushed cornflakes
Salt and black pepper, to taste
14 oz. (397 g) firm tofu, cut into ½-inch-thick strips

Directions:
Preheat the air fryer to 360°F (182°C). Grease the air fryer basket with 1 tbsp. of olive oil. Combine the flour, cornflakes, salt, and pepper on a plate. Dredge the tofu strips in the flour mixture until they are completely coated. Transfer the tofu strips to the greased air fryer basket. Brush the remaining 1 tbsp. of olive oil over the top of tofu strips. Air fry for 14 minutes until crispy, flipping the tofu strips halfway through. Serve warm.

Veggie Quinoa

Ingredients: Servings: 4 Cooking Time: 7 Mins

1 1/2 C. quinoa, rinsed and drained
1 carrot, chopped
1 C. green beans, chopped
1 potato, cubed
1 tomato, chopped
1 small onion, chopped
1 garlic clove, minced
1/4 C. cilantro, chopped
2 tsp. ginger paste
1 1/2 C. water
1/4 C. coconut milk
1 tsp. garam masala
1/2 tsp. chili powder
1/2 tsp. black pepper
1/4 tsp. turmeric
1 bay leaf
4 cloves
1 tsp. cumin seeds
2-star anise
2 tbsp. olive oil
Salt

Directions:
Add oil into the inner pot of instant pot duo crisp and set pot on sauté mode. Add cumin seeds, cloves, and star anise and sauté for 30 seconds. Add ginger and garlic and sauté for 1 minute. Add tomatoes, onions, and dry spices and sauté for 1-2 minutes. Add all the vegetables, salt, and coconut milk, water, and quinoa. Stir well. Seal the pot with pressure cooking lid and cook on high for 4 minutes. Once done, allow to release pressure naturally for 10 minutes then release remaining pressure using a quick release. Remove lid. Serve and enjoy.

Pumpkin Lasagna

Ingredients: Servings: 6 Cooking Time: 60 Mins

28 oz. pumpkin, cut into slices
1 bunch sage, chopped
1/2 C. ghee, melted
1 leek, thinly sliced
3.5 oz. kale and cavolo Nero leaves shredded
4 garlic cloves, finely grated
270g semi-dried tomatoes, drained, chopped
17 oz. quark
2 eggs, lightly beaten

Directions:
Mix pumpkin slices with sage leaves, 2 tsp. salt, 2 tbsp. ghee in a bowl. Toss leek separately with 2 tbsp. ghee, garlic, and ½ tsp. salt in another bowl. Mix kale with 1 tsp. salt, tomato, and cavolo Nero in a bowl. Now beat eggs with quark and sage in a bowl. Take a baking pan that can fit into the Instant Pot Duo. Add 1/3 of the leek mixture at the base of the baking pan. Top this mixture with a layer of pumpkin slices. Add 1/3 of quark mixture on top then add 1/3 of kale mixture over it. Top it with pumpkin slices and continue repeating the layer while ending at the pumpkin slice layer on top. Place the baking pan in the Instant Pot duo. Put on the Air Fryer lid and seal it. Hit the "Bake Button" and select 60 minutes of cooking time, then press "Start." Once the Instant Pot Duo beeps, remove its lid. Serve.

Crispy Brussels Sprouts

Ingredients: Servings: 2 Cooking Time: 16 Mins

2 tbsps. Parmesan, freshly grated
½ lb. Brussels
1 tsp. garlic powder
Caesar dressing for dipping

sprouts, thinly sliced
1 tbsp. extra-virgin olive oil
Freshly ground black pepper to taste
Kosher salt to taste

Directions:
Add oil, Brussels sprouts, garlic powder and Parmesan in a large mixing bowl. Toss to combine thoroughly. Season with salt and pepper. Put the coated sprouts in the air fryer basket. Insert trivet into your instant pot and lay the air fryer basket on top. Attach the air fryer lid and cook at 350 degrees F for 8 minutes. Toss and cook for another 8 minutes until sprouts are crisp and golden brown. Garnish with Parmesan. You can serve with Caesar salad for a dip.

Tofu Italian Style

Ingredients: Servings: 2 Cooking Time: 10 Mins

Tofu – 8 ounces, extra-firm, drained, sliced lengthwise and excess water removed
Broth – 1 tbsp.
Soy sauce – 1 tbsp.
Basil – ½ tsp. dried
Oregano – ½ tsp. dried
Onion powder – ½ tsp.
Garlic powder – ½ tsp.
Black pepper and salt to taste

Directions:
Slice the tofu into cubes and put in a Ziplock bag. Mix all the ingredients in a bowl. Add this mixture to the Ziplock bag and mix well. Preheat the air fryer at 400F for 5 minutes. Add the seasoned tofu in the air fryer and cook at 350F for 6 minutes. Open the air fryer after 4 minutes and shake the basket. Finish cooking. Serve.

Roasted Broccoli

Ingredients: Servings: 4 Cooking Time: 8 Mins

1 lb broccoli florets
1 tbsp. olive oil
Pepper
Salt

Directions:
Add broccoli, oil, pepper, and salt into the mixing bowl and toss well. Spray instant pot multi-level air fryer basket with cooking spray. Add broccoli into the air fryer basket and place basket into the instant pot. Seal pot with air fryer lid and select air fry mode then set the temperature to 350 F and timer for 8 minutes. Stir broccoli halfway through. Serve and enjoy.

Air Fryer Veggies with Halloumi

Ingredients: Servings: 2 Cooking Time: 14 Mins

2 zucchinis, cut into even chunks
1 large eggplant, peeled, cut into chunks
6 oz. (170 g) halloumi cheese, cubed
1 large carrot, cut into chunks
2 tsp. olive oil
Salt and black pepper, to taste
1 tsp. dried mixed herbs

Directions:
Preheat the air fryer to 340°F (171°C). Combine the zucchinis, eggplant, carrot, cheese, olive oil, salt, and pepper in a large bowl and toss to coat well. Spread the mixture evenly in the air fryer basket and air fry for 14 minutes until crispy and golden, shaking the basket once during cooking. Serve topped with mixed herbs.

Flavorful Mushroom Rice

Ingredients: Servings: 4 Cooking Time: 10 Mins

2 C. rice, soak for 30 minutes and drained
1/2-inch cinnamon stick
2 tbsp. vegetable oil
1/2 tsp. caraway seed
15 oz mushrooms, sliced
2 tbsp. cashews
1/4 C. coconut milk
4 cloves
2 C. of water
1/2 tsp. garam masala
1 tsp. chili powder
1/2 tsp. turmeric
4 green cardamom
2-star anise
1 bay leaf
3 garlic cloves
1 tbsp. ginger, minced
2 tbsp. green chilies
1 onion, chopped
Salt

Directions:
Add oil into the inner pot of instant pot duo crisp and set pot on sauté mode. Add cashews and sauté for a minute. Add caraway seeds, green chilies, garlic, ginger, all dry spices and sauté for 1-2 minutes. Add onion and cook for 2 minutes. Add remaining ingredients and stir everything well. Seal the pot with pressure cooking lid and cook on high for 4 minutes. Once done, allow to release pressure naturally for 10 minutes then release remaining pressure using a quick release. Remove lid. Stir and serve.

Spicy Beans

Ingredients: Servings: 4 Cooking Time: 6 Mins

1 lb green beans, ends trimmed
1 tsp. red pepper flakes
2 tbsp. garlic, minced
4 tsp. red wine vinegar
1 tbsp. soy sauce
2 tbsp. sesame oil

Directions:
Add green beans into the mixing bowl. Mix together oil, soy sauce, vinegar, garlic, and red pepper flakes and pour over green beans and toss well. Spray instant pot multi-level air fryer basket with cooking spray. Add green beans into the air fryer basket and place basket into the instant pot. Seal pot with air fryer lid and select air fry mode then set the temperature to 400 F and timer for 6 minutes. Stir beans halfway through. Serve and enjoy.

Crispy Roasted Broccoli

Ingredients: Servings: 2 Cooking Time: 8 Mins

¼ tsp. Masala
½ tsp. red chili powder
¼ tsp. turmeric powder
½ tsp. salt
1 tbsp. chickpea flour
2 tbsp. yogurt
1 lb. broccoli

Directions:
1 Preparing the Ingredients. Cut broccoli up into florets. Soak in a bowl of water with 2 tsp. of salt for at least half an hour to remove impurities. Take out broccoli florets from water and let drain. Wipe down thoroughly. Mix all other ingredients

together to create a marinade. Toss broccoli florets in the marinade. Cover and chill 15-30 minutes. 2 Air Frying. Preheat the Instant Crisp Air Fryer to 390 degrees. Place marinated broccoli florets into the fryer, lock the air fryer lid, set temperature to 350°F, and set time to 10 minutes. Florets will be crispy when done.

Squash Noodles with Spinach-walnut Pesto

Ingredients: Servings: 4 Cooking Time: 6 Mins

4 lb Spaghetti Squash
1 C. Water
For the Pesto
½ C. spinach, chopped
2 tbsp. Walnuts
2 Garlic Cloves, minced
Zest and juice from ½ lemon
Salt and ground pepper, to taste
⅓ C. extra virgin olive oil
Next, open the cooker, pour the water into it and fit the reversible rack at the bottom. Place the squash halves on the rack, close the lid, secure the pressure valve, and select Steam on High pressure for 5 minutes. Press Start.
Put the squash on a flat surface and use a knife to slice in half lengthwise. Scoop out all seeds and discard them.
Once the timer has ended, do a quick pressure release, and open the lid.
Remove the squash halves onto a cutting board and use a fork to separate the pulp strands into spaghetti-like pieces.
Return to the pot and close the crisping lid. Cook for 2 minutes on Broil mode.
Scoop the spaghetti squash into serving plates and drizzle over the spinach pesto.

Directions:
In a food processor put all the pesto

Crispy Jalapeno Coins

Ingredients: Servings: 2 Cooking Time: 5 Mins

2-3 tbsp. coconut flour
1 sliced and seeded jalapeno
Pinch of garlic powder
1 egg
Pinch of onion powder
Pinch of Cajun seasoning (optional)
Pinch of pepper and salt

Directions:
1 Preparing the Ingredients. Ensure your Instant Crisp Air Fryer is preheated to 400 degrees. Mix together all dry ingredients. Pat jalapeno slices dry. Dip coins into egg wash and then into dry mixture. Toss to thoroughly coat. Add coated jalapeno slices to Instant Crisp Air Fryer in a singular layer. Spray with olive oil. 2 Air Frying. Lock the air fryer lid. Set temperature to 350°F, and set time to 5 minutes. Cook just till crispy.

Tasty Cauliflower & Broccoli

Ingredients: Servings: 6 Cooking Time: 12 Mins

3 C. cauliflower florets
1/2 tsp. garlic powder
2 tbsp. olive oil
1/4 tsp. onion powder
3 C. broccoli florets
1/4 tsp. paprika
1/8 tsp. pepper
1/4 tsp. sea salt

Directions:
Add cauliflower and broccoli into the large bowl. Add remaining ingredients and toss well. Spray instant pot multi-level air fryer basket with cooking spray. Transfer broccoli and cauliflower mixture into the air fryer basket and place basket into the instant pot. Seal pot with air fryer lid and select air fry mode then set the temperature to 380 F and timer for 12 minutes. Stir halfway through. Serve and enjoy.

OTHER FAVORITE RECIPES

Buffalo Chicken Casserole

Ingredients: Servings: 8 Cooking Time: 30 Mins

18 oz cauliflower florets
1 C. celery, chopped
12 oz chicken, cooked and diced
8 oz cheddar cheese, shredded
2 eggs, lightly beaten
1/4 C. ranch dressing
1/3 C. hot sauce
8 oz cream cheese

Directions:
Spray instant pot from inside with cooking spray. Add cauliflower florets into the boiling water and cook for 6 minutes. Drain well and set aside. Add cauliflower florets, chicken, and celery into the instant pot. In a bowl, mix together cream cheese, hot sauce, ranch dressing, eggs, and 4 oz cheddar cheese and pour over cauliflower mixture. Sprinkle remaining cheddar cheese on top. Seal pot with air fryer lid and select bake mode then set the temperature to 350 F and timer for 30 minutes. Serve and enjoy.

Tasty Mexican Chicken Soup

Ingredients: Servings: 5 Cooking Time: 15 Mins

1 lb chicken breast, skinless and boneless
1 C. cheddar cheese, shredded
1/2 C. cream cheese
1 C. half and half
1 1/2 C. chicken stock
1 tsp. paprika
1 1/2 tsp. chili powder
1 tsp. dried oregano
1 1/2 tsp. cumin powder
1 bell pepper, chopped
1 tbsp. garlic, minced
1 onion, chopped
2 tsp. olive oil
14 oz can fire-roasted tomatoes
Salt

Directions:
Add oil into the instant pot duo crisp and set pot on sauté mode. Add onion and garlic and sauté until onion is softened. Add paprika, oregano, chilli powder, and cumin powder and sauté for 1 minute. Add stock, roasted tomatoes, and salt and stir well. Add chicken breast. Seal the pot with pressure cooking lid and cook on high pressure for 8 minutes. Once done, allow to release pressure naturally for 10 minutes then release remaining pressure using a quick release. Remove lid. Remove chicken from pot and shred using a fork. Return

shredded chicken to the pot along with bell pepper, half and half, cheddar cheese, and cream cheese and stir until cheese is melted. Serve and enjoy.

Peppery Chicken Chili (pressure Cook)

Ingredients: Servings: 8 Cooking Time: 36 Mins

2 tbsp. unsalted butter
1 medium yellow onion, peeled and chopped
½ lb. (227 g) Anaheim peppers, deseeded and roughly chopped
½ lb. (227 g) poblano peppers, deseeded and roughly chopped
½ lb. (227 g) tomatillos, husked and quartered
2 cloves garlic, peeled and minced
2 small jalapeño peppers, deseeded and roughly chopped
1 tsp. ground cumin
6 bone-in, skin-on chicken thighs (2½ lb. / 1.1 kg total)
2 C. chicken stock
2 C. water
⅓ C. roughly chopped fresh cilantro
3 (15-ounce / 425-g) cans Great Northern beans, drained and rinsed

Directions:
Press the Sauté button on the Instant Pot and melt the butter. Add the onion and sauté for 3 minutes, or until tender. Add Anaheim peppers, poblano peppers, tomatillos and jalapeño peppers to the pot and sauté for 3 minutes. Add the garlic and cumin to the pot and sauté for 30 seconds, or until fragrant. Stir in the chicken thighs, stock and water. Lock the lid. Select the Bean/Chili mode and set the cooking time for 30 minutes at High Pressure. When the timer goes off, perform a quick pressure release. Carefully open the lid. Transfer the chicken thighs to a clean work surface. Use two forks to remove the skin off the chicken and shred the meat. Use an immersion blender to purée the mixture in the pot until smooth. Stir in the shredded chicken, cilantro and beans. Serve warm.

Cauliflower Popcorn

Ingredients: Servings: 2 Cooking Time: 8 Hours

2 C. cauliflower florets, chopped
1/4 tsp. ground cumin
1/2 tsp. cayenne
1/2 tbsp. paprika
2 tbsp. hot sauce
1 1/2 tbsp. olive oil

Directions:
Add cauliflower into the large bowl. Add remaining ingredients over the cauliflower and toss well. Place the dehydrating tray in a multi-level air fryer basket and place basket in the instant pot. Place cauliflower pieces on dehydrating tray. Seal pot with air fryer lid and select dehydrate mode then set temperature to 130 F and timer for 8 hours. Serve and enjoy.

Parsnips Chips

Ingredients: Servings: 2 Cooking Time: 6 Hours

1 parsnip, cut into 1/4-inch thick slices
Pepper
Salt

Directions:
Add parsnip slices, pepper, and salt into the bowl and toss well. Place the dehydrating tray in a multi-level air fryer basket and place basket in the instant pot. Arrange parsnip slices on dehydrating tray. Seal pot with air fryer lid and select dehydrate mode then set temperature to 125 F and timer for 6 hours. Serve and enjoy.

Flavors Crab Casserole

Ingredients: Servings: 5 Cooking Time: 30 Mins

8 oz crabmeat
1 onion, sliced
1/4 tsp. garlic powder
1/4 tsp. onion powder
1 tsp. Worcestershire sauce
1 C. Swiss cheese, shredded
1 C. cheddar cheese, shredded
1/4 C. sour cream
5 oz cream cheese

Directions:
Spray instant pot from inside with cooking spray. Add all ingredients except cheddar cheese into the instant pot and stir well. Sprinkle cheddar cheese on top. Seal pot with air fryer lid and select bake mode then set the temperature to 350 F and timer for 30 minutes. Serve and enjoy.

Avocado and Tomato Egg Rolls (air Fryer)

Ingredients: Servings: 5 Cooking Time: 5 Mins

10 egg roll wrappers
3 avocados, peeled and pitted
1 tomato, diced
Salt and ground black pepper, to taste
Cooking spray

Directions:
Preheat the air fryer to 350°F (177°C) and spritz with cooking spray. Pu the tomato and avocados in a food processor. Sprinkle with salt and ground black pepper. Pulse to mix and coarsely mash until smooth. Unfold the wrappers on a clean work surface, then divide the mixture in the center of each wrapper. Roll the wrapper up and press to seal. Transfer the rolls in the preheated air fryer and spritz with cooking spray. Air fry for 5 minutes or until golden brown. Flip the rolls halfway through. Work in batches to avoid overcrowding. Serve immediately.

Tater Tot Casserole

Ingredients: Servings: 8 Cooking Time: 30 Mins

1 lb ground beef
2 lbs tater tots
1 1/2 C. cheddar cheese, shredded
1/2 C. milk
10 oz cream of chicken soup
2 C. hash browns, shredded
1 tsp. onion powder
1 tsp. garlic powder
2 tbsp. Italian seasoning
3 tbsp. onion, chopped

Directions:
Spray instant pot from inside with cooking spray. Add meat, onion, garlic powder, Italian seasoning, and onion powder into the instant pot and saute until meat is browned. Add remaining ingredients except for tater tots and stir well. Spread tater tots on top. Seal pot with air fryer lid and select

bake mode then set the temperature to 350 F and timer for 30 minutes. Serve and enjoy.

Creamy Sweet Potato Soup

Ingredients: Servings: 6 Cooking Time: 15 Mins

2 lbs sweet potatoes, peeled and diced
2 C. of water
4 C. vegetable broth
1/2 onion, chopped
1 tbsp. olive oil
1/2 tsp. cinnamon
1 tsp. paprika
3 garlic cloves, minced
Pepper
Salt
For Croissant Croutons:
1 croissant, cut into 1/2-inch cubes
2 tbsp. parmesan cheese, grated
1/2 tsp. dried oregano
1 tbsp. olive oil
Pepper
Salt

Directions:
Add oil into the instant pot and set the pot on saute mode. Add onion and sweet potato and saute for 5 minutes. Add remaining ingredients and stir well. Seal pot with pressure cooking lid and cook on high for 10 minutes. Once done, release pressure using quick release. Remove lid. Puree the soup using a blender until smooth. For Croutons: In a bowl, toss croissant cubes with remaining ingredients. Spray instant pot multi-level air fryer basket with cooking spray. Add croissant cubes into the air fryer basket and place basket into the instant pot. Seal pot with air fryer lid and select bake mode then set the temperature to 350 F and timer for 10 minutes. Stir halfway through. Top soup with croutons and serve.

Spaghetti Casserole

Ingredients: Servings: 6 Cooking Time: 30 Mins

12 oz spaghetti, cooked and drained
1/2 C. parmesan cheese, grated
1 garlic clove, minced
8 oz cream cheese
1 tsp. Italian seasoning
1 lb ground beef
26 oz jar spaghetti sauce

Directions:
Add ground beef into the instant pot and set the pot on saute mode and cook until meat is browned. Add spaghetti sauce and stir well. Add cream cheese, garlic, Italian seasoning, and cooked spaghetti and stir well. Sprinkle parmesan cheese on top. Seal pot with air fryer lid and select bake mode then set the temperature to 350 F and timer for 30 minutes. Serve and enjoy.

Apple Sweet Potato Fruit Leather

Ingredients: Servings: 2 Cooking Time: 4 Hours

1/2 C. mashed sweet potatoes
1/4 tsp. cinnamon
1 tbsp. honey
1/2 C. applesauce

Directions:
Add all ingredients into the blender and blend until smooth. Place the dehydrating tray in a multi-level air fryer basket and place basket in the instant pot. Line dehydrating tray with parchment paper. Spread blended mixture on dehydrating tray. Seal pot with air fryer lid and select dehydrate mode then set temperature to 110 F and timer for 4 hours or until leathery. Serve and enjoy.

Tasty Tomato Soup

Ingredients: Servings: 4 Cooking Time: 5 Mins

6 tomatoes, chopped
14 oz coconut milk
1 tsp. turmeric
1/2 tsp. cayenne pepper
1 tsp. garlic, minced
1/4 C. fresh parsley, chopped
1 onion, diced
1 tsp. ginger, minced
1 tsp. salt
For Cornbread Croutons:
1 1/4 C. cornbread cubes
2 tbsp. olive oil
Pepper
Salt

Directions:
Add all ingredients to the instant pot and stir well. Seal the pot with pressure cooking lid and cook high for 5 minutes. Once done, release pressure using quick release. Remove lid. Puree the soup using a blender until smooth. For Croutons: In a bowl, toss cornbread cubes with remaining ingredients. Spray instant pot multi-level air fryer basket with cooking spray. Add cornbread cubes into the air fryer basket and place basket into the instant pot. Seal pot with air fryer lid and select bake mode then set the temperature to 350 F and timer for 15 minutes. Stir halfway through. Top soup with croutons and serve.

Thyme Carrot Cauliflower Soup

Ingredients: Servings: 4 Cooking Time: 15 Mins

2 C. cauliflower florets
2 2/3 C. vegetable stock
1/8 tsp. dried thyme
1 1/2 tbsp. curry powder
1 carrot, diced
1 C. onion, diced
1 1/3 tbsp. olive oil
1/8 tsp. pepper
1/8 tsp. salt
For Italian Seasoned Bread Croutons:
1 1/2 C. bread cubes
1 tsp. Italian seasoning
1 tbsp. olive oil
Salt

Directions:
Add oil into the instant pot and set the pot on saute mode. Add carrots, cauliflower, and onion into the pot and sauté for 4-5 minutes. Add spices and stock and stir well. Seal pot with pressure cooking lid and cook on high for 10 minutes. Once done, release pressure using quick release. Remove lid. Stir in milk. Puree the soup using a blender until smooth. For Croutons: In a bowl, toss bread cubes, Italian seasoning, oil, and salt. Spray instant pot multi-level air fryer basket with cooking spray. Add bread cubes into the air fryer basket and place basket into the instant pot. Seal pot with air fryer lid and select bake mode then set the temperature to 350 F and timer for 20 minutes. Stir halfway through. Top soup with croutons and serve.

Corn Gratin

Ingredients: Servings: 8 Cooking Time: 30 Mins

2 C. corn
1 tbsp. flour

1 C. cheddar cheese, shredded
1 C. milk
1 tbsp. butter
1 C. crushed crackers

Directions:
Add butter into the instant pot and set the pot on saute mode. Add flour and milk and stir until smooth. Turn off the saute mode. Add corn and C. cheese and stir well. Sprinkle remaining cheese and crushed crackers on top. Seal pot with air fryer lid and select bake mode then set the temperature to 350 F and timer for 15 minutes. Serve and enjoy.

Cheesy Veggie Orzo Soup (pressure Cook)

Ingredients: Servings: 4 Cooking Time: 10 Mins

1 medium potato, peeled and small-diced
1 medium zucchini, diced
1 small carrot, peeled and diced
1 small yellow onion, peeled and diced
2 stalks celery, diced
1 (15-ounce / 425-g) can diced tomatoes, undrained
2 cloves garlic, peeled and minced
½ C. gluten-free orzo
5 C. vegetable broth
2 tsp. dried oregano leaves
2 tsp. dried thyme leaves
1 tsp. salt
1 tsp. ground black pepper
3 C. fresh baby spinach
4 tbsp. grated Parmesan cheese

Directions:
Add all the ingredients, except for the spinach and Parmesan cheese, to the Instant Pot. Lock the lid. Select the Manual setting and set the cooking time for 10 minutes at High Pressure. Once the timer goes off, use a quick pressure release. Carefully open the lid. Stir in the spinach until wilted. Ladle the soup into four bowls and garnish with the Parmesan cheese. Serve warm.

Lamb Stew

Ingredients: Servings: 3 Cooking Time: 30 Mins

1 lb. lamb loin, cut into pieces
2 C. chicken stock
1 chili pepper, chopped
1 C. cabbage, shredded
1 zucchini, sliced
1/2 tsp. dried thyme
1 tsp. oregano
½ tsp. chili powder
3 tbsp. olive oil
2 garlic cloves, crushed
1 tsp. salt

Directions:
Add oil into the instant pot and set the pot on sauté mode. Add garlic and meat and sauté for a minute. Season with thyme, oregano, chili powder, and salt. Stir everything well and cook for 5 minutes. Add zucchini and cook for 3-4 minutes. Add cabbage, chili pepper, and stock. Stir well. Seal pot with lid and cook on manual high pressure for 12 minutes. Once done then allow to release pressure naturally for 10 minutes then release using the quick-release method. Open the lid. Stir and serve.

Beef Chili with Onions (pressure Cook)

Ingredients: Servings: 8 Cooking Time: 19 Mins

2 lb. (907 g) 90% lean ground beef
3 large yellow onions, peeled and diced, divided
3 cloves garlic, peeled and minced
2 (16-ounce / 454-g) cans kidney beans, rinsed and drained
1 (15-ounce / 425-g) can tomato sauce
1 C. beef broth
2 tbsp. semisweet chocolate chips
2 tbsp. red wine vinegar
2 tbsp. honey
2 tbsp. chili powder
1 tbsp. pumpkin pie spice
1 tsp. ground cumin
½ tsp. ground cardamom
½ tsp. salt
½ tsp. freshly cracked black pepper
¼ tsp. ground cloves
1 lb. (454 g) cooked spaghetti
4 C. shredded Cheddar cheese

Directions:
Press the Sauté button on the Instant Pot. Add the ground beef and ¾ of the diced onions to the pot and sauté for 8 minutes, or until the beef is browned and the onions are transparent. Drain the beef mixture and discard any excess fat. Add the garlic to the pot and sauté for 30 seconds. Stir in the remaining ingredients, except for the reserved onions, spaghetti and cheese. Cook for 1 minute, or until fragrant. Set the lid in place. Select the Pressure Cook and set the cooking time for 10 minutes at High Pressure. When the timer goes off, perform a quick pressure release. Carefully open the lid. Serve over the cooked spaghetti and top with the reserved onions and cheese.

Chinese Pork Belly Stew (pressure Cook)

Ingredients: Servings: 8 Cooking Time: 42 Mins

½ C. plus 2 tbsp. soy sauce, divided
¼ C. Chinese cooking wine
½ C. packed light brown sugar
12 scallions, cut into pieces
3 cloves garlic, minced
2 lb. (907 g) pork belly, skinned and cubed
3 tbsp. vegetable oil
1 tsp. Chinese five-spice powder
2 C. vegetable broth
4 C. cooked white rice

Directions:
In a large bowl, whisk together ½ C. of the soy sauce, wine and brown sugar. Place the pork into the bowl and turn to coat evenly. Cover in plastic and refrigerate for at least 4 hours. Drain the pork and pat dry. Reserve the marinade. Press the Sauté button on the Instant Pot and heat the oil. Add half the pork to the pot in an even layer, making sure there is space between pork cubes to prevent steam from forming. Sear the pork for 3 minutes on each side, or until lightly browned. Transfer the browned pork to a plate. Repeat with the remaining pork. Stir in the remaining ingredients, except for the rice. Return the browned pork to the pot with the reserved marinade. Lock the lid. Select the Pressure Cook and set the cooking time for 30 minutes at High Pressure. When the timer beeps, perform a natural pressure release for 20 minutes, then

release any remaining pressure. Carefully open the lid. Serve hot over cooked rice.

Turkey Stroganoff

Ingredients: Servings: 8 Cooking Time: 34 Mins

12 oz egg noodles, cooked and drained
1/4 C. parmesan cheese, grated
2 C. cooked turkey, diced
1 C. sour cream
2 C. chicken broth
1/4 C. all-purpose flour
1 tbsp. parsley, chopped
8 oz mushrooms, sliced
2 tbsp. butter

Directions:
Add butter into the instant pot and set the pot on saute mode. Add mushrooms and saute for 3-4 minutes. remove mushrooms from pot and set aside. Add flour, sour cream, and broth and stir until smooth. Turn off the saute mode. Add noodles, turkey, mushrooms, and parsley and stir well. Sprinkle parmesan cheese on top. Seal pot with air fryer lid and select bake mode then set the temperature to 350 F and timer for 30 minutes. Serve and enjoy.

Cheesy Mashed Potato Casserole

Ingredients: Servings: 8 Cooking Time: 20 Mins

4 C. mashed potatoes
3/4 C. cheddar cheese, shredded
1 tsp. dried parsley
1 C. french onion rings
1 tsp. dried chives
3/4 C. sour cream

Directions:
Spray instant pot from inside with cooking spray. Add mashed potatoes, sour cream, chives, and parsley into the instant pot stir well. Sprinkle cheese and onion rings on top. Seal pot with air fryer lid and select bake mode then set the temperature to 350 F and timer for 20 minutes. Serve and enjoy.

Golden Cod Tacos with Salsa (air Fryer)

Ingredients: Servings: 4 Cooking Time: 15 Mins

2 eggs
1¼ C. Mexican beer
1½ C. coconut flour
1½ C. almond flour
½ tbsp. chili powder
1 lb. (454 g) cod fillet, slice into large pieces
1 tbsp. cumin
Salt, to taste
4 toasted corn tortillas
4 large lettuce leaves, chopped
¼ C. salsa
Cooking spray

Directions:
Preheat the air fryer to 375°F (191°C). Spritz the air fryer basket with cooking spray. Break the eggs in a bowl, then pour in the beer. Whisk to combine well. Combine the coconut flour, almond flour, chili powder, cumin, and salt in a separate bowl. Stir to mix well. Dunk the cod pieces in the egg mixture, then shake the excess off and dredge into the flour mixture to coat well. Arrange the cod in the preheated air fryer. Air fry for 15 minutes or until golden brown. Flip the cod halfway through the cooking time. Unwrap the toasted tortillas on a large plate, then divide the cod and lettuce leaves on top. Baste with salsa and wrap to serve.

Pumpkin Fruit Leather

Ingredients: Servings: 2 Cooking Time: 8 Hours

1/2 C. pumpkin puree
1/8 tsp. ground allspice
1/8 tsp. ground nutmeg
1/4 tsp. cinnamon
1 tbsp. shredded coconut
1 tbsp. honey
1/2 C. applesauce
1/4 C. coconut milk

Directions:
Place the dehydrating tray in a multi-level air fryer basket and place basket in the instant pot. Line dehydrating tray with parchment paper. Add all ingredients into the bowl and mix until well combined and spread mixture on dehydrating tray. Seal pot with air fryer lid and select dehydrate mode then set temperature to 135 F and timer for 8 hours. Serve and enjoy.

Creamy Corn Soup

Ingredients: Servings: 4 Cooking Time: 10 Mins

2 1/2 C. corn kernels
2 tsp. olive oil
1/2 tbsp. soy sauce
3/4 C. cabbage, minced
2 garlic cloves, minced
1 carrot, minced
5 C. vegetable broth
1 tsp. ground cumin
1 1/2 tsp. ginger, grated
Pepper
Salt
For Pumpernickel Croutons:
2 C. pumpernickel bread cubes
2 tbsp. butter, melted
1/4 tsp. garlic powder
1/4 tsp. salt

Directions:
Add all ingredients into the instant pot and stir well. Seal pot with pressure cooking lid and cook on high for 10 minutes. Once done, release pressure using quick release. Remove lid. Remove 3 C. of soup from the pot and Puree the soup using a blender until smooth. Return blended soup into the pot and stir well. Season with pepper and salt. For Croutons: In a bowl, toss pumpernickel bread cubes with remaining ingredients. Spray instant pot multi-level air fryer basket with cooking spray. Add pumpernickel bread cubes into the air fryer basket and place basket into the instant pot. Seal pot with air fryer lid and select bake mode then set the temperature to 375 F and timer for 10 minutes. Stir halfway through. Top soup with croutons and serve.

Creamy & Tasty Chicken Soup

Ingredients: Servings: 6 Cooking Time: 25 Mins

1 lb chicken breast, skinless and boneless
1 C. cheddar cheese, shredded
1/2 C. cream cheese
1 C. heavy cream
1 1/2 C. chicken broth
1 tsp. paprika
1 tsp. chili powder
1 tsp. dried oregano
1 tsp. cumin powder
1 bell pepper, sliced
1 tbsp. garlic, minced
1 onion, chopped
1 tbsp. olive oil
1 small jar sun-dried tomatoes, drained
Pepper
Salt

Directions:

Add oil into the instant pot duo crisp and set pot on sauté mode. Add garlic and onion and sauté for 3-5 minutes. Add remaining ingredients except for cheddar cheese, cream cheese, and heavy cream and stir well. Seal the pot with pressure cooking lid and cook on high pressure for 20 minutes. Once done, release pressure using a quick release. Remove lid. Remove chicken from pot and shred using a fork. Return shredded chicken to the pot. Set pot on sauté mode. Add cheddar cheese, cream cheese, and heavy cream and stir until cheese is melted. Season soup with pepper and salt. Serve and enjoy.

Sausage Casserole

Ingredients: Servings: 8 Cooking Time: 30 Mins

1 lb ground sausage
1/2 tsp. garlic powder
8 oz Velveeta cheese
1 C. milk
10 oz cream of mushroom soup
10 oz cream of chicken soup
2 C. cooked macaroni
Pepper

Directions:
Add sausage into the instant pot and saute until browned. Turn off the saute mode. Add remaining ingredients and stir everything well. Seal pot with air fryer lid and select bake mode then set the temperature to 350 F and timer for 30 minutes. Serve and enjoy.

Easy Chicken Soup

Ingredients: Servings: 8 Cooking Time: 40 Mins

1 1/2 lbs chicken breasts, boneless and cut into chunks
4 C. of water
4 C. chicken broth
2 tsp. thyme
2 tsp. basil
1 onion, chopped
1 tbsp. garlic, minced
2 celery stalks, chopped
5 carrots, peeled and chopped
1/2 tsp. pepper
2 tsp. salt

Directions:
Add all ingredients into the inner pot of instant pot duo crisp. Stir well. Seal the pot with pressure cooking lid and cook on high pressure for 40 minutes. Once done, release pressure using a quick release. Remove lid. Stir well and serve immediately.

Dehydrated Okra

Ingredients: Servings: 2 Cooking Time: 24 Hours

6 pods okra, slice into rounds

Directions:
Place the dehydrating tray in a multi-level air fryer basket and place basket in the instant pot. Arrange sliced okra on dehydrating tray. Seal pot with air fryer lid and select dehydrate mode then set temperature to 130 F and timer for 24 hours. Serve and enjoy.

Apple Chips

Ingredients: Servings: 2 Cooking Time: 8 Hours

1 apple, cut into 1/8-inch thick slices
1/4 tbsp. ground cinnamon
1/4 tbsp. granulated sugar

Directions:
Add apple slices, cinnamon, and sugar into the large bowl and mix well. Place the dehydrating tray in a multi-level air fryer basket and place basket in the instant pot. Arrange apple slices on dehydrating tray. Seal pot with air fryer lid and select dehydrate mode then set temperature to 130 F and timer for 8 hours. Serve and enjoy.

Crispy Chicken Egg Rolls (air Fryer)

Ingredients: Servings: 4 Cooking Time: 23 To 24 Mins

1 lb. (454 g) ground chicken
2 tsp. olive oil
2 garlic cloves, minced
1 tsp. grated fresh ginger
2 C. white cabbage, shredded
1 onion, chopped
¼ C. soy sauce
8 egg roll wrappers
1 egg, beaten
Cooking spray

Directions:
Preheat the air fryer to 370ºF (188ºC). Spritz the air fryer basket with cooking spray. Heat olive oil in a saucepan over medium heat. Sauté the garlic and ginger in the olive oil for 1 minute, or until fragrant. Add the ground chicken to the saucepan. Sauté for 5 minutes, or until the chicken is cooked through. Add the cabbage, onion and soy sauce and sauté for 5 to 6 minutes, or until the vegetables become soft. Remove the saucepan from the heat. Unfold the egg roll wrappers on a clean work surface. Divide the chicken mixture among the wrappers and brush the edges of the wrappers with the beaten egg. Tightly roll up the egg rolls, enclosing the filling. Arrange the rolls in the prepared air fryer basket and air fry for 12 minutes, or until crispy and golden brown. Turn halfway through the cooking time to ensure even cooking. Transfer to a platter and let cool for 5 minutes before serving.

Flavors Squash Soup

Ingredients: Servings: 6 Cooking Time: 8 Mins

6 C. butternut squash, peeled and cubed
1/4 C. heavy cream
1/8 tsp. nutmeg
1/2 tsp. cayenne pepper
2 tsp. thyme
3 C. vegetable stock
1 onion, chopped
2 tbsp. butter
Pepper
Salt
For Herb Garlic Croutons:
2 C. of bread cubes
1 tbsp. olive oil
1/4 tsp. dried thyme
1/4 tsp. dried basil
1/4 tsp. dried oregano
1 garlic clove, minced
Pepper
Salt

Directions:
Add butter into the instant pot and set the pot on sauté mode. Add onion and sauté for 3 minutes. Add squash, nutmeg, cayenne, thyme, stock, and salt. Stir well. Seal pot with pressure cooking lid and cook on high for 5 minutes. Once done, release pressure using quick release. Remove lid. Stir in heavy cream. Puree the soup using a blender until smooth.

For Croutons: In a bowl, toss bread cubes with remaining ingredients. Spray instant pot multi-level air fryer basket with cooking spray. Add bread cubes into the air fryer basket and place basket into the instant pot. Seal pot with air fryer lid and select bake mode then set the temperature to 350 F and timer for 10 minutes. Stir halfway through. Top soup with croutons and serve.

Potato Bisque with Bacon (pressure Cook)

Ingredients: Servings: 4 Cooking Time: 20 Mins

2 tbsp. unsalted butter
1 slice bacon, diced
3 leeks, trimmed, rinsed and diced
6 C. diced Yukon Gold potatoes
4 C. chicken broth
2 tsp. dried thyme leaves
1 tsp. sriracha
½ tsp. sea salt
¼ C. whole milk

Directions:
Set the Instant Pot on the Sauté mode and melt the butter. Add the bacon and leeks to the pot and sauté for 5 minutes, or until the fat is rendered and leeks become tender. Stir in the remaining ingredients, except for the milk. Lock the lid. Select the Pressure Cook and set the cooking time for 15 minutes at High Pressure. When the timer goes off, use a natural pressure release for 5 minutes, then release any remaining pressure. Carefully open the lid. Pour the milk into the pot. Use an immersion blender to blend the soup in the pot until it achieves the desired consistency. Ladle the bisque into 4 bowls and serve warm.

Pork Meatball Soup (pressure Cook)

Ingredients: Servings: 4 Cooking Time: 19 Mins

Meatballs:
½ lb. (227 g) ground pork
2 tbsp. gluten-free bread crumbs
2 tbsp. grated Parmesan cheese
1 tbsp. Italian seasoning
½ tsp. cayenne pepper
½ tsp. salt
1 large egg, whisked
2 cloves garlic, peeled and minced
2 tbsp. olive oil, divided
1 tbsp. olive oil

Soup:
1 medium carrot, peeled and shredded
1 Russet potato, scrubbed and small-diced
1 small red onion, peeled and diced
1 (15-ounce / 425-g) can diced fire-roasted tomatoes, undrained
4 C. beef broth
½ tsp. salt
½ tsp. ground black pepper
½ tsp. red pepper flakes
½ C. chopped fresh basil leaves

Directions:
In a medium bowl, stir together all the ingredients for the meatballs, except for the olive oil. Shape the mixture into 24 meatballs. Set the Instant Pot to the Sauté mode and heat 1 tbsp. of the olive oil for 30 seconds. Add half the meatballs to the pot and sear for 3 minutes, turning them to brown all sides. Remove the first batch and set aside. Add the remaining 1 tbsp. of the olive oil to the pot and repeat with the remaining meatballs. Remove the meatballs from the pot. Select the Sauté mode and heat the olive oil for 30 seconds. Add the carrot, potato and onion to the pot and sauté for 5 minutes, or until the onion becomes translucent. Add the meatballs to the pot along with the remaining ingredients for the soup. Close and secure the lid. Select the Pressure Cook and set the cooking time for 7 minutes at High Pressure. Once cooking is complete, use a quick pressure release. Carefully open the lid. Serve warm.

Delicious Nacho Zucchini Chips

Ingredients: Servings: 2 Cooking Time: 6 Hours

1 yellow squash, sliced thinly
1/2 tsp. tomato powder
1/4 tsp. paprika
1/2 tsp. chili powder
1/4 tsp. onion powder
1/4 tsp. garlic powder
1 tbsp. cheddar cheese, grated
Salt

Directions:
Add squash slices into the mixing bowl. Add remaining ingredients and toss well. Place the dehydrating tray in a multi-level air fryer basket and place basket in the instant pot. Arrange squash slices on the dehydrating tray. Seal pot with air fryer lid and select dehydrate mode then set temperature to 135 F and timer for 6 hours. Serve and enjoy.

Creamy Peanut Butter Carrot Soup

Ingredients: Servings: 4 Cooking Time: 15 Mins

8 carrots, peeled and chopped
1 1/2 C. chicken stock
1/4 C. peanut butter
1 tbsp. curry paste
1 onion, chopped
3 garlic cloves, peeled
14 oz coconut milk
Pepper
Salt
For Parmesan Croutons:
2 C. of bread cubes
2 tbsp. parmesan cheese, grated
2 tbs butter, melted
1 garlic clove, minced
1 tbsp. olive oil
Pepper
Salt

Directions:
Add all ingredients into the instant pot and stir well. Seal pot with pressure cooking lid and cook on high for 15 minutes. Once done, release pressure using quick release. Remove lid. Puree the soup using a blender until smooth. Season soup with pepper and salt. For Croutons: In a bowl, toss bread cubes with butter, garlic, oil, pepper, and salt. Spray instant pot multi-level air fryer basket with cooking spray. Add bread cubes into the air fryer basket and place basket into the instant pot. Seal pot with air fryer lid and select bake mode then set the temperature to 375 F and timer for 15 minutes. Stir halfway through. Toss bread cubes with parmesan cheese until well coated. Top soup with croutons and serve.

Banana Jerky

Ingredients: Servings: 2 Cooking Time: 8 Hours

2 bananas, cut into 1/4-inch thick slices
1 tbsp. fresh lemon juice

Directions:
Add banana slices and lemon juice in a bowl and toss well. Place the dehydrating tray in a multi-level air fryer basket and

place basket in the instant pot. Arrange banana slices on dehydrating tray. Seal pot with air fryer lid and select dehydrate mode then set temperature to 135 F and timer for 8 hours. Serve and enjoy.

Squash Casserole

Ingredients: Servings: 8 Cooking Time: 35 Mins

4 1/2 lbs yellow squash, cut into bite-size pieces
2 tbsp. mayonnaise
1 1/2 C. cheddar cheese, shredded
1 egg, lightly beaten
10 oz cream of celery soup
1 C. onion, chopped
Pepper
Salt
For topping:
1/2 C. butter, melted
1 C. crushed crackers

Directions:
Add squash pieces into the boiling water and boil until tender. Drain well and set aside. Mix together squash, onion, celery soup, egg, mayonnaise, pepper, and salt and pour into the instant pot. Sprinkle cheddar cheese on top. Seal pot with air fryer lid and select bake mode then set the temperature to 350 F and timer for 20 minutes. Mix together butter and crushed crackers and sprinkle on top. Seal pot with air fryer lid and select bake mode then set the temperature to 350 F and timer for 15 minutes. Serve and enjoy.

Spinach Soup

Ingredients: Servings: 2 Cooking Time: 10 Mins

3 C. spinach, chopped
3 C. vegetable broth
1 C. cauliflower, chopped
1 tsp. garlic powder
2 tbsp. olive oil
1/4 C. coconut cream
1/2 tsp. pepper
1/4 tsp. sea salt
For Hot Dog Bun Croutons:
2 hot dog buns, cut into cubes
2 tbsp. olive oil
1/4 tsp. black pepper
1/2 tsp. dried parsley
1/2 tsp. garlic powder
Salt

Directions:
Add olive oil into the instant pot and set the pot on sauté mode. Add cauliflower, broth, spinach, garlic powder, pepper, and salt and stir well. Seal pot with pressure cooking lid and cook on high for 10 minutes. Once done, release pressure using quick release. Remove lid. Puree the soup using a blender until smooth. Stir in coconut cream. For Croutons: In a bowl, toss bun cubes with remaining ingredients. Spray instant pot multi-level air fryer basket with cooking spray. Add bread cubes into the air fryer basket and place basket into the instant pot. Seal pot with air fryer lid and select bake mode then set the temperature to 375 F and timer for 15 minutes. Stir halfway through. Top soup with croutons and serve.

Chuck Roast with Onions (pressure Cook)

Ingredients: Servings: 6 Cooking Time: 1 Hour 2 Mins

2½ lb. (1.1 kg) boneless chuck roast, cut into pieces
1 tsp. salt
2 tsp. dried oregano
2 tsp. smoked paprika
½ tsp. cayenne pepper
½ C. white wine
1 (14.5-ounce / 411-g) can diced tomatoes
1 bay leaf
½ C. halved Spanish olives
2 tsp. distilled white vinegar
1 tsp. ground black pepper
1 tbsp. olive oil
2 medium yellow onions, peeled and chopped
2 medium red bell peppers, deseeded and chopped
6 cloves garlic, peeled and minced
2 tsp. ground cumin

Directions:
Season the chuck roast with the salt and pepper on all sides. Set aside. Press the Sauté button on the Instant Pot and heat the oil. Add half the seasoned meat to the pot and sear for 7 minutes on both sides, or until well browned. Transfer the browned meat to a platter and set aside. Repeat with the remaining meat. Add the onions and bell peppers to the pot and sauté for 5 minutes, or until just softened. Add the garlic, cumin, oregano, paprika and cayenne pepper to the pot and sauté for 1 minute, or until fragrant. Pour in the white wine and cook for 2 minutes, or until the liquid is reduced by half. Return the browned meat back to the pot along with the tomatoes and bay leaf. Close and secure the lid. Select the Manual setting and set the cooking time for 40 minutes at High Pressure. Once the timer goes off, use a quick pressure release. Carefully open the lid. Remove and discard the bay leaf. Stir in the olives and vinegar. Serve hot.

Cucumber Chips

Ingredients: Servings: 2 Cooking Time: 10 Hours

1 cucumber, sliced thinly
1/2 tbsp. olive oil
1 tsp. apple cider vinegar
Salt

Directions:
Toss cucumber slices with vinegar, oil, and salt. Place the dehydrating tray in a multi-level air fryer basket and place basket in the instant pot. Arrange cucumber slices on dehydrating tray. Seal pot with air fryer lid and select dehydrate mode then set temperature to 135 F and timer for 10 hours. Serve and enjoy.

Curried Squash Soup

Ingredients: Servings: 4 Cooking Time: 40 Mins

3 lbs butternut squash, peeled and cubed
3 C. of water
2 garlic cloves, minced
1 onion, minced
1 tsp. olive oil
1 tbsp. curry powder
1/2 C. coconut milk
For Caesar Croutons:
2 C. bread cubes
1/8 tsp. dried thyme
1/4 tsp. dried oregano
1/4 tsp. garlic powder
1/2 tsp. dried parsley
1 tbsp. parmesan cheese, grated
1 tbsp. olive oil
Pepper
Salt

Directions:
Add olive oil into the instant pot and set the pot on sauté mode. Add onion to the pot and sauté for 8 minutes. Add curry

powder and garlic and sauté for a minute. Add squash, water, and salt and stir well. Seal pot with pressure cooking lid and cook on high for 30 minutes. Once done, release pressure using quick release. Remove lid. Puree the soup using a blender until smooth. Stir in coconut milk. For Croutons: In a bowl, toss bread cubes with remaining ingredients. Spray instant pot multi-level air fryer basket with cooking spray. Add bread cubes into the air fryer basket and place basket into the instant pot. Seal pot with air fryer lid and select bake mode then set the temperature to 375 F and timer for 10 minutes. Stir halfway through. Top soup with croutons and serve.

Peanut Butter Banana Chips

Ingredients: Servings: 2 Cooking Time: 8 Hours

1 banana, cut into 1/4-inch thick slices
1 tbsp. creamy peanut butter

Directions:
In a bowl, mix together peanut butter and banana slices. Place the dehydrating tray in a multi-level air fryer basket and place basket in the instant pot. Arrange banana slices on dehydrating tray. Seal pot with air fryer lid and select dehydrate mode then set temperature to 160 F and timer for 8 hours. Serve and enjoy.

Banana Fruit Leather

Ingredients: Servings: 2 Cooking Time: 4 Hours

1 small banana
1 tbsp. Nutella

Directions:
Add banana and Nutella into the blender and blend until smooth. Place the dehydrating tray in a multi-level air fryer basket and place basket in the instant pot. Line dehydrating tray with parchment paper. Spread banana mixture on dehydrating tray. Seal pot with air fryer lid and select dehydrate mode then set temperature to 125 F and timer for 4 hours. Serve and enjoy.

Beef and Bell Pepper Fajitas (air Fryer)

Ingredients: Servings: 4 Cooking Time: 10 Mins

1 lb. (454 g) beef sirloin steak, cut into strips
2 shallots, sliced
1 orange bell pepper, sliced
1 red bell pepper, sliced
2 garlic cloves, minced
2 tbsp. Cajun seasoning
1 tbsp. paprika
Salt and ground black pepper, to taste
4 corn tortillas
½ C. shredded Cheddar cheese
Cooking spray

Directions:
Preheat the air fryer to 360°F (182°C) and spritz with cooking spray. Combine all the ingredients, except for the tortillas and cheese, in a large bowl. Toss to coat well. Pour the beef and vegetables in the preheated air fryer and spritz with cooking spray. Air fry for 10 minutes or until the meat is browned and the vegetables are soft and lightly wilted. Shake the basket halfway through. Unfold the tortillas on a clean work surface and spread the cooked beef and vegetables on top. Scatter with cheese and fold to serve.

Eggplant Hoagies (air Fryer)

Ingredients: Servings: 3 Cooking Time: 12 Mins

6 peeled eggplant slices (about ½ inch thick and 3 inches in diameter)
¼ C. jarred pizza sauce
6 tbsp. grated Parmesan cheese
3 Italian sub rolls, split open lengthwise, warmed
Cooking spray

Directions:
Preheat the air fryer to 350°F (177°C) and spritz with cooking spray. Arrange the eggplant slices in the preheated air fryer and spritz with cooking spray. Air fry for 10 minutes or until lightly wilted and tender. Flip the slices halfway through. Divide and spread the pizza sauce and cheese on top of the eggplant slice and air fry over 375°F (191°C) for 2 more minutes or until the cheese melts. Assemble each sub roll with two slices of eggplant and serve immediately.

Potato and Fish Stew (pressure Cook)

Ingredients: Servings: 8 Cooking Time: 28 Mins

2 tbsp. unsalted butter
2 stalks celery, chopped
1 medium carrot, peeled and diced
1 medium yellow onion, peeled and diced
2 cloves garlic, peeled and minced
1 tsp. Italian seasoning
¼ tsp. dried thyme
¼ tsp. salt
¼ tsp. ground black pepper
1 C. lager-style beer
1 (28-ounce / 794-g) can diced tomatoes
2 large Russet potatoes, peeled and diced
3 C. seafood stock
1 bay leaf
2 lb. (907 g) cod, cut into pieces
2 tbsp. lemon juice

Directions:
Set the Instant Pot to the Sauté mode and melt the butter. Add the celery, carrot and onion to the pot and sauté for 8 minutes, or until softened. Add the garlic, Italian seasoning, thyme, salt and pepper to the pot and cook for 30 seconds. Pour in the beer and scrape the bottom of the pot well. Stir in the tomatoes, potatoes, seafood stock and bay leaf. Set the lid in place. Select the Pressure Cook and set the cooking time for 10 minutes at High Pressure. When the timer goes off, perform a quick pressure release. Carefully open the lid. Stir in the fish. Select the Sauté mode and allow the soup to simmer for 10 minutes, or until the fish is cooked through. Remove and discard the bay leaf and stir in lemon juice. Serve hot.

Garlic Carrot Soup

Ingredients: Servings: 6 Cooking Time: 10 Mins

8 carrots, peel and cut into pieces
1/2 onion, chopped
1/4 tsp. ginger
1 tsp. salt
For Rosemary Croutons:
2 C. of bread cubes

1 1/2 tsp. curry powder	1 tbsp. olive oil
4 C. vegetable stock	1/2 tsp. dried rosemary
1/2 fresh lemon juice	1/2 tsp. garlic powder
2 tbsp. butter	Pepper
2 garlic cloves	Salt

Directions:
Add butter into the instant pot and set the pot on sauté mode. Add onion and garlic to the pot and sauté for 2 minutes. Add 1 C. stock, curry powder, and carrots. Stir. Seal pot with pressure cooking lid and cook on high for 8 minutes. Once done, release pressure using quick release. Remove lid. Add remaining stock and puree the soup using a blender until smooth. Add lemon juice, ginger, and salt and stir well. For Croutons: In a bowl, toss bread cubes with remaining ingredients. Spray instant pot multi-level air fryer basket with cooking spray. Add bread cubes into the air fryer basket and place basket into the instant pot. Seal pot with air fryer lid and select bake mode then set the temperature to 350 F and timer for 15-20 minutes. Stir halfway through. Top soup with croutons and serve.

Noodle Ham Casserole

Ingredients: Servings: 8 Cooking Time: 25 Mins

10.5 oz cream of chicken soup	2 C. Monterey jack cheese, shredded
3 C. ham, cooked & diced	1 1/2 C. milk
12 oz egg noodles, cooked and drained	1 C. sour cream
1/2 tsp. garlic powder	Pepper
	Salt

Directions:
Spray instant pot from inside with cooking spray. Add chicken soup, garlic powder, milk, sour cream, pepper, and salt into the instant pot and stir well. Add ham and cooked noodles and stir well. Sprinkle shredded cheese on top. Seal pot with air fryer lid and select bake mode then set the temperature to 350 F and timer for 25 minutes. Serve and enjoy.

Korean Flavor Beef and Onion Tacos (air Fryer)

Ingredients: Servings: 6 Cooking Time: 12 Mins

2 tbsp. gochujang	2 tsp. sugar
1 tbsp. soy sauce	1½ lb. (680 g) thinly sliced beef chuck
2 tbsp. sesame seeds	1 medium red onion, sliced
2 tsp. minced fresh ginger	6 corn tortillas, warmed
2 cloves garlic, minced	¼ C. chopped fresh cilantro
2 tbsp. toasted sesame oil	½ C. kimchi
½ tsp. kosher salt	½ C. chopped green onions

Directions:
Combine the gochujang, soy sauce, sesame seeds, ginger, garlic, sesame oil, sugar, and salt in a large bowl. Stir to mix well. Dunk the beef chunk in the large bowl. Press to submerge, then wrap the bowl in plastic and refrigerate to marinate for at least 1 hour. Preheat the air fryer to 400°F (204°C). Remove the beef chunk from the marinade and transfer to the preheated air fryer basket. Add the onion and air fry for 12 minutes or until well browned. Shake the basket halfway through. Unfold the tortillas on a clean work surface, then divide the fried beef and onion on the tortillas. Spread the cilantro, kimchi, and green onions on top. Serve immediately.

Coconut Red Bean Soup (pressure Cook)

Ingredients: Servings: 4 Cooking Time: 50 Mins

2 tsp. olive oil	½ lb. (227 g) dried small red beans
3 slices bacon, diced	1 (13.5-ounce / 383-g) can coconut milk
2 large carrots, peeled and diced	2 C. chicken broth
5 green onions, sliced	1 tbsp. Jamaican jerk seasoning
1 stalk celery, chopped	1 tsp. salt
1 Scotch bonnet, deseeded, veins removed and minced	4 C. cooked basmati rice
1 (15-ounce / 425-g) can diced tomatoes, undrained	1 C. chopped fresh parsley
	1 lime, quartered

Directions:
Press the Sauté button on the Instant Pot and heat the oil. Add the bacon, carrots, onions, celery and Scotch bonnet to the pot and sauté for 5 minutes, or until the onions are translucent. Stir in the tomatoes with juice, red beans, coconut milk, chicken broth, Jamaican jerk seasoning and salt. Lock the lid. Select the Pressure Cook and set the cooking time for 45 minutes at High Pressure. When the timer goes off, do a natural pressure release for 10 minutes, then release any remaining pressure. Carefully open the lid. Ladle the soup into four bowls over cooked rice and garnish with parsley. Squeeze a quarter of lime over each bowl. Serve warm.

Flavorful Fish Stew

Ingredients: Servings: 5 Cooking Time: 30 Mins

1 1/2 lbs white fish, remove bones and cut into 1-inch pieces	1 tbsp. ground cumin
1 tbsp. fresh parsley, chopped	6 oz can coconut milk
1 tbsp. fresh lime juice	8 oz fish broth
2 tbsp. coconut oil	14 oz can tomato, crushed
1/2 tsp. cayenne pepper	1 tbsp. garlic, minced
1 tbsp. paprika	1 red bell pepper, sliced
	1 onion, diced
	1/4 tsp. pepper
	1 tsp. salt

Directions:
Add oil into the instant pot duo crisp and set pot on sauté mode. Add garlic, bell pepper, and onion and sauté for 3-5 minutes. Add tomatoes, broth, coconut milk, cumin, paprika, cayenne, pepper, and salt and stir well. Seal the pot with pressure cooking lid and cook on high pressure for 10 minutes. Once done, release pressure using a quick release. Remove lid. Set pot on sauté mode and cook the stew for 10 minutes. Add fish and stir until fish is cooked, about 5 minutes. Turn off the instant pot. Add lime juice and stir well. Garnish with parsley and serve.

Crispy Tilapia Tacos (air Fryer)

Ingredients: Servings: 4 Cooking Time: 10 Mins

2 tbsp. milk
1/3 C. mayonnaise
1/4 tsp. garlic powder
1 tsp. chili powder
1 1/2 C. panko bread crumbs
1/2 tsp. salt
4 tsp. canola oil
1 lb. (454 g) skinless tilapia fillets, cut into 3-inch-long and 1-inch-wide strips
4 small flour tortillas
Lemon wedges, for topping
Cooking spray

Directions:

Preheat the air fryer to 400°F (204°C). Spritz the air fryer basket with cooking spray. Combine the milk, mayo, garlic powder, and chili powder in a bowl. Stir to mix well. Combine the panko with salt and canola oil in a separate bowl. Stir to mix well. Dredge the tilapia strips in the milk mixture first, then dunk the strips in the panko mixture to coat well. Shake the excess off. Arrange the tilapia strips in the preheated air fryer. Air fry for 5 minutes or until opaque on all sides and the panko is golden brown. Flip the strips halfway through. You may need to work in batches to avoid overcrowding. Unfold the tortillas on a large plate, then divide the tilapia strips over the tortillas. Squeeze the lemon wedges on top before serving.

Mexican Flavor Chicken Burgers (air Fryer)

Ingredients: Servings: 6 To 8 Cooking Time: 20 Mins

4 skinless and boneless chicken breasts
1 small head of cauliflower, sliced into florets
1 jalapeño pepper
3 tbsp. smoked paprika
1 tbsp. thyme
1 tbsp. oregano
1 tbsp. mustard powder
1 tsp. cayenne pepper
1 egg
Salt and ground black pepper, to taste
2 tomatoes, sliced
2 lettuce leaves, chopped
6 to 8 brioche buns, sliced lengthwise
3/4 C. taco sauce
Cooking spray

Directions:

Preheat the air fryer to 350°F (177°C) and spritz with cooking spray. In a blender, add the cauliflower florets, jalapeño pepper, paprika, thyme, oregano, mustard powder and cayenne pepper and blend until the mixture has a texture similar to bread crumbs. Transfer 3/4 of the cauliflower mixture to a medium bowl and set aside. Beat the egg in a different bowl and set aside. Add the chicken breasts to the blender with remaining cauliflower mixture. Sprinkle with salt and pepper. Blend until finely chopped and well mixed. Remove the mixture from the blender and form into 6 to 8 patties. One by one, dredge each patty in the reserved cauliflower mixture, then into the egg. Dip them in the cauliflower mixture again for additional coating. Place the coated patties into the air fryer basket and spritz with cooking spray. Air fry for 20 minutes or until golden and crispy. Flip halfway through to ensure even cooking. Transfer the patties to a clean work surface and assemble with the buns, tomato slices, chopped lettuce leaves and taco sauce to make burgers. Serve and enjoy.

Banana Peanut Butter Roll

Ingredients: Servings: 2 Cooking Time: 4 Hours

1 banana, peeled and sliced
1 tbsp. peanut butter

Directions:

Add banana and peanut butter into the blender and blend until smooth. Place the dehydrating tray in a multi-level air fryer basket and place basket in the instant pot. Line dehydrating tray with parchment paper. Spread banana mixture on dehydrating tray. Seal pot with air fryer lid and select dehydrate mode then set temperature to 135 F and timer for 4 hours. Serve and enjoy.

Cheesy Potato Taquitos (air Fryer)

Ingredients: Servings: 12 Cooking Time: 6 Mins

2 C. mashed potatoes
12 corn tortillas
1/2 C. shredded Mexican cheese
Cooking spray

Directions:

Preheat the air fryer to 400°F (204°C). Line the baking pan with parchment paper. In a bowl, combine the potatoes and cheese until well mixed. Microwave the tortillas on high heat for 30 seconds, or until softened. Add some water to another bowl and set alongside. On a clean work surface, lay the tortillas. Scoop 3 tbsp. of the potato mixture in the center of each tortilla. Roll up tightly and secure with toothpicks if necessary. Arrange the filled tortillas, seam side down, in the prepared baking pan. Spritz the tortillas with cooking spray. Air fry for 6 minutes, or until crispy and golden brown, flipping once halfway through the cooking time. You may need to work in batches to avoid overcrowding. Serve hot.

Carrot and Cabbage Beef Stew (pressure Cook)

Ingredients: Servings: 4 To 6 Cooking Time: 19 Mins

3 tbsp. extra-virgin olive oil
2 large carrots, peeled and sliced into 1/4-inch disks and then quartered
1 large Spanish onion, diced
2 lb. (907 g) ground beef
3 cloves garlic, minced
1 (46-ounce / 1.3-kg) can tomato juice
2 C. vegetable broth
Juice of 2 lemons
1 head cabbage, cored and roughly chopped
1/2 C. jasmine rice
1/4 C. dark brown sugar
1 tbsp. Worcestershire sauce
2 tsp. seasoned salt
1 tsp. black pepper
3 bay leaves

Directions:

Set the Instant Pot to the Sauté mode and heat the oil for 3 minutes. Add the carrots and onion to the pot and sauté for 3 minutes, or until just tender. Add the ground beef and garlic to the pot and sauté for 3 minutes, or until the beef is lightly browned. Stir in the remaining ingredients. Lock the lid. Select the Pressure Cook and set the cooking time for 10 minutes at High Pressure. When the timer goes off, perform a quick pressure release. Carefully open the lid. Let rest for 5 minutes to thicken and cool before serving.

Dehydrated Mango

Ingredients: Servings: 3 Cooking Time: 14 Hours

1 mango, peel and sliced 1/4-inch thick

Directions:

Place the dehydrating tray in a multi-level air fryer basket and place basket in the instant pot. Arrange mango slices on dehydrating tray. Seal pot with air fryer lid and select dehydrate mode then set temperature to 135 F and timer for 14 hours. Serve and enjoy.

Buffalo Chicken Soup

Ingredients: Servings: 6 Cooking Time: 10 Mins

1 lb chicken, cooked and shredded
1/2 C. heavy cream
5 oz cream cheese, cubed
2 1/2 tbsp. buffalo sauce
4 C. chicken broth
1 tbsp. garlic, minced
1/2 C. celery, diced
1/2 onion, diced
1 tbsp. olive oil
Pepper
Salt

Directions:

Add oil into the instant pot duo crisp and set pot on sauté mode. Add celery and onion and sauté until onion is softened about 5 minutes. Add garlic and sauté for a minute. Add shredded chicken, buffalo sauce, and broth and stir well. Seal the pot with pressure cooking lid and cook on high pressure for 5 minutes. Once done, allow to release pressure naturally for 5 minutes then release remaining pressure using a quick release. Remove lid. Transfer 1 C. of soup and cream cheese into the blender and blend until smooth. Return blended soup to the pot. Add heavy cream and stir well. Serve and enjoy.

Summer Vegetable Soup

Ingredients: Servings: 6 Cooking Time: 10 Mins

1 summer squash, sliced
1 onion, diced
1/4 C. basil, chopped
2 bell peppers, sliced
1/2 C. green beans, cut into pieces
8 C. vegetable broth
1 zucchini, sliced
1 eggplant, sliced
2 garlic cloves, smashed
3/4 C. corn
Pepper
Salt
For Garlic Buttery Croutons
2 C. of bread cubes
2 tomatoes, sliced
1/2 tsp. garlic powder
1 tbsp. olive oil
1 tbsp. butter, melted

Directions:

Add all ingredients into the instant pot and stir well. Seal pot with pressure cooking lid and cook on high for 10 minutes. Once done, release pressure using quick release. Remove lid. Puree the soup using a blender until smooth. For Croutons: In a bowl, toss bread cubes, garlic powder, butter, and oil. Spray instant pot multi-level air fryer basket with cooking spray. Add bread cubes into the air fryer basket and place basket into the instant pot. Seal pot with air fryer lid and select bake mode then set the temperature to 350 F and timer for 15-20 minutes. Stir halfway through. Top soup with croutons and serves.

Strawberry Mango Fruit Leather

Ingredients: Servings: 2 Cooking Time: 4 Hours

1/4 C. fresh strawberries
1/2 mango, peel and chopped

Directions:

Add strawberries and mango into the blender and blend until smooth. Place the dehydrating tray in a multi-level air fryer basket and place basket in the instant pot. Line dehydrating tray with parchment paper. Spread blended fruit mixture on dehydrating tray. Seal pot with air fryer lid and select dehydrate mode then set temperature to 160 F and timer for 4 hours. Serve and enjoy.

Sausage Zucchini Casserole

Ingredients: Servings: 8 Cooking Time: 45 Mins

12 eggs
2 small zucchinis, shredded
1 lb ground Italian sausage
3 tomatoes, sliced
3 tbsp. coconut flour
1/4 C. coconut milk
Pepper
Salt

Directions:

Spray instant pot from inside with cooking spray. Add sausage into the instant pot and cook on saute mode until browned. Spread shredded zucchini and sliced tomatoes on top of sausage. In a bowl, whisk eggs, coconut flour, milk, pepper, and salt and pour over sausage mixture. Seal pot with air fryer lid and select bake mode then set the temperature to 350 F and timer for 45 minutes. Serve and enjoy.

Recipe index

A

B

C

Q

R

S

T

Made in the USA
Middletown, DE
04 January 2022